MR. PLAYBOY

Hugh Hefner and the American Dream

STEVEN WATTS

WILEY

John Wiley & Sons, Inc.

Input 11/8/08

B Hefner

For Olivia Claire Watts

Library of Congress Cataloging-in-Publication Data:
Watts, Steven, date.
    Mr. Playboy : Hugh Hefner and the American dream / Steven Watts.
      p.   cm.
    Includes index.
    ISBN 978-0-471-69059-7 (cloth)
      1. Hefner, Hugh M. (Hugh Marston), 1926- 2. Journalists—United States—
Biography.   I. Title.
    PN4874.H454W38   2008
    070.5092—dc22
    [B]

                  2008009572

Printed in the United States of America

10 9 8 7 6 5 4 3 2 1

The American citizen lives in a world where fantasy is more real than reality. . . . We risk being the first people in history to have been able to make their illusions so vivid, so persuasive, so "realistic" that they can live in them.

—Daniel Boorstin, *The Image*

Humankind cannot bear very much reality.

—T. S. Eliot, *Four Quartets*

Men look at women. Women watch themselves being looked at.

—John Berger, *Ways of Seeing*

The truth was that Jay Gatsby of West Egg, Long Island, sprang from his Platonic conception of himself. . . . So he invented just the sort of Jay Gatsby that a seventeen-year-old boy would be likely to invent, and to this conception he was faithful to the end.

—F. Scott Fitzgerald, *The Great Gatsby*

When an interviewer asked my mother whether she was proud of me, she answered, "Oh, yes, but I would have been just as happy if he'd been a missionary." Later, I told her, "But Mom, I was!"

—Hugh Hefner, interview with the author

CONTENTS

ACKNOWLEDGMENTS

I have accumulated many debts in completing this book over the last few years, and it is a pleasure to acknowledge them. First, I would like to thank all of the (male) acquaintances, associates, and even strangers who have rushed forward over the past few years offering to assist me with research, carry my luggage, double-check my sources, take dictation, or wash my rental car when I visited the Playboy Mansion. This outpouring of selflessness, generosity, and friendship has revived my faith in human nature.

Several colleagues in the Department of History at the University of Missouri—Carol Anderson, Robert Collins, Catherine Rymph, Jonathan Sperber, and John Wigger—read the manuscript and forwarded many valuable comments and suggestions. Patty Eggleston, Sandy Kietzman, Melinda Lockwood, Jenny Morton, and Nancy Taube, departmental staff members all, provided various kinds of support and encouragement. A number of talented and discerning friends, including Armando Favazza, Cindy Sheltmire, Dick and Anne Stewart, Donald Tennant, Daniel Watts, Steve Weinberg, and, especially, Patricia Ward Kelly, looked over the manuscript and offered an array of useful observations. Mary Jane Edele and Catherine Damme helped ease my burden during the early going by digging up articles and transcribing interviews.

At John Wiley & Sons, my editor, Eric Nelson, expertly guided the manuscript toward its final form, while Rachel Meyers and Ellen Wright skillfully orchestrated its production. My agent and friend,

Ron Goldfarb, did his usual superb job of negotiating contracts, bolstering my spirits, and providing a sounding board on various occasions. He has my enduring gratitude for all he has done to boost my career as an author.

The librarians of Ellis Library at the University of Missouri deployed their expertise to help me gain access to various materials. At Playboy Enterprises, Inc., in Chicago, Lee Froehlich and Jessica Riddle helped me navigate the company archives. During my research trips to the Playboy Mansion, the mansion's staff treated me with great forbearance and kindness as I ransacked the files, pored through the scrapbooks, strolled the grounds, and took up more than my fair share of time at the copy machine. Among the many individuals who deserve my thanks, I note especially Steve Martinez, Norma Maister, Elayne Lodge, Joyce Nizzari, Trudy King, Amanda Warren, Alicia Boote, John Cailotto, Elizabeth Kanski, Bob Colin, Jenny Lewis, Dick Rosenzweig, and Mary O'Connor. A batch of new friends, including Elizabeth Granli, Ron McCabe, Jeremy Arnold, Lindsey Vuolo, Amber Campisi, Tiffany Fallon, and, especially, Alison Reynolds and Joel Berliner, provided enlightening conversation and companionship. Many thanks go to that intrepid band of raconteurs on Monday evenings who taught me much about old movies, bad jokes, and sharp repartee: Keith Hefner, Ray Anthony, Bill Shepard, Chuck McCann, Richard Bann, Ron Borst, Mark Cantor, Peter Vieira, Robert Culp, Johnny Crawford, and Kevin Burns.

Hugh Hefner, of course, deserves my profuse thanks. When I first approached him about this project, he graciously agreed to cooperate. He not only provided unprecedented access to his massive files chronicling the history of *Playboy* and his career, but gave me an opportunity to get an inside look at his life. He also kindly consented to sit for a battery of interviews, which eventually totaled nearly forty hours. He accepted the stricture that I maintain editorial control over the book, and while, ultimately, he took issue with some of my arguments and conclusions, he honored the agreement. For all of these things, and more, Mr. Hefner has my profound appreciation.

Two people deserve my greatest thanks. My wife, Patti Watts, reacted with remarkable good humor to my dubious proposal for doing research at the Playboy Mansion, offering only the admonition usually given to children at the toy store: "You can look, but don't touch." Subsequently, during innumerable conversations about

Playboy, American society, men and women, sexuality, and many other subjects, she has shared a wealth of insights and ideas that have enriched the book. My daughter, Olivia Claire Watts, arrived unexpectedly during the middle of this undertaking. After causing her doddering father an initial bout of terror, she has proved to be an inexhaustible source of affection, amusement, edification, and wonder. She has caused me to think harder about all of this, and the book is for her.

INTRODUCTION

The Boy Next Door

Mention of Hugh Hefner instantly evokes a host of images that dance through the imagination: visions of voluptuous women and uninhibited sex, mansion parties and celebrity entertainers, grotto hot tubs and round beds, smoking jackets and sleek sports cars. Such mental pictures, of course, stem from Hefner's role as founder and publisher of *Playboy* magazine. Over the last fifty years, *Playboy*'s monthly array of hedonistic messages, which Hefner has supported with a publicity-drenched lifestyle, has made him an impresario of sex and leisure in the United States and has brought him dazzling fame. Like Walt Disney in the movies, Muhammad Ali in sports, or Elvis Presley in popular music, Hefner has come to signify a personal style, a fantasy. Like these other larger-than-life figures, he has become an icon of modern American life who has made a significant impact on our culture.

But the climb to the pinnacle of acclaim and influence proved to be a long one. In late December 1952, a forlorn twenty-six-year-old Hefner stood on a bridge at Michigan Avenue in downtown Chicago. Bundled up against the frigid winter weather, he grimly stared out over the Chicago River. His life seemed at low ebb as he strained against the bonds of an unsatisfying marriage, flinched at

1

the unsettling prospect of parenthood, and balked at the thought of returning to an unfulfilling job with few career prospects. This unhappiness had been driven home by an event a few days earlier. He had cohosted an alumni show at his old high school where, along with his best friend, he had told jokes, performed skits, and sang a few numbers while emceeing the festivities. An enthusiastic audience had responded with laughter and applause.

That magical evening left Hefner yearning to recapture the enthusiasm, optimism, and sense of achievement of his high school years when he had been a popular and creative leader among students. But now those youthful hopes seemed far away. Standing on the bridge, he muttered, "Is this all there is? Where is my life going?" He silently vowed to do *something* to escape the ennui that threatened to suffocate him.[1]

While not quite on par with Edward Gibbon's famous reverie amid the ruins of Rome that prompted him to write *The History of the Decline and Fall of the Roman Empire*—even though critics would later accuse Hefner of starting just such a process of degeneration in the United States—this episode marked a turning point in the young man's life. A few weeks later, he started his own magazine. The results would be stunning.

Within fifteen years, Hefner and *Playboy* had taken the country by storm. From its modest beginnings in Chicago, the magazine grew spectacularly into a multimillion-dollar enterprise with a circulation of some five million readers by the late 1960s and seven million by the early 1970s. The Playboy empire expanded to include clubs, resorts, music, films, television shows, and a wide array of merchandise. Even more, like Coca-Cola or Mickey Mouse, the magazine's ubiquitous bunny logo became an international symbol of American life. During the Vietnam War in 1969, for instance, American soldiers were amused to find a dog-eared copy of *Playboy* in a captured North Vietnamese bunker. Hefner's vision of the good life, it seemed, had even piqued the imagination (or at least the libidos) of hardened communist revolutionaries.

Hefner himself became a media darling. By the mid-1960s, he had graced the cover of *Time* magazine and been featured prominently in other publications such as *Life, Look*, and the *Saturday Evening Post*. He appeared as a frequent guest on popular television programs such as *The Tonight Show* with Johnny Carson, *The Dick Cavett Show*, and Rowan and Martin's *Laugh-In*. Dozens of newspaper articles and interviews explored his social views and supplied salacious details of his outlandish love life, including the shifting bevy of girlfriends, the revolving round bed where he worked and cavorted, and the glass-walled, bathing-suits-optional swimming pool with a bar built alongside.

More significantly, however, Hefner also emerged as a serious shaper of, and commentator on, modern American values. In 1967, for instance, he appeared on an NBC prime-time special exploring America's burgeoning culture of leisure and affluence. Sitting in the library of the Playboy Mansion alongside the noted Harvard theologian Harvey Cox and William F. Buckley, the prominent conservative editor of the *National Review,* he discussed Americans' growing interest in what the show called "the pursuit of pleasure." Puffing on his trademark pipe and speaking with smooth self-assurance, he argued that an older, religious basis for morality had faded and values needed to be reformulated on a more rational basis to promote the happiness of individuals. The genuine enjoyment of life in modern America, he insisted, demanded liberated sexuality and enthusiastic, sophisticated consumption. Holding his own with these intellectual heavyweights, Hefner came across, in the words of the moderator, as "the Chairman Mao of the sexual revolution, issuing maxims for moral guerrilla warfare."[2]

In other words, within a few years of starting *Playboy* on a shoestring after begging and borrowing a few thousand dollars, Hefner became a serious, influential figure in modern culture. Yet the question of how and why the publisher of a risqué men's magazine was able to garner such influence, and even prestige, has perplexed many observers. Understanding comes with the realization that over the last half century Hefner has played a key role in changing American values, ideas, and attitudes. From the beginning, his enterprise was about more than dirty pictures, more than a girlie magazine hastily slipped under an overcoat by a guilty purchaser. It was a historical force of significant proportions.

Most obviously, Hefner and *Playboy* served as a barometer gauging the pressures of historical changes in America over a half century. In the 1950s, the magazine reflected hip, urban dissatisfaction with the stodgy conformism of the Eisenhower era as it critiqued middle-class suburbanism, the Beat Generation, and the Cold War crusade against communism. In the 1960s, Hefner helped fan the flames of the civil rights movement, the antiwar crusade, the countercultural revolt, and the emerging feminist struggle. In the 1970s, *Playboy* personified both the "Me Generation" and the economic contractions of the era, while the 1980s saw it become a foil for, and target of, the Reagan Revolution. Throughout, the editor-in-chief and his popular publication formed a kind of tablet upon which were inscribed the events shaping modern America.

But Hefner and his magazine also played a crucial part in shaping, not just reflecting, American values in the decades after World War II. Articulating some of the deepest social and emotional longings of modern Americans, this controversial publisher stood at the forefront of four upheavals that fundamentally reconfigured the United States in the last half of the twentieth century. First, he helped trigger, and then personified, a transformation in sexual values and conduct that emerged in the 1950s and swept through American society in subsequent years. *Playboy*, with its "Playmate of the Month," sexual advice columns, and array of erotic pictorials, cartoons, and jokes, moved sex out of the privacy of the marital bed and away from the responsibilities of procreation, and made it a matter of public discussion and personal pleasure. The magazine's open attitude not only loosened old-fashioned moral strictures on one of the most powerful of human urges but also promoted its commercialization. Hefner clearly stood as the most recognizable product of, and catalyst for, the modern sexual revolution.

He also served as one of the most persuasive advocates for America's postwar consumer efflorescence. As the national economy increasingly turned from production of basic goods and services to the creation of consumer products, Hefner's magazine inundated readers with symbols of material abundance. It became both a catalog for sophisticated purchasing and a guidebook for negotiating a daunting new landscape of material plenty. The pages of *Playboy*, along with Hefner's numerous public statements, articulated a credo urging unabashed enjoyment of the material goods that were flooding out to a middle- and working-class market. Addressing a simmering male identity crisis in modern society in which growing numbers of men no longer functioned as producers, the pages of *Playboy* offered the reassuring model of stylish consumer. Linking material plenty to an audacious leisure culture, Hefner helped make consumer abundance an emblem of America throughout the world.

Moreover, Hefner stood at the center of a popular culture invasion of the United States that swept all before it in the postwar decades. This sea change saw glossy magazines, television, movies, records, and entertainment of all kinds become a dominant force in most people's lives in all regions of the country. This process replaced local institutions such as churches, lyceums, reading societies, and town newspapers with large-scale, corporate media organizations that dispensed homogenized information, products, and images nationally. With his popular magazine, syndicated television shows, franchised nightclubs, and movie and musical projects synergistically broadcasting the same array of messages, the Chicago publisher personified the mass-culture overhaul of modern society in the last half of the twentieth century. Even Hefner's passionately pursued personal hobbies—swing dancing and Hollywood movies—reflected this revolutionary trend in American life. As he often observed, he was a child of popular culture who, in turn, became one of its biggest champions.

Finally, Hefner stood implicated, usually as a whipping boy, in the women's movement that swept through America beginning in the 1960s. *Playboy's* erotic images of nude young women made it an object of scorn among many emerging feminists, who complained that it depicted females as mere sexual objects. The magazine, in their view, represented the worst sort of male domination and female degradation. A distraught Hefner—he saw himself as a progressive who was unfairly indicted as a reactionary—contended that he promoted sexual freedom for women as well as men. Few women's liberationists bought the argument. As the debate ratcheted upward with bitter accusations of misogyny and betrayal, these two factions turned upon one another with ferocious animosity. As a major combatant in this battle over sexual politics and acceptable roles for women, *Playboy* illuminated one of the most profound trends in modern American social life.

While Hefner has stood at the cutting edge of these transformative trends, his influence has worked in complex ways. It often flowed through indirect channels, for instance, since what was said *about* him often proved as illuminating as what *he* said. Whether it was Harvey Cox discussing the theological implications of the "Playboy Philosophy," Tom Wolfe describing Hefner's role in the cultural ferment of the 1960s, Norman Mailer detailing the sybaritic pleasures of the Playboy Mansion, Gloria Steinem excoriating Hefner's oppression of women, Attorney General Edwin Meese denouncing *Playboy* as pornography, or Justice William O. Douglas defending Hefner's First Amendment rights, commentators have used him as a lens through which to examine a changing social landscape.

Bitter disputation has clouded the atmosphere and made it difficult to grasp Hefner's significance. Few Americans have aroused greater controversy in ascending to fame and fortune. Beginning in the 1950s, a wide variety of people—journalists, ministers, politicians, moralists, and ordinary folks writing to newspapers and magazines—disagreed violently about the merits of *Playboy* and its publisher. On one side stood Hefner denouncers who, scandalized by the magazine's pictures of nude women and its mockery of such institutions as marriage, religion, and family, condemned Hefner's appeal to degraded desires and animal instincts. Seeing themselves as defenders of respectable society, they viewed him as a dark prophet of American debauchery and decline.

Hefner disciples, inspired by *Playboy's* attacks on sexual repression and advocacy of material enjoyment, defended him with equal fervor. They acclaimed the publisher as a liberator leading the way to physical and emotional freedom from the gray-flannel fog of a repressed, conformist society still chained to the anachronistic morality of an earlier age. The magazine, in other words, became a kind of cultural litmus test for judging the positive or negative direction of modern American culture. Emotionally charged disagreement has persisted in one form or another for the last fifty years as defenders and foes of *Playboy's* values eagerly strapped on the gloves for ideological fisticuffs.

Hefner's personal life only encouraged the disputation. This fascinating story of romance, ambition, and sex revealed a young man emerging from a midwestern Methodist background who parlayed the initial shock created by *Playboy* into a powerful position as a cultural trendsetter. Constantly surrounded by a crowd of beautiful young women, he made pleasure-seeking into an art form as the Playboy Mansion became a highly publicized playground for prominent figures in the world of politics, sports, music, and movies. The private man, however, nurtured a more complicated, even mysterious personality. A set of internal contradictions—a powerful sensuality and a compulsive work ethic, a hedonistic streak and an impulse to rigidly control every aspect of his life, a compulsive desire for celebrity status and a Gatsby-like instinct for observing the merrymaking at a distance—made for a curiously driven yet detached sybarite. So, too, did his combination of restless intelligence, extreme sentimentality, and obsession with the romantic artifacts of popular culture. Hefner's personal complexities mattered little, however, to those eager to either condemn or canonize.

Ultimately, however, if understanding is to trump titillation and fervor, the controversial publisher must be approached from a different angle. While both disciples and demonizers of Hefner are likely to be disappointed by this perspective, Hefner must be analyzed as a historical figure, not merely a controversial celebrity. Viewed in this rightful context, at first glance, he appears as a rebel. Wave after wave of attacks throughout his career—from anti-obscenity zealots, defenders of decency, religious moralists, conservative politicians, feminist activists—have positioned him as a dissenter in modern America. Indeed, Hefner himself has embraced the role of heroic insurrectionist seeking to overturn outdated, stultifying, Puritan traditions in American culture. In fact, this scenario contains a kernel of truth. As a crusading reformer, he has done much, in the face of often virulent opposition, to loosen restrictions on sexual expression.

But the image of Hefner as rebel also misleads. In more profound ways, he has expressed many of the deepest impulses of mainstream American culture. For example, he appeared on the cultural skyline as champion of a venerable tradition in American life, the self-made man. Rising to great heights from modest circumstances by dint of hard work and a new idea, he romped up the path to success as Benjamin Franklin in bunny ears.

More importantly, Hefner has presented a compelling vision of the good life in modern America. In so doing, he occupies a crucial position in a longer historical trajectory. In the early 1900s, as historians have emphasized in recent decades, the Victorian restraints of the nineteenth century steadily eroded as the mass of Americans gradually replaced a traditional code of self-control with a new creed emphasizing emotional, physical, and material gratification. Then the privations of the Great Depression and World War II stunted the process, creating a great cultural reservoir of pent-up material and emotional desires. In the postwar era it shot forward once again, and Hefner emerged as perhaps the leading popular philosopher of a revived, intensified culture of self-fulfillment for an audience yearning for gratification. He seductively portrayed the pursuit of happiness as a combination of physical pleasure, leisure entertainment, and consumer enjoyment. Brilliantly commingling sexual liberation and material abundance, *Playboy* captured the essence of modern American desire.

In this sense, Hefner's historical influence has been, quite literally, fantastic. The *Playboy* dream is the stuff of fantasy, conjured from the realm of desire by a kind of cultural alchemy. While often flowing from Hefner's personal experiences—"My life has been the fulfillment of a fantasy," he likes to say—his vision of happiness also resonates powerfully in the broader culture. The notion of having few limits on personal pleasure is the modern American dream as well as Hefner's. As the historian Daniel Boorstin observed, the enormous abundance of modern America has created "a world where fantasy is more real than reality. . . . We risk being the first people in history to have been able to make their illusions so vivid, so persuasive, so 'realistic' that they can live in them."[3]

Whether we like it or not, Hefner's vision of America as the land of self-fulfillment has been realized in many ways. His notions of sexual happiness and material comfort, pleasure and leisure, maleness and femaleness, of individuals freed from many of the restraints of family and religion have become commonplace, though often in diluted form. We see in Hefner and *Playboy* many of our own perceptions of modern life. We see reflections of what we have become, both personally and collectively, glimpses of where we might be going, for good or ill. We see many of our hopes and fears about our culture, often hopelessly mingled together.

But the process of analyzing the impact of Hefner and *Playboy* on American life must begin by returning to the past. There, in the halcyon days of the late 1920s before the trauma of the Great Depression, a middle-class couple only recently removed from the rural hinterland faced the future in a dynamic midwestern city. Their oldest son, the typical boy next door, would find opportunities and restrictions in equal portion, and each would provide its own enticements.

PART I

BEGINNINGS

1

A Boy at Play

Hugh Hefner grew up in a repressive, "Puritan" atmosphere in which his family discouraged shows of affection. The strict religious code of his parents forbade emotional displays, drinking, swearing, or sexual candor, and he yearned to break free and find love, romance, and emotional connection. This desire finally drove him to outright dissent in young adulthood and he founded *Playboy* as a proclamation of freedom and sexual liberation. In Hefner's words, "In many ways it was my parents who, unintentionally, developed the iconoclastic rebellion in me." This personal struggle not only provided the seedbed for his later career, Hefner argues, but framed larger issues in modern America that explained the enormous appeal of *Playboy*. "Puritan repression is really the key that unlocks the mystery of my life," he wrote. "It is the 'Rosebud' that explains what my life is really all about."[1]

Such is the story that Hefner has told interviewers countless times over the last forty years, and it provides an unshakable foundation for his own understanding of his life. He has constructed a kind of personal mythology. Like all of us, only more self-consciously and publicly, he has constructed a view of his past that explains and justifies his present. But Hefner's rendering of his youth simplifies a complex situation. Like all myths, it strikes a chord with its dramatic narrative of a young hero overcoming obstacles and triumphing. Also like all myths, it is only partially true. As D. H. Lawrence once warned, "Don't trust the teller. Trust the tale." And the real tale of Hefner's youth suggests a somewhat different story that is compelling in its own way.

In fact, Hefner was the product of a moderately progressive family where traditional, Victorian reticence about emotional display and sexuality, while certainly present, was rapidly giving way to a more modern notion of juvenile self-fulfillment. Only recently removed from the rural culture of the Great Plains, his college-educated parents had adapted themselves to the bustling urban life of Chicago. Growing up in the 1930s, Hefner was doted on by his mother while an emotionally absent father deprived the boy of a male authority figure. Left to his own devices, the imaginative child immersed himself in the popular culture of the era—movies, music, radio, and cartoons—and created a rich fantasy life that gradually took on a reality more vibrant than his actual, lived experiences. The product of indulgence as much as restraint, the boy's fantasies mirrored larger patterns in America's emerging culture of self-fulfillment and its desire for leisure, entertainment, and emotional satisfaction. They made him a creature of modern values in ways that he never fully appreciated.

But the origins of Hefner's early life were found far from the city lights and urban crowds of Chicago and Los Angeles where he would spend most of his days. The family into which he was born, and the values that he found so stifling, were shaped on the distant, windswept prairies of turn-of-the-century Nebraska.

I

At the conclusion of a young people's party at the Methodist church in Holdrege, Nebraska, in 1911, Glenn Hefner asked Grace Swanson if he could walk home with her. She agreed, and thus began a long courtship between the two rural teenagers. This small town of some thirty-five hundred people sat in the south-central part of the state, about 120 miles from Omaha. Born in a sod house, Glenn had been shaped by a father who flitted from job to job—barber, insurance agent, real estate salesman—in a vain attempt to keep his family out of poverty. Grace enjoyed more prosperous circumstances. She had been born in 1895 to a farm family and experienced a typical rural childhood punctuated by chores, animals, and domestic dramas. Her mother was a religious woman, while her father, although a good provider, was a man of harsh temperament and an authoritarian bent. This stern disciplinarian rarely concerned himself with the progress or well-being of his children. Once as she came home from grade school, Grace recalled, "he passed me in the yard and hit me with a black snake whip . . . because he thought I hadn't come right home from school." She confessed, "I did not think I loved my father, just feared him." Moreover, he refused to attend church like his pious wife, drank at local taverns, and swore vigorously.[2]

Grace, who would be an important influence on her eldest son in subsequent years, imbibed the religious values of her mother. When an older brother tormented her, she would shout, "Sinner, you are a sinner," which was the worst epithet she knew. She sang in the church choir, won a public speaking contest sponsored by the anti-liquor Women's Christian Temperance Union, and socialized with other young people at the local church. Glenn displayed a somber temperament as a young man—"Life was a serious business for him," Grace explained—but moderated it with a tonic of jovial good humor. His parents were respectable churchgoers, and he followed their example.[3]

Glenn and Grace first became acquainted through basketball in high school. They both played avidly, and one day the school principal, as he observed the boys' and girls' teams practicing, remarked, "I think Glenn Hefner and Grace would make a good couple. They ought to get together." And indeed, after their encounter at the church party, the two young people dated steadily throughout high school. They were serious students who appeared comfortable in each other's company. Grace was particularly scholarly, serving as editor of the school yearbook and becoming class valedictorian. After graduation, Glenn went on to Nebraska Wesleyan University in Lincoln, while Grace taught at a country school for two years before joining him there. She studied chemistry and math at Wesleyan while Glenn took business and accounting courses. The young couple socialized by going to movies, fraternity parties, and football games. Upon graduating from college in 1918, Glenn joined the navy to serve in World

War I while Grace remained to finish her degree while working as a part-time schoolteacher. He returned to Nebraska after the cessation of hostilities and taught in high school and worked at a small-town bank before moving to Chicago to join some friends. He found a job with a railroad company and then in an accounting office. Grace soon joined him and they were married at a Methodist church in 1921.[4]

The newlyweds took up lodgings on the West Side near the Austin district, where several friends and relatives already lived. Glenn worked as an accountant while Grace took jobs as a telephone operator and bookkeeper before joining the World Service Commission of the Methodist Church, where she dealt with young people working as prospective ministers or in the Home Missionary Society, the Women's Home Missionary Society, and the Deaconess Society. In the spring of 1926, however, Grace quit her job because she was expecting her first child.[5]

Hugh Marston Hefner was born on April 9, 1926, and enjoyed a healthy infancy. His parents socialized with other young couples, playing pinochle and checkers, sharing potluck suppers, and occasionally going to the movies. On rare occasions they would return to Nebraska to visit farm relatives. In 1929 a brother, Keith, arrived, and the following year the family moved to a new house at 1922 North New England Avenue in Austin, which would remain the family home for many decades. The Hefners soon acquired a new Model A Ford, and within a few years Hugh and Keith possessed the accoutrements of a typical middle-class childhood—bicycles, a sandbox in the backyard, and a dog named Wags.[6]

Hugh's boyhood unfolded happily. His neighborhood offered nearby fields and streams, and the Hefner house became a gathering place for boys such as Harold and Russell Saewert, Don Harper, Jimmy Bachman, Warren Tellefson, and Hugh's best friend, Jimmy's brother Curtis Bachman. They would play in the backyard, ride their bicycles, or roam their rustic surroundings conducting war games and encountering snakes, birds, and crawdads. "Mine was the house where they came to play, and she made us all welcome," Hefner noted of his mother. In the early 1930s Grace took her sons and their pals to see the Field Museum, the Aquarium, and the Chicago World's Fair with its proud slogan, "The Century of Progress." Hugh and Keith had a close boyhood relationship, playing constantly and sharing a bedroom. "We did everything together as kids. I worshipped him," Keith recalled later. The boys felt quite grown up when given their own bedrooms, only to discover that they had been separated because their nightly talking and giggling was keeping their parents awake.[7]

Hugh developed a special love for animals. "When he was a kid," remembers Keith, "he wanted to be a veterinarian, [it] was the first job that he ever thought of, I think." At age eleven, Hugh received a prize from the Illinois Humane Society for his poem "Be Kind to Dumb Animals," which included these stanzas: "To all animals please be kind / Then faithfulness you will find / Feed cat and dog when they need to be fed / Then them to happiness you have led." An interesting animal-related incident occurred around age six. Throughout his childhood, Hugh had treasured a special blue-and-white security blanket featuring a bunny pattern. When he came down with a mastoid infection, he received a present from his parents to speed his recovery—a wire-haired fox terrier that he named Brows. A little box was set up in the basement, and the boy donated his "bunny blanket" for the dog to sleep on. Unfortunately, Brows died about a week later and the blanket had to be burned. Hugh was heartbroken, but the imagery seems to have stuck with him at some level. Later he would note the "*Citizen Kane* kind of connection here of the burned blanket" as he went on to create the bunny empire.[8]

In physical terms, Hugh developed slowly. While active and boisterous with his friends, he was not athletic and shied away from organized sports. He tended to be reserved in formal situations at school or home and hated to answer the telephone. A close childhood friend recalled an incident from the second grade when the shy boy was called upon to read aloud. "He stood up to read and lost his place. I can still see him standing there looking confused and embarrassed. From then on, all the way through high school, he read line-by-line, using his finger."[9]

Even as a boy, however, Hefner displayed an unusual creativity. Fascinated with drawing, he spent countless hours sketching crude cartoon strips such as *Cranet*, an adventurer who flew from Earth to Mars; *Jigs and Spike*, cowboy outlaws; *Jim Malt*, a youthful detective; and adventure characters named "Marvel Man," "the Mystic," and "Metallic Man." He wrote fantasy stories such as "The Haunted Castle" and "Ratty," the "story of a big rat who couldn't be caught until nature took a hand," based on a real rodent who roamed the neighborhood. At age nine he published a one-page neighborhood newspaper called the *Bi-Weekly News,* which he sold for a few cents to the parents of his pals. In grammar school, he created two unofficial class newspapers that sold for a penny each, before moving on to create a school-sanctioned newspaper called the *Pepper,* which proudly announced his role as "Editor and Tiper." Recalled a childhood friend, "From the sixth through the eighth grades, I have a mind's eye view of Hef at his desk, dashing off drawings and circulating them to me and other classmates for our amusement. He was always inventing comic strips."[10]

In fact, throughout grammar school Hefner's preoccupation with drawing and story-writing exasperated his teachers. Absorbed in his imagination, he often neglected his studies. "He doesn't do his arithmetic, geography, or spelling unless I stand right at his elbow. He constantly draws," his fourth-grade teacher wrote to Grace Hefner. "I've about reached the end of my patience with him. . . . Perhaps you can help. He will not pass if he doesn't do his work." After being called to task, the boy tried to buckle down to the academic duties at hand and composed two contrite poems, complete with imaginative spelling:

Why I Waist Time
I think I get to dreaming
Of something I might do.
And I forget my studies,
And what I'm supost to do.

What I'm Going To Make of Myself Next Semester
I will not make my teacher mad,
Because that would make me sad.
I will not draw at all in school,
And I won't brake a single rule.

But the problem persisted, calling forth yet another signed promise the following year: "I will not do the things below. 1. I will not talk to my neighbor. 2. I will not play in school. 3. I will not cause my teacher any trouble and I will work my very best."[11]

Young Hefner, however, could not mend his ways. In his early teenage years he continued drawing cartoon strips—eventually they would number about seventy different series—and to write and illustrate stories. He had begun to read fiction by Edgar Allan Poe and H. G. Wells and became a devotee of Sax Rohmer's Dr. Fu Manchu tales and Sir Arthur Conan Doyle's Sherlock Holmes. His own stories, with titles such as "The End of the World," "The Lizard Men from Under the Earth," "Dr. Claw's Invisible Hound," "The Mansion of Madness," and "Out of the Fog," increasingly focused on the macabre, the supernatural, horror, and science fiction. In 1940, Hefner formed and became president of "The Shudder Club," which, as expressed in his youthful syntax, aimed "to bring together all lovers of chills and horror and enjoying good mystery together." Like all self-respecting clubs for boys, it offered an official handshake, password, membership pin, and special "decoder circle" that permitted members to untangle secret messages. Hefner, doing all of the work, published five issues of *Shudder* magazine, which offered original mystery and horror stories. The boys were delighted when Bela Lugosi, Boris Karloff, and Peter Lorre replied to their solicitation and accepted honorary positions in the club.[12]

By 1940, Hefner's creations were reflecting the pressure of world events. "Photoplays" consisted of photographs of costumed characters, shot on the family Kodak, that were captioned to tell a story. While two of them were Sherlock Holmes parodies, the other pair were stories about World War II titled "Bill Dodgely and Troop 31" and "The Kid's No Coward." A 1940 comic strip told the story of three French brothers escaping from a Nazi prison in occupied Europe, while a ten-page tale imagined a German invasion of the United States that was heroically rebuffed near Chicago.[13]

Indeed, throughout childhood Hefner created vivid fantasy worlds in which he immersed himself, a trait that would prove to be lifelong. The boy who wouldn't answer the telephone or venture alone to the dentist's office a few streets away preferred to inhabit a reality he had created and to entice others to join him there. "I was a dreamer and people referred to me as a dreamer," Hefner later admitted of his childhood. "I had these flights of fantasy."[14]

This tendency had appeared in him at a very young age. Along with his brother and his pals, he organized a game he called "Clay" that they played day after day for years. Using modeling clay on a large table, they created dozens of small human figures and elaborate settings—battlefields, haunted mansions, mysterious ships—that were like miniature movie sets. He invented stories the boys would bring to life as they would bend and twist the clay figures and speak for them. Grace later would recount how her eldest son "liked to fantasize and tell stories and play with these clay figures."[15]

In fact, Grace was repeatedly struck by Hugh's insular creativity. "As a child, he found it very difficult to make new friends. When he was in school, he was a dreamer, and sort of lived his own life in his own mind," she observed. "I would ask him who some of his class-mates were, and he wouldn't know the names of very many of them." But he could relate the plots of his stories and comic strips down to the tiniest detail. "You couldn't always tell what was making Hugh feel unhappy, because he was very much a loner," a baffled Grace admitted. "He always lived in a fantasy world."[16]

Keith Hefner observed the same impulse in his older brother. Hugh preferred to spend time in his room, writing stories and draw-ing cartoons, when he wasn't playing. Often shy and insecure with other people, the boy did not like venturing out. "His fantasy life really began with the stories he wrote as a child in grade school and the cartoons he drew," Keith said. "He could really make his life what he wanted it to be." Even as a kid, noted the younger Hefner, Hugh wanted "his world to stay exactly as he made it, and doesn't want to go anywhere else where that isn't the reality."[17]

Hefner's fantasies did not appear sui generis, however, but were shaped by a cluster of influences. Family dynamics and reli-gious instruction played an important role in channeling his cre-ative instincts, as did the popular culture milieu of Depression-era America. These factors converged to prod his imagination and create a yearning that would motivate him throughout his life.

II

Like many middle-class children in the 1930s, Hugh Hefner was molded by traditional forces of family and religion. Since the early nineteenth century, respectable American families had drawn upon evangelical Protestantism and Victorian ideology to sustain them in a fluid, dynamic society of opportunity. The revivals of the Second Great Awakening had swept through the United States in the early 1800s, creating a Protestant tradition of "moral free agency" that made the individual the arbiter of his own salvation. The crystallization of Victorian culture around the same time had enshrined a set of moral principles devoted to individual self-control. As late as the Great Depression, these traditions informed the way middle-class parents raised their children.[18]

This mind-set was changing dramatically, however, both in the larger culture and in the Hefner household. New leisure activities such as amusement parks and the movies had helped break down Victorian self-control in the early 1900s, while the explosive growth of a consumer economy gave rise to an ethos of material and emotional self-fulfillment. The Hefner family proved susceptible to such modernizing influences. To a marked degree, and contrary to Hugh's memories later in life, not just "Puritanism" but progressive notions of morality and childrearing influenced the proceedings at New England Avenue. So too did American popular culture, every variety of which colored the outlook of the eldest Hefner son. Glimpses of the man who founded *Playboy* could be seen in a youngster frustrated by the reticence and nose-to-the-grindstone ethic of his parents. They also manifested in a boy who was never disciplined without explanation, who chafed at even the mild restraints put in place by his parents, who argued with Sunday school teachers, and who whiled away countless hours in the company of cartoonists, mystery writers, and movie directors.[19]

As Hefner would recall throughout his life, restraint and repression colored the atmosphere of his family as he came of age. Orderly rules and sobriety muffled expressions of emotion. Hugh and Keith had to be at home and in bed earlier than their playmates, and they were not allowed to play with friends on Sunday, which was set aside for church and family activities. Grace and Glenn also shied away from displays of affection to each other and to their children. Little kissing and hugging occurred in this emotional climate of cool reserve. Keith remembered, "There was a period that lasted about two weeks when I was quite young, when I thought it would be nice to kiss my father on the cheek good night and that lasted about a week. I could tell how embarrassed he was by it." In fact, Grace and Glenn buried emotions so deep that feelings of any kind—anger, affection, disputes—seldom came to the surface. There was much calmness and kindness among the Hefners, but little passion. "His parents are very controlled people," Hefner's first wife reported. "In the three years we lived there, I never heard them raise their voice. Never."[20]

This atmosphere was reinforced by the temperaments of the boys' parents. Glenn, a straitlaced, hardworking CPA, had carved out a career at the Advanced Aluminum Company and also kept the books for the Austin Methodist Church, where the Hefners attended. About five foot eight with broad shoulders and a trim waist, the former basketball player had kept himself in good shape into middle age. Although taciturn, he had more of a sense of humor than Grace and was known to joke on occasion. He found it hard to talk to his sons, but occasionally joined them in pitching horseshoes or playing ball.[21]

But Hugh and Keith seldom saw their father because he was addicted to his work. Glenn left in the morning before his sons arose and returned near midnight after they were in bed. This grinding schedule resulted partly from his fascination with bookkeeping and partly from the Depression, when working extra hours could mean the difference between keeping a job and unemployment. He left the raising of his children to his wife, which pleased none of them. The boys sensed a vacuum in their lives because their father was seldom around for bonding experiences. When Keith told his dad how much he had missed his presence in boyhood, Glenn responded, "I didn't think I had to [be present]. My father never did anything with me." Grace also felt pangs of loneliness and worry, often walking around the block near midnight when he still had not appeared at home. An industrious, remote figure who was respected, even admired, in the Hefner family, Glenn was negligible in his personal impact. He was "a very nice husband" and a hard worker, said Grace, but as a father "he wasn't there." [22]

Glenn's reserve influenced his attitudes toward physical issues and sexuality. When the family went to a local swimming pool, he carefully hid his body from his sons as he stood behind a locker door and changed into his swimming trunks. He never discussed sex in any fashion with his sons. Decades later, Keith was stunned when his father asserted that he had never masturbated in his entire life, even as a teenager. Grace shared this Victorian aversion to sexuality. Later in life she confessed that she never had much use for sex. Glenn was very shy, but "he always liked it more than I did."[23]

Grace shared her husband's religiosity, kindliness, lack of pretension, and undemonstrative nature. Of medium height and sharp-featured, with wire-rimmed glasses and a habitually serious expression, this soft-spoken woman wore no makeup, dressed simply, and kept her long hair carefully twirled up in a bun. As a young woman she had decided that if Glenn did not come back from World War I, she was going to become a missionary or a teacher in a mission school. A deeply felt code of Protestant values caused her to endorse virtuous, plain living, to view wealth with suspicion, and to see displays of emotion as unseemly.[24]

As a mother, Grace followed the same path trod by religious middle-class women for decades. Although college-educated, she stayed at home and devoted herself to the upbringing of the children. She handled all domestic matters, kept a house that was tidy if somewhat stark, and prepared meals of common midwestern fare: fried chicken, pot roast, pork chops, and fried fish. She enforced rules of behavior, counseled restraint, and set a tone of moral uplift in her household. She tried to raise children who were, in her own words, "very moral, kind, giving, social beings, treating other folks the way they want to be treated." Religious instruction played a significant role in her childrearing efforts. As Hugh noted throughout his adult life, this "repressed Midwestern Methodist home" overseen by his mother produced a "Puritanical upbringing."[25]

Yet Grace and Glenn Hefner were not simply hidebound traditionalists. Vestiges of old-fashioned principles certainly remained, but they had drifted far away from the values of provincial Nebraska. In certain ways they had embraced modernity. Not content to be a farmer or village storekeeper, Glenn had attended college and created a career in the corporate world of Chicago. Uprooted from the countryside, the Hefners had abandoned the extended family network that supported a traditional worldview. There was little contact with family as the Hefner boys were growing up. "I always felt as if the family on both sides, there was a remoteness," Hugh recollected. "We were not close to our relatives at all." Moreover, the Hefners had surmounted their modest economic origins, remaining relatively prosperous even during the dark years of the Depression. In fact, on occasion, Grace and Glenn sent money to help relatives back in Nebraska. "I was only vaguely aware of it. I never felt in danger in terms of anything economic," Hugh recalled of the Depression.[26]

In addition, Grace displayed a modern side that was never appreciated fully by her eldest son. Although a moralist, she was a progressive, educated woman who nurtured a liberal social vision and a view of childrearing attuned not only to religion but to the latest theories put forward by psychology. These impulses would shape young Hugh's character quite as much as, and perhaps more than, the residue of "Puritan repression."

Grace had a remarkably liberal worldview in many ways. She was a pacifist who "didn't think there should be any war, and didn't think there should be any implements of war," according to Keith. Far in advance of her time, she denounced racial prejudice and taught her sons tolerance. Once, when they were at the train station, another passenger warned them to avoid an orange juice stand because a black person was squeezing the oranges. "Some people think that black people are different from us and aren't as clean as us and so forth, and that isn't right," Grace immediately told the boys. "Don't pay any attention to that."[27]

Grace's progressive views also surfaced in her opinions on childrearing. As a young mother, she fell under the sway of *Parents* magazine. She subscribed to this journal and relied upon its expert advice on everything from what movies were acceptable for children, to sex education, emotional training, and hygiene habits. What Hugh later interpreted as the fruits of a stern, cold "Puritan" ideology—not kissing on the mouth, skimpy displays of affection, strict rules about bedtime—came, in fact, from the pages of *Parents*. There mothers were told that kissing on the lips spread germs, that sentimentalizing children undermined scientific training, and that children did most of their growing during the sleep hours. As she explained, "I was very sure that what was recommended by *Parents* magazine should be done."[28]

Grace's reliance on this publication reveals much. *Parents* had been founded in 1926, with funding from the Rockefeller Foundation, to promote the most recent scientific findings in the new field of child development. Within a few years it became the largest-selling educational magazine in the world. This publishing venture was part of a larger Progressive crusade in the early twentieth century to utilize modern social science in many areas of education—in schools, among parents, in social work—to create a rational, efficient social order. As the historian Ann Hulbert has written, "A contingent of professional men and progressive-minded women led the way in spreading a new gospel that the child's fate would no longer be entrusted to God or mere custom." They joined in "calling on science to come to the rescue."[29]

Psychology, particularly behaviorism, dominated research in child development in the 1920s, and its strictures filled the pages of *Parents* magazine: enhance your child's development by molding behavior at a young age, pursue strict habit formation, rely on science rather than sentiment. The crack-up of the traditional Victorian family in the decades around the turn of the century had created great emotional and social strains in the American family. Now, with its impressive battery of social science experts, this publication promised to help young, isolated mothers like Grace Hefner shape a new generation of well-adjusted, confident citizens for an efficient modern society.[30]

Thus Grace's parenting, while influenced by her own Victorian upbringing, had a strong progressive element. Her letters to Hugh's teachers adopted psychological language in addressing his difficulties with concentrating on academic subjects. A mastoid infection around age six, she explained to an instructor, had created problems with his hearing and sight but she did not discuss this "handicap" around him for fear that he would "feel inferior." "He is unusually sensitive and whether he has been ridiculed in front of other children and is fearful of its being repeated, or what, I do not know," she wrote to another teacher. "I have been greatly troubled by his lack of adjustment." When Hugh's academic problems persisted and he remained reluctant to answer the telephone or travel to the dentist, she did not react like a good Victorian mother with punishment or admonitions. Instead, Grace concluded that this behavior "was not normal" and took him to an expert for testing. The doctor decided that, again in the language of the new behavioral sciences, his IQ was quite high and "his mind was ahead of his social development."[31]

In fact, Grace's psychology-tinged approach created an atmosphere of indulgence and rationality regarding her children. They "should have their own likes and dislikes, follow their own wants, their own inclinations," she maintained. She listened carefully to Hugh and Keith and tried to discuss issues in a nonthreatening way. While stressing the need for rules, she avoided punishing her children (especially corporal punishment) and offered explanations for parental decisions rather than just imposing her authority. In Grace's words, "I always had a strong sense of duty—you know, this should be done because it was the right thing to do. But I at least tried to explain *why*."[32]

Hugh was Grace's favorite—"If we were both drowning, there was never a question in my mind who she would save, if she could only save one," Keith once said—and her indulgence shaped his character. She listened carefully to his ideas, took him seriously, and nurtured a special bond of communication between them. "I was a kid who, from very early on, was always asking 'why,' and she encouraged that," Hugh would say later. This penchant for independent thinking produced a kind of self-regard that was striking even in his childhood. From a young age, he resented doing anything that he saw as an "obligation," such as going to the neighbors for a social visit or joining parents and brother for a ride in the car. He resisted such things if he saw no purpose in them.[33]

A striking example of Grace's modern childrearing methods involved sexual education. It illustrated how her progressive attachment to psychology was undermining her old-fashioned moralism. In the best Victorian tradition, she found the topic of sexuality to be acutely embarrassing. Her parents had never discussed sex and reproduction with her, she viewed sex outside of marriage as unthinkable, and she found sensuous figures such as Mae West to be offensive. Nonetheless, her modern instincts dictated a scientific approach to the issue. So after consulting *Parents* magazine and a friend trained in child development, she steeled herself, procured an illustrated book, and explained the facts of reproduction to Hugh and Keith. She even answered a couple of questions from one of the boys' playmates, whose outraged mother subsequently telephoned and asked Grace to avoid the topic with her son. Hugh would complain later that all he learned about was the biology of reproduction, and not physical and emotional aspects of sexual intercourse, but Grace believed that she was proceeding according to the latest expert advice: "I thought I was progressive."[34]

Hugh's education in sexual matters received a jolt, however, from a family scandal that even his mother's progressive approach couldn't explain. In 1931, Glenn's father, James Hefner, was arrested in Burlington, Colorado, and tried on four counts of taking "indecent liberties" with three girls aged ten and eleven. The charges accused the sixty-one-year-old man of "willfully and feloniously placing his hands under the clothes of . . . and upon the private parts of" the girls. He was convicted and spent over a year in jail, while his wife rented a room nearby so she could visit him. Grace was so horrified by this crime and fearful of having married into a bad family that she briefly considered taking the two boys and leaving. But Glenn, after visiting his family, came home so completely mortified by the incident that she immediately abandoned such thoughts. Hugh's reaction to this incident was tangled when he learned of it a few years later. He felt disgust at the crime and intense sympathy for his father. Yet he wondered what had caused such aberrant behavior. Somehow, emotional and sexual repression seemed to be at fault. He blamed those who "were trying to control our lives in terms of sexuality," concluding that "the real sinners were people who were trying to make the rules. They were the Puritans."[35]

Thus the family dynamic in the Hefner household—its juxtaposition of Victorian restraint and modern science, moral principles and psychological techniques—had a complex impact on Hugh during his boyhood. Naturally sweet-natured, he loved his parents. While in college, for instance, he wrote Grace and Glenn, "Had I the ability to choose two perfect people for my parents, I don't think I could have found a pair better for me than God did. I shall always love you, and more than that, respect you, for what you are and have been." But as a boy he yearned for greater displays of parental affection. Unaware of *Parents* magazine and its psychological directives, he blamed the repression of a Protestant culture. He also grew sensitive to the pain caused by his parents' emotional reticence. He listened sympathetically when his mother, complaining about Glenn's absences, said "she was very much alone, and couldn't understand why he would have to work such long hours." But he also sympathized with his father's attempts to insulate himself from an impassive wife. "Her children were her life, as in many homes," Hugh explained. "What was there for the father? What was there for the husband?" This convergence of emotional yearnings, both his own and his parents', sent the sensitive boy in search of ways to fill the void.[36]

The Hefner family dynamic, however, also created a child who was extraordinarily self-absorbed. Doted on by his mother and lacking a firm male authority figure, he pursued his own interests with a passionate determination. "Even when Hugh was growing up, he was always so intense [and] he'd be miserable if he couldn't do the thing he wanted," Grace once noted. His parents allowed the boy to have his way with most things and seldom punished him. The only time he was ever spanked was when he once refused to leave his room and join the family to go swimming. Because it occurred so seldom, Hugh felt even more keenly the weight of punishment or restraint when it did occur.[37]

Religion also played a crucial role in shaping the sensibility of the eldest Hefner boy. The family was steeped in traditional Protestantism, regularly attending the Austin Methodist Church while Grace reinforced its messages at home. "We didn't have family prayers, formal devotions, and all that, but . . . we judged our actions by what we thought we should do according to our religious upbringing," she explained. Hugh was a pious child, although subject to the usual juvenile confusions. At age three, he asked his mother, "What is God?" Grace explained that God was a loving father over all of us, so when Glenn came home that evening, the boy said, "Hello, God!" Once, in a moment of tension, Grace overheard Hugh reassure Keith that God would take care of them. "I was pleased to hear of his faith," she reported. Hugh occasionally composed religious poems, such as a 1937 effort titled "Easter" that described Christ's ascension to Heaven.[38]

But boyhood piety gave way to adolescent skepticism. Grace and Glenn insisted that the boys attend Sunday school, but a teenage Hugh resisted after arguing with his teacher about stories or doctrines he found to be nonsensical. He asked, for instance, where the other people came from in the Bible when it explained only Adam and Eve, Cain and Abel. Once again, Grace's modernity triumphed over her traditional Protestant loyalties. She tolerated Hugh's dissent and encouraged him to think for himself. She even allowed the boys to decide whether they would be baptized when they became teenagers. Keith decided to do it, but his older brother did not. And when Hugh refused to attend church a short time later, his mother agreed, provided that he attend the Church League for teenagers on Sunday evening. Hugh admitted that "even though my parents were very religious, it wasn't dogmatic religion." Nonetheless, young Hefner was growing uncomfortable with the moral universe of the Methodist Church.[39]

As much as family and religion, American popular culture molded Hugh Hefner's boyhood character. "Pop culture was my other parent," he described later. "The movies and the music, particularly, were the alternative where I escaped into other dreams and fantasies." He went to movies as early as age five and recalled seeing in the early 1930s *Smoky,* the story of a horse, the Flash Gordon serial with Buster Crabbe, and Mickey Mouse cartoons. Detective stories, horror fiction, comic strips, and adventure tales all inspired his juvenile imagination as images of Little Orphan Annie, Jack Armstrong, Tom Mix, Buck Rogers, and Dick Tracy danced in his head.[40]

Hugh cherished particular favorites. He idolized the cartoonist Milton Caniff, creator of the comic strip *Terry and the Pirates.* Pat Ryan, the protagonist, was a debonair adventurer whose pipe-smoking later inspired Hefner to take up the habit. The movie *Tarzan and His Mate* also left a big imprint. The boy imbibed its images of virtuous nature, rapacious white hunters, and benevolent jungle creatures. "What do you get from animals that you don't get from people all the time?" Hefner explained. "Non-judgmental love."[41]

Indeed, movies became his greatest boyhood passion. He would go to local theaters two or three times a week, sometimes seeing a double feature in the afternoon with his brother and then another with his parents in the evening. He loved mystery films, horror films, and westerns, but musicals inspired his greatest devotion. Throughout the 1930s and early 1940s he sat enthralled by Fred Astaire and Ginger Rogers, Nelson Eddy and Jeanette MacDonald, and the Busby Berkeley films. He had boyhood crushes on stars such as Alice Faye, Betty Grable, and Deanna Durbin. The reason musicals had such a powerful impact, he later concluded, was that "you could say things in the lyrics of songs that you couldn't express any other way—to begin a romance, to express lost love, and . . . to feel the dreams and the yearnings." In musicals, he believed, "What you are trying to do is fill that yearning to be loved."[42]

Popular culture filled an emotional void in the boy's life. Craving more affection than he was receiving at home, he embraced the intensely romantic images and music found in the Hollywood musicals of the Depression era. This bright, sensitive child saw the movies as a way to connect with life. In the darkened theater, he recalled years later, "You could be transported to another world—the world of the imagination. And that, in turn was then reflected in the life that was most important to me, which was the life of my own imagination."[43]

Thoroughly caught up in America's modern culture of self-fulfillment, this midwestern youth moved toward adulthood. Entering high school, he did not yet know that it would be a golden age in his life, one he would ever after try to recapture.

III

Hugh Hefner enrolled at Steinmetz High School in January 1940. Although colored by typical adolescent angst, it unfolded as a remarkably positive period, with two events proving crucial. First, he became the leader of a social group of close friends, and second, around age seventeen, he created the persona of an imaginative, romantic figure whose fantasies dominated the endeavors of his pals. In important ways, this became a template for his life.

Bursting with energy, the teenager plunged headlong into numerous school activities that allowed his creativity to flower. Journalism provided one outlet. As a sophomore he started a small paper called the *Hour Glass,* and the following year he began working as a reporter, cartoonist, and circulation manager for the regular school paper, the *Steinmetz Star*. Theater also attracted Hefner, and he appeared in several school plays. He also wrote, directed, and appeared in a fifteen-minute horror film titled "Return from the Dead" that was shot with a 16-millimeter camera borrowed from a neighbor and featured two of his best friends.[44]

More importantly, however, he created a gang of close friends. It began with Hefner's strong friendship with Jim Brophy. The two boys had known one another since grade school, but in high school the bond between them became unbreakable. They presented different personalities. Brophy, a whiz at science and an excellent student, pursued ham radio as a hobby and won several science awards at Steinmetz. He would graduate fourth in a class of just over two hundred and would go on to forge a career as a physics professor. Hefner, while very bright, tended to be a lackadaisical student who poured his energy into creative endeavors such as writing, acting, and cartooning. But the pair shared great intelligence along with an absurd, slapstick sense of humor. "[We] thought each other to be hysterically funny," Brophy recalled. "Our personalities were very different, but we sparked each other's imaginations." Hefner described them as the "Hope and Crosby" of Steinmetz High as they played off of one another with jokes and gags. They even dressed similarly with flannel or checkered shirts and saddle shoes.[45]

The Hefner-Brophy friendship became the focal point of a Steinmetz group who began hanging out together by 1942. Composed equally of boys and girls, the gang included Hefner and Dorothy

Novak, Jim Brophy and Janie Borson, Betty Conklin and Bob
Clousten, and Dorothy Diephouse and Bob Haugland. They went
to movies and dances, played jazz records, threw parties with innocent kissing games, and drove around in cars borrowed from parents,
and Hefner's identity became wrapped up in what he described as
"the whole beautiful gang." But little of the fun happened at the
Hefner household. According to Brophy, it was "dark and dull . . .
[and] there was not warmth or real interchange in that household.
I think that's one reason why Hef lived so intensely in our little circle
of friends."[46]

Then came a dramatic change in Hefner's life. In the summer
before his junior year, he had become interested in Betty Conklin, an
outgoing girl who played the drums and idolized Gene Krupa. He saw
her as the ultimate coed and they learned to jitterbug together, but
when school started, she invited someone else to a hayride. Hefner
was crushed and carried a torch for many years. Determined to make
himself more attractive and popular, he decided on a personal overhaul. He began to refer to himself as "Hef," adopted a more stylish
wardrobe and suave manner, improved his dancing, began using hip
expressions, and, in his words, "became the imaginary adolescent,
the teenager that I wanted to be." Writing in 1942, he described this
new persona as

a lanky, Sinatra-like guy with a love for loud flannel shirts and
cords in the way of garb, and jive for music. He looks and acts a
lot like a High School kid you'd see in a movie. A very original
fellow, he has his own style of jiving and slang expressions. . . .
He calls everyone "Slug" or "Fiend" and his pet expression is
"Jeeps Creeps."[47]

This personal reinvention made Hefner one of the most popular
students at Steinmetz High. Teaming with Jim Brophy, he emerged
as a social leader whose gang became an elite group. "To be associated with the famous team of 'Hefner-Brophy' was, for me, to be at
the highest social pinnacle in the school," Janie Sellers wrote Hefner
many years later. "Together, I felt that you ran the whole school."
Indeed, Hefner took center stage at Steinmetz. Increasingly popular, he parlayed his energy and creativity into election as president
of the Student Council at the start of his senior year. Eventually, his

classmates voted him among the top three in the categories of "Most Likely to Succeed," "Most Popular Boy," "Class Humorist," "Best Orator," "Best Dancer," and "Most Artistic."[48]

At this time, Hefner also began a project that would preoccupy him for the rest of his life. He began to chronicle his experiences in a cartoon autobiography. Inventing a character for himself called "Goo Heffer," the youth composed dozens of comic strips that followed every twist and turn in his gang's activities in funny, charming, and occasionally poignant style. Sometimes he fictionalized their encounters a bit to add drama or humor. Hefner would pass the strips around among the group, who enjoyed them immensely, before carefully pasting them into scrapbooks. The adolescent justified the project on several grounds: he liked to draw, he often found school to be boring, it would entertain his friends, and it would provide an interesting record of his teenage years to look back on in later life.[49]

But there were also deeper impulses at work. Quite self-consciously, the cartoons centered on the author, self-described variously as "our hero," a "Sinatra-type of guy," or "the type of high school kid you would see in the movies." They made Hefner the pivot around which the gang revolved, and his descriptions of their life became the prevailing ones. "Hef always had a strong interest in self," noted Brophy. "He loved living in his imagination." At some level, Hefner was aware of this self-promotion. "In the comic book, you create a world in which the hero of the story is you, and you include your friends in the story," he observed later. "And you pass it around, and you are the center of that little world that you created." Hefner's vibrant imagination also came into play. While based on real people and events, the stories offered a narrative where, in his own words, "The truth is twisted to make a better comic. . . . And with the characters the same thing is true." This blurring of fact and fantasy, he admitted, "may be confusing, especially since photographs of a lot of them [his friends] are put here. And we'll admit it is difficult to photograph a fictional character. Well, I'm confused too."[50]

Hefner's talent for imaginative recreation gained strength from his immersion in popular culture. His adolescent interests ran the gamut of pop culture venues in 1940s America: swing dancing and music, cartoons and radio plays, slick paper magazines, and Hollywood movies. The teenager loved the big band music of Glenn Miller, Tommy Dorsey, and Harry James and even wrote a swing tune titled "The A-Card Blues." He became a crusader for student rights regarding music and dancing, complaining publicly about the staid school dances. "The majority of the students who dance prefer jive, but the moment you start even a simple jive break, someone steps up and stops you," he grumbled. "If the Friday night dances are for us students, why not give us the kind of music we enjoy?" As president of the Student Council, he worked unsuccessfully to have a jukebox placed in the cafeteria so students could dance during lunch hour. An article titled "A Saga in Jive" by "Hep Hef" playfully related a story in jive talk. "If you Stein studes are really hep you ought to be able to dig the jive talk," he wrote. "I say you are a bunch of squares. Well, let's see."[51]

Hefner also began exhibiting a trait that would define much of his adult life—a powerful attraction to females. He displayed a dawning awareness of sexuality that, while steeped in innocence and romance, veered close to obsession. The introverted youngster had several schoolboy crushes on various girls before finally taking one of them to see a movie in eighth grade on his first real date. During his first two years of high school, Hefner was attracted to a pretty girl named Beverly Allen, whom he fell for when she kissed him while playing Post Office at a party. The next few years saw a parade of high school girlfriends: Betty Conklin, Edith Biowski, Dorothy Novak.[52]

As his interest in the opposite sex flowered, the adolescent Hefner bridled at social restrictions regarding the mysterious, yet compelling area of sex. A 1938 article in *Life* magazine, titled "A Tragedy of Youth," had made a deep impression. It told the sad tale of a teenage boy and girl in New York City who, after she became pregnant, made a suicide pact that produced one death and a murder trial for the survivor. The story resonated with twelve-year-old Hefner, who, while not completely understanding the issues, saw it as an example of social rules that created misery rather than happiness. The following year he saw the rerun of a pre-code film with his mother. When one of the female characters made a suggestive remark, Grace whispered, "Well, they couldn't get away with that today." Hugh thought silently, "Gee, I wish they could." In high school, he argued with his mother about the wisdom and propriety of having sex with girls. Grace insisted that "you run the risk of bringing a life into the world that you have no way of taking care of, and you don't have the right." Her eldest son contended that since pregnancy could be avoided, sexual relations should be permitted. Even as a teenager, Hefner chafed against authority and its proscription of sex.[53]

Meanwhile, Hefner's growing interest in females and sexuality found an enticing outlet. In the eighth grade he discovered *Esquire* magazine in the basement of a girlfriend's house—her father was a subscriber—and started to read old copies of this men's magazine. He became particularly fascinated with the pinup drawings by George Petty, whose lush, idealized depictions of women in various states of undress had begun to appear in the magazine in 1933. He started collecting "Petty Girls" and hanging them on the walls of his bedroom. A bit later he discovered pinups drawn by the artist Alberto Vargas, also in *Esquire,* and began adding "Vargas Girls" to his collection. Grace disapproved, but her modern sensibility overcame her religious scruples and she did not make him take them down. Keith, interested in acting, had tacked up posters of movie stars in his bedroom, and she decided that both her boys should be allowed to pursue their own ideas. "I think for a supposedly narrow-minded person, I was rather broad minded to allow them to do those things," she observed later. One of Hefner's favorite Petty Girl drawings portended the future—an attractive young woman whimsically outfitted in a pink bunny suit complete with long ears.[54]

Hefner's actual romantic life, however, failed to meet the *Esquire* standard. Instead, it reflected a typical teenage pattern of awkward advances, flashes of euphoria, occasional rejection, recurrent confusion, and fun. It also embodied his consuming desire to be in love. As Brophy explained, "Hef was constantly falling in love. . . . If he wasn't in love, he felt incomplete and unhappy." But Hefner was no teenage lothario. Often shy and awkward with girls, he offered a bright, sweet, energetic temperament and an underwhelming physical presence. He "was unusually skinny," said Janie Borson, one of the gang. "That was his problem with the girls. We were looking for Tyrone Power." But as "Goo Heffer" philosophized in the cartoon autobiography, "If ya don't get mixed up with wimmen, ya don't have no fun. So you're miserable. If ya do, their friends get sore if ya hit the rocks. And with no friends, you're miserable. So it's evident that wimmen are gonna cause ya misery no matter what. But I love 'em anyway."[55]

By the last year of high school, Hefner had gained a little sexual experience. Going steady with a couple of girls had led to kissing and petting, and occasionally he even got into trouble with his mild-mannered parents for going too far. Glenn became furious one evening when Hugh arrived home in the early morning hours after a late date. His father burst out, "'Where the god-damn hell have you been?' And it was the one and only time in my entire life that I ever heard him swear," Hefner recalled. Another time he cuddled with a girl in the rumble seat as he was out driving around with friends. When the father warned sternly that such behavior was not acceptable, the son observed that the edict "of course, gave the whole idea of a rumble seat a very romantic connection."[56]

Thus during childhood and adolescence Hugh Hefner immersed himself in a fantasy world that he created from available elements in his young life. A family atmosphere of emotional repression created longings for emotional connection. As Victorian tradition vied with modern social science in the Hefner household, he encountered vestiges of restraint while enjoying a general atmosphere of indulgence and encouragement. Authority appeared distant, abstract, and vaguely defined. When strictures were imposed by parents, school, or church, they seemed all the more severe because of their infrequency.

For this bright, creative child, popular culture promised happiness. Movies, cartoons, magazines, swing music, and dancing presented visions of self-fulfillment where romance, adventure, and intense personal experience were the norm. By the time he became a teenager Hefner viewed his life in terms of a movie plot and himself in terms of a cinematic character. Restless, ambitious, and increasingly committed to his own fantasies, he desperately sought emotional satisfaction. Like growing numbers in the culture of modern America, he felt entitled to it.

But the key question, of course, was how to find such gratification. As he left the warm cocoon of high school in 1944, Hugh Hefner entertained vague hopes of being a cartoonist with his own strip, or of working for a magazine as a writer. But first he was forced to confront an international crisis that had swept through the lives of all Americans, even those living sheltered lives in midwestern cities.

2

Boot Camp, College, and Kinsey

As Hugh Hefner prepared to graduate from high school in early 1944, he faced an uncertain future. On the one hand, he had deep misgivings about abandoning the golden days of late adolescence and his gang of pals at Steinmetz High. On the other hand, the wider world beckoned. Since late 1941, World War II had dominated American life, and respectable young men were expected to enter the military during this national crisis. Young Hefner felt the obligation keenly. With determination, and a bit of trepidation, he joined the army and prepared for a new stage in his life.

I

It began with girls. As with so many other episodes in his adulthood, Hefner's embrace of military life became entangled with his romantic relationships. Just as he was about to graduate, he fell into an intense, if innocent, love affair with Janie Borson. The girlfriend of his best pal, Jim Brophy, she had idolized Hefner and admired his creative talent for years and the two had maintained a close friendship throughout high school. By accident, they found themselves alone together in early 1944 a couple of times and several long, soulful talks produced a passionate kiss. They wrote anguished letters to one another trying to sort out their feelings, but both were reluctant to betray Brophy. An unexpected solution appeared when Hefner met someone else.[1]

Shortly after graduation, Hefner attended a party of Steinmetz High kids and met a young woman who had been a classmate. He recognized the face but did not really know her. Mildred Williams was the type of girl he found attractive—cute, vivacious, with dark hair, bangs, and bobby socks. The two talked for a long time, flirted a bit, and eventually she sat on his lap. Later he discovered that she had done so to make another boy jealous, but there was a mutual attraction. By the end of the evening they had made plans to see each other again.[2]

Millie played the violin, was athletic, and came from a blue-collar family. Her mother was a housewife and devoted Catholic who regularly shepherded Millie and her four sisters to Mass. Her father, a streetcar conductor and later a bus driver, had left the Catholic Church years before. An avid reader, he had educated himself and became an avowed communist, often commenting to his daughter, "We should have it as good as they do in Russia." He also tended to be very strict, even authoritarian, with his family and absolutely refused to allow his daughters to date until they were sixteen.[3]

Hugh and Millie had several dates during the two weeks between the time they met and the day he left for military service. He picked her up from her job at the Mars candy company and they would have a soda or see a movie. Eager to be in love as always, Hefner fell hard for this young woman and promised to write her faithfully while he was away. She promised to do the same, although with less conviction. True to his deepest instincts, Hefner enveloped Millie in a romantic fantasy. This relationship, which existed largely on paper except for a couple of brief furloughs when he returned to Chicago, would sustain him over the next two years.[4]

Hefner, still a boy at age seventeen—he stood about five foot ten inches and weighed 115 pounds—started his stint in the armed services as a cadet in the Army Specialized Training Reserve program.

As his alter ego, Goo Heffer, noted in the comic autobiography, he was leaving comfortable surroundings and would soon "be carrying a gun as are so many of his age in this age. Goo doesn't like this change, any more than most of us but he's 'stuck with it' and so will try to make the most of it."[5]

He left Chicago in March 1944 for the University of Wisconsin campus to undergo initial training. Arriving with several suitcases containing all the amenities of home, including typewriter, alarm clock, and clothes hangers, he bunked with two new roommates in the three-to-a-room dormitories. Over the next several weeks, the new enlistees studied academic subjects, participated in an ROTC curriculum, and practiced marching. Hefner also lugged along the several volumes of his comic autobiography, which he shared with his bunkmates and other cadets in the evenings. Drawn into the orbit of his life, the trainees enjoyed the comic strips so much that they would grill Hefner about his high school experiences and pals. One even asked about the possibility of writing to one of the girls depicted in the comic.[6]

Like many young men in the service away from home for the first time, Hefner grew sentimental and homesick. On May 14, 1944, for example, he wrote a long letter to his mother and father baring his emotions:

> There is a great deal that I feel that I have never said. There's a great deal of gratitude that I have never really expressed. There are things that I never really appreciated fully until I came here to Wisconsin—they are the things you've done and sacrificed for me. I've felt them more in the last few months than ever before. . . . When I look back I realize how very lucky both Keith and I have been to have grown up in a home with so much love and fairness. In what I would term a "democratic" home. . . . When I learn of how some fellas or girls have been brought up with too much discipline or not enough love it makes me feel plenty sorry for them and plenty grateful to you. . . . I want you to be proud of me. I think you're the best mom, and pop's the best dad, that a fellow could have.

This letter illustrated Hefner's sweet temperament, but also suggested that serious disgruntlement with his childhood was the product of later life.[7]

One aspect of the army shocked Hefner, however. For the first time in his life he encountered social attitudes far different from the liberal values he had imbibed in childhood. In particular, outbursts of anti-Semitism and racism punctuated discussions among the cadets and he found the bigotry hard to digest. He heard nasty cracks about fellow soldiers who were Jewish and derogatory comments about a local Jewish girl he took to a few dances, incidents that caused him to confront the speakers a couple of times. While there were no African Americans in his training group, Hefner also heard racist slurs, such as references to the jazz he liked as "nigger music." In a letter home, he acknowledged that out in the world "you meet all kinds of prejudices and hatreds and it makes me glad and proud to know I have no such hatreds." But when he came home on furlough, he complained that his mother had "created a fairy land" and overprotected him from the real world during his childhood. She had taught him that "all people are good people, and all people have the same values and the same noble thoughts and ambitions," Keith Hefner reported. "So that you're not prepared when—wham!—it isn't so."[8]

After several months at Madison, Hefner was processed through the Fort Sheridan reception center in Illinois in June 1944 and began a typical, nomadic army stint. He departed first for basic training at Camp Hood in Texas. Things now had become deadly serious, as he noted in his comic autobiography: "Schooling for death, or for the preservation of his own life." He did well in basic training, suffering injury only from a serious sunburn gained in the oppressive climate. He won a sharpshooter badge for firing the M1 rifle and made it through "Killer College" at the end of basic training where troops went through maneuvers while throwing real grenades, hearing live ammunition zinging overhead, and completing a twenty-five-mile hike with full equipment. He also did extensive antitank training during the last period of his stay at Camp Hood.[9]

After a brief furlough in Chicago, Hefner reported to Fort Chaffee, Arkansas, in October 1944 for additional training as an infantry rifleman. After more instruction at Camp Gruber in Oklahoma, he was ordered to Fort Meade, Maryland. There he awaited processing to go to a port of embarkation for active overseas duty. Then came news that changed his army life enormously. He had been assigned to the "Chairborne Infantry" by getting a desk job as a clerk in S-1, or personnel, because of his typing skills. A delighted Hefner appreciated this "dandy break" because, in his words, he liked "Washington's women very much." A series of clerk assignments followed in Camp Adair near Salem, Oregon, and Camp Pickett, Virginia.[10]

Throughout his army days, Hefner pursued creative endeavors. He drew numerous cartoons for the army newspapers and wrote a satirical song titled "I'd Make a Hell of a Good Civilian" that his company sang and marched to. He regularly attended dances at his various postings and found diversion in his favorite boyhood hobby, noting, "My escape, always, throughout the army days, was the movies." The army showed first-run movies to the troops almost weekly and he frequented theaters in nearby towns whenever possible. And, of course, he worked steadily on his comic autobiography, drawings dozens of strips depicting Goo Heffer and his life in the army. Hanging over Hefner's head, however, was threat of active deployment either for combat or, by the summer of 1945, as part of a force occupying Japan. In early August 1945, he commented in his comic autobiography that Hiroshima and Nagasaki "marks the beginning of an age, the Atomic Age. . . . Where does Goo go from here? Home or overseas for occupation?"[11]

Meanwhile, Hefner courted Millie Williams from afar. From March 15 to August 27, 1945, for example, he wrote her over eighty letters. Addressed to "Dearest Millie," they combined gushy expressions of romantic feeling with confessions of loneliness and boredom. In a letter of March 27, 1945, he described how hearing a popular song on the radio titled "I've Said It" made him think of her:

> Music like that, and some of these wonderful nights, really put me into moods. I dream of being with you. Of being far out in the country on a cool spring evening in the car, with the radio turned on softly. Or out on some hillside on a beautiful spring evening with not a care in the world and no one to bother us. Of course, being a fella in love, I guess I think of some slightly different things than you do at times. Quite a bit on the physical side.[12]

Hefner's infatuation with Millie, however, did not keep him from dating many other girls while in the army. In Wisconsin, he met a local high school girl and took her on several dates. He wrote many long letters to Janie Borson, with whom he kept a strong friendship, and in one confessed that his relationship with Millie might not last. "We're too different in too many ways and every now and then I know I'm still the same old wolf 'cause I get other femmes on the mind," he wrote. While in Washington he dated several girls, and upon arrival in Salem, Oregon, a college town, he attended dozens of dances and became involved with at least two young women. As he would note later, during his army days he "created this world of romantic adventure" that saw many casual dates but no serious emotional involvement.[13]

Hefner's military career finally ground to a halt with the general demobilization after the conclusion of World War II. Early in 1946 he made corporal and a few months later received an honorable discharge from the U.S. Army. In May 1946 he returned to Chicago to get on with his life.[14]

II

Like many other young men after World War II, Hugh Hefner was at loose ends after his discharge from the military. He attended a couple of dances at Steinmetz High School to recapture some of his high school glory, but his pals were gone and things weren't the same. He revisited Salem to see the girls he had dated, but once again was unable to recapture the fun times he had enjoyed there. Finally, he took an art class in anatomy drawing at the Chicago Art Institute in summer 1946. But overall, as he confessed, "in Chicago I felt really lost."[15]

Millie, in the meantime, was attending the University of Illinois at Urbana, some ninety miles south of Chicago. Although neither she nor Hefner was quite sure about their relationship—she also had dated others during his army service—she had accepted his pin. So Hefner made a decision that met several objectives. He enrolled at the university on the GI Bill, which allowed him to escape the aimlessness of Chicago, take steps toward finding a career, and be with his girlfriend. Moreover, after taking several tests administered by the government, he discovered that he could get advanced credit that would, in combination with a heavy course schedule, allow him to graduate in two and a half years.[16]

So in September 1946, Hefner embarked upon a college career. His expectations were somewhat unrealistic. As with so many other things, his vision of college life had come out of the movies and centered on "raccoon coats and dances and jalopies," as he put it. But the influx of GIs after the war was changing the atmosphere at American universities as they became more crowded, more serious, and more career-oriented. After spending a semester living in a university-approved house, he was accepted into the Granada Club, an independent rooming house for young men off Green Street. He became roommates with Bob Preuss, established a fresh circle of friends, and threw himself into a new round of experiences.[17]

Hefner had vague hopes of being a cartoonist or writer. But he decided to major in psychology because of his fascination with human behavior and motivation. "I felt that if I could unlock those secrets and understand that, then it would serve me very well as a writer and in life." Minoring in creative writing and art, he performed quite well scholastically, and was pledged by Phi Eta Sigma, the freshman scholastic honorary society, and initiated into Chi Gamma Iota, the veterans' scholastic honorary society. At the end of his freshman year, he received recognition for "excellence in scholarship" at the Annual Honors Day convocation. By his senior year, he was ranked in the top 10 percent of his class and allowed to do some independent study.[18]

Hefner also pursued artistic endeavors. He regularly published cartoons both in the *Daily Illini,* the official student newspaper at the university, and *Shaft,* a campus humor magazine. He crossed paths with Gene Shalit, who worked as the sports editor of the newspaper and editor of the magazine. His favorite class in college was a writing course offered by Samson Raphaelson, the prominent screenwriter and playwright, who was visiting the campus. He had authored *The Jazz Singer* and several comedies for Ernst Lubitsch and later would write *Suspicion* for Alfred Hitchcock. This writing seminar had only a handful of students and it met regularly at Raphaelson's home, where he would talk intimately with students about his craft. Hefner was enthralled by this liberal Jewish intellectual. "He was like a mentor for me, and an inspiration because of what he stood for," he said later.[19]

Plunging into his studies and experiencing the intellectual excitement of university life, he received a quiet gesture of support from his mother. Perhaps sensing a lack of confidence in her oldest son, Grace decided to inform him that a boyhood intelligence test had disclosed a genius IQ of 152. On Mother's Day 1948, an appreciative Hefner wrote a long letter expressing a renewed faith in his abilities and appreciation for loving parents:

> First, a confession: not since high school have I had any real faith in my own ability, or in the future. The news about my I.Q. has given me the spark I lost so long ago. I cannot express to you the difference it has wrought in my outlook, in my innermost feelings. Egotism is a dangerous thing, but self confidence in one's own ability is so very necessary to happy living. . . .
>
> My childhood, my growing into manhood, were wonderfully happy years. No one is more responsible for that happiness than you. I remember the long hours spent with both Keith and me; the time and energy you sacrificed. . . . There is no way in which I can ever adequately repay you for all that you have done for me.[20]

No bookworm, Hefner pursued a variety of extracurricular activities during his college years. Football became a passion, and the 1946 Fighting Illini team had no greater fan as it won the conference title. He filled his scrapbook with enthusiastic descriptions of the games and heroic sketches of key players. After Illinois beat UCLA in the Rose Bowl by a score of 41–14, he even exclaimed, "Who cares if communism is moving across Europe and Palestine is caught in the throes of civil war?" At the Granada Club, Hefner achieved a reputation as an intense but fun-loving guy. He loved playing long games of Monopoly, gin rummy, and bridge with his housemates. He also developed an interest in airplanes and by 1947 had taken enough lessons and logged enough flying time to get his private pilot's license.[21]

Music also occupied much time and energy. Hefner subscribed to *Down Beat*, listened faithfully to Dave Garroway, an influential DJ, and followed the twists and turns of taste in popular music. His record collection, based on singers such as Billie Holiday and Peggy Lee, became legendary in the Granada Club for its size and avant-garde quality. Hefner built and painted a pair of cabinets to house his collection, which he expanded at every opportunity. Dances, of course, occurred frequently on campus and he attended regularly with Millie. During his last year at the University of Illinois, Hefner even sang in a combo with a couple of friends from the Granada Club accompanying him on bass and guitar. Advertisements described him as "The Boy with the Bop in his Voice" and the "Campus Ballad King." He imitated the style of a popular singer, Frankie Laine, and performed his songs, such as "My Desire" and "A Sunday Kind of Love."[22]

In reflective moments, Hefner wrestled with the religious legacy of his childhood. For his final project in Raphaelson's writing seminar, he presented a gothic play with a religious theme. Its plot focused on a biochemist's claim that he had stumbled across proof that God did not exist, a discovery that led to anguished debates with his son and, eventually, patricide and suicide. The story represented "a conflict over whether the world is better off with or without the knowledge," the author explained. "Is truth all important, or is the world better left in ignorance?"[23]

Hefner also continued a years-long debate with his parents over the validity of Christian doctrine. After Grace sent him a pious article titled "Goodness and Decency Belong on Top," he replied politely but skeptically. Traditional religion was "trying to sell an absolute standard in moral and spiritual life, and fact seems to strongly suggest that no such thing exists—that morals are a relative thing, etc.," he wrote. While he continued to believe in God, he doubted whether a just deity would judge people living in the wilds of South America or the cities of China according to Western Christianity. "I have a much better philosophy of my own—an altruistic seeking for happiness on this earth," Hefner added. "No absolute standards—instead, the judgment of each act measured in terms of the amount of happiness or unhappiness it will bring to people."[24]

Throughout college, Hefner poured much of his emotional energy into his relationship with Millie Williams. They went steady during his entire two and a half years in Urbana. She lived in Colonial Manor, an independent house for women, and was already a junior when he arrived. "Millie and I are going great guns at the moment," Hefner wrote to Janie Borson just a few weeks before starting college. "When she finds out about all my G.I. romances she'll probably never speak to me. But then again, mebbe' she will for I've learned she's had several of her own since I went away."[25]

Indeed, the relationship was somewhat tenuous from the outset. They had spent very little time together during Hefner's military service, relying on a "paper romance" while dating other people. She was pinned to another boy in Urbana when she accepted Hugh's pin. In practical terms, the two had very different interests—she liked athletics and classical music while he favored dancing and jazz— and when they played as bridge partners, bickering always seemed to occur. Both expressed misgivings about the relationship, and a despondent Hefner once kept a chart of how he felt about her over a several-month period. He found the highest ratings came when she was away.[26]

But their lust was bubbling furiously. Throughout their college years, Hugh and Millie would drive into the country and pet heavily. The sexual frustration became palpable as he would pull back at the last minute from actual sexual intercourse because she was afraid of becoming pregnant and failing to graduate. Occasionally they engaged in oral sex. But both found these intimate encounters—racing to the edge of consummation, then throwing on the brakes to avoid disaster—to be emotionally draining. Millie saw it as "destructive." Hugh described it sardonically as "a relationship held together by two and a half years of foreplay." Finally, as Millie was about to graduate in the spring of 1948, they decided to lose their virginity and went away for the weekend to the nearby town of Danville. Predictably, it was a letdown. They stayed in a seedy hotel, saw a lousy movie on Sunday, and found the actual sexual act to be disappointing after such an enormous buildup. "It was not a very romantic weekend," Hefner recalled.[27]

But Hefner, true to his nature, remained determined to be in love. Despite misgivings, he propped up the relationship and talked regularly of marriage. Millie, equally uncertain, went along because "I didn't see any alternative to it, to be perfectly honest. . . . He kept insisting that I was the one he wanted to spend his life with." Hefner created a fantasy of romance and placed Millie at the center of it, even when both of them sensed it was overblown. By the time she graduated in the late spring of 1948, they were talking seriously of marriage. Even though he harbored doubts about the relationship, whenever Millie hesitated he would reassure her and insist that she was "just being nervous about the wedding coming up," she recalled.[28]

In the meantime, however, Hefner had become enthralled with one of the most controversial books to appear in postwar America. It dealt with a subject that increasingly fascinated him both personally and intellectually—sex.

III

In 1948, Alfred Kinsey published *Sexual Behavior in the Human Male*. Described by one critic as "the most talked about book of the twentieth century," it sold some 200,000 copies within two months of its release. Reviews appeared everywhere—newspapers and magazines, journals of opinion, literary and professional journals—and the pollster George Gallup reported that one out of five Americans had read or heard about the book within a short time after its publication. As one scholar has put it, "Overnight 'Kinsey' became a household word, his name forever embedded in popular culture."[29]

Why did Kinsey galvanize the popular imagination? Confident that the erosion of Victorian standards had prepared Americans to engage sexuality more frankly, he examined sexual behavior dispassionately and presented his results as scientific fact "divorced from questions of moral value and social customs." Kinsey and his staff interviewed several hundred men at great length, asking dozens of detailed questions, and analyzed a host of variables—social class and ethnicity, age, marital status, geographical location, religious affiliation, educational level, job or profession—that influenced sexual activity. Kinsey found a widespread violation of traditional sexual standards with regard to masturbation, petting, and premarital or extramarital sex. He delved into more controversial subjects by introducing his famous heterosexual-homosexual continuum, suggesting that premarital chastity hindered sexual fulfillment, and exploring the nature of orgasms. When a companion study, *Sexual Behavior in the Human Female*, was published in 1953, it showed American women sharing in the same varied sexual behavior. By bringing discussion of sexuality out into the open, Kinsey signaled a new era of sexual frankness in American life.[30]

Americans reacted immediately. The Kinsey Report, as it became known, reflected a loosening of sexual mores that had been occurring since early in the twentieth century. Supporters stressed that this researcher had merely exposed to view the actual behavior of Americans and that these facts must be faced in order to forge realistic moral principles and social policies. But Kinsey's findings also shocked a middle-class society committed to consumer conformity and traditional morality. Critics of *Sexual Behavior in the Human Male* denounced it for encouraging a degradation of American morality and mounting an attack on the family structure. More sophisticated critiques chided Kinsey for focusing on the biology of sex while neglecting important cultural, psychological, emotional, and social dimensions. But regardless of attitude, a majority of Americans probably agreed with *Time* magazine that Kinsey's most striking achievement had been his "open discussion of sex . . . which got such matters as homosexuality, masturbation, coitus, and orgasm into most papers and family magazines."[31]

Hefner was primed for reaction to the Kinsey uproar. His personal frustrations with Millie and their physical relationship had created emotional agitation over issues of sexuality. In addition, his healthy interest in girls and sex since adolescence had grown into a preoccupation during his college days. Even as he prepared to depart for the University of Illinois in August 1946, he joked to Janie Borson, "Finished my course of drawing nekkid women at the Art Institute last Friday. Considered continuing my study at the Rialto [burlesque theater] but the gals move around too much there." Over the next couple of years, Hefner became fixated on sex as an expression of both his thwarted physical desires and his emotional inclination to create fantasies of self-fulfillment.[32]

Many of Hefner's collegiate cartoons for the *Daily Illini* and *Shaft*, for instance, had sexual themes. One showed a cop approaching a male and female student necking in a car parked along the street. The guy looks out and says, "Whatsamatter? Whatsamatter? I paid my nickel [in the parking meter]!" Another displayed two guys drawing a naked young woman in an art class on anatomy, as one says incredulously, "And we get three hours credit for it too?" A more elaborate cartoon featured one panel where a guy is chasing a gal as the caption says, "In the spring a young man's fancy lightly turns to . . ." A second panel shows her turning around and chasing him as the caption reads, "What a girl's been thinking of all year long!"[33]

Shaft, for which Hefner became managing editor during his second year at Illinois, became a particular venue for his sexual enthusiasms.

He introduced a new feature to the humor magazine titled "Coed of the Month" that was a prototype for the *Playboy* Playmates. It offered an enticing photograph along with a brief description of her activities, hobbies, interests, and plans for the future. In an editorial column, he noted that while some students had lobbied for a special "sex issue," he found the suggestion redundant: "Every issue of *Shaft* is a sex issue." In April 1948, *Look* ran an article on college humor magazines and omitted Hefner's publication. In a subsequent letter to the editor, he complained, "You neglected the lustiest, bustiest of them all—Illinois' *Shaft!*"[34]

Hefner's behavior also suggested a growing preoccupation with sexual matters. Bob Preuss, a roommate at the Granada House, was struck by his candor in talking about sex. "I remember him talking about coming and penetration—he was open," Preuss recalled. "He would talk about stuff I'd never say." Hefner also deployed sexual frankness in his relationship with Millie, telling her about liaisons with girls during his army days. Once, he even revealed that he had petted with one of her roommates, as well as with a couple of other young women, during the summer when she was gone. Hefner thought he was being honest, but she saw it as an attempt to gain emotional advantage in their relationship.[35]

Like nothing else, however, Kinsey's *Sexual Behavior in the Human Male* electrified Hefner. It confirmed his growing sense that sex was central to the human experience and that Americans had enshrouded it in mists of superstition and hypocrisy. In a brief review in *Shaft* of "what may be 1948's most important book," he noted that Kinsey's results indicated that "if American laws were rigidly enforced, ninety-five percent of all men and boys would be jailed as sex offenders." Hefner reported that the book was disturbing because it "makes obvious the lack of understanding and realistic thinking that have gone into the formulation of our sex standards and laws. Our moral pretenses, our hypocrisy on matters of sex have led to incalculable frustration, delinquency, and unhappiness."[36]

Hefner's fascination with Kinsey colored his cartoons. A summer 1948 offering in the *Daily Illini* depicted a furtive guy in a dark trench coat sidling up to the desk of the campus bookstore. A clerk says to another, "He wants to know if we'd be interested in handling an illustrated version of the Kinsey report." Another showed a guy and gal sitting in a parked convertible. Wearing a low-cut dress, she is looking angrily out of the car while he holds his reddened cheek and pleads, "Aw, c'mon baby, I'll never make the Kinsey Report if you act like that."[37]

But Kinsey also became a catalyst for Hefner's thinking in a larger sense. This scientist, in his view, had demonstrated that more sex was going on than polite American society ever admitted, and that ordinary people routinely flouted rules and conventions. Fascinated by Kinsey's findings, Hefner read everything about the book that he could get his hands on. "Kinsey had a tremendous impact on me," he recalled later. "It supplied the evidence that proved the things that I had been feeling for so many years, which was that what we said about our sexuality was not what we did. That we were hypocrites, and out of that came a good deal of hurt." Kinsey spoke directly to important issues in the young man's life, illustrating that "'they' made those laws and 'they' wouldn't let me be intimate with my girlfriend."[38]

Kinsey's revolutionary report, however, failed to prepare Hefner for an aspect of the sexual revolution that hit much closer to home. Millie graduated from the University of Illinois in June 1948 and got a job teaching high school at Lee Center, Illinois, in the fall. She would visit Urbana periodically throughout the autumn, and the couple became officially engaged on Christmas Day 1948. A few weeks later, however, a crisis developed that shook Hefner to the core.

While in Chicago, the couple went to a Loretta Young movie called *The Accused*, which told the story of a schoolteacher who was harassed by a bright, aggressive student who offered her a ride one evening and then forced himself on her in the car. She resisted and hit her assailant on the head, accidentally killing him. Terrified, she rolled the body off a cliff, pulled herself together, and tried to resume her normal life. But discovery of the body and escalating guilt caused her to unravel emotionally. Millie looked increasingly uncomfortable during the movie, and when they went to the car afterwards she began sobbing hysterically. "I've done something terrible," she gasped, but then refused to elaborate. After a confused Hefner insisted on an explanation, she finally confessed to a sexual liaison with a coach at the school where she was teaching. Still sobbing, she said that they had done it once, that it was not romantic or satisfying, and that she was consumed with guilt. Hefner was stunned. Although nearly speechless from shock, he told Millie he could forgive her and offered assurances that that they would still get married. But privately, his equilibrium was shattered.[39]

Hefner was deeply hurt by Millie's revelation. Later he described it as "the single most devastating experience of my entire life." He sat in his room for days afterward playing records, especially the Billy Eckstine song "Fool That I Am," over and over. When visiting her in the small town where she taught, he would drive extremely fast—sometimes hitting ninety miles per hour and once getting a traffic ticket for speeding—as pain and resentment welled up. Overall, Millie's affair had a profound, if complex, impact on Hefner's attitudes. On the one hand, the rational side of him tried not to blame her and held society accountable for holding people to impossible sexual standards. But on the other hand, his emotional side felt betrayal and pain. "The episode hung like a cloud over me until the marriage," he said. "Nothing was ever the same between us again." The affair, it seems clear, encouraged Hefner to distrust women and the notion of commitment to, and from, them. Even though he had necked and petted with other girls in college, he had never had sex with them. Bruising his male ego and, even more importantly, deflating the romantic fantasy he had built up around Millie, the affair scarred him for life.[40]

Thus Hefner graduated from the University of Illinois on February 6, 1949, with his personal life on shaky ground and his professional prospects uncertain. Evidence of disarray appeared in a decision to halt his beloved comic autobiography. He admitted that giving up this record of his experiences "wasn't an easy decision to make. It has been an intimate part of my life for more than six years. . . . It will be like losing an old friend." But finishing school and preparing to marry marked a new stage in his life. "It seems like a fitting place to write finis. I want to try my hand at professional cartooning; I want to write a novel and some short stories," he wrote.[41]

Little of this would come true. Hefner married Millie but he did not become a professional cartoonist, did not write a novel or short stories, and did not give up his autobiography. He could not foresee that over the next few years he would struggle mightily with shaping a career and fending off unhappiness before finally carving out a path in the society of postwar America. Only after a period of drift would he create something that combined his obsession with popular culture, his criticism of American moral values, and his growing interest in sex. Then neither his life nor that of the larger society would ever be quite the same.

3

The Tie That Binds

In the fall of 1948, a few months before graduating from the University of Illinois, Hugh Hefner wrote an apologetic letter to his parents. He admitted that he had been distracted and morose in recent weeks as concerns about career and livelihood pressed heavily. "This worry about my ability to earn a decent living in work for which I am suited, to gain a home and the things I want for my own future family, has given rise to this seeming lack of interest in what those about me are doing, and hence it seems at times that I just don't care about anyone else," he confessed. But such anxiety was normal, he assured his parents. It would pass.

Hefner's situation was not unusual. Male malaise, of course, had been rampant after World War II as millions of servicemen reentered domestic life and struggled to find jobs, reconnect with family, and find a direction for their lives. Hefner had postponed this crisis temporarily with college, but now he faced the world with hazy plans and half-formed goals. He knew that he wanted to get married, that art and journalism appealed to his imagination, and that becoming a writer or cartoonist would be nice. Beyond that, however, there was nothing concrete. The next few years would witness several episodes

of false starts and dashed dreams before Hefner finally found his
footing and created a vehicle to express many of his deepest impulses
and values.[1]

I

On June 15, 1949, Hugh Hefner married Millie Williams in a ceremony held in the rectory next to Saint John Bosco Church. They
had agreed to a Catholic ceremony to please her mother, but because
Hefner was not Catholic they could not be married in the church itself.
It was a modest, blue-collar event: the reception was held in the local
VFW hall with food prepared by friends and family members. The
newlyweds honeymooned for a few days at Styza's Birchwood Lodge
in Hazelhurst, Wisconsin. Upon returning to Chicago, they moved in
with his parents on New England Avenue because of limited funds
and the persistent postwar shortage of affordable housing.[2]

But things did not go smoothly. This was "a time of confusion and
uncertainty," in Hefner's words, as he spun his wheels in trying to
start a career. He initially sought work in Chicago's newspapers and
magazines, but with little experience and no contacts, "I didn't have
a clue of how to get started, how to make a connection." Desperate,
he finally took an unattractive job with the Chicago Carton Company
on the South Side in April 1949 as an employment manager at a salary
of $45 a week. He hated the job, and because he didn't have a car,
his father had to drive him to the train to go to work. Discouraged
with his mundane tasks and disgusted by the company's discriminatory hiring policies toward African Americans and Jews, he quit after
only five months.[3]

Hefner remained unemployed throughout the fall of 1949 as he
tried to develop and sell a pair of comic strips for newspaper syndi-
cation. Finding no takers, he enrolled at Northwestern University
in early 1950 with dreams of earning a graduate degree and starting
a career as a college professor. "With a masters or doctors degree,
I could teach (Sociology, I think) and write and draw to my heart's
content in all the free time a school teacher (particularly at the college level) finds himself with," he noted. After one semester, however,
he left and reentered the workforce. He found a job as a copywriter
at the Carson Pirie Scott department store in the Loop at a salary of

$40 a week. "I've got a job writing—it's copy writing to be sure, but it's real, honest-to-goodness, creative writing with art and layout on the side," he wrote excitedly. "It doesn't pay much to start, but there's a fine future in advertising, I'm learning plenty, and it's something I really enjoy working at."[4]

Six months later, Hefner landed a position at *Esquire* writing promotional copy at $60 a week. But the magazine that had enthralled him during boyhood as a paragon of sophistication and glamour proved disappointing. "It was not fulfilling," he reported. "You actually had to check in and punch a clock when you came in and then for lunch. So it was just a job." Moreover, *Esquire* was closing down its Chicago operation and the editorial staff had already moved to New York. When the promotion and circulation staff prepared to do likewise, the magazine offered Hefner a cost-of-living increase but refused his request for an additional $5 a week. So he quit. In some vague way, he had decided that his future, no matter how undefined, lay in the Windy City.[5]

In January 1952, Hefner began work at Publisher's Development Corporation, a company that published *Modern Man, Art Photography,* and *Modern Sunbathing*. These small magazines contained nude photos and had no subscriptions because of fear that the post office would pull them from the mail as obscene material. As manager of sales promotion and circulation, Hefner got to know newsstand dealers, distributors, printers, and the magazine market. But he found it an unpleasant place to work, even though he was earning $80 a week, because George Von Rosen, the hard-bitten owner, made his employees constantly fear for their jobs. So in early 1953, Hefner went to work for *Children's Activities* as circulation promotion manager at a salary of $120 a week. This monthly children's magazine was published by the Child Training Association and had a circulation of some quarter of a million.[6]

Thus Hefner shuffled through a series of unfulfilling jobs following college and found little to engage his interests, talents, and passions. His complaint about his first job at the Chicago Carton Company— "I'm going around in psychological circles. There's no kick in the work, no feeling of accomplishment"—was repeated many times over the next four years. But throughout this period of distress, he tried to express his artistic and journalistic impulses in other ways. He launched several projects that lay nearer and dearer to his heart.[7]

Hefner nourished a deep love for drawing, writing, popular music, and the movies, and yearned to express himself creatively. "I think he would have liked being an artist," Millie observed. "I think that was his first love, art." Thus in 1949, right out of college, he was delighted to secure an assignment writing movie reviews for a small local magazine titled *Dale Harrison's Chicago*. "Offering us the opportunity to do a movie column is like picking an alcoholic for the job of saloon editor. It just ain't work," he wrote in his first review. A bit later, he worked hard to develop a couple of comic strips. One, titled *Gene Fantas, Psycho-Investigator,* created a character who probed deep into the psychology of human motivation to solve crimes and problems. A second, more lighthearted strip with the title of *Freddy Frat* focused on the misadventures of college life. He had no luck in selling them.[8]

Periodically, Hefner tried to muffle these creative urges and reconcile himself to a staid, middle-class existence. In a long letter dated Christmas 1950, he noted that "Millie and I have bought and paid for a used car and a new television set. I'm nicely settled in a job writing men's store advertising for Carson Pirie Scott & Co." But discontent kept bubbling up. "He was depressed when he couldn't find out what he was going to do," Millie explained many years later. "You know, his cartoons weren't selling. . . . And then when he decided to go back to school at Northwestern, he thought at least he could teach school. But he wasn't real happy with that idea."[9]

Hefner achieved one notable creative success, however, that charged his emotional batteries and made him a minor celebrity in Chicago. In the spring of 1951, he published *That Toddlin' Town: A Rowdy Burlesque of Chicago Manners and Morals*. He had been working on this book of original cartoons offering a satirical, risqué look at the Chicago social scene for months and was overjoyed when it appeared. The front cover featured a sketch of a stripper dancing on a table surrounded by smiling men with drinks, while the cartoons themselves took a jaunt through the saloons, clubs, and theaters of the city, offering commentary on its "manners and morals." Local newspapers took notice. The *Chicago Daily Tribune* described it as "a book of cartoons irreverently satirizing Chicago's mores . . . with a collection of drawings that look like the kind *Esquire* might judge were too racy for its picture readers," while the *Chicago Herald-American* noted that it would "make you laugh if you know the city." "I hope it'll make me a pot full of money," Hefner wrote excitedly. "But even if I just break even on the darn thing, it's a start, the beginning of getting a reputation, the all important step in the right direction—the direction I most want to go!"[10]

One Michigan Avenue bookstore featured a window display of *That Toddlin' Town,* while promotion for the book allowed Hefner to rub shoulders with Chicago's entertainment establishment. He was interviewed on several radio shows and appeared on local television shows such as Hugh Downs's *Luncheon Date* and Ernie Simon's *Curbstone Cut-Up.* The latter featured a zany publicity stunt. As Simon prepared to interview Hefner outside a movie theater, a man in a gorilla suit came by carrying a beautiful young woman, which replicated one of the cartoons in the book. The book's success thrilled the author. It earned a couple of thousand dollars' profit and a curator from the Chicago Historical Society requested some of its original cartoons for a special exhibition in its museum. "A nice prestige-type thing," Hefner noted.[11]

The following year, Hefner embarked on another project more indicative of the future. In the fall of 1951, he began exploring the possibility of going into business for himself. Along with Burt Zollo, a copywriter with whom he shared an office at *Esquire,* he developed a prospectus for *Pulse: The Picture Magazine of Chicago,* and began contacting potential investors. They were unable to raise money, however, and the project fizzled out. Nevertheless, by late 1951 the idea for a magazine of his own had clearly begun to percolate in Hefner's head.[12]

While searching for vocational direction in the early 1950s, Hefner also struggled to shape his views of the world into some kind of cohesive form. In typical adolescent fashion, this bright young man had soaked up a mishmash of ideas and theories during his high school and college years, ranging from Hollywood movies to Freud, popular cartoons to Darwin, Protestant theology to Tarzan. He had come out of college with more questions than answers, however, and upon entering the adult world he attempted to integrate a jumble of images and thoughts into a worldview that would help him find his way within the larger society. Increasingly, he drew together several elements—Ayn Rand and heroic individualism, popular psychology, Alfred Kinsey and sexual liberation, and sentimental images from popular culture, particularly the movies—and molded them into a whole. They became the building blocks of a social fantasy.

As part of his flight from the religious values of his parents, Hefner had turned to psychology to explain human behavior. He concluded from his college studies that deep-seated impulses in the human psyche, not sin, explained behavior. "The reason I was majoring in psychology at Illinois and then in postgraduate work at Northwestern was because it all had to do with trying to understand *why*," he explained. "If I was going to be a writer, I should understand why we behaved the way we do." Hefner developed a broad appreciation of how human instincts and impulses, often buried or twisted into strange shapes, helped determine behavior. Freud, he recalled, was one of his idols.[13]

He also wrestled with psychological and sociological theories that portrayed human beings as creatures of larger, powerful social or psychic forces. He learned, in his own words, that "man was pretty much an expression, a sum total, of his heredity and his environment. He could not be blamed for a damned thing. He was just a victim, nothing more." Hefner bridled at this determinism, arguing that if it was widely accepted "we would all sit on our asses and do nothing." In a similar vein, he saw McCarthyism and its pressures for political and social conformity as forcing Americans to become "security-conscious, committee-conscious, afraid to be different from anybody else, afraid to express a different opinion." He concluded that all of these ideas and trends were undermining "the free-enterprise system" and "a free democratic society." In his view, "Eliminate the importance of self, drag everyone else down to the common denominator, and you are walking right into the society that George Orwell warned us about in *1984*."[14]

Ayn Rand's *The Fountainhead* became a catalyst for his individualist inclinations. This novel, with its philosophy of "objectivism," or the notion that morality consists of rational self-interest, resonated powerfully with the young man. Its hero, Howard Roark, a determined individualist, galvanized Hefner's sense of self. "It began to come clear to me for the first time that if you took the importance of the individual out of society, eliminated his personal importance, his integrity, his personal point of view, his right to be different, for the sake of what you referred to as the Common Good, it could *never* be a common good—it could only be a common evil," Hefner reflected. He became convinced that individualism lay at the heart of a free society while communism, socialism, and fascism offered a suffocating collectivism. In later years, after running an interview with Rand in *Playboy*, Hefner would be shocked to discover that she was a Barry Goldwater conservative. But in the early 1950s, Rand's powerful message of unfettered individualism carried a powerful appeal for a young man anxious about McCarthyism and middle-class conformity.[15]

Hefner's individualist creed, like other aspects of his life, increasingly came to focus on sexual behavior and standards. The 1948 Kinsey Report had inflamed his adolescent resentments about sexual hypocrisy and repression. So when he was required to do a long research paper during his brief stint in graduate school at Northwestern in the spring of 1950, a natural topic beckoned. Written for a class in social pathology and carrying the title "Sex Behavior and the U.S. Law," the seventy-eight-page paper examined the wide array of laws governing American sexual behavior. Hefner looked at a variety of sexual practices such as intercourse before, during, and outside of marriage; intercourse with prostitutes; incest, homosexuality, and the statutes and punishments that applied to them. There existed, he concluded, not only a gap between American principles and behavior regarding sex, but a state of affairs where "much of this hypocrisy has been legislated into the statutes of the various states." Common practices such as premarital sex, oral sex, masturbation, and "lewd cohabitation" had been deemed illegal, and if enforced, in Hefner's words, "these laws would send close to ninety per cent of our male population to prison." This situation, he concluded, revealed that modern freedoms had not been extended to sexuality. Hefner blamed Christianity, which had denounced carnal urges and idealized celibacy, as the culprit. He offered as a counterpoint the light of reason, which, if allowed to shine on sexuality, would lead to the decriminalization of many activities that hurt no one. "Man's moral life, as long as it does not harm others, is his own business, and should be left to his own discretion," he concluded.[16]

Even more important was the emotional conviction that Hefner brought to this project. He threw himself into research and writing, in his words, "with the all-consuming passion of the true believer." It provided not only a focus for his intense, Rand-style individualism, but a kind of catharsis for coming to terms with his personal pain over Millie's infidelity and the perceived repressions of his Protestant childhood. With its twin messages of sexual freedom and individual liberation, the paper captured central impulses in Hefner's emerging worldview and presaged many of the themes that he would address in his later career. The grade he received for the paper—an A for research, but only a B+ for the conclusions—reinforced his conviction that sexual repression and hypocrisy had warped American sexual attitudes.[17]

Hefner's emotional and ideological maturation received an added boost from American popular culture. He continued to nurture sentimental dreams of affection, romance, and passion that were rooted in popular music and movies. Cinematic images of simple, strong men of integrity and principle who persevered through difficult circumstances, as portrayed in movies such as *Mr. Smith Goes to Washington*, *Meet John Doe*, and in various characters played by Humphrey Bogart, influenced him. He secured an underground copy of D. H. Lawrence's banned book *Lady Chatterley's Lover* and devoured Budd Schulberg's *What Makes Sammy Run*, the popular novel about Sammy Glick and Hollywood. He also became enthralled with the work and life of F. Scott Fitzgerald, reading *The Great Gatsby* and Schulberg's *The Disenchanted*, a fictionalized treatment of the sad last stages of Fitzgerald's life. "I didn't want to grow up and be my parents. There had to be something more," he explained. "And that something more was hinted at somehow in the dreams and the movies and the books I read."[18]

Thus by the early 1950s Hefner had forged an individualist, liberationist mind-set that was committed to unfettered expression, sexual freedom, and personal autonomy. He may not have known exactly where he was going, but he knew the ideas that were going to take him there. At the same time, his search for vocation and direction in young adulthood was far more than an intellectual exercise. It lay intertwined with his personal life, particularly an unsatisfying marriage and a growing sexual restlessness.

II

Hugh and Millie Hefner began their married life in 1949 in awkward circumstances. Forced to live with his parents because of economic pressures, they converted the largest bedroom in the house into a small apartment. The younger Hefners' appreciation, combined with the elder Hefners' emotional restraint, made for a congenial household. The only point of contention concerned Hugh and Millie's enthusiastic lovemaking, which occasionally could be heard by both his parents and their longtime neighbors. An embarrassed Grace took her son aside one day and asked for more restraint, or at least less noise. Such minor problems aside, the youthful couple settled in as Hugh pursued various jobs and art projects and Millie worked at the Mars candy factory. Hefner seemed content, noting on Christmas 1950 that "I find myself more in love with Millie than I was on our wedding day."[19]

Change came in the early spring of 1952, when Millie discovered she was pregnant. Within a few weeks the young couple had found a five-room apartment at 6052 South Harper on Chicago's South Side, and throughout the summer they threw themselves into a redecorating project. For Hugh, it was an opportunity to realize a fantasy—living the life of a hip, young urban couple. Seeking to create a Greenwich Village–style environment, Hefner designed a dark gray living room accented with white, yellow, and black draperies, Picasso prints, and spare, modernist furniture, including an orange Knoll womb chair. The bright dining room had three walls painted rust orange and one covered in Philippine grass paper. A long hallway featured some of Hefner's cartoons along with a playful touch—framed his-and-her chest X-rays. The bedroom had yellow walls and dark green bamboo shades, while the baby's bedroom was decorated with Pogo cartoons. The *Chicago Daily News* ran a brief picture story on the apartment as Hefner acknowledged he was trying to "create a sort of bohemian life that I imagined was going on out there that I wasn't a part of."[20]

Yet Hefner's carefully cultivated image was belied by the reality beneath. In fact, Hugh and Millie had begun to drift apart. Both had harbored doubts about the relationship, but they hoped that the marriage bond would overcome them. Like many young couples in 1950s America, they had felt pressure to get married and have children because, in Hefner's words, "it was simply the thing that you did." But they were ill-suited to one another, and the frustrations grew stronger, rather than weaker, over time.[21]

Disappointment had surfaced early on. The wedding ceremony had been pleasant, but the honeymoon at a lakeside lodge in Wisconsin fell victim to extremely hot weather and boredom. Their sexual relationship had cooled gradually, and when a tight emotional connection failed to develop, they settled into a calm but dispassionate relationship. Friction flared only when they played as bridge partners and inevitably bickered. Much like Grace and Glenn Hefner, they coexisted with little fighting but little affection either. A friend observed, "I saw them more as good friends than as lovers because I never saw them display any affection, hugging or kissing or touching."[22]

Gradually, a quiet discontent grew as each partner felt a lack of fulfillment. "It was a charade. We were playing roles," Millie admitted later. Hugh added, "I have always had the capacity to find the bright side of almost anything. I don't think I was ever really happy in the marriage, but I think that I managed to convince myself that I was." The stalled union, along with the stalled career, seemed to signal the death of his youthful dreams. In looking back at the early years of his marriage to Millie, he later described the period as "one in which I was really lost."[23]

For Hefner, two issues grew particularly frustrating. First, he claimed that Millie had little interest in sex. "He told me Millie was unresponsive in bed and that he had tried everything he knew to stimulate their sex life, but nothing succeeded," Eldon Sellers, a close friend, reported. Second, Hefner was emotionally unprepared to be a parent. He had agreed to a family because of social pressures to have children, and the arrival of daughter Christie on November 8, 1952, had delighted him. But at heart, Hefner was no family man and, in his words, "all this togetherness seemed meaningless. I went through the motions, but my heart wasn't in it." The responsibilities of fatherhood had little appeal and the arrival of a second child, David, in 1955 only exacerbated the situation. Millie had wanted another baby and Hugh was reluctant, so she arranged the biological schedule without consulting him. "The second child was planned, but I wasn't in on the plan," he noted ruefully.[24]

In the meantime, the troubled marriage faced growing pressure from Hugh's increasingly active sexual imagination. His strong erotic drive had become evident on the afternoon of their wedding when, on a very hot day at Millie's parents' house with relatives scattered about, he wanted to have sex in her bedroom. She refused. In subsequent years, Hefner's fascination with sexual themes and issues grew stronger. His snapshots of the new apartment included a from-the-back, waist-up picture of Millie as she stood in the shower. A 1952 letter to posterity in his autobiography was decorated with miniature photographs of scantily clad and nude women. Hefner eagerly collected sexual tidbits from the news, noting in a letter the following year, "Sex made a couple of big headlines this month as margarine heir Minot Jelke was convicted as a panderer for $50 to $200 a date call-girls—and Christine Jorgensen returned to the U.S. after a series of famous operations that turned her from a man into a woman." As Eldon Sellers put it, "he was obsessed with sex."[25]

Hefner's preoccupation did not remain ethereal. He became a connoisseur of sexual experimentation in a group of young married friends. He hosted parties at the Hefner apartment featuring stag films, which titillated the group, and kept up a running commentary of one-liners to remove any embarrassment. He organized risqué games such as strip poker and strip charades where, while consuming hefty amounts of alcohol to remove inhibitions, husbands and wives would end up stripping down to their underwear. These boisterous parties, according to Sellers, produced a bunch of half-naked people running around laughing and cavorting. "Nothing sexual happened but it was titillating," he said.[26]

Hefner also went further. One night after he and Millie watched a stag movie with Janie and Eldon Sellers, he suggested that the four of them make love on the same bed, each husband to his own wife. They did so and, in Sellers's words, "It was different and exciting." According to Millie, Hugh began to hint at switching partners, apparently suggesting it with the Sellerses, although the swap never materialized. But it did happen with his brother, Keith, and his wife, Rae, one evening at the apartment. While Millie ultimately backed out of having sex with Keith, Hugh slept with his sister-in-law.[27]

Soon Hefner became even bolder. After procuring the necessary equipment, he made his own stag film. Titled "After the Masquerade," it was shot at a friend's apartment where Hefner and a female acquaintance had sex while wearing masks to protect their identity. On another occasion, Hefner shared a partner with Eldon Sellers, whose own sexual experimentation also was accelerating rapidly. When he took a young woman home to make love, she said she wouldn't mind a friend, "so I called Hef and he came right over." Hefner's thirst for sexual experience became so strong that he even had a one-time homosexual encounter. One evening in downtown Chicago he was propositioned and, according to Sellers, he "thought what the hell. Found it an interesting experience. As far as I know, the guy just gave him a blow job."[28]

Hefner's blossoming sense of sexual liberation, however, did not extend to Millie. When Eldon Sellers divorced his wife, his friendship with the Hefners intensified and he would drop by to visit, sometimes when Hugh was not home. Hefner bridled. "He told me about a friend of his who lost his wife to his best friend," Sellers recalled. Hefner's fears were well grounded, because Sellers had become attracted to Millie. "I thought she was very sexy and once when we played a kissing game [at a party], she had kissed me kind of passionately, a French kiss," he confessed.[29]

Amid these sexual shenanigans, however, Hefner maintained a fascinating posture. While organizing, staging, even choreographing the revelries, and contributing much wit and good cheer, he stayed a step removed. He enjoyed participating in new sexual adventures, but never abandoned himself to them. As Sellers observed, he never got drunk at the couples' parties but carefully maintained his self-control. Millie agreed, noting that her husband "stages things. But he's not part of it." She believed that Hefner's reserve, in part, protected him from feeling vulnerable. But Millie also concluded that her husband, at a deeper level, somehow created an alter ego who could act out his deepest desires while his real self remained as an observer. "I kept thinking it's like he's two people. He's this fantasy character. He's this viewer of life," she explained. "It's this other person that is doing all the fantasy things that he would like to be able to do but he can't do." In a sense, Hefner's creation of a social fantasy contained a fantasy of himself.[30]

Not surprisingly, Hefner's restless sexuality finally culminated in a full-blown affair. While working at Publisher's Development Corporation, he started an affair with a nurse that lasted for about a year. She was an attractive, earthy woman whose vigorous erotic appetite contrasted with Millie. "She managed to give me back my sexual self-respect," Hefner said. "She was attracted to me in a way I didn't feel that Millie was." He justified the illicit relationship as not being unfaithful, but merely compensating for Millie's lack of sexual interest. Moreover, the affair demonstrated Hefner's growing discontent with America's repressive code of sexual conduct. "I don't remember having any guilt," he said later. "I just felt that I was, in effect, breaking the rules that I'd been raised with."[31]

Thus the wheel-spinning lack of momentum in Hefner's career was matched by discontent and sexual adventurism in his personal life. His various forays—the affair, the bohemian apartment, the stag films, the risqué parties—expressed a common desire to jettison the social conventions of postwar America. "It was all part of the same thing. It was somehow trying to get out of that life," he noted. "Somehow to just not keep marching in lockstep to the abyss." Disparaging American society as a hive of *Father Knows Best* conformity, he yearned for liberation. But in both his career and his private life, the fog of frustration refused to lift. In Hefner's words, "I was really not a happy guy, either professionally or personally, at that point in my life."[32]

III

Hefner's discontent, ironically, came to a head in a moment of great joy. In December 1952, he and Jim Brophy wrote and directed the *Revue of Stars,* a fund-raising variety show, for the Steinmetz High School Alumni Association. The old school chums served as masters of ceremonies and performed several song and comedy numbers, including a hilarious "Walking My Baby Back Home," where Hefner serenaded Brophy, who was dressed as a woman. The crowd loved the show, and Hefner, showered with applause and laughter, was ecstatic. As he noted in his cartoon autobiography, "Who says you can't turn back the clock? For the past two hours we've been plunked right back in the middle of 1943!" The alumni show "reinspired my faith in myself. It reminded me of my high school days when I truly believed I could do anything."[33]

But this moment of euphoria quickly turned to ashes. As the glow of success faded, the experience of the show only highlighted the angst that had enveloped the rest of his life. He grew acutely despondent about his stalled career and his unhappy marriage, and the feelings almost overwhelmed him a few days later. Standing on a bridge over the Chicago River in the middle of a typically frigid winter, he looked out over the water and felt a desperate desire to recapture those warm feelings of high school life when he had been the esteemed leader of a gang, romance was in the air, and everything seemed possible. "I stood on the bridge . . . and I felt as if my life was over. I had put away all my dreams from childhood and I was miserable." But misery inspired decision as Hefner thought to himself, "I've gotta do something."[34]

Within weeks he moved to start his own magazine. He had toyed with the idea earlier, but now he threw himself into a project that would express all of his interests, ideas, and passions. Its centerpiece would be the subject that increasingly captured his imagination: sex. "I just decided to do it all on my own. Nobody else, just do it," he said. He knew there was a market for photographs of nude women from his experience with Publisher's Development Corporation, whose low-quality magazines still appealed. *Esquire,* he believed, had deteriorated by removing many of its pinups and cartoons. "I thought I could really actually put together a *good* magazine. I felt with absolute certainty that I knew exactly what I was doing."[35]

Hefner began talking up the idea with close friends. He and Eldon Sellers had taken to playing ping-pong in the basement of his apartment building, and amid the games Hefner began discussing his plans for a magazine. "He had it all figured out—and the way he explained it, I got very excited and wanted to be a part of it," Sellers explained. Hefner also contacted Burt Zollo, his accomplice from *Esquire,* who was now working for a public relations firm, and laid out his plan:

> I'd like to produce an entertainment magazine for the city-bred guy—breezy, sophisticated. The girly features would guarantee the initial sale—but the magazine would have quality, too. . . . Give the reader reprint stories by big name writers, top art by local artists, cartoons, humor, maybe some pages in full color to really give it a classy look. . . . Later, with some money in the bank, we'll begin increasing the quality, reducing the girlie features, going after advertising, and really making it an *Esquire*-type magazine.[36]

In the spring of 1953, Hefner took concrete steps to bring his fantasy to life. He spent his evenings at a card table in the living room of his South Side apartment, laboring into the early morning hours as he blocked out the elements of the magazine he decided to call *Stag Party*. He formed HMH Publishing Company and enlisted Eldon Sellers to raise funds. Meanwhile, he contacted distributors all over the country, whom he had come to know from his days with Publisher's Development Corporation, and solicited advance orders for the new magazine. His letter announced "a deal that should make some money for both of us. STAG PARTY—a brand new magazine for men—will be out this fall." Every issue of the magazine, he promised, "will have a beautiful, full page, male-pleasing nude study—in full, natural color! Now you know what I mean when I say this is going to be one of the best sellers you've ever handled."[37]

Thrilled with his new endeavor, Hefner threw himself into the work. He sat for long hours at the card table pounding out copy for the magazine, combing through available articles and cartoons, and sorting the orders from wholesalers that were arriving steadily. "He didn't really sleep much because he was working practically all night," Millie reported. Hefner's enthusiasm became contagious. Burt Zollo, who had expressed reservations initially, was won over and described Hefner as "a highly creative guy who was nevertheless highly realistic. He would be successful."[38]

Much effort went into raising money with family and friends. A wealthy girlfriend of Sellers's invested $2,000 [and] Hefner borrowed $200 from a local bank and hocked his furniture with a loan company for $600 more. Zollo invested $300, while Keith Hefner contributed $1,000 to his brother's venture. Grace Hefner, even though she had reservations about the magazine, invested another $1,000. A grateful Hugh wrote to his mother, "Because of the spontaneity of it and because it was made with the knowledge that much of the magazine, like my book, will not be material that you fully, personally approve of, this is just about the nicest thing you have ever done for me." Eventually, Hefner gathered just over $8,000 to put out the first issue of the magazine.[39]

Meanwhile, enough orders had come in from distributors for Hefner to make an arrangement with a printer he knew in New Rochelle, Illinois. With a new press and some open time, the man agreed to print *Stag Party* on credit with half down in thirty days and the other half in sixty days. Hefner also made an important decision to hire an art director to handle the visual side of his new magazine. He contacted a Chicago graphic artist named Art Paul about illustrating a story, but was so taken by the illustrations on display that he pressed him to assume a larger role. Hefner had arrived at the artist's studio with a growth of beard, wrinkled clothes, and a harried look, but enthusiasm for the new magazine bubbled out of him. "I thought, for God's sake, he's either got to be an exceptional person, or he's got to be crazy," Paul recalled. But the artist agreed to work part-time on the magazine's visuals, and Hefner paid part of his fee in cash and part in stock from the new company.[40]

Hefner made his most crucial move, however, when he purchased the rights to a nude photograph of perhaps the hottest, sexiest young actress in Hollywood. Marilyn Monroe had rocketed to movie stardom in 1952 on the basis of the movies *The Asphalt Jungle*, *All About Eve,* and *Niagara*. In the subsequent flurry of publicity, it came to light that a Los Angeles photographer had shot several nude photos of her in 1949 for use in a calendar. Monroe joked that during the shoot she had "nothing on but the radio." Hefner read that the John Baumgarth Calendar Company of Chicago now owned the rights to one of the photos, but was reluctant to send its calendar through the mail because of the Post Office taboo on nudity. Knowing that he needed a gimmick to sell the first issue of his magazine, Hefner quickly drove to the company. He persuaded John Baumgarth to sell him the rights to the photos, which featured the actress sitting seductively against a red velvet backdrop.[41]

As the magazine moved nearer to publication, however, an unexpected crisis loomed. In September 1953 Hefner received a letter from a law firm representing *Stag* magazine. This publication considered *Stag Party* to be an infringement on its title and threatened to sue. Hefner convened a frantic meeting with Millie and Eldon Sellers and they began tossing around other titles: *Top Hat, Bachelor, Gentleman, Sir, Satyrs, Pan*. But none seemed suitable, and Sellers finally offered *Playboy*. Millie thought it sounded outdated and made people think of the 1920s. But Hugh, who associated the Roaring Twenties with "high living, parties, wine, women, and song—the things we want the magazine to mean," loved the name and adopted it immediately. A logo had already been completed by the cartoonist Arv Miller—a stag bedecked in smoking jacket, standing against a fireplace with a cigarette holder and martini glass—and it required a quick substitution of a rabbit head. A bit later, Art Paul would create the famous rabbit head silhouette logo with its "elegant, on-the-town look."[42]

In November 1953, everything was set to launch the first issue of *Playboy*. Advance orders for seventy thousand copies had rolled in over the past several months, but no one knew if the magazine would really sell. The first issue rolled off the presses without a publication date because its youthful editor and publisher, while convinced he had an attractive product, remained uncertain whether sales would support a second issue. Hugh Hefner had gambled everything on the venture, both materially and emotionally, and now he could only wait and see how it would play out.

PART II

ASCENT

4

How to Win Friends and Titillate People

In the first week of November 1953, a nervous Hugh Hefner walked the streets of downtown Chicago, haunting the newsstands for a glimpse of his new magazine. The first issue of *Playboy* had just appeared, and like an anxious father he fretted about the status of his offspring. A few weeks earlier Hefner had negotiated a good deal with a distributor, Empire News, based on advance orders for the magazine. Then in mid-October he had driven the seventy-five miles to Rochelle Printing in his beat-up 1941 Chevy, along with Eldon Sellers and Art Paul, and spent several hours copyreading the page proofs. When the presses delivered the final product, and it was covered and bound, Hefner felt a surge of emotion. He described it as "one of the great moments of my life."[1]

Now Hefner watched as browsers picked up a newsstand copy of *Playboy*, curiously looking at the table of contents before sneaking a peek at the Marilyn Monroe pictorial. He thrilled when a customer bought a copy, and his heart sank when they set it down and moved on. When the newsstand proprietors were not looking, Hefner even walked over and moved *Playboy* to a more prominent position in the display. Over a period of several days, he brooded that if his magazine did not sell, the prospect of shattered dreams and bankruptcy loomed in the near future.[2]

Hefner need not have worried. Within a short time, landslide sales made the new product a winner. Experts had predicted sales of about 60 percent of copies published, a respectable result. But *Playboy* sold nearly 80 percent, about fifty-four thousand copies—an astounding figure for a new publication that had been launched on a minuscule budget with little publicity or advertising. The second issue, which already had been blocked out when the first appeared, hit the newsstands in early December, and a more confident Hefner now included his name on the masthead. The second issue outsold the first by about two thousand copies.[3]

Even Hefner seemed a bit taken back by the powerful response to *Playboy*. The magazine appeared to strike a nerve almost immediately as not only readers, but American culture, or at least much of its male portion, seemed ready for it. The magazine's appeal radiated from its very first issue. Daring, provocative, even naughty, but not dangerous or subversive, *Playboy* expressed many of the mainstream values of postwar America while giving them an invigorating new form. Aimed at men who were trying to navigate the unfamiliar waters of a prosperous new social and economic milieu, the magazine offered an exciting vision of the good life for a society that, without totally being aware of the fact, was yearning to lead it. *Playboy* began bringing a submerged collective social fantasy to the surface.

I

While proud of his new publication, Hefner knew that it was far from what he envisioned in terms of quality and style. The first *Playboy* was lively and vibrant, crudely composed and not very sophisticated-looking. The editor joked that its cobbled-together format consisted of "something old, something new, something borrowed, something blue." Behind the rough edges, however, lay all of the basic components that the magazine would refine and expand upon in the future.

As Art Paul observed, the inaugural issue was "a sketchbook for what the magazine was really going to be."[4]

A smiling, waving Marilyn Monroe sat on the cover along with a promise that the reader would find within "For the First Time, in any Magazine, Full Color," the famous nude photo of the actress. Readers then encountered a jaunty introduction that announced a new kind of magazine for a new kind of male reader:

> If you're a man between the ages of 18 and 80, PLAYBOY is meant for you. If you like your entertainment served up with humor, sophistication and spice, PLAYBOY will become a very special favorite.
>
> We want to make clear from the very start, we aren't a "family magazine." If you're somebody's sister, wife, or mother-in-law and picked us up by mistake, please pass us along to the man in your life and get back to your *Ladies Home Companion.* . . .
>
> Most of today's "magazines for men" spend all their time out-of-doors—thrashing through thorny thickets or splashing about in fast flowing streams. We'll be out there too, occasionally, but we don't mind telling you in advance—we plan on spending most of our time inside.
>
> We like our apartment. We enjoy mixing up cocktails and an *hors d'oeuvre* or two, putting a little mood music on the phonograph, and inviting in a female acquaintance for a quiet discussion on Picasso, Nietzsche, jazz, sex. . . .
>
> Affairs of state will be out of our province. We don't expect to solve any world problems or prove any great moral truths. If we are able to give the American male a few extra laughs and a little diversion from the anxieties of the Atomic Age, we'll feel we've justified our existence.[5]

There it was in a nutshell—the promise of sophisticated amusement for young, urban males who sought relief from the stresses and strains of workaday life, and who felt more comfortable (or, perhaps more accurately, *wanted* to feel more comfortable) pursuing modern art, films, and foreign cuisines rather than wily trout, smoky campfires, and recalcitrant do-it-yourself projects. The magazine would be, in Hefner's memorable phrase, "a pleasure-primer styled to the masculine taste."[6]

A quick scan of the first issue's contents elaborated the nature of the young Chicagoan's magazine. Sexual titillation pervaded. One article explained how to enliven a boring party with a provocative game, "strip quiz," while another depicted nude swimming festivities in California. A selection from the *Decameron* provided "a humorous tale of adultery." Ribald themes dominated the many cartoons—one showed a shapely young woman about to write in her diary, asking a friend, "What is the past tense of virgin?"—as well as "Playboy's Party Jokes." Other articles explored "The Return of the All-Purpose Back," "The Dorsey Brothers," and "Desk Design for the Modern Office." "The Men's Shop" displayed the latest in consumer amenities for young men, while "Matanzas Love Affair" explained the delights of Cuban food and drink. Reprints of stories by Arthur Conan Doyle and Ambrose Bierce offered mystery and adventure. "Miss Gold-digger of 1953" denounced greedy women who manipulated the legal system for alimony.

The centerpiece of *Playboy*'s first issue, however, was its "Sweetheart of the Month." As promised on the cover, it showcased the sensual attractions of Marilyn Monroe. "She's as famous as Dwight Eisenhower and Dick Tracy, and she and Dr. Kinsey have monopo-lized sex this year," said the text. "She is natural sex personified. It is there in every look and movement. That's what makes her the most natural choice in the world for our very first *Playboy Sweetheart*." Several photos of Monroe, including a nude shot of her posed against red velvet, provided proof for the assertion. The magazine assured readers, "We'll be running a beautiful, full color unpinned pin-up in each new issue of PLAYBOY."[7]

What drew men to this potpourri of offerings? The attractive bundling of sexual images, of course, highlighted by the Monroe pictorial, initially hooked a male audience whose previous encoun-ters with erotic material likely consisted of grimy, grainy photos in underground venues. But *Playboy*'s appeal was rooted more deeply in the broad social and cultural milieu of postwar America.

Middle-class life in the 1950s had emerged from the cauldron of the Great Depression of the 1930s and World War II in the 1940s, traumatic events that had devastated the economic institutions of the country in the first case, and dislocated it socially and psychologi-cally in the second. Memories of bankruptcies and lost mortgages, of battlefield scars and aching separations, lingered painfully in the American psyche. Millions of ordinary citizens had entered the postwar period yearning to replace uncertainty with security, volatility with stability, need with possession. The United States' victorious position in the world—what pundits increasingly described as "The American Century"—provided the means to do so.

Coming out of World War II as an economic colossus, the United States had changed direction from a military to a consumer agenda. By the 1950s, prosperity had become the hallmark of American life. Middle-class citizens enjoyed an economy of abundance that brought an unprecedented flow of goods. Supported by the mortgage provision of the GI Bill, a vast new army of homeowners prompted a boom in housing construction that produced swelling suburbs such as Levittown, Long Island, that built and sold seventeen thousand homes beginning in 1949. The automobile industry boomed as Detroit companies, led by General Motors, produced ever larger, more stylish, and more powerful cars for average-income buyers. High employment and steady growth in income encouraged leisure activity with a resulting boom in vacation travel and television sales. The flood of consumer products to the middle class led *Fortune* magazine to proclaim in 1956, "Never has a whole people spent so much money on so many things in such an easy way as Americans are doing today." The historian David Potter, in a much-discussed book titled *People of Plenty* (1954), concluded that material abundance, the key factor in American development over two centuries, had reached an apex in the postwar era. In a special 1959 double issue titled "The Good Life," *Life* magazine marveled that in modern America, "suddenly what used to be the small leisured classes became the big leisured masses."[8]

The American family emerged at the center of this new consumer economy. Riding the crest of the ballyhooed "baby boom" of the late 1940s and early 1950s, it achieved newfound prominence in the postwar period. A new cultural code of family togetherness idealized life in suburban ranch houses, cruising about in station wagons, and gathering in family rooms to watch television shows such as *Father Knows Best* and *Leave It to Beaver*. Americans embraced the promise of a new kind of family experience that, in the words of one historian, "would fulfill virtually all its members' personal needs through an energized and expressive personal life."[9]

This environment of material abundance and family togetherness forced a reshaping of the basic American tenet of individualism. Earlier periods had stressed a rugged personal code where the citizen had marshaled hard work, determination, and self-control to blaze his own path to success. But in the heady days of the postwar era, a new socioeconomic atmosphere demanded revisions. An economy increasingly dominated by large corporations made bureaucracy, not entrepreneurship, the new field of play. Here a "personality" composed of attractive images and compelling personal skills—not an old-fashioned "character" of rigid moral values—would foster "teamwork" and ascent up the corporate ladder. New avatars of success, such as the clergyman-therapist Norman Vincent Peale, in his wildly popular *The Power of Positive Thinking,* urged readers to call upon a "Higher Power" to gain confidence and strengthen mental health as the basis for securing happiness and prosperity.[10]

The pressures of the Cold War molded these elements of abundance, family, and teamwork into a compelling American Way of Life. Economically, government defense contracts underwrote a significant portion of 1950s prosperity. Rhetorically, the United States trumpeted a creed of anticommunism that juxtaposed American bounty and family, bureaucratic efficiency and vibrant personality against drab Stalinist collectivism. Pressures for conformity emerging from corporate bureaucracies, national advertising campaigns, and the suburban ethos gained additional power from an anticommunist ideology that demanded solidarity against the Red Menace. In 1959, *Life* ran a lighthearted story—complete with several photos—about newlyweds who spent their weeklong honeymoon in a bomb shelter, surrounded by a cornucopia of consumer amenities.[11]

But as the 1950s unfolded, challenges arose to this American Way of Life that showed widening cracks in its imposing edifice. Much of it was covert. By mid-decade, Elvis Presley and rock 'n' roll music were shaking middle-class restraint with depth charges of sexuality and emotional rebellion. The Beats, through novelists such as Jack Kerouac and poets such as Allen Ginsberg, bitterly criticized middle-class materialism and created a bohemian counterculture devoted to unfettered personal expression. Critics attacked the conformity and unimaginative quality of bourgeois America in works such as William H. Whyte's *The Organization Man* (1956), David Riesman's *The Lonely Crowd* (1950), and Dwight Macdonald's "A Theory of Mass Culture" (1957). Macdonald's words typified the critique: "There is slowly emerging a tepid, flaccid middlebrow culture that threatens to engulf everything in its spreading ooze."[12]

In the heart of the Eisenhower era, it was the genius of *Playboy* and its editor to articulate an approach that tapped *both* mainstream aspirations and marginal unhappiness. While rebellious, Hefner's magazine did not challenge the basic tenets of postwar American life. Instead, it channeled the restlessness of ambitious, irreverent, often accomplished young men toward eliminating its stodgier features and loosening its most restrictive demands. It expressed a dissent based on lifestyle. *Playboy,* and its readers, sought to make hard play the equal of hard work in the American creed. They sought to remove barriers to pleasure in order to enjoy the full bounty of the new American wealth. Through this shared fantasy of self-gratification, they aimed to enhance the American dream of an abundant life, not overthrow it.

Thus *Playboy,* while scandalizing old-fashioned defenders of religion and morality, appealed to growing numbers of people intoxicated with abundance and eager to throw off restraints. Hefner had a partial awareness of his magazine's cultural role. "I wanted to create a breezy, class entertainment magazine for the city-bred guy," he explained in early 1954. At the same time, he believed that his desires were shared by others. "The whole focus of the magazine was the notion of living unmarried in a city with your own apartment, with a nice car, with good food and drink, where you'd actually prepare something for a romantic dinner. It was all in the first issue." Indeed, this cultural agenda for the good life proved to be a bond between Hefner's magazine and its readers.[13]

II

Looking back from a vantage point many years later, Hugh Hefner saw his magazine standing at the ramparts battling against 1950s conformity and repression. "Before *Playboy*, the only moral, proper way for a middle-class person to live their life was to get married, settle down, have babies and live happily every after, whatever that meant," he explained. "We dared to suggest that there were other ways of living your life." He believed that a pernicious alliance of religion and politics had created a censorious public morality and a rigid creed of family virtue in the postwar period. He also blamed Red-hunting McCarthyism for making a mockery of World War II's democratic aims and turning anticommunism into a recipe for political and social repression. *Playboy,* Hefner concluded, struck a blow for cultural freedom by promoting a freer expression of eroticism. "We knew that we were obviously ringing some kind of a revolutionary bell by simply running nude pictures in the magazine," he noted.[14]

But *Playboy* played a more complex, even ambiguous role, as it went out to the American public in the mid-1950s. Its dissenting impulses, while real, were hardly revolutionary. In many ways, perhaps even more powerfully, it affirmed postwar American values. Seeking to loosen the system from within rather than assault it from without, Hefner served as an agent of regeneration for the American Way of Life. "*Playboy* is dedicated to the enjoyment of 'the good life' that is every American's heritage, if he's willing to display a little of the initiative and derring-do that made the country great in the first place, instead of settling for job security, conformity, togetherness, anonymity, and slow death," he told Cold War America. "And just incidentally, while trying to climb that ladder of success through creativity, thought, initiative, and daring to be different, Americans supply the only chance this country has of moving back into a position of world leadership." In various ways, *Playboy* consistently articulated a goal of individual success and social prosperity.[15]

The magazine urged its readers to enjoy life by embracing leisure, entertainment, and material comforts. *Playboy* encouraged people to partake of exciting new opportunities instead of delaying gratification. "Our readers believe in The Good Life, and so do we," it told aspiring authors in 1954. "Hence, free-lancers will make us happy by submitting material that stresses wine, women and song rather than rod, reel, and bait-bucket." Editorial asides in the magazine assured readers that "The Good Life" consisted of "good food and drink, first-rate reading matter, and a compliable young person of feminine gender."[16]

Playboy repeatedly connected its vision of pleasure pursuits to upward mobility in 1950s America. On its first anniversary, it reported that "the average PLAYBOY reader has a little better education, position, and income than his non-PLAYBOY-reading brother." The following year, the magazine ran a piece in *Advertising Age* that quoted a composite *Playboy* reader: "Don't get me wrong. I'm a hard-working guy and I'm well on my way to the top in business. But I like to have fun. I like nice clothes, great food and drink, women. No, I'm only 29. I'm college educated, I earn a good living and I expect to earn a good deal more. I have faith in myself and the future. I'm not worried about tomorrow. I'm *living now*."[17]

A 1955 survey of *Playboy* readers uncovered statistical evidence supporting its appeal to the youthful, ambitious, and affluent. Conducted by the market research company of Gould, Gleiss, and Benn, Inc., it reported that the great majority of readers were between the ages of twenty and thirty-four, over 70 percent had attended college, almost 63 percent were business and professional men or students studying to enter those fields, 88 percent owned automobiles, and nearly all took regular vacations. Most pursued hobbies such as photography, reading, or music, smoked a wide variety of tobacco products, and consumed various brands of hard liquor and beer. Its average reader, the magazine concluded, was "a young man-about-town who enjoys good, gracious living."[18]

Playboy's argument that social success and a hunger for the good life went hand in hand found its clearest expression, however, in a 1956 ad campaign that asked, "What is a Playboy?"

> Is he simply a wastrel, a ne'er-do-well, a fashionable bum? Far from it: he can be a sharp-minded young business executive, a worker in the arts, a university professor, an architect or engineer. He can be many things, providing he possesses a certain *point of view*. He must see life not as a vale of tears, but as a happy time; he must take joy in his work, without regarding it as the end and all of living; he must be an alert man, an aware man, a man of taste, a man sensitive to pleasure, a man who—without acquiring the stigma of the voluptuary or the dilettante—can live life to the hilt.

The *Playboy* reader, in other words, was someone who was determined both to find economic success and enjoy its material and emotional fruits.[19] But Hefner also grasped the more subtle point that *Playboy* embodied social fantasy as much as reality. While his magazine affirmed the appetites of well-connected stock traders, shrewd young lawyers, and au courant architects, it also provided a kind of wish fulfillment for weary salesmen or aspiring young middle managers who desperately wanted to believe they were on the fast track. As Hefner admitted in a 1955 interview, *Playboy*, in a sense, was "an escapist magazine" projecting "the kind of life part of the reader would like to live." It offered him "an imaginary escape into the world of wine, women and song," he said. "Then the other part of him says he has to go back to his family responsibilities and his work."[20]

Central to *Playboy*'s fantasy of the good life, of course, was a loosening of traditional restrictions on sexuality. Early issues of the magazine suggested that sex was a healthy, natural human impulse, not a dirty endeavor to be repressed or a sacred one to be elevated. An array of erotic photographs, pictorials, cartoons, jokes, and articles drove home the message. "Nudity and the Foreign Film," for instance, with text and photographs, contrasted American and European movies in terms of depicting nudity. "The movie censors of America have considered the human body and concluded that it is immoral," the magazine declared. But no one was justified in "forcing its opinions, tastes, and attitudes on the rest of us. We make a habit of thumbing our noses at censors, because we feel they have no place in a democracy."[21]

Hefner defended *Playboy*'s sexual thrust. "It's one of the things our guy is interested in, and there's no reason for us to apologize for it," he told an interviewer in 1955. He scorned the notion that his magazine's sexuality might corrupt the nation's youth. The idea that one must bring "our literature and entertainment down to the level of twelve-year-olds is incredible," he argued. Healthy sex was part of the good life, Hefner insisted, and *Playboy*'s expression of that sentiment "reached the young city man in a way that makes him feel a real identification with the magazine."[22]

The first issues of *Playboy* also called for male liberation from the demands of marriage and family life. Preaching the gospel of bachelorhood, the magazine offered articles such as "Miss Gold-digger of 1953," which warned that greedy women, backed by the courts, were using divorce settlements to stick an "ex-spouse for a healthy chunk of his earnings from that day forward, for the rest of his unnatural life." When an irate woman sent a letter complaining that most men were unscrupulous seducers who "*ought* to pay, and pay, and pay" when fleeing a marriage, *Playboy* replied, "Ah, shaddup!" "Open Season on Bachelors" examined marriage traps laid by women for unsuspecting men, while "A Vote for Polygamy" came to the breezy conclusion that "the end of the ignoble experiment in monogamy may be near." Hefner and his early readers, resisting the powerful pull of family ideology of the 1950s, fantasized sex as a form of play released from its ties to marriage and procreation.[23]

Beyond sex, *Playboy* advocated a wide variety of leisure activities to enhance the good life. Smart, flattering clothing became a must in articles such as "That Brooks Brothers Look," which proclaimed, "Burn my zoot suit, mother. Conservative eastern dress is a must this season." Elegant cuisine became another necessity as the magazine took on a "food and drink editor" in early 1954, Thomas Mario, who expounded upon the "Pleasures of the Oyster" and explained "the manly art of outdoor cooking" to aspiring male sophisticates. Sex, of course, was never far from the flame. In Mario's words, when "you deliver the thick, browned steaks, charred and crisp on the outside, rare inside" and then hand her an ear of roasted golden bantam corn on the cob you "detect in her eyes a kind of yielding rapture. Are any further stratagems necessary?"[24]

Playboy supplied a steady diet of entertainment. It offered sketches of celebrities such as Orson Welles, Steve Allen, and Frank Lloyd Wright, while brief tours of music recordings, films, books, and sports kept readers conversant with the latest turns in popular culture. The renowned musician Dave Brubeck explained "The New Jazz Audience." "Playboy After Hours" began in 1955 with reviews of restaurants in Chicago and New York, the new British musical *The Boy Friend*, records by Mabel Mercer, Frank Sinatra, and Billie Holiday, the movies *Mister Roberts* and *Pete Kelley's Blues*, and books by Harold Robbins and George Axelrod. The annual College Issue surveyed the male student with his "dreams of the future bachelor apartment, the hi-fi set, the well-stocked liquor cabinet, the sports car—and the bedroom-eyed beauties who will help him enjoy it all. These are the dreams, of course, that PLAYBOY is made of."[25]

This process of pleasure-priming saw *Playboy* preparing readers to face the challenges of upward mobility. Shepherd Mead, in "How to Succeed in Business Without Really Trying," deployed satire to mask shrewd advice on how to thrive in the corporate world. As he explained, "It is the ability to Get Along, to Make Decisions, and to Get Contacts that will drive you ahead. Be an 'all-around man' of no special ability and you will rise to the top." For the aspiring gourmand, articles explained a long list of "common menu terms found in restaurants with a continental background." Essays such as Evelyn Waugh's "The Death of Painting" assessed the impact of photography and abstract expressionism on modern art.[26]

Playboy's fictional offerings tried to sharpen readers' appreciation of the finer things in life. Top writers responded to generous payments, and the magazine began publishing short stories by distinguished writers such as Ray Bradbury, W. Somerset Maugham, Charles Beaumont, John Steinbeck, and James Jones. Some offered gems, such as Bradbury's "Fahrenheit 451," a chilling futuristic tale, and Beaumont's "Black Country," a gripping story about a jazz horn player, but others did not hand over their best material. That was fine with *Playboy*. Indeed, a solicitation in *Writer's Digest* revealed the type of writing sought by the magazine. "Fiction should be modern, aware, sophisticated, highly literate but not 'literary'; articles should treat subjects of interest to the city-bred 'operator' who knows his way around, and should be handled in a breezy, comfortable, unpedantic style; humor should be ribald and/or satirical"; and "Sex, being a part of The Good Life, will have an important place in all three categories." In other words, the cultural curriculum taught at the *Playboy* schoolhouse aimed to provide a veneer of sophistication rather than the real thing. Compiling a cultural *Cliffs Notes* for those who had earned gentleman's C's in college (or for many others who had only dreamed of enrolling), the magazine tossed them aesthetic tidbits that were challenging, but not *too* challenging.[27]

Thus Hefner and *Playboy* defined the central obstacles facing 1950s America as matters of lifestyle and taste. He did not stand alone. As the historian Jackson Lears has pointed out, most highbrow cultural critics in this period also focused on aesthetics, making their critiques of American life "a matter of taste" as they excoriated the bland conformity and tasteless consumption that had swallowed up the middle class.[28] But instead of elitist chastisement, Hefner utilized "can-do" midwestern uplift. Mixing two parts eroticism to one part intellect, and adding a dash of irreverent humor, he cheerfully concocted a cultural cocktail that eased ambitious young men into a fuller enjoyment of American abundance in all of its material and emotional dimensions.

III

The attraction of Hugh Hefner's road map to the good life became evident in *Playboy's* sales. The print run—70,000 copies for the first issue—grew steadily and after one year stood at 185,000. It exploded to 500,000 by the end of 1955, and at 1.1 million copies a month passed *Esquire* by the end of 1956, with gross sales of some $3.5 million and a net profit before taxes of around $400,000. These quick, quantum leaps in readership made the magazine an unprecedented success in American publishing history.[29]

Hefner was elated. As he wrote a couple of months after the magazine's first issue:

> What do you say when a dream comes true? . . . I own a magazine—a magazine of my very own. . . . Certainly much of my life, and especially the last three or four years, has been a preparation for this. For there is nothing on earth I would rather be doing than editing and publishing this magazine called PLAYBOY. . . . Perhaps I'll wake up in a few months and it will all be gone. But in this January of 1954, life is just a little more wonderful than I ever really believed it could be.[30]

But Hefner did not rest on his laurels. *Playboy's* initial success drove the young editor to work at an even more frenzied pace. "Hef's reaction to the first issue? Going full blast," recalled Eldon Sellers. He worked nearly around the clock and barely saw his wife and daughter. Hefner wrote, "PLAYBOY consumes seven days of every week, more than a dozen hours a day, and I knock off at 1:30 or 2:00 in the morning"[31]

His personal identification with *Playboy* became almost total. "I've always edited the magazine for myself, on the assumption that my tastes are pretty much like those of our readers. The concept of the magazine should grow and broaden with me," he informed a local reporter. The growing profits were gratifying, but his real pleasure came from editing and publishing the magazine. It was a labor of love that reflected, in his words, "a yearning to communicate, to express one's talents and ideas." Moreover, Hefner began formulating plans for expansion—opening *Playboy* to advertising, publishing a compilation book, *The Best from Playboy,* and licensing specialty items like calendars and cards.[32]

Impressive sales also brought institutional expansion. Hefner had prepared the first three issues of *Playboy* on his apartment card table, but in early 1954 accumulating profits allowed him to rent office space in a four-story town house at 11 East Superior Street on the

Near North Side, directly across from Holy Name Cathedral. Hefner was delighted with this location in the bohemian section of Chicago that mingled office buildings, boutiques, antique stores, apartments, and a teeming nightlife of saloons, strip joints, and clubs. *Playboy* began with one floor of offices, but expansion led to the acquisition of all four floors in little more than a year.[33]

The magazine's profits also rescued the young editor and his family from debt. Sales from the first couple of issues permitted them to get their furniture out of hock, and Hefner bought a new Studebaker for his family on Christmas 1953. In mid-1955, he had the money to purchase a new Cadillac Eldorado for himself. He and Millie also prepared to move into a large, comfortable lakeshore apartment. When dreaming of his own magazine, he wrote, "I didn't realize that it would make me rich, but that's what it's doing."[34]

Even more importantly, however, *Playboy*'s skyrocketing popularity put the young editor in the public eye. He became a celebrity, first in his hometown, then gradually throughout the rest of the country. He emerged as a subject of discussion and speculation. "His angular features usually have a solemn, almost haggard look, though occasionally they break into a whimsical grin," described a feature article in *Chicago* magazine. "He speaks rapidly and evenly, punctuating a robust dictionary vocabulary with contemporary slang." Brief pieces on Hefner and *Playboy* appeared in *Time* and *Newsweek* by mid-1956, and the editor appeared as a guest on Mike Wallace's *Night Beat*, a popular New York television show. He became an American success story in the best Horatio Alger tradition. As he told a reporter, "From the time I left high school until the magazine succeeded, I was never a very happy guy. Now it's something like being in high school all over again, but on a much greater scale."[35]

Hefner's newfound success also inspired a surge of controversy. As *Playboy* began attracting attention, censorship problems arose. In October 1954 the magazine applied for a permanent second-class mailing permit—it had been operating with a temporary one up to this point—typically issued to periodicals. The U.S. Post Office delayed, and then denied, the application on the pretext that *Playboy*, which had skipped an issue because of production problems, was not regularly published. Then a reapplication was denied, this time on the grounds of obscenity. Postmaster General Arthur Summerfield informed Hefner that a revision of the magazine's contents might gain approval. So HMH Publishing brought a civil action against Summerfield in federal court in the District of Columbia in November 1955.

Hefner sought an injunction to keep the Post Office from interfering with the delivery of his magazine and asked the court to enjoin the granting of a second-class permit. He challenged the "censorship powers" claimed by the Post Office and presented a ringing declaration of principle. "We don't think Postmaster Summerfield has any business editing magazines. We think he should stick to delivering the mail," Hefner proclaimed indignantly. "This isn't a new fight. It never is. Yesterday it was Anthony Comstock, today it is Arthur Summerfield." Hefner won a complete legal victory. The court issued an injunction restraining the Post Office from interfering with the magazine's distribution and ordered it to grant second-class privileges. Eventually, the court awarded *Playboy* $100,000 in compensation.[36]

A couple of months later, a ruckus arose when Chicago's Northwestern University banned *Playboy* from its bookstore. It claimed that protests had come in from English professors, a navy ROTC officer, a women's service group, an assistant football coach, and a fraternity housemother. Upon investigating these "letters of complaint," however, the *Daily Northwestern*, the student newspaper, discovered that the writers were fictitious. Meanwhile, Hefner wrote a letter to the university objecting to the ban. Censorship was particularly disturbing "in a large university dedicated to the principles of democracy and freedom of speech and press," he wrote. "Of course, these would-be censors may feel that college students aren't yet capable of choosing what to read or see or listen to. . . . These same 'censors' might next logically lead a raid on the Northwestern university library, which undoubtedly includes a great many books not quite suited to the adolescent mind."[37]

With both controversy and success swirling around *Playboy*, Hugh Hefner emerged as a cultural bellwether in postwar America. *Playboy's* agenda of sensual and material enjoyment reflected the nation's massive, ongoing shift from a work culture to a leisure culture. In a climate of unprecedented and widespread abundance, fresh desires for play were surmounting traditional demands for labor. Burdened too long by the deprivations of economic depression and the sacrifices of war, growing numbers of young Americans wanted to have fun and enjoy the good life. A restless young midwesterner appreciated those desires—indeed, he shared them—and created a venue for their expression. Over the last half of the 1950s, his magazine would go on to create a full-blown fantasy formula designed to fulfill them.

Playboy's rapid success, however, quickly overwhelmed its crude bureaucratic structure. Within months of the first issue, it became evident that a single editor and a few assistants, no matter how dedicated, would not suffice. With typical energy, Hefner threw himself into building a larger operation.

5

Hedonism, Inc.

A s *Playboy* took off in its first year of publication, Hugh Hefner faced a happy problem: he was overwhelmed with work. The explosion of sales created editorial and production tasks that Hefner and a few part-time assistants could not handle. The young editor moved to address that need by hiring several individuals—editors, artists, photographers, promotions experts, businessmen, support staff—to flesh out the publication team.

This influx brought a number of forceful, talented people to Hefner's side and made his operation a beehive of creative ferment. Expansion came in two stages. First, in 1954, the nucleus of the *Playboy* operation took shape with the arrival of a tiny group of longtime editorial operatives. Then in 1956 came a second, larger wave of hiring that included a group of staffers who would reshape further the basic structure and look of the magazine. Throughout this growth process, Hefner put his creative stamp on nearly everything in *Playboy*. By the late 1950s, the young publisher had created an organizational structure that became the foundation for the magazine for decades.

I

The early days of *Playboy*, like those of any successful new venture, were marked by a great sense of excitement and anticipation. As sales of the first few issues of the magazine rose steadily, Hefner put together the skeleton of a publication staff throughout 1954 and early 1955. Art Paul came on board as a full-time art director, Ray Russell became associate editor, and Vince Tajiri took over as head of the photo department. Joe Paczek assumed the duties of paste-and-layout man. Marjorie Pitner became an all-purpose reception-ist, subscription manager, and bookkeeper, while Eldon Sellers took on the tasks of advertising, circulation, and business manager. Pat Pappangelis was hired as Hefner's secretary, and John Mastro joined the organization as production manager.

The tiny group was energized by a powerful feeling of creating something fresh and interesting. Working in the small Superior Street town house in an atmosphere marked by common purpose and cama-raderie, they felt a sense of mission. "In those early days, it was really a team effort. We were all in on the creation of something exciting and important," Pitner reported. "We were there because we loved what we were doing."[1]

With such a small and close-knit staff working in tight quarters at the brownstone on Superior Street, there was little division of labor. Recalled Pitner, "In those days, I handled everything from tracking artwork and editorial material back and forth to the typesetter and the printer, to depositing checks from subscribers and labeling their copies for mailing." She also typed manuscripts for the magazine and even lent a hand to choosing risqué jokes for the "Party Jokes" page, until Hefner raised an eyebrow at her awful choices and took her off the job. During *Playboy*'s first Christmas, the entire group gath-ered to stuff magazines into envelopes, affix labels, and rush them out to mailboxes to get to subscribers on time while listening to Frank Sinatra's *In the Wee Small Hours* album.[2]

A sense of closeness marked the office atmosphere. According to John Mastro, "We were a family together, we all knew what the job was, we had a common goal, and we all knew that if this thing goes, it was good for all of us." When Hefner got his first Cadillac, the whole staff gathered to congratulate him, while he personally handed out bonus checks and thanked them for their hard work at the office

Christmas party. An early staffer observed, "There was a closeness there, and I guess a lot of it was just because of the fact that we were involved in a new adventure."[3]

Amid this warm atmosphere, several individuals emerged to play particularly important creative roles in shaping different parts of the magazine. When Art Paul initially joined *Playboy*, he had worked on an hourly basis as Hefner shuttled photos and artwork between his kitchen and Paul's small studio. The artist received only partial payment. But as the magazine flourished, he agreed to join *Playboy* as full-time art director and took part of his back payment in stock. He quickly began to create the cool, sophisticated, slightly irreverent graphics that became a hallmark of the magazine.[4]

Paul had been born and raised in Chicago and was trained at both the Art Institute and the Institute of Design. A freelance designer in his early career, he maintained a strong interest in jazz, classical music, and films. Upon his joining *Playboy*, he and Hefner talked extensively about design, communication, and how to say what you wanted to say. They collaborated closely on early issues of the magazine, often working frantically with Paul doing layout and Hefner writing copy right up to press time.[5]

The art director, like Hefner, was determined to create a distinctive look for the magazine. In his words, "I really wanted to see if I couldn't create a whole new visual kind of language." He sought a clean, fresh design style with, in his phrase, "a keen sense of drama." Paul had a hand in shaping every visual component of *Playboy*: choosing artwork and arranging photographs, directing layout and type styles, consulting on cartoon art and reproductions, and conceptualizing special features. He played a key role in designing the magazine's cover, which not only had to convey what the issue was about but also include the *Playboy* rabbit symbol (the latter quickly developed into a game as readers tried to find the often cleverly hidden head-and-ears logo). But whatever the specific project, Paul always aimed for a strong relationship between language and graphics. He believed that visuals must somehow "broaden the scope of the story or get the reader to exercise curiosity."[6]

While Paul worked with Hefner to shape the distinct graphic image of *Playboy*, Ray Russell arrived to help with a host of editorial chores. He also had grown up in Chicago, studying acting at the Goodman Theatre and music at the Chicago Conservatory of Music before serving a stint in the air force during World War II. He was working as an editor at the *Walgreen Pepper Pod,* the house publication of Walgreen Drug Stores, when he saw the first issue of *Playboy* in a local bookstore. Noticing the reprinted articles obviously secured on the cheap, he sent off a couple of his stories to the magazine along with a humorous note recommending that it "wise up and start printing a few stories written later than 1889." To Russell's surprise, he received a phone call a couple of days later from "a young man obviously pitching his voice very low in an attempt to sound fifty years old." They set up a meeting at a bar in January 1954, Russell hoping to secure a writing assignment or two. But Hefner, who arrived carrying his usual oversized briefcase full of artwork and layouts, was so impressed that he offered the writer an editorial position on the spot. Russell accepted immediately.[7]

He joined Hefner and Paul at the Superior Street offices a couple of weeks later. "The three of us constituted the entire editorial and art staff of *Playboy*. There weren't even any secretaries. Hef and I typed our own letters," Russell related. "Hef and Art and I were constantly in and out of each other's offices, conferring, very occasionally arguing, bubbling over with ideas and enthusiasm." Russell became involved with every aspect of the magazine dealing with words. He screened submissions, edited those chosen for publication, wrote photo captions and subscription pitches, reviewed books and movies, and "retold" Ribald Classics from Boccaccio and Balzac. He even wrote original articles on current personalities such as Frank Lloyd Wright and Dave Garroway. One of his most enduring contributions was the subscription pitch titled "What is a Playboy?" that became a key expression of the magazine's philosophy for many years.[8]

Looking like a miniature Orson Welles with his rotund figure, beard, cigar, and theatrical personality, Russell threw himself into the multitude of tasks facing the tiny staff. When boxes of new magazines from the bindery arrived, he helped Hefner lug them up the stairs and weigh them on a baby scale (it was Hefner's own, donated by his mother) before they were sent out to distributors. He emptied the wastebaskets. He scrambled to meet publication deadlines as he, Hefner, and Paul often drove to the printing plant in Rochelle once a month and stayed up all night amid the roar of machinery correcting proof pages as they rolled off the presses still wet. But Russell loved his work. The early magazine "was crude but vital, full of amateurish blunders but also full of freshness and wide-eyed enthusiasm," he noted.[9]

Hefner's third important hire was Vince Tajiri, who became photo editor. Of Japanese American background and a native of Southern California, this self-taught photographer had served during World War II with the famous 442nd Infantry before moving to Chicago to shoot weddings and assignments for small magazines. He was employed at Publisher's Development Corporation when he befriended Hefner. He declined to invest in *Playboy* because of the risk, but responded to Hefner's job offer a couple of years later. "When I arrived, the photo department was me, one file cabinet, a secretary and two desks," he recalled. Tajiri also wondered aloud if there would be enough work to keep him busy—Hefner never let him forget the remark—but soon began to focus on creating a distinct photographic style for *Playboy*. He described it as "slick but candid, a cross between advertising photography and photo journalism—not only for the nude layouts but for fashion, food and drink, all the lifestyle elements that are such an integral part of the magazine's identity."[10]

Something of a perfectionist, Tajiri took great pains to choose just the right photos from among the hundreds he took or were submitted to him. Photographers sometimes went through eight or ten shoots before Tajiri would accept their work. "We always overshoot our layouts," he explained. "For example, we usually shoot about 120 sheets for each Playmate. . . . We only use about one out of every fifty shots." Tajiri also proved very sensitive to Hefner's aesthetic preferences, especially regarding young women. In his words, the publisher liked a natural feeling where the girl was "caught in a moment of her life when she was doing something, or has just done something, and then looks up at the camera and presumably associates with the reader." This approach also carried over into photographs of clothing and meals, where Tajiri proved adept at conveying "the fun you could have or enjoy, the tastes of foods, the taste of wines." His photographic style became a hallmark of *Playboy*. "It is rather slick but we try to bring into it a candid, alive, realistic feeling," he explained.[11]

In 1956, a second stage of staff expansion came as *Playboy* profits funded the move to a four-story office building on Ohio Street. As Hefner wrote to his brother in April, "On the business side, everything I have to report is tremendous. Each month proves incredibly better than the last and this obviously cannot go on forever, but the end of the growth is not yet in sight." This continued success of the magazine allowed for payment of an annual lease of about $500,000 following a complete remodeling of the building at a cost of about $325,000. It also allowed Hefner to hire several important figures who would play major roles in taking *Playboy* to a new level of popularity and influence.[12]

His most important move came with the hiring of A. C. Spectorsky. In July 1956, *Playboy* announced that this distinguished New York journalist and literary figure would be joining the magazine as Hefner's second-in-command. The publisher had decided that someone carrying credentials with the East Coast establishment would help *Playboy* to gain increased respectability. *Playboy* had published one of Spectorsky's stories, "Some Guys Get It," under a pseudonym, and when Hefner decided to hire a literary editor his name surfaced. The young publisher set about luring Spectorsky to Chicago. After a phone call established that he might be interested, Hefner flew to New York to discuss the situation and offered the job. After a trip to Chicago to check out the *Playboy* operation, Spectorsky accepted.[13]

Arrangements were soon made—a salary of $35,000 a year, an expense account, stock options, moving expenses, an advance against salary to escape one apartment lease and sign another. Hefner was delighted with his new editorial director. Impressed with Spectorsky's literary credentials and connections to writers, he described the New Yorker as "a real heavyweight" who would "handle a lot of the issue by issue problems and free me to plan more of the special features, handle long-range planning, etc." Spectorsky appeared equally pleased with his new job. Convinced that his talents and Hefner's would complement one another perfectly, he told the publisher, "With your instincts and my taste, there's nothing we can't accomplish." Equally important, he was content to remain in the background and support Hefner as the public symbol of the magazine. "I think Hef, the young sparkplug and head of the whole operation, is the guy who should be kept in the foreground," he wrote in a staff memo.[14]

Auguste Comte Spectorsky did much to bring a more sophisticated, polished air to the upstart Chicago publication. He came from a cosmopolitan background, having been born in Paris in 1910 to Russian émigrés, and spoke French exclusively for the first four years of his life, before his parents fled to New York City to escape the onrush of World War I. He graduated from New York University after majoring in physics and mathematics, but a gift for writing led to a stint on the *New Yorker's* editorial staff. He then became the literary editor at the *Chicago Sun* for six years in the 1940s, before returning to New York to work as a writer and editor in movies, television, and journalism. In the early 1950s, he authored a much-discussed book, *The Exurbanites*. A tall man with short-cropped hair, large eyes, and languid manner, Spectorsky had an elegant, world-weary persona that underlined his urbanity, while his age (he was ten or fifteen years older than the others on the *Playboy* staff) contributed further to his authority.[15]

Almost immediately, Spectorsky put the magazine in touch with the literary culture of the East Coast. Soon after signing on, he and his wife, Theo, hosted several parties in New York City to introduce Hefner to important authors, publishers, and agents. "Hef knew no one, so I took him by the left arm so his right arm was free to shake hands, and introduced him to every single person," Theo related. "I couldn't just introduce him, then leave him on his own because he was so shy he'd just shut up." Moreover, Spectorsky began to exploit his literary contacts to bulk up the fiction and nonfiction offerings in *Playboy*. Ken Purdy, for instance, a personal friend, soon became a regular contributor, along with an impressive list of fiction writers such as John Steinbeck, James Jones, Jack Kerouac, Ray Bradbury, P. G. Wodehouse, and Charles Beaumont. Nonfiction authors such as Vance Packard, Philip Wylie, Ralph Ginzburg, and Arthur C. Clarke joined them.[16]

Equally important, Spectorsky began to construct a talented and hardworking staff. Although an imposing figure, he was a pleasant, considerate man whom nearly everyone grew to love as well as respect. Ray Russell, for instance, initially resented the New Yorker's arrival but soon came "to really like and admire Spec." Arlene Bouras, who joined the magazine as a highly skilled copy editor, found him to be an excellent line editor and a wonderful discussant on larger questions of style, content, and language. Commented an assistant editor, "He's not only the most professional editor I've ever met, but he also can write. He dictates most of his prose, right into the machine with hardly a change." Spectorsky shouldered many tasks at *Playboy*—from securing writers to reading every word that went into the magazine, from integrating the various editorial functions to serving as a liaison between editorial and circulation, from coordinating with graphics and photographs operations to okaying the layouts before they went to Hefner for final approval. "If there is a man behind the scenes at *Playboy*," he told an interviewer several years later, "I suppose I am it."[17]

Publicly, Spectorsky expressed contentment with his position. "I am a much better writer than when I came to *Playboy*," he told an interviewer about five years after joining the magazine. "It helped me clarify a lot of my thinking about the relationship of the sexes and what makes some people happy and others unhappy . . . [and] loosened up a lot of rather rigid ideas I'd had without realizing I had them." He also enjoyed the affluence the job brought him, buying a big apartment, a sailboat, a yacht club membership, and a big house in St. Croix.

Privately, however, Spectorsky developed profoundly ambivalent feelings about working for *Playboy*. He never got over the idea that the magazine, somehow, was beneath his talents. The reasons were complex.[18]

In part, Spectorsky viewed his position at the magazine as a sign of his failed literary career. "He wanted to write something that would last in history," recalled his wife. "He wanted to achieve stature—and he felt that he would never achieve it at *Playboy*." Bouras, his good friend and colleague, agreed. "He aspired to an awful lot more than he ever achieved in life," she reported. "And I think he knew he was capable of original work and he hated himself for never having achieved it." Spectorsky aspired to be editor of the *New Yorker*, and developed a kind of self-contempt when he failed to do so. He would tell a story, for instance, about contacting Lionel Trilling, the famous literary critic, when Hefner offered him a job. Spectorsky was worried that it would be viewed as selling out, but he reported that Trilling replied, "You have nothing to sell out." Spectorsky meant the story to be self-deprecating, but most listeners found it to be embarrassing, sad, and all too revealing of the teller.[19]

Spectorsky's ambivalence also appeared in his complicated, love-hate connection with Hefner. Publicly, and often privately, he praised his boss for his intelligence and described him as "that rare creature in this business, a publisher who is primarily editorially-oriented rather than business oriented." He believed that Hefner had an unerring instinct for what was right for his magazine, and a broad streak of generosity in his personal makeup. At the same time, Spectorsky became contemptuous of what he saw as Hefner's deficiencies—bad aesthetic taste, an unwillingness to be intellectually challenged, an emotional distance from friends and colleagues, an intense selfishness, an unpredictability in his work hours and decision-making process. Sometimes his frustrations boiled over. "You want every article to be the way you'd handle it if you were writing it. You refuse to accept an article writer's own approach to his subject," he complained to Hefner in 1957. *Playboy's* progress must be judged comprehensively, not by "you alone-at-night, vaguely terrified, with frustrated feelings about one article." Spectorsky began referring to Hefner (behind his back) as "Godzilla" and emerged from many encounters, according to Ray Russell, with "an exasperated gaze heavenward or a weary shake of the head, or a sigh of *weltschmerz.*"[20]

Nonetheless, he yearned for his boss's approval. "He had a very strange relationship with Hefner," Spectorsky's wife reported. "Almost father-son, but the wrong way around. I don't know why he had this tremendous need to please Hefner but he did." When the magazine's popularity soared and the publisher credited the editorial staff, Spectorsky was elated. But when his teenage daughter died from a medical complication in the mid-1960s and Hefner was the only staff member who failed to offer condolences, he grew despondent. "There have been times when I've hated Hef more deeply than anybody I don't love," Spectorsky once confessed. "To hate him as much as I've hated him, you really have to love him."[21]

Around the same time that Spectorsky arrived on the scene, another man joined *Playboy* who would become one of the most influential, and controversial, figures in the organization's history. Victor Lownes met Hefner at a party hosted for the up-and-coming comedian Jonathan Winters. The two hit it off immediately and began going out to clubs and taverns together. Within a few weeks Hefner offered Lownes a job at his magazine, and the young Chicagoan became head of promotions. Over the next decade, he also would become promotions director for the Playboy Clubs.[22]

Victor A. Lownes III came from a silver-spoon background. He grew up in Florida as the son of an affluent building contractor, while his grandparents on both sides of the family were quite wealthy. "There were chauffeured Pierce Arrows and things like that in my background," he once told an interviewer. After attending prep school in New Mexico, he matriculated at the University of Chicago, married the daughter of a rich cattle rancher from Arkansas, and took a job with one of his grandfather's companies. Although ensconced in a fashionable Chicago suburb with a beautiful home and two small children, he grew to hate his life. He felt trapped in a tennis-club and cocktail-party society while his career stalled in a series of dead-end promotion and advertising jobs. So in 1953 Lownes left his family, divorced his wife, and moved into a bachelor apartment where he began to date showgirls and host boisterous parties. It was at one such gathering that he met Hefner. According to Eldon Sellers, a friend of both men, Lownes began "romancing" the young publisher because he was impressed with him and *Playboy* and wanted to be a part of it.[23]

Lownes's charm and sophistication appealed greatly to Hefner. He was everything Hefner aspired to be—handsome, debonair, witty, and elegantly attired in Brooks Brothers clothing as he seduced countless women who crossed his path. "Hef emulated Victor—he really wanted to be Victor," Theo Spectorsky observed. *Playboy* staffers commented that "when Vic talks, Hef sees it in technicolor." The two developed a real camaraderie, eating at the East Inn and spending late-night hours at clubs on Rush Street such as the Cloister Inn, the Black Orchid, and Dante's Inferno.[24]

Lownes's oversized personality and outrageous sense of humor quickly made him a legend at *Playboy*. While working late at the magazine, he discovered that a local radio show called *The Bishop's Study*—a Catholic clergyman would advise callers on personal problems—had a telephone number one digit off from that of his office phone. So frequently he received the radio show's calls by mistake. Claiming to be the bishop's assistant, Lownes dispensed scandalous advice, urging women to leave their families or counseling young people to live together before marriage. One evening when a caller asked where the bishop was, Lownes replied, "He's out getting drunk." After mounting complaints, the church program finally changed its number. Another time, Lownes successfully convinced a beautiful but rather dim young woman that before she bought a dog, she should contact "Hertz Rent a Puppy" for a test run. The staff choked back laughter as she earnestly paged through the phone book looking for the business's number.[25]

Lownes's love life seemed a fantasy lifted from the pages of *Playboy*. A dedicated womanizer and suave bon vivant, he attracted numerous young women for sexual flings. "Quantity was more important than quality in those days," he admitted later. Lownes and Eldon Sellers became roommates and their residence became party central. Lownes bolted together four double beds into what he called a "playpen" and covered it with a huge bedspread, while he and Sellers made a large bowl of punch with grapefruit juice and grain alcohol. Female dancers from the nearby Empire Room would drop by after work, and the group would play strip games into the wee hours of the morning. Hefner often dropped by to join in the bacchanals.[26]

Lownes poured an enormous amount of energy and creativity into *Playboy*'s promotions department. He convinced Hefner to set up a network of college reps to take advantage of the tremendous popularity of the magazine among male students on campuses. Developing a large staff that soon occupied a whole floor of the Ohio Street offices, he produced subscription ads, promotional pieces, and items for newspaper and magazine columns. He became famous as a fountain of new ideas at staff meetings. "He worked like a shotgun," noted one associate. "He'd fire off twelve different ways to do something, and one of them would hit." One of his greatest achievements came with Hefner's pet projects, the 1959 "Playboy Jazz Festival." At his boss's request, he organized and produced the entire affair—a three-day music concert that brought such luminaries as Count Basie, Ella Fitzgerald, and Stan Kenton to some twenty thousand jazz fans at Chicago Stadium.[27]

At the same time, Lownes's freewheeling style and flamboyant personality caused problems. Unable to delegate authority and tremendously egotistical, he intimidated subordinates and spread confusion. "I had been so successful with so many ideas that I guess I began to feel that they must all be good, and people should accept them unquestionably," he confessed later. "And when they didn't I'd try to browbeat them into it." When the promotions department became mired in dissension or confusion, Hefner scolded Lownes for sacrificing competence to creativity. "You've got to give me more than devotion and more than creative genius," he wrote. "I also need organization and efficiency, a meeting of deadlines, a following of procedures."[28]

Moreover, Lownes indulged dark impulses in his personality. Displaying a cruel streak that alienated even his admirers, he often turned dictatorial. A master of the putdown, he zeroed in on people's personal weaknesses and tormented them with sarcastic jibes.

"He was just an abrasive man with everybody," Theo Spectorsky said. "He mistreated everybody, ranted and raved, screamed at people." Colleagues described him as "brutal," "vicious," and a "rat." Part of this arrogant behavior stemmed from his background as a spoiled rich kid, but another part was rooted in tragedy. As a boy, Lownes had shot and killed a young friend in a hunting accident. A *Playboy* colleague believed that he treated people so badly because, subconsciously, he wanted them to hate him because of that terrible mishap.[29]

Lownes's abrasive behavior caused severe problems in the promotions department. Displaying the classic sign of the bully by picking on the weak, he "ruled by outright terror" over subordinates, according to one colleague. Instead of politely approving or disapproving proposals from subordinates, for example, he pounded a reply on their memos with a special rubber stamp, one of which had, Roman style, a closed fist with the thumb pointed up and the other with it pointing down. On occasion his rudeness would cause his entire staff to "quit *en masse*—the whole floor—and just walk out the door. Hef would run out to calm everyone down." Once, when his maltreatment of employees caused a momentary pang of guilt, Lownes put a jar of quarters on his desk and told everyone to take a coin whenever he said something nasty to them. The jar was soon empty.[30]

Lownes's impulse to belittle and dominate others found a particularly unpleasant outlet in his treatment of women, producing boorish behavior and social agitation. He enjoyed sexual conquest, discarded women at his pleasure, and expected girlfriends to obey his every whim. According to one, "You wore what he said. And you did just what he said." Once, he concocted a late-night plan to have Hefner go to his apartment, crawl in bed with his sleeping girlfriend, and pretend to be Lownes as he made love to her. Things backfired, however, when the drowsy young woman excused herself to use the bathroom and instead called the police to report a "weirdo" who had broken into the residence. Officers arrived soon, and a highly embarrassed Hefner had to explain his way out of this predicament. When friends, in recognition of Lownes's bad treatment of women, presented him with the Golden Prick Award at a party, he began a mock acceptance speech: "I would like to thank the members of the academy . . ." Despite such outrageous, egocentric behavior, he became one of the brightest stars in the *Playboy* organization by the late 1950s.[31]

Other influential figures joined the magazine around the same time. Jack Kessie stepped in as associate editor in 1956, helping to establish the magazine's signature style under the pseudonym of "Blake Rutherford," author of numerous men's fashion pieces over the next decade. He personified the *Playboy* vision of the good life. Always tastefully attired, he "had the bachelor pad, the hi-fi and the wet bar, dined at all the elegant restaurants, drank the right wines, drove the right sports car," in the words of a colleague. Around the office, his frequent lunches with Ray Russell—the two would trade witticisms, barbs, and bons mots as they liberally lubricated their food with martinis—became much-discussed social events.[32]

Anson "Smoky" Mount, a friendly, pipe-smoking Tennessean, became the magazine's expert on college football. He supervised the college bureau, created the famous "Pigskin Preview" each fall, and began selecting *Playboy*'s All-American players. From a deeply religious background, he also emerged as the magazine's spokesman and toured the country giving talks and debating fundamentalist critics of Hefner's philosophy. Like Kessie, he identified totally with the *Playboy* lifestyle, wearing rabbit-ear cuff links and pins and talking up the magazine to anyone who listened.[33]

Artist LeRoy Neiman joined the staff. An old acquaintance of Hefner's from his Carson Pirie Scott days, he had studied at the Chicago Art Institute, painted murals in the army, and eventually moved into fashion illustration. In 1954 he illustrated his first story for *Playboy*, a Charles Beaumont tale titled "Black Country," and over the next year he contributed sketches for other stories and did a cover. By 1956, Neiman's paintings and sketches had become recurring features in the magazine. A couple of years later, he made his enduring mark on *Playboy* with "Man at His Leisure," a series covering the most glamorous, exclusive social and sporting scenes in the world. Neiman's stylish illustrations of grand hotel suites in London and Venice, Maxim's restaurant in Paris, the Cannes Film Festival, the Grand National Steeplechase in England, the Grand Prix in Monaco, and bullfights in Madrid became identifiable symbols of the *Playboy* lifestyle. In later years he would create the magazine's famous "Femlin," the illustrated long-haired pixie female wearing only long black gloves and black stockings. His artistic style—impressionistic with elegant, elongated figures and bold, slashing colors and an aura of sophisticated elegance—was well suited to the young magazine.

Neiman's personal appearance as a fashionable street tough with a brusque, profane manner, an ever-present cigar, and a shock of black hair and extravagantly large mustache made an equally strong impact in the magazine's offices.[34]

With the expansion of the *Playboy* staff, the atmosphere at the magazine gradually changed. The close-knit ambiance became more corporate and turf battles began to emerge. According to one insider, Spectorsky, Paul, Lownes, and Tajiri "spent more time infighting and backbiting and jockeying for position than they did working together for the good of the magazine." But the feeling of excitement survived; a sense, in Hefner's phrase, of "riding a rocket." In this freewheeling social atmosphere inhabited by young, vibrant, talented men and women, the air became thick with eroticism. "There was a lot of sexual high jinks at *Playboy* in the 1950s," Hefner recalled later. "Sex in the office was commonplace."[35]

Thus, by the mid-1950s, Hefner had begun building an organization but remained clearly atop it. Absolutely devoted to *Playboy,* he imprinted his personality and tastes on every aspect of the publication. He combined boyish enthusiasm with a ferocious work ethic to lead, and occasionally herd, a talented and strong group of subordinates in the direction he envisioned. He had hired people, in his own words, "who could do something you wanted even better than you could do it yourself." As the creative force driving the magazine, his life and his work became indistinguishable.[36]

II

From the very beginning, when *Playboy* sold out its first few issues and scrambled to its feet financially, Hugh Hefner immersed himself in the publication of the magazine. When he and his tiny staff moved into the house on Superior Avenue in early 1954, he ensconced himself in his fourth-floor office. With a small bedroom and kitchenette appended to the office, he frequently slept there and his family saw him less and less. Quite literally, he lived his work.

Hefner followed a work schedule that awed his subordinates. Marshalling incredible amounts of energy, intensity, and enthusiasm, he threw himself into publishing *Playboy*. A staffer described him as "monomaniacal" and noted, "Women may have been his pastime, but

Playboy was his *life.*" Essentially, he lived at Superior Street, running out for bites to eat, catching a few hours of sleep in his office bedroom, and then beginning again. "He's a very intense, dedicated individual," observed Vince Tajiri. "He goes along with maybe a 1000 rpm's while most of us are going at 400 and there's this intensity, and also this impatience." He became famous among the secretaries for forgetting names, dates, and various peripheral matters because, in the words of one, "his mind was too full of things he was working on."[37]

With the move to the Ohio Street offices, Hefner's work schedule maintained its exhausting pace while becoming more eccentric. His new office suite also had a small bedroom, as well as bathroom and dressing room, and he would work deep into the early morning hours, catch some sleep, and begin his workday sometime after noon the following day. "Every afternoon, he would come barreling out of his office as if shot from a cannon, and all hell would break loose," Arlene Bouras described. "He would ricochet from office to office issuing orders, finding out why yesterday's orders hadn't been carried out, always demanding more than he was getting from everyone who worked with him." As the start of his workday began moving toward midafternoon, production manager John Mastro kidded, "Hef, I haven't figured out if you're a day ahead of us or a day behind us." Several celebrated habits began to emerge. First, Hefner took to working in his pajamas as the boundary between personal life and job dissolved. Second, he began to fill his office—floor, desk, tables—with stacks of material. "His own office is a huge, cluttered room awash with copies of magazines, books, cartoon roughs, proofs, records, and prints of past and future Playmates," noted a newspaper story. According to the cartoonist Shel Silverstein, visitors "really did have to step carefully to get over and around everything."[38]

Hefner also grew more jaded. In *Playboy's* early days at Superior Street, for instance, the jazz musician Stan Kenton, one of the publisher's idols, stopped by to thank the magazine for honoring him in its first jazz poll. When Hefner heard, according to LeRoy Neiman, he charged down the stairs to meet his hero because "that's the kind of gee-whiz guy he was in those days." Only two years later, however, after the move to Ohio Street, Kenton dropped by to be photographed when Hefner strolled through the studio looking at some papers and drinking a Pepsi. He glanced over and saw Kenton "sitting there on a stool under the floodlights, and he says, 'Oh, hi, Stan,' and wanders out again."[39]

But all of Hefner's personal quirks faded before his perfectionism, which drove him to involvement in every facet of *Playboy*. He expected everyone to share his passion for the magazine and created daunting standards of achievement. "He asked more of us than we were capable of giving, and that brought out the best in us," Bouras explained. When Mastro once complained that a production revision would be too expensive, he replied, "John, you worry about getting it right; let me worry about the cost."[40]

Hefner's exacting standards, however, did not prevent him from being a generous boss during *Playboy*'s early years. He took time to talk with employees such as Marge Pitner and Pat Pappangelis about personal difficulties and in one case advanced an employee a large sum of money to pay for several months of treatment for an emotional problem. While a workaholic, he was no slave driver to his staff. "Hef, I just can't work any harder," John Mastro once told him. "I know it, John," Hefner answered. He had a special ability to convey enthusiasm and inspire subordinates to give their all. His "power of persuasion," Eldon Sellers commented, "almost got you into a hypnotic state." A sly sense of humor often lightened the mood. Hefner once quipped to the dignified Spectorsky, "I've figured out why you and your wife are so sophisticated. You practice fidelity for kicks." Spectorsky observed that his boss was "able to detect the limitations and drawbacks of a person as well as his virtues and advantages," chew him out if necessary, "then re-inspire him and make him feel good and loved about his work."[41]

At the same time, Hefner could become distant and impatient. While forbearing with lesser staffers, he would grow testy with lieutenants, snapping, "Come on. Get to the point." The publisher's intense focus and high expectations also made him reluctant, perhaps unable, to compliment members of the *Playboy* staff. Art Paul, for instance, observed Hefner struggling to commend editors, artists, photographers, and production people, noting, "You can almost see him working on it." Hefner simply expected others to share his single-minded devotion to, and high standards for, the magazine.[42]

Yet his leadership style allowed input from talented subordinates when it served the larger purposes of improving the magazine. When Hefner disagreed with Art Paul over graphics issues, he usually backed down, saying, "You're the art director." He also swallowed his own judgment and allowed Ray Russell to push ahead with "The Contaminators," a 1959 nonfiction article dealing with the dangers of radioactive pollution. Hefner feared that such an article would be too controversial and weighty for an entertainment magazine, but when the piece elicited much praise, he was delighted to have been proven wrong. As Hefner described later, he tried to direct his organization by "more leading than pushing—getting people to where I wanted them to be—whether it was a cartoonist or an art director."[43]

As *Playboy* grew in the mid-1950s, Hefner increasingly focused on a central task—shaping the magazine's point of view. He sought to have all features revolve around a central theme of enjoying the pleasures of the good life, and to do so with a consistent tone of irreverent sophistication. In a 1956 memo to the staff, he outlined this goal:

> I don't want anything in *Playboy* that runs counter to the basic editorial attitude of the magazine. . . . [We want] not only features within the magazine that are in themselves entertaining, but also service features on such things as food, drink, fashion, and travel that help make life entertaining. . . . In our critical columns, where more than anywhere else we give some definition to our point of view, we offer opinions on music, classical as well as popular and jazz, on books and plays and theatre and films, and we often try to say rather important things about all this (although we hope to say it entertainingly). . . . Our non-fiction can sometimes have something to say just a bit deeper than it is fun to pinch girls in crowds and still not run counter to the fundamental policy of the magazine. . . . I don't want articles that preach, or are pompous, or primarily concerned with international affairs, religion, or racial friction.[44]

Hefner directed his energies into molding every element in *Playboy* around its "basic editorial attitude." According to Vince Tajiri, he scrutinized every photograph that went into the magazine with "the perfectionism of a diamond cutter" to make sure it fit the house style. Arlene Bouras received voluminous memos on appropriate type style, copy-editing, punctuation, and proofreading that became the basis of the magazine stylebook. His insistence that bullets rather than white space be used to separate sections in a manuscript became gospel. "If Jesus Christ himself ever came down and asked for white space, we wouldn't give it to him," he declared. Hefner directed that ads for tawdry products, no matter how profitable, would not be allowed: "We won't accept anything as an advertisement with sex as its primary appeal."[45]

Hefner's attention to detail penetrated every nook and cranny of the operation. He monitored articles on men's clothing to make sure they represented "the new and unusual in fashion." He scrutinized photographs for their sophistication, declaring, "I don't want *Playboy* to simply follow fashion—I want it to create trends, to point directions." Hefner critiqued drafts of movie reviews for excessive artiness. "Because *Playboy* is not edited for the select, super-brow. . . . I think we should be trying a little harder to fit our reviews to the editorial point of view of the magazine," he instructed. "Instead, we're getting a lecture on cinematic art." He demanded a more sympathetic article on Charlie Chaplin, one that reflected *Playboy's* recognition that "the dreamer and idealist [was someone] who may not always conform, who may not always be right . . . who may do things of great artistic brilliance followed by things of uneven or even inept quality, for such is the nature of genius."[46]

Music lay especially close to Hefner's heart and drew special attention. He hired the distinguished jazz writer and critic Leonard Feather, and solicited a series of pieces on the history of jazz. He requested articles "that will explain the differences in the kinds of jazz, how they developed and something about the men and circumstances responsible for them." When the soundtrack for the movie *High Society* was released, he asked for a review combining sentimentality (a Hefner trademark) with the usual hip commentary. The record had "kept me in a warm, romantic glow all evening," he told Spectorsky. "Let's mix a little sweetness with the sulphuric acid you guys are brewing. . . . The songs are all originals by Cole Porter, there are some real beauties here." He also mandated increased attention to television as a growing form of entertainment.[47]

Always, of course, Hefner relentlessly promoted *Playboy* to the public. In a long letter to old friend Burt Zollo, whose company was publicizing the magazine, he complained about a lack of results. He insisted that the magazine should be easy to promote. "A bunch of Chicago guys have put together the craziest publishing success in a decade and not a single Chicago newspaper has done a feature story on it," he groused. "The special services that we might expect from a public relations organization with many contacts and much know-how just aren't coming off." Within a short time, Hefner signed on with a new public relations firm.[48]

Ultimately, however, the key to Hefner's approach was that he edited *Playboy* for himself, aiming it at his own tastes and values. "Hefner used to tell us that he had the book done for his satisfaction and that if he liked it others would, too," Jack Kessie reported. Said Victor Lownes, "It was a guidebook for him, just as it was for millions of young college men." Spectorsky concurred: "The reason he's so good at his job is he's schizophrenic enough to be editor and publisher and, at the same time, audience." Hefner usually asked for opinions and input, but in the final analysis he always went with his own sense of what was appealing. When asked about this, he replied simply, "It's a very personal book and a very personal business." Later, he explained in more depth. "I was doing the magazine for myself, but it was . . . my perception of a young urban guy in a connection with the opposite sex. I created a kind of romanticized, idealized young urban bachelor and aimed the magazine at this figure."[49]

In 1956, an evaluation revealed just how well suited he was to his job when Hefner hired a firm to administer psychological audits to all executives at the magazine, including himself. The report described him as "well qualified for your present position as Editor-Publisher of *Playboy* magazine" and affirmed his great mental ability, a broad streak of creativity, tremendous drive, and zest for his work. But the evaluators also noted several dangers in Hefner's makeup: a weaker sense of planning and administration, an element of impulsivity and immaturity in formulating actions, a habit of working to the point of physical exhaustion, and an inability to delegate authority that portended trouble when the organization grew larger. Overall, however, the audit concluded that Hefner would thrive when administering "creative programs. This direction should be satisfying to your high needs for self-expression."[50]

Clearly, Hefner was doing something right. One of the great success stories in American publishing, *Playboy* surged upward in 1956 from eightieth place to become the forty-ninth largest-selling magazine in the country, passing *Esquire* in the process and posting a 102 percent gain, the largest in the industry. It had net sales of just over $3 million. By the end of 1959 its circulation had climbed to over one million copies a month while total revenue swelled to

$5.5 million. The magazine's growing size and complexity reflected its popularity. While the January 1957 issue was eighty pages long with nineteen features and articles, the December 1960 issue was almost double that size, with 150 pages and twenty-eight features.[51]

As the magazine grew, so did Hefner's confidence. When he offhandedly expressed an interest in making foreign movies, a lieutenant replied, "The only trouble with that, Hef, is that you'll have to be in a foreign country." The publisher replied, "Okay, in that case we'll start our own." But Hefner also clearly appreciated his success. In December 1958, on *Playboy*'s fifth anniversary, he expressed his gratitude:

> When I sit at my desk here in the PLAYBOY building, looking back to that day in the fall of 1953 when all this began, it all seems quite unreal. When I put together that first thin issue of PLAYBOY . . . I hoped only that the magazine might be successful enough to permit me to continue working at what I loved instead of wasting a life away at something else that I didn't really care about. But this labor of love has turned into the most spectacular magazine success of our generation, has brought me in five years more recognition and wealth and purpose than I ever dreamed of having in an entire lifetime. I am—I think—one of the luckiest men in all the world.[52]

But what had fueled the skyrocketing popularity of *Playboy*? Hefner believed that people sensed "right away, very early, it wasn't just a magazine. It was a projection of people's fantasy life." Yet what was the *content* of this fantasy? What exactly were people responding to in *Playboy*'s imaginative vision? In fact, Hefner's magazine captured perfectly two powerful trends in postwar American culture: sexual liberation and consumer abundance. From these elements *Playboy* created an enticing dream world of physical and material pleasure for a society grown increasingly impatient with restraint.[53]

6

The Pursuit of Happiness

In the fall of 1956, Hugh Hefner appeared on *The Mike Wallace Interview*, a popular television show in New York City. The host, who would become famous in a few years as a national reporter for CBS, was already building a reputation as a tough interviewer. He confronted his guest immediately. "Tonight our guest is the thirty-year-old brain behind the hottest property in the publishing world," Wallace began. "And we'll try to find out why he really did start *Playboy* and whether or not it is just a smutty book." Noting that the magazine presented pictures of girls in various states of undress, he asked Hefner if he enjoyed the profits from this "oversexed" endeavor.

Hefner defended himself. Sex, he admitted, was an important component in *Playboy* because it was important to his audience of young, urban males. But he noted that the magazine also included much material on clothing, music, automobiles, and food and drink as well as literature by distinguished authors. When Wallace suggested that what he was really selling was "a high-class dirty book," Hefner replied, "There's nothing dirty in sex unless we make it dirty. A picture of a beautiful woman is something that a fellow of any age ought to be able to enjoy," he maintained. "It is the sick mind that finds something loathsome and obscene in sex." But Wallace refused to relent, and the publisher finally grew annoyed. "I would estimate that no more than 5% of any issue of PLAYBOY is concerned with sex, and we seem to be devoting an entire half-hour program to it tonight," he snapped at one point.[1]

This rhetorical exchange reflected the first stirrings of what came to be called the "sexual revolution." As middle-class America enjoyed a great wave of prosperity in the 1950s and older habits of self-denial withered, a new commitment to pleasure penetrated into the most intimate, personal realm of human life: sex. Increasingly, many beneficiaries of the culture of abundance challenged older ideas about proper sexual values that had been in place since the nineteenth century. This movement emerged as a coalition of those pursuing a sexualization of culture, those advocating a reconfiguration of family life and gender roles, those deploying sex as a political tool to assault bourgeois life, and those seeking greater tolerance for diverse sexual practices. These groups found a common enemy in traditions of sexual restraint supported by church, state, and middle-class values. As pressure mounted from dissenters and agitators, cracks appeared in the edifice of sexual propriety that dominated American culture in terms of music, movies, popular literature, and dating etiquette.[2]

Playboy, with its erotic photographs and dissenting editorial stance, offered one of the earliest open displays of rebellion. Arbiters of mainstream culture took note. In 1957, a playful cartoon in the *New Yorker* featured a drawing of a sultan surrounded by dozens of beautiful harem girls as he sat reading a copy of *Playboy*. That same year, a long article in the *Nation* examined the growth of sophistication in America by examining magazines such as *Vanity Fair, Esquire, Vogue,* and *Harper's Bazaar*. It also noted a new arrival. "The recent phenomenon of the sophistication business is *Playboy,*" it explained. "Starting bawdily and naively, it has grown progressively subtler" with its photographs of fresh, attractive young women from ordinary avenues of American life. "I must applaud a brand-new invention in eroticism which grew out of the free-wheeling, ebullient attitude of the editors," noted the author.[3]

While the sexual revolution would not arrive full-blown until the middle of the next decade, the 1950s saw initial rumblings. Perhaps more than any other single individual, Hefner represented the first stage of rebellion as *Playboy* expressed a growing, if inchoate, yearning for a new sexual code.

I

In later years, Hefner often asserted that a desire to overthrow prevailing American attitudes about sex in the 1950s had prompted him to start *Playboy*. The culprit creating this prudish, hypocritical climate, he believed, was America's Puritan past. He himself had been taught as a youngster that sexuality reflected humans' animal instincts and, as such, was something to be distrusted and repressed. "I began questioning a lot of that religious foolishness about man's spirit and body being in conflict, with God concerned primarily with the spirit of man and the Devil dwelling in the flesh," he wrote. "I wanted to edit a magazine free of guilt about sex." *Playboy,* with this agenda, provided a voice for those beginning to search for a new sexual morality.[4]

While Hefner's appraisal of *Playboy*'s liberationist role contained much truth, he misidentified the enemy. The publisher followed the lead of H. L. Mencken, the literary and social critic, who had launched hilarious, mocking attacks on the abiding heritage of Puritanism in the 1910s and 1920s. But the cultural opposition actually came from a different source. The sexual atmosphere that Hefner found to be so suffocating, in fact, was the legacy of nineteenth-century Victorian ideology rather than the Puritan theology of the seventeenth and eighteenth centuries. The belief that desires required self-denial and bodily appetites demanded self-control, while rooted in centuries-old Christian principles, had emerged wholesale from Victorian moralists in the nineteenth century, whose worldview had been shaped in the nexus of a rapidly expanding market capitalism and a vibrant evangelical Protestantism. Victorians insisted that passions, if unrestrained, would undermine the capacity for hard work, a virtuous private life, and a benevolent public one. Sexuality, of course, stood high on their list of sensual delights to be repressed. Popular advice writers like Sylvester Graham instructed young men and women that sexual indulgence led to moral decline, physical dissipation, and social disaster. By the late nineteenth century, sexual orthodoxy had produced a host of anti-vice statutes, such as the Comstock Act (1873), which banned obscene materials from the mail. Anthony Comstock, an intrepid foe of erotic materials as well as contraceptives and abortifacients, was appointed a special agent of the U.S. Post Office and spent the next three decades removing sexual materials from avenues of public exchange, including stores and shops. He became the ultimate symbol of Victorian rectitude on sexual matters.[5]

Victorian ideology, however, was tottering by the early decades of the twentieth century. Advocates of an emerging consumer economy encouraged the embrace of leisure, pleasure, and play and the abandonment of self-denial. A new ethos of self-fulfillment inspired advertising messages promising personal happiness through the purchase of goods; new amusement parks such as Coney Island showcased the delights of recreation; and new advice literature, such as Dale Carnegie's *How to Win Friends and Influence People,* stressed the necessity of sparkling personality instead of upright character. Yet Victorianism, while desiccated in many areas, maintained a powerful hold on sexual culture well into the middle decades of the twentieth century. Ensconced in small-town America and bolstered in urban areas by Catholic and Protestant churches, sexual orthodoxy actually received a new boost after World War II from a popular credo of "family togetherness" that made domestic harmony a hallmark of American life, and defined it as a key source of strength in the larger Cold War struggle against communism.[6]

Thus Hefner, indeed, faced a powerful, long-standing opposition in the Eisenhower era. In sexual matters, Victorian restraint and repression still loomed large in American culture. As one historian has put it, middle-class respectability "provided a clear set of rules about sexual behavior. At its heart was a simple stricture: no sex outside marriage." Propriety made dating into a complex series of stages (going steady, pinned, engaged), with an attendant hierarchy of carefully negotiated physical intimacies (necking, petting above the waist, below the waist, through clothes, under clothes). Parents and schools limited opportunities for young people to have sexual contact by imposing curfews, controlling use of the car, and encouraging double dating.[7]

Yet scattered challenges to the sexual orthodoxy sprang up in the 1950s. The Kinsey Reports, with their analysis of male and female sexual practices, created a storm of controversy by revealing the extent to which actual conduct violated official values. Much popular reading material—Grace Metalious's salacious best-seller *Peyton Place,* tell-all scandal magazines such as *Confidential,* Mickey Spillane mysteries pulsating with violence-tinged eroticism—broached parameters of sexual propriety. Rock 'n' roll, unforgettably symbolized by Elvis Presley and his gyrating hips, blared rhythmic sensuality and suggestive lyrics to dancing teenagers. Gradually, a powerful assault on traditional notions of sexual restraint began gathering momentum.[8]

Hefner and *Playboy* particularly popularized an ideology of sexual liberation in the 1950s that began to erode traditional values. A Thomas Paine for the mid-twentieth century who distilled complex ideas into bright prose and vivid images, Hefner entered public life as the pamphleteer of the sexual revolution. He stressed several themes in his rhetorical and visual assault on the palisades of propriety.

Hefner propagated the deceptively simple idea that sex should be fun. Throughout the first decade of *Playboy*'s publication, he attacked the traditional formulation that sex must be either sacred or sinful and rejected the cultural dictum that it should be strictly relegated to the realm of marriage. In the modern world, he argued, sex could no longer be linked exclusively to procreation and the sanction of church and state. It existed for a variety of purposes. In his words, "it could be recreational, a sense of identity in terms of who you are, an expression of love." Hefner sought to make the erotic legitimate on its own terms.[9]

Throughout the 1950s, *Playboy* promoted the notion that sex was for human pleasure. As Hefner once quipped, "We believe sex should be enjoyed right along with nasty pleasures like drinking and gambling." A host of articles, stories, and images followed his editorial lead. "Don't Hate Yourself in the Morning" reassured virile readers that young women also sought erotic experiences outside marriage. "Many women are beginning to adopt the sexual attitude of bachelors, in that they want physical pleasure—or relief, if you prefer—without having to pay for it by signing up for a lifetime." "Contour Contact: The Gentle Art of Laying Hands on Lasses All About You" instructed young men in techniques of delicately stroking the arm of a young woman, helping her into or out of a taxi, or leaning over to smell the perfume she had dabbed behind her ear. Such subtle physical contact provided a "sadly undervalued means for discharging pent-up emotion." "The Big Bosom Battle" disagreed with a physician who recently had called for a deemphasis on female breasts because they threatened to make women neurotic and create a cultural fixation. "We just can't go along with this bosom deceleration," noted the magazine. "We agree that there's a lot of interest in the things, but we say there can never be too much. Such interest is healthy and adds to the gaiety of nations."[10]

Pictorials in *Playboy* elaborated the sex-is-fun theme. A feature titled "Playboy's Yacht Party" displayed four scantily clad (and occasionally unclad) young women going out for a relaxed vacation on a yacht accompanied by an attentive crew of sailors, while "Playboy's House Party" depicted a similar group romping through a sensual day and evening at a beachside home in Miami. Other typical features focused on females from various regions of the United States, such as "The Girls of Hollywood," which offered intimate glimpses of some fifteen attractive women where the "sun-kissed strip of California coast known as Hollywood draws unto itself the most beautiful girls in the world." "Minsky in Vegas" described the burlesque king Harold Minsky and his popular lineup of seminude showgirls at the Dunes Hotel. *Playboy* also ran revealing pictorials on a whole series of Hollywood starlets eager for exposure—Sophia Loren, Kim Novak, Jayne Mansfield, Brigitte Bardot, Stella Stevens, Marilyn Monroe.[11]

Disregarding the sacrosanct quality of traditional discussions of sex, *Playboy* consistently used humor to lighten the atmosphere. "Some people seem to think it's all right to joke about robbing a bank, when you wouldn't actually do it, but they don't apply the same reasoning to adultery," Hefner observed. He penned a humorous article, "Virginity: An Important Treatise on a Very Important Subject," in which he joked that most men saw virginity as an unpleasant matter to be disposed of quickly. Unfortunately, he added, "this important information has been withheld from a large part of our female population." Hefner then offered a lighthearted analysis of various arguments that men could present to reluctant female partners. He confessed partiality to the "Freudian Approach," which emphasized the dangers inherent in frustrating the libido, and the "Atomic Age Approach," which posited that the threat of nuclear destruction made it imperative to live for tonight.[12]

Shepherd Mead's "How to Succeed With Women Without Really Trying" series satirized the lifelong male search for female companionship. In one installment, he observed that a boy noticing physical changes in his body was ready to become a man but must "go through a period which may *seem* long, but which will actually last no more than ten or twelve years." Mead continued, "Never in all the march of civilization have so many had to wait for so long. But you will say, as others have before you, that it was surely worth it." *Playboy's* cheerful take on sexuality also flavored cartoons by Jack Cole, Erich Sokol, John Dempsey, and Gardner Rea. A typical cartoon showed a red-faced, pleasantly befuddled tippler who inquired of two Salvation Army crusaders beating on a bass drum, "You mean if I sow liquor & dames, I'll reap liquor and dames?" Regular features such as "The Ribald Classic," a series of short, humorous tales of seduction and romance, and the risqué "Party Jokes" page, also sought to replace sexual solemnity with laughs.[13]

Playboy reformulated seduction in the 1950s, depicting it as neither improper nor immoral, but a social ritual full of romance, excitement, and anticipation. Hefner filled the magazine with images and instructions regarding the accoutrements of sexual attraction. Food editor Thomas Mario articulated the seductive role of fine food and wine in articles such as "The Breaking of the Fast: Morning Menus for Two," which instructed a young man on the proper way to prepare and present breakfast for a woman the morning after. Blake Rutherford (the pseudonym of associate editor Jack Kessie) presented a long series of pieces on the sexual appeal of elegant, understated clothing. Numerous articles on hi-fi systems, the correct way to mix a martini, and the most powerful, current sports cars underlined the connection between worldly goods and sexual allure. "Playboy's Penthouse Apartment," a lavish text-and-sketches article appearing in September and October 1956, showed how stylish living quarters provided the ideal setting for attracting and entertaining winsome young women. In November 1955, Hefner initiated "Playboy After Hours," which surveyed a host of entertainment establishments with an eye toward their romantic ambience. Overall, the *Playboy* picture of seduction stressed romance, sophistication, and pleasure.[14]

Hefner's calls for rethinking sex repeatedly emphasized the social need for a "healthy heterosexuality" in America. Modern pressures of fashion had converged with traditional repression, he argued, to warp images of female beauty. Confusion about gender images had blurred the visual and emotional lines separating men from women and created a kind of social neurosis. In Hefner's view, a regeneration of vigorous sexual intercourse between men and women promised to restore vitality to American society. *Playboy,* as he stressed repeatedly, was "very much a heterosexual magazine." The magazine refused to be "embarrassed by the male-female relationship" and pledged that "we will vote in favor of a heterosexual society until something better comes along."[15]

In this crusade for heterosexuality, Hefner took special aim at women's fashion magazines as architects of androgyny. For several decades, he noted, they had promoted the ideal of the tall, slender, angular woman with small bust and thin hips. Many females emulated this model, but most men recoiled because it was "devoid of sex." The male ideal of female attractiveness, Hefner argued, accented a "full figure, narrow waist, full hips, a very robust and healthy looking gal." *Playboy* devoted itself to portraying this vision of the "fully feminine—round, soft, and with a maximum emphasis on the beauty of being female."[16]

In Hefner's view, homosexuality joined with the fashion industry androgyny to construct another barrier to healthy relations between men and women. He was no homophobe, and in fact urged toleration for this sexual behavior. But, like even the most progressive figures in the 1950s, he saw homosexuality as an aberration, a sign of maladjustment. "It is the normal, healthy heterosexual thing for men to be interested in the full, well-rounded female," he told one magazine. Why did men like to drive sports cars, wear fashionable suits, listen to a new stereo, and enjoy good food and drink? he asked rhetorically. "To sit in a corner with a fellow? I rather doubt it." *Playboy,* he made clear, was devoted to "the boy-girl relationship, to heterosexual activity in modern society." This provided a contrast to outdoor men's magazines, which recommended leaving women at home while you hunted, drank beer, and bonded with other men. "On a Freudian level, you could consider them blatantly homosexual," he declared.[17]

Hefner elaborated in a roundtable discussion on a CBS television show in Chicago. He complained bitterly that fashion magazines had idealized the tall, thin woman—a "Vogue mannequin" type—and suggested another influence:

If you want to take the next step and see how really sick it's getting . . . You also know, and the theater in New York is very much involved in this, where a great deal of this concept of beauty comes from. This whole fashion thing comes largely from men. But it's not a heterosexual concept. And I feel basically that it is an anti-female concept.

Another participant asked, "You mean a homosexual concept?" Hefner replied, "Darn right, darn right."[18]

"The Playboy Philosophy," the early 1960s work summarizing Hefner's early thought on the sexual revolution, clarified this point. A leading sex researcher, he pointed out, had commented upon "the prevalence of homosexuality and perversion in the United States" and insisted that a greater emphasis on male-female sex provided the only antidote. "If we desire a healthy, heterosexual society, we must begin stressing heterosexual sex; otherwise, our society will remain sick and perverted," Hefner agreed. So while Hefner was not anti-homosexual, he clearly saw *Playboy*'s healthy heterosexuality as an antidote to androgyny and gender confusion, one that promised to restore American vitality.[19]

Hefner's notion of "clean sex" promised a healthy alternative to prevailing, tawdry images of vice and transgression, sin and sensationalism. Religion, he contended, handcuffed sex to procreation with any escape eliciting an all-points bulletin describing the offender as obscene. A similarly twisted state of affairs pervaded popular women's magazines, as a *Playboy* article titled "The Pious Pornographers" revealed. *Redbook, Ladies' Home Journal,* and *Cosmopolitan* overflowed with sensational articles on topics such as sexual dysfunction, failed marriages, and scandalous affairs. This "sick, sad sex kick of the ladies magazines" offered readers a steady diet of "Virginal Wives," "Jealousy-Crazed Mates," and "perverts and child-molesters." Titillation reigned supreme. "What we were trying to do was promote a healthier attitude toward sexuality," Hefner explained. *Playboy* suggested that "clean sex, healthy sex in the 1950s was a prerequisite for a healthy society in America."[20]

For all his passionate proclamations of sexual liberation, Hefner insisted that *Playboy* stay within the bounds of good taste. He championed the erotic and avoided the pornographic. Images and words evoking healthy sexual urges were fine, he believed, especially if they emitted an aura of romance, but sensational, sadistic, and prurient aspects of sex were out of bounds. But it was not always easy to find the line of demarcation. When an advertiser threatened to close the account over some nude photographs, Hefner asked him to reconsider in light of a changing sexual culture in America:

> There is a transition taking place in society today that is very evident in the movies and in books and magazines, too, for that matter. The nation is becoming more mature and able to discuss and view openly what was taboo ten or fifteen years ago . . . *Playboy* isn't interested in being sensational—it never has been. . . . If we took the sex out of *Playboy,* we would be a fraud, and we know it. At the same time we are concerned with staying well within the bounds of good taste. . . . However, treating sex in an adult manner on the one hand—and not overstepping the bounds of good taste, on the other—is not as easy a proposition as it might appear.[21]

Thus Hefner labored as a popularizer of sexual revolution in the postwar era. His conviction about "modern man's need for a new, more realistic, rational, human, and humane sexual morality" had been in place long before he even dreamed of starting a magazine, he explained. But he used *Playboy* to tirelessly pursue this goal, and signs were appearing of "a transition from guilt, shame, and hypocrisy to a new honesty, a new permissiveness, a new willingness to talk about sex in a frank and open way—a freedom to examine, to express, to enjoy."[22]

As the old saying goes, however, a picture is worth a thousand words. The most celebrated element in the *Playboy* crusade for sexual liberation, of course, was visual. The "Playmate of the Month," whose revealing fold-out portrait graced every issue of the magazine, became an American icon. As Hefner noted many years later, "The Centerfold, in its own way, was as much of a statement in terms of the sexual revolution as the 'Playboy Philosophy.'"[23]

II

Marilyn Monroe, in her famous nude pose against a lush backdrop of red velvet, adorned the first issue of *Playboy* as its "Sweetheart of the Month." By the next issue, the feature had become the "Playmate of the Month" with a regular format—several photographs of an attractive young woman, a portion of them erotic, surrounding a nude fold-out centerfold in full color. It quickly became the magazine's signature item. At first, Hefner called upon professional models, but soon he began to look for another type of Playmate—fresh, wholesome "girls next door" from the byways of ordinary American life. Readers responded eagerly to this type, prompting the humorist Mort Sahl to quip that a whole generation of American men came of age believing that young women had a staple in their midsection.

Hefner did not have to go far to secure the prototype Playmate of the 1950s. In the spring of 1955, he asked Charlaine Karalus, the magazine's subscription manager, to pose for the magazine center-fold. During bantering negotiations, she agreed to be photographed if he would buy an Addressograph machine to ease her duties at the office. It was an inspired agreement. Karalus, an elegant, full-figured blonde with healthy good looks, appeared in the July issue as "Janet Pilgrim." Hefner came up with the name as a sly dig at his Puritan forbearers, and actually appeared in her centerfold as a tuxedoed figure in the background, back to the camera. This recurring hint of a man in the centerfold photos implied sex and seduction. *Playboy* explained its Playmate concept:

> We suppose it's natural to think of the pulchritudinous Play-
> mates as existing in a world apart. Actually, potential Playmates
> are all around you: the new secretary at your office, the doe-
> eyed beauty who sat opposite you at lunch yesterday, the girl
> who sells you shirts and ties at your favorite store. We found
> Miss July in our own circulation department, processing sub-
> scriptions, renewals, and back copy orders. Her name is Janet
> Pilgrim and she's as efficient as she is good looking.[24]

Reader response was so enthusiastic that Pilgrim also appeared as a Playmate two more times, in December 1955 and October 1956, establishing a record that still stands. She became something of a celebrity as admiring cards and letters poured into *Playboy* from all over the country. In the fall of 1956, Pilgrim's popularity became evident when she accepted an invitation for an appearance at Dartmouth College. She met with an English class, was interviewed on the campus radio station, held a press conference at the offices of the student newspaper, and attended a faculty tea held in her honor. *Playboy* took advantage of her fame with a special advertisement. "A lifetime subscription to *Playboy* brings a personal call from Janet Pilgrim," it promised; "we could think of nothing more special than to have *Playboy*'s famed Playmate of the Month call him person-to-person anywhere in the U.S. on Christmas Eve or Christmas Day." Thus was born the girl-next-door image that became the hallmark of the magazine's centerfolds.[25]

A long tradition of pinup art existed in the United States dating back to the early 1900s. Around the turn of the century, the Gibson Girls—pen-and-ink drawings by the illustrator Charles Gibson— represented the height of female beauty with their lush dresses, tiny waists, and elaborate curled hair piled atop their heads. By the 1920s, posters publicizing the scantily clad Ziegfeld Girls had per- meated popular culture while the following decades saw *Esquire*'s Petty Girls—sleek, stylized drawings of nude young women by the artist George Petty—and Vargas Girls, lush illustrations of well- endowed young women by Alberto Vargas. During World War II, movie-star pinups of actresses such as Betty Grable also became a popular feature of soldiers' and sailors' lockers around the globe. All of these erotic images shared a common characteristic. They were highly stylized, idealized renderings of women who were enticing, yet unattainable.[26]

The Playmate of the Month transformed this tradition. Instead of focusing on movie queens or showgirls, *Playboy* humanized the female pinup by presenting young women from everyday life who (at least theoretically) were attainable, non-intimidating, and possessed of a healthy sexual appetite. The Playmates were "attractive girls that we find all over America," Hefner explained to Mike Wallace in 1956. "In the past year, one Playmate was an airline stewardess, one a New York telephone operator, and one a Phi Beta Kappa." Their typicality was matched by their modern attitudes. The *Playboy* centerfold appeared as an icon of sexual liberation in the 1950s, suggesting that, as Hefner liked to put it, "nice girls like sex, too."[27]

Hefner described his goal in a 1956 memo to *Playboy* photographers:

> The Playmate should be posed in a *natural* setting, not the sterile surroundings of a studio. The model herself should

look relaxed and natural. . . . Some simple activity like reading, writing, mixing a drink, trying on a new dress—the variations are endless—will add tremendously to the appeal. . . . Obviously the Playmates should be attractive in both face and figure, but more specifically, we like a healthy, intelligent American look—a young lady that looks like she might be a very efficient secretary or an undergrad at Vassar. We prefer fresh, new faces . . . a natural beauty.

In a letter that same year, he explained to a corporate client that his magazine featured "the freshest, most all-American looking girls we can find." The Playmates had become, he argued, "the photographic dream girls for a large part of our male population."[28]

The stories accompanying the photos reinforced this natural, realistic appeal. They noted the Playmate's job or activities and discussed her interests, hobbies, and attitudes. This "personalizes the girl; she's not just a rag a' bone and hank o' hair. She's a living, breathing human being," Hefner explained. "Playmates are real people and they are one of the good things in life that you can enjoy when you get up there and work hard and play hard." The whole girl-next-door idea, he noted later, "was intended to make the Playmates more a part of real life for our readers."[29]

At the same time, important elements of fantasy went into the presentation of these "real" young women. The photos were artfully posed to create the *illusion* of being unposed. The texts accompanying the photos were verbal creations (often highly exaggerated) designed to enhance the "natural" quality of the Playmates' lives and underscore their sexual interest. Thus *Playboy* subtly created an erotic vision. After all, the vast majority of young American women were not quite *that* pretty, *that* healthy, *that* well-endowed, or, to be honest, quite *that* enthusiastic about sex in an age of crude birth control measures. The Playmate as represented, a workaday yet fetching young woman who joyfully sought sex, was the *fantasy* of the girl next door.

Playmate features in the 1950s embodied this mix of the real and the unreal. They were about six pages long, including a double-page spread that expanded to a three-page foldout in 1956 as the word "centerfold" entered the popular lexicon. The photographs themselves were relatively modest. They always featured some kind of drapery at the waist or were taken from the side or back to avoid revealing the pubic area. Breasts were bare but seldom showed nipples. Brief stories described the Playmate as an actress, salesgirl, student, waitress, legal secretary, or in some other kind of normal occupation. Overall, a relaxed, lighthearted, spontaneous atmosphere prevailed. While sex in traditional men's magazines like *Esquire* had a leering quality "like the old goats who chased showgirls in their cartoons," as one *Playboy* staffer put it, Hefner's centerfolds projected a playful, even innocent quality. As a real, attainable female who was nonetheless a two-dimensional image on a page, gazing directly at the male reader with an alluring smile, the Playmate offered a promise of sexual fulfillment.[30]

Two Playmates typified the centerfold feature during the early years of *Playboy*. A perky platinum blonde named Lisa Winters graced the magazine's pages as the December 1956 Playmate, and the text described her as "the kind of fresh, young beauty that photographers all across the country are constantly looking for." It noted that she loved to read and was partial to the poems of Elizabeth Barrett Browning and the fiction of Poe, Hemingway, and Kipling. Ms. Winters, a self-described "home girl," liked plain food such as spaghetti and chocolate ice cream and preferred young men who had a sense of humor and avoided pettiness. The pictorial featured five black-and-white photos of her fully clothed in various settings in her hometown, two color photos of her nude wearing a sheer nightgown, and a centerfold shot of her climbing out of a swimming pool, her breasts carefully hidden behind her arm with her face upturned to soak up the sunshine.[31]

Virginia Gordon appeared in a January 1959 pictorial titled "Girl Who Wears Glasses." *Playboy* confessed that the old notion of librarians as killjoy spinsters, "as well as a Dorothy Parker couplet about girls who wear glasses, have hitherto prevented us from scouting the libraries of our land in search of gatefold glamour. A little unbiased cogitation, of course, should have led us to the conclusion that there's no reason why a librarian can't be as lovely as any other lass, as dewy as a decimal system, as stacked as the stacks she supervises." The text noted that Ms. Gordon enjoyed "water sports, chess and charades, and she admits to a secret longing to own a Corvette."

Grace and Glenn Hefner with
their sons, Hugh and Keith, in
the early 1930s

Hefner at age eight

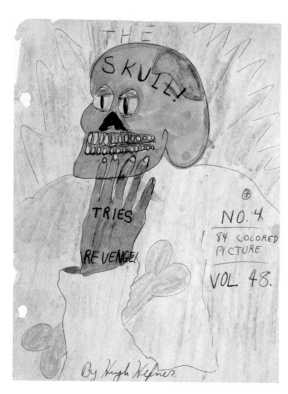

The Skull Tries Revenge,
one of many series of
adventure and horror
cartoons that Hefner
drew as a boy

A teenage "Hep Hef" with two female friends from Steinmetz High School

Hefner during his stint in the United States Army (1945–1946)

Hefner and girlfriend Millie Williams at a college dance

One of Hefner's ribald cartoons for *Shaft*, a publication run by students at the University of Illinois

Hefner as a crooner—the "Campus Ballad King"—during his college days

The youthful editor at his desk during the early days of *Playboy* in 1954

A staff meeting with (left to right) Art Paul, Joe Paczek, Hefner, Ray Russell, and Jack Kessie at *Playboy*'s offices at 11 East Superior Street

Hefner with A. C. Spectorsky, *Playboy*'s influential editorial director

"What Sort of Man Reads *Playboy*?"—a promotional campaign that stressed the magazine's vision of the good life for young, upwardly mobile young men

WHAT SORT OF MAN READS PLAYBOY?

A young man sure to cast an appreciative eye in the direction of a new model, the PLAYBOY reader looks for qualities in a car that will set him apart at a stoplight or on the superhighway. And it isn't just his trend-setting enthusiasm for the new and different that makes him an ideal prospect in the automobile market – it's his proven ability to buy the car of his choice. Facts: According to the leading independent magazine survey, a larger percentage of PLAYBOY families bought an automobile during the last 12 months than can be claimed by any other magazine. (55.1% of PLAYBOY households purchased a total of 473,119 cars last year.) Not too surprising when you know that 95.7% of all PLAYBOY households own one or more cars, 30% own two or more, and 6.2% own three or more. There are, in fact, 131.9 automobiles owned by every 100 PLAYBOY families – the highest concentration of automobile ownership reported for the readers of *any* magazine. (Source: Consumer Magazine Report by Daniel Starch & Staff, August 1958.)

PLAYBOY ADVERTISING DEPARTMENT · 232 E. Ohio St., Chicago, MI 2-1000 · 720 Fifth Ave., New York, CI 5-2620

Hefner on the set of his first television show, *Playboy's Penthouse*, in the late 1950s

Hefner pounding out "The Playboy Philosophy" for the magazine in the early 1960s

Hefner and girlfriend Cynthia Maddox at the opening of the New York Playboy Club in December 1962

Hefner and guests dancing at a Playboy Mansion party in Chicago

Four black-and-white photos showed her fully clothed at work, while the color centerfold depicted her nude, drying her hair with a bath towel marked "His," with one leg raised demurely to screen her waist while her elbows carefully masked the tips of her breasts.[32]

While the Playmates captured a restless erotic energy emerging in the early stages of the 1950s sexual revolution, they also served another important purpose. The publisher deployed his battalions of All-American girls to fend off what he perceived as a looming threat in postwar society: women seeking to entrap men in marriage. The domestic ideal of family togetherness, so dear to the heart of Eisenhower's America, seemed little more than a prison to Hefner. He urged young men to a spirited resistance. The *Playboy* agenda of sexual liberation, in part, aimed to separate the pleasure of sex from the entangling obligations of the woman-dominated family.

The very first issue of the magazine launched an attack on female manipulation of marriage in America. Burt Zollo's "Miss Gold-digger of 1953" denounced alimony as a weapon used by greedy women to strip men of their livelihood. The courts, ignoring the fact that modern divorce often was no one's fault, routinely ordered ex-husbands to pay ex-wives up to half of their salaries for support. A long list of outrageous cases should make men aware that "All-American womanhood has descended on alimony as natural heritage." Zollo sharpened the attack on marriage a few months later in a piece titled "Open Season on Bachelors." Modern women sought economic and social security above all else, he argued, and were "perfectly willing to crush man's adventurous, freedom-loving spirit to get it." The evidence could be seen in "the sorry, regimented husbands trudging down every woman-dominated street in this woman-dominated land." With male freedom at risk, Zollo argued, the true playboy must "enjoy the pleasures the female has to offer without becoming emotionally involved."[33]

Throughout the 1950s, *Playboy* continued to mock traditional notions of wedded bliss. In 1955, for example, a tongue-in-cheek article, titled "A Vote for Polygamy," described monogamous marriage as a historical anomaly. This practice had been brought into Western civilization by barbarians who attacked the Roman Empire, its author contended, and "has since been rejected by Mohammedans, Buddhists, and residents of Southern California." With "varietistic" males naturally seeking many sexual partners and women rapidly outnumbering them in the general population, the future was clear: "a return to an older and more practical form of social-sex organization—polygamy." In 1958, *Playboy* surveyed its readership and reported the mix of husbands and bachelors in this fashion: "Approximately half of PLAYBOY's readers (46.8%) are free men and the other half are free in spirit only."[34]

Hefner contributed to this skeptical critique of marriage. Throughout the decade, he suggested that men should marry later rather than sooner, if at all. When a reporter asked if he would want his sister to marry a *Playboy* editor, he fired back, "I don't want my editors marrying anyone and getting a lot of foolish notions in their heads about 'togetherness,' home, family, and all that jazz." He believed that social pressures forced people to marry too early and offered himself as an example. "I had never really been out on my own, never really been free, which is maybe a part of why this independent, free spirit thing is as important to me as it is," he said. When his marriage ended a bit later, he celebrated his "freedom to do what I want to do, when I want to do it, and to be able to go where I want to go, when I want to go there."[35]

In "The Playboy Philosophy," published in the early 1960s, Hefner explained his objections to marriage American-style. "The extensive Puritanism that still exists in American society with its moral prohibitions against sex outside of wedlock, is one of the powerful pressures leading to early marriages," he claimed. Heartache often resulted. A more relaxed, realistic acceptance of "a justifiable place for sex outside of marriage" would help, as would greater sensitivity to the emotional needs of young adults. "The typical male selects a mate and marries her—supposedly for a lifetime—before he has fully developed, himself, into the adult human being he will be for the rest of his years. It's no better than a game of marital blind-man's bluff, it seems to me," he wrote. "If, on the other hand, those first years were devoted to work and play, as a single adult—then when marriage did come, a young man would be far better prepared for it."[36]

Hefner's notions of sexual liberation struck a chord with many male readers in postwar America. *Playboy*'s fun-filled visions of attractive, willing females and unfettered sexual pleasure piqued the imagination of young bachelors operating in an atmosphere of material abundance. The Playmate, in contrast to the grasping woman who had secured a husband merely to provide economic and social support, also offered a fantasy of sexual adventure to older men already caught up in the gray-flannel world of family and children, station wagons and backyard barbecues. Hefner's vision of sexual revolution in the 1950s appealed to male angst as well as male freedom, frustrations as well as desire.

Ultimately, however, *Playboy's* eroticism promoted a larger cultural development. It helped drive the final nails into the coffin of traditional Victorian morality, with its notions of self-control, delayed gratification, and character formation. It encouraged instead a new idea that happiness came from sating appetites and gratifying desires. This culture of self-fulfillment had emerged during the early 1900s but flowered dramatically after World War II. As one historian has described this process, an old-fashioned, Protestant ethos of "salvation through self-denial" gave way to a new mind-set "stressing self-realization in this world—an ethos characterized by an almost obsessive concern with psychic and physical health defined in sweeping terms." Hefner's ideology of sexual liberation played a crucial role in Hefner's important historical shift. The material abundance of 1950s America—"a period of growth and affluence unequaled in the past," Hefner called it—had created a new appreciation for life's pleasures. In Hefner's words, "with the social revolution has come a sexual revolution as well."[37]

The *Playboy* fantasy depicted unfettered individuals romping across a social landscape seeking, and finding, physical pleasure and emotional fulfillment. It presented images of sophisticated young men and fetching young women enjoying exuberant sexual experiences, unencumbered by the drudgery of marriage. Hefner reassured readers that in the modern culture of self-fulfillment, sex could be "quite properly, an end in itself. And if sex can serve as a means of self-realization, this is purpose enough and justification enough for its existence." It was the quintessential expression of what one social scientist, writing in the 1950s, termed "fun morality." In the transforming morality of modern America, she argued, "fun, from having been suspect, if not taboo, has tended to become obligatory. Instead of feeling guilty for having too much fun, one is inclined to feel ashamed if one does not have enough."[38]

Hefner's fantasy of sexual liberation embodied this new outlook. "I think the magazine includes portions of the real world and portions of the world of dreams, as well," he observed. "And I think it is probably a good thing to include both. Without our dreams and aspirations, life would be a rather drab affair." Happily for Hefner's readers, the *Playboy* agenda for sexual revolution promised a world that would be anything but drab.[39]

7

An Abundant Life

The encouragement of pleasure, Hugh Hefner believed, lay at the heart of *Playboy*. The sexual element was obvious, of course, but he always added another theme when discussing his magazine's agenda—a desire to boost "the benefits of materialism" as another way "to put some of the play and pleasure back into life." Hefner believed that the enjoyment of material abundance, like sex, had aroused guilt for generations in a culture carrying the burden of Puritan tradition. He wanted to change that. While money could not buy happiness it could be used, he contended, "to enhance life— for oneself and others—and that's what we tried to promote in the magazine."[1]

Hefner used his "pleasure primer" to promote upward mobility, worldly success, and material prosperity, creating a full-fledged endorsement of the consumer-goods explosion in the post–World War II American economy. "People had money for the first time in their lives. They were coming out of the war. There were many new things to own. People had more leisure," Vic Lownes explained.

"The living standards of the country, the productivity of the country was zooming upwards, and *Playboy* was a remarkable reflection of all this. The sexuality, the materialism, it all came at the same time."[2]

Instructing ambitious young men on how to choose from among the dizzying array of products made available by this dynamic economy, *Playboy* helped them navigate through the unfamiliar sea of material prosperity facing middle-class America. In the same way that etiquette books had taught prosperous Americans genteel manners in the nineteenth century, *Playboy* served as a guidebook for enjoying the consumer cornucopia of the 1950s. Monthly, Hefner insisted that the savoring of abundance, like the enjoyment of sex, promised to remove older strictures of self-denial and increase human happiness.

I

The first issue of *Playboy* enticed readers with visions of material plenty. A section titled "The Men's Shop" offered a calfskin-covered ice bucket "trimmed in high polished aluminum," a mahogany "Silent Valet" for hanging suits, a portable bar with "black Formica top trimmed in red, green, ivory, or chartreuse Duran plastic," and a stylish brass coat and hat rack. Soon "Playboy's Bazaar," a self-styled "buying guide," appeared to display the latest consumer items available to the fashionably prosperous. Indeed, in a host of ways, the magazine promoted the consumption of fashionable clothing and good food, sporty cars and fine liquor, urbane leisure and hip entertainment as the essence of the good life in modern America.[3]

This was no voice crying in the wilderness. As the historian Lizabeth Cohen has noted, a full-blown "Consumers' Republic" emerged in the 1950s from a "shared commitment on the part of policymakers, business and labor leaders, and civic groups to put mass consumption at the center of their plans for a prosperous postwar America." This project shaped everything from social aspiration to residential patterns, advertising strategies to notions of citizenship, market maneuvers to political formulations. But this list of contributors contained another important type—cultural figures who articulated how the pursuit of material goods brought happiness. Hugh Hefner stood at or near the front of this line.[4]

Playboy guided readers through the new postwar society of consumer abundance, pointing out opportunities for enjoyment and warning of pitfalls. Its features, advertisements, and symbolic messages presented the array of goods available to successful young men. Then, even more importantly, it encouraged them to partake as a way to achieve joyous fulfillment. "With increasing affluence, how one spends one's leisure time and finds value in it is more important than ever," Hefner noted of this new era. Benjamin Franklin had written a guidebook for coping with life when a more frugal, work-oriented ethic was essential to survival in a frontier society. But now "*Playboy* came along and offered a new set of ethical values for an urban society." The magazine's editorial message was succinct: "Enjoy yourself." So at the same time Hefner labored as a pamphleteer of the sexual revolution in the 1950s, he also served as a popular moralist for the consumer revolution, busily reassuring his audience that it was okay to feast on the fruits of materialism.[5]

Playboy's campaign for consumption focused on several themes. It stressed the importance of style in purchasing and enjoying goods as it nurtured an appreciation of the finer things in life among its young male readers, many of whom were facing the conundrums of consumer choice for the first time. As the magazine noted of its typical reader in 1955, "You can find him at the theatre, a concert, or small jazz spot. He is in the midst of the biggest buying spree of his life. Cars, cameras, and hi-fi cabinets. Clothes, cognac, and cigarettes."[6]

Playboy directed that buying spree, becoming an arbiter of taste for young men on the make in an American land of plenty. "The Basic Bar" provided directions on how to equip a bar in order to "serve the right drinks, in the right way, at home." "The Compleat Fidelitarian" and "The Stereo Scene" offered pointers on the latest developments in hi-fi equipment," while "The Verities of Vino" explained the protocols of wine appreciation. On the automobile front, "The Compleat Sports Car Stable" surveyed the fastest, most elegant American and European cars on the road. "The Playboy Sports Car" invited readers to join in the planning of the perfect sports car for today's prosperous, sophisticated young man. *Playboy* took the role of consumer adviser seriously, so much so that occasionally it poked fun at itself. In 1955, for example, it offered the facetious "Mixing the Perfect Martini," where a maniacally fastidious butler poured gin and dry vermouth from a test tube to get the precise number of cubic centimeters, measured olives with a caliper to get an exact millimeter reading, stirred the drink exactly twenty-five revolutions, and twisted a lemon peel over the cocktail for effect even though no juice came out.[7]

One of the most popular *Playboy* consumer features appeared in 1956. Over two issues, "Playboy's Penthouse Apartment" took readers on a tour of the ultimate bachelor pad, dispensing advice on how to create a sophisticated urban apartment. "PLAYBOY has designed, planned, and decorated from the floor up, a penthouse apartment for the urban bachelor—a man who enjoys good living, a sophisticated connoisseur of the lively arts, of food and drink and congenial companions of both sexes. A man very much, perhaps, like you." A series of color sketches showed views of a sleek Scandinavian-style dining room, state-of-the-art kitchen with dishwasher and glass-domed oven, spacious living room with fireplace and elaborate stereo system, elegant home office, and master bedroom suite with bedside controls to operate lights, drapes, and music throughout the apartment and a bathroom complete with a giant sunken tub and shower. Skylights, an illuminated aquarium, recessed Swedish fireplace, and a cork tile floor added to the apartment's "sense of masculine richness and excitement." Abstract art adorned the walls, a plethora of large windows allowed abundant light, and chic modern furniture by Noguchi, Bruno Mathesson, Saarinen, Eames, and Knoll graced the rooms. The apartment appeared "a bachelor haven of virile good looks, a place styled for a man of taste and sophistication. This is *his* place, to fit his moods, suit his needs, reflect his personality."[8]

The subject of clothing occupied a special place in *Playboy's* ongoing tutorial on consumer purchasing. Throughout the 1950s the magazine counseled readers on the newest male fashion trends and what to wear in every type of social situation. "The Well-Clad Undergrad" advised the well-dressed young man on campus, while the ubiquitous Blake Rutherford addressed myriad fashion issues throughout the decade with his preference for Continental styling. Throughout such informational articles, of course, *Playboy* gently mentored its audience on appropriate tastes and standards. A 1959 article on formalwear, for instance, instructed readers on how to choose "elegant, good-looking formal attire" for warm-weather occasions:

A black or white dinner jacket is, of course, still correct for summer or tropical wear. . . . Formal trousers, of course, are never anything save midnight blue or black. . . . Black patent leather or dull calf shoes or pumps are always worn. Your hose, of course, should always be black. . . . No time of year puts more emphasis on your formal wardrobe than the season coming up. Why? Because this June, July, and August, the country clubs, yacht clubs, beach clubs, and just plain clubs are going [strong]. . . . Also, if your vacation plans carry you to a resort, large hotel, or aboard a cruise ship, you'll find that a dinner jacket is mandatory for evening wear.

Despite the element of fantasy—one wonders how many *Playboy* readers actually frequented yacht clubs or cruise ships—the magazine's advice reflected a new sensibility in the middle class. Consumption demanded a modicum of style, or it became little more than a crass hoarding of goods, a crude triumph of quantity over quality.[9]

Advertising in *Playboy* reinforced the editorial message of stylish buying. In fact, the magazine's advertising policy guaranteed an aura of upscale consumption. Determined to distance his publication from the normal run of girlie and pulp magazines, Hefner rejected ads for products that emphasized tawdry or proletarian themes. He spurned over 75 percent of advertisers who sought to peddle such items as "guns, correspondence courses, hair restorers, and trusses" because they failed to comport with the desired image of prosperity and success. "We agreed early on to accept only advertising that seemed to be consistent with the editorial attitude of the publication," Hefner wrote to a company whose ads he had turned down.[10]

Hefner stuck to his guns, even though it meant a loss of profits in the short term. In 1955, the magazine landed its first major advertising account with Springmaid sheets. The initial ad depicted an eloping couple crawling down a ladder as the buxom bride-to-be proclaimed to her flustered young man struggling to balance a hope chest, "Certainly we're taking it . . . they're Springmaid sheets and I have a full chest, too." *Playboy* continued pursuing mainline advertisers, and after several years of limited success—many companies were skittish about identifying with such a risqué publication—it began to reel them in more and more as the magazine prospered.[11]

By the late 1950s, Hefner had successfully linked *Playboy* to upscale consumption. The June 1959 issue was typical. Advertisements appeared for over twenty items of male apparel, including After

Six dinner jackets, Frank Brothers clothes, and "the cool comfort of Hush Puppies." More than ten liquor ads appeared, including Walker Straight Bourbon Whiskey, Bacardi rum, and Rainier Old Stock Ale. On the transportation front, readers came upon ads for BMW, Autotourist European Rental Cars, and the Silhouette Mark II sailing boat.

Home amenities also abounded, with promotions for everything from Crosswinds House beach towels and robes to Scintilla Satin Bedsheets, Lektrostat Kit record cleaners to Mansfield Holiday II 8-mm. cameras, Leslie Record Racks to the Electro-Voice Musicaster (an outdoor "high-fidelity speaker system for relaxed enjoyment at the patio or pool"). Personal accessory plugs included the Ronson Electric Shaver, Max Factor crew-cut hair dressing, Rogers "Rocket Flame" cigarette lighter, Merrin Gold Jewelry, and English Leather aftershave and toiletries. Ads focusing on romance promoted such items as Coty Perfume ("Nothing makes a woman more feminine to a man") and the Batch Book, "a new and modern address book that lets you list every pertinent detail—the surest way to avoid social errors."

Playboy iced the commercial cake with advertising for a new consumer appurtenance: the credit card, which promised added convenience and buying power. It claimed that the Diners Club credit card "is nearly universal in its use. It can be used to buy thousands of items and services—clothing, dinner, hotel rooms, boats, liquor, tires, cars, plane trips, luggage, stenographic services, recordings, cameras, fishing equipment, gifts, flowers—many, many things."[12]

By urging its readers to buy "many, many things," *Playboy* emerged at the center of a consumer bonanza in 1950s America. It even established a special service in 1957 to assist readers with purchasing goods. Interested consumers could contact the "Playboy Reader Service," which would then provide "the local shopping information you need to purchase any of the hundreds of interesting items you find featured in PLAYBOY (Playmates excepted). All you have to do is check the item listed in the Index of Advertisers in which you are interested." Always keen to underline the pleasure connection between sex and abundance, the magazine noted that this service was supervised by Janet Pilgrim, who was pictured painting footsteps on a floor as a pair of anonymous men's legs stepped along in the prints.[13]

Hefner correctly sensed, however, that American consumer society, as it evolved to a more advanced stage in the postwar era, involved more than just buying goods. It was intimately connected to a larger ethos of pleasure, leisure, and entertainment. Uninhibited consumption depended on the emotional joys of self-fulfillment, not the moral satisfactions of self-denial. *Playboy,* in a host of 1950s articles and features, encouraged just such a creed of gratification.

Recreation took the lead. "Playboy on Poker" explored winning strategies for the card game, while "The Art of Travel" taught inexperienced travelers how to move about the country and the world "with special ease and grace." It explained guidebooks, travel agents, how to assemble an itinerary that suited individual tastes, and how to evaluate tour packages. "Invitation to Yachting: Playboy's Guide to Fun Afloat" perused luxury watercraft and their deployment for the weekend sailor. Advertisements plugged a host of nightclubs for the sophisticated young man and his date: Chicago favorites such as Morton's, Sardi's East, Blackhawk, and the Cloisters, and out-of-town nightspots such as Rendezvous of the Stars in L.A. and the Sands in Las Vegas.[14]

Musical entertainment featured prominently in *Playboy's* recipe for recreation. Hefner was a longtime fan of jazz, and promotion of this genre abounded. "Bird" described the saxophone virtuoso Charlie Parker and his fantastic, wailing performance style. The noted jazz critic Leonard Feather penned many features, including "Ella Meets the Duke," a look at icons Ella Fitzgerald and Duke Ellington, and "Sinatra," an analysis of the most influential vocalist of the era. The Playboy Jazz Poll debuted in 1957, with readers voting annually on the best singers and instrumentalists at every spot in the typical band. Some twenty thousand ballots selected such luminaries as Stan Kenton as bandleader, Louis Armstrong and Dizzy Gillespie on trumpet, J. J. Johnson and Jack Teagarden on trombone, Benny Goodman on clarinet, Dave Brubeck on piano, Lionel Hampton on vibes, and Gerry Mulligan and Paul Desmond on sax. Sinatra and Fitzgerald won out as male and female vocalists.[15]

Sports regularly moved into the *Playboy* spotlight, especially Hefner's two favorites, boxing and college football. The magazine offered an annual ring preview such as "Boxing 1956," which weighed the prospect of fighters like Rocky Marciano, Archie Moore, Floyd

Patterson, and Sugar Ray Robinson. In September 1957, *Playboy* introduced its first college football forecast as Anson "Smoky" Mount, who had been running the College Bureau, took over the job for the next fifteen years. He proved himself to be one of the most accurate football prognosticators in the country as "Pigskin Preview" became an annual feature. Throughout, *Playboy* seized every chance to connect sport with consumption, promoting an array of sporting goods including Abercrombie and Fitch golf clubs, Hedland water skis, and skin-diving masks and underwater cameras.[16]

Movies, another Hefner pastime, attracted much attention in *Playboy.* "Playboy After Hours" reviewed the latest American and European film releases while articles on movies, actors, and the Hollywood scene cropped up regularly. "The Horror of It All" explored the popular appeal of Hollywood horror films, while "Chaplin: The Chronicle of a Man and His Genius" examined the career of the brilliant comedic actor. Billy Wilder, Hollywood's hottest writer-producer-director, received a close analysis in "Charming Billy." Attention also focused on theater. In December 1956, two veteran critics—Wolcott Gibbs from the *New Yorker,* and Ward Morehouse from *Theatre Arts*—offered their assessments of "Broadway: The Season Just Past, the Season to Come."[17]

Playboy fed its readers a nourishing diet of humor. Cartoons, again reflecting the publisher's own taste and background, emerged as a magazine stalwart. Early contributors such as Jack Cole and Gardner Rea were joined by a new cadre of hip funsters by mid-decade. In 1956, Shel Silverstein brought his irreverent sensibility to the magazine with a series of globetrotting cartoons, one of which pictured him talking to a stern butler at Buckingham Palace, who said, "I believe I can say with assurance, sir, that Princess Margaret will not be interested in appearing as January's Playmate of the Month." In August 1958, *Playboy* introduced "The Sick Little World of Jules Feiffer," describing the cartoonist as someone with "more than a touch of the psychoanalyst and the social critic in his makeup." Feiffer specialized in visually minimalist, conversation-heavy encounters between men and women that pointed out human foibles and hypocrisies. The grotesque, macabre work of Gahan Wilson also became a *Playboy* favorite. A typical cartoon depicted a disheveled scientist in a lab coat straining to hold a laboratory door shut against a giant, multicolored blob pushing it open, as he told a superior, "It turns out, we'll have no trouble producing the new drug in large quantities, sir!" Hefner worked with all the cartoonists, particularly inspiring the *Babs and Shirley* series—it featured a pair of single, sexually adventurous roommates—drawn by the cartoonist Al Stine.[18]

Playboy's growing reputation for presenting high-quality fiction moved down the same path. As the *Los Angeles Times* noted in 1957, "Some of the best short fiction written in America today is being published in *Playboy*. These short stories are gutty and imaginative, skillfully written, and—perhaps most important—experimental." Indeed, writers such as John Steinbeck, Jack Kerouac, Arthur C. Clarke, Ray Bradbury, P. G. Wodehouse, and Charles Beaumont appeared in its pages throughout the late 1950s. Yet much of the writing fit more comfortably into an entertainment than a literary mode. The magazine presented morsels of fiction that were usually digested easily, providing a greater portion of pleasure than thought. Typically, it described the lead fictional piece in January 1958 as "a yarn that has all the elements of exciting story telling—suspense, ironic humor, a pip of a plot, and a twist ending—written with flair and flavor." The same issue also contained the magazine's annual $1,000 prize for fiction, which it awarded to "the past year's most entertaining story."[19]

Playboy's promotion of a leisure culture of consumer self-fulfillment went beyond the abstract. Throughout the 1950s, Hefner's enterprise cashed in on the pleasure-oriented message of the magazine. It developed a multifaceted merchandising campaign—clothing, albums, books, personal accessories—devoted to the enjoyment of abundance. By 1957, a leatherette Playboy Binder for collecting issues of the magazine and Playboy cuff links had appeared along with three books: *The Third Playboy Annual, Playboy's Party Jokes,* and *Playboy's Ribald Classics.* Soon neckties, tie tacks, bracelets, sport shirts, sweaters, playing cards, and bar accessories came forward, all adorned with the magazine's rabbit head logo. By 1959 a line of jazz albums, the Playboy Model Agency, and Playboy Tours joined the list. Hefner also branched out with a syndicated television show and a national chain of nightclubs. In much the same way that the postwar Walt Disney Company utilized synergy to meld movies, television, merchandising, and theme parks into an entertainment empire, Playboy, Inc., integrated various projects into a cohesive enterprise to promote its vision of leisure, pleasure, and material abundance.[20]

Not all Hefner's expansion activities were successful, however. *Playboy's* growing profits inspired him to launch a satire magazine titled *Trump* in late 1956, but sales lagged badly. Other money leaks opened around the same time. Hefner had invested a large amount of funds in the new offices on Ohio Street when his banker unexpectedly pulled his line of credit. With no working capital, a financial crisis ensued. Hefner took strong measures: cutting 25 percent from all executive salaries, giving up his salary entirely, discontinuing *Trump*, and temporarily giving up 25 percent of his company's stock to help secure a bank loan for $250,000. As he confessed in July 1957, "This has been a rough six months—months of difficult decision and of payment for some wrong decisions in the past."[21]

But the setback was only temporary. The magazine righted itself by the end of 1957, secured a major national distributor, and continued its long-term trajectory of growth. *Playboy* and Hefner steadily established themselves as symbols of the new prosperity, and nowhere did this appear more clearly than in a successful campaign to link pleasure with upward social mobility.

II

In April 1958, *Playboy* proudly reported the results of a study of American magazine readership. Conducted by Daniel Starch & Staff and published in the annual *Consumer Magazine Report*, the survey assembled economic and social statistics on the readers of all major magazines in the country. It concluded that *Playboy* had a younger, more affluent, and better-educated audience than any other of the fifty magazines surveyed, jostling with the *New Yorker* and *U.S. News and World Report* in many categories. Its readers not only led the pack in spending on travel, automobiles, liquor, and tobacco but bought more "electric coffee makers, food mixers, fans, irons, and toasters." Its typical reader was "at the peak period of purchasing" and highly attuned to success, *Playboy* noted proudly. As the magazine concluded, "It's gratifying to know that this constellation of attributes, this orientation of the personality, is possessed by the men who are—statistically—the leaders in their liking for, and ability to attain, the good things of this life."[22]

Hefner immediately began featuring the Starch Report in advertising his magazine, launching a campaign around the familiar slogan, "What Sort of Man Reads Playboy?" According to the ads, the Starch survey "shows the average *Playboy* reader has a higher income than the reader of any other men's magazine. The *Playboy* reader is younger, too. 75.5% of all *Playboy* readers are between 18 and 34, the acquisitive age when every purchase is a brisk step ahead." Ads stressed readers' extensive education, high professional and business standing, taste for liquor, fine cars, travel, clothes, and entertainment. In sum, the typical reader was successful and poised to consume: "Although they're younger—the median age of the *Playboy* reader is 28—they have a higher household income than the readers of any other men's magazine. And *Playboy* ranks highest of all men's magazines in consumer statistics for tobacco, beer, whiskey, wine, wearing apparel, photographic equipment, automobiles, and radios."[23]

Clearly, Hefner had achieved one of his fondest goals by the late 1950s—to make *Playboy* synonymous with a modern ethos of prosperity and social attainment. The Starch Report seemed to prove his contention that pleasure-seeking paved the road not to dissipation but to worldly success. Now Hefner sought to cement his victory by addressing one of the most publicized cultural upsurges of the era.

The "Beat Generation" had attracted much attention by the late 1950s for its posture of detached, cool, hipster alienation. Led by writers and poets such as Jack Kerouac and Allen Ginsberg, the movement disdained the bland conformity of middle-class, suburban life and celebrated primal experience, drugs, and personal freedom. *Playboy* covered the Beats as well as any magazine in the country. It published a 1958 symposium on "The Beat Mystique," exploring "aspects of the new nihilism—frozen-faced, far out, devoid of normal meaning"—and analyzing the emotional deadness resulting from "the great triumvirate disease of the American male—Passivity, Anxiety, Boredom." Kerouac himself probed "The Origins of the Beat Generation," suggesting that the movement he had christened came out of a revulsion against middle-class norms, a search for genuine emotional experience, a fondness for popular culture icons like the Marx Brothers and the Three Stooges, and an indigenous "old American Whoopee."[24]

In one sense, *Playboy* tried to co-opt the movement. It presented Yvette Vickers in the July 1959 issue as the "Beat Playmate" who hung out at hip coffeehouses and clubs in Los Angeles exchanging ideas and discontent with like-minded souls. "She's interested in serious acting, ballet, the poetry of Dylan Thomas," noted the text. "She has strong opinions and is more than a bit of a rebel, frowning prettily on conformity." The centerfold photograph depicted her lying on her stomach on a sofa, nude from the waist down, wearing only a man's shirt. With a frazzled look on her face, an empty bottle of wine, a full ashtray, and an open book of poetry sitting next to her on the floor, she reached down to spin albums on a hi-fi.[25]

Mainly, however, Hefner made the Beats a foil for his efforts to define the *Playboy* audience. While sharing their discontent with the dowdy, "square" aspects of traditional American values, he found their style appalling. Disillusionment, drugs, and despair had little kinship with the *Playboy* ideal of sophisticated style, social achievement, and material prosperity. So Hefner coined a phrase to describe his readership and its effort to reform and revitalize, not reject, mainstream American society. "PLAYBOY has become, in its first five years, the voice of what might be aptly called the Upbeat Generation," he announced in 1958.[26]

Hefner returned to this phrase again and again in discussing his loyal, and growing, audience. "When the Beat Generation became a cause célèbre and we reported on it, and Kerouac wrote for us, I made a case for what I called the Upbeat Generation," he recalled years later. Instead of dropping out of society, the Upbeat Generation sought to "embrace the play and pleasure aspects of life along with the work. So we were rejecting the notion of conformity, but turning life into a celebration that incorporated capitalism."[27]

In a private letter, Hefner asserted that if *Playboy* "is to truly be a much-needed rebel voice for the Upbeat Generation—then it's got to holler long and loud about all those sacred cows" of sexual repression and asceticism. In a radio interview, he suggested that while the Beat Generation had attracted much publicity, a "much larger portion of the same generation is also equally unwilling to conform to the old ideas and ideals, but wants to do something about it—and we refer to them sometimes as the Upbeat Generation. These are the guys for whom *Playboy* has meaning. We suggest that life can be an awful lot of fun, if you work hard and play hard, too."[28]

In a long statement to a Chicago magazine, Hefner embedded the Upbeat Generation in a broader reading of American history. After World War II, he contended, many people had moved to the suburbs and become obsessed with security and conformity.

> But now from behind the generation of static, controlled people came a new generation. We now have two generations—one behind each other—with the biggest gap between them of any other two generations in the history of this country. I'm convinced that the present generation, we like to call it for reasons of promotion the Upbeat Generation, is our true salvation. And *Playboy* fits that generation more than any other magazine.[29]

Ultimately, the agenda of the Upbeat Generation represented a revamping of the old American creed of opportunity and mobility. *Playboy*'s message expressed a "strong belief in the wonderful opportunities that exist in this country if a person is willing to work to achieve something and make something of himself," Hefner wrote to a friend. "*Playboy* says to its readers, the world is a wonderful place; enjoy it, live it to the hilt, work hard and play hard, and you will make this a better world for yourself and for those around you." He was confident of victory, telling a reporter, "Kerouac's got a few beat guys over in his corner, but we've got all the rest."[30]

In 1959, Hefner hosted an event that seemed to celebrate the vitality of the Upbeat Generation. The Playboy Jazz Festival took shape as a gala concert that gathered the biggest jazz luminaries in America for three days of performances. Victor Lownes undertook the organization and promotion of the event and originally booked it at Soldier Field. Then the city fathers reneged on the agreement because of pressure from the local Roman Catholic Church, which denounced any city affiliation with *Playboy*. After receiving much support in the local press, Hefner and Lownes were able to secure a new venue at Chicago Stadium.[31]

From August 7 to 9, a who's who of American jazz took the outdoor stage at the stadium: Louis Armstrong, Duke Ellington, Count Basie, Dave Brubeck, Miles Davis, Ella Fitzgerald, Dizzy Gillespie, Coleman Hawkins, Stan Kenton, Oscar Peterson, and many others. Comedian Mort Sahl emceed the festival, and some eighteen thousand listeners attended every night. A jubilant Hefner sat in the front row as Sahl quipped, "This should prove to skeptics that *Playboy* magazine is interested in more than one thing." When Hefner was introduced at the intermission on the last night, he asked if there should be another festival next year and the crowd roared its approval.[32]

Playboy made no money from the event, turning over all proceeds above expenses to Chicago's Urban League. But it gained something much more valuable: an upgrading of its reputation. As *Variety* observed in a highly favorable assessment of the concert, "there's little doubt the affair did enhance *Playboy*'s institutional status." In comments to *Billboard,* Victor Lownes revealed just how much.

> Our main object is to improve the image of the magazine in the eyes of those advertisers who have not yet stopped to read it, but who judge it merely by the centerfold. We want to bring home to these advertisers that *Playboy* covers all the interests of the smart, young American male. Accomplishing this is worth a considerable bit of money to us.

By pulling off this prestigious event, the magazine took a large step forward in establishing itself in the mainstream. Connecting itself to images of sophisticated entertainment, leisure, and upward mobility, it demonstrated that it was hip but not beat.[33]

Hefner's upbeat message of social success and material abundance showcased one final dimension. "The emphasis on hi-fi, sports cars, good food and drink, good entertainment, good literature and music is to stimulate our young men to educate themselves so they can make enough money to enjoy these benefits," he told the *Saturday Evening Post.* "In this way we can help overcome the educational gap between ourselves and the Russians. Our mission is to make this the Upbeat Generation instead of the Beat Generation, and thus perform a service for America." This desire to help his country in the prevailing atmosphere of Cold War tension revealed an ideological dimension in Hefner's enterprise. Engaged in a confrontation with the global forces of communism, the United States attempted to define and defend an American Way of Life based on consumer prosperity as well as democratic freedom. On this front, *Playboy* stood prepared to play a heroic role.[34]

III

In the summer of 1959, Vice President Richard Nixon journeyed to Moscow as the head of a delegation to open the American National Exhibition at a trade fair. While touring the model of a suburban home from the United States, he engaged Soviet premier Nikita Khrushchev in the famous "Kitchen Debates." Nixon maintained that the prosperous standard of living for ordinary citizens in the United States would fuel its long-term triumph, insisting that television sets, washing machines, vacuum cleaners, and other consumer amenities were the weapons that ultimately would win the Cold War. Khrushchev mocked this notion. But Nixon's rhetoric revealed much about the tight link between the desire for economic security and national security. The ability to choose from among an abundant array of material items set off the United States from the gray, drab, uniform existence of communist societies and defined its notion of the good life.[35]

In many ways, *Playboy* embodied this ideological impulse. In terms of style, of course, the magazine could not have stood further from the stodgy Eisenhower administration, whose leader once allowed that his favorite band was Fred Waring and the Pennsylvanians. But on matters of political economy, Hefner stood shoulder to shoulder with Nixon and a vast majority of his fellow citizens. America's ability to produce and consume an array of items represented the essence of the modern free enterprise system.

Clearly, Hefner and his magazine lay in the mainstream of Cold War corporate liberalism. Like both major political parties, *Playboy* displayed an essential belief in modern consumer capitalism along with an endorsement of government controls to keep its excesses in check. To this consensus, Hefner and his magazine added strong elements of free expression and nonconformity regarding cultural issues. *Playboy*'s politics in the 1950s were capitalist in their endorsement of entrepreneurial free enterprise, progressive in its belief in the necessity of government regulation, and libertarian in its emphasis on individual freedom on social and cultural matters. While usually proceeding indirectly—the Upbeat Generation tended to find political disputation distracting and uncool—the magazine positioned itself as a defender of the American Way of Life. Far from being subversive, as some of its more hysterical critics contended, *Playboy* insisted that adoption of a pleasure ethic would strengthen America in its struggle with communism.

At the heart of Hefner's ideological message lay a total commitment to individual freedom. This bedrock belief emerged in part from his reading of American history, which concluded that an optimistic, rags-to-riches, success-seeking creed had animated its citizens until the Great Depression brought an obsessive concern with protecting the average, ordinary individual:

> Because of a very valid concern for the average man, for the common man, who was in trouble, little by little, much of the viewpoints expressed in the mass media began to emphasize not only concern for the common man, but almost a kind of idealization of him. . . . Then on into the war years for another half-dozen years, beginning in the Forties, conformity of another kind took hold. . . . Well, out of all this came a tremendous de-emphasis of the importance of the individual and individual initiative, and a tremendous de-emphasis on education. . . .
>
> All of a sudden we realized, and on a very practical level, too, that the country had almost stood still for 20 years. All of a sudden the world's greatest power was a long way short. . . . But with the new generation, there seemed to be an unwillingness to accept a lot of these old taboos, old traditions, old concepts. . . . I think *Playboy* is a part of this.[36]

Hefner consistently stressed that "individual freedom in terms of sexual behavior was of a piece with individual freedom in the free enterprise system." He believed, in his own words, that the genius of capitalism allowed "the best ideas and the best people rise to the top, or at least have a chance to compete. And everyone benefits from that on every kind of level."[37]

At the same time, Hefner firmly supported government regulation of the economy. In the tradition of twentieth-century progressivism, he asserted that a free, competitive society would not "remain free or competitive very long . . . without some controls; complete laissez-faire capitalism wouldn't give us free enterprise any more than anarchy would give us political freedom." While competition and profit-seeking should be encouraged, "you need government to control, to referee the game." So while Hefner endorsed the free play of individual ambition, he also contended that it should be kept from mutating into destructive greed and power-mongering. He was, in his own phrase, a disciple of "enlightened self-interest."[38]

Moreover, in the 1950s Hefner was clearly anticommunist. In a memo on a Charlie Chaplin story for *Playboy*, he observed that the comic genius had made a serious mistake in endorsing leftist radicalism during the 1930s when "Communism was not clearly seen as the totalitarian dictatorship it is today." In a private letter, he again denounced communism as "a totalitarian dictatorship that permits no opinion but its own, and I happen to be a boy who believes fervently in democracy and freedom of expression."[39]

Hefner's stubborn libertarian streak also pushed to the fore, particularly in issues involving free speech. He denounced any kind of censorship, either from interest groups or from the government. In 1959, for instance, controversy arose when the police chief in a San Francisco suburb banned *Playboy* because of "obscene" pictures. A newspaper storm erupted, with Congresswoman Kathryn E. Granahan (D-Pa.), chairwoman of the Subcommittee on Postal Operations, denouncing the "billion dollar a year smut racket" and claiming a connection among lewd materials, juvenile delinquency, and communism. Hefner vigorously defended free expression. "If the reading material of the citizens of any community is to be pre-selected—a pretty abhorrent thought in itself—I can't think of anyone less qualified to do it than a local police chief," he told the Associated Press.[40]

Hefner also raised the banner of free speech in defending against McCarthyism. Although anticommunist, he was disgusted by the Red-hunting crusades initiated by Senator Joseph McCarthy and his ilk. After a reader complained about *Playboy*'s willingness to publish articles by leftist writers, Hefner offered a ringing defense of free expression in a democracy:

> PLAYBOY sincerely believes that this nation is big enough, strong enough, and right enough to give free expression to the ideas and talents of every man among us without fear of being hurt by any man's individual weaknesses or follies. . . . [America] prides itself on fair play and believing a man innocent until proven

guilty. But that's really beside the point—for we appreciate Picasso as one of the world's greatest living artists, and we *know* he's a Communist. Politics may be important in government, where national security is a vital consideration, but it has no place in art and literature. Not if America's art and literature, and indeed the country itself, are to remain free.[41]

Hefner's libertarian positions on matters of sex and politics aroused the ire of the FBI. In 1957, he reported that FBI agents visited the offices of *Playboy* to inquire about a pictorial being shot called "Photographing Your Own Playmate." They also visited Millie's apartment, asking about her husband's activities, and put the publisher under surveillance. According to documents in Hefner's FBI file, agents were combing through *Playboy* as early as 1955 looking for obscenity and unfavorable references to the Bureau or the director.[42]

Nonetheless, the magazine maintained a mainstream political posture that was reflected in Hefner's own political loyalties. In 1952, he vacillated between Eisenhower and Adlai Stevenson. "Millie and I belong to that happy group known as independent voters, and this year we're pulling for Ike," he noted initially. But then he switched to Stevenson, contending that "his unusual qualifications for the job outweigh all other considerations." At the end of the decade, he observed that if *Playboy* were a political magazine, "it would probably be Republican in almost all of its national views. I know that I am. I don't dig Socialism—I think it's unworkable and tends to make men sit on their asses instead of working hard to better themselves." This posture continued well into the mid-1960s.[43]

Hefner's centrist politics influenced his love of the "New Comics," humorists who eschewed gags and one-liners for satirical musings on contemporary mores and issues. He first encountered this free-form comedy in the improvisational shows of the Compass Players (later Second City), a Chicago group that satirized the stodginess and hypocrisy of mainstream America. Then Mort Sahl, who styled himself "America's only working philosopher," appeared. Wearing a sweater and brandishing a rolled-up newspaper in one hand, he developed an intellectual, stream-of-consciousness style that skewered prevailing shibboleths in politics, foreign policy, ommunism, and religion. On the issue of segregation, for instance, Sahl noted that

"Eisenhower says that we should approach this problem moderately. But Stevenson says we should solve the problem gradually. Now if we could just hit a compromise between those two extremes . . ." Hefner also became a fan of Lenny Bruce, the outrageous "sick" comedian who used a stream of four-letter words to caustically dissect the age of Eisenhower. Commenting on everything from funeral homes to dope addiction to homosexuality, Bruce typically observed of the newspaper headline "Flood Waters Rise, Dikes Threatened," "It's always the same. In times of emergency they pick on minority groups."[44]

Hefner promoted Sahl and Bruce heavily in *Playboy*, believing them to be allies in a common cause—"questioning the conformity and repression of the times." The publisher shared a political sensibility with the New Comics that was more a matter of cultural style than policy pronouncements. Sahl and Bruce had no real quarrel with the Cold War or capitalism. With their jazz vocabulary, sophisticated urbanism, and irreverence for authority, these comics, much like Hefner and *Playboy*, represented a movement to loosen the system culturally and morally rather than revamp it politically or economically.[45]

Playboy's vaguely progressive political temperament prompted a gradual engagement with social issues. It published Vance Packard's "The Manipulators," a scathing critique of corporate researchers who studied people's hidden needs and anxieties in order to sell products. "Eros and Unreason in Detroit" criticized the American auto industry for producing shoddy, tasteless cars that appealed to the "one great fault with most American males: an irrational fear of impotence." "The Cult of the Aged Leader" questioned the geriatric domination of all branches of government. In 1959, *Playboy* issued a special editorial sounding the alarm about nuclear testing and the dangerous, perhaps deadly, release of the radioactive element strontium-90 into the atmosphere. A responsible, reformist political sensibility dominated all these pieces.[46]

Perhaps the most remarkable testament to Hefner's mainstream politics, however, came in a 1960 letter to Ronald Reagan, then president of the Screen Actors Guild. The publisher had learned from a mutual friend that Reagan had been upset by an article in *Playboy* authored by Dalton Trumbo, one of the blacklisted "Hollywood Ten." So he wrote to the actor assuring him that "We, here at *Playboy*, don't dig Communism and don't dig Communists—I don't like

Communism and the fundamental things it stands for." However, Hefner continued, censorship and blacklisting represented a "step toward tyranny" and was "precisely what this country is fighting against and what all totalitarian nations, Communist Russia included, have always stood for." A free society, he argued, demanded a "process of freely exchanging divergent ideas, instead of trying to shut up the ones with which we do not agree."[47]

The letter encapsulated *Playboy's* politics in the 1950s: pro-entrepreneur, anticommunist, pro–individual expression, anti-censorship. As a voice of a respectable opposition, Hefner sought to loosen the restraints of the system while staying firmly within it. Navigating a course between the stultifying conformity of the Eisenhower age and the jagged alienation of the Beats, *Playboy* and its publisher represented an official counterculture. Much like Theodore Roosevelt and his crusade for a "vigorous life" at the dawn of the twentieth century, *Playboy* mounted a revitalization movement that sought to inject sexual energy, social style, and masculine power into a tired mainstream society in order to strengthen it for struggle against hostile foes. As Hefner expressed it beautifully in a newspaper interview at the end of the decade, "We're trying to project an acceptable rebel voice."[48]

Promoting consumer abundance as well as sexual liberation, *Playboy* provided a powerful boost to the full-blown culture of self-fulfillment that was sweeping away the last vestiges of Victorian self-denial. As Hefner once put it, launching *Playboy* "was like a mission—to publish a magazine that would thumb its nose at all the restrictions that had bound me."[49]

Hefner and *Playboy*, in defying older rules of restraint, gave voice to his era's yearning to meet all needs, satisfy all desires, sate all appetites. This crusade, he explained, aimed at "challenging the two greatest guilts our society has: materialism and sex." Hefner had gambled that his own desire to partake of sexual and material abundance was shared widely in postwar society. He had presented a magazine reflecting his interests, his tastes, his desires, himself, "not exactly as I exist, but as my dreams existed. The kind of guy that I aspired to be." The bet paid off. *Playboy's* popularity revealed that many others had similar visions of the good life and wanted to be the same kind of guy.[50]

8

Living the Fantasy

The signs were hard to miss. As *Playboy* took off in the mid-1950s, its youthful editor and publisher began to spend increasing amounts of time with shapely females who regularly appeared in the magazine's offices. Ray Russell raised his eyebrows one day when a young woman showed up and stayed a long time in his boss's office. "I realized she wasn't there on business. It shows you how naïve I was in those days that I was shocked, because after all, Hef was *a married man*," he observed. "I wised up soon enough in the years to come as the stream of young ladies filed in and out of Hef's office."[1]

Victor Lownes stumbled across another indicator of his boss's sexual adventures. A common female acquaintance let slip about Hef's "little black book" she found on his night table. It listed girls he dated and "there were some coded markings" that apparently "referred to various specialties in the sex department." It also listed one of the older, dowdier females on the *Playboy* staff as one of his past conquests. When Lownes asked Hefner if he had really slept with her, the publisher admitted he had. Lownes inquired mischievously,

"Was she better looking in those days?" Hefner thought for a moment and replied, "I hope so."[2]

Such was the emerging pattern of Hefner's private life in the 1950s. As *Playboy* gathered steam, its young publisher gradually adapted his own life to the new atmosphere of fantasy he had invoked. In many ways, it was not an easy process. Shy, sentimental, and largely uninterested in fashionable clothes, fast sports cars, and fine food and liquor, Hefner did not gravitate naturally to sophistication. Moreover, he was married with two small children. So his embrace of a *Playboy* lifestyle emerged only in fits and starts, beginning with a series of girlfriends and liaisons that contributed to the steady crumbling of his marriage.

Near the end of the decade, however, Hefner fully reinvented himself. Publicly, and with great fanfare, he adopted the *Playboy* ethos of sexual revolution and material abundance. He also undertook several projects involving television, nightclubs, and a fantastic mansion that brought to life the magazine's fantasies of pleasure.

With his keen intuitive sense, Hefner grasped the growing importance of celebrity in postwar America. In a consumer culture devoted to leisure and entertainment, celebrities from the world of movies, television, sports, and glossy magazines—those, according to Daniel Boorstin's famous quip, who were "well-known for their well-knownness"—assumed central places in popular consciousness. Mass communication broadcast larger-than-life images of people on the television screen or glossy magazine page and created an illusion of actually knowing them. As Richard Schickel has observed, in this muddle of public and private life these "intimate strangers" gained a powerful influence. As arbiters of manners and opinions, celebrities became "the chief agents of moral change in the United States." In the 1950s, Hefner emerged as just such a celebrity. As Mr. Playboy, projecting images of a dream-come-true life of sexual and consumer plenty, he emerged as the impresario of the pleasure ethic in postwar America.[3]

I

With the founding of *Playboy*, work and play became inseparable elements of Hefner's life. With increasing regularity, he collapsed from exhaustion in the small adjoining bedroom at his Superior Street office and stayed overnight. Subsequently, his Ohio Street office suite contained a separate bachelor apartment with a bedroom, dressing room, and bathroom. Both settings hosted dalliances with a series of young women. Steadily distancing himself from a strained marriage and a family in which he had declining interest, he threw himself into a life he felt had been denied him in young manhood. Hefner became a playboy about town.

The nightclub scene on the Near North Side, not far from the magazine's Ohio Street offices, formed the background for Hefner's revitalized social activities. While Chicago was an old-fashioned, machine-run city under the domination of Mayor Richard Daley and heavily influenced by the Catholic Church, the Near North Side flourished as a bohemian haven full of artists and art galleries, newspapers and journalists, restaurants and clubs. The area around Rush Street was particularly boisterous, filled with nightclubs such as Mr. Kelly's, the Black Orchid, the Cloisters, and the Chez Paree. With a gang of buddies—Victor Lownes, Shel Silverstein, comedian Don Adams, agent Lee Wolfberg, and club owners Shelly Kasten, Skip Krask, and John Dante—Hefner prowled the nightspots of the area in the early morning hours after leaving his office around midnight. The group played poker and gin rummy, shared drinks and music, and often went out for breakfast as the sun came up. "Chicago was the swingingest town in the entire world," Adams noted of the atmosphere. "It was like New Year's Eve every night."[4]

Casual sexual conquests punctuated these boisterous male gatherings. The nightclubs were full of women, and Hefner, like the others, successfully wooed, according to Kasten, "show girls, waitresses, hat check girls, gals off the street." One night they all had too much to drink and, in Krask's words, they "organized an orgy." During the revelry, he and Kasten snapped a picture of Hefner in bed with two girls. Several nights later, as a prank, they gave him an envelope they claimed some guy had dropped off. It contained a print of the salacious picture along with a note demanding $500 to keep it out of the newspapers. The publisher looked stricken and turned so pale that they quickly stopped the joke.[5]

The *Playboy* offices, bubbling with sexual intrigue, provided an equally vibrant social atmosphere. In a setting where breaking down walls of sexual restraint was company business, vigorous young men and women, unsurprisingly, developed attractions. Affairs flourished. Ray Russell fooled around with girls in the office "with some regularity," according to a colleague. Bev Chamberlain and Vince Tajiri had an extended affair. Janet Pilgrim hooked up with advertising executive Phil Miller. Eldon Sellers and Anson Mount began socializing with their wives and, according to Sellers, "these get-togethers often took the form of wife-swapping hanky-panky." Staff parties often turned libidinous. On Ohio Street a version of the "play-pen" at the Lownes-Sellers apartment—four beds bolted together side by side—was erected in the photo studio for physical encounters. At one wild Christmas gathering, two usually staid staffers spent several hours necking and petting heavily on a couch in the middle of the room. "Their concentration and their stamina were amazing," remembered Arlene Bouras. As Russell once cracked, "At most companies you'd be fired if you fooled around on the job with somebody you worked with. At *Playboy* it was grounds for promotion."[6]

Hefner surged far ahead of the pack with his sexual escapades. By 1955 he had begun dating a series of young women. First came Shirley Delancey, who along with her roommate, Mary Ann LaJoie, was a dancer at the Empire Room in Chicago's Palmer House. (They served as the inspiration for *Babs and Shirley*.) He went out with Connie Chancellor, ex-wife of then Chicago television broadcaster John Chancellor. He had flings with several magazine employees: Playmate Janet Pilgrim, personal secretary Pat Pappas, and assistant photo editor Bev Chamberlain. In 1956, Hefner began seeing Sheila Browning, who worked at Chicago's Gaslight Club, as well as the popular Playmate Lisa Winters. Upon visiting Hollywood for the first time, he attended a party at photographer Earl Leaf's home in the company of starlets Suzanne Sidney and Joan Bradshaw that, in his words, "ended in a multi-partner orgy." He even had a one-night stand with Janie Sellers, an old high school friend who had had a crush on him for years. There were others—many others—as Hefner estimated he had around fifteen to twenty liaisons a year.[7]

Some of the publisher's colleagues did not approve of his sexual adventures, especially with coworkers at the magazine. Art Paul derided his boss's pursuit of many women on the staff as "the old sophomoric notches on the bedpost" mentality. Marge Pitner also disapproved because it created personnel problems. Female staffers he dated "figured they didn't have to show up for work on time anymore, like they were privileged characters or something," she observed.[8]

Not surprisingly, Hefner's marriage grew strained. Millie lost patience, concluding that his sexual pursuits were an obsession dating back to adolescence. Her husband did not try to hide his affairs, spending little time at home and confessing when Millie confronted him. The couple had a rocky relationship for the five years after *Playboy* started, with long interludes of separation punctuated by brief reconciliations. "The fault is all mine, of course, and I'm in that unhappy state where I seem to be unable to live either with or without her," Hefner told his brother in 1956.[9]

But from among the dozens of sexual dalliances that Hefner had in the last half of the 1950s, three young women emerged as special girlfriends. They were companions with whom he had genuine relationships, and their experiences revealed much about the man behind the masthead. Betty Zuziak was an eighteen-year-old coed at Northwestern in 1957 when she met Janet Pilgrim and got a job at *Playboy* in the subscription department. A cute, perky girl with an affectionate manner and relaxed style, she met Hefner at the staff Christmas party, felt an instant attraction, and lost her virginity to him. "I fell hard, and was very much in love—my first major romance," she described. The publisher saw her steadily over a four-year period from 1957 to 1960. He went to her apartment several times a week—accumulating stacks of parking tickets in the process—where they would spend quiet evenings listening to records, watching television, and eating home-cooked meals. Hefner described Zuziak as "a warm and comfortable companion" and their relationship as a "shelter from the storm, an escape from all my responsibilities into our own private little world of simple pleasures and pastimes." For her part, Zuziak was content to be "with him because I cared for him."[10]

While seeing Zuziak, Hefner met a teenage model and beauty-contest winner named Joyce Nizzari while visiting Miami in 1958. They felt an immediate attraction and spent several nights together "imagining we were falling in love with one another," in Hefner's words. He invited her to Chicago, and over the next couple of years they saw each other frequently. With medium dark hair, lovely features, and a lithe figure, Nizzari accompanied Hefner to the Cannes Film Festival and Kennedy Inaugural Ball and they had an intense relationship at various periods from 1958 to 1961. Hefner described her as a "special lady" in his life and even visited her parents' home in Miami during one trip there. Nizzari became a Playmate in the December 1958 issue of *Playboy*.[11]

In 1959 Hefner met Joni Mattis. She came from a troubled background, having spent part of her childhood in a Baptist orphanage after her mother died and her father entered the service during World War II. When her father returned home from the service, he sexually molested her. As a teenager, she became pregnant and gave up the baby for adoption, then lived with a sternly Christian foster couple before marrying a rigidly religious man who treated her harshly. She began modeling and met Hefner while serving as an usherette at a movie theater, dressed in a French maid's costume. A petite, demure young woman with enormous dark eyes and pale skin, she resembled a Dresden doll and exuded a sense of intense vulnerability. Mattis and Hefner were mutually smitten and enjoyed passionate interludes from 1959 to 1961. She would appear as a Playmate in November 1960. When the romance ended, the two remained close friends and Mattis would go on to work for Hefner until her death in 1999.[12]

Hefner's serious relationships with Zuziak, Nizzari, and Mattis revealed much about his mental and emotional qualities. They brought to light competing, even contradictory impulses in his personality—on the one side a sweet nature, romantic sentimentality, and endearing lack of sophistication, and on the other a tendency toward distrust, possessiveness, and egotism.

Hefner's shy, simple nature struck all of the young women with whom he became involved. Unpretentious and a homebody, he veered toward card games with his buddies, fried chicken dinners, films, and pasting pictures in his scrapbook. "He had a little-boy quality about his enthusiasms that I found utterly charming," said Zuziak. He exhibited a basic shyness, noted Mattis, and even a kind of vulnerability. He loved to sit home and watch television shows such as *The Twilight Zone,* or dash out for a late-night movie followed by a cheeseburger at a local diner. Dressing respectably, but with little concern for fashion, he always wore white socks because of a foot fungus he had picked up in the army.[13]

Hefner had a warm, sweet temperament. "He was extremely romantic and I ate that up," Zuziak reported. "He was constantly sending me flowers and gifts." On one occasion he presented her with a piece of jewelry containing a white pearl set with a diamond chip and a smaller black pearl. The pearls embodied their relationship, he told her, with the smaller black one, representing unhappiness, being totally dominated by the larger white one, standing for love and affection. "We held hands a lot and did a lot of hugging and cuddling," Zuziak noted. Mattis had a similar experience, as Hefner displayed great concern for her feelings and treated her, according to that archaic phrase, like a lady. During their romantic evenings or weekends, he would order champagne, play jazz records, and talk quietly with her. As she once put it simply, "he was real sweet."[14]

But alongside these romantic qualities stood less attractive ones. Hefner felt a need to maintain dominance in his relationships with women, an impulse, according to Zuziak, that was rooted in a fear of female betrayal from Millie's affair with the coach many years before. He controlled relationships because giving up power meant showing weakness and demonstrating vulnerability. Exposing chinks in one's emotional armor to women, who could wound you emotionally, was dangerous and unacceptable.[15]

This instinct to dominate produced a powerful egotism in Hefner's romantic relationships. When one of the staffers at *Playboy* opined that he was seeing women who weren't good enough for him, he replied frankly, "Well, if I start going out with movie stars then I wouldn't have someone who was more interested in me than in herself." All his girlfriends noted that he focused on his own needs, while they were forced to adapt to his schedule, desires, and preferences if they wanted to see him. Some feared losing themselves completely from being swallowed up in his world. "His relationships are basically I, I, I, I. . . . It was very, very difficult," said Zuziak.[16]

Hefner also could be possessive, even callous, toward women who were close to him. He felt free to see any attractive female who caught his fancy, but wanted exclusive devotion from his girlfriends. According to one, "He had a total double standard. He served notice that he would be seeing others, but he expected me to be totally loyal to him." Moreover, Hefner could be remarkably insensitive to his girlfriends by exhibiting obliviously his latest conquest. "Hef broke my heart. You know, he'd parade them right in front of me," Mattis complained. "I'd be sitting there, and then he'd have a girl, and he'd just walk right in front of me. Take the girls into his room."[17]

Occasionally, Hefner's girlfriends would grow frustrated and strike back at him. Zuziak arranged a casual date every once in a while to make him jealous. Mattis adopted more extreme tactics, such as one time when at a party where Hefner was showing too much attention to Ann Richards, a singer in Stan Kenton's band, she sidled up and nudged her into the swimming pool. She also began spending time with Frank Sinatra to make Hefner angry.[18]

Hefner's affairs in the 1950s had predictable domestic consequences as his marriage, already on shaky ground, began to crumble. He was almost never at home, and awkward episodes involving Millie and his girlfriends mounted steadily. On New Year's Eve in 1955, when she was pregnant with their second child, Millie went to a *Playboy* party and "there was Hef sitting over there with a girl, and necking with her," she recalled later. "I just walked out, hailed a cab, and went home." Another time, Millie came up to the magazine offices with the children. Janet Pilgrim, who had been having an affair with her boss, became visibly upset and left. According to a coworker, a few weeks later she hastily married and it "lasted about a month."[19]

Hefner had concluded that his marriage, because of basic incompatibility, was hopeless. After their official separation in the summer of 1957, he ruminated that "in the end, she has suffered the most from it, for I have the magazine to keep me going." An embittered Millie complained that her husband lacked the capacity to be faithful. "This is the way he's behaved all the time I've known him," she said. "There was never a time that I knew him where I felt we had a one-to-one relationship." His disregard of parenthood became a particularly painful point of contention. "He didn't particularly want children," Millie noted. "He went along with it. But he was not a father." As weeks went by during which Hefner would not see Christie or David, she nonetheless assured the children that "Daddy was good, and Daddy was caring, and he was so busy he didn't have a lot of time, but he loves you." But he did visit periodically, and, Millie admitted, "In his way, he cared, too."[20]

Finally, the marriage ended. In March 1959, after reaching agreement in advance with her husband, Millie sued Hefner for divorce on the grounds of desertion. She asked for custody of the children and alimony, receiving both, while he received rights of regular visitation. The pair had negotiated the terms on an amicable basis and they accepted the divorce in a positive light. Millie made plans to remarry. "Hef has no marriage plans, thinks the publisher of PLAYBOY should be a bachelor, hopes to remain that way for a long time," Hefner noted in a letter. "All remains more than friendly on all sides and the new marriage should be best for everyone—Millie, the children, and all." And, indeed, Hugh and Millie would stay on fairly good terms over the next several decades.[21]

These private adventures set the stage for a seminal event in Hefner's life. In the late 1950s he transformed himself, much as he had done before his senior year in high school, when he dropped the nice, middle-class, boyish Hugh for the jive-talking, swing-dancing, saddle-shoed Hef. Now, with his marriage over, his magazine enjoying boom times, and new social vistas opening up, Hefner remade himself. From a private cocoon where he labored as a workaholic and lothario, he emerged onto the public stage as a pipe-smoking social butterfly with a string of beautiful women on his arm. He became Mr. Playboy.

II

Readers opening the June 1957 issue of *Playboy*, expecting to find the usual preview of the magazine's articles and features in the "Playbill," were surprised. "This month we'd like you to meet Editor-Publisher Hugh M. Hefner, the man responsible for the pulse, the personality, and the very existence of this magazine," began a different introduction. The piece described a night owl who arose just before noon and worked into the early hours of the morning, a man who shouldered many tasks as the head of a dynamic men's magazine. Above all, it stressed how his personal style reflected that of his readers:

> His dress is conservative and casual, he always wears loafers, and a bottle of Pepsi-Cola, which he consumes at the rate of two dozen a day, is never far away. There is an electronic entertainment wall in his office . . . [and] Brubeck, Kenton or Sinatra is usually on the turntable when Hefner is working.
>
> He is essentially an indoor man. . . . He likes jazz, foreign films, Ivy League Clothes, gin and tonic, and pretty girls— the same sort of things that PLAYBOY readers like—and his approach to life is as fresh, sophisticated, and yet admittedly sentimental as is the magazine's.

A full-page picture of Hefner showed him standing on the bottom stairs at the entrance of the Ohio Street offices, looking coolly upward as an attractive blonde a few steps below stared flirtatiously at him.[22]

In such fashion, Hefner stepped out from behind his desk and into the public limelight as he remade his image in the late 1950s. His motivation was personal, but the makeover reflected a larger trend in American popular culture as the decade ended. The ideal of the team-oriented business executive, the family man in the gray flannel suit, moved to the sidelines before a new ideal of the vibrant, vigorously heterosexual male who was bold, irreverent, hip, and successful. The new type popped up everywhere—in fictional figures such as James Bond, in politicians such as John F. Kennedy, and in entertainers such as Sinatra and the Rat Pack. In the public imagination, Hugh Hefner joined this group as he personified the *Playboy* lifestyle.[23]

In fact, the magazine incessantly promoted the icons of the new male ideal. Nowhere was this more obvious than in *Playboy's* idolization of a suave, handsome fictitious secret agent from Her Majesty's Secret Service. When Kennedy, the glamorous new president, announced that he was a fan of Ian Fleming's spy novels with their fictional hero, James Bond, he confirmed a *Playboy* favorite. The magazine had introduced Fleming's character in March 1960 with "The Hildebrand Rarity," a short story, and over the next few years the dashing spy would become a mainstay of the publication. With his casual elegance, beautiful women, fast sports cars, and space-age gadgets, Bond embodied the magazine's fantasy appeal for men. Fleming actually visited the *Playboy* offices in 1960, and the magazine proudly reported his comment: "I'm sure James Bond, if he were an actual person, would be a registered reader of PLAYBOY." Hefner was a big fan, once writing Fleming to offer the environs of his magazine as a setting for a future story. The Bond phenomenon, both in book and movie form, as well as the sexy women who adorned the films, would appear regularly in *Playboy,* while Fleming and Sean Connery (the cinematic Bond) would be the subjects of interviews.[24]

Similarly, the magazine offered admiring treatments of Frank Sinatra and the Rat Pack. Hefner had idolized the popular singer for many years, and a 1958 *Playboy* profile describing him as "the most potent figure in show business today, the most spectacularly popular singer of popular songs, the most sought after movie star, the most successful wooer of women." By the late 1950s, Sinatra, along with his sidekicks—singer/dancer Sammy Davis Jr., comedian Dean Martin, actor Peter Lawford, and comic Joey Bishop—had become the epitome of modern male celebrity with their suave manner, sophisticated wisecracks, undeniable talent, and womanizing reputations. A 1960 *Playboy* feature on the Rat Pack described how they filled the Sands nightclub in Las Vegas every evening while filming the movie *Ocean's Eleven*. Calling them "the innest in-group in the world," it characterized the Rat Pack as "a very special gang of Hollywood rebels . . . [who] possess talent, charm, romance, and a devil-may-care nonconformity that gives them immense popular appeal."[25]

Around this time, Hefner began hanging out with Sinatra and his cronies. Sammy Davis, who frequently performed at the Chez Paree, a Near North Side club directly across the alley from the *Playboy* offices, became a frequent visitor and a good friend of the publisher. In September 1960 Hefner hosted a party for the Rat Pack after one of their performances in Chicago, and two months later Hefner and Lownes were invited to attend a Hollywood stag party for Davis, an African American who was about to enter a controversial marriage with the blond Caucasian actress May Britt.[26]

Hefner's endorsement of the new male paradigm also surfaced in his involvement with John Kennedy's bid for the presidency in 1960. He donated money to the campaign under the auspices of Sinatra, who had gained entry into Kennedy's circle through Lawford, Kennedy's brother-in-law, and subsequently championed his cause among Hollywood entertainers. Hefner was attracted to the youthful senator's sympathy for civil rights, a special cause for him, and saw him as a progressive figure eager to overturn the stodgy traditionalism of the Eisenhower era. Typically, he looked through the prism of the movies, perceiving in Kennedy "a Frank Capra view of society that I strongly supported. He was, to me, a 'Mr. Smith Goes to Washington,' 'Meet John Doe' president." But Kennedy's vigorous masculine aura also appealed. Hefner admired the young senator for being "a handsome swinger," in his words. "He had personal karma and sex appeal that was appealing on both the political and personal fronts. The joke at the time was that Kennedy would do for sex what Eisenhower had done for golf," Hefner recalled later. "He was one of us."[27]

After Kennedy's election, Hefner secured tickets and went to Washington, D.C., to celebrate the new president's taking office.

On January 20, 1961, he and Joyce Nizzari, along with Victor Lownes and a date, attended an Inaugural Ball organized by Frank Sinatra for Hollywood, Broadway, and entertainment stars. Hefner rented a Georgetown town house and limousine for the occasion. A few days after the inauguration, Hefner and Lownes flew to New York City for a tribute to Martin Luther King Jr. at Carnegie Hall, which featured entertainment by Sinatra and his Rat Pack.[28]

Thus Hefner associated himself with Bond, Sinatra, and Kennedy as a prototype of the new male in the popular imagination. After returning from the Cannes Film Festival in the summer of 1959, where he rubbed shoulders with a host of film stars, the publisher was primed to project a new celebrity image. He began to dress more fashionably, started smoking a pipe, and gave numerous interviews elaborating on his personal life. Purchasing a Mercedes-Benz 300SL convertible, he appeared in an ad for the car where he posed comfortably leaning against it in front of the entrance to the *Playboy* offices. Hefner also pursued self-promotion in the pages of *Playboy,* reassuring a skeptical associate that "as a living personification of the magazine I can't quite see where my presence within the book is anything but positive."[29]

The press picked up the signals as stories stressing Hefner's celebrity status began to appear. The *Chicago American* presented a big spread in June 1960 with a piece called "The Playboy Behind Playboy." "For all practical purposes, Hefner IS Playboy," it said. "Its personality is Hefner's and vice versa." Others followed quickly. A feature in the *Minneapolis Sunday Tribune* described Hefner as "the country's hardest working playboy." Surveying his daunting editorial routine and personal endeavors, it concluded, "As he works, he manages to live the life glorified by his magazine." By 1961, press accounts routinely elaborated this theme. The titles revealed all: an AP story called "Playboy's Playboy Hugh Hefner Lives American Male's Dream" and a UPI story titled "Serious 'Playboy' Built an Empire with Pretty Girls."[30]

The public creation of Mr. Playboy, however, was difficult. Not a natural sophisticate, Hefner remained a hardworking, quietly intense, sentimental, and introverted guy with a fondness for the simple things in life. The quest to become a polished, urbane role model often only highlighted his ordinary tastes in food, drink, and clothing. The ironic picture of "the publisher of a magazine devoted to the sophisticated life, fine wines & haute cuisine, etc. subsisting almost exclusively on Pepsi and fried chicken" amused his friends, as well as Hefner himself, according to Ray Russell. Similarly, girlfriend Betty Zuziak described Hefner as "a very simple, honest, totally unsophisticated man ... prior to the pipe and all that, when they began to push his image."[31]

Thus the appearance as Mr. Playboy demanded a makeover of much of Hefner's personality. Zuziak sensed a fraud. She believed that, in fact, he became "caught up in a monster he created" and began "playing a part" to meet public expectations. "At what point do you separate reality and the fantasy?" she asked. However, this plausible contention overlooked the fact that *Playboy*, from the very beginning, was an exercise in sexual, emotional, and material fantasy. So if Hefner was playing a role, it was one he believed in wholeheartedly. It brought him front and center stage in American society, where he could convince his audience that fantasy could be more powerful, more *real*, than reality. He utilized the props of cars, clothes, women, interviews, and publicity, but the real opportunity to shape a persona came with a trio of projects that provided an even larger stage for projecting the *Playboy* dream of the good life.[32]

III

In the few months from October 1959 to February 1960, Hefner launched a television program, bought a magnificent Gilded Age mansion in Chicago, and opened the first Playboy Club. These initiatives changed his life forever. They made him not just a spokesman for but the major practitioner of the *Playboy* lifestyle. Transforming his daily life into, in his words, "a fantasy perception of bachelorhood that had heretofore merely been reflected in my magazine," Hefner, indubitably, became Mr. Playboy.[33]

In the late summer of 1959, the publisher began developing a syndicated television show titled *Playboy's Penthouse*. It would be "a 'Playboy Party' complete with our 'Playmates' and outstanding personalities from the fields of entertainment and the arts," he told the *Chicago Sun-Times*. He commissioned Cy Coleman, noted songwriter of tunes such as "Witchcraft," to compose a theme song for the show, and created a format based on a cocktail party held in a chic bachelor apartment.[34]

The first segment was broadcast in the late evening of October 24, 1959. Hefner, outfitted in tuxedo and pipe, welcomed several famous guests—Ella Fitzgerald, Nat King Cole, Lenny Bruce, and author Rona Jaffe—to his "apartment," which was set off with sleek modern furnishings. Surrounded by beautiful young women, he traded small talk with the entertainers before their seemingly impromptu performances. Joyce Nizzari and Eleanor Bradley discussed their experiences as Playmates, Shel Silverstein described his worldly travels doing cartoons for the magazine, and A. C. Spectorsky explained his "Kitchenless Kitchen" for the modern bachelor quarters. The latest fashions, witty repartee, elegantly dangling cigarettes, and clinking martini glasses embellished the proceedings.[35]

In part, a business rationale lay behind the program. While the Jazz Festival had upgraded *Playboy* as a viable advertising medium, Hefner hoped that "the syndicated television show would do the same on a national basis." The magazine had an image problem with many general readers and needed to distance itself from any taint of "filth and obscenity," Victor Lownes told *Sales Management*. The television show would help. With its vibrant images of the good life, the program promised to be "an ideal showcase for our advertisers as well as for the talent on the show," he explained.[36]

But the program also had a larger aim—bringing the *Playboy* vision of happiness to life. Hefner insisted on a format and content that would draw the magazine's "particular editorial personality and point of view into the show." In so doing, of course, it would showcase Hefner and his new image. Everything reinforced this gambit, from the opening, which rolled credits over a filmed background of him driving his Mercedes convertible around Chicago at night, to the setting in a sophisticated bachelor pad, to his debonair appearance. As Lownes confirmed, the show was a "logical extension of the magazine into a new medium—the *Playboy* lifestyle brought to life. With [Hefner] himself as Mr. Playboy, of course."[37]

But the project faced a recurring difficulty—Hefner was not a very good host. He would open the door to the camera and say rather grimly, "Good evening, I'm Hugh Hefner. Welcome to the party." Surrounded by pretty girls, he labored gamely, attempting small talk and witticisms with the entertainers, venturing insights and observations with the intellectuals. He even adopted the pipe as a prop because, in addition to lending an air of elegance, it occupied his hands. But he came across as awkward, wooden, and tense, more Gary Cooper than Cary Grant. "I was stiff, ill-at-ease and ill-prepared for the role of a performer," he confessed later. "I was an amateur and my on-camera performance made Ed Sullivan look like a polished pro."[38]

Nonetheless, the show became a vehicle for Hefner's growing celebrity. The power of television—bringing live images of the publisher and his lifestyle into living rooms throughout the country—enhanced his public renown. Advertising also contributed to the self-promotion. *Playboy* plugged the show and its host while an ad released to national media outlets carried a large photo of Hefner with a text describing its setting: "swank surroundings high above the city's throng, you'll meet the stars of show business, famous authors and artists, celebrities and, of course, PLAYBOY's lovely Playmates of the Month." A *TV Guide* promotion contained a picture of Hefner against a mass of Playmates and a breathless text: "EVERYONE IN CHICAGO KNOWS THIS MAN! Bevies of beautiful women surround him! Headliners from the entertainment world are his guests, and enliven his sophisticated parties! Handsome, suave, urbane—he's the envy of every man, the idol of every woman!"[39]

While not a huge hit, *Playboy's Penthouse* did well. Shot in Chicago at WBKB, it was syndicated to twelve other cities, including New York and Los Angeles, and got respectable audience numbers. The reviews were generally positive, although most noted Hefner's limitations as a host. *Variety,* for example, observed that the show "has freshness, some degree of sophistication, and some good talent along with it," while Hefner was "somewhat awkward as an emcee but is excellent as a conversationalist." For participants, the show was fun to shoot. A genuine party atmosphere prevailed much of the time, even to the extent that guests drank real liquor to keep things loose through multiple takes. On more than one occasion, Hefner recalled, "performers were somewhere between tipsy and inebriated when they appeared."[40]

The twenty-six-week first season included guests such as comedians Bob Newhart and Don Adams; musicians Sarah Vaughan, Stan Kenton, Tony Bennett, and Count Basie; and author Carl Sandburg. A second season began in September 1960—Sammy Davis Jr. starred in the opening—with a new hourlong format. Reviews were even more positive. "In most respects this is a highly improved product in the area of production and presentation, notably where host Hugh

Hefner is concerned," stated the *Chicago Sun-Times*. "Hefner is more relaxed. Last season he reminded me of the stuffy neighbor who unbends once annually to let in the kiddies on Halloween night. Now he seems more composed, more deliberate about showing off something he wants to share (I mean the cats, silly, not the girls)." Nevertheless, at the conclusion of the second season, Hefner and WBKB decided the show had run its course.[41]

Around the same time, Hefner undertook a second project that became a crucial part of Mr. Playboy's mystique. He created a fantasy home, the Playboy Mansion, in which he could actually pursue, with great fanfare, a lifestyle of bachelor freedom and abundant living. For the last few years, he had been living at his office, while keeping a small apartment on Astor Street that he rarely used. By late in the decade he grew determined to occupy a home suitable for the new public image he was shaping. He first planned to build a four-story town house on the Near North Side, but he ran into problems with city regulations and spiraling estimations of cost. So Hefner began to look for an existing structure that could be remodeled, and he soon located the perfect one.[42]

A. C. Spectorsky and his wife, Theo, were in their apartment reading and listening to music on a Sunday afternoon in December 1959 when the doorbell began ringing frantically. It was Hefner, who came running up the stairs to announce that he had just bought the house across the street. He led them over for a quick tour of the huge structure, much of which was unoccupied, dingy, and full of dust and cobwebs. But the excited editor convinced them that he would soon make it into a show-place. He did so, and about a year later, according to Theo, as they sat in the great room by the fireplace, he "looked over at me like a little boy and said, 'the greatest thing I ever did was to buy this house.'"[43]

Hefner's dream home sat at 1340 North State Parkway, on Chicago's famed Gold Coast and two blocks from Lake Michigan. The four-story, brick-and-limestone mansion had been built in 1899 for Dr. Henry Isham, a prominent Chicago physician. A social center in the city during the early part of the century, it had welcomed famous guests such as Theodore Roosevelt and Admiral Richard Byrd before being divided into apartments during the Great Depression. The size of a small hotel, it sat behind an ornate iron fence and offered a mod-est lawn, driveway, and annex. Its most prominent feature was a huge ballroom on the second floor about the size of a basketball court with an enormous marble fireplace at one end and imposing French doors at the other. Two stories tall, with open beams on the ceiling and two enormous bronze chandeliers, the room was adorned with pillars and decorative features of carved wood. Two suits of armor would soon guard the entryway, while several modern masterpieces of abstract expressionism would enhance the paneled walls. Hefner refurbished the numerous apartments and bedrooms in the mansion, many of which had marble fireplaces.[44]

The editor installed two unique features that soon became legendary. First, below the ballroom he built an indoor swimming pool decorated with palms, and a recessed grotto. On one side of the pool sat a bar with a glass wall allowing visitors to look directly into it, with the entire complex accessible either by stairs or by a fireman's pole from the floor above. Second, in a suite off the ballroom on the second floor Hefner designed his famous master bedroom. The centerpiece was a large, rotating round bed that had controls for television, stereo, tape machines, lights, and music in the headboard. As the proud owner noted, this gadgetry "helped give it a James Bond mystique." The bed became not only the nest for Hefner's romantic trysts, but command central for his organization as he soon littered it with memo drafts, page proofs, and photo stills. Once again, work and play became inseparable elements in his life.[45]

After several weeks of renovation and decoration in early 1960, Hefner quickly established a party scene at the baronial Playboy Mansion as the make-believe revelries of *Playboy's Penthouse* became the real thing. A. C. Spectorsky gave him a brass plaque for the front door that read in Latin, "Si Non Oscillas, Noli Tintinnare," translated as "If You Don't Swing, Don't Ring." Hefner hosted the first big party in May 1960 and others soon followed. "Major parties at the mansion became an almost weekly event, with a couple of hundred people invited. They usually started around midnight and went until dawn. The parties were centered in the ballroom, and included an extensive buffet, drinking, dancing," Hefner explained. After the renovations were completed, the parties spread into the swimming pool, the adjoining game room, and the underwater bar. The mansion's kitchen remained open twenty-four hours a day for guests, and the ballroom had a theater-sized movie screen that descended out of the ceiling, allowing Hefner to show 35mm films, both old and current, to dozens of his friends.[46]

The mansion soon attracted enormous publicity. The *Chicago Tribune* ran a big spread in its Sunday magazine early in 1961, and major stories on Hefner and his home soon appeared in *Time* and the *Saturday Evening Post*. The most striking publicity, however, came in the pages of *Playboy*. In December 1961, Hefner ran a lavish ten-page feature in the form of a pictorial on a "gala house party" held in honor of the magazine's eighth anniversary. Opening the doors of the Playboy Mansion to his readers, Hefner showed visiting Playmates around "his opulent digs." Readers caught glimpses of nude girls cavorting in the famous pool and grotto, while the pipe-and-slippered host explained his elaborate stereo and collection of abstract expressionist paintings by modern masters such as Pollock and de Kooning. The article also carefully noted the many celebrities who had visited the mansion, including Frank Sinatra, Sammy Davis, Hugh O'Brian, Stan Getz, Mort Sahl, and Tony Curtis.[47]

If *Playboy's Penthouse* provided Hefner a public forum, and the Playboy Mansion a private one, for presenting himself as Mr. Playboy, a third undertaking invited his audience into the picture. On February 29, 1960, the first Playboy Club opened at 116 Walton Street in Chicago. "It will be an attempt, endorsed by these editors, to project the plush and romantic mood of the magazine into a private club of good fellows interested in a better, more pleasurable life," Hefner explained in an internal memo at *Playboy*. Victor Lownes explained it more simply: "the idea was to bring the magazine to life." The Playboy Club, which soon would spread to cities all over the United States, vividly framed Hefner's new celebrity lifestyle by permitting others a brief taste of it.[48]

The publisher had entertained the idea for a club when he and his club-hopping pals discussed the fantasy of having their own place to hang out. "Having our own club would be a real kick and a great way to meet chicks," Hefner recalled. As the magazine became popular, the idea broadened to include the *Playboy* lifestyle. An article on Chicago's Gaslight Club in the magazine—thousands of readers wrote in asking about gaining membership—gave a direct prod to begin the project. Hefner and Lownes realized there was a large market for a nightclub centered on the *Playboy* idea of pretty girls, fine food and drink, and sophisticated entertainment. They began to formulate plans.[49]

The first step involved bringing in someone with practical experience. They contacted an old friend, Arnold Morton, who owned a club that Hefner and Lownes frequented on their nocturnal rambles. He agreed to join the project, and the trio divided responsibilities— Hefner and Lownes developed the concept and were responsible for overall management while Morton, in his words, handled the "meat and potatoes." They also divided the shares of the new company with Lownes getting 25 percent, Morton 25 percent, Hefner 25 percent, and the magazine 25 percent. When the doors of the first Playboy Club swung open, it reflected Hefner's recommendation: "The main thrust of our creativity is to bring the pages of *Playboy* to life."[50]

The five-story club wove together thematic strands from Hefner's magazine and television show. It offered good food, generous drinks, and hip entertainment in a sophisticated atmosphere. Drawing upon the bachelor apartment fantasy, it contained dining areas styled the Living Room and the Playmate Bar, and large rooms for music and comedy shows called the Penthouse and the Library. The Cartoon Corner offered framed cartoons from *Playboy*, while an elaborate stereo system piped jazz throughout the structure. Wood-paneled walls, rich colors, and leather furniture enhanced the ambiance. A crucial aspect of the lifestyle formula lay in the illusion of exclusivity. Members paid an initial fee of fifty dollars to become a lifetime keyholder and received a Playboy Key stamped with the familiar rabbit head logo. "The Playboy Club is a meeting place for the most important, most aware, most affluent men of the community," the magazine observed. A special publication for members appeared called *VIP: The Playboy Club Magazine* that carried stories about personnel, entertainers, and coming attractions. Such stratagems encouraged members to believe that they were part of a sophisticated urban elite. Even James Bond became a member, as revealed in *Diamonds Are Forever*.[51]

Throughout, of course, the club highlighted images of beautiful women and liberated sexuality. Its most notable feature became the Bunnies, young women who served as waitresses and hostesses in the various sections of the establishment. Chosen for their good looks and vivacious personalities, they included models, working girls, and a number of Playmates from *Playboy*. The Bunnies became a magnet for hordes of men eager to see magazine images in the flesh. Their attire did not disappoint. Originally, Hefner had wanted to present the Bunnies in short nightgowns or modified undergarments. But after discussion with Lownes, he decided to go with the rabbit theme. A seamstress prepared a prototype Bunny outfit: a one-piece, satin, swimsuit-style garment that was low-cut on top and steeply raised on the sides to accentuate long legs. The later addition of bunny ears, a fluffy bunny tail, and bow tie and cuffs completed the ensemble.[52]

The Bunnies quickly emerged as key symbols in the diversifying *Playboy* empire. The fourth floor of the Playboy Mansion was converted into a dormitory where many of them found lodging while also ornamenting the weekly parties. Hefner's brother, Keith, joined the organization to manage the female workforce. He developed an extensive list of protocols in the *Playboy Club Bunny Manual*, inventing the famous "bunny dip," the unique maneuver whereby the waitress faced away from the table, arched her back, bent her knees and delivered drinks with a graceful arm motion. Bunnies were encouraged to project a healthy sexuality, much like the girl-next-door aura of the Playmates, but were not allowed to see patrons after hours or even give out their phone numbers. Hefner needed to be extraordinarily careful to avoid any taint of sexual impropriety, and scandal would quickly produce accusations of lewdness or even prostitution. "If any of our girls date a customer, she gets fired," Hefner told a newspaper. "We've got to keep it that way or the whole thing could come down around our ears."[53]

The Chicago Playboy Club was an immediate hit. Patrons lined up around the block to get in, and within a year it had enrolled over fifty thousand keyholders. Over the next few years the clubs would expand into fifteen American cities and gain a membership of half a million. Such popularity reflected the growing appeal of the *Playboy* lifestyle to urban men, especially in such a three-dimensional, flesh-and-blood form. As Keith Hefner observed, the clubs represented "the excitement of the pages of *Playboy* and . . . let people get a glimpse of what the fantasy world was really all about." The Playboy Club, of course, also magnified Hefner's stature. Mr. Playboy featured prominently in news stories about these popular nightspots which not only represented *Playboy*'s fantasy of the good life but extolled the celebrity of the man who personified it.[54]

But not all of Hefner's efforts to promote himself as Mr. Playboy were successful. His expansion of a lifestyle empire with him at the center experienced two notable failures. Around the same time as these other endeavors, he set in motion *Show Business Illustrated,* a magazine devoted to entertainment. Covering films, theater, recording, nightclub acts, television, and books as well as gossip reports on the comings and goings of the stars, the magazine reflected Hefner's long-standing fascination with America's mass culture. "It will do for show business what *Time* does for news and *Sports Illustrated* for sports," Hefner told the newspapers. He hired an editorial staff from New York and published the first issue in September 1961. The publication flopped almost immediately. A cluttered smorgasbord of entertainment news, brief reviews of every production under the sun, and sexy photos of beautiful women (but no nudes), the magazine appeared encyclopedic but it had no personality, no editorial stance, no special spark. After six months and only eight issues, he sold the magazine to a competitor and absorbed a loss of $1.5 million.[55]

A second failed project revealed much more about Hefner's personality and aspirations. In 1961, he became involved in a venture to make a Hollywood movie about his life and amazing success as publisher of *Playboy*. He had become friends with the actor Tony Curtis, and their conversations spawned the idea. Curtis was enthusiastic; Hefner was ecstatic. After preliminary negotiations, *Playboy* announced the forthcoming movie in November 1961, and *Variety* confirmed that Columbia Pictures would finance and release the film, while Stanley Margulies would produce and Bernard Wolfe would write the screenplay. Curtis spent a couple of weeks in Chicago hanging around the magazine offices to observe Hefner in preparation for the role.[56]

It quickly became apparent, however, that the participants were not on the same page. Curtis and the studio envisioned a light comedy about a guy with six girlfriends who constantly had to scramble in organizing his life to avoid embarrassing conflicts. Hefner had more serious themes in mind—Curtis sarcastically referred to the editor's desire for "Dostoevsky in the nude"—and began to bombard the actor, writer, and producer with missives. Unused to the publisher's massive memos, they were stunned when thirty-pagers began to arrive at their offices with disturbing regularity. They would explicate "the entire Playboy Philosophy, which he wants to dramatize in a six-hour movie, paragraph by paragraph," said Curtis. "And I don't even have to read them, I just have to *weigh* them to know that we're never, ever going to make this movie."[57]

The memos spoke volumes about Hefner's perception of himself. He envisioned the film as a vehicle for a romanticized rendering of his own life—the young man from modest circumstances who overcame the odds, liberated American society from life-choking prudery, and walked off into the sunset. Hefner outlined this triumphant fantasy, with himself as the star, in a memo to Curtis:

> It is the middle 1950s in Chicago, and a young man in his mid-twenties, a rather down-at-the-heels Brooks Brothers type, with button-down shirt frayed at the edges and buttons coming loose on his overcoat, is working for $60 dollars a week for a big, plush men's magazine. The young man is unhappy—but he has wild dreams for the creation of a magazine for the urban man. . . . [He successfully launches the publication and a national do-good group says the magazine is obscene; the Playmate of the Month is little better than a streetwalker. The group sues and there is a dramatic trial.] We get a chance for a wonderful court scene that has many of the emotional values of the beautiful court ending in "Mr. Deeds Goes to Town," and a similar judicial-type climax set in the Washington Senate in "Mr. Smith Goes to Washington." This climax offers all the opportunities for the evils and hypocrisy of censorship, prudery, and the bluenose view of life pitted against freedom, youth, a notion that sex is beautiful rather than dirty. . . . Through the stress and strain of it all, our hero has come to his senses and realized that it is truly the little secretary that he loves, and they wander out of that courtroom to live happily ever after.

Hefner wanted to present to the public the film version of his life that he had already created in his own imagination. He wanted to make a movie about a movie running in his head.[58]

Hefner's associates in the film venture were unreceptive. They plunged ahead with their own screenplay. Hefner disapproved. Two new writers, Bud Yorkin and Norman Lear, came aboard to rework it and they turned in a revised version that Hefner also rejected, subsequently firing off several long memos promoting his version. In early 1963, a "final" draft of the screenplay appeared and production was set to begin. Hefner again objected, claiming that he had been shoved aside, and refused his approval. After several testy exchanges, the publisher and the studio agreed that shooting should be postponed. The project quietly faded away.[59]

Despite the failure of the movie, Hefner's larger transformation into Mr. Playboy succeeded in creating a kind of fantasy fulfillment at the dawn of the 1960s. By remaking himself into an ideal young male sophisticate walking out of the pages of *Playboy,* he realized a dream of what his life should be that had been slowly taking shape since adolescence. But the public ramifications loomed even larger. By publicizing his exploits he stimulated a fantasy among a large audience that such a life was possible. Like a fictional British secret agent, a gang of hip Hollywood entertainers, and a charismatic young president, Hefner symbolized a growing desire among American men to grab the good things in life—sex, material abundance, style, success. In turn, this fed the desire of many women to grab on to such men.

Hefner could not have been happier. As he wrote in a December 1961 letter, "What does it feel like, being a living legend? Well, it feels just great!"[60]

PART III

TRIUMPH

9

The Philosopher King

The crisp black-and-white film showed a young man with dark hair and an intense manner driving through the rainy streets of Chicago in his sleek white Mercedes convertible. As he sped along with windshield wipers clearing his vision and the vinyl top protecting him from the elements, his words came out to listeners in a voice-over. Noting that he was thirty-five years old and the creator of a $20 million empire centered on *Playboy* magazine, the driver exclaimed, "I wouldn't trade places with anyone else in the world." He contended that people should work and play hard because "you only get one time around in this old world, and if you don't make the most of it you have no one to blame but yourself."

For the next twenty minutes, the film juxtaposed recurring images: on the one hand, a bash at the Playboy Mansion with loud music, sumptuous food, dancing revelers, and bikini-clad young women cavorting in the indoor swimming pool; on the other, an inspection of the *Playboy* offices, a survey of its publisher's work routine, and brief interviews with colleagues. Throughout, the young man offered his views on liberated sexuality, the virtues of enlightened self-interest and the good life, and his own role as the spokesman of a new, restless generation. Radiating self-satisfaction, he concluded, "I consider myself to be, quite possibly, the luckiest human being in the world."

The Most, a 1961 documentary produced by a Canadian group, won several awards for its flashy, slightly satirical treatment of Hugh Hefner, the publishing sensation who had made *Playboy* an icon of modern, youthful urban sophistication. The film seemed to capture Hefner's energy, focus, and sensibility while subtly suggesting in a variety of ways—his girlfriend repeatedly struggling with the word "intelligent" while being interviewed, several bored men dozing at the mansion party—a vacuous element in the perfect life. But Hefner's enormous self-confidence left the most powerful impression. Appearing as someone who saw himself as the very embodiment of the hip, swinging, trendy life in America, he proclaimed, "I have come to be seen as emblematic of the 1960s."[1]

Not everyone was so impressed. "That man, strutting, preening, posing, and spouting nonsense, is a new kind of animated cartoon, a sort of mental Magoo," said a venomous review in *Newsweek*. "The prince of playmates lives in an unspeakably vulgar playhouse with a swimming pool, and apparently, a perennial party." But impressed or not, people were paying attention. A spate of publicity in newspapers, magazines, and television put Hefner firmly in the public spotlight early in the 1960s.[2]

Throughout these appearances, Hefner often elaborated his lifestyle message of sexual pleasure, material abundance, dedication to work, and enjoyment of leisure from the 1950s. But he also began to turn his magazine in a new direction in the early 1960s, addressing a number of controversial social, cultural, and political issues. Taking himself and *Playboy* more seriously as an influence on American values, he began a lengthy, serial exposition of his worldview that raised extended commentary from many corners, especially the religious community. Ensconced in the comfort of the Playboy Mansion in the early 1960s—indeed, withdrawing deep into its pleasurable confines—the young editor became a kind of philosopher king.

I

With the success of *Playboy*, *Playboy's Penthouse*, the Playboy Mansion, and the Playboy Club serving as a springboard, Hefner vaulted into the national limelight as major media outlets rushed to describe and assess his remarkable success. In this great glare of publicity, debates about the significance and merit of his ideas flared up as critics lined up to support or condemn. Hefner became the talk of the country.

The big national magazines took the lead. Most often they combined disdain for the *Playboy* enterprise with grudging recognition of its popularity. In March 1961, *Time* ran a feature article that outlined Hefner's successes with his magazine, clubs, and licensed products, while at the same time dismissing *Playboy* as sophomoric, "a sort of editorial whee," and its publisher as "a living promotion stunt." The *Saturday Evening Post*'s "Czar of the Bunny Empire" was even harsher. This in-depth examination recognized Hefner's growing legend, but portrayed him as a fraud who traded on sleazy pictures of naked women while proclaiming high-minded ideals, crafted a debonair image to hide the social tastes of a rube, and projected a public persona of charm and wit while privately engaging in querulous outbursts of temper. Such stern disapproval, however, did not stop the magazine from running full-page ads in the *New Yorker* and the *New York Times* promoting its "Hef profile" of "*Playboy*'s boy wonder of the publishing world."[3]

The *Wall Street Journal* offered a more detached analysis. It concluded that a formula of sex and sophistication, producing a strong identification with a young, growing audience, had created Hefner's $20 million empire. The *New Yorker*, in one of its famous cartoons, offered another kind of affirmation. As a bride and groom stood at the altar preparing to take their vows, and a pair of rabbit ears poked up from the top of her veil, a seated guest turned to another and remarked, "He met her in some Chicago key club, I understand." Smaller publications also joined the journalistic chase. *Pageant*, a celebrity magazine, and the *Realist*, an offbeat journal of culture and opinion, also profiled Hefner. His story gained an international dimension as stories popped up in Italy's *L'Espresso* and *L'Europeo*, Germany's *ER*, England's *Queen*, and the *Time* magazine of South America, *Visión*.[4]

Another sign of Hefner's prominence came in the send-ups of *Playboy* that began to appear. The humorist Art Buchwald surveyed the Bunny kingdom's expansion in his nationally syndicated column—"Some people are afraid that Hefner may try to take over the United States, if not by force, at least by sex," he wrote—while *Mad* magazine presented a parody issue called *Playkid*. It featured a "Hideaway Clubhouse for Little League Bachelors," surveyed the latest fashions in space helmets and baseball cards that "sophisticated first through fourth graders will want to include on their after-hours 'must list' for the school season," and included a letter from a future Playmate who described herself as having "golden hair, hazel eyes, ruby-red lips, and sparkling silver braces on both my upper and lower teeth." *Aardvark*, the collegiate satire magazine, published a fake Christian number titled *Prayboy*. Supposedly edited by Hugh M. Holy, it contained a food feature called "One Part Bread, Two Parts Wine," a clothing piece titled "Black Is the Color of My Preacher's Suit," and a pictorial on "The Girls of the Holy Land." An interview with "The Lord"—described as the star of the King James Bible and Milton's *Paradise Lost*—had him telling the questioner, "I know exactly what I'm going to say. In fact, I know exactly what you're going to ask."[5]

The Hefner media flurry also came on the airwaves. A variety of documentaries, profiles, and interviews appeared in venues such as the Canadian Broadcasting Company, NBC's early morning *Today* show, a CBS talk show in Chicago called *At Random, The Jack Paar Show,* and Mike Wallace's popular *PM East,* which included interviews with Hefner, Spectorsky, and Lownes as well as taped footage from inside the magazine's offices. A comedic high point came on *The Steve Allen Show* when a Playboy Bunny appeared in a skit where she trained the host to serve in her job. As a mincing, wisecracking Allen donned the rabbit ears, learned to walk correctly with an enticing stroll, and practiced the "bunny dip," the studio audience howled.[6]

By the early 1960s, news of *Playboy* and its publisher was reaching a vast new audience. Some treatments were hostile, but even unfavorable publicity has its merits, as the showman P. T. Barnum once observed. "Now and then some one would cry out 'humbug' and 'charlatan,' but so much the better for me," he wrote. "It helped to advertise me, and I was willing to bear the reputation." In fact, in this flood of stories, the allure of the forbidden appeared to have a more powerful appeal than righteous exhortations. In a modern culture pulsating with messages of individual self-fulfillment, chastisements of *Playboy*'s licentiousness from stuffy cultural arbiters often had the ironic effect of encouraging what they condemned.[7]

At the center of this whirlwind of attention stood Hefner himself. In stories and interviews he stressed the Upbeat Generation's desire for upward mobility and leisure, the virtues of unfettered individualism, and the need for a vigorous pleasure ethic in modern American life. *Playboy*, he insisted, was the voice of a restless, aspiring new spirit in the country that sought to embrace a life of abundance even as it sidestepped demands for middle-class, suburban conformity. "Life is a wonderful, exciting adventure, if we allow it to be. If we savor and fully enjoy each day of it," he typically declared in one of his television appearances. "Trouble is, we too often defeat our own best chances for finding real satisfaction and happiness in life. There is a great tendency in our culture to live continually for tomorrow. And when you do that, tomorrow has a way of never coming."[8]

Hefner advocated a code of robust sexuality. Reciting his by-now familiar formulation, sex meant pretty girls, romantic nights on the town, and physical and emotional joy. His magazine and the Playboy Clubs urged the open embrace of wholesome sex rather than conveying vulgar images of strippers, illicit liaisons, and shameful vices. "The guy brings the dream with him—he supplies the most important ingredient of all," Hefner told a British journalist. "And the majority of guys are not looking for the kind of action that breaks up that dream. . . . Clean sex has a greater appeal than tawdry sex." As he summarized in a 1962 appearance, "Anything that makes sex seem clean, healthy, desirable, and beautiful is good."[9]

But the familiar proselytizing contained a new element of self-confidence that bordered on egotism. At various times, Mr. Playboy described himself as "without doubt the most successful man I ever met," a "living legend," and a modern F. Scott Fitzgerald who was "typical of the present generation." Perhaps his most breathtaking comment came in *The Most*. Pondering his influence and achievements, he concluded, "Genius is kind of a funny word. I suppose by definition I consider myself one—both intellectually and in terms of creativity."[10]

Playboy's growing prominence also triggered a backlash of negative criticism. "Is the American man emotionally retarded, a perpetually snickering adolescent?" asked the conservative writer Russell Kirk. "The abuse of sexual images and enticements is a symptom of decadence in American life." The *Saturday Review* derided Hefner's "bunny-tailed utopia" as "the country of arrested adolescence." Benjamin DeMott, a professor of English at Amherst, sneered at *Playboy*'s "vision of the whole man reduced to his private parts."[11]

Such denunciations touched a nerve. Convinced that *Playboy's* critics were misrepresenting his views, Hefner decided to strike back. He began to ponder more deeply what he saw as his mission in American society. Inspired by the acclaim and fueled by the attacks, he decided to explain the philosophy behind his enterprise.

II

In December 1962, readers of *Playboy* encountered a new editorial series. The magazine's rabbit head logo sat atop the title, "The Playboy Philosophy," while below it sat the author's name: Hugh M. Hefner. He noted that while his magazine had become the subject of much recent discussion, its views and images had been distorted. He vowed "to state our own editorial credo here, and offer a few personal observations on our present-day society and PLAYBOY'S part in it." As he observed in a private letter, "If PLAYBOY was to be either praised or damned for what it represents and believes in, I would rather have it for what we really do believe than what someone else says that we believe."[12]

"The Playboy Philosophy" became the phrase that launched a thousand pages. Originally intended as a fairly brief statement, the project soon became an obsession and swelled beyond all proportion. The author holed up in the Playboy Mansion, poring over dozens of files filled with research material and staying up for days on end writing, and rewriting, endless drafts of his thoughts on an array of social, cultural, political, legal, and sexual issues facing American society. By the time it ground to a halt, Hefner's "statement" had appeared in twenty-five installments over a three-year period.

A genuine sincerity and idealism initially prompted this undertaking. Convinced that mainstream American values needed to be examined and reformed, Hefner sought dialogue and debate. "It is simply a pleasure—and a considerable one—to try to spell out one's guiding principles," he told a correspondent. "I hope that we can offer some ideas about moral responsibility, ethics, the importance of the individual, the need for greater emphasis on . . . the humane side of life that may start people thinking about some of those things."[13]

But then a kind of mania set in as Hefner turned creation of the Playboy Philosophy into the journalistic version of the Bataan death march. Hidden away in his bedroom and writing for days without sleep, he became afflicted with a growing compulsion to explore every aspect, dig up every detail, and express every thought about the social or sexual problem at hand. The essays ballooned. Working at his bedroom desk on a Royal Standard typewriter, or perched atop his round bed surrounded by piles of documents, the author consulted elaborate files on birth control, womanization, the law and obscenity, divorce, abortion, and a host of similar topics. Several research assistants combed through books looking for relevant discussions and quotations. Hefner sent a stream of his infamous memos demanding information on various topics ranging from the arcane to the impossibly vast:

> Please get me as much research as possible on earlier Catholic attitudes on sex—the Church used to be very liberal in the area of sex in earlier European days.
>
> Will you please have a staff member gather for me a nice list of famous men of history who, in addition to their other accomplishments, were noted for their high degree of sexual activity, either in or out of marriage?
>
> Can we tie the Renaissance in with sexual freedom and sexual vigor? If so, I would like some specifics not only in terms of sexual freedom and sexual totalitarianism, but also specific examples of what was accomplished in periods like the Renaissance in Europe, and what failed to occur during the Dark Ages and the Victorian period.[14]

New associate editor Nat Lehrman, who had been assigned to head the research staff, witnessed the process first hand. With an irreverent sign saying "If Hef Likes It, It's Art" tacked behind his desk, the young journalist struggled to assist the publisher with his essays. Hefner agonized over every word, once subjecting Lehrman to a twenty-four-hour writing session where, near the end, he considered verbs, alternately writing and crossing out "said," "stated," "remarked," and "observed." An exhausted Lehrman muttered each time, "Sounds good to me." Finally Hefner said sharply, "You're not just trying to get out of here, are you?" Hefner's haphazard use of others' work also caused problems. He was particularly taken with two books—one titled *Sex and the Law* and the other *Sex and History*—and quoted great chunks from them with little or no attribution. Eventually, both authors grumbled about having their work cribbed, but Lehrman headed off disaster by paying them in lieu of a lawsuit for plagiarism.[15]

Indeed, Hefner's painstaking labors created exasperating problems for *Playboy*. Preoccupied with his writing and locked away in his mansion bedroom, the publisher neglected other important decision-making with the magazine. His installments of the Philosophy often arrived so late that they pushed the magazine over production deadlines, driving the editors to distraction. A. C. Spectorsky, upon whose shoulders fell many of the difficulties, turned bitter, describing the mansion as "the Bunker," the philosophy as "a grinding, endless bore," and his own struggles as "the tortures of the damned." According to Theo Spectorsky, Hefner spent "two years repeating himself, working at a snail's pace, fussing over every comma, weeks past deadline almost every month, squirreled away inside his quarters at the Mansion, with Augie trying frantically to pry the word loose."[16]

What did this Herculean labor produce? Mostly, Hefner elaborated themes he had been discussing for years in interviews—the liberated individual's need to enjoy material abundance, economic opportunity, leisure fulfillments, and sexual freedom; the emergence of a restless Upbeat Generation eager for such things; *Playboy*'s mission to promote this agenda. All the while, he ransacked history for examples and unloaded bushels of quotes from philosophers and social thinkers to buttress his opinions.

The first few installments meandered through discussions of American history and the cult of "the common man," the influence of religion on modern values, capitalism versus communism, the history of sex in Western civilization, and disputes over obscenity, pornography, and censorship. Then Hefner turned to even broader questions of the competing claims of the individual and society, the role of reason and self-interest, the historical evolution of religious morality, and the history of sexual mores. During the concluding installments of the Playboy Philosophy, the author, obviously running out of steam, printed transcripts from four radio roundtables on "The American Sexual Revolution" in which he had participated.[17]

The final result was an enthusiastic, if rather pedestrian and unsystematic, recycling of ideas common to modern humanist liberalism. Hefner followed a well-trodden path in arguing that the good of the individual trumped most social considerations, worldly human affairs were more important than the afterlife, and traditions or institutions that unduly restricted individual expression should be dismantled. An unusually strong libertarian position defending the pursuit of self-interest, and an unusually daring emphasis on sexual freedom made for the most novel features of his essays. The Hefner credo was part John Stuart Mill, part Adam Smith, part Ayn Rand, and part popular Freudianism.

If the content of Hefner's essays was unremarkable, their style could be exasperating. While his unadorned prose could be crisp and illuminated with flashes of insight and passion, more often it was turgid and repetitive. The Hefner style incorporated great chunks of quotation (three pages verbatim of a description of Supreme Court justice Hugo Black's views on free speech) and presented generalizations that reached galactic proportions ("Modern American morality is an amalgamation of the superstitious paganism and masochistic asceticism of early Christianity; the sexual anxieties, feelings of guilt and shame, witch-hunting sadism and sex repression of the medieval Church; the desexualized courtly love of the troubadours; England's Romantic Age, wherein love was presumed to conquer all; and the prohibitively strict, severe, joyless, authoritarian, unresponsive, book-banning, pleasure-baiting dogma of Calvinist Protestantism, Puritanism, and Victorianism."). His consistent use of the "imperial we"—"we've decided it's time to speak out ourself [sic] on what we believe in, and what we feel PLAYBOY represents in present-day society"—quickly became annoying as it imparted a pretentious quality to the essays. As Mort Sahl quipped, "Hef always wanted to impress upon me that he was writing the Philosophy himself. Which I had no doubts of after reading it."[18]

The Playboy Philosophy elicited widespread commentary. *Playboy* readers offered much sympathetic appreciation, flooding the magazine with letters supporting the publisher's attempts to construct a moral foundation for a modern lifestyle. They praised Hefner for presenting life-affirming views that, in the words of one, discredited the notion that "sex is evil, that pleasure is evil, that physical comfort and the accumulation of wealth is evil." Another reader characterized the Playboy Philosophy as "a 20th century version of Thomas Paine's *Age of Reason*." A third saw in Hefner's musings "the hunger for a new philosophy as great as that which is inspiring the Sexual

Revolution itself." Distinguished commentators also weighed in affirmatively. Albert Ellis, writer on psychology and sexual morality, praised Hefner for his "highly consequential and well-thought-out views" while Ralph Ginzburg, the provocateur and editor of *Eros,* offered congratulations on a weighty series that was "dealing the single most significant blow to the forces of censorship of any publication in the history of the United States."[19]

But Hefner's controversial views also inspired much denunciation. Some critics focused on what they saw as rampant hypocrisy in the Playboy Philosophy, arguing that he was straining to create a serious rationale for an enterprise obviously fueled by sex and profit. A newspaper columnist asked, "I wonder what your circulation figures would be if you were to eliminate some of the more arresting features such as, say, the monthly Playmate, the Party Jokes page, the Ribald Classic, the fashion studies and automobiles." An essayist in the *Realist* observed brutally that Hefner's theorizing could not obscure the central appeal of his magazine, "namely, that Americans will pay a lot of money to look at tits." *Playboy* was really a monument to "clever commercialism," another critic noted, and Hefner's philosophy would remain "semi-fraudulent" until he addressed that fact.[20]

Other critics took a more philosophical bent. They argued that Hefner's stress on individual self-fulfillment overlooked the need for obligation and responsibility in society, while his stress on style and possessions ignored the more important virtues of love, respect, and soul. Reflecting "a certain emptiness that is the emptiness of necessity," wrote one critic, Hefner propounded "an empty materialism and cellophane hedonism." Others excoriated his social ideal as "a fairyland of distorted values" and his pleasure-seeking as "a form of infantilism and narcissism." Writing in the *Antioch Review,* an English professor described the Playboy Philosophy as a compendium of half-digested ideas, a sophomoric "hit-and-run gallop through psychology, economics, morality, education, religion, and sociology."[21]

A long, thoughtful essay in a Sunday edition of the *Chicago Sun-Times* encapsulated many of these critical suspicions. "Bunnies in a Tinseled Thinksville" took Hefner to task for peddling a sunny vision of life that ignored elements of pain and despair, without which there could be no understanding of happiness. With sex, the author maintained, Hefner presented a false choice between stuffed-shirt prudery and recreational seduction. "Could it be that neither approach suggested by Hefner is the healthy, the natural and the right one?" he wrote. "Can a man be all for sex and all against Hefner's brand of sex?" Citing William Faulkner's observation that a view of life that did not take into account "love and honor and pity and pride and compassion and sacrifice" was doomed, said the author, "it is interesting that not one of them is discussed in the Playboy Philosophy."[22]

Many critics also found the Playboy Philosophy's literary style off-putting. The repetitive, bloated structure of the essays prompted the complaint that Hefner "has succeeded quite admirably in compressing a few ideas into many words." *Playboy's* old nemesis, *Esquire,* awarded one of its 1963 Dubious Achievement Awards to Hefner in the form of "a delicately fashioned, hand-embroidered sampler, embellished with warm and homely symbols in each corner surrounding these words: SHUT UP." A scathing assessment in one journal noted mathematicians' contention that if you place a monkey in front of a typewriter and give him an infinite amount of paper and time, sooner or later he will accidentally type out Shakespeare's *Hamlet.* "A comic we know has a time-saving suggestion: get an infinite number of monkeys to do the job instantaneously," it continued. "Now we find that an infinite number of monkeys *do* exist and that they are employed as researchers by Hugh M. Hefner, editor of *Playboy* magazine."[23]

Hefner responded to such attacks with typical seriousness. He established the Playboy Forum as a new venue in *Playboy* to discuss issues raised by both critics and defenders. It made its debut in July 1963 and soon was filled with supportive letters from readers, along with responses from Hefner. In the spring of 1965, because of interest expressed by many college students and faculty, Hefner went on a campus speaking tour to defend his philosophical speculations. He appeared to packed auditoriums at Cornell, Johns Hopkins, Northwestern, and the University of North Carolina to discuss the Playboy Philosophy, usually in a panel-discussion format that included local professors, writers, and moralists. Finally, in 1965 Hefner founded the Playboy Foundation, a nonprofit agency that became an activist arm of the Playboy Philosophy. Involving itself in several landmark endeavors—freeing a West Virginia man who had been imprisoned for having oral sex, funneling hundreds of thousands of dollars to the Kinsey Institute and Masters and Johnson for sex research, assisting with the *Roe v. Wade* case that established women's abortion rights—the foundation proved that Hefner's philosophy was more than mere rhetoric: it was a heartfelt manifesto of social reform.[24]

Meanwhile, Hefner engaged in an extended battle of wits with a powerful enemy: the American religious community. The Playboy Philosophy had fingered Christianity as the source of most modern emotional and social woes, and many religious spokesmen responded in kind. The resulting debate between *Playboy* and the preachers provided a glimpse of the cultural ferment beginning to bubble in 1960s America.

III

In the first installment of the Playboy Philosophy, Hefner focused attention on two religious writers: Harvey Cox, the famous theologian and author, who had denounced the magazine's advocacy of "recreational sex" in *Christianity and Crisis*; and the Reverend Roy Larson, who accused *Playboy* of misleading young men in defining their goals, character, and values in the Methodist magazine *Motive*. When Hefner ended the series over two years later, he did so with several radio roundtables featuring himself, a priest, a minister, and a rabbi. This persistent engagement with religious figures made clear that the publisher's ideas about religion lay at the heart of both his formulations and the resulting controversy.[25]

Indeed, the *Playboy* editor minced few words in identifying Christianity as the bogeyman in the evolution of stultifying moral codes in Western civilization. The Playboy Philosophy blamed both Catholicism and Protestantism for nurturing repressive, restrictive, hypocritical attitudes that had denied physical needs and stunted emotional health. Hefner contended that Christianity, while sometimes engendering sympathy, understanding, and charity, more often had inspired "bloody wars," kept millions "in abject poverty," and promoted "the tyranny of man over his fellow man." This indictment of Christianity reflected *Playboy*'s twin preoccupations—sex and material abundance.[26]

Christian doctrine, Hefner argued, had cultivated a prejudice against material accumulation and prosperity by opposing worldly things—possessions, money, success—to the ultimate goal of salvation. Since Christianity taught that poverty was holier than wealth, the pauper was more likely to receive God's grace than the prosperous man. Such doctrines may have been compelling in an earlier age of material want, Hefner argued, but "they make very little sense in America today, however, where every man had ample opportunity to better himself."[27]

Moreover, Hefner contended, Christianity had nurtured a poisonous hostility to human sexuality. Its roots lay in a dualistic paradigm that posed the body and flesh as evil, and spirit and soul as virtuous. From the time of Saint Paul onward, sex was seen as a sinful bodily activity tolerated only for procreation. "By associating sex with sin, we have produced a society so guilt-ridden that it is almost impossible to view the subject objectively," he noted of Christian culture.[28]

The Christian abhorrence of sinful flesh, Hefner continued, produced something even worse—repression and censorship. Since bodily temptation could not be transcended, the church sought to regulate it with elaborate moral codes. Medieval Catholicism had been stringent, but it was Calvinism, according to the *Playboy* publisher, that turned repression into an art form in America. It first clamped down on pleasure-seekers in the colonial era, and then persisted as a repressive force throughout American history. This Puritan heritage, Hefner believed, had created a monstrous alliance with the state to create anti-pleasure outrages such as blue laws, anti-evolution statutes, and Prohibition. Sex became a special target as Christian zealots imposed severe legal restrictions on fornication, cohabitation, adultery, and sodomy, as well as erotic literature, divorce, abortion, and birth control. In his view, it was "in our laws related to sex that we find the greatest church-state intrusion upon our personal freedom."[29]

Ultimately, Hefner confronted religion in the name of reason. A humanist and rationalist, he disdained what he saw as the blind faith and superstition driving Christian doctrine. "We believe in a moral and law-abiding society," he noted at one point in the Philosophy, "but one in which the morality and the laws are based upon logic and reason rather than mysticism or religious dogma." Sexuality provided a telling example. Irrationally insisting that sexual activity be strictly limited to marriage, he contended, the church overlooked the obvious sexual desires and needs of unmarried people. By simply saying that "sex for all these people is wrong, is taboo, in truth, religion has not satisfactorily come to grips with the problem as it exists," he wrote.[30]

Christianity, in Hefner's worldview, ran counter to the American Way of Life with its values of democracy, self-reliance, and success-seeking. As he argued passionately in the Playboy Philosophy,

> Religion is based upon faith; democracy is based upon reason. America's religious heritage stresses selflessness, subservience to a greater Power and the paying of homage to Him in long-established, well-defined, well-organized ways; democracy teaches the importance of self, a belief in oneself and one's own abilities. Religion teaches that man should live for others; our democracy's free enterprise system is based on the belief that the greatest good comes from men competing with one another. . . .
>
> Most organized religion in the U.S. is rooted in a tradition that links man's body with evil, physical pleasures with sin and pits man's mind and soul against the devils of the flesh; the principles underlying our democracy recognize no such conflict of body, mind, and soul.[31]

In part, Hefner's animus toward Christianity flowed from a rejection of his religious upbringing. As an adolescent, he had become disenchanted with his parents' beliefs and "I'm still reacting," he confessed in an interview. But his broadsides also reflected a broader ferment in American Christianity as the 1960s unfolded. In a growing leisure culture of abundance since World War II, growing numbers of mainstream Protestants and Catholics began to question traditional religious strictures against material and sexual pleasure. Moreover, a dissenting sensibility associated with the civil rights movement and progressive politics created pressures in behalf of social activism within churches. The result was a swelling crisis as many believers began to question the relevance of traditional Christian values for modern society. Such controversy culminated in the dissident "God is Dead" movement at mid-decade. Amid this turmoil, powerful defenders of Christianity marshaled their forces and lashed out at critics.[32]

Hefner became a key target. In the early 1960s, Christian traditionalists attacked the Playboy Philosophy in such numbers that an article in the *Columbia Journalism Review*, titled "Playboy and the Preachers," concluded, "If *Playboy* has not exactly discovered religion, religion has discovered *Playboy*." Some religious critics simply blasted Hefner as a purveyor of "barnyard morality," but others proceeded more thoughtfully.[33]

They took the *Playboy* publisher to task for a superficial understanding of theology. They complained that he failed to grasp the influence of Neoplatonism in medieval Christianity and seemed totally unaware of Martin Luther's "earthy appraisal of man's sexual nature." He failed to appreciate that the New Testament affirmed that "life in the flesh" was good, even delightful as long as sex took place within the institution of marriage. But critics were most distressed by Hefner's treatment of Puritanism. They contended, often heatedly, that since American Christianity had jettisoned Puritan ideas in all of the mainstream denominations by the early 1800s, Hefner was tilting at theological windmills. The publisher, concluded one writer, was "willing to tell the religious tradition of the West to go to hell, even though he badly misunderstands that tradition."[34]

In fact, some traditionalists contended that Hefner had attempted to create a "substitute religion" for his young, urban audience: *Playboy* served as its Bible, the bunny logo as its sacred symbol, the Playboy Clubs as its "sacred temples," and the Bunnies as its "priestesses." *Playboy* even had a Lord's Prayer, said one critic:

Our Fathers, who art in Madison Avenue and Ohio Street, hallowed be thy names. May Thy work and influence flourish, and may Thy will be done, in Peoria as well as in Manhattan.

Give us this day our daily Martini—dry and smooth—and forgive us our goofs, even as we try to overlook the goofs of others. And, for heaven's sake, our Lords, take us into temptation and deliver us from the Puritans.

For thine is the Kingdom and the Power and the Glory—if not forever, at least until someone sharper than you comes along. Amen and Amen.[35]

Hefner's secular religion, according to its opponents, promoted a frivolous hedonism. Clerics contended that pleasure and recreation were the only good in the *Playboy* moral universe. Sex served as a form of entertainment and women became merely "the grandest of all consumer goods." As a chaplain summarized in the *Catholic World*, the Playboy Philosophy represented "the elevation of the flesh and the material to the level of the end in itself—a contemporary idolatry."[36]

The Playboy Philosophy also dehumanized people, according to many religious critics. By worshiping materialism and the body while ignoring matters of the spirit and soul, Hefner reduced people to less than fully human. Moreover, his philosophy isolated the individual and weakened the possibility of genuine, meaningful relationships with others. Real sex, one essayist argued, reflected a yearning for emotional connection combining "*eros* (which loves the worth of the other person) and *agape* (which loves the 'authentic being' of the other person)." Hefner's view of sex, to the contrary, reflected only a sterile, selfish individualism, fueled by bodily desires, that was unable to make a broader human connection. As one critic inquired pointedly, "Is it not curious that a magazine so interested in sex is singularly silent on the family?"[37]

Other religious commentators rushed to Hefner's defense. About half of the clergymen who wrote in to the Playboy Forum supported the Playboy Philosophy, with a significant portion being Unitarian ministers, a small, liberal denomination. A Methodist college chaplain exclaimed, "The position you take is more authentically Christian than much that is heard from pulpits today." A Pittsburgh Theological Seminary professor proposed that Hefner endow a Playboy Chair of American Church History and noted, "I would be delighted beyond measure to occupy such a chair." A minister praised the publisher from his pulpit in 1964, arguing that he had "dared to question the life-denying philosophies" of the Western tradition. In his view, the Playboy Philosophy had converged with a "liberal religious ideal" to affirm that "the chief end of life is to glory man and enjoy him forever."[38]

The religious reactions, both positive and negative, thrilled Hefner. He concluded that he was being taken seriously, noting that his essays had provided "a catalyst for a new discussion and examination of American social and sexual mores" that involved "newly acquired theological, philosophical, medical, psychological, and sociological insights." He also took action. He offered steep discounts to any clergymen who subscribed to *Playboy*. He also sent Anson Mount to study at the Episcopal Theological Seminary in Sewanee, Tennessee. Mount emerged as an official spokesman in a long series of public appearances where he defended the theological implications of the Playboy Philosophy.[39]

By the mid-1960s, religious hostility to Hefner and his Playboy Philosophy began to wane as a growing tide of social activism pushed liberal Protestantism in his direction. A 1964 radio roundtable in New York City, for instance, emerged as an exercise in searching for common ground. Three local clerics—Father Norman O'Connor; Reverend Richard Gary, an Episcopal minister; and Rabbi Marc Tannenbaum—joined Hefner for a discussion of religious morality and premarital sex, adultery, and birth control. A delighted Hefner celebrated their lack of moral certainty. "Whatever difficulty each of you may have had in delineating an absolute sex standard or code of conduct for your respective religions is a positive reflection, I think, of the soul-searching and re-evaluation taking place within *both* religious and secular society," he declared.[40]

The pages of *Playboy* reflected this rapprochement with liberal Christianity. In 1966, the Reverend William Hamilton contributed an article on "The Death of God" that acclaimed this liberating event for empowering humans to solve their own problems, based on the example of Jesus of Nazareth. The following year, the magazine convened "The Playboy Panel: Religion and the New Morality," which brought together a distinguished group of progressive clergy. They ranged widely over the contemporary landscape, agreeing that modern life demanded a reformulation of religious morality to include situational ethics and greater latitude for sexual expression.[41]

Harvey Cox, however, perhaps best represented liberal Christianity and its accommodation with *Playboy* in the 1960s. An early critic of the magazine with his influential 1961 essay, "Playboy's Doctrine of Male," by 1967 he appeared in the conciliatory Playboy Panel. Meanwhile, he had become a sparring partner for Hefner at several public forums. In an appearance at Cornell, he noted that he had become a fan of the magazine because of its committed engagement with moral questions in recent years. Cox became a contributor to *Playboy*, penning an article on the "Revolt in the Church," which insisted "that theological doctrines and religious forms we have inherited from the past have reached the end of their usefulness," and "For Christ's Sake," which urged Christians to embrace "the revolutionary portent of Jesus."[42]

Hefner's "Playboy Philosophy" and his extended encounter with the tribunes of American Christianity denoted a serious new role for the upstart publisher and his magazine in the 1960s. No longer just a venue offering entertainment for men or a tour guide for jaunts through America's leisure culture, it was becoming a journalistic seismograph measuring deeper rumblings beginning to shake the cultural foundations of postwar America. Within a short time, as *Playboy* confronted a host of social and political issues, that seismographic needle would swing full tilt.

10

The Happiness Explosion

The prose was alternately elegant and jarring, the tone slightly surreal, the punctuation wild and swirling, the phrases cracking like staccato rimshots. Tom Wolfe, avatar of the "New Journalism," had come to Chicago in 1965 to explore the singular world of Hugh Hefner. He spent time at the Playboy Mansion observing the editor in his bedroom headquarters, trying to capture the essence of one of the blazing new symbols of what he called "The New Life Out There" in modern America. He published the result in the Sunday magazine of the *New York Herald Tribune*.

According to Wolfe, Americans had chased wealth and social advancement for generations before jettisoning the old status games in the economic boom of the 1950s and early 1960s. "They're using a combination of America's great postwar mass luxuries—time, money, and technology," he wrote, "to create avant-garde styles of living that make New York's culturati and fashionati look like leftovers from a 19th-century Rumanian card dance." They had turned their households into consumer havens and created "discreet and rather marvelous electronic worlds."[1]

Hugh Hefner exemplified this new lifestyle. Perched on an enormous, revolving bed and dressed in pajamas, slippers, and robe, he kept at his fingertips dozens of dials and switches to move the bed, operate the television, adjust the hi-fi, dim the lights, and manage the videotaping system. According to Wolfe:

> Hefner's genius has been to drop out of the orthodox status competition and to use money and technology and to convert his habitat into a stage and to get on the stage, not in the spectator seats, and to be the undisputed hero himself. Through the more and more sophisticated use of machines, Hefner, and to a lesser degree millions of . . . *homemakers* outside of New York have turned their homes into wonderlands, almost complete status spheres all their own. . . .
>
> What Hefner has been offering is not merely a fantasy of some kind of potentate's serving of sex but also a fantasy of a potentate's control of the environment—all of a sudden made possible by the new lumpen middle-class style of life.

As a new kind of royalty—Wolfe dubbed him the "King of the Status Drop-Outs," the "Consumer King"—Hefner represented a new kind of American. Rejecting many traditional norms of behavior and mobilizing affluence to pursue personal contentment and gratification, he, like many of his fellow citizens, had detonated a "Happiness Explosion."[2]

Many others agreed that Hefner represented a mutinous spirit arising in America. He had lured Americans to "enjoy what they have always frowned upon: hedonism . . . unmarried sex . . . and suave pseudo-intellectualism," said *Life. Look* disapprovingly quoted his declaration that publishing *Playboy* was like "waving a flag of freedom, like screaming 'rebellion' under a dictatorship." The cultural critic Malcolm Muggeridge concluded that Hefner sought "the abandonment of the Judeo-Christian view of sex." In other words, the *Playboy* publisher increasingly appeared as not just a purveyor of illicit pictures, but as a social subversive.[3]

Hefner's evolving image was an early sign of a larger discontent in American society. A spirit of rebellion was growing by the mid-1960s that combined impatience with traditional restraints, disapproval of long-standing hierarchies, and desires for personal fulfillment. According to the historian David Farber, America's restless affluence had brought the belief that "the old rules of scarcity and traditional values of thrift and delayed gratification no longer held. . . . Cultural authority—the power to set the rules of proper conduct and behavior—was up for grabs." A cultural cauldron of ferment had begun to bubble in 1960s America, and no one seemed to know whether the end result would be intoxicating, explosive, or both. Hefner didn't know either, but he sensed that *Playboy* would be in the thick of the action.[4]

I

Throughout the early 1960s, *Playboy* continued addressing familiar concerns with sex, consumption, and entertainment. Erotic themes, of course, remained front and center stage as readers encountered many old standbys—the Playmate of the Month, the Ribald Classic, Playboy's Party Jokes, the Vargas Girls drawings. Special features included "The Girls of New York," "The Girls of the Riviera," and, as the magazine's contribution to Cold War thaw, "The Girls of Russia." "A Toast to Bikinis" showcased the female form, as did celebrity pictorials on "The Nudest Jayne Mansfield" and "Brigitte Bardot: The Sex Kitten Grows Up." The adult cartoon strip *Little Annie Fanny* debuted in October 1962, while "Sex in the Cinema," a yearly roundup of erotic vignettes from the movies compiled by the film critics Arthur Knight and Hollis Alpert, began in April 1965.

In similar fashion, the magazine continued its advocacy of refined consumption and stylish living. Instructional articles on French cooking, stereo equipment, and purchasing modern art appeared alongside old favorites such as "Attire" by Robert L. Green, "Food" by Thomas Mario, and "Man at His Leisure," by LeRoy Neiman. A new feature in 1960, "The Playboy Advisor," promised to "answer your questions on a wide variety of topics of interest to the urban man—from fashion, food and drink, hi-fi and sports cars to dating dilemmas, taste and etiquette." *Playboy's* advertisements, as they had done for years, enhanced the fantasy of bountiful modern living, as ads for Ballantine scotch, Wembley ties, Renauld sunglasses, Kaywoodie pipes, and Munsingwear pajamas and robes adorned the magazine.[5]

On the entertainment front, "Playboy After Hours" continued previewing movies, plays, and music while pieces on figures such as Tony Curtis, Elizabeth Taylor, and Richard Burton kept readers abreast of the hottest celebrities. "On the Scene" focused on new, young entertainers and artists such as Jean-Paul Belmondo, Stanley Kubrick, and Bob Dylan. The "Pigskin Preview" and the "Playboy Jazz Poll" remained popular annual features. The October 1963 issue began the serialization of Lenny Bruce's controversial autobiography, *How to Talk Dirty and Influence People.*

Playboy enhanced its literary reputation for short fiction through-out the early 1960s. Old friends Arthur C. Clarke, Ray Bradbury, Charles Beaumont, and Ken Purdy were joined by younger writers such as Bruce Jay Friedman, Irwin Shaw, Philip Roth, and John le Carré. Pieces by prominent artists and authors such as Henry Miller, Pablo Picasso, and Bertrand Russell also graced the magazine's pages, while provocative cultural criticism came from the likes of Alfred Kazin and Leslie Fielder.[6]

But *Playboy*'s traditional formula also expanded significantly from 1960 to1965. "The Playboy Panel," inaugurated in November 1960, presented a venue for debating controversial public issues. Under its auspices, Ralph Ginzburg, Norman Mailer, and Otto Preminger pondered "Sex and Censorship in Literature and the Arts," while Marquis Childs, Senator Jacob Javits, and Vance Packard traded views on "Business Ethics and Morality."[7]

The famous "Playboy Interview," which debuted in September 1962, used a lengthy question-and-answer format to attract not only entertainers—Miles Davis, Billy Wilder, Frank Sinatra, Richard Burton—but figures in politics, arts and letters, journalism, and philosophy. Indian head of state Jawaharlal Nehru, philosopher Jean-Paul Sartre, labor leader Jimmy Hoffa, and pop sensations the Beatles all became subjects. "The Playboy Forum," a new feature created in July 1963 to encourage debate over Hefner's serialized Playboy Philosophy, underlined *Playboy*'s growing engagement with contemporary social issues.[8]

The magazine's growth spearheaded a larger expansion of the company. A second Playboy Club opened in Miami, a third in New Orleans, and by 1965 additional venues had appeared in Phoenix, New York, Los Angeles, San Francisco, Detroit, Baltimore, Boston, Atlanta, and Kansas City. A minor disruption came when Victor

Lownes departed the company in late summer 1962 after clashing with Keith Hefner, who had assumed a managerial position with the Playboy Clubs. The volatile Lownes, ever jealous of his favored position, went after Hefner's younger brother. After a particularly rancorous tirade accusing Keith of mismanagement, the older brother put his foot down. "You know, Victor," he said, "if you have nothing else to do with your time but do this kind of horseshit, you must not be doing your job." Not long after that, Lownes resigned.[9]

The New York club sounded the only sour note. A city commission, headed by a devout Catholic, refused to grant a cabaret license because of scantily clad waitresses. After an appeal, a state Supreme Court judge ordered the issuing of the license, observing that "it is not incumbent upon the petitioner to dress its female employees in middy blouses, gymnasium bloomers, turtleneck sweaters, fisherman's hip boots, or ankle-length overcoats" to satisfy the commissioner's personal moral code. A few months later, *Life* magazine broke a story exposing the New York State Liquor Authority for engineering shakedowns and payoffs from bars, clubs, and liquor stores. It emerged that the Playboy Club had been forced to pay a tribute of some $79,000 to get a liquor license. Hefner issued a statement explaining that his company had paid out of necessity, but then subsequently exposed the wrongdoing to the district attorney and a grand jury. In a trial on corruption charges brought against several state officials, *Playboy* was vindicated as being the victim of extortion and blackmail. The club had a gala opening on December 8, 1962.[10]

Other Playboy projects flourished. Playboy Tours offered vacation packages while *The Playboy Gourmet* appeared as a handbook for food and drink. The bunny logo emblazoned a long list of items: jewelry, clothing, calendars, bar accoutrements, keychains, lighters, and golf equipment. *The Bedside Playboy* collected the best articles and stories from the magazine, while the *LeRoy Neiman Portfolio* and the *Alberto Vargas Portfolio* presented a collection of the artists' drawings from the magazine. On September 28, 1964, the Playboy Theatre opened in Chicago after a complete refurbishing of the old Surf Theater. The following spring, Hefner purchased the lease on the famous Palmolive Building on Michigan Avenue in Chicago for $2.7 million. After extensive renovation, *Playboy* occupied about 25 percent of the thirty-seven-floor building, rechristened it the Playboy Building, and made the huge beacon that swept out over the city from atop it the magazine's calling card. A few months later, Helen Gurley Brown, author of *Sex and the Single Girl*, reshaped *Cosmopolitan* into a female version of *Playboy*.[11]

Hefner's synergistically expanding empire produced soaring profits. The 1964 annual report indicated that magazine sales had reached $2.4 million and were expected to reach $3 million by early 1965. Advertising sales climbed dramatically as *Playboy* roped in new mainstream clients such as Goodyear Tires, Falstaff Brewing, Admiral TV, Fabergé, and Schick Razors. Total sales from magazine circulation, advertising, and subsidiary products totaled nearly $21 million; from the Playboy Clubs over $12 million; and from Playboy products a bit over $1 million. This represented an increase of 43 percent over the previous year.[12]

Hefner maintained his position atop *Playboy*'s hierarchy. As publisher, editor, and guiding light, he controlled everything about the magazine, from editorial policies to visual images to every aspect of the operation. Nothing about *Playboy* escaped his attention, and a barrage of lengthy memos disclosed a perfectionism bordering on compulsion.

Hefner initiated the Playboy Advisor in 1960 with a full set of instructions on how to formulate answers to problems of dating, dining, and dressing. He rode herd on the column, critiquing both the answers (they often required more punch and color) and the editing of the letters (a pathetic overtone often needed to be scrubbed). He also monitored special projects such as the "Playboy Pads" series and "Sex in Cinema" series.[13]

Hefner regularly tackled visual issues in the magazine. In a long 1962 missive on Playmate photos, he instructed that the reader should "feel as though he really knows the girl—he understands something about her inner thoughts, her hopes and dreams, her fears, and her aspirations." Around the same time, he composed a nineteen-page, single-spaced critique of the graphics and design of the previous year's magazine. Proceeding issue by issue, picture by picture, drawing by drawing, he analyzed in incredible detail every image that a reader had seen and suggested improvements.[14]

Hefner's attention extended into all areas of the *Playboy* empire as well. He kept an eye on the management of the Playboy Clubs and personally approved every piece of Playboy merchandise and every Playboy Books project. Even minor undertakings like the Playmate

Calendar prompted him to chastise the photo and art departments for failing to work more cohesively and carefully.[15]

The tiniest detail drew his attention. One memo dictated that "for all receptionists, on all floors, in all of the Playboy Buildings, absolutely no gum chewing is to be allowed during the working day while they are at their desks." Another instructed that two suits of armor at the Playboy Mansion needed to be cleaned and remounted, while "some chain mail for the front pelvic area should be placed on the older suit in place of the velvet skirt that is now on it." He went through every bedroom and apartment in the mansion providing directions on how each should be set up in terms of décor, furniture, painting, towels and washcloths, ashtrays, keys, and rental fees.[16]

Under Hefner's leadership, *Playboy* grew bigger, more influential, and more profitable in the early 1960s. In so doing it relied upon many familiar elements to provide "entertainment for men," but it also began to modify its traditional agenda in significant ways. Few would have predicted it in earlier years, but the publisher slowly entered the world of public affairs.

II

As the new decade unfolded, Hefner, in his words, decided that if the magazine was to grow "then we should be paying attention to major social issues that were keeping a good number of people from enjoying the life we were espousing in the rest of the magazine." The Playboy Philosophy reflected this new concern with matters more weighty than techniques of seduction, dining etiquette, and the latest cut of evening wear. But Hefner and his magazine also caught a larger liberationist spirit that was blowing through America in the early 1960s and shaking the shutters of tradition. The magazine began to promote a liberal activism that advocated not a radical overhaul of the socioeconomic system, but breaking down barriers to provide greater, freer access to it. *Playboy's* positions represented an official counterculture of the enlightened, sophisticated, and affluent.[17]

The arrival of several new, youthful editors helped sharpen *Playboy's* new profile. In the early 1960s, Spectorsky hired Sheldon Wax, Murray Fisher, and Nat Lehrman to bring fresh perspectives and energy to the magazine. They reinforced its new social and political sensibility and influenced its liberal bent. "We were doing very interesting things, particularly in the sexual area and in the civil liberties and civil rights area in the early Sixties," Lehrman recalled later. "There were things happening, ideas were opening up. *Playboy* was always a step ahead of those ideas."[18]

New kinds of articles began to appear. Paul Goodman wrote a scathing critique of the nation's school system and J. Paul Getty penned a series of articles on business; both agreed that the quest for economic security had created a conformity that was choking initiative and creativity in America. In "The Age of Overbreed," Sir Julian Huxley warned that population growth was threatening to overwhelm both physical resources and social structures around the globe.[19]

In cultural affairs, Terry Southern, the controversial author and playwright, contended that movies had supplanted the novel because of their superior sensory capabilities and willingness to tackle contemporary problems. The burgeoning drug culture attracted attention. Dan Wakefield examined the history of marijuana use, suggesting its virtues as well as vices, while Richard Carter explored Americans' love affair with pharmaceuticals—pills, potions, capsules, ointments—as the pathway to perfection in body and spirit.[20]

Playboy turned its attention to politics. In 1963, William F. Buckley and Norman Mailer jousted over "The Role of the Right Wing in America Today." Buckley defended conservatives' perception of unraveling moral values and a willingness to coddle communist authoritarianism in mainstream society while Mailer characterized conservatism as little more than a "contradictory stew of reactionaries and individualists, of fascists and libertarians." In "The Liberal Dilemma," the noted commentator Marquis Childs argued that modern progressives needed to venture beyond the comfortable confines of the New Deal tradition in addressing modern problems.[21]

Perhaps the most striking aspect of *Playboy*'s heightened social awareness came in the area of race relations. Hefner's longtime support for racial equality and the civil rights movement laid the groundwork. In his television show, *Playboy's Penthouse,* he had insisted on booking black acts and mixing white and black guests. Conversing on the air with the Gateway Singers, a music group with three white men and a black woman, he discussed their inability to get network bookings because of the racial mix. When several southern television stations refused to carry the show, Victor Lownes told the press,

"Hefner and I aren't going to back down on this issue. Television can be a great force in ending discriminatory nonsense. . . . Most of the complaining letters we get about it are from idiots."[22]

In the early 1960s, Hefner supported Sammy Davis Jr.'s controversial marriage to May Britt, a white woman. He attended a benefit for Martin Luther King Jr. in New York City and made a significant contribution. With the launching of the Playboy Clubs, Hefner put a firm policy of racial integration into place. Black keyholders were welcome and black comedians such as Dick Gregory, George Kirby, Slappy White, and Flip Wilson were booked regularly. Controversy flared in 1961 over the admission of blacks to the newly opened New Orleans club. An article in the *Village Voice* exposed the fact that the nightclub, which had been franchised to local owners, was refusing admission to African Americans. Hefner fired off a long letter to the editor explaining that *Playboy* was "a liberal organization that is being *forced* to comply with a local situation" in New Orleans. He reassured that all efforts were being made to integrate the club as soon as possible. Indeed, within a short time the parent company had repurchased the New Orleans club, as well as the Miami club, from the franchise holders and put integrated policies into place.[23]

African Americans, especially in Chicago, voiced their appreciation. Articles in the black press praised *Playboy's* nondiscriminatory hiring policies and quoted Hefner: "I personally accept other human beings, in both my personal and business world, on the basis of individual merit and without regard to their race, color, nationality, or religion." In 1962 Hefner received the "Brotherhood Award" from one Chicago group and the "Good American Award" from another for his commitment to "the fundamental right of equality of opportunity in employment without regard to color, creed, sex, or national origin."[24]

Hefner's relationship with Dick Gregory, the controversial black comedian, exemplified his racial stance. The Chicago Playboy Club hired Gregory, then an unknown local comedian, to do a show in 1961 and he quickly became a favorite with his irreverent routine focusing on American racial tensions. "Segregation isn't all bad," he would say. "Have you ever heard of a wreck where the people on the back of the bus got hurt?" Or, "I wouldn't mind paying taxes if I knew they were going to a friendly country." Hefner remained a friend and supporter when the comedian became an outspoken civil rights activist, and wrote the introduction for Gregory's book *From the Back of the Bus*

(1962). In the summer of 1964, Hefner even "guaranteed" a $25,000 reward offered by Gregory for information leading to the discovery of three missing civil rights workers in Mississippi.[25]

Hefner's civil rights stance was replicated in *Playboy* in the early 1960s. He encouraged staffers to solicit African American Playmates. "If a girl is really beautiful, I think she ought to prove popular with our readers, whatever her race," he wrote. The first black Playmate, Jennifer Jackson, appeared in March 1965. Playboy Interviews with prominent figures on the civil rights scene such as Gregory, King, and Cassius Clay appeared.[26]

The most dramatic *Playboy* interviews came with two figures standing as ideological bookends on the race issue. In May 1963, Malcolm X aired his militant message of black separatism, declaring, "I don't know when Armageddon is supposed to be. But I do know that the time is near when the white man will be finished. The signs are all around us." Then George Lincoln Rockwell, leader of the American Nazi Party, expounded his vicious creed of white supremacy. Interviewed at his compound by the African American journalist Alex Haley, he kept a pearl-handled revolver sitting on the table next to him as he denounced blacks and Jews. The exchanges were both chilling and memorable:

> *Rockwell:* It's nothing personal, but I want you to understand that I don't mix with your kind, and we call your race "niggers."
> *Haley:* I've been called "nigger" many times, Commander, but this is the first time I'm being paid for it. So you go right ahead. What have you got against us "niggers"?
> *Rockwell:* I just think you people would be happier in Africa back where you came from. . . . Equality may be the stated purpose [of the civil rights movement], but race mixing is what it boils down to in practice, and the harder you people push for that, the madder white people are going to get.[27]

Playboy's sensitivity to racial issues particularly influenced two articles. In July 1962, Nat Hentoff presented "Through the Racial Looking Glass," an impassioned plea for understanding the new militancy emerging in the African American community. It explained "the spiraling pride of race among American Negroes" and their bitterness about the slow progress on civil rights and the persistence of economic discrimination. In a very different kind of piece, James Baldwin, the eminent black writer, discussed his artistic efforts to explore the subject of race. "The reality I am trying to get at," he concluded movingly, "is that the humanity of this submerged population [of African Americans] is equal to the humanity of anyone else, equal to yours, equal to that of your child."[28]

Hefner and *Playboy's* social and political orientation in the early 1960s reflected a Kennedyesque sensibility. Promoting energy, youth, and boldness, it played up the theme of a new generation and affirmed liberal causes. Sympathy for human freedom, *Playboy* suggested, was another mark of the sophisticated modern male. Ironically, however, the publisher's growing public engagement was accompanied by a private withdrawal. Rarely leaving the controlled environment of the Playboy Mansion, he labored for days on end with little sense of time and had ever fewer encounters with the outside world. Hefner's fantasy, while still vivid to the outside world, seemed to turn inward and become a private dream.

III

The social scene at the Playboy Mansion became everything Hefner had dreamed of when he moved into the residence. He had refurbished the wonderful old house with an eye toward entertainment, and in the early 1960s it became packed with lavish parties, movie screenings, and famous guests. Those in attendance often felt swept up in "a timeless, spaceless sensation," as Norman Mailer described it. "One was in an ocean liner which traveled at the bottom of the sea, on a spaceship wandering down the galaxy along a night whose duration was a year."[29]

The festivities were enhanced by sexual encounters between young men and women who cavorted in the huge ballroom, indoor swimming pool, or underground bar. "We were all enjoying the sowing of wild oats—men and women alike . . . with absolutely no strings attached," described Keith Hefner. "Old rules didn't apply," said Murray Fisher. "It was like going to some infant's paradise, where you could eat all the candy you wanted and you wouldn't get fat." The mansion's atmosphere simply bowled over many who experienced it.

As Bob Hope quipped about Hefner's parties, "It's this guy's world. He just lets us live in it."[30]

But this joyful, uninhibited picture became blurred in a peculiar way as Hefner increasingly retreated from the hedonistic scene he created. He holed up for long stretches in his private quarters at the Playboy Mansion, attending movie screenings and making cameo appearances at many parties. But just as often he stayed out of sight. By the time he started writing the Playboy Philosophy, he had abandoned his corporate office for his bedroom, where he worked in his pajamas, ate junk food and swilled Pepsis by the dozen, and drew thick curtains across the windows to keep out sunlight. He slept and ate as he felt the need, regardless of the time of day or night. He became a recluse. "I rarely went out. But why should I?" Hefner said of his unconventional lifestyle. "Everything I wanted was already there."[31]

But there was more to it. Hefner's physical and emotional withdrawal, in many ways, had a chemical basis. By the late 1950s, he had slipped into a habit that would corrode his editorial skills over the next decade. In 1957, he complained that an exhausting work schedule was putting him to sleep at his desk and Victor Lownes suggested Dexedrine, an appetite suppressant that kept you awake and alert. Hefner tried one and was delighted when it boosted his energy and concentration. He began gobbling dexies and, according to Lownes, was soon staying up "for three or four days, without sleeping or eating, hardly blinking, working feverishly around the clock with the single-minded intensity of a maniac."[32]

By 1958, Hefner had developed a drug dependency. "Can we get a new supply of Dexedrine to fortify the troops during the next all-night mission?" he wrote in a June memo. A few months later he requested: "Can we get a new supply of Dexedrine to the fourth floor—our present quantity is running low and, as you know, the total operation of *Playboy* is now dependent on those little orange pills."[33]

Not surprisingly, Dexedrine made Hefner's professional judgment increasingly erratic. Spectorsky complained to Hefner that his dexie-induced schedule made it nearly impossible for the staff to consult with him while fostering an unfortunate preference for purple prose. "I think that by the time you do buckle down to reading a piece, it's got to be in neon to hold your attention, it's got to be like headlines," Spectorsky wrote. "It makes it damn hard for those of us who live more conventionally to know what you'll respond to, and how you'll respond."[34]

By the early 1960s, Hefner's Dexedrine habit was causing severe problems. While Ray Russell resigned in 1960 from a desire to become a freelance writer, he also had lost patience with his boss's "distortion of perception and judgment. . . . Hef had always been a great guy to work for, but now I could never be sure when I was working for him or for the pill." Dick Rosenzweig, who became Hefner's executive assistant in 1963, was shocked as his boss came to look like "he had popped out of Dachau. He was skin and bones because, among other things, the dexies take away your appetite."[35]

The dexies influenced everything. They produced gargantuan memos where Hefner would stay up all night, talking into his Dictaphone, with the results subsequently transcribed and distributed to long-suffering staffers. "Hefner made a point of never saying anything in 10 words if he could use 100, never saying anything once if he could repeat it three or four times," Lownes noted. "The joke we all told at the time was that you had to take a dexy just to *read* those goddamn memos." Editorial meetings were erratically called, frequently canceled, and invariably late starting. Executives called Rosenzweig to see where Hefner was positioned in the drug cycle before they scheduled an appointment, knowing that he could be explosively ill-tempered when he was coming out of a binge. Dexies also shaped the manic composition of the Playboy Philosophy. Associates described him as a "demonic" recluse in his bedroom bunker, speeding like crazy as he covered the material from every imaginable angle, then crashing into a sleeping stupor before beginning the cycle all over again.[36]

The ultimate dexie ordeal came with the writing and publication of "The Chicago Mansion," a story on his residence composed in the fall of 1965. Hefner cherished the project and its composition became a drug-driven obsession. He began firing off Tolstoyan memos on early drafts, and more revisions brought more memos. After several weeks, Spectorsky threw in the towel. "Here is the fruit of weekend and Monday work by the entire staff with the help of 57 pages of single-spaced memos from you," he wrote Hefner. "Hef, I have lost all judgment on this. . . . I do not recall a time in my life when I felt so defeated by a job that I have lived with, awake and in my dreams, for days. . . . You can reach me at home; I am ill and going to bed."[37]

With only a week before deadline, Hefner took over the writing and brought Murray Fisher in to assist. An unforgettable ordeal unfolded as Fisher sat next to the publisher for several days and nights, stopping only to grab a sandwich or catch a couple hours of sleep. "I matched him Pepsi for Pepsi, Dexie for Dexie, and the more I took the more reasonable he seemed to me," Fisher recalled. For endless hours Hefner painstakingly examined each sentence, crossing out nearly every word and agonizing over its replacement. "By the fourth day, we were both hallucinating vividly—unfortunately, not always the same thing," Fisher described. They finally finished the piece as the sun came up on Thanksgiving Day, and the assistant editor confessed he "had a lot to be thankful for: somehow, I had survived."[38]

But Hefner's reclusive habits did not tarnish his image. Paradoxically, his withdrawal only seemed to increase the mystique surrounding him. Controversy also contributed, as with a headline-grabbing trial that brought him before a Chicago jury on charges of obscenity in November 1963. After a complaint by Chicago Citizens for Decent Literature, a Catholic group first offended by his stalwart defense of Lenny Bruce after his recent arrest for obscenity, Chicago police had arrested Hefner for a *Playboy* pictorial on Jayne Mansfield. Widely covered by newspapers, radio, and television and packed with spectators, the proceedings in the Chicago Municipal Court became a circus. A *Playboy* press agent handed out copies of "The Playboy Philosophy." The consultation room for Hefner and his attorney displayed a full-color picture of the pope. Prosecution experts testified that the Mansfield pictorial inflamed the sexual appetite, while Hefner's attorney countered with a discussion of Benjamin Franklin's "Letters to Young Men on Choosing a Mistress" and termed him "a playboy of 1776." Hefner, accompanied by a beautiful Playmate, testified that only 5 percent of the material in his magazine was devoted to nude or seminude women. After a hung jury refused to condemn the publisher, the prosecution was dropped and Hefner emerged from the trial with an enhanced image as a defender of free speech.[39]

Hefner's love life in the early 1960s fed the public's fascination. The *Playboy* publisher pushed the erotic pedal to the floor, observing, "I remember quite clearly the first time I realized that I had slept with a different girl every night the previous week. Wild, crazy, wonderful. . . . At long last, I had managed to find my Jazz Age, the Roaring Twenties of my dreams." The mansion became "a bachelor's paradise" for the fulfillment of his fantasies and, in his words, "I couldn't have been more pleased with myself if I had discovered fire or invented the wheel."[40]

Hefner had dozens of casual sexual liaisons with Playmates. During the shooting of the "Playmate Holiday House Party" for the December 1961 issue, he was involved with eleven of the twelve participating Playmates, according to Joni Mattis. Hefner gloried in his Don Juan image, noting that "reputation actually made you more attractive to women." A notorious fling came with Donna Michele, a sultry eighteen-year-old ballet dancer and actress who became Playmate of the Year in 1963. She accompanied Hefner to the Mansfield obscenity trial—she sulked when the Kennedy assassination interrupted Chicago nightlife and preempted television—and then to Jamaica for a week's vacation in early 1964, but soon departed to pursue a movie career.[41]

Throughout this period, however, Hefner steadily dated two young women. Cynthia Maddox served as his regular girlfriend from 1961 to 1963 and Mary Warren from 1963 to 1968. He became very close to both, and their relationships with the *Playboy* editor revealed much about his state of mind. Exhilarated by the atmosphere of sexual liberation and determined to dominate his romances, Hefner molded these young women into the larger pattern of his life and work.

Cynthia Maddox had begun working at *Playboy* in 1959 as a receptionist, and slowly worked her way up to become an editor in the cartoon department. Strikingly beautiful, she was, in Hefner's words, "the blond, blue-eyed, pink-skinned beauty with the knockout body that you mooned over at your desk in high school." Maddox originally had caught the eye of Victor Lownes, who pursued her relentlessly. When he put his hand on her knee under a table at lunch, she would stare coldly, grab the hand, and slap it back on the tabletop. Hefner found Lownes's public humiliation hilarious.[42]

Hefner set his own sights on Maddox. He found her stern resistance to Lownes admirable, and relished a challenge in the fact that she was "the company virgin. Everyone knew she was a virgin because she made such a point of it," he said. The two began dating and developed a starry-eyed romance. When Maddox finally decided to consummate the relationship, he arranged a trip to the West Coast and rented a bungalow at the Beverly Hills Hotel. Upon returning to Chicago, she moved into an apartment in the Playboy Mansion.[43]

The pair had a smooth working relationship. As assistant cartoon editor, Maddox worked side by side with Hefner for a long session each week and they "absolutely agreed about cartoons," in her words.

They spent weekends together as well as an evening or two a week, and she accompanied Hefner to New York for the Playboy Jazz Awards, and to Los Angeles for a visit with the artist Alberto Vargas and his wife. Maddox's beauty made her a natural for the magazine and she ended up as *Playboy* cover girl five times from 1962 to 1966.[44]

The couple shared many interests, watching old Nelson Eddy–Jeanette MacDonald movies from the 1930s and consulting on the purchase of modern paintings for the mansion. But Maddox had a strong streak of jealousy that made Hefner uncomfortable. At the opening of the New York Playboy Club in 1962, a pretty brunette followed the editor back to his room uninvited. He was politely trying to get rid of her when Maddox came in and, convinced he was fooling around, exploded in anger. "When Cynthia got mad she threw things," Hefner said. "She started with a book and was reaching for a lamp when the phone rang. . . . She locked herself in the bathroom for a time, before accepting my innocence and making up."[45]

Maddox adored Hefner's sweet and funny side and found mansion life tremendously exciting with its music and parties, celebrities and brilliant guests. It was "just like being a movie star," she told a journalist. At the same time, she increasingly felt trapped in her famous boyfriend's life. All their activities revolved around him and she complained that he dominated any discussions or disagreements that they had. "Sometimes, God, I don't feel like I have any identity of my own," she confessed in a newspaper interview. "I would like someone who really notices me, really can respect me, really can remember things about me—some man who thinks about me when I'm away from him."[46]

Maddox also grew increasingly disturbed over Hefner's dalliances with other women. "I've been dating Hef for about a year. He dates other girls and I don't like it. He knows that I don't like it," she complained in *The Most*. (She also created an indelible image of the ditzy blonde, telling the interviewer, "Discussions go on back and forth and we try to work things out very intelligubly . . . uh, intellijub . . ." as she stumbled over the word "intelligently." Laughing embarrassedly, she dropped her prop, retrieved it as the shoulder strap on her dress slipped down, and tried to recover with a breathy Marilyn Monroe–style "Hi!") She resented his double standard where he expected to date others while she remained faithful. In public she acted unconcerned, but "inside, it was killing me." Sometimes when the anger boiled up, she stomped on material he had laid out for the magazine.[47]

Finally, a frustrated Maddox engaged in several affairs of her own and the romance with Hefner began to cool by the summer of 1963. She also began to see a psychiatrist in hopes of recovering her self-regard. The two drifted apart, although they would reconnect amiably in later years. As Maddox said, "When I walked out, I was ready to leave and I didn't miss it."[48]

In late summer 1963, Hefner met Mary Warren, a tall, stately twenty-year-old with green eyes and a great figure. They were immediately attracted to each other, and after the publisher's fling with Donna Michele ended, they settled into a long relationship. Warren worked at the magazine as a receptionist, and then became a door Bunny at the Chicago Playboy Club. Like Maddox, she was a virgin when she met Hefner. Such innocence always attracted the publisher, who confessed that he became caught up in "the feeling that the girl could love you. Only you. And that it was all-encompassing."[49]

Warren possessed an uncommonly sweet temperament—a quiet, friendly, unspoiled quality—that struck many who met her. "There was something special about Mary," said Nat Lehrman. "She had no hard edges." This may have stemmed from her religious background. Her mother was appalled when she joined *Playboy*, predicting, "The next thing, you'll be sleeping in Hefner's round bed!"[50]

When Warren moved into the mansion, she utterly devoted herself to Hefner. Her dedication to him became legendary. "If home, work, TV, and the time of day are all geared to his needs, it is understandable that he would have a woman that molds her life to his," said Shel Silverstein. "Mary did that." She secluded herself in the mansion with him and appreciated the few occasions when they ventured out together: a long walk through the neighborhood in the rain, a jaunt to the Old Town Art Festival, an evening at a nightclub, and a skiing trip to Aspen. Hefner appreciated her dedication, describing her as "one of the sweetest, most devoted women I've ever known."[51]

But Warren's devotion came at a price. Beset by insecurities, she floundered in establishing a sense of self-worth amid the constant attention focused on Hefner. A 1965 story in *Life* magazine described her sitting in his bedroom performing perfunctory tasks as she waited for him to break from work. "I wouldn't think of interrupting Hefner," she said. "I would never have anything that important to say." When asked if she was happy in her life with the publisher, she replied dutifully, "I regard it as an honor, a pleasure, and a wonderful experience." Perhaps as a reflection of her uncertain identity, Warren changed her hair color many times—from blonde to chestnut to brunette—during her years as Hefner's girlfriend.[52]

Despite her best efforts, Warren also had trouble accepting her boyfriend's womanizing. Sally Bealls, Hefner's administrative assistant, took Warren under her wing and often heard the young woman pour her heart out about her desire to settle down with Hefner, who regularly saw other women. Bealls tried to joke that the publisher was merely "doing research," but Warren found little consolation in the humor. Hefner, with his usual honesty, did not try to hide the situation. "Right now, my special girl is Mary. It has lasted three and a half years," he told *Look* magazine in 1965. "But in the meantime, I have had many less important relationships." In fact, he reveled in his many sexual liaisons. Growing restless around the holidays in late 1964, he turned elsewhere for female attention. "There was a delicious decadence in spending Christmas day in bed with three girls," he reported.[53]

Warren's desire for marriage and family found a temporary surrogate with Humphrey, a lovable St. Bernard puppy she and Hefner adopted and named after his favorite actor, Humphrey Bogart. She hosted a mansion party for the newborn pup in July 1964. A 1965 magazine story painted a rather sad picture of her keeping the puppy in a playpen in the master bedroom, addressing him as "Baby" and Hefner as "Daddy" and herself as "Mommy." While Hefner worked on his bed, Warren tried not to disturb him while cuddling and playing with Humphrey.[54]

Slowly, Warren assumed a quiet air of sadness. While photographs appeared to show a happy, beautiful young woman on her famous boyfriend's arm, a closer look revealed hollow smiles and melancholy eyes. A series of cards and notes to Hefner offered glimpses of her insecurity and resignation. One said, "In this modern world of blasé sophistication, it's certainly a relief to know someone like you, who derives pleasure from the simpler things in life. Like me! Love, Mary." A 1964 birthday card contained a poem in her handwriting: "Although I nag you so very much—Please don't evict me from your rabbit hutch! Love, Mary." A late 1965 card contained this mournful note: "My heart is blue,'cause I don't know if you love me like I love you. Love, Mary."[55]

In the fall of 1965, Warren moved out of the mansion. Living in an apartment less than a block away, she continued to date him for more than two years as they went to mansion parties, opened Playboy Clubs, and occasionally went skiing. In 1967 she quit *Playboy* to become executive secretary for a medical researcher at Michael Reese Hospital as the relationship wound down. In July 1968, Warren sent a final, bittersweet anniversary card to Hefner. The front said, "As long as we've got each other . . ." and then opened to read, "Who needs happiness. Love forever, Mary."[56]

Hefner's romantic life in the early 1960s displayed what would become a lifelong pattern. He maintained a primary relationship with a young woman over several years, all the while seeing other comely females on a regular basis. In love with love but determined to avoid commitment, he openly, honestly adhered to a double standard: he could date others but his girlfriends could not. Like the social concerns appearing in his magazine, Hefner's love life defied the norms of respectable middle-class America as he created a lifestyle tailored to his own desires. Yet, as Tom Wolfe pointed out, many average Americans also were seeking fulfillment by challenging traditional restrictions on the pursuit of happiness. Once again, it seemed, the publisher had positioned himself at the cutting edge of social change.

But the unruly spirit that energized Hefner, *Playboy*, and American society in the early 1960s would soon appear tame. The brisk winds of dissent in that period within a short time would build into a hurricane of rebellion that threatened to tear apart the social and political fabric of the United States. Like many Americans, Hefner would find himself caught up in an upheaval dwarfing anything he could have imagined. With typical shrewdness, he maneuvered himself and his magazine right into the heart of the storm.

11

Make Love, Not War

In the summer of 1966, Hugh Hefner returned to the United States
flush with excitement. Journeying to England for the opening of
the London Playboy Club and Casino, he had been galvanized
by the creative energy pulsating throughout the city. In fact, "Swinging
London" had captured much of the world's imagination as the center
of a popular culture renaissance in the mid-1960s featuring the pop
music of the Beatles, the daring "mod" fashions of Mary Quant, the
films of Tony Richardson, the acting of Terence Stamp, the photography of David Bailey, the experimental theater of John Osborne,
and the hairstylings of Vidal Sassoon. Permeating the atmosphere
was a spirit of liberated sexuality. "London today is in many ways
the cheerful, violent, lusty town of William Shakespeare," wrote *Time*
magazine. Hefner believed that the city's spirit of cultural ferment
soon would appear in the United States.[1]

Little did he know. Even as his plane touched down in Chicago,
dissatisfaction with traditional values was building explosively. Dissent
over American military involvement in Vietnam was mushrooming,
the civil rights movement was becoming militant, and restless college
students were questioning the bureaucratic structures dominating

modern life. Even more broadly, growing numbers within an affluent middle class were turning rebellious in the name of personal freedom and fulfillment. Challenges to old-fashioned American values of self-control, piety, and respect for authority seemed to materialize on every front.

Mainstream media registered the social discontent. In a 1967 cover story titled "The Permissive Society," *Newsweek* explored America's growing agitation. Probing a zeitgeist in flux, the article noted that "old taboos are dead or dying" as American movies, novels, plays, music lyrics, and advertising were adopting wholesale a vocabulary of frank language and sexual images. An even larger collapse of restraint regarding obscenity, premarital sex, and nudity left many Americans bewildered and confused. "The shattering of taboos on language, fashion, and manners generally is part of a larger disintegration of moral consensus in America," *Newsweek* concluded. Hefner figured prominently in the story as a symbol of the new sexual openness, asking, "Why are laughter, anger or pity legitimate reactions [among adults], but not sexual excitement?"[2]

The journalist and historian Max Lerner ruminated similarly. In a 1967 newspaper column he argued that America had evolved from a "production society" into a "swinging pleasure society" marked by a plethora of consumer items and pulsating desires for personal freedom, fulfilling experiences, and "expressive lives." Lerner also cited Hefner, arguing that the publisher was trying "to provide a frame for a hedonic life—a frame of reasoned principle" in *Playboy*.[3]

Over the next few years, Hefner would figure even more prominently in a period of turbulence that stretched American society to the breaking point. As racial rioting, political pandemonium, massive civil disobedience, and bitter clashes over cultural values became common fare, he and his magazine stood at the center of the action. Indeed, the half decade from 1966 to 1971 marked the peak of the *Playboy* ascendancy. As the sexual revolution now exploded full force as part of a larger cultural upheaval, Hefner remained its most prominent advocate and symbol. At the same time, he moved to the left politically and became a spokesman for nuclear disarmament, racial reconciliation, personal liberation, and an enlarged welfare state.

But an internal tension characterized *Playboy's* new agenda of social and political activism. As some observers noted, Hefner's magazine maintained an uncomfortable conflict between its promotion of hedonism and material affluence—sports cars, fine wines, fashionable clothing, chic apartments, fancy stereos—and its espousal of a political ethos that attacked corporate profit-making, denounced "the establishment," and demanded uplift of the downtrodden. To certain of his allies on the left, Hefner increasingly seemed to be upholding with one hand the very system he was attacking with the other. He seemed to reflect, in the memorable phrase of Tom Wolfe, a species of 1960s "radical chic"—the glib embrace of political radicalism by social elites firmly ensconced within the system.[4]

But such tension would not bear fruit for some time. Meanwhile, the *Playboy* editor became what he had always dreamed of being—not only a full-fledged popular culture celebrity but a serious player in the shaping of modern American values. Heeded as never before, he emerged as the prince of 1960s hedonism.

I

Hefner's growing prominence appeared unmistakably on the cover of *Time* magazine on March 3, 1967. Under a diagonal yellow slash announcing "The Pursuit of Hedonism," a wooden sculpture by fashionable avant-garde artist Marisol rendered the publisher as an "All-American boy" in red, white, and blue on two blocks of wood. The feature story inside proved equally provocative, if less flattering.

While *Time* presented Hefner as "prophet of pop hedonism," it scarcely concealed its tone of contempt. The feature described him as an "impresario of spectator sex," a fanatic who spread "the gospel of pleasure with a dogged devotion that would do credit to any missionary," and a juvenile who appealed to "the undergraduate who wants to act like a sophisticate." Nonetheless, *Time* grudgingly concluded that he reflected something significant in modern life. *Playboy*'s popularity indicated that "the puritan ethic was dying, that pleasure and leisure were becoming positive and universally adored values in American society."[5]

Over the next few months Hefner seemed to be everywhere. He gave scores of newspaper and magazine interviews and appeared as a guest on *The Tonight Show* with Johnny Carson, *The Joey Bishop Show* on ABC, and the syndicated *Bill Dana Show*. NBC News gave him a starring role in its May 8, 1967, prime-time special *The Pursuit of Pleasure,* which examined the growing hunger for affluence, leisure, and self-gratification among ordinary Americans. The host, Sander Vanocur, described him as "the Chairman Mao of the sexual revolution, issuing maxims for moral guerrilla warfare," and characterized *Playboy* as "the McGuffey's reader of the sexually literate." Hefner sat alongside the noted conservative commentator William F. Buckley and the Harvard theologian Harvey Cox, in the library of the Playboy Mansion. Puffing on his trademark pipe, he insisted that the old religious basis of morality had faded and a new foundation was required. Quick on his rhetorical feet, he held his own with these intellectual heavyweights.[6]

Meanwhile, Hefner's enterprise flourished. By 1968 the magazine's circulation stood at five and a half million, its clubs and merchandising operations were flourishing, and plans were afoot for a new syndicated television show. Statistics revealed that from 1963 to 1969, the company's yearly sales rose from $26 million to $96 million as *Playboy* remained at the center of what *Newsday* called a "budding real estate, publishing, entertainment conglomerate." Arbiters of American business sat up and took notice as *Business Week, Generation: The Magazine of Young Businessmen,* and *Barron's* all ran flattering stories on the dramatic growth of the Playboy empire.[7]

Hefner displayed his growing wealth and influence in two highly publicized moves. First, in the spring of 1967, after a lengthy renovation, *Playboy* occupied its chic new headquarters in the recently christened Playboy Building. Second, in the summer of 1967 Hefner ordered a personal Douglas DC9 jetliner for $4.5 million. Dubbed the Big Bunny, it was painted black because "it epitomized elegance, the kind of elegance once associated with a limousine," in Hefner's words—and had the magazine's bunny logo emblazoned in white on the tail. He spent an additional $1 million on remodeling that brought large, cushioned seats that transformed into sleeping berths, a videotape system and retractable screen, television monitors, a discotheque and bar, conference areas separated by fiberglass partitions, and a galley capable of preparing an eight-course meal for thirty diners. Its interior decoration utilized hand-rubbed rosewood, black leather, and oiled bronze. Hefner's private quarters in the rear of the plane housed a six-by-eight-foot elliptical bed complete with special seat belts and a Tasmanian opossum spread, a stereo and videotape system, a motorized swivel chair, and a shower with two nozzles.

A crew of eight "jet bunnies" dressed in black miniskirted uniforms with knee-high boots served as stewardesses. This extravagant "*Playboy* pad with wings," as *Look* magazine described it, quickly became the supreme symbol of Hefner's pleasure-filled lifestyle.[8]

As Hefner and his enterprise flourished, *Playboy* expanded its reach. The magazine continued to serve up healthy portions of erotic pictorials, ranging from nude photographs of Jane Fonda on the set of a French film to "The Bunnies of Missouri." On the literary front, a growing crowd of notable writers flocked to the magazine. From 1966 to 1970, Jean-Paul Sartre, Isaac Bashevis Singer, Saul Bellow, Kurt Vonnegut Jr., John Updike, Graham Greene, and Joyce Carol Oates contributed stories and essays.[9]

The *Playboy* "pleasure-primer" of stylish consumption expanded in accordance with the rapid growth of a consumer economy in the 1960s. Features explored topics such as the merits of various small aircraft available to the busy entrepreneur, the building of a modern business wardrobe, and the rewards of continental travel. The magazine continued to survey the entertainment world of music, movies, and comedy, frequently turning to high-profile celebrities such as Federico Fellini, Bob Dylan, Woody Allen, Michelangelo Antonioni, and Stanley Kubrick for "Playboy Interviews."[10]

Most significantly, however, *Playboy* threw itself wholeheartedly into politics. The first tentative forays in the early 1960s now became a full-scale charge into a public arena grown volatile by mid-decade. Racial tensions exploded with African American rioting in America's cities during the "long hot summers," which in turn generated a strong white backlash. American involvement in the Vietnam conflict triggered the first waves of antiwar protests. A more generalized discontent with prevailing social and economic power structures swept through college campuses. Hefner's magazine responded by becoming a standard-bearer for liberal causes.

In 1966, James Farmer, the black leader of the Congress of Racial Equality, praised the transformation of the civil rights crusade into "a full-fledged revolutionary movement." *Playboy*'s panel discussion on "The Crisis in Law Enforcement" pondered the rise in crime, growing conservative animosity toward "bleeding heart" judges, and liberal fears about the expansion of government police powers. Max Lerner offered a long, carefully reasoned essay advocating admission of communist China into the United Nations.[11]

The following year, *Playboy* examined the growing wave of protests in the United States and concluded that "dissent is an obligation that everyone opposed to the status quo owes himself and society." It analyzed domestic disturbances and suggested that an American proclivity for violence stemmed from poverty, excessive repression, and a boundless individualism. A critique of police policies and practices informed readers that "despite new Supreme Court safeguards of our civil rights and liberties, police brutality prevails and the police mentality assumes guilt until proven innocent."[12]

Playboy Interviews became particularly political. A 1966 session with the historian and political adviser Arthur Schlesinger Jr. explored his views on America's Vietnam involvement, domestic policies, and the civil rights movement. An interview with Fidel Castro focused on America's rift with Cuba and larger ideological issues at work in the Cold War. Meanwhile, the magazine's cultural commentary began to highlight the growing assault on American middle-class values. An extensive discussion with the drug guru Timothy Leary focused on LSD, psychedelics, and legal restrictions on their use. A long analysis of the "underground press" surveyed the "always uninhibited, often outrageous, sometimes unintelligible anti-establishment newspapers" that had sprung up as venues for dissent.[13]

In December 1967, *Playboy* showcased its expanded profile. The issue—some 320 pages long with a psychedelic cover of wavy, distorted lettering set against a bright background of purple, bright green, and orange—seemed to take in everything going on in contemporary America. Readers encountered erotic pleasures ranging from the monthly Playmate, Lynn Winchell, to "Art Nouveau Erotica" and "The Wicked Dreams of Elke Sommer"; stories by Isaac Bashevis Singer, P. G. Wodehouse, and Irwin Shaw; celebrity features on television host Johnny Carson and actor Walter Matthau; sophisticated consumer pieces on traveling to the Winter Olympics in Grenoble, France, and shopping for the latest high-tech gifts and gadgets for Christmas. They also found a range of political pieces. One related how a dean at Harvard left to become director of freshman studies at Miles College, a small, unaccredited Negro college near Birmingham, Alabama. John Kenneth Galbraith presented a proposal for extracting America from Vietnam, while Justice William O. Douglas examined "Big Brother" governmental intrusions into Americans' private lives.[14]

Playboy's final 1967 issue captured the sensibility of that era—politically engaged, yet optimistic, inclusive, and high on the "peace and love" possibilities of a new age. Much like the Summer of Love in 1967 and the March on the Pentagon, it reflected a widespread attitude of hope that reasonable, open-minded people of goodwill could work to resolve pressing problems. But this optimistic tone would not last, either in America or in *Playboy*. Within a few weeks, the country seemed to explode.

II

Shortly after midnight on August 27, 1968, Hefner, Max Lerner, Jules Feiffer, John Dante, and Bobbie Arnstein ventured out of the Playboy Mansion and walked toward Lincoln Park. They wanted to observe firsthand the battleground occupied by police and protestors as the Democratic National Convention convened in Chicago. Violent clashes had erupted as thousands of antiwar protesters had converged on the city and the police had responded with beatings and mass arrests. Film accounts of the bloody confrontations had dominated national network news and the pungent smell of tear gas had wafted through large areas of the central urban area. Hefner, increasingly political, had been absorbed in the growing controversy.[15]

In fact, some dissidents in the Democratic Party had made the Playboy Mansion their unofficial headquarters for the convention. A few days before it convened, Hefner had cosponsored (along with John Kenneth Galbraith and George Plimpton) a black-tie, $100 per ticket fund-raiser at his home for the insurgent peace candidate, Senator Eugene McCarthy. Subsequently, he hosted what the *New York Times* described as a "week-long party for the beautiful people" of the Democratic Party. Liberal activists such as Cleveland mayor Carl Stokes, Boston mayor Kevin White, civil rights leader Jesse Jackson, California industrialist Ed Pauley Jr., and actor Warren Beatty frequented the mansion, shaping strategy and enjoying the hospitality.

But now the seriousness of the situation confronted Hefner directly. As his little group glimpsed a large crowd of demonstrators approaching with an escort of angry police, they sensed danger and headed back to the mansion. Just then, a police car pulled up and several officers jumped out, pointing shotguns and yelling at them to go home. When Hefner explained that was precisely what they were trying to do, an officer whacked him across the buttocks with a billy club, causing a large bruise to form. When news of the incident appeared, one wag suggested that the police had seen a pajama-clad figure and mistook him for a Viet Cong, but Hefner was not amused. He called a news conference at the mansion to denounce unprovoked police brutality. "The squad car almost ran us down. We saw an uptight establishment. Goading people, looking for something to attack," he described. Hefner vowed to become more politically involved in light of his experience. "Last night I saw so-called law and order, without any consideration for justice or democracy," he said. "That doesn't separate us very far from totalitarian society."[16]

Hefner's experience offered a snapshot of the divisions threatening to tear the United States apart at the end of the decade. The uproar in Chicago capped several months of domestic disruption in America probably unequaled since the Civil War a century earlier. Throughout America, youths were flocking to the standard of the counterculture with its ethos of "sex, drugs, and rock 'n' roll." The Tet Offensive by communist forces in Vietnam revealed a military stalemate and triggered massive antiwar demonstrations and campus revolts. The dominant Democratic Party splintered under the pressure as challenges from two peace candidates, Senators Eugene McCarthy and Robert F. Kennedy, caused President Lyndon B. Johnson to announce his withdrawal from the race. Meanwhile, a powerful conservative backlash developed as Republican Richard M. Nixon gained support for his "law and order" campaign and Alabama governor George Wallace, a third-party candidate, promised an even stronger crackdown on civil rights and antiwar agitators. By early summer 1968, anger, despair, and rioting swept through the country in the wake of the stunning assassinations of Martin Luther King Jr. and Robert Kennedy, which occurred within a few weeks of each other. The country stood polarized between radical advocates of change and staunch defenders of authority and stability, while many in the middle remained confused, resentful, and frightened.[17]

In this atmosphere of public turmoil, Hefner clearly positioned himself as a voice of left-liberal dissent. His critique of American authority, of course, began with the sexual revolution and its potential for creating a new, liberated world of personal happiness.

Birth control had separated sex from reproduction and allowed it to be "considered as purely pleasurable," he argued, and people were finally overcoming their tendency "to make something hidden and presumably evil out of the human body."[18]

But sexual revolution was only part of a larger movement aimed at dismantling barriers to personal fulfillment and promoting human liberation, he continued. As he told the *Saturday Evening Post,* "Exactly the same things that are causing the sexual revolution in this country are also causing the civil rights revolution and the dissent on Vietnam and the student protests." Sexual freedom was one aspect of a broader crusade linking "racial freedom, social freedom, political freedom, liberality." The common enemy was an insidious, repressive, outdated Puritanism and at stake was American self-government. The question of forbidding erotic material for private enjoyment, he claimed in 1969, went to a larger question of "whether you want a democracy or some form of authoritarian society that is predicated on the premise that man is weak and can't rule himself politically, can't rule himself socially, can't rule himself sexually."[19]

As Hefner veered left politically in the late 1960s, he condemned America's anticommunist foreign policy, denounced its involvement in the Vietnam War, and advocated United Nations control of its nuclear arsenal. He endorsed the use of recreational drugs such as marijuana and LSD, maintaining that in a democratic society "you must be free to make your own decisions in terms of control over your own mind and body." In 1969, in a long series of interviews with the writer Malcolm Boyd, he stressed his political commitment to individual rights, a "more socialized capitalism" with government regulations on a market economy, and the necessity of world government. He also expressed sympathy for youthful dissent, asserting that "there are far more men of goodwill under twenty-five than over."[20]

Hefner summarized his political credo in a few brief maxims: "International law instead of warfare to control the possibility of nuclear holocaust. An end to racism. An end to poverty around the world. [To] the population explosion. [To] the pollution of our natural resources. Then, all that remains is disease. If we spent our money on these things instead of war, by the year 2000 we could be moving into a real golden age." As he reminisced later about this period, "I yearned for a world without boundaries in which men of varying political, ethnic, and religious persuasions lived together in a free and just society. That was the sort of idealistic bleeding-heart liberal I was."[21]

The late 1960s version of *Playboy* mirrored both the heightened political sensibility of its founder and the confrontational mood growing in the United States. From 1968 to 1970 the magazine launched a barrage of social criticism aimed at undermining bourgeois virtues and Cold War values. This campaign materialized on several fronts.

The magazine endorsed a cultural politics of full-blown sexual liberation, offering sympathetic portrayals of "The Sexual Freedom League" and partner-swapping "swingers." It surveyed college campuses with an eye to discovering whether schools stood "in the vanguard or on the sidelines regarding the abolition of restrictions on life, liberty, and the pursuit of heterosexual happiness?" (The University of Wisconsin ranked first while Bob Jones University ranked last.) It presented in-depth interviews with medical researchers Drs. William Masters and Virginia Johnson, whose book *Human Sexual Response* unexpectedly had become a runaway best-seller, and Dr. Mary Calderone, the pioneering advocate of sex education.[22]

Playboy also closely examined the new sexual freedom in entertainment. A long look at the avant-garde "theater of the nude" analyzed recent productions such as *Hair, Dionysus in 69,* and *Futz!* and concluded that "eclipsing even Hollywood, the New York stage is taking it off—taking it all off." The magazine presented a text-and-photo feature on *Oh! Calcutta!* a controversial off-Broadway nudist romp that "unabashedly satirizes—and celebrates—contemporary sexual mores, hang-ups, and diversions."[23]

Editorially, the magazine denounced censorship of erotic materials and advocated birth control and reform of divorce laws to allow for easier, less contentious breakups. It also appealed for a more sympathetic consideration of homosexuality, presenting letters from liberal clergymen in the Playboy Forum arguing that "a genuine Christian spirit demanded toleration and redemption, not moral condemnation." *Playboy* took the progressive position that a "sickness" formulation should be dropped in favor of the more scientific "deviance," and that homosexuals, since they followed "a compulsion based on phobic reaction to heterosexual stimuli," should be encouraged to seek therapeutic help.[24]

More broadly, *Playboy* advocated a hip cultural politics in the late 1960s that favored the abandonment of traditional restraints in favor of personal freedom. Its fashion advice urged young men to embrace a new sartorial freedom by abandoning coats and ties for Nehru jackets, chains and pendants, and "leisure suits." As one piece put it, fashionable males should be "more involved in doing their own thing than in being caught up in any specific fashion trend."[25]

The magazine sympathetically portrayed the swelling drug culture as another venue for self-exploration. Articles explored the links between drugs and sexual ecstasy, advocated the decriminalization of marijuana, and urged the loosening of legal restrictions on drugs of all kinds. As a Playboy Panel on "The Drug Revolution" noted, drugs had moved to the forefront in "the war between freedom and repression, youth and age, powerlessness and power."[26]

Playboy became a bastion of left liberalism in its politics. It defended the growing wave of youthful dissent and acclaimed the recent student revolt. It denounced intrusive government power, called for the end of Cold War military actions such as Vietnam, and advocated a staunch environmentalism and expansion of social welfare programs. It sought to make Christianity a force for ending social ills as spokesmen such as Harvey Cox called for the resurrection of Jesus as "a joyous revolutionary" who would unlock "the radical potential in Christianity."[27]

Increasingly, *Playboy* enticed a distinguished list of liberal officeholders and public figures to appear in its pages. They included Senators J. William Fulbright, Jacob Javits, and Frank Church, who wrote on such issues as the need for gun control, lowering the voting age, and reconfiguring American foreign policy. Supreme Court justices William O. Douglas and Arthur J. Goldberg also contributed articles, the former on the increase in water pollution and the latter on the dangers posed to the Bill of Rights by advocates of law and order. Martin Luther King Jr., who visited the mansion in October 1967 to discuss public issues, published the last piece he ever wrote in the magazine.[28]

The Playboy Interviews became a friendly forum for many liberal activists. The list included war critic and draft counselor William Sloane Coffin, consumer advocate Ralph Nader, civil rights spokesman Jesse Jackson, and radical lawyer William Kunstler. The magazine even glamorized Marxist intellectuals such as Herbert Marcuse, described in a profile as a "septuagenarian superstar" who toured the college lecture circuit attracting hordes of adoring young acolytes.[29]

Even *Playboy's* monthly centerfolds periodically displayed a new political sensibility. "Turned On" Playmate Debbie Hooper campaigned for Senator Eugene McCarthy, dedicated herself to "helping her generation unwind our uptight society," and "grooves on sunshine, sculpture, and progressive politics." Playmate Gloria Root was a "full-time radical" who determinedly protested the Vietnam War while remaining "always on the move, always ready to challenge authority, and always eager to have a good time." Another Playmate, "Tuned-In Dropout" Elaine Morton, rejected "establishment modes of living" and dropped out of college to live in a converted milk truck along the west coast of Baja California.[30]

At decade's end, *Playboy* reached the height of its political activism. In 1969, it presented a tandem tribute to the recently assassinated Robert Kennedy and Martin Luther King Jr. that glorified their martyrdom to liberal causes. It also offered two long blueprints for social and political change—they were drawn up by a who's who of liberal public figures, including Theodore Sorensen, Mayor John Lindsay, William Sloane Coffin, Senator Charles Percy, César Chávez, Julian Bond, and Senator George McGovern—that aimed to solve problems of war, injustice, poverty, and pollution. In the fall of a 1970, "Playboy's Political Preference Chart" appeared for the fall elections, grading candidates in key races around the country based on the extent of their liberal views.[31]

Thus the late 1960s politics of Hefner and his magazine lobbed grenades into the camp of the political establishment and displayed a libertarian streak dedicated to protecting the individual against displays of governmental power, whether in the bedroom, the draft board, or on city streets. But for all its radical rhetoric, *Playboy's* politics were not revolutionary. While the magazine and its editor sought to enhance personal liberation and social justice, this agenda did not challenge America's basic social and economic system. In fact, as a number of critics pointed out, a certain tension emerged between Hefner's advocacy of sweeping social and political reform, on the one hand, and his espousal of hedonism, material affluence, and corporate success, on the other.[32]

The *Detroit Free Press*, for instance, contended that the *Playboy* scene appealed mainly to "Richard Nixon's silent majority." An academic article argued that *Playboy*, far from challenging the standing order, represented the very spirit of modern American capitalism.

In the same way that Benjamin Franklin's Protestant ethic of thrift and hard work had provided the productive drive for an infant capitalism in the late 1700s, Hefner's "ethics of consumption" set the foundation for a mature capitalism. Franklin's "productive industry" had given way to Hefner's "strenuous leisure" in the evolution of the American socioeconomic system.[33]

Some youthful radicals were less polite. Upon hearing that his teacher was writing an article on Hefner, a Yale student launched a profanity-laden denunciation of the publisher as the enemy. "Jesus, he's so materialistic. *Playboy* glorifies everything that is lousiest about America," said the young activist. "Those hairless, frozen blondes—made up to look like the girl next door, and photographed in a phony, out of focus way. And those goddamn conformist ads. Everybody is sort of supernigger, with his unbelievable chick, his goddamn expensive car, his shitty correct suit and shaving lotion and pad. Christ." Another young radical told a radio interviewer, "*Playboy* today is practically the voice of the establishment. Young guys today are interested in more than cars and hi-fi sets and carefully posed pictures of balloon-bosomed bunnies."[34]

Such tensions produced a confrontation in the pages of the Playboy Forum. In 1969, a correspondent accused the magazine of hypocrisy, professing to be for liberal change and social progress while doing "everything you can to perpetuate the American upper-middle-class way of life." If genuine revolution ever came, he said, "the image of the good life you hold up to Americans will be the first thing to go." *Playboy* replied angrily. It accused the reader of not only seeking a future inhabited by gray-uniformed monks, but failing to grasp the magazine's position. "While the luxuries we portray may today be enjoyed only by a fraction of the world's peoples, we do not think true social progress consists of sweeping those luxuries away but, rather, in extending them to all (a possibility technology is making both feasible and desirable)," it indignantly noted. "We see the good life and social progress as vitally connected."[35]

This critique of *Playboy*'s faux radicalism found some confirmation in the magazine itself. Throughout the late 1960s, it uneasily juxtaposed its anti-establishment rhetoric with a celebration of consumer abundance. César Chávez, Jesse Jackson, and Tom Hayden, railing against the oppressions of the system, appeared alongside J. Paul Getty, the billionaire businessman who tutored readers on success in the corporate world. Such tension produced awkward moments. The November 1970 issue, for instance, positioned "West of Eden," a sympathetic account of hippie communes (they were seeking "new ways to live humanely with nature and one another") immediately next to "Presents Perfect," a slick survey of the newest amenities available to prosperous consumers. Accented by young women with scant clothes and sultry stares, the glossily photographed bounty of goods included a "three-screen TV, by Sony, for $695"; a "Volante 3000 transistorized polystyrene wall clock, from Design Group, $40"; and an "eleven-channel mobile phone featuring compact transmitter-receiver and easily mounted handset, by Symetrics, $1645." Questions of how communes and Cuisinarts, César Chávez and J. Paul Getty could be reconciled remained unanswered.[36]

Hefner grew sensitive to such criticism. When pressed on his simultaneous belief in affluence and radical politics, he replied, "I've showed that it's possible to be a liberal and anti-establishment and still be very successful." Moreover, he insisted, youthful dissenters erred in adopting "an anti-materialist mood." "Many of them resent *Playboy* because it espouses the virtues of materialism. The real problem is how to get the benefits of materialism to the most people possible." He insisted that "materialism isn't—and shouldn't be—a dirty word," and provided no barrier to developing a "strong social conscience." Hefner tried to steer a careful course between the old and the new: "*Playboy* has the establishment status symbols yet we are iconoclastic and anti-establishment in our questioning of the old mores."[37]

In another sense, however, the tension between Hefner's defense of material abundance and his political attack on the establishment was less than his critics imagined. For much 1960s radicalism, in fact, was less radical than it appeared. As Christopher Lasch observed, this movement tended to view politics as street theater, a public performance that valued style over substance and adopted "dramatic gestures," media manipulation, and "self-promotion." Significantly, most young radicals of this era were themselves the children of postwar affluence whose commitment to self-gratification equaled that of the establishment they attacked. The radical slogan "the personal is the political" revealed a focus on consciousness-raising that, much like the modern consumer capitalism it opposed, sought a goal of self-fulfillment. Also like their opponents, dissenters rejected such outmoded traditions as self-denial, duty, sacrifice to the common good, and higher loyalties, all of which faded before the pressing demands of personal transformation. Thus it was no accident that Jerry Rubin, radical hero as one of the "Chicago Seven," followed an easy path from radical politics to a series of therapies in the 1970s (Est, Rolfing, Gestalt, Esalen, meditation) to, finally, Madison Avenue as a marketing analyst and venture capitalist. In other words, the profound personalism of 1960s radicalism, almost as much as the capitalist structure it denounced, reflected the modern historical shift from a society of scarcity and self-control to one of abundance, leisure, and self-fulfillment.[38]

This same overarching desire for self-fulfillment clearly fueled much of the late 1960s politics of Hefner and his magazine. In 1969, he argued that Americans no longer gained identity through work but through avocation and recreation. Thus the most pressing modern issue was to "get beyond the guilt that goes with pleasure" and forge happiness based on play and satisfying desires. "Our basic thing is about how to enjoy your leisure," Hefner explained of the *Playboy* ethos. Harvey Cox praised countercultural dissenters for rejecting outdated notions of "work as the sole means of achieving human fulfillment" in favor of "devising a new leisure life style." At the end of the 1960s, in an article titled "Leisure in the Seventies," *Playboy* highlighted its commitment to self-fulfillment. Events of the last decade, it contended, had revealed a profound struggle to adapt to a new world where technology had created "more leisure time for almost all of us—a prospect that frightens as many as it pleases." This demanded new strategies for "using our new time more creatively, adopting personal pursuits that will become as much a part of our identities as our jobs." Ultimately, *Playboy* reassured, "the potential pitfalls of the new leisure are outweighed by the promise of self-exploration and discovery."[39]

So in many ways Hefner stood as a fitting symbol of 1960s rebellion, although in ways neither he nor his critics ever fully understood. Whether in politics or culture, the antagonists of this contentious era—political radicals *and* aspiring executives, seekers of emotional experience *and* seekers of material wealth, both the establishment and its critics—endorsed the deeper claims of the self. In a modern American culture where the demands of self-realization infused everything, notions of commitments above and beyond personal need failed to register. As *Playboy*'s editor recognized perhaps better than anyone, quenching inner desires comprised the logic of modern American life. This powerful, expanding impulse of self-fulfillment animated not only Hefner's politics in this age of rebellion, but his private life as well.

III

In some sense, the personal always had been the political for Hefner. He had lived out his private rebellion against middle-class mores since founding *Playboy* in 1953, personifying the pleasures of sex and materialism that he believed had been stifled by a heritage of Puritanism. American culture seemed to catch up with him by the mid-1960s as middle-aged suburbanites reveled in consumerism and relaxed sexual standards while youthful rebels threw restraint to the winds and rejected most forms of authority. The Hefner Doctrine of hedonism with a social conscience went mainstream, and the publisher's private life reflected the search for self-fulfillment under way in the permissive atmosphere of late 1960s America.

But the problem of Hefner's legendary reclusiveness lingered. Abundant publicity had informed the public about his isolation in the mansion for months, if not years, at a time. Wired on dexies and addicted to work as much as revelry, given to terrible eating habits and scrupulously avoiding sunshine and exercise, Hefner had become dangerously underweight and his teeth had begun bothering him from massive, daily sugar doses in soft drinks. Nothing better illustrated this peculiar exile than his comical initial visit to the new Playboy Building. "The first time was in the middle of the night when it was raining. I was out walking," he ruefully told an interviewer. "We'd laid out millions and I hadn't yet wandered over, even though it's only a few blocks from the Mansion. It turned out the guard didn't know who I was—but he finally let me in."[40]

By early 1967, at age forty-two, pale and weighing a gaunt 135 pounds, Hefner was ready for a change. His 1966 trip to London, and his observation of a new liberationist ethic sweeping through America shortly thereafter, had inspired him to consider a change of habit. "When a fellow moves into his forties, it's time he takes stock of his life, undergoes a reevaluation, and perhaps revamps things a bit," he told the *Chicago Tribune*. As he admitted to *Time*, "I finally woke up to the fact that I had the world by the tail, and if I wanted to enjoy it, I'd better start taking care of myself."[41]

He decided to act. In one of those bold transformations by which he periodically altered his life, Hefner reinvented himself. He began to sleep regularly and eat a healthier diet. Giving up amphetamines, he embarked upon a moderate exercise routine—mostly on a slant board and stationary bicycle—and gradually added thirty pounds to his frame. "It's part of a new image called living longer," Hefner told one magazine. Affected by the new sense of freedom sweeping through men's fashions, he also purchased a new wardrobe. Abandoning the white shirts, restrained ties, and trim, dark-colored business suits from earlier days, he hired a tailor and spent $10,000 on a new Edwardian wardrobe of wide-lapeled, double-breasted suits, colorful shirts, flashy ties, and leather overcoats, as well as Nehru jackets and pendants.[42]

He also decided to delegate more editorial responsibility at the magazine to subordinates. As *Playboy* had expanded, the tasks involved with overseeing its publication had grown enormously and Hefner's burden became backbreaking. He began turning over more responsibilities to Art Director Art Paul, Photo Director Vince Tajiri, and Editorial Director A. C. Spectorsky and his young associate editors. Hefner explained his decision in terms of confronting Frankenstein: "I found that I had built this marvelous machine, but far from being master of that machine, the machine was ruling me."[43]

Thus Hefner, both physically and psychologically, left the cocoon of the mansion and ventured out into the vibrant, experimental atmosphere of the late 1960s. His own, personal sexual revolution became central to this new engagement with the world. He had continued to have sex with a variety of Playmates and Bunnies throughout the mid-1960s, but now his encounters proliferated. He enjoyed flings with "Personal Playmates" such as Cynthia Myers, Jill Tewksbury, Gale Olson, and Carol Imhoff. He even had a brief affair with one of his daughter's teenage friends in late 1968. "When my more reclusive Mansion years ended, they ended with a bang," he recalled later. "The number of my new sexual partners increased ten-fold that year [1968]—from 4 to 40—as I enthusiastically participated in the pleasures to be had in this sensual society."[44]

In July 1968, while visiting Los Angeles, Hefner participated in what he called a "Hollywood orgy that Cecil B. Demille would be proud of." About seventy Hollywood swingers came to his apartment on Sunset Boulevard in an atmosphere resonating with sexual adventurism. The result startled even Hefner:

> The scene that night is not easy to describe. It began as a very conventional cocktail party, but before long couples had started fondling one another, pulling off their clothes, making out on the couches, on the floor, in the living room, bedroom, and bath. Couples turned into threesomes, foursomes, moresomes—combinations that boggle the imagination. . . . I'm right there in the middle of it all.

The next evening, a few friends came over to discuss the events of the previous night. Suddenly, a strange couple came in, ordered drinks, and began making out on the couch on the other side of the room. "They'd been invited to the orgy, but got the date wrong," Hefner discovered.[45]

Meanwhile, at the mansion, a vibrant new social scene flowered. Large, boisterous parties had continued throughout the 1960s, of course, but now they were invigorated by a new atmosphere of liberation as well as Hefner's actual participation. A long list of celebrities from every walk of life frequented the festivities. On any given night, one might encounter Bishop Pike and David Susskind, astronaut Scott Carpenter and Mort Sahl, jockey Billy Hartog and Johnny Carson, Woody Allen and Alistair Cooke, Danny Kaye and Vic Damone, Michael Caine and Mel Tormé, Wilt Chamberlain and Steve McQueen, or dozens of others.[46]

A high point in the new mansion social environment came on February 23, 1968, when Hefner hosted "The Happening," a grand gathering devoted to the new psychedelic age. Dozens of guests arrived dressed in the latest groovy garb—miniskirts, Nehru jackets, fringed leather jackets, flowered shirts, love beads—and playfully waved signs saying "Love," "Charlie Brown for President," "Flower Power," and "War Is Bad for Children and Other Living Things." As rock music from a live band blared through the house, dancers and spectators alike were blanketed with a swirling, throbbing light show.

Playmates adorned with body paint roamed through the crowd, as did a robed guru. Behind a large buffet table groaning with food sat a sign reading "Psychedelicatessen."[47]

A coterie of male companions invigorated Hefner's active new life. The group included old friends Shel Silverstein, the cartoonist, author, and songwriter; John Dante, former club owner and now *Playboy* employee; plus Bill Cosby, the comedian and actor starring in the television hit *I Spy*. The quartet spent much time hanging out at the mansion, talking and joking, pursuing women, and playing games into the early morning hours. They also ventured up to Playboy's new Wisconsin resort at Lake Geneva, which opened in May 1968. This facility had been created as part of the company's synergistic plan, aimed at the leisure needs of "affluent pleasure seekers" with its fine restaurants and bars, stage shows, shops, game rooms, twenty-five-acre lake, tennis courts, ski runs, and golf course. Hef and his three buddies loved to fly up to the resort, catch a show, and throw a party for the Bunnies and performers.[48]

Hefner's reemergence into the world also inspired a new television project, *Playboy After Dark*. Shot at CBS studios in Los Angeles and syndicated nationally, the show started taping in the summer of 1968. Hefner had been inspired to reenter television as part of his personal makeover. "The whole thing represented a change in lifestyle for me. For the last several years I have been, well, a sort of recluse," he told the *Los Angeles Times*. "Now I'll be spending every other week out here taping the show."[49]

Like his first television project a decade earlier, *Playboy After Dark* took the form of an apartment party hosted by Hefner. Presenting a variety of singers, comedians, dancers, and celebrities, it adopted a casual, personal tone and attempted, in Hefner's words, to "use the camera as a third person at our party." It offered an entertainment blend of old and new: comedians Jack E. Leonard and the Smothers Brothers, musicians Buddy Rich and the Grateful Dead, filmmakers Otto Preminger and Roman Polanski. Hefner was eager to display the current interest in sexual liberation. "The Playboy Philosophy advocating more permissive behavior in sex will be implicit in the show," he told *Variety*. "But we'll do it in good taste and with sophistication."[50]

Then Hefner fell in love. At the third taping of *Playboy After Dark* on August 7, 1968, he met an eighteen-year-old UCLA coed named

Barbara Klein, who was an extra. He was immediately struck by her schoolgirl looks—button nose, large dark eyes and long dark hair, dazzling smile, purple miniskirt. According to Lee Wolfberg, who later introduced them, when Hefner first spied her, it was "like a movie scene, across a crowded room, he sees her and lights up like a light bulb." When she danced frenetically to the music of the guest band, Iron Butterfly, "I almost fell out of my chair," Hefner recalled later. They shot another episode the next day, and he finally had a chance to talk with the young beauty. He invited her to join him and a few friends at a post-show jaunt through some Los Angeles discos, which prompted a legendary quip. Klein said, "I've never dated anyone over twenty-five." "That's okay," Hefner replied. "Neither have I."[51]

That night, after slow-dancing with Klein to Herb Alpert's hit song "This Guy's in Love with You," Hefner began to fall for her. Klein, on her part, found her suitor to be bright, funny, and charming, but was worried that "he was old enough to be my father." They had dinner the next several evenings, went dancing, and concluded their dates in dark corners of the clubs cuddling and smooching like teenage sweethearts. "All of a sudden, he didn't seem so old to me anymore," said the coed. Hefner admitted, "I hadn't felt like this since high school. I flew back to Chicago in a happy haze."[52]

Over the next several months, a smitten Hefner pursued Klein relentlessly during his trips to Los Angeles. At first, a Playboy limousine would pick her up at her dormitory, but as other students began to buzz about the situation she decided to drive her own car to meet the publisher. Klein became a regular on *Playboy After Dark*, increasingly appearing on camera at Hefner's side, and between segments they would sit and hold hands. "It was very exciting for both of us. I remember when he sent flowers to the dormitory. He sent so many flowers that I was able to give one to every girl in the dormitory," she said. "It was all a new experience to be with somebody who knew how to handle women. He really does make a woman feel special."[53]

In September, Klein accepted Hefner's invitation to come to Chicago, staying at the mansion and accompanying him to the Lake Geneva resort. They spent much time kissing and petting but Klein refused to give up her virginity. For her that meant total commitment, and she was still unsure about the gap in age between them. Hefner grew intensely frustrated by the situation, but he was so smitten that patience triumphed over desire. He took the shocking step of meeting her parents in Sacramento, then flew with her to Aspen for a Christmas ski vacation, followed by a New Year's celebration in Las Vegas. The publisher's friends were amazed at his ardent yet restrained courtship. "He really romanced this lady," noted Cosby.[54]

This went on for months. Finally, on Valentine's Day in 1969, the two consummated their relationship on Hefner's round, rotating bed at the Chicago mansion. "The next thing I knew, we had done it, and I was in shock," Klein recalled. "I don't even remember how it was, I was so taken aback by the whole thing. I remember thinking at the time, well, at least we've got that out of the way." With her inhibitions finally overcome, Klein threw herself into the relationship and became the key figure in Hefner's life.[55]

She had an immediate impact on the publisher, inspiring a flurry of travel that shocked his friends and associates. In February they went to Acapulco with three other couples for a seaside vacation where Hefner went parachute-sailing high over the bay even though he couldn't swim a stroke and didn't like the water. They procured some marijuana from the locals, got delightfully high, and spent an evening giggling and gorging themselves on Kentucky Fried Chicken. The following month the couple traveled to Hawaii, followed by an early summer trip to Puerto Rico. When Klein got a starring role in a movie, *How Did a Nice Girl Like You Get into This Business,* Hefner accompanied her to Rome, Monte Carlo, Paris, and London for several weeks of filming. At the publisher's suggestion, she changed her name to Barbi Benton because it would look better on a theater marquee. At a press conference, Hefner even went public with his bliss: "I think I can say this is the first time I've ever been in love."[56]

At home, Hefner displayed a new zest for activity in the company of his girlfriend, especially in California. They spent the day at Disneyland, went bowling with Sonny and Cher, and even took up tennis. "We used to play at public courts because we didn't belong to a club," she explained. "We were about the same in terms of ability, which was beginners, but sometimes we'd get to the court and have to wait. . . . Can't you just see Hef waiting in line? It was fun; we held hands."[57]

Benton found the luxurious lifestyle to be an important part of the Hefner appeal. Having grown up as a doctor's daughter and accustomed to the finer things in life, she appreciated that the house wine at the Playboy Mansion was Château Lafite Rothschild. "I was *meant* to be a Jewish-American princess," she admitted. "That was a lifestyle a girl could get used to." She also slid into the *Playboy* orbit and was featured in a nine-page pictorial in 1970 titled "Barbi Doll." Originally reluctant to pose nude, she overcame her reservations because the magazine "upholds really good taste." Pursuing her career as a model, toying with the idea of becoming a singer, and enjoying the attentions of her famous boyfriend, Benton lived in the moment. "I really honestly thought I'd probably only stay with Hef as long as we were having fun," she said.[58]

Thus Hugh Hefner reached the height of happiness and influence in the late 1960s. More widely read than ever before, *Playboy* was shaping public opinion while his company was raking in tremendous profits. His celebrity status had reached the top tier as America caught up with, and celebrated, his advanced notions of pleasure-seeking through sexual liberation and consumer enjoyment. His unabashed liberal political crusading seemed to embody the spirit of this tumultuous age. Finally, and no less importantly, he seemed to have found the girl of his dreams.

But then Hefner, like the hero in a Greek tragedy warned of hubris, was blindsided and knocked from his pedestal at the point of his greatest triumph. Certain of his liberal allies grew troubled over an issue becoming increasingly explosive in the radicalizing world of late 1960s America. Many women had never been comfortable with *Playboy* and its depiction of females, and now they sharpened their weapons and went after its editor with a vengeance. Things would never be quite the same.

12

What Do Women Want?

At the end of the decade, 1960s social activism blew up in *Playboy*'s face. In February 1969, during a talk by Bruce Draper, the magazine's college promotion director, at Grinnell College in Iowa, a cadre of protestors burst into the gathering. To the astonishment of those present, about ten of the interlopers—mostly females but including a few men—completely disrobed as they shouted and waved signs reading "Liberated Women Are More Fun" and "Playmeat of the Month." Then they fanned out through the audience, handing out fliers reading "We protest *Playboy*'s images of lapdog female playthings and their junior-executive-on-the-way-up possessors." The protesters identified themselves as members of the Grinnell Women's Liberation Group and the Guerrilla Theater.[1]

This proved to be the opening salvo in a rapidly escalating war. At Antioch College in Ohio, protestors disrupted *Playboy* photographers who were there to take pictures of new men's fashions. About three hundred people chanted slogans, taunted the visitors, and took their clothes off to protest the magazine's "mindless flaunting of the female body." Even the Playboy Mansion became a target later that year. At a benefit party for the ACLU hosted by Hefner, Mrs. Wayne

Parsons, a member of the organization's board of directors in Illinois, expressed her disgust at *Playboy* by taping political flyers over valuable works of art hanging on the walls. As security men escorted her out, she shouted that Hefner's magazine "portrayed women as mere sexual objects."[2]

In such agitated fashion, a highly emotional and divisive dispute ensnared Hugh Hefner at the moment of his greatest success. Acolytes of the women's liberation movement, one of the freedom-seeking crusades emerging from the political ferment of the 1960s, put the publisher and his magazine in the ideological crosshairs and pulled the trigger. Hefner, they accused, was an exploiter of women. The publisher, who saw himself as a great emancipator, felt a profound sense of betrayal as a growing segment of the left began portraying him as an agent of oppression. The controversy escalated into full-scale conflict that occasionally waned but never disappeared. It would plague him for the rest of his career.

Up to this point, Hefner had been at the center of several great social transformations that remade post–World War II America: the sexual, consumer, and media revolutions. Now another great wave of social change—the movement for women's rights—threatened to engulf the *Playboy* ship and capsize it. But the issues proved to be as complicated as they were emotional. Hefner's and *Playboy's* attitude toward, and role in, the struggle for women's rights proved less salutary than the publisher would ever admit, but also less incriminating than his feminist critics claimed. The situation overwhelmed simplistic attacks and defenses and ultimately, as with just about everything else in his career, it focused on sex. Moreover, it involved an evolution of ideas and attitudes about women's role in society, as Hefner and his magazine changed from the 1950s to the 1970s. The same held true for the vast majority of Americans, and his story, like theirs, revealed much about a difficult sea change in modern social and cultural values.

I

In the 1950s, women were assigned a particularly important place in the structure of American society. After the enormous dislocations in personal life caused by the Great Depression and World War II, the postwar era repositioned women at the center of a revitalized domestic ideal. The traditional family reemerged with renewed vigor as women assumed positions as stewards of large, "baby boomer" families and domestic managers of increasingly affluent households. Awash in a consumer bonanza, urban and suburban families became hubs of what one historian has termed "domestic containment"— stable entities that cultivated sound values and nourished security as part of a larger ideological struggle. In the postwar definition of femininity, it became women's civic duty to sustain the family as a bulwark of the American Way of Life in the struggle with a hostile communist foe.[3]

But social and economic developments soon placed enormous new pressures on female domesticity. First, women entered the workforce in unprecedented numbers to help support America's growing consumer tastes, and by 1960 roughly 30 percent of American wives were laboring for wages. They faced inequalities in pay, however, and, if married, a growing burden from piling housework on top of an outside job. Second, young women attended college in growing numbers after World War II and the notion of careers outside the home took root. Third, as the Kinsey Report on *Sexual Behavior in the Human Female* made clear in 1953, restrictions on female sexuality appeared to be loosening in postwar society, a trend that accelerated rapidly with the introduction of the birth control pill in 1960. Finally, from within the confines of the idealized American home, a slow-simmering discontent began to emerge among many women who felt trapped by an endless round of childcare duties, PTA meetings, shopping, and housecleaning. Betty Friedan, in *The Feminine Mystique* (1963), famously described this sense of frustration as "the problem that has no name." In other words, many women ensconced in the American home were growing restless by the early 1960s.[4]

Playboy, of course, emerged precisely during this period. Over its first decade, from the early 1950s through the early 1960s, the magazine reflected both the dominant expectations and the growing discontent regarding women's position in postwar America. Hefner upheld certain long-standing attitudes about males and females, but he disrupted others. Partly by design, but largely by accident, he helped set the stage for a revolution in attitudes about women.

Playboy presented itself as a strident opponent of the 1950s domestic ideal. It called for a loosening of the model of middle-class conformity binding young women (as well as young men) and applauded the notion that they should postpone marriage, work for a time, and explore the world before settling into motherhood and family. The magazine also contended that females should be freed from "Puritanism" and allowed to experience erotic pleasure just like their male counterparts. In other words, women should be liberated for sex.

Playboy's Playmate of the Month typified this message. She represented not only the girl next door who demonstrated that "nice girls enjoy sex, too," as Hefner liked to put it, but the adventurous female who had left the neighborhood to experience the world. The Playmate embodied, literally, the notion of the liberated young woman who stood outside marriage and motherhood as a student, stewardess, model, secretary, or librarian. So did the popular cartoon series *Babs and Shirley,* which humorously portrayed two single, working young women who shared an apartment as well as a spirit of carefree sexual freedom. A typical cartoon pictured the two bachelorettes sprawled on the sofa chatting, as Shirley observed, "Ordinarily I never chase after a man, Babs, but this one was getting away."[5]

In many public statements, Hefner maintained that a healthy society encouraged a robust female sexuality. *Playboy's* ideal of "full-figured, fresh faced . . . natural female beauty" protected against the identity confusions of an "asexual society." Moreover, the magazine promoted the notion of sex with no strings attached. In embracing this fantasy, many young men sharpened a tendency to see females mainly as sexual prey. Throughout *Playboy's* first decade of existence, women usually appeared as attractive creatures who were fair game for the wiles of seduction. In part, of course, this scenario updated the erotic game of enticement and pursuit between men and women that was as old as humankind. But it also encouraged men to see women primarily as sexually alluring creatures to be bedded and enjoyed serially.[6]

This attitude toward women appeared consistently in the early years of *Playboy.* In a playful series of pieces on "how to succeed with women without really trying," Shepherd Mead urged young men to play the field and avoid hasty marriage. "You can have only one wife at a time, but the bachelor can be surrounded by girls of all kinds," he joked. "Surround yourself." He suggested ploys for breaking marital engagements: "I'm afraid of us, Ethel." "Of us, Davie?"

"Of our passions. Burn us both to ashes." Another version surfaced in "The Playboy Coloring Book," a satire that presented line sketches and directions as if to a child poised with a box of crayons. One said, "Here is the playboy with his two favorite toys. The one on the left is called a sports car. Color it fast. The one on the right is called a playmate. Color her pretty." On another page: "This is the playboy's office. . . . The playboy's secretary cannot type, or spell, or take shorthand. Color her hair yellow, and her eyes green, and her lips red, but leave her mind blank." At another point: "These are extra playmates. . . . It does not matter which is which. The girls' hair colors are interchangeable. So are the girls."[7]

Playboy, like nearly everyone else in 1950s America, also upheld the primacy of men in society. It defended male dominance in the workplace, arguing that single women should take jobs but avoid "competing" with men for plum positions. If the young woman's place was not necessarily in the home, neither was it in the executive suite. As Shepherd Mead half-jested, "The woman executive must not be allowed to spring up—and, once having sprung up, must be suppressed as quickly as possible." Married women also were expected to know their place. An advertisement in *Playboy* for "The Pink Pedestal" offered a certificate with an illustration of a woman in ancient garb standing atop a classical column holding a broom. "Put the little woman in her place," read the text, and give her this award "that shows your appreciation of her daily slaving. Personalized with her name. A constant source of inspiration on kitchen or laundry-room wall." "I guess we do express an antifeminist point of view, and we might be somewhat in error in not giving the exceptional woman full credit," Victor Lownes told the *Saturday Evening Post* in 1962. "But we firmly believe that women are *not* equal to men."[8]

Hefner agreed that gender roles went "back to the very beginning of time. The man goes out and kills a saber-toothed tiger while the woman stays at home and washes out the pots. Fair, unfair, good, bad, or indifferent, the roles were clearly defined." He asserted, "No sane woman would really want equality. . . . There are an endless number of special advantages, considerations, courtesies, laws that protect womankind. They would no more want to do without these than the man in the moon." As he explained to a friend, "If PLAYBOY sometimes seems to be saying that women belong in the bedroom and not in the office, it is because so many publications are trying to divest women of all natural womanly charms, to make them competitive with, and almost indistinguishable from, men."[9]

In fact, *Playboy* and Hefner frequently raised the alarm against the danger of growing female power. Throughout the 1950s and early 1960s, the magazine often portrayed women as grasping, competitive, and dominating as they appropriated power in the home and secured growing leverage in the consumer marketplace. Men, the magazine warned, needed to assert their position before they became completely emasculated.

In its very first issue, *Playboy* warned against gold-digging women who manipulated the divorce system to keep them in the high life. "All-American womanhood has descended on alimony as a natural heritage," it said. "Even the simplest wench can make a handsome living today." In subsequent years, it exposed additional schemes concocted by domineering women, such as the manipulation of language: "*Femalese:* 'Oh dear, I feel so foolish, coming out without my purse this way.' *Translation:* 'Out with the wallet, sweetheart, and hold still—this won't hurt a bit.'" Another lamented the disappearance of the old-fashioned "all-girl girl" in the face of newer, more aggressive types. This older ideal "never permitted a few belated civil liberties to transform her into a Susan B. Anthony Memorial Shrew."[10]

Playboy's early crusade against overweening women reached its apex in a series of biting articles from Philip Wylie. This controversial journalist and novelist had first gained attention with *Generation of Vipers* (1942), a vitriolic best-seller that attacked "Momism." Modern mothers, he accused, were typically cloying, manipulative shrews who weakened American society by browbeating their husbands and sissifying their sons. Now Wylie penned several pieces in Hefner's magazine that denounced more generally the sway of modern females. In "The Abdicating Male" (1956), Wylie claimed that women had captured "more than 80% of America's buying," a trend mercilessly manipulated by Madison Avenue and shamefully accepted by stifled men. In "The Womanization of America" (1958), he decried a modern "taffeta tide" that was flooding over social clubs, teaching, entertainment, and the arts. When men had granted female rights and emancipation, he argued, women took advantage because "to them equality meant the tyrant's throne." In "The Career Woman" (1963), Wylie took special aim at females— "perfumed pirates," "girl-guillotiners," "she-tycoons"—who were invading business management and the professions. This type represented an "obscene compulsion: she must compete with and, if necessary, cripple manhood and masculinity on earth."[11]

In 1962, *Playboy* gathered eight spokesmen for a Playboy Panel on Wylie's "The Womanization of America." "In many ways, women's meteoric ascendancy has been entirely laudable; we are not male chauvinists," *Playboy* professed at the outset. But it also claimed that "women are being masculinized even faster than the country is being womanized. Or is it, perhaps, that men are being effeminized?" Most of the panel endorsed this view. Two commentators described women's growing influence as a healthy move toward equality, but the others agreed with Norman Mailer, who contended that "women are becoming more selfish, more greedy, less romantic, less warm, more lusty, and more filled with hate." As Alexander King, playwright and *Life* editor, observed, "I haven't the slightest doubt that this absolute, unquestioned equality [of women] is a great mistake and in violation of all natural laws. It is a mistake because democracy is all right politically, but it's no good in the home."[12]

Like the panel, Hefner endorsed Wylie's "womanization" thesis. He complained about the modern "submergence of the male" beneath a growing female authority and linked *Playboy*'s success to a male reaction against the threat of "a female-oriented society." He criticized women's influence in magazines, movies, and television with its "castrated, female view of life—one example out of many of the growing womanization of America." His rallying cry: "We think it's a man's world, or should be."[13]

Hefner fully aired his resentment of female domination, and the need for a reassertion of male authority, in a 1962 radio program:

> In the last 20 or 30 years, we have a female dominated and oriented society, with the roles of man and woman so similar that it is now quite difficult for a woman to discover exactly what her real identity is, or a man, either. We've wound up with an almost asexual society, with women competing with men instead of complementing them. . . . I mean, it's sick! Now, we think women are the most wonderful thing in the world. But we think they should be *women.* . . .
>
> For *Playboy,* the roles of the sexes are clearly defined. Society remains essentially masculine. Otherwise, neither men

nor women know exactly what's expected of them in personal relations or in life. You'll note that our girls in *Playboy* are called "Playmates" . . . and they complement and suit a man and his needs. And in the process, of course, they fulfill their own needs and desires. Have you ever known a really happy woman who was domineering and competitive? I haven't.[14]

In a 1962 television panel, Hefner confronted the issue of gender equality. There was no distinction between the sexes in terms of "all the important intellects and capacities," he granted, but problems arose when women abandoned complementary roles. Females' competitive capacities lagged, as even a quick survey of great writers, artists, actors, and scientists revealed. "Granting Sands and the Bronte sisters and Elizabeth Barrett Browning—do these few names compare, either in size or stature, with Shakespeare, Shaw, Poe, Hemingway, Chekhov, Dostoevsky, Melville, Ibsen?" he argued. "Against Madame Curie you've got to place Pasteur, Darwin, Galileo, Newton, Edison, Einstein. It's like putting Grandma Moses in with Picasso, Van Gogh, Renoir, Gauguin, and Matisse." Hefner drew a clear conclusion: "If a woman is, bit by bit, denouncing her own femininity, then she is moving, step by step it seems to me, towards a denial of her own person."[15]

Thus two contrary impulses regarding women vied with one another in the world of *Playboy* from the 1950s to the early 1960s. First, Hefner and his magazine sought to restrict females to "complementary" roles in American society, welcoming them into the workplace as long as they did not threaten male jobs and prestige. This position, of course, reflected mainstream opinion in this prefeminist era. Second, *Playboy* campaigned to liberate young women from domestic roles to enjoy sexual pleasures long denied them by traditional American morality. Here Hefner's publication articulated a position that undermined orthodox values in far-reaching ways. This ambiguity reflected the first strains of a massive shift in sensibility regarding women's roles in modern society as Hefner, like his fellow citizens, entered unfamiliar territory.

But notions of polite debate about the proper place for women in modern America soon crumbled. As the 1960s unfolded, opponents of *Playboy* grew increasingly outraged by its images of women and mobilized their forces for attack. An exchange of views disappeared in a cacophony of accusation and recrimination.

II

In the spring of 1970, during two appearances on the nationally televised *Dick Cavett Show*, Hefner felt the full impact of feminist fury. The first segment placed him alongside the activists Susan Brownmiller and Sally Kempton to discuss the new movement for women's liberation. In Kempton's blunt assessment, men "oppress us as women. And Hugh Hefner is my enemy." He tried to be conciliatory, blaming religion for the oppression of women and contending that *Playboy* had supported women's rights by endorsing equal job opportunities and abortion rights. The real progressive goal, he maintained, was to expand "human rights" for women *and* men. Brownmiller retorted scornfully that she would believe that "on the day that you are willing to come out here with a cotton tail attached to your rear end." An audience laced with supporters applauded and cheered.[16]

A few weeks later, a second segment moved from the contentious to the riotous. This time Hefner confronted the feminists Holly Tannen and Diane Crothers. He goaded them with the term "lib ladies" and condemned "militant women's lib, which I find anti-feminine and anti-sexual." His antagonists returned fire. Crothers and Tannen denounced *Playboy* for presenting women as "mindless sex objects" who were expected to serve men while "looking incredibly nineteen forever." Hefner retorted that radical feminists simply endorsed the old prejudice that "if a woman is beautiful then she is brainless." *Playboy,* he declared, "exploits sex like *Sports Illustrated* exploits sports." Then things got out of hand. Several dozen feminists in the audience began shouting, "We're oppressed people," "This is a fascist country," "We are here to demand reparation." Two of them stormed the stage yelling "Fascist" and "Off the pig" before security officers escorted them from the studio. An angry Cavett declared, "We have two representatives of your movement up here. Now if you don't want to let them talk, get the hell out of here."[17]

Such confrontations revealed the intense emotion suffusing discussions of *Playboy* and women's rights by the end of the 1960s. The liberationist movements of that decade, which Hefner had embraced, now seemed like a Pandora's box as a horde of activists turned on their benefactor. Hostile encounters became frequent as feminists bombarded Hefner and his magazine with fusillades of pent-up hatred at every opportunity. This campaign, however, had been gathering force for several years. It first had established a beachhead in the early 1960s when a young female journalist had infiltrated the world of the Playboy Clubs and written an exposé.

Gloria Steinem was a bright, ambitious freelance journalist in New York City in 1963 when she accepted an assignment from *Show*, an arts and culture magazine, to go undercover at the New York City Playboy Club and write about her experience. She secured a position as a Bunny and worked at the club for several weeks. "A Bunny's Tale" appeared in two parts in the May and June issues, and its scathing account of women in the *Playboy* world raised themes that would fuel the feminist attack for years.[18]

Written in the form of a daily diary, Steinem's article offered no breathtaking revelations or scandals about life inside the Playboy Clubs. Instead, in an understated, detailed style she characterized a Bunny's work as degrading drudgery. Steinem portrayed the Bunnies as cinching one another into excruciatingly tight outfits while stuffing the ample bosom cavity with any material they could get their hands on—gym socks, plastic bags, foam rubber, silk scarves, absorbent cotton, and many others—to meet the *Playboy* ideal. She denounced a system of rules that made Bunnies pay a daily fee for cleaning and upkeep of their outfits, forbade them from sitting, and awarded demerits for messy hair, coming back late from a break, or addressing the room director by his first name. She condemned guidelines from the *Playboy Club Bunny Manual*—"You should make it seem that the customer's opinions are very important" or "Always remember, your proudest possession is your Bunny Tail. You must make sure it is white and fluffy"—as demeaning. But most importantly for an emerging feminist critique, Steinem asserted that Bunnies were overworked and underpaid, earning far less than the advertised $200 a week. She claimed that Bunnies worked long hours with few breaks and little food for a meager paycheck of $108 to $145 a week. This accusation touched a nerve as working women were beginning to resent unequal pay, unfair treatment, and stifled opportunity.[19]

Steinem also raised another issue—sexual objectification and harassment—that would become central to an emerging feminist critique. Her work stint in the Playboy Club, she maintained, consisted of an endless round of sexual abasement. She claimed that club managers expected her to accompany Number One Keyholders—*Playboy* executives, VIPs, influential media members—when they were in the club and date them if asked. She contended that male customers directed a constant stream of salacious comments, sexual innuendo, and lewd propositions her way: patrons handed her keys to their hotel rooms, leeringly asked her to serve drinks at a "private" party, or queried, "If you're my bunny, can I take you home with me?" She asserted that many of the Bunnies bought into their own exploitation, quoting one who praised a customer because he "he treats you just the same whether you've slept with him or not." Steinem offered a melodramatic conclusion. Upon leaving after a work shift, she saw a hooker sitting in a car. "She looked at me and smiled. I smiled back. She looked available and was. Of the two of us, she seemed the more honest."[20]

Many Bunnies were outraged by Steinem's depiction of their labors as sordid and financially unrewarding. They insisted that their positions in the Playboy Clubs provided not only respectable pay and a taste of glamour for ambitious young women, but also a foundation for their later successes as business owners, entertainers, and physicians. To many of them, Steinem was an elitist with a political agenda. "The fact was, Gloria Steinem couldn't identify with the rest of us and didn't care to," wrote one. "At that point in her life, she would never have considered working as a waitress, let alone a waitress with Bunny ears, except as research for an article. Her viewpoint was that of . . . a privileged professional." Deborah Harry, a Bunny turned rock star, described her life in the club as "a rare combination of women in the workplace—beauty, femininity, sexuality, and at the same time, ambition and intelligence." Lauren Hutton, the future supermodel, described her sister Bunnies as "pre-feminist pioneers and extraordinarily brave for the time. . . . We were like sisters learning together how to take charge of our own lives."[21]

Moreover, Steinem herself displayed considerable ambivalence regarding feminist issues in this period. She wrote for *Vogue*, *Glamour*, and *Ladies' Home Journal*, not exactly progressive beacons for women, and recently had published *The Beach Book*, which extolled oceanside fantasies about Cary Grant and martinis, Aristotle Onassis's yacht, and sunbathing. Interestingly, she also had engaged in a mild flirtation with Hefner himself. Put in touch by a mutual friend, they tried unsuccessfully to meet up in New York City and Hefner sent a note of dismay over having missed her. "There's the possibility that I should leave things as intriguing and mysterious as they are. Nothing you can say, as a novelist friend once pointed out to me, is nearly as good as what the readers will imagine," Steinem wrote back. "Still, I would like to meet you sometime when you're in town, so I'll take the chance and to hell with the novelist."[22]

By the mid-1960s, dissenting voices were growing louder in denouncing women's second-class status in American society. Complaints mounted about discrimination and inequities in the workplace, restricted opportunities, and sexual exploitation. Critics had begun blasting *Playboy* for portraying women as one-dimensional sexual playthings. *Cosmopolitan* accused Hefner's magazine of promoting the view that women served as "an accessory for the well-dressed bachelor. Of course, she is discarded when she reaches age twenty-five, or before that, if she exhibits any intelligence." *Life* took a similar tack: "In Hefnerland, a woman is simply another aspect of the status-symbol mania that is stamped all over *Playboy*. She is no more or less important than the sleekest sports car or the most expensive bottle of Scotch." A sarcastic article in *Mademoiselle* contended that real women were attracted by a man's mind, character, and "faith in some values beyond the latest Italian cut in tuxedos."[23]

Hefner reacted calmly, if defensively, to such criticism. He moderated his earlier views, dropping complaints about womanization and stressing that *Playboy*'s crusade for sexual liberation had released women from their real oppressors—a religious heritage that repressed their sexuality and made them chattel. "It is odd how many feminists fail utterly to understand the extent to which the emancipation of women and the sexual emancipation go together," he explained in 1966. "Historically, the idea of women remaining chaste while men philander freely obviously stems from the notion that they are chattel, and that used property is not as good as unused property; and this idea is one that Playboy vigorously opposes."[24]

By 1968, however, Hefner had grown testy in the face of growing attacks. He complained that some women were so consumed by their grievances that they had lost sight of how the sexes "have everything to offer each other." When asked if he was ever attracted to a woman who was smarter than he was, he snapped, "I never met a woman who was my intellectual superior. The most intellectually stimulating people are not women, they're men." He described protesters against *Playboy* as "ridiculous" and insisted that "sexual liberation is a major part of female emancipation," he said. "I think *Playboy* has done more for that than just about anyone."[25]

Meanwhile, *Playboy* adopted a two-part strategy in dealing with feminist critics. First, it sidestepped them by defining the modern woman as seeking a new lifestyle based on freedom and fun. "The New Girl," for example, described a fresh type of "postfeminist" young woman who embraced an active life of "sexual freedom and psychedelics, skindiving and the swim, Bobby Kennedy and Bobby Dylan, the New Left and Civil Rights." A photo and text article on "The No-Bra Look" argued that this trend combined "both a feminist rallying cry and a chic contemporary fashion trend." A piece on "The Abortion Revolution" argued that obsolete laws against terminating pregnancy should be abolished in the name of female freedom.[26]

Second, the magazine positioned itself as an advocate of women's rights but an opponent of radical women's liberation. In a long statement in 1970, the magazine clarified its stance:

> Though we are opposed to the destructive radicalism and the anti-sexuality of the extremist fringe of militant feminism, our position on women's rights, we feel, is as consistently liberal as our position on all human rights. We've been crusading for a long time for universal availability of contraceptives and birth control information, as well as for the repeal of restrictive abortion laws; we believe a woman's right to control her own body, in sexuality and in reproduction, is an essential step toward greater personal freedom. Likewise, we reject the Victorian double standard, which applauds sexual experience in men and condemns it in women. . . . We are also opposed to the traditional stereotype that relegates women to domestic drudgery. We certainly believe that any woman who wants to shun the homemaker's role for a career, or who wants to combine both, should have the opportunity. . . . It should be needless to add that we believe women ought to be given equal pay for work of equal value.[27]

Strident feminists, however, branded Hefner and *Playboy* as the supreme symbols of male oppression of women. Campus demonstrations flared up, as in April 1970 at the University of Southern California where a group of activists carried signs reading "We Won't

Take Playboy Lying Down," heckled a magazine spokesman during a talk, and finally rushed the auditorium stage and tried to take over the microphone. Ti-Grace Atkinson, a prominent feminist, gave speeches describing *Playboy* as "middle-class pornography. We all know Hugh Hefner is a pig." Militants picketed the Playboy Club in Boston and demanded that Bunnies come out for consciousness-raising discussions. The manager refused, saying, "I think you'll agree they're not exactly dressed for the occasion."[28]

A dramatic moment came when Gloria Steinem arrived at the Chicago mansion in 1970 to interview Hefner for *McCall's*. They clashed immediately. Her article, titled "What *Playboy* Doesn't Know About Women Could Fill a Book," mocked the publication as a 1950s relic peddling fake 1960s progressivism. Steinem, by now a leading feminist, laid into the publisher in the best New Left style, accusing him of promoting a shallow, retrograde consumerism that made women into another commodity like liquor, hi-fi sets, and sports cars. Hefner disagreed strenuously, defending his belief in "capitalism with a social conscience," women's rights, and sexual freedom for males and females. As the two sparred over female images in Hefner's magazine, Steinem declared, "There are times when a woman reading *Playboy* feels a little like a Jew reading a Nazi manual." He heatedly retorted, "I think the militant feminists want to be men."[29]

Finally, Hefner struck back at his political tormenters. At his instigation, *Playboy* solicited an article on feminism and approached the freelance writer Susan Braudy. She joked that she wanted to write such a compelling piece that the *Playboy* editors would soon be "renaming their magazine *Play People*." Her original draft analyzed the women's liberation movement and argued that stereotypes for both sexes were breaking down under the impact of feminism. The magazine accepted the piece but asked for revisions that stressed the differences between "the radical crazies and the moderates." Then Hefner demanded a stronger critique of militant feminism. When Braudy refused to make wholesale changes, *Playboy* killed the article while paying her the writer's fee. The magazine then reassigned the project to Morton Hunt, who presented "Up Against the Wall, Chauvinist Pig!" in the May 1970 issue. It recapitulated the main lines of Hefner's critique: while progressives agreed on ending discrimination in terms of legal rights, workplace equity, and sexual freedom, these proper reforms were being overshadowed by "militant man-haters who do their level best to distort the distinctions between male and female and to discredit the legitimate grievances of American women."[30]

Just as the Hunt article was about to appear, controversy exploded. On April 15, 1970, the Vietnam Moratorium Committee held a fundraiser at the Playboy Mansion, but as the guests arrived, they were greeted by some three hundred anti-*Playboy* protesters organized by the Chicago Women's Liberation Union. The picketers waved signs reading "Peace, Not Piece" and "Sign Your Check But Don't Go In," and jeered at guests who entered the house of "sexploitation." Several dozen police arrived to cordon off the entrance and ended up arresting several of the protesters. Inside, against a backdrop of antiwar speechmaking, traumatized liberals compared notes on running the gauntlet outside. "I've crossed picket lines before, but never one as vicious as that," said Rod Serling. "I felt like I was walking into the Twilight Zone." Then Shelly Schlicker, a secretary at *Playboy,* began to loudly criticize the magazine and its attitude toward women. As reporters gathered around, she complained that the upcoming Hunt article "puts down women's lib" and that two secretaries had been dismissed for refusing to type it. "I'll probably get fired for saying all this," she added.[31]

A few days later, Schlicker secretly copied and released to the press the in-house Hefner memo that had fueled the Hunt article. Its heated reaction to the original Braudy piece revealed the publisher's state of mind:

> [W]hat we have is a well-balanced, objective article, but what I want is a devastating piece that takes the militant feminists apart. . . . What I'm interested in is the highly irrational, emotional, kookie trend that feminism has taken in the last couple of years. . . . These chicks are our natural enemy. It is time to do battle with them. . . .
>
> We certainly agree that a woman's place is not in the home, that a woman should enjoy a career. . . . But the militant feminists want much more than this—essentially she wants to play a role exactly comparable to the male's, to compete with him not simply in the business world but emotionally, and in every other way. The only subject related to feminism that is

worth doing is on this new militant phenomenon and the only proper PLAYBOY approach is one that devastates it.[32]

An uproar ensued. *Playboy* fired Schlicker for publicly circulating a confidential corporate communication, and she responded by joining feminist groups to protest outside the Playboy Building. Raising a clenched fist for television cameras, she declared, "I am joining with my sisters to fight Hugh Hefner, *Playboy*, and everything they stand for. . . . We will no longer sell ourselves in return for a pair of ears and a tail and a condescending pat on the behind." As *Newsweek* noted, while Hefner refused to retract anything, he was "surely hunkering down in anticipation of even more trouble."[33]

The infamous memo cemented Hefner's reputation among women's liberationists as the Antichrist. *Playboy* later would provide a forum to feminist critics such as Germaine Greer and Betty Friedan, but the hostility remained. Hefner felt hurt, even betrayed by this vilification. Knowing that *Playboy* had carried the flag for progressive reform in behalf of civil rights, disengagement in Vietnam, and sexual liberation, he could not fathom why many liberals now branded him a villain. "*Playboy*'s been on the side of humanity and reason in all the causes that are important, so you'd think that female emancipators would separate their friends from their enemies," he asserted in 1969.[34]

But Hefner's public pronouncements on feminism provided only one perspective on his views of women. His private experiences offered another. As much as any debating points in public exchanges, the nature of his close relationships with females over the first four decades of his life revealed much about his attitude toward women and their place in society.

III

Hefner's understanding of women had taken root during his boyhood in rather barren emotional soil. He had imbibed emotional repression from his mother, Grace, who had withheld affection even as she indulged most of his whims. At the same time, through an addiction to the movies and popular music, he absorbed exaggerated notions of female beauty and highly sentimental notions of romance.

Then during late adolescence, he had been stunned when Millie Williams, his fiancée, betrayed him by having a sexual affair with a coworker. Hefner never got over these youthful influences. He reached adulthood with a complex, ambivalent view of women and their motives and inclinations. It was in equal parts adoring and suspicious, loving and manipulative, lusty and resentful. He relentlessly pursued and bedded women as the sweet side of his nature searched for "a place where the lyrics to the songs are true," as he often described, yet the controlling side sought to keep the upper hand emotionally. At some level, he was aware of these internal conflicts, once telling an interviewer that "intellectually, I may think in a certain way; practically, I may act in another way. . . . I am and I remain a combination of incoherences that I uselessly try to reject."[35]

This ambiguous sensibility shaped Hefner's lifelong habit of establishing relationships with much younger women. From Betty Zuziak and Joyce Nizzari in the 1950s to Cynthia Maddox and Mary Warren in the 1960s and Barbi Benton in the late 1960s (not to mention countless others for shorter duration), he gravitated toward beautiful females in their early twenties. In one sense, this impulse expressed the mysterious compulsion of male lust and the unique opportunities for venting it that appeared in the *Playboy* world. But the attraction to young women also met deeper emotional needs. On the one hand, they provided the publisher a strong dose of nonthreatening affection that made his world seem warm and safe. On the other hand, their youthful inexperience allowed him to maintain emotional control. Hefner expressed this ambivalent urge perfectly in a 1966 interview. "I pick good-looking, young girls because I get something very good out of the innocence and sweetness that exists at that level," he admitted, then added a revealing addendum: "Most of the girls I have gone out with have benefited because I give them an identity and, when they come out of the machine, they are better for it."[36]

This sensibility also led Hefner to avoid involvement not with smart women, as his critics often accused, but accomplished ones. "I don't feel uncomfortable with an intelligent woman. Simply, I do not know what to do with her," he confessed. The publisher wanted to adore and protect women, and to enjoy their devotion in return, while pitting himself against men. He perceived males in terms of intellectual stimulation and competitive accomplishment, saw females as sources of affection and love, and grew uncomfortable when either gender transcended those familiar confines. "In a lot of ways, I'm a very dominant guy and am attracted to a very feminine, submissive kind of woman. The truly competitive female leaves me cold," he noted in 1968. Thus women who sought to be like men—such as militant feminists, in his perception—turned his emotional universe on its head. As he told an interviewer, "It's not brains that turns me off a girl; it's that emotionally castrating thing."[37]

Hefner's internal impulses also made him a firm believer in the double standard. While he proclaimed that the sexual revolution had liberated women for sexual experiences just like men, his actions fell short of his words. As Cynthia Maddox described, "Of course, I was always theoretically free to do as I pleased, but I abided by Hef's rules. If I was on a date with another boy, heaven help me if he even kissed me." Hefner admitted that while he wanted to play around, when his girlfriends did so "I was rather hurt." He blamed his upbringing for the hypocrisy. "You know, I still have some of the Puritan heritage that I grew up with. There are gaps between what I intellectually believe in and the man I am," he admitted in the late 1960s. "I'm afraid I believe in a double-standard for men and women in actual situations far more than I want to admit."[38]

Thus for Hefner the traditionalist, affectionate and attractive young women provided companionship, fun, and sexual satisfaction and would adapt to the contours of his life. They would be bright enough to be interesting, but not so accomplished as to threaten his domination of the relationship. They would remain sexually true to him, while he retained the option of sleeping with others. This represented, of course, a heightened version of mainstream male attitudes toward women in a pre-feminist age: women were expected to support and "complement" men. Hefner, like almost all American males, struggled to accommodate new notions of female equality.

But for Hefner the rebel, sex moved front and center stage. The issue of the "sexual objectification" of women became *the* dividing line as feminist critics insisted that *Playboy* reduced women to objects of physical desire and downplayed their intelligence, character, and achievements. Hefner disagreed passionately. "*Playboy* treats women—and men, too, for that matter—as sexual *beings*, not as sexual objects," he countered, and the cause of sexual liberation "helped women step down from their pedestals and enjoy their natural sexuality as much as men." He denied portraying women as a kind of consumer item, like a sports car or fine wine. "Far from being an accessory to the good life, women—and the romantic liaison between them and our male readers—are the very point and purpose of what *Playboy* espouses as a guide for living," he insisted.[39]

There seemed to be little common ground for understanding between Hefner and his feminist foes. But a broader historical perspective suggests otherwise. The antagonists—caught up in a profound transformation that reached to fundamental questions of status, biology, identity, and social organization—shared more than they knew in laboring to direct and grasp this sea change. Their common struggle illuminated several historical issues.

First, *Playboy* and the feminist movement worked in tandem to undermine the domestic, suburban "family togetherness" model of 1950s America. The noted feminist Barbara Ehrenreich accused Hefner of employing the rhetoric of sexual revolution to mask his real goal: encouraging men to abandon marriage and family in a "flight from commitment." This argument, however, overlooks the fact that Betty Friedan, and many other feminists, focused on a similar target. *The Feminine Mystique* maintained that women had been imprisoned in the American home by the demands of childrearing, homemaking, and marriage. Unhappy, anxious, even depressed, they desperately sought escape from this "comfortable concentration camp." In this goal, *Playboy* and feminism shared more than either would ever admit.[40]

Moreover, both *Playboy* and modern feminism were part of a larger crusade promoting an ethos of self-fulfillment in modern America. Since the early decades of the twentieth century, mainstream culture had steadily jettisoned traditional Victorian values of self-control and self-denial for a new agenda of finding happiness by fulfilling, not suppressing, appetites. Hefner's version of self-fulfillment, as Ehrenreich has described, focused not only on "the Playmates in the centerfold . . . but a wealth of other consumer items . . . imported liquor, stereo sets, men's colognes, luxury cars, and fine clothes." Yet her indictment overlooks feminism's own agenda of self-gratification. Feminists did not focus explicitly on consumer prosperity because they assumed it. As Friedan observed, much of women's postwar conundrum stemmed from "our abundant society" where middle-class people had unprecedented leisure time. *The Feminine Mystique* instructed that feminism should focus on helping women to find "'self-realization' or 'self-fulfillment' or 'identity' . . . break out of the housewife trap and . . . [start] fulfilling their own unique possibilities as separate human beings." In terms of this broad historical development, Hefner and women's liberationists again shared more than they ever recognized.[41]

In addition, both *Playboy* and its feminist critics overemphasized the power of sexual imagery. For Hefner, erotic representations of the female body pointed the way to human freedom and happiness, while for feminists they inscribed a kind of slavery for women. Both sides exaggerated. While sex is a vital part of human life, it is far from being the most important. In trying to make it so, along with the visual images that arouse it, both disputants distorted real life. Their extreme positions—Hefner defining unfettered sex as the road to nirvana with *Playboy* photos as signposts; many early feminists denouncing the sex act as inherently exploitive and female nudes as posters of oppression—granted undue power to a single aspect of human endeavor. Both overlook the likelihood that erotic imagery, whether evocative or scandalous, pleasurable or annoying, is often relatively inconsequential.

Finally, both Hefner and his feminist critics evolved on the issue of the struggle for women's rights. The publisher changed from a romantic paternalist and denouncer of "womanization" in the 1950s to an equal-rights liberal by the 1970s. He came to endorse a mainstream agenda similar to that of Betty Friedan and the National Organization for Women (NOW): integration of women into the public sphere, equal pay for equal work, and abortion rights. Feminism also evolved as it began splintering into contending factions by the early 1970s. "Equity feminism," or the movement for legal and social equality of women eventually endorsed by Hefner, made steady gains in the culture and legal system. "Gender feminism," a newer, more revolutionary movement inspired by books such as Kate Millett's *Sexual Politics* (1970), contended that women were prisoners of a patriarchal system and engaged in a gender war with their male oppressors. This smaller, more radical movement mainly influenced academe and the intelligentsia. By the mid-1970s, Hefner and many equity feminists stood together, albeit uneasily, in the liberal mainstream, and in later years feminists such as Christina Hoff Sommers, Camille Paglia, and even Friedan herself would come to the publisher's defense.[42]

Ultimately, the flashpoint issue of sexual objectification revealed the shortcomings of both Hefner and early women's liberationists. The problem was not so much portraying women as sexual objects. In one sense, women *are* sexual objects for men, in the same way that men, perhaps to a lesser extent, are for women. The problem comes in portraying them *only* in this light. Early feminists pinpointed *Playboy*'s penchant for superficial sexuality, but exaggerated both the intent and the impact. At the same time, Hefner reasonably defended his magazine's erotic portrayal of women as a legitimate aspect of the sexual revolution, but refused to recognize that *Playboy* often underplayed other aspects of female humanity. This tendency appeared on the March 1972 cover, which depicted a woman in the shape of a liquor bottle with a Playboy corkscrew lying alongside.

Perhaps the most reasonable conclusion came from the writer Joyce Carol Oates, who reported that she had received an appeal from NOW asking her to boycott *Playboy* as a future publication venue. Hefner's magazine, it said, mocked "the central message of the women's movement, that women are and should be treated as human beings." While admitting some sympathy with the entreaty, this distinguished writer ultimately rejected it in an eloquent reply:

> I cannot claim to have much interest in the pictorial aspect of PLAYBOY, but I see no reason to focus upon certain pages and deliberately to neglect the very real presence of others. PLAYBOY has published exceptionally fine interviews in recent years (one of them with Germaine Greer, who was allowed to be as frank and insulting and critical of PLAYBOY as she pleased), some important articles, and . . . some very interesting fiction. The stories of mine that appeared in PLAYBOY dealt with male/female conflicts—and in nearly every case, I dramatized the continuing cruelty of the myth of male superiority in such a way that any reader, male or whatever, should have felt some sympathy and understanding for women. . . .
>
> I have never published anything in any magazine on the basis of my agreeing, entirely, with every page of that magazine. In a democratic society, there must be avenues of communication in publications that appeal to a wide variety of people, otherwise writers with certain beliefs will be read only by people with those same beliefs, and change or growth

would come to an end. PLAYBOY is astonishingly liberal, and even revolutionary in certain respects. . . .

My personal belief is that worship of youth, flesh, and beauty of a limited nature is typically American and is fairly innocuous. . . . [Y]our anger over PLAYBOY and its hedonistic philosophy is possibly misdirected.[43]

Indeed, the protests against *Playboy* gradually died down. But animosity among women's liberationists remained strong, resurfacing a decade later in a strange alliance with social conservatives in the Reagan administration. But as the 1970s unfolded, *Playboy*'s guerrilla war with feminism moved off center stage as more pressing issues arose to demand Hefner's attention. They would challenge both his personal well-being and his professional survival.

13

Down the Rabbit Hole

As the 1970s began, Hugh Hefner, in his own words, "had the world on a string." The Chicago publisher spread the gospel of personal freedom and material abundance to countless converts as much of his Aquarian Age dream actually seemed to materialize. In 1972, *Playboy* reached a zenith of popularity with sales of seven million magazines while Playboy Enterprises, Inc., expanded not only into Playboy Clubs but hotels, resorts, filmmaking, books, and records. Hefner personified the lifestyle he promoted. Surrounded by beautiful women and celebrities in the Chicago mansion, he now commuted regularly to Los Angeles and soon would purchase a second estate in the Beverly Hills area. Moreover, he had fallen in love with a beautiful young woman. Personally happy and professionally triumphant beyond his wildest dreams, Hefner stood poised in the early 1970s for coronation as the monarch of a Disney-style leisure empire. He celebrated with his own version of the Roaring Twenties, an exuberant era he always resented having missed.[1]

Before long, however, Hefner and *Playboy* became caught up in the complex cultural and political dynamic of the decade. Flowing between the revolutionary 1960s and the conservative era inaugurated by Ronald Reagan in 1980, the 1970s were marked by a gradual but inexorable process of polarization. On the one hand, this period saw the fulfillment of 1960s liberation as many disciples of the sexual and cultural revolution carried their crusade to full maturation. On the other hand, a growing backlash gathered momentum as much of Middle America increasingly drew back from radical excesses to embrace traditional social and political values.

To complicate matters further, ordinary citizens beset by political exhaustion from Watergate, "Rust Belt" deindustrialization, international weakness in the wake of the Vietnam debacle, and social dislocation from a powerful shift from the urban Northeast to the "Sun Belt" of the South and West, fled the public realm. With a new sense of limits and loss of optimism, many people—from evangelical Christians to therapeutic liberals to New Age reformers—began turning inward to personal experiences and self-exploration. Increasingly skeptical of remaking the world, Americans, in the words of one historian, "chased new pasts, new futures, new Gods—and they chased them by and for themselves."[2]

Hefner and his magazine stood at the convergence of these trends. Symbolizing liberation, fueling reaction, and promoting a preoccupation with self, they reflected the powerful countercurrents of the age. Even as the publisher reveled in the liberationist excesses of the Swinging Seventies, he was forced to confront its positive and negative consequences. New challenges appeared in his struggles with an upstart magazine competitor, a volatile business atmosphere, and a drug scandal that placed him and his enterprise in mortal danger. But perhaps the first sign of commingled possibilities and problems came with romantic turmoil in his private life.

I

Since mid-1968, when Barbi Benton had captured his heart, Hugh Hefner had never been happier. To be near the young UCLA coed, he gradually abandoned Chicago to spend increasing amounts of time in Southern California. He overcame his dislike of traveling to spend several weeks in 1969 and 1970 escorting her and a group of friends on tours of Europe and Africa. By the following year, he was residing nearly half the time in a second home in an exclusive area of Los Angeles.

But in the spring of 1971 Hefner put everything at risk. He met a voluptuous young blonde in Chicago who attracted his romantic attentions, and within a few months he found himself involved in a love triangle that stretched across half the country and demanded a precarious balancing act of emotions and energy. Always the film fan, Hefner compared his situation to *The Captain's Paradise,* the 1953 comedy where Alec Guinness portrayed a ship captain sailing between Gibraltar and Tangier with a lover in each port. "In the movie, the arrangement ended in disaster with both loves leaving him. Could I hope for any better conclusion?" Hefner asked rhetorically. The answer, of course, was no. The situation unraveled, but not before a series of events, exhilarating and stressful alike, threw his personal life into tumult for several years.[3]

Barbi Benton, in many ways, was Hefner's dream girl. Cute, energetic, and charming, this former cheerleader and Miss Teenage America contestant embodied his vivid adolescent fantasies of femininity. The allure was irresistible. "Barbi was the sort of girl you had a crush on in high school or college who was invariably pinned to the captain of the football team or some other BMOC," the publisher observed.[4]

More subtly, another aspect of Benton's personality came to fascinate Hefner. The perky brunette proved to have ambitions that almost equaled his. Savoring the limelight, she loved her new high-profile status and used it as a springboard to launch a brief film and television career and, more successfully, a singing career. "She wanted to model, be in the movies, become a celebrity, become a somebody," Hefner observed. "I saw this yearning in Barbi and encouraged it." Within a few years, after several singing tours and several recurring television roles, she was delighted when a group of fans approached the couple at a public event and "more wanted her autograph than mine," Hefner reported. She also enjoyed the opulence of the Playboy lifestyle. Once, when giving a tour of Hefner's home, a visitor asked about the material in a large chandelier. She replied (Hefner took to calling these "Barbieisms"), "Bronze or brass, whichever's better."[5]

But the relationship began to exhibit strain as Benton increasingly sought to escape Hefner's shadow and establish her own public identity. They disagreed over her attempt to start a musical career. He made her cry after hearing a practice session and commenting that she would never become a singer. "He said, 'I'm not telling you this, darling, because I want to hurt you. It's because I *don't* want to hurt you,'" Benton related. "I took it as a challenge." And indeed, despite her thin voice, Benton became a fairly popular country singer within a few years, and Hefner became supportive. She also made strides as a comedic actress on television, joining the cast of the popular comedic revue *Hee Haw*, and securing a recurring role on *The Love Boat*.[6]

Hefner's dalliances with other women also created tensions. While Benton was his special girl, the publisher was far from monogamous. In the early 1970s he had flings with many Playmates, including Marilyn Cole, Janice Pennington, Sharon Johansen, Lillian Mueller, and Hope Olson. He also enjoyed countless casual sexual encounters. On a trip to St. Tropez in August 1971, for example, he spent several days on a rented yacht and concluded his stay, in his own words, "by bedding two British Bunnies in a *ménage a trois*." Two years later, during one of Benton's absences, a friend "brought over three cute chicks on Saturday night to cheer me up and we had a little scene in the grotto and the bedroom." Benton tried to be stoical about the situation. "I object to it, but I don't hassle him; a girl just has to accept it—guys fool around," she told a *Cosmopolitan* reporter. "It doesn't mean he loves the other girls."[7]

But Benton remained ignorant of the fact that Hefner had become deeply involved with another woman. He met Karen Christy when she arrived at the Chicago mansion in May 1971. A twenty-year-old Texan from Abilene, she had attended North Texas State University as an art student, worked as a model and corporate secretary in Dallas, and won a local Playboy Bunny Hunt in Dallas. She agreed to move north and work in the Chicago Playboy Club because it would get her closer to her dream—attending the Chicago Art Institute. As she settled into the mansion dormitory, the other girls "thought I was a hick from the sticks. And I was." She met Hefner at a party and was struck by his casual, friendly manner and wonderful sense of humor.[8]

Hefner was smitten by this blonde bombshell. Christy had a baby face with large eyes, upturned nose, full lips, and a stunning figure. Partial to flashy, revealing clothes, she was wearing a pink, one-piece hot-pants outfit that highlighted her voluptuous physique. They spent the rest of the evening together, joking and flirting, playing pool and pinball, munching on a midnight supper, then descending to the mansion's underwater bar for drinks and a long, quiet conversation. Their evening culminated with a movie in his bedroom and an embrace on his round bed. "I can still remember the magic moment when I started to slowly unzip the front of her outfit and she didn't stop me," Hefner recalled later.[9]

Hefner found the young Texas beauty enormously seductive. "I don't think I was ever more physically attracted to anyone than Karen Christy," he said later. "She was sweet, soft, and sensual, all at the same time" and displayed an "erotic playfulness" that triggered his sexual ardor. If Barbi Benton embodied Hefner's high school cheerleader fantasies, Christy represented another, cinematic set of images from his youth. In his words, "she looked like she'd stepped out of one of those Busby Berkeley musicals from the early Thirties." Their sex life became, even by his standards, particularly passionate.[10]

This shy southern girl appealed to Hefner with her sweet drawl, down-home charm, and a self-deprecating sense of humor. She shared his enthusiasm for movies and games and they spent hours watching films in the mansion ballroom and playing backgammon, Monopoly, Risk, and pinball with a small group of mansion regulars: Shel Silverstein, Bobbie Arnstein, Gene Siskel, and John Dante. She proved ingenious at giving him unique gifts. For their marathon Monopoly games, she commissioned small board figurines of him and her—he was depicted in a bathrobe smoking a pipe, she in a hot-pants outfit—as well as the other four regular players. Another time she presented him with a lifelike portrait of herself as a reclining nude painted in the Vargas style with a special hinge in the frame that exposed her pubic area.[11]

At Hefner's request, Christy soon moved into a first-floor apartment at the mansion. As their relationship deepened, the publisher showered the Texas beauty with outlandish gifts: a full-length white mink coat, a white Mark IV Lincoln automobile, a five-carat diamond cocktail ring from Tiffany's. He also chose her as *Playboy's* Miss December 1971. Christy returned this affection, becoming his steady companion in Chicago and accompanying him on jaunts to Walt Disney World, the Caribbean, and a backgammon tournament in New York City. She patiently awaited his return from trips to Los Angeles, once decorating the Chicago mansion trees with yellow ribbons in a reference to the hit song "Tie a Yellow Ribbon," which celebrated a lover's homecoming in such a fashion. Hefner delighted in these sentimental gestures. By the end of 1972, he confessed, "my love for her had become every bit the equal of what I felt for Barbi."[12]

Thus throughout 1972 and the first half of 1973, Hefner found himself in a full-fledged love triangle with two beautiful young women. Trying to balance them, he flitted from the Midwest to the West Coast on an every-other-week schedule, alternately spending time with either Benton or Christy while making long-distance calls to the other. The stress of the situation occasionally turned to comedy. He wrote a memo instructing that Christy's pinball scores be erased from the tote board in the game room when Benton was on the premises, and then put back when she left. Another time, when Hefner had Christy over at his Los Angeles mansion while Benton was gone, he instructed his security people to detain the mistress of the manor at the gate should she return and signal him by cutting off the piped-in music. As the publisher and his blonde girlfriend were consorting in the grotto, the music suddenly stopped and Christy, wrapped in a towel, dashed to a waiting limo to be whisked out the back gate. A few minutes later, Hefner realized that it had been a false alarm from a simple gap in the tape. Sitting alone, he heard the music resume.[13]

Each point on the love triangle offered a different perspective. Benton realized that her famous boyfriend saw other women but remained in the dark about her new rival. Christy, who knew about Benton, of course, faced things realistically. She accepted Hefner's reassurances that the Benton relationship was nearing an end, noting "you'd have to be a real idiot to believe something a man says to you about another girl. I mean, I was naïve but I wasn't stupid." Hefner rationalized what he was doing as a variation on the old wife-mistress fantasy of sustaining a comfortable, harmonious relationship in public and an exciting, illicit relationship in private. As for his efforts to hold it all together, he used the old vaudeville quip about using every available minute in a show: "I'm dancing as fast as I can."[14]

In the summer of 1973, the situation finally exploded. Earlier, Benton had grown suspicious of Hefner when she found white bobby pins in his bathrobe and saw one of his assistants walk by with a notepad upon which was a scribble about "a mink coat for Karen Christy." When Benton inquired, Hefner reassured her it was nothing and that "you're the girl I *love*." But then came an unmistakable, public sign of betrayal. An article in *Time* on men's magazines blew his cover with this description: "Long a two-of-everything consumer,

Hefner has lately extended the principle to his romantic life. Former Playmate Barbi Benton, his longtime escort, lives in the California mansion; blonde Karen Christy, an ex-Bunny in the Chicago Playboy Club, is ensconced in his Chicago quarters. Somehow the arrangement continues to work." It also featured an incriminating photograph of Hefner with his arm around Christy watching a movie at the Chicago mansion. A furious Benton confronted Hefner and moved out of the Playboy Mansion West in a huff and got her own apartment. In Benton's words, "I didn't want to have anything to do with him. I just thought he was a cheat and a liar." After several weeks, she surrendered to his entreaties and moved back in the mansion, but she kept the apartment for insurance.[15]

The situation grew increasingly stressful as Benton and Christy sniped at one another, and at Hefner, in the press. In *People* magazine, Benton described Christy as "just another girl who lives in one of the bunny dorms" and added, "I thought it was a bit tacky of [Hefner] to allow a photographer to shoot a picture of him with his arm around another girl when I have been living with him as his wife for five years." Christy dismissed Benton. "Why should I be jealous? She used to live in the Mansion. Now she doesn't," she told a reporter. At Thanksgiving 1973 tensions escalated when Benton and Christy both sought to spend the holiday with the publisher. Benton began to see other men, having an affair with a fellow cast member on *Hee Haw* and sleeping with an old boyfriend on a ski trip.[16]

Then things began to crumble with Christy. She confessed to an affair with Val Lownes, Victor Lownes's son, when she was lonely during Hefner's many absences. They reconciled, but things were never the same. The couple began to quarrel, and Christy became increasingly spunky in asserting herself. She began to demand parity in the relationship, and he responded angrily. "[He would] stomp his feet and beat his pipe on the table and turn purple in the face," she described. "I just thought he was spoiled, he's always had everything he wants for so many years, that he really doesn't remember what it's like to have to compromise." But Christy stood her ground and Bobbie Arnstein, Hefner's executive secretary, said, "She didn't think anybody could talk back to him . . . the way I did and get away with it."[17]

The young Texan, for all of the blonde-bimbo stereotypes, was no dummy. While deeply fond of her older lover and the mansion lifestyle, she always saw the arrangement as temporary and grew weary of his domineering ways and escapades with other women. "I loved Hef but he's very manipulative . . . I resented it," she explained. During one particularly bitter quarrel, Christy claimed that she loved him more than he did her. When he replied that she *should* love him more, she furiously exclaimed, "Why should I love you more? Because you're rich and famous? You're always saying you don't want people to love you because you're rich and famous and that's the only thing about you that makes you more loveable than me." She stalked out of the room and left the mansion. The distraught publisher learned that she had gone to a girlfriend's nearby place and, even though it was after midnight, he went throughout the apartment building ringing doorbells until he located her. Standing outside the door, he pleaded with her to return, and appeared so contrite that she finally agreed.[18]

By early 1974, however, Christy concluded that her life with Hefner had reached a dead end. She realized "he would do anything in the world for you as long as it didn't inconvenience him in any way. In other words, what Hef needed came first to Hef, and what you needed came second." In March she finally left for good. In order to escape the bodyguards who accompanied her in public, she went to a favorite dress shop, slipped out through the rear service entrance, and took a cab to a girlfriend's, who had "borrowed" her white Lincoln the day before. Christy drove to Texas, and while Hefner called several times to convince her to come back, she refused. Over the next few years they would have several brief rendezvous, but the relationship was over.[19]

Benton and Hefner patched things up and stayed together a few more years, but their romance slowly withered. Not only did her career keep her away for great stretches of time, but the issue of marriage and children drove a wedge between them. While Benton wanted to get married and have children, Hefner balked. They discussed the topic many times but disagreed on what was said—Benton claimed that Hefner proposed to her, while he adamantly denied doing so. The relationship finally collapsed in 1976 when she accused him of having an affair with one of her close friends. Bemused, he demanded who had told her, and when Benton named the informant, he said, "Oh, she did, huh? Well, I had an affair with her, too." That was the last straw for Benton, and she moved out for good. But she never got over Hefner completely. Years later she still reminisced fondly about their years together: "Wherever I go or whoever I end up with, that's a torch I'll always carry. Hef was the love of my life."[20]

The complications of Hefner's romantic life in the early 1970s proved to be portentous. At the very time he was struggling to maintain simultaneous relationships with two girlfriends, a much more serious situation arose. A drug scandal erupted in the heart of his world, the Chicago mansion, as agents of the federal government began to circle. Accusation, arrest, suicide, and banner headlines followed and threatened to destroy the fantasy life that he had created.

II

On December 9, 1974, the front-page headline in the *Chicago Tribune* blared, "Federal Drug Probers Zeroing in on Hefner." The exclusive story informed readers that the publisher had become "a prime target of a federal narcotics investigation" and was suspected of harboring illicit drug activity at his mansions and ordering a cover-up when drug agents closed in. According to one source, "he's in a helluva lot of trouble. There is no doubt about it." The next day, a *Chicago Sun-Times* headline fed the uproar by claiming "Hollywood Figures Tied to Playboy Drug Probe," especially a prominent movie actor who allegedly had transported illegal drugs to Hefner's Los Angeles mansion.[21]

While shocking to the public, these stories did not surprise those close to the situation. For the last two years, in fact, federal drug agents had been stalking Hefner. It had begun in September 1972 when the federal Drug Enforcement Agency (DEA) contacted Bobbie Arnstein, Hefner's executive assistant at the Chicago mansion and one of his closest friends. Agents accused her of participating in a drug-carrying venture on a trip to Miami with her boyfriend, Ron Scharf, about a year earlier. Over the next two months, they interrogated her three more times. In December, DEA agents arrested Scharf and two other men and indicted them on charges of transporting cocaine to Chicago. Meanwhile, they continued to grill Arnstein, accusing her of conspiring in a drug-running operation, goading her to testify against Scharf, and, most importantly, pressuring her to finger the ultimate recipient of the illegal drugs. From the beginning, they made it clear that they were after bigger game—namely, her boss—and dangled the prospect of immunity in return for her cooperation. Protesting Hefner's utter innocence, she steadfastly refused.[22]

Over the next fifteen months, government lawyers—they included James Thompson, the U.S. attorney, and Douglas P. Roller, attorney for the Justice Department's special strike force—built their case. Finally, on March 21, 1974, DEA agents arrested Arnstein on the sidewalk as she exited the Playboy Mansion on charges of conspiracy to distribute and sell cocaine. As newspaper photographers snapped pictures, officers handcuffed her and looked through her purse, where a vial of cocaine was discovered. As they took her away, she quipped, with a burst of black humor for which she was known, "But I haven't had lunch." The ordeal that began, however, would be anything but funny.[23]

After being released on bond, Arnstein suffered mounting government pressure to implicate Hefner. This investigation, while aimed at the *Playboy* publisher, in a larger sense represented a counterattack against 1960s rebellion. Never popular with local Chicago authorities, who were offended by his social and cultural values, Hefner had made Richard Nixon's infamous "enemies list" as a representative of 1960s liberal degeneracy. Antidrug zealots in the government, representing a conservative backlash from Middle America, viewed him as an outlandish symbol of that decade's dissenting lifestyle. Given the sex-and-drugs values of many countercultural figures, and the increasing popularity of cocaine among the beautiful people in entertainment circles, it was not surprising that the Playboy Mansion came under suspicion. When a young woman close to Hefner surfaced in a drug sting, representatives of the Silent Majority saw their chance to bring him low.[24]

But one problem sullied this scenario: Hefner, despite the prosecutors' suspicions, was no drug-culture enthusiast. For many years, of course, he had habitually used amphetamines because they kept him awake for marathon work sessions. By the late 1960s, he also occasionally smoked marijuana, primarily for its salutary effect on lovemaking. But he notoriously avoided harder drugs of all kinds. As Hefner explained later, "Everyone close to me knew that I was more conservative in my attitude about drugs than most of my friends. I had never used cocaine . . . I had never seen anyone use cocaine precisely because my friends knew my attitude, my prejudice against hard drugs."[25]

Nonetheless, the DEA and federal prosecutors were convinced that Hefner presided over a cocaine emporium at the Playboy Mansion. And the fact that some of his friends were indulging in the stylish new drug made him vulnerable. Arnstein was caught up in this larger struggle. The authorities relentlessly pressured her to provide evidence of a drug pipeline to her boss. Knowing of Hefner's innocence, and racked with guilt over the torrent of trouble she had brought down on him, she adamantly resisted but suffered severe emotional convulsions. A couple of weeks after her arrest, she took an overdose of sleeping pills but friends rushed her to the hospital in time to save her life. This proved to be a temporary respite. The drug scandal exposed a mental fragility that sent her into an inexorable spiral of decline.[26]

Arnstein's troubled personality had deep roots in an unpleasant childhood. She had been born in 1940, along with her twin brother Eddie, into a comfortable Chicago family, but when she was ten her father died suddenly and the family was forced to move in with relatives. Although a bright student with a keen sense of humor, Bobbie did not take school seriously and became a rebellious, street-wise teenager with bleached blond hair who loved television and movies, drank a bit, and dated unpopular boys whom she found interesting.[27]

Once out of high school, Arnstein held a series of low-paying jobs before becoming a receptionist at *Playboy* in 1960. She took to her new environment and by 1962 had risen through the ranks to become Hefner's executive secretary. Arnstein grew close to her boss and they became lovers for a short time before settling into a deep friendship. She also became close friends with Cynthia Maddox, with the two women sharing an apartment for several months.[28]

Then disaster struck. Bobbie had fallen in love with Tom Lownes, Victor Lownes's younger brother, a Harvard-educated journalist with literary talent and a warm personality who had joined *Playboy* as an editor after working for the *Miami Herald* and *Show Business Illustrated*. After dating for several months, they discussed marriage and in the summer of 1963 drove to Florida in Lownes's Volkswagen to visit his mother. In southern Indiana, Arnstein took the wheel for a stretch, but at some point she lost control of the car and skidded off the road. While she was thrown from the vehicle in the wreck and suffered lacerations and a broken arm, Lownes was killed. Consumed by guilt, Arnstein never drove again and told anyone who would listen that she had killed Lownes and wished she had died instead. When she returned to the mansion for a long convalescence, friends worried about her state of mind and monitored her closely. She began drinking too much and attempted suicide once, but slowly seemed to regain her equilibrium. She eventually began dating again, but the relationships always remained casual.[29]

Arnstein found a creative outlet, however, as Hefner's executive assistant. She had moved into the mansion in 1961 and had assumed a host of duties. She scheduled Hefner's business meetings, communicated his editorial decisions to *Playboy* executives, shopped for his clothes and gifts, ran interference with his girlfriends, supervised gardeners and technicians and secretaries at the domicile, regulated the guest list for movies and parties, handled his mail, and performed countless sundry tasks. Loyally protecting her boss's privacy, she told callers, "I'm sorry, but Mr. Hefner does not receive telephone calls. He speaks on the phone only when he specifically originates calls himself." She appeared often at his side, notepad in hand, ready to handle any situation. "It was clear that she was his link to the world. This was no ordinary secretarial relationship; she was more like an ambassador," an observer described.[30]

Arnstein's energetic, efficient presence matched the intense demands of her job. Small of stature, with shoulder-length auburn hair and a dazzling smile, she managed Hefner's schedule with a combination of intelligence, quick wit, and impatience with pretense. Many friends considered her to be the funniest person they had ever known, and her repartee became legendary. She collected comedy albums and loved the dark, irreverent humor of Lenny Bruce, and later, Richard Pryor. While suspicious of most compliments, she glowed when a close friend, Shirley Hillman, once remarked that she was as funny as Bruce. Arnstein occasionally would walk by Hillman and say with a laugh, "Tell me that Lenny Bruce line again."[31]

Arnstein's humor flashed out unpredictably. When a preoccupied waiter at an Indian restaurant asked, "Can I get you something, sir?" she immediately pulled up her sweater to expose her breasts and said, "Do I look like a guy to you?" The startled waiter regained his dignity and replied in his most proper manner, "No charge." The group broke into laughter, and they received no bill for the meal.

Another time she composed a "Memo to New Bunny Mothers" that mercilessly mocked the rigid rules at the Playboy Clubs:

> Bunny Mothers and General Managers should not socialize with Bunnies; Floor Managers and Bunnies should not socialize with General Managers; Bunny Mothers and Room Directors can socialize with Floor Managers, but not with two or more General Managers present; Cooks and Busboys can't socialize with anyone and neither can the hatcheck Bunny; Hugh M. Hefner, when present or absent, can or cannot socialize with anyone, depending on how he feels some of the time; the rest of the time he can do whatever he likes. You will come to love the freedom of your new job.

She delighted in skewering self-important *Playboy* executives. When she saw one approaching, a favorite tactic had her engage Hefner in conversation about his sexual adventures in previous days, which she knew he liked to talk about. She would ask him question after question, seeming to hang on every word as the executive waited, fuming, in the next room. Then she would turn and make a face to a grinning audience of secretaries who had witnessed the performance.[32]

Arnstein's relationship with Hefner became the centerpiece of her life. She always carried a bit of a torch and idolized her boss even as she became aware of his faults. Close friends believed that Arnstein's powerful emotional ties to Hefner stemmed from her father's early death and that she loved him, yearned for his approval, and resented his hold over her all at the same time. "She worshipped Hef," explained one of these friends. "For the most part, he was daddy. He filled that place up in her that she needed in order to feel like a whole person."[33]

Humor and her skillful reading of his moods sustained their relationship. Arnstein and Hefner both possessed a keen wit, and their exchanges of quips and jibes became legendary around the mansion. "I thought she could give and take with him better than anyone I've ever seen. And I think he enjoyed her company so much for that," noted Karen Christy. When Hefner showed up at her desk to exult that he had finally convinced Barbi Benton to have sex with him, for instance, Arnstein replied, "Well, Hef, why don't you rent the Goodyear Blimp and tell the world. I'm sure everyone will be just as thrilled as I am." A laughing Hefner responded, "But you can't talk that way to a man worth a hundred million dollars!" She did an uncanny imitation of an angry Hefner, and when the publisher was chewing someone out she loved to stand behind him and mimic his actions while the poor victim struggled not to laugh. At the same time, Arnstein excelled at reading her boss's state of mind, shrewdly sensing when she should vanish, hang out with him, or maneuver him into a bout of serious work as she took notes and efficiently dealt with issues. Hefner deeply appreciated the talents of his right hand woman, once describing her as "the brightest, wittiest, most insightful, sensitive, insecure, caring, craziest, most contradictory female I've ever known. . . . I loved her."[34]

As all of Arnstein's friends came to realize, however, her bravado and wit masked a deeply troubled soul. In fact, she may have suffered from a manic-depressive disorder. In her teens, she had contemplated suicide and as an adult often sank into deep, black emotional holes and talked repeatedly about wanting to die. Friends observed her intense feelings of inadequacy, heartwrenching descriptions of life as unbearably painful, and witnessed expressions of self-hatred. They convinced her to see a psychiatrist—predictably, she began to do hilarious riffs on how worthless psychiatrists were—and worried when she began to rely increasingly on speed and sleeping pills to regulate her highs and lows. At least one suicide attempt in the late 1960s only exacerbated the concern. She was "a tragedy waiting to happen," said Michelle Urry, a close friend. "She was so funny, and she could be so vulnerable. The vulnerability was terrifying sometimes when you saw it."[35]

Arnstein's emotional problems gradually became entangled with Hefner, the central presence in her life. She constantly sought his approval as a way to help bolster her identity and self-worth. Given his narcissistic bent, Hefner was ill-suited to provide such psychological reinforcement, but even if he had been it would have been insufficient. "Nobody could have filled her up," observed Urry. "Bobbie needed to do it for herself."[36]

For all of her hero worship of Hefner, Arnstein also felt harried, frustrated, and occasionally unappreciated in her job. She complained about its pressures and talked about resigning. In 1973, she complained to Dick Rosenzweig about being underpaid and unacknowledged. She observed that while she loved Hefner, her sensitivity to his needs "is the very same thing that can cause such anxiety." She complained that he was incredibly demanding and took her for granted.[37]

By the early 1970s, Arnstein was acting more erratically. Mortified by weight she had put on her slight frame over the past few years, she checked into a facility in Texas for several weeks and dropped forty pounds. Exhilarated by her success, she returned to Chicago with a penchant for health food, gave up liquor and marijuana, and purchased a flashy new wardrobe of platform shoes, tight jeans, feathers, scarves, chains, and jewelry. She also began dating younger men on a regular basis and experimented with lesbianism, having at least one affair with a female coworker. At times she seemed on top of the world, ensconced in Hefner's inner circle in Chicago and a regular at the marathon game-playing sessions along with Shel Silverstein, Gene Siskel, John Dante, and Karen Christy. Other times the depressive episodes would intrude and she would return to her old reliance on drugs.[38]

Then Arnstein met someone who would send her life onto a crash course. Ronnie Scharf was a good-looking, charming young man seven years her junior who was also a small-time drug dealer. As her infatuation grew, so did her drug usage—cocaine, Quaaludes, Placidils, and eventually heroin. She strained to keep Scharf's attention and he began spending many nights in her mansion quarters, where they would get high in the early morning hours. In 1971 came the fateful trip to Miami with her boyfriend and his roommate, Ira Sapstein. While she lounged by the pool and soaked up the tropical sunshine, Scharf and Sapstein purchased cocaine from a dealer and transported the drug back to Chicago.[39]

A subsequent chain of events sent her life spiraling downward—the initial contact from DEA agents in the fall of 1972, Scharf's and Sapstein's indictment at the end of the year, several months of interrogation and pressure, and Arnstein's own indictment and arrest in March 1974. As drug agents and prosecutors cajoled her to finger Hefner, she began to crack under the pressure and attempted suicide. She was despondent that she had drawn Hefner, the man she idolized, into great danger when he was completely innocent. Relentless prosecutors mocked her for "taking the fall" for her boss, denigrated her as a whore, and threatened a long jail sentence if she didn't hand him over. U.S. Attorney James Thompson even called her into his office to say that he had received word that a contract had been put out on her life and that she should trust neither friend nor foe. The clear, if ludicrous, implication was that Hefner might have her killed. Arnstein's depression deepened and her drug use grew.[40]

Meanwhile, Hefner and *Playboy* were sucked deeper into the maw of the drug investigation. The Chicago Strike Force circled the publisher, looking for an opening. It sent girls to infiltrate the Playboy Mansion and spy on Hefner and his guests, and secured inside informants in Allan Crawford, the mansion's security chief, and William Noel, the publisher's personal valet. The DEA dug into Hefner's procurement of Dexedrine, discovering an improper process involving a local pharmacy where amphetamine prescriptions were written for mansion employees and then delivered for the publisher's use. But this was small stuff. Despite what Hefner termed "the Inquisition," the government uncovered no evidence connecting him to the procurement, use, or sale of hard drugs.[41]

On October 22, 1974, Bobbie Arnstein's trial began. It was a disaster. Over several days government prosecutors implicated her in the Miami drug deal, with their star witness being George Mathews, the convicted narcotics dealer in Miami who now claimed that he had seen Arnstein put the cocaine in her purse to carry it to Chicago when she, Scharf, and Sapstein departed. This represented a change from his initial story, when he said that only Scharf and Sapstein were involved, and Mathews admitted that prosecutors had promised him a reduced jail term if he cooperated. Arnstein vehemently denied his testimony, and indeed, Mathews appeared to perjure himself in order to get his sentence reduced from fifteen years to three months. But her lawyers refused to let her testify, fearing that she would fall apart under cross-examination. They also rightly perceived that Arnstein would alienate a working-class Chicago jury with her wisecracking persona and expensive wardrobe of knee-length boots, flashy vests, and wild-print skirts and blouses. She acted self-destructively in the courtroom, passing notes and giggling with Scharf. Once, her close friend and attorney, Keith Stroup, became furious when he observed that one folded-up note actually contained a small pinch of drugs. The jury found both Scharf and Arnstein guilty of cocaine trafficking, and the judge sentenced the former to a six-year prison term. Incredibly, he handed Arnstein a provisional fifteen-year sentence that had a double purpose: it allowed for several weeks of psychiatric evaluation to be followed by a resentencing, and it gave prosecutors more time to pressure her to say that she was supplying Hefner as a way to save herself from the prison term she dreaded.[42]

In the wake of Arnstein's conviction, a torrent of bad publicity engulfed *Playboy* and its publisher. Front-page newspaper headlines blared that a broadening federal investigation was closing in on Hefner and had uncovered a drug link to a prominent Hollywood celebrity, who later proved to be Peter Lawford. Accompanying stories noted that *Playboy* employees had been subpoenaed to testify before a Chicago grand jury, and that a former security chief at the mansion claimed that marijuana and cocaine were regularly used at the Playboy Mansion. Then a state's attorney decided to reopen an investigation into the death of former Bunny Adrienne Pollock, who had died in 1973 from an overdose of alcohol and Quaaludes. Even though she had expired in her own apartment, a Cook County grand jury began to look into a possible link to drug use in the Playboy empire.[43]

Hefner's troubles attracted national attention. The *Los Angeles Times* detailed his emergence as a "Drug Probe Target" while *Newsweek* probed "The Playboy Connection." In the *Village Voice*, Alexander Cockburn asked, "Who's After Hef?" and noted that the Chicago Strike Force and the DEA seemed out to get Hefner, warning that he would discover that "after all those years of parties and hospitality and of famous names in the guestbook, how few true friends he has." Friendly observers in Chicago were reduced to grim jokes. "Anyone who wrote the 25-part, 200,000 word 'Playboy Philosophy' doesn't need any drugs, he's a one-man Nembutal factory," quipped the columnist Bob Greene. "Reliable sources confirm that a platoon of *Playboy*'s top photo retouching artists have been on overtime, with orders to airbrush Hefner's pipe out of all existing photographs."[44]

A string of publicity blunders by Hefner and *Playboy* personnel exacerbated the situation. A few weeks before Arnstein's trial, the publisher hosted a fund-raiser for NORML (the National Organization for the Reform of Marijuana Laws) while the police stopped the manager of the Playboy Club in Los Angeles for suspected drunk driving and found cocaine in his car. Then the executive secretary of the Playboy Foundation was arrested in Chicago for possession of a quarter pound of marijuana in her automobile trunk. Then, incredibly, the January 1975 issue of *Playboy* carried an article promising "The Truth About Cocaine." It noted that "a blizzard of cocaine is blowing over us" as it "has spilled from the ghetto and the mansion to become the illegal drug of choice, second only to marijuana, of many prosperous middle-class Americans." While the piece offered a dispassionate depiction of the attractions and dangers of cocaine, it seemed to spotlight *Playboy* as a symbol of the drug culture.[45]

Meanwhile, Arnstein, terrified by the prospect of a jail sentence and horrified at having dragged her beloved boss into a widening scandal, fell apart. Huddled in the Chicago mansion, she alternated between panic and depression. For his part, Hefner was caught in a bind. He had paid all her legal bills, refused to blame her, and offered personal encouragement whenever the opportunity arose. But with Playboy lawyers insisting that he keep a distance to protect himself, he offered no public statement on her behalf. Having moved to California, he encouraged her to come west and continue her regular job but refused to let her live in the Playboy Mansion West. A profoundly depressed Arnstein plummeted emotionally. Friends worried that she was in "very, very bad shape" as she cried, talked of suicide, and repeated that she did not want to be an imposition on Hefner and the Playboy organization.[46]

Finally, Arnstein cracked. On the evening of January 11, 1975, she had dinner with Shirley and Richard Hillman at their apartment and seemed in reasonably calm spirits. She left their place late in the evening, took in a movie with a boyfriend, and then returned to the mansion. Gathering a few personal items, she then left in the early morning hours of January 12 and walked a few blocks to the Hotel Maryland on Rush Street, where she procured a room on the top floor, hung out a "Do Not Disturb" sign, and locked the door. The next afternoon, when the maid could not get in to clean the room, hotel managers broke the lock and entered to find Arnstein sprawled on the bed, dead. She had ingested a massive quantity of barbiturates. Authorities discovered an envelope propped up with one last wisecrack scrawled on the envelope: "Boring note of explanation within." The long, rambling suicide note said, in part:

> It was I alone who acted and conceived of this act. . . . I am innocent of the charges. Despite the *perjured* testimony of the government's "star" witness, I was never part of any conspiracy to transport or distribute the alleged drugs. . . . I don't suppose it matters that I say it, but Hugh M. Hefner is—though few will ever realize it—a staunchly upright, rigorously moral man—I know him well and he has never been involved in any criminal activity which is being attributed to him now.[47]

When Hefner took a telephone call in Los Angeles and heard of Arnstein's suicide, he was stunned. But as the shock wore off, anger took its place and he dismissed advice from his attorneys that he sit tight and withhold comment. Instead, he instructed aides to schedule a news conference at the Chicago mansion for the following afternoon and to prepare the Big Bunny for a quick flight. He immediately began preparing a statement, writing in longhand on a yellow legal pad, and continued working through the night on the long flight to Chicago. A limousine took Hefner and his party directly to the mansion, and after a quick bite of breakfast and more revision, he faced over one hundred reporters and a battery of microphones, television cameras, and flash bulbs at 1 P.M. on January 14. Disheveled and deeply distressed, struggling to contain his emotions as tears threatened to roll down his haggard face, Hefner struck back at a government he believed had crossed the line of legality and decency—a government so determined to get him that it had hounded a close friend into killing herself.[48]

"You'll excuse me if I look a little harried," he began hesitantly. "I'm quite upset." But he gathered himself and launched an attack on what he described as "not a legitimate narcotics investigation at all but a politically motivated, anti-Playboy witch hunt." He passionately asserted his own innocence of any connection with hard drugs and condemned the government's relentless pressure on Bobbie Arnstein. He accused drug agents and the court of using an extremely harsh jail sentence "in an attempt to force Bobbie Arnstein to falsely incriminate me." Asserting that "the enemies' list mentality of Watergate" was alive and well in the government, he argued that the forces of "authoritarian repression" continued to threaten a free society. Arnstein was "one of the best, brightest, most worthwhile women I have ever known," the publisher said, his voice breaking. "She will be missed by me and a great many others as well."[49]

Hefner drew blood. In subsequent days, James Thompson tried to brush off his accusations, describing the publisher as "off the wall" and declaring, "I'm not sure that what Hefner stands for these days is all that relevant, or that any prosecution of him would mean much." But a wave of sympathy slowly built for the *Playboy* publisher as a subject of government persecution. Supportive articles appeared in the *Chicago Sun-Times* and *Washington Post,* while both *Newsweek* and *Time* gave full vent to Hefner's accusations. Most notably, the conservative columnist William Safire, writing in the *New York Times*, questioned the tactics of prosecutors in going after celebrities such as Hefner. Regarding Arnstein's fifteen-year jail term, he wrote, "What clearer invitation to perjury can there be than such a 'provisional sentence'? It is one thing to give a cooperative witness a break, entirely another to threaten to let a defendant rot in the slammer until he or she tells the story the prosecution wants."[50]

Over the next several months the drug case against Hefner collapsed completely. When the Chicago Strike Force sent its final report to Washington, it was obvious they had no real evidence against the *Playboy* publisher and the Justice Department did not move to prosecute. Meanwhile, the DEA came under attack for unethical, even illegal tactics and the attorney general in the new administration of President Gerald Ford launched an internal investigation of "possible mismanagement or corruption." In May 1975 the head of the DEA was asked to resign. Later in the summer James Thompson resigned as U.S. attorney to run for the governorship of Illinois, and his successor, Samuel K. Skinner, decided to drop the case. "No evidence of unlawful acquisition or distribution of cocaine or other hard drugs by Mr. Hefner, the corporation, or its employees has been adduced," he said in a public statement accompanying the conclusion of the inquiry. In a personal letter to Hefner, Skinner came close to an apology. "I am aware that the last year was not an easy one for you or your associates, and I truly wish it could have been avoided," he wrote. "I have always felt that any investigation should be conducted without any publicity whatsoever in order to protect the individuals involved."[51]

So Hefner finally was vindicated in a drug case that seemed to have been driven mainly by an anti-*Playboy* political agenda. But much damage had been done. Most disturbingly, a young woman lay dead. The *Playboy* image also had been sullied as, in a sense, Hefner won a Pyrrhic victory. While he was exonerated from any personal involvement in drug trafficking, his name had been blackened for the better part of two years by media stories depicting his lifestyle as a hotbed of drug use and depravity. Such images created serious, lasting damage. They fed a growing concern in Middle America that a climate of permissiveness had created moral dry rot in the structure of American values. The Illinois electorate, significantly, chose Jim

Thompson as governor in 1976 with 65 percent of the vote and then reelected him for three additional terms.

Hefner's ordeal in the drug scandal was accompanied by mounting financial problems in his company by the mid-1970s. Early in the decade, Playboy Enterprises Inc.'s profit potential seemed almost limitless. In 1972, a long, glowing piece in the *New York Times* described it as a "manifold 'leisure time' industry which sprawls voluptuously across the game board of American life." It compared Hefner's operation to the Disney entertainment empire and pointed to several new foreign-language editions of *Playboy*, a new magazine titled *Oui*, seventeen Playboy Clubs, three gambling casinos, four large resort hotels, two movie theaters, a book division, a film division, a record company, modeling and limousine agencies, and dozens of merchandise items emblazoned with the bunny logo. *Forbes* magazine agreed, noting that Hefner had gone "far beyond selling entertaining fantasies as an escape from life's cares; now *Playboy* wants to sell its fantasy as a way of life."[52]

At the same time, financial trouble loomed on the horizon. Caught up in the company's growth and eager to create a multifaceted entertainment empire, Hefner and his lieutenants had indulged in overexpansion. They failed to create a suitable management structure for their far-flung endeavors and by the mid-1970s stresses and strains were becoming evident. The magazine continued to turn a profit, but many Playboy Clubs had begun losing money—the British clubs, because of gambling revenue, were an exception—while hotel and resort ventures were floundering. The Great Gorge resort in New Jersey, for instance, which opened in 1972, was a disaster from the beginning. This giant luxury hotel of over six hundred rooms cost PEI over $30 million to build, and it never came close to the 60 percent occupancy it required to break even. Playboy's movie projects also fizzled. Roman Polanski's 1971 *Macbeth* enjoyed critical success but generated little box-office appeal, while the company's follow-up, *The Naked Ape*, flopped both artistically and financially.[53]

PEI's problems could be seen in its volatile stock prices. The company had gone public in late 1971 with an initial burst of enthusiasm, but over the next few years the value of its shares fell sharply. Fallout from the drug scandal contributed to the negative mood, as two members of the company's board of directors resigned to avoid staining their reputation while some advertisers backed away from commitments to the magazine. In 1974, PEI's two-decade anniversary, the respected business journal *Dun's Review* offered a grim conclusion: "On recent performance, the record of Playboy at twenty seems one of careless squandering that promises a dismal future."[54]

Part of the problem was Hefner himself. Increasingly bored with financial aspects of his enterprise, he had withdrawn from corporate affairs throughout the late 1960s and early 1970s. While formulating broad goals for PEI, he had turned over the empire to associates to run. "I'm out here playing backgammon. I don't want to hear from anybody," he admitted later. But lacking a strong hand at the helm, the company had begun to meander off course as it proceeded on its corporate journey. Criticism of Hefner's absentee status began mounting as business experts decried the publisher as being "far removed from the business side of his empire." Some PEI executives concurred. Robert Gutwillig, a vice president for marketing who was helping run the company, wrote a blistering 1974 memo that described Hefner as "a chief executive with a whim of iron, disregard for the welfare of the company, contempt for his employees, and a lifestyle second only to Louis the Sun King." At the height of the drug scandal, Gutwillig and Robert Preuss, president of PEI, even took the extraordinary step of asking Hefner to step down until the investigation was complete. In early 1975, Hefner finally was forced to act, establishing a temporary Office of the President, overseen by himself and composed of six executives, to run PEI while a search was launched to secure an experienced business figure to become president and COO.[55]

Thus the first half of the 1970s saw Hefner facing romantic turmoil, drug scandal, and financial difficulties in his company. But like much of America, he stepped back from public problems and turned inward to concentrate on his personal life. During these same years he had created a new private refuge far from the Midwest where he had grown up and launched his career. Success had created fresh wishes for self-fulfillment, and California now presented a rich new environment in which to realize them. There Hefner would nourish the most elaborate, heretical fantasies that he could concoct.

14

Disneyland for Adults

In mid-June 1972, the Rolling Stones interrupted their North American tour for a brief layover at the Playboy Mansion. Even by the jaded standards of Mr. Playboy's abode, it was an impressive performance as Mick Jagger, Keith Richards, and friends engaged in a nonstop, four-day orgy of sex, drugs, and partying. A string of incidents soon became legend: Jagger flipping up his bathrobe at poolside and replying "Have at it, luv," to a lustful girl who had just blurted out, "I want to bite your ass"; Richards at the center of an orgy under the dining room table; a bacchanalia in Hefner's huge Roman bath. When the band stumbled off to its next concert dates, Mary O'Connor, one of Hefner's key assistants, assessed the damage in a long memo: a heap of irretrievably burned towels, bedsheets, and rugs; chairs, couches, and bedspreads stained to ruination; bathroom fixtures knocked askew and drapes pulled down and destroyed; plumbing so blocked in one room that plumbers had to cut into the walls to clear the pipes. But the publisher shrugged off the carnage. Proud of his friendship with the band, he put up a framed poster inscribed "To Hugh Hefner, for his warm hospitality—from Mick Jagger and the Stones."[1]

Such incidents typified the revelry of Hefner's life at the mansion, but he had grown restless in Chicago. The shooting of his television show, *Playboy After Dark,* took him to Los Angeles for frequent stints and his developing relationship with Barbi Benton kept him there. Then Bobbie Arnstein's suicide, along with his breakup with Karen Christy, further loosened ties to the Windy City. But most importantly, the allure of Hollywood proved irresistible. He purchased an estate near Sunset Boulevard to house him during the long West Coast stays and increasingly gravitated to the sunny, starstruck climate of Southern California. By 1975, he was living there permanently and the Chicago mansion, shuttered with a skeleton staff, gradually became a relic of his past.

The Playboy Mansion West, with its stately manor house and beautiful grounds, became Hefner's new personal paradise, a Shangri-La where he and a steady group of friends cavorted in what he termed a "Disneyland for adults." For the publisher, this new atmosphere represented a psychological as well as a geographical shift. "California is the *avant garde* of everything that is happening in this country," he said. As the new center of Hefner's world, the residence became more than a home. It served as a kind of social and cultural greenhouse for the cultivation of his reputation. Embracing private pursuits with even greater zeal, Hefner threw himself into group sex with a coterie of female friends and marathon game-playing sessions with an informal fraternity of male friends. Facing an American public landscape marked by Watergate-era political cynicism, economic recession, and weariness with social crusades, the publisher retreated into his private realm and played even harder. Like many Americans in this era, Hefner turned inward after the public storms and stresses of the 1960s.[2]

I

Early in the new decade, Hefner made a decision that changed his life. Tired of staying in his apartment during frequent sojourns in Los Angeles to tape his television show in the late 1960s, he decided to buy a house. In late 1970, Barbi Benton found an unusual estate that immediately captured his imagination—a thirty-room mansion on six acres in the heart of Holmby Hills, an exclusive residential area of Los Angeles, and only a block off the fabled Sunset Boulevard. Originally built in the 1920s for the family of Arthur Letts, the founder of Broadway department stores, it now was unoccupied, having been used for several years by the city as a hospitality center for visiting dignitaries. Hefner visited the estate with Benton, and immediately fell in love with it. He purchased it on February 3, 1971, for the price of $1,050,000.

The house and its grounds offered several attractions to the *Playboy* publisher. He was struck immediately by the beautiful marble panel on the hillside just inside the main gate, with its apt depiction of Aurora, the Roman goddess of dawn, leading a group of beautiful young women into a new day. The Tudor Gothic mansion sitting atop the hill featured a façade of gray granite adorned with towers, crenellations, and bay windows with leaded glass. The hand-carved oak door opened into a two-story great hall flanked by ornate dining rooms on one side and a large living room with fireplace and library on the other. A curved double staircase led to the second floor, where a huge master bedroom suite occupied one end, while a string of smaller bedrooms swept the length of the mansion. At the far end of the structure another wing of rooms bent at a right angle to form an L shape. One of Hefner's favorite features was a secret panel that led down to a hidden wine cellar, an architectural component reflecting the fact that the house had been built in 1927 during Prohibition.[3]

Surrounding the mansion were six acres of land with a greenhouse, gamehouse, guesthouse, sweeping lawns in front and back, and the largest stand of redwoods in Southern California. Almost immediately, however, Hefner decided to extensively renovate the grounds to create a personal fantasy setting. He wanted a swimming pool and tennis court, but also sought to create "a veritable Eden with waterfalls, fish ponds, and a variety of birds and animals running free," as he put it. Ron Dirsmith, a landscape architect who brought Hefner's vision to life, created a hill at the rear perimeter of the backyard to hide the adjoining property and placed in front of it a complex of waterfalls, streams, koi pond, and meandering swimming pool, all seemingly connected. The pool enclosed a rock grotto, while surrounding it was a tiered flagstone patio with a bar and a bathhouse built of natural stone. Everything in Dirsmith's design reflected Hefner's desire to maintain a natural landscape and create what he called "a little piece of paradise." The effect was heightened by the addition of a menagerie of flamingos, peacocks, African cranes, macaws, monkeys, rabbits, llamas, and dogs, most of which wandered freely among the lawns and trees.[4]

Hefner also ordered a redecoration of the house to create "the ultimate baronial bachelor's pad." He erased any feminine details he found. He replaced the original French crystal chandelier in the great hall, for instance, with a masculine bronze one and enlarged the master bedroom, adding walnut paneling and a beamed ceiling. A new, hand-carved circular stairway led up to an attic office that was also wood-paneled. Nude female figures were incorporated into a carved stone fireplace and an enormous bed, surrounded by movie and television screens and electronic gadgetry, became the centerpiece of the room.[5]

Hefner forged a strong emotional identification with his new abode. The man who avoided sunlight in Chicago now "became entranced with the beautiful azaleas, rhododendrons, and the ferns and marvelous pines and the various plants that were out there," reported Dirsmith. Determined to maintain a natural, organic ethos on the grounds, Hefner and Dirsmith modeled the grotto on prehistoric caves in France, embedding in the glass ceiling panels designs of prehistoric objects and insects trapped in amber. The publisher demanded paths, walkways, and isolated niches throughout the property to encourage an atmosphere of intimacy for his friends. The final result delighted him. "This property seemed to have been meant for me," Hefner said later. "A new Playboy Mansion for a new decade, interconnected to nature as the Chicago Mansion had never been."[6]

The public opening of the Playboy Mansion West came on November 20, 1971, at a benefit fund-raiser for the ACLU. Studded with celebrities such as Burt Lancaster, Anthony Quinn, Beverly Sills, Walter Matthau, Angie Dickinson, Richard Widmark, Yul Brynner, George McGovern, and Arthur Schlesinger Jr., the event prompted a *Los Angeles Times* reporter to complain, "You could get a pain in the neck from all the head swiveling." But such large-scale social events soon caused disgruntlement among Hefner's new neighbors. In 1972 they drew up a list of complaints—loud music, walkie-talkie noise at all hours, late-night use of the tennis court, large numbers of parked cars clogging the streets, nude young women standing atop the backyard hill disrupting golfers on the adjacent course—and hired an attorney to negotiate with the publisher prior to taking legal action. Hefner declared his intention to be a good neighbor and agreed to modify the offensive practices.[7]

As the mansion got up and running, unaccustomed problems tormented the staff. Not long after it opened, for instance, Hefner's troop of squirrel monkeys created an uproar. Following training advice from experts at the San Diego Zoo, groundskeepers initially kept them on long ropes and fed them at regular times at the base of a huge redwood in the backyard. After several weeks, they released them and the monkeys hung around in anticipation of the feeding. But then the simian brigade, perched high in the redwood branches, alertly observed a huge buffet table being set out in a neighbor's yard for a wedding. A furious phone call informed mansion personnel that some two dozen hairy raiders had come swinging out of the trees and were eating everything in sight, and a posse of gardeners, butlers, security people, electricians, and carpenters went charging down the hill to retrieve the miscreants. Fortunately, Hefner's large kitchen was able to replace the pilfered food, but the monkeys were put in giant enclosures thereafter.[8]

Despite such mishaps, nearly all visitors to the Playboy Mansion West saw it as a fantasy come to life. A jaded reporter for the *Los Angeles Herald Examiner,* who had seen many beautiful residences in Beverly Hills and Bel-Air, admitted that "seldom do you see anyone short of the aristocracy living in such baronial splendor." Anthony Haden-Guest, in a 1973 article for *Rolling Stone,* described

> a mullioned slab of Old Englishry, a gray gleam of ersatz granite in the Southern California sunlight. To the back the image dissolves, re-forms. Sexy vicarage metamorphoses to miniature Versailles. Gibbons swing and chatter in the trees while a couple of house guests foozle with croquet hoops; a quintet of East African cranes lope up a handmade hill and an associate movie-producer hopefully pursues a trio of cuties. Mottled Japanese carp float on one side of a bridge, and on the other, in the bathing pool, another cutie, with the left cheek of her bikini bottom cut into a heart shape, floats on an air mattress.

The actor Peter O'Toole, after strolling the grounds with Hefner, Paul Newman, and Joanne Woodward, offered a snappier summary: "This is the way God would have done it if he had the money."[9]

Hefner adored his new residence. While savoring its sheer physical beauty, he also imagined it radiating a mystique that was equal parts erotic freedom, material affluence, and old Hollywood glamour. The publisher saw it not only as a haven for pleasure, but as his ticket into the movie-star community that he had idolized since childhood. He planned for his new abode, with its spacious grounds and sumptuous manor house, to become a site for recapturing some of the charm and allure associated with the golden age of American filmmaking. Indeed, as Hefner threw lavish parties and cultivated the celebrities of the silver screen, he became a Hollywood fixture.[10]

Profoundly satisfied with his new California dwelling, he once answered a query about vacations by saying, "I go from the house to the Jacuzzi." In 1975 he lovingly shepherded into the pages of *Playboy* a long article titled "Playboy Mansion West." Describing the property as a "new paradise by the Pacific, a contemporary Shangri-La for work and play," it took the reader on an extended, step-by-step tour through the house and grounds. Replete with evocative prose and dozens of lush photographs, it reflected Hefner's emotional blueprint for his new home. The article stressed its atmosphere of liberation and fantasy, and its "ethereal, dreamlike quality." It described Hefner's circle of friends, "a free-form floating family— maybe 30 or 40 regulars, who come and go, group and regroup in ever-changing combinations"—as they made the residence "a second home." It pointed out Hefner's new affinity for nature, sunshine, and daytime working hours, joking that "Hef discovered he couldn't do a thing about the ridiculous hours the sun kept so he decided to meet it halfway." In both pictures and prose, it illuminated the mansion's attraction for movie stars and entertainers by noting the presence of figures such as Sammy Davis Jr., Peter Lawford, Raquel Welch, Tony Curtis, Jim Brown, Jack Nicholson, Groucho Marx, James Caan, Clint Eastwood, and many others. Finally, of course, the article rounded out Hefner's vision of the mansion by depicting the beautiful, unclad, and uninhibited young women who pervaded the property. Visitors to the Playboy Mansion West, it concluded, "have nothing to do but relax and enjoy the wonders of this Disneyland for adults."[11]

In fact, the *Playboy* publisher hosted innumerable gaudy social events at the mansion throughout the 1970s. Hefner's longtime love of boxing led to elaborate "Fight Night" parties for bouts such as the 1974 Muhammad Ali–George Foreman contest in Zaire (where Ali thrilled Hefner by saying hello on the air), and the "Thrilla in Manila" contest between Ali and Joe Frazier in 1975. Hefner's birthday also provided the occasion for yearly parties. One of the most notable came on his fiftieth in 1976, when his friends put together a surprise roast where a group of comedians and close friends made fun of the publisher before a large crowd. Two years later, Hefner's birthday prompted the "Schlong Show," a bawdy send-up of Chuck Barris's television hit, *The Gong Show*. A number of mansion regulars sang, danced, told jokes, and entertained as a panel composed of Hefner, Peter Lawford, and comedian Alan Kent awarded points and rang the gong on particularly awful acts. On his fifty-fifth birthday, in an elaborate set in the backyard, friends presented the Calamity Awards, a satire on the Academy Awards that focused on the foibles of mansion insiders. Roman Polanski, for example, received the "Outstanding Achievement in Box Office Disasters Award" for a recent movie. The director had fled the country because of a scandal involving an under age girl, so his award was accepted by James Caan's eleven-year-old daughter, who walked up to the microphone and brought the house down with this line: "I'm sorry, my husband couldn't make it tonight."[12]

A long string of parties and social events shaped the regular calendar of life at Hefner's mansion. New Year's Eve, Valentine's Day, Halloween, and the announcement of the Playmate of the Year became standard fare while a pajama soiree, the Midsummer Night's Dream Party, became a particular favorite of many mansion regulars. Hefner was especially thrilled by the Playmate Reunion, on the twenty-fifth anniversary of the magazine's founding, when 136 former Playmate centerfolds gathered at the California mansion for a weekend celebration in September 1979. Weekly movie nights, attended by several dozen guests, filled out the mansion's social schedule, as did numerous fund-raising events for charities. Hefner had special enthusiasm for a gathering in the summer of 1978 to restore the famous Hollywood sign that sat in the hills north of Los Angeles, which he described as "Hollywood's Eiffel Tower."[13]

As its mystique spread, the Playboy Mansion West became the setting for several ABC-TV specials focusing on Hefner and the

Playboy lifestyle. In April 1977, for instance, ABC televised *Playboy's Playmate Party,* hosted by the comedian Dick Martin and featuring appearances by Bill Cosby, Robert Culp, James Caan, and Arnold Schwarzenegger as well as Hefner and an assortment of Playmates. Two years later, in November 1979, Richard Dawson hosted *The Playboy Roller Disco and Pajama Party* on ABC. With musical entertainment provided by Chuck Mangione and the Village People, most of the activity focused on Hefner and several dozen skimpily clad Playmates roller skating to disco music on the tennis courts, dancing in the mansion's great hall, and lounging by the swimming pool and grotto. Such shows drew high ratings, but many critics found them to be little more than extended commercials for Hefner and *Playboy.*[14]

The mansion also hosted many political events that reflected its owner's attraction to liberal causes. In the spring of 1976, he hosted a fund-raiser for California governor Jerry Brown during his race for the presidency in the Democratic primaries. The following year he did the same for Los Angeles mayor Tom Bradley, who swept to a reelection victory. The National Organization for the Reform of Marijuana Laws (NORML) also continued to attract Hefner's support with several fund-raisers while the publisher received NAACP Image Awards in the latter 1970s. In 1978, a Playboy Foundation gathering in behalf of the Equal Rights Amendment brought in thousands of dollars and featured Dr. Benjamin Spock as the guest of honor.[15]

Thus a public image began to take shape of the Playboy Mansion West as a gathering place for Hollywood's beautiful people and a private playground for the *Playboy* publisher, his friends, and a legion of beautiful female companions. But the popular impression of Hefner's hedonistic Eden in Southern California, no matter how extravagant, could not match what actually happened behind its walls. In real life, Mr. Playboy enjoyed a private realm of sensual indulgence and exuberant play in the 1970s that dwarfed anything he had experienced in earlier years. It would have boggled the imagination of his public.

II

The December 1977 issue of *Playboy* featured "Playboy's Playmate House Party," which described the beguiling "party after the party" following a recent ABC television show. It followed seven Playmates as they cavorted about the mansion grounds, often in the nude, having pillow fights, sunbathing, relaxing in the sauna, shooting pool, and finally joining Hefner to enjoy a lobster and wine buffet. But then came the pièce de résistance—a "champagne celebration" in the grotto Jacuzzi where the publisher and the naked females relaxed in the bubbling waters, casually intertwined with chilled champagne at hand. The article described this scene as "a perfect candlelit capper to what has been a vintage day for Hef and the girls." With broad winks to the reader, the article hinted at what had become a reality: Hefner had emerged at the center of a group-sex scene.[16]

The editor had slept with a host of women over the last two decades, of course, and often concurrently, but seldom together. In the case of his "serious" girlfriends, they never shared his bed with other females. Now, however, group-sex scenes became the norm at his West Coast Shangri-La. At the same time, Hefner intensified his long interest in game playing—card games, board games, pinball and video games—into a passion. The new mansion became, in his words, "both a swinger's paradise and a sanctuary" where fun and games, quite literally, became the stuff of his life. Later, he described this period as "part of the 'if that's all there is, then let's keep on dancing' attitude that took hold after Bobbie Arnstein's death." During this escapist interlude, "I was celebrating my survival, if nothing else."[17]

The unrestrained sexual atmosphere at the 1970s mansion quickly achieved legendary status among those privy to its daily life. By about 1973, Barbi Benton was absent for long stretches doing television spots or touring with her band, and "there were plenty of Playmates and Bunnies eager to fill my time," Hefner noted later. An atmosphere of sexual abandon began to envelop the mansion grounds as notorious lotharios such as Warren Beatty, Jack Nicholson, and James Caan were regular visitors along with a constant stream of Playmates, ambitious models, and aspiring actresses. Unending seductions and uninhibited sex became the normal order of things. Beatty, for example, was notorious for his sexual conquests. According to an observer, the stunningly handsome, soft-voiced movie star would simply approach a young woman, shake her hand, and quietly say, "Hi, I'm Warren," at which point she would melt. The filmmaker Michael Trikilis once was having sex with a beautiful young woman in one of the gamehouse bedrooms when the door suddenly opened and Hefner stood there. Trikilis froze, fearing that the publisher might be angry, but he calmly walked by, patted him on the butt, and said, "Hi, Mikey." "Couples could be found coupling on the Mansion grounds at almost any time of the day or night," Hefner described. "It was an Eden that prompted pleasure seekers to leave their inhibitions at the gate."[18]

The grotto became the erotic shrine at the center of this pleasure temple. Its sensual atmosphere presented both an outdoor feeling of nature and an intimate feeling of cavelike seclusion. With soothing jets of water, an array of overstuffed cushions scattered about, soft candlelight, and piped-in music—all hidden behind a waterfall masking the entrance to the larger pool outside—the grotto appeared like a set from a romantic movie. Guests responded to the allure of this magical spot, and it was not unusual in the 1970s to see people making love there in various combinations at all hours.[19]

But the real erotic energy at the mansion radiated from Hefner and a bevy of young women who established a highly unconventional relationship throughout the late 1970s. The "Mansion Misses," as he termed them, became his regular sexual partners in group scenes occurring occasionally in the grotto but most often upstairs in his master bedroom. This steady group of young women included Hope Olson, Patti McGuire, Marilou York, Marcy Hanson, Daina House, Susan Kiger, Alison Reynolds, Debbie Svensk Jensen, and Monique St. Pierre. Hefner felt excited and liberated by a situation where "instead of having to choose one girl over another on any given evening, I simply chose them all—and the more the merrier."[20]

His consorts agreed. The Mansion Misses saw the group sex as an exciting erotic adventure that freed them from traditional moral restraints. "It was a once-in-a-lifetime opportunity to act out the fantasies we all have," explained Svensk. Marcy Hanson described it as "a dream world" where participants "could just have fun and experience everything without any rules to follow," where they had "the freedom to express ourselves in every way that felt good to us, without being labeled evil or promiscuous."[21]

Monique St. Pierre was especially eloquent on this point. Upon joining Hefner and several girls in his bed for the first time, she was overwhelmed:

> I remember holding hands . . . and one another. And gradually the warmth grew and grew into a tremendous sexual energy

that finally swept us along faster and faster, and finally over the edge. I didn't even know what I was doing, I wasn't even aware of myself as being separate from the others. . . . It was the most amazing sex I've ever had. But the most amazing thing about it was that it wasn't really about sex. It was about life.

St. Pierre experienced a kind of euphoria where she "felt so free to let down every guard that you had ever learned in your entire life. Nothing seemed wrong." It made her feel intensely alive and she described a kind of spiritual experience—"a feast, a festival, an adventure, an awakening. It transformed me."[22]

The female participants in this unusual erotic arrangement experienced a special bonding that created intimate relationships and blunted jealousies. With no strings attached to this experiment in physical pleasure, they became close friends and enjoyed one another's company with no one having a special claim on Hefner. Several of them described it as "a big happy family" or a "big happy sorority" where the ultimate agenda was to break the rules and have fun. "We were such good friends with each other that we were just showing our love for one another, not in a lesbian way at all, but just in that we cared so much for each other and for Hef," explained Alison Reynolds. "We all became really close friends up there in Hef's bedroom." In fact, the friendships were so strong that they would go on to last for decades thereafter.[23]

But Hefner did not limit himself to the Mansion Misses. Throughout the late 1970s he regularly engaged in sporadic sexual encounters with a variety of "Personal Playmates," as he liked to call them. This group consisted of women he dated seriously for a short time, such as Lillian Mueller, the sultry Norwegian beauty who became the 1976 Playmate of the Year. It included a number of young women who posed for *Playboy*—Ashley Cox, Nikki Thomas, Janice Pennington, Christie Maddox, Michelle Drake, Gig Gangel, Sivi Aberg, among them. It contained others who were simply attracted to the sexual excitement of the mansion, such as a beautiful University of Michigan undergraduate who sought out Hefner as a kind of fantasy fulfillment and spent several sensual weekends with him at the mansion. Moreover, the publisher sporadically engaged in "swinging" sessions that included his favorite girlfriend of the moment along with couples such as Orson and Denise Mozes. As Hefner observed, after breaking up with Barbi Benton he devoted himself "to a far more open lifestyle, not to any one person, but to many. There were too many delicious possibilities for me to contemplate limiting myself to only one or two."[24]

Throughout this uninhibited period, however, Hefner did maintain a serious romantic relationship of sorts. In the fall of 1976, just after the final departure of Benton, he met a shy, nineteen-year-old blonde from a very traditional background. Sondra Theodore had been born and raised in San Bernardino, where she had been in the Girl Scouts, taught Sunday school, and acted in local theater productions. After a year in college she had moved to Los Angeles to pursue an acting career when she accompanied a girlfriend to a party at the Playboy Mansion. Awkward and nervous, she was quietly nursing a drink at the bar when Hefner appeared and put her at ease with his calm, joking manner. After a tour of the grounds, they played pinball for a time and then danced to a slow, romantic song. Then the publisher left her to attend to his other guests but promised to return. He did, saying, "Well, I've looked the whole party over and can't think of anyone I'd rather spend the rest of the evening with." Swept off her feet, Theodore spent the night with Hefner and over the next several weeks began a romantic relationship that would last for five years.[25]

Theodore became a fixture at the mansion. Hopelessly in love with Hefner, the vivacious young woman attended to his wants and needs in every way possible. She developed an interest in old movies and big band music, faithfully accompanied him to social gatherings and public appearances, and played his favorite tunes on the big Steinway piano in the living room. She gushed about her boyfriend to the press, recounting that he had "such a boyish charm you just want to cuddle him up and love him. He's witty, he's funny, he guides you, takes care of you, yet he's the keeper of his house." Hefner responded to her sweet, romantic nature, describing her as a "fresh faced, wholesome, gawky kid with a tomboyish charm that captured my heart—that made me feel like a boy again." He bought her an expensive necklace that spelled out "Baby Blue" in diamonds, after the Barry White song of the same name that they had danced to that first evening. He also chose her as *Playboy*'s Playmate of the Month in July 1977.[26]

But Hefner had no intention of giving up the other women in his life. "I was really committed to non-commitment," he said, and while he cared for Theodore, it was not deep enough to create a serious, long-term love affair. "She was a special girl, but not the only girl," Hefner noted bluntly. The publisher had no intention of committing one-on-one to *anybody*, and it reflected his desire to avoid the burden of obligation that went with a steady, exclusive girlfriend. "It was the same kind of thing that you get with marriage. Then you have to make decisions not simply on the basis of what you want to do, but what you're expected to do," he explained. "I don't think I was avoiding emotional involvement, but I was avoiding some of the responsibilities of a one-on-one relationship."[27]

Theodore tried to take this in stride, accepting Hefner on his own terms and overlooking his dalliances with other women. But it was not easy. She told others—and obviously, herself—that she knew what she was getting into and that sex with many women was part of his lifestyle, his very identity. "I love him too much to throw it out the window over a silly thing like him seeing another girl once in a while," she told a newspaper interviewer. "The others are just adventures." At the same time, she yearned for a deeper, more permanent relationship. "If he were to ask me to marry him tomorrow, I'd do it," she admitted publicly. Thus she found herself caught between conflicting desires—to be happy or to make Hefner happy. "I shed a lot of tears, and it was very painful at times," she admitted, but she gamely acknowledged a basic fact: "I knew I wasn't going to change him, so if I was going to love a man like him, I had to accept what he was all about."[28]

Theodore also struggled to be accepted by the other females in Hefner's bedroom coterie. Initially, they saw her as an interloper who was conniving to have the publisher all to herself. They played mean tricks on her and froze her out at every opportunity. But Theodore persisted, constantly telling the others that "if we love him we will try to make him happy, and he likes harmony." She soon won them over and became a full-fledged member of the sorority. In fact, so complete was her devotion to Hefner that she began to set up group sexual activities to please him. According to another member of the sorority, "She would almost be his little gofer. He would want to get someone, and she would get the girl into the scene."[29]

Eventually, however, the strain of sharing Hefner began to wear on Theodore. With the man she adored sleeping with many other women, often in her presence, the jealousy and pain began to build up. His relationship with Heather Waite, a gorgeous blond beauty queen, became especially distressing from 1978 to 1980 as the two women took turns, with one being at the mansion on certain days and the remaining days reserved for the other. Theodore's crying spells became more frequent, as did her arguments with Hefner, and she gradually began to dull her bubbly personality with alcohol and drugs. She had maintained her own apartment since dating Hefner, and increasingly she went there to escape. Her close friends in the sorority grew worried as she numbed her pain chemically. Theodore admitted that "the lifestyle started to take a bit of a toll on me," and when they finally broke up in 1980 "it was very difficult on me, very difficult. And I had a lot of anger and I felt betrayed."[30]

Despite such emotional complications, Hefner radiated a vibrant, magnetic sexual vitality throughout the last half of the 1970s that seemed to overwhelm all problems. He appeared as a man with an insatiable appetite for sex and little respect for erotic boundaries. At the same time, his physical intensity was accompanied by a gentle, romantic quality that made sex more than just physical pleasure. "Hef was the catalyst, he was the power source of all that energy. He was exuding it, generating it, building it, orchestrating it," Monique St. Pierre recounted. "He was incredibly gentle and loving, but also incredibly wild." Marcy Hanson described him as "like a little boy under a Christmas tree when it came to sex—so playful and adventuresome, so enthused by every new creative thing you came up with in bed."[31]

Hefner's sexual passions occasionally produced curious situations. His love of slathering baby oil on his girlfriends during lovemaking would create problems for them in removing the sticky mess in their hair the next day. During a raucous lovemaking session with Sondra Theodore, he accidentally swallowed one of her "Benwa Balls," a sexual toy that consisted of two metal balls inserted inside a woman to enhance her physical sensations. He fell back on the bed, choking and unable to breathe, and was about to lose consciousness when she squeezed his chest and finally dislodged the sphere. The incident frightened them, but later that evening he made light of the trauma with friends. At the point of expiring from inhaling a sex toy, he joked, "The first thing that went through my mind was, is this what it has all led to? The second thing was, what will all the newspaper headlines in the world say tomorrow morning? The third was, are we getting this on videotape?" A short time later, Theodore had the offending Benwa Ball framed against a velvet purple heart with a caption: "Lest We Forget."[32]

The aura of Hefner's sexual prowess allowed him to enhance his public persona at every opportunity. Delighted by the growing legend, he observed, "It wasn't difficult to figure out that the most successful sex object I'd created was me. It was a role I was very comfortable playing." When commenting to the press about his reputation as a Casanova, pride occasionally shaded into vanity, even crassness. "I have built here what could be viewed as a perpetual woman machine," he commented in a 1978 interview with the *Chicago Tribune*. "Women, although they say they like a faithful and monogamous man, are very attracted to a man who has had a lot of romantic experiences. The more experienced you are, the more desirable you are to a woman." Reveling in the transgressions, the uninhibited pleasure-seeking that defined his sexual life in the late 1970s, Hefner described it as the period when "I was least my mother's son."[33]

But Hefner's grand experiment in liberated sexuality made up only one side of mansion life in the 1970s. His other passion consisted of game playing, which he elevated to the level of obsession. Along with a fraternity of male friends dubbed "The Rabbit Pack" by one wag—it included John Dante, Joe DeCarlo, Bernie Cornfeld, Shel Silverstein, Gene Schacove, Jim Brown, Lee Wolfberg, John Rockwell, Berry Gordy, Billy Eisenberg, Michael Trikilis, and James Caan—he engaged in competitions that would last for hours, or even days. Monopoly was a favorite, but pinball became an even bigger addiction. The gamehouse on the mansion grounds soon grew stuffed with the latest pinball machines—Bally even issued a special model with images of Hef, Theodore, and Patti McGuire—and became the site of marathon tournaments. Competition and conviviality mixed in equal measure. "You rotated and there were so many machines, and people would sit on the couch and talk and you could run back and forth and talk and play the game," a girlfriend described.[34]

In Hefner's hierarchy of pastimes in the 1970s, however, backgammon moved to the very top. He had been introduced to this ancient game early in the decade and his interest inspired a quartet of articles in the March 1973 *Playboy* that explored the history of the game, its contemporary attraction, strategies of play, and the most stylish boards and gear. Hefner really got hooked, however, after attending a 1972 world championship tournament in Las Vegas. Attracted by the intense, rapid-fire competition of the game and its veneer of jet-setting glamour and cosmopolitanism, he began to play seriously. Backgammon became a significant part of life at the mansion with games of varying size and duration going on almost all of the time. Celebrities, friends, high-rolling gamblers, and serious players joined Hefner in these activities and large amounts of money were won and lost.[35]

The mansion soon attracted world-class players such as Billy Eisenberg, Tom Gilbert, and Oswald Jacoby. Hefner also began frequenting tournaments and enjoyed some success, once beating Tim Holland, a world-ranked player. As backgammon mania set in, according to Eisenberg, a group of regulars competed constantly as "Hef and the boys started playing for 12, 18, 24, 36, 48 hours at a time." Some of the games got out of hand, with unskilled players losing great amounts of money and debts going unpaid. Eventually, Hefner was forced to end such games in the interests of harmony at his Southern California Eden. At the same time, he became a major investor in Pips, a private backgammon club in Hollywood that flourished for several years.[36]

The game became a consuming passion for Hefner. He found it exciting, noting that it had "a confrontational quality about it that really got the adrenaline going." Focusing both his considerable powers of intelligence and energy, he threw himself into the games and grew adept at many of its subtle strategies. Friends marveled at how, on more than one occasion, he would sit at the backgammon board for two or three days straight without food or drink except for a steady supply of Pepsis and an occasional dexie. "Hef had the focus of a laser in those days," reported one observer. Backgammon even trumped sex on occasion in the Hefner universe. One time a beautiful blond Playmate spent several hours lolling about as she read magazines, munched on snacks, and chatted with the staff as she waited for some romantic attention from the publisher. But he stayed holed up in the library engaged in a marathon backgammon contest. She finally gave up around 5 A.M., gave him a goodnight kiss, and left to go to bed. Hef looked up briefly to quip, "Greater love hath no backgammon player," and went back to rolling the dice.[37]

Hefner's obsession with games in the 1970s reflected, of course, *Playboy*'s broader social philosophy of pleasure-seeking. But it also appealed to more personal impulses. First, they provided lighthearted distraction to a man who had been utterly absorbed in his work for two decades. "The ability to enjoy such frivolous pastimes is part of what life ought to be all about," he said in 1974. But pinball and back-gammon also offered a framework for sociability to someone whose shy nature did not make for a natural bon vivant. "He was great with games and fun with games. That's when you get him relaxed and his personality really comes out," Sondra Theodore commented. "He shares himself with his friends." Nor was it surprising that Hefner, one of the great business and journalistic successes in postwar America, savored the competition and relished winning. Finally, games pro-vided an outlet for the publisher's burning energy. Having pulled away from much day-to-day direction of the *Playboy* enterprise, he found that backgammon offered, in the words of Eisenberg, an opportunity to deploy his "restless imagination and intellect, and . . . a flight from boredom."[38]

Thus Hefner's private pursuit of pleasure in the 1970s marked a shift, both in intensity and in kind, from his earlier style of life. While the revelry at the Chicago mansion in the 1960s had aimed to revitalize American society, the hedonism of his California Shangri-La during the following decade seemed to map out an escape route. Personal life had become not an enhancement to public life, but an alternative. Once more, however, Hefner's growing preoccupation with private endeavors and states of mind had a larger cultural reso-nance. As many commentators noted, not only the *Playboy* publisher but large segments of the American population seemed to be turning inward.

III

In 1976, Tom Wolfe published an essay that captured an essential impulse of the new era. The 1970s, he wrote, "will come to be known as the Me Decade." In the aftermath of the upheavals of the 1960s, great numbers of Americans had embraced spiritual revivals, popular therapies, physical fitness, self-help movements, hippie communes, and sexual liberation in a cultural groundswell promoting personal self-fulfillment. This powerful wave of introspection involved "changing one's personality—remaking, remodeling, elevating, and polishing one's very *self* and observing, studying, and doting on it," wrote Wolfe. Seeping from the discourse of religion, counseling, physical exercise, and many other endeavors were the phrases of the age: "Let's talk about me . . . Let's find the Real Me . . . Let's get rid of all the hypocrisies and impedimenta and false modesties that obscure the Real Me." Self-gratification had become the order of the day.[39]

Many social observers concurred, seeing in the 1970s a great shift toward the cultivation of personal life. Books with revealing titles—*The Culture of Narcissism, America's Quest for the Ideal Self, The Pursuit of Loneliness, Habits of the Heart: Individualism and Commitment in American Life, The Fall of Public Man*—poked and prodded the American psyche and produced similar diagnoses: Americans were displaying all the symptoms of an advanced case of self-absorption. As one critic put it, the modern citizen increasingly "demands immediate gratification and lives in a state of restless, perpetually unsatisfied desire."[40]

In many ways, Hefner and his increasingly indulgent Playboy lifestyle became a symbol of the "Me Decade." Instead of writing the Playboy Philosophy or speaking at public forums on the moral implications of *Playboy*, he now played marathon backgammon games, orchestrated group-sex sessions, and convened charity fund-raisers featuring Hollywood's beautiful people. Instead of taking to the airwaves to debate William F. Buckley and Harvey Cox on changing social values, he now headlined televised Playboy parties that celebrated his celebrity lifestyle. To many, Hefner embodied the modern culture of personal self-fulfillment.

Hefner's statements in the 1970s certainly encouraged the connection. He intoned the "Let's talk about me" mantra, telling one interviewer, "I know there's a tremendous amount of fascination, projection, and fantasy [among the public] related to the life I'm living" and describing it as "an adventure in finding a better lifestyle." He insisted that material wealth and pleasures of the flesh, in fact, *would* bring contentment. "What really produces happiness is self-fulfillment, doing what you really enjoy doing," he claimed, then added that he "didn't know anybody who was fulfilling their personal aspirations to the extent that I've been able to." In a 1974 Playboy

Interview, he insisted that personal needs trumped social expectations. "What I'm saying is that every one of us needs a personal sense of identity and self-worth in order to function satisfactorily in society." And to those who might disapprove of his lifestyle, he offered a blunt rejoinder: "My feeling, frankly, is that I earned it and I have a right to do with it exactly as I damn please."[41]

In 1979 Christie Hefner, by then working for *Playboy*, confirmed her father's link to the "Me Generation" impulse. "It is now perfectly acceptable to say, out loud, what I care about is myself," she contended in an interview. "I think what Wolfe calls the 'me decade,' the whole sense of self-emphasis, self-enrichment, all of that is very much . . . inherent in the original concept in the magazine and the life that Hefner's been living." As her father put it, the 1970s was an era when "I was savoring my personal life as never before."[42]

A steady stream of publicity highlighted his hedonistic life of personal pleasure. The 1972 *New York Times Magazine* quoted his description of his glamorous new Hollywood mansion: "My house is an extension of me and my personality. It's a controlled environment which lets me do the things I like to do." According to *Newsweek*, Hefner had shaped his magazine into "a mainstream guide to living well in the me-decade." The *Chicago Sun-Times* argued that Hefner's secret for well-being lay in the fact that "he has thought about the way he would like to live and then has gone ahead and lived that way." *People* magazine, in a 1974 cover story, observed that the continuous round of fun and games at the mansion embodied his "deliberate change in lifestyle."[43]

Playboy itself increasingly became a showcase for Hefner's personal life. The twentieth anniversary issue in January 1974 showcased him as a larger-than-life subject of the Playboy Interview. "I can say that in many ways, he is even a more remarkable figure than his legend," related the interviewer, who went on to describe his "staggering" energy, "overwhelming" powers of concentration, and "incredibly compelling personality." Growing numbers of feature articles, such as the "Playboy Mansion West" and "Playboy's Playmate House Party," revolved around his private endeavors. Most strikingly, in July 1977 *Playboy* debuted a regular new feature, "The World of Playboy," which focused on Hefner and his activities—meeting celebrities, appearing in the media, partying at the mansion. In September 1978, for example, it described him arriving in the Bahamas for the opening of a new Playboy casino and his fifty-second gala birthday party with glowing prose and abundant photographs.[44]

Ultimately, Hefner strode out of the pages of *Playboy* in the 1970s as a swinging icon of self-gratification. Even more than in earlier decades, he became, in his words, "a guy people can fantasize about and see as a representative of the good life." While the press characterized his hedonistic lifestyle as *Playboy*'s "most important fantasy— or is it reality?" a delighted Hefner fed the hype, declaring, "Well, the major sex object created by *Playboy* over the last 25 years happens to be me."[45]

Hefner's personal image reached a new high when he hosted *Saturday Night Live*, NBC's hip, satirical new comedy revue, on October 15, 1977. From the opening monologue, when he sang a sly version of the old hit song "Thank Heaven for Little Girls" while decked out in red silk pajamas, through his appearance in several skits—trying to seduce skeptical cast member Jane Curtin on his famous round bed, dispensing the Playboy Philosophy to attentive students while dressed as Socrates, leading a space mission as Captain Macho—Hefner validated his central position in American mass culture. His appearance proved to be one of the most popular in the history of the show, and it took him to a new level of personal celebrity.[46]

Yet the reaction to Hefner's brand of personal hedonism reflected the polarization emerging in American society by mid-decade. The continued appeal of *Playboy* indicated substantial public approval, as did Hefner's *Saturday Night Live* role and a host of awards and other appearances. *Playboy*'s twenty-fifth anniversary in late 1978 and 1979 also reflected its popularity. An extravagant anniversary issue was over four hundred pages long, filled with advertising, and loaded with pieces by heavyweights such as John Updike and Gore Vidal and an interview with Marlon Brando. It also crowned the aptly named Candy Loving as the twenty-fifth anniversary Playmate. ABC televised two prime-time specials—one a history of Hefner and *Playboy*, narrated by George Plimpton, and another titled *Playboy's Roller Disco and Pajama Party*—that pulled down high ratings. The mansion hosted a Playmate Reunion that garnered much publicity, while Hefner accepted a star on the famous Walk of Fame from the Hollywood Chamber of Commerce.[47]

In addition, commentators offered positive assessments of the *Playboy* legacy. They placed Hefner alongside Elvis Presley as a giant figure in modern popular culture, praised him as an embodiment of the American dream, and commended his leadership of the modern sexual revolution. *Newsweek* described *Playboy* as "an institution" after years of "cheerleading for sex and the good life." Chicago mayor Michael A. Bilandic even proclaimed a "Hugh M. Hefner Day" in a tribute that acclaimed his "ideas and determination and . . . outstanding contributions to the business world."[48]

At the same time, Hefner's flamboyant 1970s image found a frostier reception than in earlier decades. Growing numbers of critics viewed Mr. Playboy's opulent lifestyle as a cruel hoax in an era when many Americans were struggling to maintain a decent standard of living amid economic recession and inflation. Faced with shrinking jobs, rising prices, and a mounting energy crisis, many Americans saw Hefner's hedonism, in the words of one, as "out of touch with today's reality, a decadent, indulgent relic of easy times and easy money." *Playboy's* vision may have been attractive in the past, but in "these days of hunger, war, terrorism, joblessness, economic hardship, and despoliation of the planet," wrote one columnist, "*Playboy* and the materialistic American Dream it is selling are becoming anachronisms." Even Bob Greene of the *Chicago Sun-Times*, an old Hefner friend, suggested that the publisher's lifestyle proved only that "you never really had to grow up if you didn't want to."[49]

More ideological critiques also took aim. Conservatives, who had begun to organize throughout America at the grassroots level by the mid-1970s, offered particularly strident attacks. Holding aloft an old-fashioned standard of personal character and rectitude, they assailed Hefner for fomenting moral decline, social degeneration, and personal licentiousness. M. J. Sobran blasted the publisher in the *National Review* for promoting a shallow narcissism and insidious moral relativism that undercut firm notions of right and wrong. That so many Americans had come to see their moral standards as "subjective" and grown reluctant to "impose" them on the rest of society "is a measure of Hugh Hefner's success," he lamented. George Will rebuked Hefner as a purveyor of vulgar "adolescent fantasies." In a long 1975 interview, the conservative columnist sparred with Hefner over the question of displaying sexuality. Was *anything* out of bounds? Will inquired. Would *Playboy* depict bestiality? When Hefner replied that such a scene would be degrading, the interviewer pressed him: "There are some things that are objectively degrading? . . . I'm trying to find something that will cause Hefner to put his foot down. And I want to know on what ground it is."[50]

Other conservatives embroidered these complaints. They vilified *Playboy* for prompting readers to "imagine the insanely debauched good time Hef is having." They portrayed Hefner as an antique hipster mouthing the slogans of 1960s-style liberation, with one cartoon depicting a Playboy Bunny as a wrinkled old woman sitting in a rocking chair. Others waxed indignant about the modern epidemic of divorce, illegitimate births, alcoholism, welfare abuse, venereal disease, and drug abuse that could be traced to *Playboy's* message of "instant gratification; if it feels good, do it." Even worse was his profit-making from pushing "gay rights, legal abortions, legalization of pot, and a myriad of other social sicknesses." Ultimately, conservatives agreed, Hefner symbolized the moral degradations of animal sex: "the girls—unblemished, defying gravity, they are kneeling, bending, reclining declarations of all *Playboy* was or probably ever will be." In the face of this onslaught, the publisher could only lament, "For some tradition-oriented people I represent the devil without horns."[51]

But certain progressive analysts also criticized Hefner by the mid-1970s, describing his sex-and-games sensibility as vacuous, materialistic, and chauvinist. *Rolling Stone,* the official voice of the counterculture, sneered at Hefner's world of "adolescent fantasy," while some liberal newspapers mocked *Playboy's* "acquisitive chic" and "consumerism run amok." The advance of the women's movement had rendered Hefner's sexual ethic "absurd, embarrassing, or irrelevant," contended one editorial. Even the sexual revolution had gone sour under *Playboy's* leadership, concluded the *Christian Science Monitor.* The crusade for freedom to enjoy sex had deteriorated into "a mass-media venture in the skin trade" and a frivolous pursuit of thrills as "D. H. Lawrence was succeeded by Hugh Hefner, and Lady Chatterley ended up as a centerfold."[52]

Thus Hefner's quest for self-fulfillment in the 1970s came at a price. For much of the previous two decades, Mr. Playboy's lifestyle had reflected many mainstream hopes and aspirations in an expanding, affluent, optimistic America. But now it triggered disgruntlement as much as desire. To be sure, his devotion to personal experience reflected the spirit of the "Me Decade," but the growing intensity of his sexual radicalism and conspicuous consumption increasingly appeared elitist. While some found it exciting and inspiring, many working- and middle-class people facing job loss and inflation, a sex-saturated media, a surging rate of illegitimate births, and an eroding family structure, grew resentful of the *Playboy* ethic. Many ordinary citizens looked not admiringly but askance at the country's most notorious symbol of hedonistic pursuit. Hefner, protected in his Shangri-La cocoon, remained largely oblivious to such outside pressures. As one of his friends quipped about him in the 1970s, "Luxury corrupts. And absolute luxury corrupts absolutely." The joke revealed more than it intended.[53]

As Hefner devoted himself to play with single-minded zeal in the 1970s, moreover, problematic issues with his magazine and his company moved to the fore. Playboy Enterprises, Inc., encountered financial reverses while *Playboy,* the anchor of Hefner's professional and personal life, was faced with redefining itself in the liberated culture it had helped create. Hefner, preoccupied with the physical and emotional delights of his private fantasyland, had walked away from the direction of his enterprise. Getting it back on course proved to be a difficult process.

PART IV

MALAISE

15

A Hutch Divided

As Hefner frolicked in the sybaritic atmosphere of his Southern California Shangri-La in the 1970s, *Playboy,* the backbone of his enterprise, faced unprecedented challenges. The magazine had climbed to a high point of circulation in 1972 with some seven million monthly readers, but its readership began to slip as a spate of imitators intruded on its territory. This brought not only revenue losses but a crisis of identity. No longer the daring trailblazer on the sexual frontier, the magazine struggled with a growing perception that time had passed it by. Ironically, the success of the sexual revolution in the Swinging Seventies made *Playboy* appear quaint to acolytes of sexual openness.

Moreover, to many ordinary Americans struggling daily with economic decline during the decade, the magazine's message of unfettered consumerism seemed a mocking reminder of the halcyon days of an earlier era. Ideological polarization also whipsawed *Playboy.* Progressives drawn to women's liberation and economic redistribution saw its images of naked women and conspicuous consumption as retrograde, while conservatives viewed it as a symbol of the 1960s threat to family values, social stability, and moral certitude.

Hefner and his associates struggled to reposition *Playboy* in this new atmosphere of sexual liberation, cultural and political disarray, and economic contraction. The task proved daunting. A central question loomed—what would *Playboy* be in a post-1960s society marked by an economic nosedive, "Me Decade" personal preoccupations, and a growing division between a sexually liberated, urban, bicoastal elite and a family-oriented, religiously-inclined "Middle America" in the heartland worried about the nation's decline? The continued success of Hefner and his magazine depended on the answer.

I

At the dawn of the 1970s, *Playboy* occupied a lofty spot among influential American magazines, as a gathering of authors indicated. On October 6–8, 1971, Hefner and A. C. Spectorsky hosted the Playboy International Writers Convocation at the Playboy Towers Hotel in Chicago. Many luminaries of American letters who had published in the magazine attended: David Halberstam, Alan Watts, Studs Terkel, Arthur Schlesinger Jr., Arthur C. Clarke, John Kenneth Galbraith, Harvey Cox, Art Buchwald, James Dickey, John Cheever, Alex Haley, V. S. Pritchett, Gay Talese, Calvin Trillin, Tom Wicker, Garry Wills, and others. In fact, so many literary aristocrats showed up that the *Atlantic* termed it the "Gathering at Bunnymeade." For the better part of three days, these distinguished writers mingled with *Playboy* editors and each other to critique the magazine, participated in panels on subjects such as "The New Journalism," and partook of lavish banquets. Most of the writers seemed delighted, and occasionally awestruck, to meet fellow authors whose achievements they respected. The Writers Convocation, by gathering under one roof so many distinguished authors, confirmed *Playboy*'s prestigious position in the world of American letters.[1]

The convocation proved to be a turning point in *Playboy*'s history. Only a few months later, on January 17, 1972, Spectorsky died of a stroke at his winter home in St. Croix, Virgin Islands. The suave New Yorker had been in ill health for a couple of years, suffering a serious heart attack in 1970 that kept him away from the magazine offices for several weeks. Vague discussions had begun about a possible successor, but the sudden demise of the man who had provided strong editorial leadership since the mid-1950s sent a shock of uncertainty throughout the organization.

Several dynamic young editors—Arthur Kretchmer, Sheldon Wax, Nat Lehrman, and Murray Fisher—had come to the magazine in the mid-1960s and stood ready to assume leadership. Intelligent, energetic, and ambitious mavericks of leftist political disposition, each had carved out a fiefdom. In the exhilarating atmosphere of profit and acclaim for *Playboy,* each pursued his own projects as publication decisions were reached through byzantine negotiations or hammered out in chaotic, occasionally confrontational editorial meetings. "Spec seemed increasingly overwhelmed by a staff heady with success," Hefner recalled later. "I was the only one who could go into that lion's cage of creativity without a whip and a chair." After Spectorsky's death, Hefner chose Kretchmer as *Playboy's* new executive editor and appointed Wax and Lehrman as associate editors.[2]

Thirty-one-year-old Arthur Kretchmer had been with the magazine for five years after an education at the University of Pennsylvania and City College of New York, a stint with *Cavalier,* a *Playboy* imitator, and a short period doing freelance writing for publications such as the *Village Voice*. A tall, thin New Yorker with a thick shock of long black hair, a beard, and thick wire-rimmed glasses, he often displayed the morose expression of a disaffected intellectual. Kretchmer saw himself as a bohemian radical, an impression reinforced by his fondness for blue jeans, boots, and T-shirts emblazoned with slogans such as "Trotsky Youth." The contrast with the elegant, urbane Spectorsky could not have been more striking. "In another time and place, Spec would have been a member of the aristocracy and Kretch a revolutionary," Hefner commented. Indeed, Kretchmer fancied himself a counterculture radical and planned to stay at the magazine for only a couple of years. But Spectorsky saw something in the young man— incisive intelligence, sound judgment, tough-mindedness, an eye for good writing—and began to groom him as his heir apparent. The two had a falling out over Kretchmer's strong independent streak and leftist politics, but shortly before Spectorsky's death they reconciled. Hefner believed Kretchmer was the best man for the job, and the new executive editor quickly brought a boost of youthful energy to the magazine.[3]

The new editorial leadership at *Playboy* inspired confident talk about a bright future. A few months after taking the helm, Kretchmer told the *New York Times* that "many months we think we're publishing the best magazine in America. Spec had to prove that *Playboy* was the kind of magazine Jean-Paul Sartre gave interviews to. We don't have to prove anything now." Editors joked confidently about their preeminence, with one wisecracking that his idea of the perfect *Playboy* would "feature articles by West Coast models interlaced with the genitalia of famous writers." Despite the confidence, however, *Playboy* faced one of the biggest challenges in its history. A rival had arisen in the men's magazine field and launched an all-out assault on Hefner's publication, beginning a war that bit into the older magazine's profits and prestige.[4]

The conflict had begun in the summer of 1969, when a series of audacious ads for a new magazine, *Penthouse,* appeared in major urban newspapers and advertising trade journals. The initial one pictured the famous *Playboy* rabbit logo lined up in the crosshairs of a telescopic rifle sight over the caption, "We're going rabbit hunting." Another pictured the rabbit reading the new magazine and declared, "*Penthouse* envy. Has the aging playboy gone soft?" The ad campaign reflected the brash sensibility of *Penthouse*'s editor, Robert Guccione. An Italian American from Brooklyn, Guccione had moved to Great Britain in the late 1950s where, after dabbling with odd jobs, cartooning, and editing for several years, he started *Penthouse* in 1965. It quickly amassed a circulation of several hundred thousand, and he decided to challenge Hefner's position on his home turf with an American edition.[5]

Penthouse shamelessly parroted *Playboy* in its format, offering a fold-out "Pet of the Month," an introductory page termed "Housecalls," a monthly interview, a letters-to-the-editor column called "Forum," and the same mix of nude features, fiction, cartoons, and articles on food, fashion, and public affairs. Guccione shrugged off guilt, contending that "We took no more from *Playboy* in the end than *Playboy* took from *Esquire* and other magazines." More importantly, *Penthouse* presented an explicit, "hot" treatment of sexuality—revealing poses, women fondling themselves, lesbianism, fetishism, threesomes, letters to the editor detailing kinky sexual adventures—that went far beyond anything found in the older magazine. Representatives of *Penthouse* contrasted this "international" sexual flavor to the fresh-faced, all-American, cheerleader style favored by Hefner's publication. They made a shocking argument: *Playboy* had fallen behind the times in terms of sexual liberation.[6]

Guccione pushed this impression by relentlessly attacking his more established rival as old-fashioned, even anachronistic. He decried *Playboy* pictorials as "artificial" with images shaped by art directors, hairstylists, and fashion photographers and contended that his photos conveyed a natural, earthy, real atmosphere of sexuality. "We give our readers the pictures without the lectures. The pinups without the hang-ups. Writers yes, philosophizers no," declared his ads. He derided Hefner's magazine as "uptight" and outdated in a liberated new age. "*Playboy*'s reader profile gets older every year while ours gets younger," he proclaimed.[7]

The clash between Guccione and Hefner gradually took on a nastier, more personal edge. The flamboyant *Penthouse* editor, habitually dressed in tight leather pants, boots, open-necked shirts, and gold rings and medallions, sniped at the older man's style and image. "*Playboy* projects the sexual identity of Hugh Hefner, which is the closest thing to a closet queen that I know of," he told *Rolling Stone*. Hefner dismissed his outspoken rival as a self-promoter who, for all of his derisive comments, aped the Hefnerian lifestyle with his New York mansion full of beautiful women and plans for Penthouse clubs. "I don't really object to this energetic impersonation of his," Hefner commented sharply. "If I were he, I'd want to be me, too." Hefner snubbed Guccione the only time they met. After the publishers ran into one another at the house of a common friend, Bernie Cornfeld, and stiffly shook hands, Hefner invited Cornfeld to the mansion the next day to see a movie. But then Hefner's secretary called Cornfeld to say that Hefner preferred that Guccione not come with him.[8]

The so-called "Pubic Wars" between *Playboy* and *Penthouse* ignited over the issue of pubic hair in nude photographs. Playboy had quietly crossed this sexual frontier in an August 1969 piece showing the Broadway dancer Paula Kelley, but Guccione did so more boldly in an October 1970 feature on a former Miss Holland. Hefner met this new standard of revelation in January 1971 with Playmate Liv Lindeland, insisting that the decision had been made long before *Penthouse*'s pictorial. The move raised eyebrows, and when pressed on whether average Americans were truly ready for pubic Playmates, Hefner grew testy. "You better ask God about that. He put it there, and it's time that society grew up and recognized that pubic hair exists," he replied. He also composed staff memos explaining the new parameters: "Remember, pubic hair is no longer a taboo at Playboy—as long as it is handled in good taste." In January 1972, *Playboy* took another step by presenting Marilyn Cole, a statuesque brunette from Great Britain, as the first full-frontal nude Playmate. One wag, noticing that the magazine began selling shares on the stock exchange around the same time, quipped that PEI "was the first company to go public and pubic in the same year."[9]

Other than these maneuvers on the follicle front, *Playboy* maintained a public pose of haughty indifference to its upstart challenger. But the numbers began to flash a warning. The first American issue of *Penthouse* in September 1969 sold 235,000 copies. Over the next two years sales skyrocketed, with the magazine attracting 1,280,000 readers in August 1971 and breaking the 2 million mark in mid-1972. *Playboy* remained far ahead as its readership also climbed—6.5 million copies a month in 1971, and a high-water mark of over 7 million in 1972—but the gap was narrowing. In the fall of 1973, *Penthouse* would be up to 4 million a month, while *Playboy*'s sales numbers leveled off and then began to fall. By 1976, the two magazines would be running close, with *Playboy* at 5–6 million and *Penthouse* at 4.5–5 million.[10]

As the competition intensified, Hefner realized that he must confront the threat more directly. In the fall of 1972 he upped the erotic ante by launching a new magazine titled *Oui*, in partnership with the French publisher Daniel Filipacchi. Envisioning a Continental complement to *Playboy* that would blunt the *Penthouse* attack, Hefner described the new monthly magazine as having "a European accent in its humor, reviews, and approach to photography." *Oui* started off strongly, but never showed a profit, and it gradually became disconcertingly clear that it was taking more readers from *Playboy* than from *Penthouse*. After several years of mounting red ink, PEI quietly sold *Oui* in 1981.[11]

Further complicating matters, other rivals began challenging *Playboy*'s hegemony. Throughout the early 1970s a proliferation of skin magazines brought increased competition for attention on newsstands. Publications such as *Gallery, Touch, Voir, Genesis, Dude, Cavalier, Viva,* and *Coq* blatantly imitated the Hefner formula but offered more explicit, kinkier photos. Raunchier publications such as *Screw* and *Hustler* specialized in extremely explicit, almost gynecological images of female genitalia. This explosion of sex magazines, *Time* observed, saw publications "locked in battle to zoom in on ever more explicit poses and privacies." When *Esquire* appraised the skin-book boom—its cover featured a perplexed Hefner surveying an issue of *Hustler*—it exclaimed, "What have they done to the girl next door?" The article concluded sardonically that in many of the raunchy new magazines, she "comes on so strong that you're tempted to move to a quieter neighborhood."[12]

As the Pubic Wars became a multifront struggle in the first half of the 1970s, Hefner found himself fighting a growing impression that *Playboy* had become antiquated. He defended his publication as the standard that was attacked by rivals even as they copied it. "They say that imitation is the sincerest form of flattery," he noted tartly, "so I guess I've been flattered more sincerely—and blatantly—than any other magazine publisher in history." He noted that *Playboy* encompassed the entirety of the modern man's interests while his competitors represented a tawdry throwback to the "Victorian-porn approach." Some observers agreed, however, with Guccione's declaration that "*Playboy* has become part of the Establishment." The *Los Angeles Times* portrayed *Playboy's* modesty as "going the way of the 1950s *Esquire*," and *Time* observed that while *Penthouse* centerfolds "glory in showing off their buxom bodies, moles and all, *Playboy's* Playmates seem unreal, plasticized, and antiseptic." The *Wall Street Journal* suggested that Hefner and his magazine had become devoted to "striving for acceptance by the conventional world of commerce and letters."[13]

In a sense, *Playboy* had become a victim of its own success. After cracking open the door in American society that prohibited public displays of nudity in the 1950s, the magazine had knocked it off its hinges during the following decade. By the 1970s, a great wave of sexual images—not only magazines but graphic movies, massage parlors, adult bookstores, strip clubs and "girlie shows," and sex shops peddling erotic paraphernalia—washed over the American landscape and stretched the limits of popular acceptance. Indeed, the decade witnessed the appearance of what the *New York Times* termed "Porno Chic." X-rated movies such as *Deep Throat, The Devil in Miss Jones,* and *Behind the Green Door* attracted vast popular audiences and made celebrities of porn actors such as Harry Reems and Linda Lovelace. Commercial sex districts, filled with erotic clubs and theaters, mushroomed in big cities throughout the country, *The Joy of Sex,* a sex manual, became a huge best-seller, and sex clubs such as Plato's Retreat and Sandstone sprang up to meet the desires of sexual adventurers. While the new sexual openness tended to focus on an urban, bicoastal audience, it spread into Middle America. As *Time* observed in its 1976 cover story on "The Porno Plague," Mason City, Iowa (population 32,000), offered five bars featuring nude dancers. "The concept of a loosened, public, open sexuality has become part of mainstream American life," noted a *Newsweek* columnist in 1975.[14]

Indeed, *Playboy*'s own survey on sexual behavior underlined the significant shift in American mores since the Kinsey research two decades earlier. Titled "Sexual Behavior in the 1970s," the study was funded by the Playboy Foundation and published in six monthly installments in 1973–1974. It examined the sexual attitudes and behavior of about two thousand people in a variety of cities and towns and reported that "we are now surrounded by evidence that people are openly doing things that a generation ago were unthinkable, or at least among the most guarded of personal secrets." Investigators found that Americans engaged in sex more frequently and increasingly endorsed premarital sex, oral sex, and the end of the double standard for men and women. Statistics revealed a marked increase in every category of sexual practice since the Kinsey Reports. Moreover, the *Playboy* survey reported that this sexual sea change had become highly visible in the media and a major issue for the public. Data suggested that "sexual liberalism is the emergent ideal that the great majority of young Americans—and a fair number of older ones—are trying to live up to," the survey concluded.[15]

For Hefner and his magazine, ironically, the triumph of the sexual revolution created uncertainty. With sexual expression running rampant, erotic images available everywhere and in every form, and the lines of permissiveness being pushed to the point of obliteration, *Playboy*'s role appeared increasingly blurry. As Hefner acknowledged in a 1973 interview, his magazine was "not nearly as avant-garde, or on the forefront of the fight for sexual freedom in terms of content, as it once was." But what territory could it stake out in a new world where there was no longer a repressive establishment to hurl brickbats against? Seeking to avoid the raunchiness of *Penthouse* and *Hustler* while remaining sexually relevant, *Playboy* struggled to steer a course in this unfamiliar situation.[16]

Initially, Hefner and his editors adopted a strategy of making the erotic content of their magazine "hotter." By 1974 *Playboy* was displaying a variety of more explicit photographs and features and the Playmates began to appear in more provocative poses. Even the magazine's cover began to broadcast this new aesthetic. The October 1975 cover portrayed two women, both with dress straps pulled down and one with a breast exposed, embracing warmly beside a headline that said, "Sappho: Stunning Portraits of Women in Love." This rather shocking departure into lesbian sex proved only a warm-up for the following month's issue. The November 1975 number crossed another line with its cover photo showing a young woman in a theater watching a film. Sprawled in her seat wearing spike-heeled shoes, she had her blouse open and her skirt pulled up with legs spread apart. With one hand, as *Newsweek* archly described it, "to give her the benefit of the doubt, [she] seems to be plumbing the depths of her bikini panties for a stray kernel of popcorn."[17]

This strategy misfired. *Playboy*'s forays into explicit shots, lesbianism, and female masturbation triggered outrage among advertisers, who deluged its offices with complaints about obscenity. A furious Howard Lederer, director of advertising, told Hefner that some $40 million of annual advertising revenue was in danger of disappearing over the raunchier content and threatened to resign. In an interview, Arthur Kretchmer admitted that *Playboy* needed to be more careful about crossing the line "separating sensuality and vulgarity." Even Hefner was uncomfortable. "I wasn't interested in publishing pornography," he recalled of this period in later years. "My intent, from the outset, had been to make sex and nudity acceptable in America."[18]

So in November 1975, Hefner ordered a strategic retreat. In a series of meetings and memoranda, he made it clear that *Playboy* was pulling back from lewd and lascivious displays. At an editorial conference held at the mansion in Los Angeles, he announced, "Gentlemen, we have lost our compass. The magazine has lost sight of what it was meant to be. . . . *Playboy* has to present the sensuality without the coarseness. We're going to make this a class act again." News releases went to outlets such as the *Gallagher Report,* which reported that Hefner had decided it was "folly" to compete with newer magazines in terms of sexual explicitness. Arthur Kretchmer was dispatched to New York City, where he reassured nervous advertisers that *Playboy* had no intention of becoming an outlet for pornography. "Hefner doesn't want to be known as a smut publisher," he declared. "We're not fighting a crotch war at *Playboy*." In December 1975, Hefner reassured PEI shareholders at their annual meeting that *Playboy* was pulling out of the explicitness sweepstakes. The magazine also promised newsstand wholesalers an end to nudity or explicit images on its cover, thus ensuring that it could be presented openly and not wrapped in brown paper or shielding.[19]

So after this traumatic episode of *raunchus interruptus*, *Playboy* reestablished its ethic of tasteful eroticism. But "taste" did not exactly offer a blood-stirring new agenda, and Arthur Kretchmer understood the dilemma. In 1974, he had told Hefner that *Playboy* needed an overhaul and the publisher had agreed. Two years later, Kretchmer mused about "tilting it toward a younger, brighter and hipper readership" and making it once again an indispensable item for smart, sophisticated young men. "We're not only going to be more attuned to the reality of living in the 70s, but we're going to ask questions and challenge premises as well," he promised. But revamping *Playboy* for a new age, it soon became evident, was easier said than done.[20]

II

After abandoning "this gynecological, who-can-be-more-explicit race" among men's magazines, as Hefner put it, *Playboy* groped for fresh identity throughout the latter 1970s. But the process of evolution was a subtle one. In fact, readers of the magazine encountered a comforting array of familiar features as articles explored stylish clothes, fast cars, domestic amenities, and popular pastimes. Newfangled technology such as "videocassettes" came in for attention, as did the hottest new pinball and video games. Entertainment trends and sports attracted the usual attention, ranging from Norman Mailer's two-part article on the Muhammad Ali–George Foreman "rope a dope" fight in Zaire to a fascinating piece on Francis Ford Coppola, Hollywood's trendiest young film director. Two other traditions, "Playboy's Annual Jazz and Pop Poll" and "Playboy's Annual Football Picks" also remained firmly embedded in the magazine's format.[21]

Playboy kept up its tradition of distinguished writing. Old friends such as John Updike, Vladimir Nabokov, and Kurt Vonnegut contributed pieces as did a galaxy of new contributors that included Doris Lessing, Gabriel García Márquez, Michael Crichton, Nadine Gordimer, Susan Sontag, Larry McMurtry, Mario Puzo, and Günter Grass.

In October 1976, *Playboy* ran a preview excerpt of Alex Haley's new book, *Roots,* edited by the magazine's Murray Fisher, which went on to become a huge best-seller and popular television mini-series. Reviews of current books, records, and movies continued, as did the Playboy Forum with its discussion of a wide array of social issues. The Playboy Interview presented scintillating discussions with figures ranging from Marlon Brando to Germaine Greer, Jack Nicholson to Joan Baez, Norman Lear to Anita Bryant, Albert Speer to Erica Jong.

Sex, of course, stayed front and center stage in *Playboy* throughout the 1970s. The Playmate of the Month remained the primary erotic attraction, although with a few minor alterations. Hefner further personalized Playmates by adding their signature to the centerfolds in 1975, and by introducing two years later the Playmate Data Sheet with its vital statistics, ambitions, and "turn-ons" and "turnoffs." Traditional celebrity pictorials included old favorites such as Elke Sommer and Raquel Welch as well as rising young starlets such as Valerie Perrine, Melanie Griffith, and Barbara Bach. Readers also encountered the customary photographic surveys of beautiful coeds from around the country, such as "The Girls of the Pac 10" or "The Girls of the Ivy League."

But a new explicitness marked these erotic presentations. While *Playboy*'s cover was toned down and photographs never tilted the raunch meter like *Penthouse* and *Hustler,* its sexual ethic became more daring and explicit than ever before. Playmate photographs were increasingly revealing, with full-frontal nudity a standard feature and spread-legged poses more common. An uninhibited sexual aesthetic also influenced the "Playboy Advisor," which increasingly described intense or unusual sexual experiences, often with graphic details, and discussed sexual techniques such as oral sex and the use of sex toys. By 1977, *Playboy* was examining X-rated movies as part of its film reviews. Articles ranged further afield as in 1976's "Me and the Other Girls," by Kathy Lowry, which offered a confessional account of experimentation with bisexuality. The following year saw both Dan Greenburg's "My Weekend of Flashy Orgasms," which detailed his stay at Sandstone, the notorious California retreat specializing in multipartner sex, and "Swingers Scrapbook," a text and photo feature on the sexual frontier of orgies, threesomes, and every variety of fantasy fulfillment. In 1978, the magazine presented "The Great Playboy

Sex-Aids Road Test." This consumer survey, which certainly would have made Ralph Nader blush, recruited three couples to test the reliability and performance of vibrators, dildos, massagers, stimulators, and other kinds of sexual paraphernalia.[22]

Despite the intensified eroticism and popular, time-tested features, *Playboy's* standard formula appeared stale to some observers, a middle-aged rendering of what *seemed* to be hip rather than the real thing. Arthur Kretchmer believed that the problem stemmed from post-1960s malaise. Following the social turmoil and political crusading of the Aquarian Age, he observed later, "*Playboy* was as aimless for a while as I think the culture was. . . . Society cooled off and, to be frank, we cooled off."[23]

Hefner grew aware of these difficulties. "I think *Playboy* is a very good book, but it has lost some of its vigor," he confessed to the *Village Voice* in 1975. When pressed on whether time had passed *Playboy* by, he admitted that "after twenty-two years, the magazine had become repetitive." But revisions were coming, the publisher promised, as he and his editorial staff were "exploring and examining the editorial product, and making some changes to revitalize the book, make it more contemporary, make it more part of today."[24]

Indeed, the mid-1970s saw Hefner and his lieutenants laboring to revitalize the venerable publication. They kept intact *Playboy's* basic formula of sex and consumerism, but experimented with features that would distinguish it from its competitors. As Kretchmer described it, the magazine sought to define and embody "the cutting edge of the mainstream."[25]

One editorial project sought to integrate *Playboy's* sexual themes into a broader emphasis on the modern male lifestyle. "We are going to re-emphasize what the magazine is first and foremost: a lifestyle book in which sex is one part of a total package," Hefner announced. Or in Kretchmer's pithy phrase, *Playboy* intended to be "the indispensable magazine to the urban male reader whose psyche is 28 years old."[26]

In part, this attempt to "relate to contemporary lifestyles," as Hefner described it, involved a trendier tone. It also involved modifications to the format, as two new lifestyle sections appeared in 1977. "Playboy's Pipeline" consisted of short pieces on contemporary trends that promised "tips on keeping your lifestyle in high gear," while "Playboy on the Scene" pledged to cover "what's happening, where it's happening, and who's making it happen." In the April 1978 issue, for example, they examined a variety of topics: importing foreign cars, surviving tax audits, rehabbing historic houses, the newest microwave oven technology, and European influences on men's fashion. In Hefner's words, these modifications "reemphasized what the book is first and foremost: a lifestyle magazine devoted to how one spends one's leisure time."[27]

Playboy's reinvigorated lifestyle orientation inspired a new promotional campaign. With great fanfare, the magazine began running a series of ads in 1977 titled "The Playboy Reader: His Lust Is for Life." They presented *Playboy* as representative of a cohort of prosperous, under-thirty-five young men who had rebelled in the 1960s but now sought to work within the system. "Good news for American business: those young men who wouldn't sell out in 1967 are buying-in in 1977," said one ad. The campaign depicted a cadre of sensitive, educated, upscale Baby Boomers as "new materialists" who thoughtfully consumed items that promised to create a richer, emotionally satisfying life. "These life-embracing young adults have kept the best of the 60s, leavened it with their own maturity and invented a whole new thing for the 70s," touted another ad. "Faded jeans. Now pre-faded and with a designer name at $40 a pair. Leather boots. *Soft* leather boots." Photos reinforced the text, showing *Playboy* subscribers jogging in fancy running suits, scuba diving, sitting down to a gourmet meal, and snuggling with their "lady" to watch the sunset at their summer house. After being eclipsed by the social agitation of the 1960s, the good life reappeared at the center of the *Playboy* lifestyle in the "Lust for Life" campaign.[28]

Playboy also recast itself as a venue for investigative journalism in the mid-1970s. Operating in a cynical atmosphere shaped by the Vietnam debacle and the Watergate scandal, the magazine increasingly labored to expose public life as a sordid mass of corruption, ignorance, and greed. In 1974, *Playboy* set the trend with its serialization of Carl Bernstein and Bob Woodward's *All the President's Men,* the blockbuster exposé of the Nixon administration's crimes and demise. In subsequent years, articles examined "Big Brother" surveillance of citizens by the federal government, incompetence and financial fraud in the American health-care system, pervasive safety violations in the airline industry, the looming bankruptcy of the Social Security system, and rampant corruption in modern labor unions. A particularly shocking article appeared in 1976, when

"The Puppet and the Puppetmasters: Uncovering the Secret World of Nixon, Hughes, and the CIA" accused Howard Hughes of using his multibillion-dollar empire to manipulate President Richard Nixon and the CIA into illegal, covert intelligence operations that resulted in Watergate.[29]

Playboy's new emphasis on nonfiction included healthy doses of the "New Journalism." By the late 1960s and early 1970s, journalists such as Tom Wolfe, Hunter S. Thompson, Joan Didion, and Gay Talese were reformulating traditional practice by replacing "objective" reporting, "balanced" analysis, and narrative description with abundant dialogue, dramatic scenes, and the author's participation in the story. *Playboy* embraced this flashy, dramatic, highly personalized style, describing it as "a writer telling a story that he or she has lived with little pretense of objectivity." It offered Richard Rhodes's personal account of the destruction of the Mississippi River by economic developers and his exploration of the modern cocaine culture, which featured him buying and using the drug, contacting sellers and distributors, and carefully avoiding the police. Dan Greenburg's "My First Orgy" humorously related his own fumbling participation in several group-sex parties. *Playboy* even ran "The Great Shark Hunt," the story of a drug-soaked deep-sea fishing tournament in Cozumel by one of the genre's founders, Hunter S. Thompson.[30]

Playboy directly engaged with political issues as never before. Throughout the 1970s, the magazine consistently appeared as a leftist gadfly, although growing into the role had been painful. A. C. Spectorsky had clashed with his younger, more radical assistant editors over the political drift of the magazine in the late 1960s, describing their dissenting articles as just "do-good indignation." He furiously objected to a draft article on environmentalism condemning vacation resorts, noting that it began "with a putdown of Tahoe, a resort that we are covering favorably in our upcoming travel feature for March." Hefner often agreed, writing one memo that urged the editors to avoid "thinking of ourselves, and of our readers, as a bunch of young hippie activists. They're not—and we shouldn't attempt to be." In the spring of 1970, amid a long, favorable report on the state of *Playboy* and its immediate future, Spectorsky issued a warning. "It would be very easy—and very dangerous—to revolutionize PLAYBOY, to make it the voice of the growing edge of anti-establishment youth," he wrote.[31]

Hefner working on his famous revolving bed in the Chicago Mansion

Hefner and girlfriend
Barbi Benton shortly
after they met in 1968

Hefner hosting a fundraiser for the antiwar presidential candidate Eugene McCarthy at the Chicago Mansion in 1968

Hefner with Karen Christy, the other point in the love triangle with Barbi Benton, in the early 1970s

Bobbie Arnstein playing Monopoly with Hefner aboard the Big Bunny before her tragic demise

Playboy's 1977 "Lust for Life" campaign, which attempted to reconnect the magazine to a post-1960s, post-political activist generation

Left to right: Hef's girlfriend Sondra Theodore, Playmate of the Year Monique St. Pierre, and Hefner playing pinball on the new *Playboy* machine

Shooting a 1977 ABC television special, *Playboy's Playmate Party*, poolside at the Playboy Mansion West

Playboy Enterprises president Derick Daniels addressing a stockholder's meeting

Left to right: Hefner, Playboy Clubs International president Arnie Morton, and Victor Lownes touring the Great Gorge Resort Hotel in New Jersey

investigative report

By ROBERT SCHEER

*how a group of zealots took aim at pornography
and ended up in a war against sex itself*

THE MEESE COMMISSION

DOWN IN Arlington County, Virginia, the lady dancers at what the locals call "tittie bars" had best be wearing pasties, or prosecutor Henry Hudson will bust them. He once was quoted as saying, "I live to put people in jail."

For the past six years, Hudson has also been going after video stores and threatening to shut them down for renting movies depicting nonsimulated intercourse. "Our vice squad has a reputation," he has told me, "for checking periodically in the stores, and the people are careful about what they sell in the county; yes, sir, they are. I don't apologize for that; I'm proud of that. We have a good family community here."

That stand-up-to-porn spirit caught the attention of the President of the United States, who commended Hudson for his actions and vowed to keep his eye on the young prosecutor.

One day in the spring of 1986, I find myself in Hudson's bailiwick in the Arlington civic center, in a cubbyhole at the end of a corridor decorated with WANTED posters. I am there because Hudson has now become a national figure as the chairman of Attorney General Edwin Meese's Commission on Pornography,

whose activities I am tracking for my newspaper, the *Los Angeles Times*. We are sitting in his cluttered office, discussing more variations on a single theme—sexual conduct—than I have ever discussed with anyone. The topics range from the limits of anal sex to the many varieties of sodomy. Hudson talks about the proliferation of pornography and how he sees it as his obligation to return this country to the clean good old days.

I ask him, "By good old days, do you mean when they banned James Joyce's *Ulysses* or the novels of Kurt Vonnegut, Jr., and D. H. Lawrence, all of which have been censored?"

"I can't say I've read or seen the items in question," says Hudson. "I don't have time to read books or go to the movies."

"What is this thing called pornography you're now investigating?" I ask.

"Pornography, to a degree, is like the word love; it means different things in different contexts."

"Great," I observe, "but you're head of a commission that wants to get rid of it, so what is the *it?*" Hudson then rifles through the search warrants and *Miranda* confessions in his briefcase but can't find the *(continued on page 157)*

ILLUSTRATION BY STEVE BRODNER

Playboy's blistering 1986 attack, "Inside the Meese Commission" (complete with a caricature of attorney general Edwin Meese)—part of Hefner's battle with the Reagan Administration

The 1985 press conference where Hefner publicly denounced Peter Bogdanovich for his reaction to the Dorothy Stratten murder

Hefner and his fiancée, Kimberly Conrad, in an 1989 interview

Hefner and his "Manly Night" buddies in the mid-1990s

Hefner and Gloria Steinem being inducted into the Magazine Hall of Fame in 1998

With Spectorsky's death, the rift over politicizing *Playboy* ended as the magazine became an unabashed advocate of leftist political positions. In 1971, it announced a three-part symposium on "A New Set of National Priorities" that claimed, "The decay of our cities, the deterioration of the environment, and the enduring poverty suffered by 15 percent of the population are the three major challenges the U.S. must meet when it divests itself of the burdens of Vietnam." The experts mustered to discuss these crises were a who's who of liberal spokesmen, including Senator Gaylord Nelson, Mayor Carl B. Stokes, and the writer Michael Harrington.[32]

Playboy elaborated its leftist critique of American social and political ills throughout the 1970s. It derided the evangelist Billy Graham for promoting "the unswerving belief that God, the flag, and the president are an immutable trinity." It showcased liberal senator Philip Hart's denunciation of modern corporate crime, presented E. L. Doctorow's jeremiad on American nuclear weaponry, and featured a long, sympathetic Playboy Interview with radical icons Tom Hayden and Jane Fonda. Other articles analyzed Nelson Rockefeller as "the true Godfather of American politics" and described Nixon's appointees to the Supreme Court as architects of "police-state verdicts" and governmental tyranny. In 1977, "The Playboy Enemies List" spoofed the infamous file kept by the Nixon administration by amassing its own register of conservative villains, including Phyllis Schlafly, Charles H. Keating Jr., George Gilder, and Frank Rizzo.[33]

At the same time, *Playboy's* politics, while firmly leftist, displayed a streak of cynicism. The whole system was corrupt, the magazine often seemed to suggest. In 1972, a skeptical article observed that supporters of the presidential campaign of George McGovern "consistently confused their elitist youth constituency—college students—with youth itself. There were damn few gas-station attendants on the floor of the Democratic National Convention in Miami Beach." Pieces skewered insurgent icons from the 1960s such as Rennie Davis, a radical leader who had become the chief proselytizer for an Indian religious guru, and Timothy Leary, who betrayed many of his old friends to the federal government in the 1970s. The magazine went after Jane Fonda, observing that her multimillion-dollar Hollywood career often seemed at odds with her outspoken political radicalism.[34]

Playboy's political engagement produced one of the biggest journalistic coups of the decade: the notorious Playboy Interview with

Jimmy Carter in the fall of 1976 that created a political firestorm
on the eve of the presidential election. Throughout the summer,
Robert Scheer had interviewed Carter several times on assignment
for *Playboy*. In the final session at Carter's home in Plains, Georgia,
the candidate was asked about the fear among some voters that his
Baptist piety and moralism might unduly influence his political judgment. Carter replied with a long soliloquy about his religious convictions. Christianity taught that everyone was a sinner, he said, and
it was God's place to judge sin. The righteous Christian should not
haughtily condemn the person who "leaves his wife and shacks up
with somebody out of wedlock," nor should you "consider yourself
better than someone else because one guy screws a whole bunch
of women while the other is loyal to his wife." He confessed, "I've
looked on a lot of women with lust. I've committed adultery in my
heart many times. This is something that God recognizes I will do—
and I have done it—and God forgives me for it."[35]

Carter's comments caused a national uproar. "The Great Playboy
Furor," as *Newsweek* described it, saw "newspapers throughout the
country making whoopee with Carter's over-candid confessions."
Traditionalists and religious conservatives denounced him for hypocrisy, pointing to his willingness to talk to a girlie magazine while claiming that his Christian character was the basis of his campaign. They
condemned his use of salty language—"screw" and "shack up," in
particular—as degrading and unworthy of a national leader. While
some ministers defended Carter for his "judge not lest ye be judged"
position, many more attacked him for undermining the need for
moral judgment. In the indignant, if linguistically challenged, retort
of one, "It is not holier-than-thou to condemn another man for shack-
ing down [*sic*] with another man's wife." Even some Democrats and
liberal supporters questioned the lack of judgment and unseemliness
that colored this episode. Max Lerner, an old friend of Hefner and
Playboy, chastised the candidate for using "locker-room language"
and misjudging presidential standards of decorum.[36]

Carter's interview delighted cartoonists. One depicted a Playboy
Bunny sitting on the lap of the leering candidate as he said, "I'm
Jimmy Carter. I'm running for President." Another showed a tooth-
some Carter staring at the Statue of Liberty, while in a balloon above
his head appeared an image of Lady Liberty in the nude. In a takeoff

on the Jimmy Stewart movie *Harvey,* a cartoon depicted Carter standing next to a giant rendering of the Playboy rabbit logo as the candidate asked innocently, "Rabbit? . . . What rabbit? I don't see any rabbit." His opponent, President Gerald R. Ford also took advantage of the Georgian's *Playboy* problem. By mid-October, some 350 newspapers in twenty-two states were running an ad that juxtaposed Ford's recent appearance on the cover of *Newsweek* with the Carter interview on the cover of *Playboy* next to Playmate Patti McGuire, who was seductively unbuttoning her shirt. The caption said, "One good way to decide this election." By late October, Carter ruefully admitted to the press, "I would not give that interview if I had to do it over again," but he held on to narrowly win the election.[37]

Playboy's vigorous investigative and political journalism in the 1970s sat alongside a softer editorial theme: romance. Hefner urged his editors to make it the new touchstone of the magazine, declaring, "When there is romance, the sex connection is difficult to attack. Romance is both traditional and contemporary. Romance is blue collar and white collar. We have always been more romantic and therefore more corny, than our contemporary magazines. . . . If the public could be made to see our concept of ourselves, any image problems that we've been having would be over." Kretchmer urged the staff to infuse romance into fashion pieces, service features, travel articles, even the "Playboy Advisor," which should increase its focus on letters involving romantic situations and problems.[38]

This theme brought a new flavor to the magazine. A feature titled "The Rousing Return of Romance" announced, "The signs are everywhere. Men and women are wearing softer colors and dressing up. On the beaches, couples walk hand in hand. In sidewalk cafes, they sip Perrier or white wine. Candlelight is replacing electricity in some restaurants." It guided readers through the romantic features of cities such as San Francisco and New Orleans, offered tips for choosing romantic gifts, gave pointers on the art of romantic conversation, and suggested romantic products such as massage oils, silk pajamas, and fluted champagne glasses. *Playboy* began running a regular column titled "Man and Woman" that focused on romantic issues. In its twenty-fifth anniversary issue in January 1979, a cartoon even departed from the usual sex-and-frolic themes. It pictured a middle-aged man reading *Playboy* in bed while his wife stood naked before the mirror as she prepared to put on a negligee. He looked up and said affectionately, "You know something, sweetheart? *Playboy* isn't the only thing that's still great after twenty-five years."[39]

Perhaps most tellingly, however, Hefner and his editors reshaped *Playboy* to capture the "Me Decade" zeitgeist of the 1970s. The magazine, with its long-standing agenda of sexual and consumerist satisfactions, saw the "Let's talk about Me—let's find the real Me" as a reemergence of its natural constituency. The present generation "is closer to what *Playboy* is all about and has been talking about for 25 years than at any time since we've been publishing," Hefner explained. "It's interesting that we live in what has been called a me generation . . . [with] an appropriate appreciation of living one's own life and getting the most out of it."[40]

Playboy's "Lust for Life" promotional campaign in 1977 epitomized the new sensibility. An early ad in the series described a typical subscriber as "very much focused into today and what he can do for himself. . . . Expressing himself to the world. Without denying himself the world." Another quoted a subscriber who said, "My reaction to things now is how do I feel, not so much how the world feels." Another described the value system of the typical modern *Playboy* reader. "First, it's a lifestyle of fierce loyalty. To himself. And to any product that helps him to be himself," it reported.[41]

A host of *Playboy* articles fanned out to explore the personal terrain of the "Me Generation." "Leisure in the Seventies" concluded that any potential pitfalls involved with the growth of nonwork time "are outweighed by the promise of self-exploration and discovery—it affords anyone with the energy and imagination to fill—rather than kill—his free time." In 1971, *Playboy*'s "Student Survey" concluded that college youth were "turning away from social concerns toward more personal pursuits." In 1974, "I'm OK, You're So-So," by editor G. Barry Golson, parodied self-awareness programs and popular psychotherapies as guides for "how to achieve self-fulfillment through mental discipline, positive thinking, and a firm belief in other people's mediocrity." Other pieces described the new physical fitness craze as enhancing "your ability to use your body to live life as you want to," and the "inner game of sex" as a Zen strategy shifting emphasis "from outward success to inner growth."[42]

The Playmates, always a mirror of social values, reflected the turn toward introspection. "The greatest luxury in my life is solitude," avowed Linda Beatty, Miss August 1976. "The days I have to myself I spend on myself: reading, exercising, and meditating. . . . Working out our differences [with men I date] teaches me about myself." Pamela Jean Bryant, Miss April 1978, described herself as a dreamer and a loner. "I spend hours at the beach or chain myself to my desk, just writing in my journal. . . . I've stopped listening to others and started listening to myself."[43]

Perhaps the ultimate expression of the magazine's "Me Decade" orientation, however, came in "The Playboy Report on American Men." At mid-decade, Hefner commissioned Louis Harris and Associates to conduct a survey of American men to discover their values and attitudes. Over a five-week period in late 1976 and early 1977, researchers questioned 1,990 men between the ages of eighteen and forty-nine to discover their views on family, love, drug use, work, leisure, religion, money, health, friends, peace of mind, changes in women's roles, and politics. When released to the public in 1979, the report concluded that American men could be divided into four groups along a continuum: "Traditionalists," who defended time-honored values of the past; "Conventionalists," who were prepared to consider new alternatives after they had gained acceptance; "Contemporaries," who preferred fresh values as part of a continuity with the established order; and "Innovators," who embraced change and a willingness to experiment with alternative lifestyles.[44]

But cutting across these categories, the "Playboy Report" claimed, was a powerful endorsement of personal self-fulfillment. "The increased emphasis men are placing on self-fulfillment, pleasure, and doing one's own thing is dramatically altering America's traditional value system," it concluded. "The emerging self-oriented values represent a new personal liberalism. It stands apart from the traditional, conservative-radical distinctions based on social and economic issues. Its concern is for the conduct of one's personal life." A project spokesman explained that this was not mere selfishness or greed, but a demand for "personal relevance," a "quest for self-realization." The use of money, work, and leisure to find private meaning was "very much what this 'me generation' is." This was music to *Playboy*'s ears. It was "now perfectly acceptable to say, out loud, what I care about is myself," a spokesperson for the magazine noted when the report was released. The drive for self-enrichment was "inherent in the original concept in the magazine and the life that Hefner's been living."[45]

The adjustments to *Playboy* made by Hefner and his editors in the mid-1970s stabilized its identity after the drift of the Pubic Wars period. But journalistic success, of course, depends on profits as well as product. The larger financial picture of Playboy Enterprises, Inc., grew hazy in the 1970s as the magazine's readership slid and most company endeavors lost money, causing concern about the future among investors and in the business community. These nagging monetary problems made it clear that the future of Hefner's enterprise demanded financial reforms as well as editorial rethinking. The result was one of the biggest shake-ups in the history of the company.

III

In early 1976, Playboy Enterprises, Inc., quietly removed the "Playboy" moniker from two of its largest facilities. Its New Jersey resort west of New York City became the "Great Gorge Resort Hotel," while its hotel in downtown Chicago transformed into "The Towers." "What we did," said a company vice president, "was admit that the Playboy name and rabbit-head emblem were a detriment to business. That's quite an admission for an outfit that a few years ago was sure it was going to conquer the world."[46]

The change revealed much. By the mid-1970s, Hefner's company was facing a financial crisis as *Playboy* and the London casinos continued turning a profit while its other far-flung endeavors—clubs, hotels and resorts, films, records, and books—were losing prodigious amounts of money. Pretax profits of some $20 million in 1973 had sunk to $2 million in 1975 and rose only slightly to $5 million in 1976. In an interview with *Advertising Age,* Hefner blamed part of the problem on a weak economy but also admitted that his company had been "growing without really getting on top of the individual areas, departments, and divisions." Many company insiders were more cynical, joking darkly that PEI leaders "pushed a wheelbarrow full of money down to the basement every night and burned it."[47]

In the summer of 1975, Hefner initiated a draconian measure. He brought in Victor Lownes, his old sidekick, who had left Chicago in the early 1960s to run the profitable Playboy casino operation in England. Lownes became head of Playboy Clubs International, the biggest money drain in the company, with instructions to reform the operation. Lownes, who quickly became known as "Jaws," brought his inimitable flair and notorious mean streak to the Windy City. He announced his plans for "getting rid of the potted plants and all the people hiding behind them," joking that he might move operations back to the old headquarters on Ohio Street and hold a footrace where "anyone who can get down there and claim a desk we'd keep. Everyone else would be out." Within a few weeks he brutally fired dozens of people. But Lownes went too far when he announced that "Hefner's personal image is not that useful of a promotional vehicle anymore," and the publisher reined him in. "I've got egg on my face and I guess I was moving faster and farther than Hef wanted me to," said a chastened Lownes. But the damage had been done—company morale lay shattered.[48]

In 1976, the *Wall Street Journal* offered a bleak assessment of Hefner's empire: a drop in circulation and advertising with the magazine, a flood of red ink with hotels and resorts and domestic Playboy Clubs, the record and film divisions losing money, the First National Bank of Chicago withdrawing two lines of credit totaling $6.5 million because of the drug scandal, a hostile IRS leveling a $7.7 million bill for back taxes, PEI stock bottoming out at a price of $4 a share. Ironically, the article contended, many problems stemmed from the perception that the sexual revolution had passed *Playboy* by. "Nobody gets that excited about looking at a Bunny anymore," it noted. But difficulties also came from the company's "reputation for poor management" and its disdain for business expertise. Overall, the *Journal* concluded, it was clear that "Playboy's days of booming growth have ended."[49]

Hefner had grown painfully aware of looming problems. Usually bored by business details, he listened closely to his 1975 task force and its recommendations for corporate reorganization. While initially resisting proposals to fire people and jettison company projects, he gradually grasped the magnitude of the economic difficulties facing PEI. After a hard-nosed appraisal, Hefner committed himself to organizational restructuring, no matter how difficult.[50]

He moved dramatically in the spring of 1976. Hefner announced that he was stepping aside as president and chief operating officer of PEI and had launched a search for a replacement who would focus on the day-to-day operation of the company. He would remain as chairman and chief executive in charge of major policy decisions. Hefner had finally come to terms with not only his own limited business acumen but that of the friends he had entrusted to run his company. Respect and communication between the founder and his lieutenants had broken down. "One of the things that bothered me the most was their attitude toward Hefner," said one task force member. "I saw everything from contempt to just total disregard to casual dismissal. . . . I think they were perceiving an ineffective leader and that was an accurate perception. He was, at that time, an ineffective leader."[51]

By the summer, Hefner found his man in Derick Daniels, a forty-seven-year-old vice president of the Knight Ridder newspaper chain. The son of a patrician North Carolina family, he had grown up in Washington, D.C., and attended the University of North Carolina before going into journalism. Daniels worked for the *Durham Morning Herald, St. Petersburg Times, Atlanta Constitution,* and *Miami Herald* and got his big break in 1967 when he became city editor of the *Detroit Free Press,* just in time to direct the paper to a Pulitzer Prize for its coverage of the devastating race riots of that year. In 1974, he became a vice president and chief of news operations for Knight Ridder, Inc., with its chain of thirty-two newspapers nationwide.[52]

When an executive recruiter first approached him, Daniels recoiled. "I told the headhunter, 'No, no, no,' that I really didn't want to talk about it," he admitted to *Business Week.* But curiosity got the best of him, and when he met Hefner they clicked immediately. After five or six hours talking together, Daniels was struck by the publisher's intelligence and honesty. "He was a guy who knew what he wanted, he knew what the problems of the company were, and knew something had to be done with it, and he was ready to do it," Daniels recalled later. He became convinced that Hefner genuinely wanted an infusion of managerial expertise. In his words, "He wasn't going to be looking over your shoulder every moment—[he was] a man who had recognized that he had built something that had outgrown his own interest in continuing to try to run day to day."[53]

So Daniels accepted the position and joined the company on October 1, 1976. He took the helm with characteristic confidence and disarming wit. He told the press that Hefner "made it clear to me that he understands the need for a professional manager with an

entrepreneurial flair. He wants that place run and I intend to run it."
Revealing his plans to move into a Chicago penthouse apartment near
PEI headquarters, he quipped, "I've done my duty to the suburbs,
back lawns, home repairs." When asked if his own sexual education
had prepared him to enter the notorious *Playboy* scene, he joked,
"Like everyone else my age, I learned about the female anatomy from
the Sears catalogue."[54]

In terms of style and appearance befitting a Playboy president,
Daniels appeared right out of central casting. Slightly built, urbane,
and impeccably tailored, he had an unusual pair of mismatched
eyes—one blue and one hazel—topped by stylishly barbered locks
that spilled down over his ears and collar. His tanned and deeply lined
face—a friend once compared it to the façade of a North Carolina
beach house—wore an intense, brooding, occasionally bemused
expression. A four-packs-a-day smoker, he deployed the constant
Benson & Hedges cigarette in his hand as a prop to accent words or
phrases uttered in a smoky drawl. Somewhat reserved in social and
professional situations, he cultivated stylized mannerisms that reinforced an impression of incisive intelligence, idiosyncratic style, and
understated toughness. "First impression is John Wayne trapped in
Joel Grey's body," noted a reporter upon meeting him.[55]

Daniels emerged quickly as an articulate spokesman for *Playboy*.
He painted a bright future, describing it as "a magazine that celebrates life" and a purveyor of dreams. "I see the need for fantasy
in a complicated, difficult world," he said. "If you don't dream about
things that can be, what hope is there?" He linked *Playboy* to "the
upscale reader—the upwardly mobile man, open to new ideas and
experiences" who had "a feeling for quality" both in life and in his
consumer preferences.[56]

But Daniels got off to a controversial start. A few months after
starting his new job, he held a belated farewell party in Miami that
sent jaws dropping throughout the Playboy organization. Held at the
spacious home of a sculptor friend in Coconut Grove, the gathering featured male butlers and bartenders dressed in leather-and-
leopardskin outfits with bare buttocks. Female attendants wore black
thong panties and no tops. In the middle of the festivities, a shapely
young woman performed a striptease to reveal her pubic hair shaved
in the shape of a heart. Moreover, Daniels appeared on the cover of
the *Miami Magazine* reclining against his twenty-two-year-old female

companion and dressed in his garb for the evening: a gold lamé jumpsuit unzipped to the waist and gold neck chain and medallion. When Lee Gottlieb, PEI's public relations director, saw the story and cover photo, he scrambled down the hall to ask Daniels to suppress any more publicity. While the company was striving to create an image of seriousness and fiscal responsibility, he complained, this story appeared showing "the new president in this bizarre get-up at some kind of orgy." As Hefner recalled later, "If I was afraid of hiring someone who was too stuffy, I didn't have anything to worry about with Derick."[57]

As Daniels took up the presidency of PEI, his personal style did little to reassure nervous investors and executives. He married the young woman on the magazine cover, M. J. Taylor, the day before assuming the presidency. A tall, self-confident, articulate young woman with a full figure often on display with see-through blouses, she was a free spirit who once attended a corporate reception barefoot. The Danielses quickly acquired a reputation in Chicago for outlandish parties in their Towers penthouse apartment that spawned rumors of sexual "swinging." The new president's personal eccentricities—daily consumption of up to thirty cups of coffee, fasting for two days every week—added to his mystique, as did his flamboyant wardrobe. He would appear at the office in an elegant blue pinstriped suit, or a white suit with matching white shoes, or leather pants with sweater and scarf and loafers with no socks, or a flying suit with red cowboy boots. At a welcoming party held in the Playboy Mansion, he wore a billowing white blouse, tight white trousers, and white high-heeled boots, with a white silk scarf draped around his neck. As Daniels told one of his new colleagues, at Knight Ridder he had been "a closet freak. . . . Now I work in a corporation where I can be what I want to be."[58]

Many company executives found this unseemly for a corporate president. One feared that Daniels was "absolutely, personally out of control, and that we had hired a nut." Victor Lownes was particularly contemptuous. "Go up to your room and have a party, Derick, and don't bother me with this nonsense," he was overheard replying to a Daniels directive. In fact, as rumors spread about the social antics of the new president and his wife, Lownes coined a moniker for the couple that soon spread throughout the Playboy organization: "The Bizarros."[59]

But Hefner and Daniels mutually supported one another. Publicly, Hefner lauded his new lieutenant's business and administrative skills, while Daniels praised the publisher at every opportunity. Much of America had repressed sexual impulses, he told the *New York Times*, until "Hugh Hefner taught his readers that it was healthy to be a human sexual creature." To the *Chicago Tribune*, he described the publisher as "the classic entrepreneur" and "the single most important promotional entity that Playboy has."[60]

Daniels, with Hefner's support, used his first six months as president to formulate a basic strategy for saving PEI: focus on strengths and get rid of liabilities. The company had started with a strong core—the magazine and the clubs—but then caught a bad case of "conglomerate fever," expanding into "hotels and resorts and movie theatres and record companies . . . with very little knowledge of the businesses they were getting into," he observed. Daniels's plan was simple: "to trim off some of the things that were not working and . . . build the core strength of the whole company."[61]

In the spring of 1977 Daniels amputated several unprofitable PEI enterprises, closing the Playboy resort hotel in Jamaica and the Baltimore Playboy Club. He soon sold off theaters in New York and Chicago, franchised several new Playboy Clubs, suspended motion picture production, and reached a partnership agreement with Columbia Records regarding the company's ailing record division. "We are organizing, planning, training, head-hunting and, especially, professionalizing our approach to multiple businesses," Daniels told the press. In a widely publicized "hutch cleaning" in September 1977, he terminated some seventy PEI employees from the bloated payroll. These cutbacks were necessary, Daniels stated, because "over the years a sizable number of functions and jobs grew up which did not contribute directly to the profitability of the company."[62]

Nearly everyone, both inside the company and out, agreed that such reforms were overdue. Within a short time, the cutbacks had stopped the financial slide of Hefner's enterprise as fiscal years 1977 and 1978 showed a modest rebound in profits and the price of PEI stock rose. Financial analysts responded, with *Forbes* headlining "The Bunny Battles Back" and the *New York Times* judging that "Playboy Settles Down to Work: Glamour Gone, Profits Revive." The company, most observers agreed, had righted itself but was not totally out of the woods. "The bunny is back, no denying that," said one analyst. "But it's not clear whether it's merely shot up with a lot of cortisone or has truly regained its health."[63]

Thus Hugh Hefner and Derick Daniels were able to stabilize PEI's financial condition. But as the 1970s ended, *Playboy* occupied a more uncertain position than it had at the beginning of the decade. In an increasingly polarized America, some critics on both the left and right took aim at the Hefner agenda. During the twenty-fifth anniversary celebration in 1978–1979, Mike Royko, the cranky populist and longtime columnist for the *Chicago Sun-Times*, scathingly described the publisher as a self-promoter whose idea of sophistication was to "jiggle pinball machines in his rec room, drink a case of Pepsi a day, and play backgammon with those of his companions intelligent enough to understand the game." The liberal commentator Richard Cohen dismissed Hefner as a man desperately trying to concoct his own legend out of the need "we all have to justify our lives, to give it meaning—to say that it has been more than just pleasures and luxuries." The radical *Guardian* denounced *Playboy* for promoting "consumerism run amok."[64]

On the right, critics excoriated *Playboy's* "leering, voyeur's view of sex from the men's room wall" and its "obsession for materialism and personal pleasure. It is shallow and greedy." Colorful denunciations of Hefner and his magazine piled up: "embarrassingly hedonistic," "an overdose of ostentatious materialism," "flesh-peddling spiffed up with name brand contributors," "sexual junk." Perhaps the unkindest cut came from the town newspaper where Hefner had gone to college, which concluded that "*Playboy,* which has gone from bad to worse in portrayal of the female anatomy and in usage of language of the gutter, has done little but degrade the society in which it has prospered over this fourth of a century."[65]

But much worse was to come. As a new decade opened, a conservative political and cultural revolution that had slowly gathered momentum throughout the 1970s took the United States by storm. Opposed to nearly everything that *Playboy* represented, it drove Hefner and his enterprise into a desperate defensive posture. Within a short time, what had been merely disconcerting became horrendous as Mr. Playboy entered a long, nightmarish era in his life.

16

The Dark Decade

On August 15, 1980, Hefner and a group of his friends were playing in the mansion gamehouse when a curious phone call arrived. When the publisher's appointments secretary, Cis Rundle, picked up, the caller identified himself and asked to speak to Hefner. Cis told the publisher, who, annoyed at being interrupted, said she should take a message. The caller replied, "Well, he better come to the phone. He's got a dead Playmate on his hands," and mentioned the Playmate's name. Rundle gasped. The victim was Dorothy Stratten, the recently crowned Playmate of the Year, a transcendently beautiful, innocent young woman who had won the heart of everyone in the *Playboy* organization since arriving in Los Angeles from rural Canada only two years before.[1]

Rundle rushed to Hefner's side and blurted out the news. In her words, "Hef turned slate grey. I first thought he might faint, but he didn't. He was just in shock. He went right to the phone and spoke for a bit. Everyone was just standing there frozen." The detective reported that the young woman had died from a shotgun blast to the face, and the body of her estranged husband also lay at the scene, apparently having killed himself after shooting his wife. Hefner was stunned. Another aide, who had rushed in, reported that "Hef was standing there and looked sort of like a stone. He was ashen. His face was all white. . . . I put my hand on his arm and it was like his skin was moving." As the reality of the terrible event sank in, Hefner gathered himself and began orchestrating calls to the victim's friends and family as well as to key figures in the magazine. Disbelief mingled with horror and grief at the news.[2]

While a tragedy in its own right, of course, Dorothy Stratten's tragic death symbolically marked the beginning of nearly a decade of profound trouble for Hefner and the *Playboy* enterprise. Like a stampede, a host of problems—political, cultural, economic, personal—pounded down upon the publisher and his entertainment empire and threatened to demolish it. A trio of problems flared up in 1980, foretelling that Hefner would enter the darkest period of his life, both professionally and personally. As events unfolded, it was far from certain whether he would survive.

I

In mid-October 1980, a series of newspaper and television ads appeared in the Chicago media. Sponsored by the National Heritage Foundation, a Christian consortium, they denounced Hefner as a smut peddler spreading a message of "low-commitment sex, recreational drugs, selfish materialism, and adolescent irresponsibility." They pointed to lascivious features in the twenty-fifth anniversary edition of *Playboy*, quoted anti-Christian passages from the Playboy Philosophy, and noted an epidemic of teenage pregnancies, divorces, venereal diseases, fatherless children, and abortions sweeping through modern America. "*Playboy*, perhaps more than anyone else in the past 20 years, has called America to self-indulge as never before and it appears that we are now reaping the results," the ads stated. "It's becoming evident that popular hedonism will eventually wreck a society."[3]

The timing of these media messages was no accident. They came about two weeks before the presidential election, a contest in which the Republican candidate, Governor Ronald Reagan of California, had emerged at the head of a powerful new conservative movement.

Aiming to create a stronger American posture in foreign affairs, trim the welfare state, and renew commitment to the nuclear family, religious standards, personal responsibility, and sexual restraint, this crusade sought to reestablish traditional political, moral, and cultural values at the center of American public life. The Reagan Revolution had quietly taken root in the 1970s as a reaction against the widespread political dissent, cultural rebellion, and social turmoil that characterized 1960s America. As many Americans first grew befuddled, then angry, a gathering backlash saw local organizations spring up around the country, often in the suburbs, in a grassroots political network for the so-called New Right. Fervent opposition to the permissive morality of 1960s radicalism among disgruntled traditionalists led to a parallel mobilization on the cultural front. Groups such as the Moral Majority, founded by the Reverend Jerry Falwell in 1979, emerged determined to reassert Christian morality in the American political process.[4]

A series of clashes in the 1970s had established *Playboy* as a key target of the conservative insurgency. The dispute over passage of the Equal Rights Amendment in Illinois, for instance, put Hefner's magazine at odds with the conservative activist Phyllis Schlafly. She composed a ditty mocking *Playboy*'s support for the ERA and sang it on the steps of the capitol to the tune of "Here Comes Peter Cottontail": "Here comes Playboy Cottontail, Hopping down the capitol trail, Trying to buy the votes for ERA, / Telling every girl and boy, / You can only have your joy, / By becoming gender free or gay." *Playboy*'s defense of the porn actor Harry Reems, *Screw* magazine editor Al Goldstein, and *Hustler* publisher Larry Flynt, all of whom had been prosecuted by local communities on charges of obscenity, also rankled traditionalists. While Hefner had rallied behind the defendants on First Amendment grounds of opposing censorship, angry conservatives saw the episodes as confirmation that he was a pornographer at heart. In their minds, *Playboy* became associated with hardcore magazines and films.[5]

In the 1980 election, conservatives made cultural issues of personal morality and responsibility a keystone of the Reagan run for the presidency. Drawing upon the famous phrase of the Puritan leader John Winthrop, Reagan declared his hope that America would "uphold the principles of self-reliance, self-discipline, morality, and—above all—responsible liberty for every individual so that we will become that shining city on a hill." In his trademark smooth and earnest speaking style, the former California governor repeatedly posed a wholesome family life, personal responsibility, and traditional morality as antidotes to social decay. He recruited Robert Billings, an organizer of the Moral Majority, to join his campaign staff and in August 1980 journeyed to Dallas to address some fifteen thousand followers of the Religious Roundtable, an organization of conservative Christians. "I'm sick and tired of hearing about all of the radicals and perverts . . . coming out of the closet. It's time for God's people to come out of the closet," he declared. Two months later, speaking at the annual meeting of the National Religious Broadcasters, Reagan stated, "I don't believe we should have ever expelled God from the classroom." While Reagan never mentioned *Playboy* directly, other conservative spokesmen did. William F. Buckley excoriated Hefner during the campaign as a man who sought "to justify the superordination of sex over all other considerations—loyalty to family, any principle of self-discipline, any respect for privacy or chastity or modesty."[6]

The Moral Majority swung into action with particular force during the 1980 campaign. These cultural conservatives rallied in support of a traditional way of life under siege, seeing pornography, abortion, the ERA, homosexual rights, and denial of school prayer as "a matter of conscious plots [directed] at the traditional family and the peaceful neighborhood." In this eruption of activism, Hefner appeared as an agent of immorality and national decline. Falwell lashed out at the publisher angrily and often. In his 1980 book *Listen America!* the minister denounced the "cult of the playboy" as a threat to the family while in speeches he declared, "People like Hugh Hefner and Larry Flynt ought to be in the penitentiary." He attacked "the Hugh Hefners and the Jane Fondas, who weave their immoral philosophies into the moral fabric of this country" and described the publisher as "making a living from smut." The *Moral Majority Report* even accused Hefner's magazine of standing at the center of a national pornography-and-drugs network—supposedly, it also included NORML founder Keith Stroup, Timothy Leary, Abbie Hoffman, and Paul Krassner of *The Realist*—called the "Aquarian Conspiracy."[7]

While Hefner was not surprised by the conservative resurgence—he had expected it since seeing public support for the police crackdown during the 1968 Democratic Convention in Chicago—its vehemence galvanized him and inspired a spirited counterattack.

Hefner portrayed his conservative detractors as revivalists for the 1950s sensibility he had opposed in founding *Playboy*. "We're fighting some of the same fights again: abortion, censorship," he argued, with the Moral Majority aiming to regulate the content of school libraries and television shows. Christie Hefner, now working for PEI, supported this libertarian position, claiming that the Moral Majority sought "to return women to the kitchen and prayers to the schools." Moreover, with their talk of boycotting *Playboy* advertisers and screening the content of television shows, Falwell and his followers were threatening the First Amendment. "I've got to believe that the majority of people, in fact, respect the right of others to choose what they want to read and what they want to see," she argued.[8]

Hugh Hefner used *Playboy* to launch a full-bore attack on the Moral Majority and the new conservative movement. It ran a scathing piece, titled "The Reagan Question," that accused Reagan of being a hypocritical, communist-obsessed simpleton who pandered to Moral Majoritarians, threatened nuclear war, repeated apocryphal stories from notecards, and submitted to the directives of his drill-sergeant wife. "The Astonishing Wrongs of the New Moral Right" blasted the Falwell crowd as radicals who sought "to restructure the entire framework of American society to fit a set of rigid, doctrinaire political and religious beliefs." "Inside the New Right War Machine" revealed the fund-raising and organizational maneuvers of the conservative activists Richard Viguerie, Howard Philips, and Paul Weyrich. The 1980 campaign represented "a religio-political attack on personal freedom," *Playboy* declared melodramatically. "There's a war going on and the bad guys are winning."[9]

Playboy also employed mockery. A parody titled "Prayboy: Entertainment for Far-Righteous Men," contained a pictorial on "The Girls of the Moral Majority" and an article titled "Public Libraries—Must They Contain Books?" The "Prayboy Advisor" answered a query from a puzzled, pious couple about the nature and location of loins, often mentioned in the Bible: "All we can say is—you do have loins. One set each. But, unfortunately, we can't tell you where they are." In the "Prayboy Interview: GOD," when the Almighty was asked how to cleave to the path of righteousness, he replied, "By struggling against the wicked wiles of Satan, by following My commandments, and by getting back the Panama Canal." "Prayboy's Purity Jokes" began with the following: "Seems two liberals went back to her place and indulged in fornication. Just as the two sinners reached that moment of sexual union which is only permitted in holy matrimony, a truck crashed into her house and killed them dead and they both went to hell." A highlight of the mock issue was its centerfold, "Mrs. December," Norma-Beth Ewan, who posed in a pink housecoat with her five children under a sampler reading "Stand by Your Man." Her data sheet noted that turnoffs included "people who call me Ms. and the UN"; her favorite books were Deuteronomy and *The Joy of Cooking;* her favorite musician was Lawrence Welk.[10]

But Hefner's maneuvers, like those of the Democratic Party, had little impact as Reagan crushed President Jimmy Carter in the 1980 election. This dawning of a new political age would reshape American public life in profound ways for the next quarter century. In the process, Hefner and *Playboy* became identified, by all sides, as the antichrist of the newly triumphant conservatism. With the battle lines clearly drawn, the only question concerned when all-out war would begin.

The Reagan Revolution was accompanied by a second discomfiting development for *Playboy* that same year—the publication of a controversial book that placed Hefner and his magazine at the center of a cultural firestorm. For the better part of the 1970s, fueled by a $3.8 million advance for publication and movie rights, noted "New Journalist" Gay Talese had been engaged in a book project examining America's sexual revolution. Amid intense press interest, Talese explored the changing sexual landscape as a participant observer who delved into X-rated movies, massage parlors, erotic literature, infidelity and experimentation, swinging, and controversial new sexual resorts and clubs such as Plato's Retreat and Sandstone. The result was *Thy Neighbor's Wife,* a volume that appeared to tremendous fanfare in 1980. Through a wealth of descriptive stories, the book suggested that since midcentury, Americans gradually had abandoned taboos to embrace a new ethic of sexual freedom. A liberated atmosphere had been created, Talese concluded, by "America's new openness about sex, its expanding erotic consumerism, and the quiet rebellion . . . within the middle class against the censors and clerics that had been an inhibiting force since the founding of the Puritan republic."[11]

Hefner appeared as a central figure in *Thy Neighbor's Wife.* Talese had spent a good deal of time interviewing the publisher and hanging out at the Playboy Mansion, and he presented Hefner's life as emblematic of the sweeping liberation of American sexual values since the 1950s. In the three long biographical sections, Talese examined Hefner's childhood, the early stages of his career with *Playboy*, and his more recent endeavors, particularly the tangled romance with Barbi Benton and Karen Christy and the drug scandal that took Bobbie Arnstein's life. Full of colorful anecdotes and striking prose, Talese's biographical account suggested Hefner's success demonstrated that "Americans everywhere were becoming increasingly tolerant of, if not preoccupied with, various forms of sexual expression." At the same time, Talese portrayed the publisher as a restless, isolated, immature, somewhat neurotic figure whose search for happiness remained unfulfilled.[12]

While *Thy Neighbor's Wife* quickly moved onto the best-seller lists, it proved a huge critical disappointment. Reviewers generally found it to be a tedious, sanctimonious, even grim account written by a zealot for the cause of sexual liberation. "Dull as a double-feature of x-rated movies," said one. "*Thy Neighbor's Wife* read like a history of the Soviet Union written by Leonid Brezhnev," said another. Critics complained that Talese presented sex as a form of physical gymnastics devoid of emotional meaning or human connection, and dismissed the book as "the work of an undeniably aroused libido, but a limp mind."[13]

Moreover, most reviewers concluded that the book distorted modern American sex life. The mass of ordinary Americans—those who "enjoy sex as a wonderful part of life but do not make it a *cause celebre,* who are neither appalled nor entranced by their bodies"—were ignored in favor of a tiny fringe of erotic experimenters. This focus on radical dissenters made the book appear anachronistic, a cultural relic from the age of "flower children and psychedelic drugs." As one critic noted, "what might have been groundbreaking five years ago is now as moribund as poor Sandstone, which, although Talese typically neglects to mention it, is no longer open for business."[14]

Ideology colored many of the evaluations. Liberal commentators scoffed at Talese's chauvinist focus on middle-aged men looking for action and his neglect of women, homosexuals, children, and many others impacted by the changing social mores of the sexual revolution. The more sophisticated, such as Alexander Cockburn, cited Michel Foucault and lectured Talese for ignoring the likelihood that instead of striking a blow against the system, "the ruses of sexuality" constituted merely another form of subjugation in late capitalist society. Conservatives were even more hostile, portraying *Thy Neighbor's Wife* as a manifesto for social recklessness. Talese, they complained, simply ignored the heavy social costs of the sexual revolution: the undermining of love, marriage, and the family structure and an increase in divorce, venereal disease, abortions, teenage pregnancies, and the sexual exploitation of females. His own stories confirmed that the sexual revolution produced mostly "emotional impoverishment and desperate boredom," wrote one reviewer. "Perhaps the merit of *Thy Neighbor's Wife* is that it laid bare the desolate spectacle."[15]

Hefner was caught in the critical crossfire. Many commentators skewered Mr. Playboy as the supreme symbol of the shallow sexual hijinks described in this overblown book.[16] Far from being a social revolutionary, Hefner appeared to most reviewers as an overgrown adolescent committed mainly to his own pleasure. The publisher and his ilk, according to one, were "distressingly shallow," with "self-gratification their only concern." Ellen Goodman ridiculed Hefner and his acolytes for being "pathetically stuck in the traditional male mode; stuck in sad old fantasies; stuck as eternal adolescents proving they can do what mommy told them was naughty."[17] Critics took special aim at Hefner's life at the mansion, which they characterized as a portrait in insipidity: the publisher "on his circular rotating bed, surrounded by half a dozen nude bunnies, each one of whom is gently massaging him with oil, while a TV camera records the love session for future reference and his butler stands by to play and replay 'Tie a Yellow Ribbon.'" As one critic concluded derisively, this "adolescent utopia" consisted of "bunnies, backgammon, and Pepsi-Cola—what a life."[18]

Hefner, too, was unhappy with Talese's depiction of him. He complained that the book underplayed his crucial role in the sexual revolution while wildly distorting his romantic escapades. Talese also made him appear frustrated and unhappy, Hefner groused, when in fact he loved his life. A hostile review in *Playboy* caused Talese to conclude that Hefner was out to get him, and Hefner only confused matters when he agreed that his magazine's assessment of *Thy Neighbor's Wife* was unfair. "I'm sorry that it ever appeared in *Playboy*," he said publicly, while in a private note he apologized to Talese for the review not only because it "attempts to trivialize an important work, but because I think *Playboy* should applaud any serious effort of this sort that attempts to humanize our sexuality."[19]

Ultimately, the intellectual street fight prompted by the publication of *Thy Neighbor's Wife* in 1980 left Hefner bruised. He and Talese appeared as partners in cultural crime, as hucksters peddling an elixir of "liberated" sexuality brewed in the Swinging Seventies. Observers of every ideological stripe interpreted their message of sexual freedom not as inspirational, but as an embarrassing exercise in juvenile, narcissistic hedonism. Caught between a conservative Scylla, who loathed him for his undermining of traditional morality, and a progressive Charybdis, who scorned him for failing to replace it with anything meaningful, the *Playboy* publisher found himself in an increasingly isolated position. Symbolically, *Thy Neighbor's Wife* seemed to bring the curtain down on the drama of sexual insurrection played out during the 1960s and 1970s. Much of the audience turned away, more from distaste than hostility.

However jarring Reagan's election and Talese's book were in 1980, they receded before the upheaval caused by Dorothy Stratten's tragic murder that same year. This horrible event struck very close to home, traumatizing Hefner personally and throwing his circle of friends and associates at the mansion into an emotional tailspin. He had known the young woman well, and entertained high hopes for her success, and her senseless killing unnerved him. To make matters worse, as details gradually emerged about the train of events leading to her death, a troubling picture emerged—of rapid, dazzling success leaving a vapor trail of manipulation and frustration, marital infidelity and frustrated ambition, jealousy and sadistic revenge.

Stratten first arrived at the Playboy Mansion West in 1978 at age eighteen, a gorgeous but unsophisticated girl who had never been on an airplane before. Born and raised in Vancouver, Dorothy Ruth Hoogstraten came from a difficult family background. Abandoned by her father, the girl and her family had lived in a succession of rough neighborhoods, supported by her mother's labors as a housekeeper, before finally securing a house in a working-class suburb. At age fourteen, Dorothy began working at the Dairy Queen to help pay the bills and gain a bit of spending money. Within a couple of years, the tall, skinny, awkward girl began to fill out, with her Dutch heritage producing a striking physical package of blond hair, blue eyes, high cheekbones, and a voluptuous figure. During her senior year in high school, the young beauty met Paul Snider, the man who would become the central figure in her short life. He came into the Dairy Queen one afternoon, driving a Datsun sports coupe, wearing a long fur coat and lizardskin boots with spurs, and flashing a variety of gaudy rings and neck chains. Struck by his blond waitress, he got her phone number and after several tries procured a date.[20]

Snider was a small-time hustler who had dropped out of school as a teenager. Variously a pimp, car show promoter, and narcotics dealer, he saw in Stratten both a romantic prospect and a potential meal ticket. Perceiving the beauty blooming beneath the dowdy clothes and sweet temperament, he quickly set himself to winning the young blonde's devotion. Over the objections of her family, Snider wooed Stratten romantically, showering her with presents and impressing her with inflated talk about his career. A Svengali figure, he chose her clothes and makeup while looking for an opportunity to market her striking beauty. His chance appeared in the summer of 1978.[21]

As part of *Playboy*'s Great Playmate Hunt to find a centerfold for its twenty-fifth anniversary issue, the Vancouver photographer Ken Honey, who had discovered several Canadian Playmates over the years, was scouting for prospective candidates. Snider convinced Stratten to go for a test shoot, and after the session Honey sent about a dozen color shots to Marilyn Grabowski, *Playboy*'s photo editor in Los Angeles. Struck immediately, Grabowski called Honey and had him arrange a flight for Stratten to Los Angeles while she set up a shoot with glamour photographer Mario Casilli. Snider was annoyed because it had been arranged for Stratten to travel alone, but he relented and his girlfriend set off on the adventure of her life.[22]

Stratten's shoot went beautifully, and for several days she resided at the guesthouse at the Playboy Mansion. Although overwhelmed by the stately residence and nervous at meeting Hefner and mingling with celebrities, the young woman made a memorable impression with her sweet temperament and good looks. Grabowski assured her that a Playmate appearance was certain, so Stratten flew home to Vancouver, quit her job, and returned to Los Angeles for an extended stay at the mansion. Snider, suspicious that Dorothy was slipping away from him, called three or four times a day to Stratten, Grabowski, and Casilli. When the photographer and his crew accompanied Stratten back to Vancouver to do some location shots, Snider met them at the airport in a rented limousine and snapped, "You guys take the cab.

The limo is for Dorothy and me." He began to pressure Stratten to get married, and after much hesitation she reluctantly agreed to an engagement. The couple moved to Los Angeles.[23]

Stratten began a magical rise. She came in second for *Playboy's* twenty-fifth anniversary Playmate—primarily because of her inexperience—but was slated to appear as the August 1979 Playmate. Meanwhile, she and Snider took up residence in a small Westwood apartment. Stratten worked as a Bunny in the Los Angeles Playboy Club and took acting lessons, and he pushed several unsuccessful promotional schemes: wet T-shirt contests, male strippers, a "handsomest man in LA" contest. In June 1979, she succumbed to Snider's pressure and married him in Las Vegas, having told Grabowski, "I owe it to him. I was a nobody when he found me." A few weeks later, with her Playmate issue on sale, Stratten signed with an agent and secured several small parts in films and television shows. She appeared prominently in the October 1979 ABC broadcast *The Playboy Roller Disco and Pajama Party*. Selected as the 1980 Playmate of the Year, Stratten won the title role in the feature film *Galaxina,* a science fiction satire, a few weeks later.[24]

Throughout this period, Stratten and Snider drew contrasting reactions at the mansion. Hefner and his friends loved her and, universally, viewed him as a "creep." Snider, with his satin shirts, flashy gold chains, mink coat, and grandiose manners, alienated those with whom he tried to ingratiate himself. Hefner, who had become something of a father figure to Stratten, loathed Snider on sight and had him checked out with the Vancouver police. He urged the young woman to avoid rushing into marriage, even when she asked him to give her away at the wedding, and banned him from the mansion grounds unless he was with Stratten.[25]

As Stratten's prospects soared, Snider's hold over her unraveled. His various plans to market her image—a poster of her roller skating in a skimpy outfit, a perfume, a photo book—floundered even as he became more insistent on handling her financial affairs. He commandeered her income, pocketing most of her paychecks and purchasing a Mercedes 450SE for his own use while she drove a 1967 Mercury Cougar. Such high-handed treatment finally alienated his wife, who hired her own financial manager, Robert Houston. He set up Dorothy Stratten Enterprises, and thereafter her income was deposited into a corporate account from which she, but not Snider, could withdraw funds. Only a monthly stipend was placed in a joint checking account. An infuriated Snider bullied and berated Stratten to tears and the relationship crumbled.[26]

Tensions reached a crisis point when Peter Bogdanovich, one of Hollywood's hottest young directors, chose Stratten for a part in his new film, *They All Laughed,* a romantic comedy with John Ritter, Ben Gazzara, and Audrey Hepburn. They had met at the mansion and Bogdanovich had asked her to read for the part. Smitten by her beauty and impressed with her acting instincts, he had put her in the film in the part of the love interest for Ritter. In March 1980, Stratten flew off to New York City for several weeks of shooting and, unbeknownst to everyone, began an affair with Bogdanovich. By all accounts, the two fell in love and Stratten determined finally to end her relationship with Snider. First, she asked for a separation in a letter, writing, "I want to be free. Let the bird fly. If you love me, you'll let me go." In June, she saw an attorney and declared their physical and financial separation, even though she wanted to arrange a generous monetary settlement for Snider.[27]

Her husband reacted with rage and desperation. He hired a private detective to tail his wife and Bogdanovich, trying to get evidence for an alienation-of-affections lawsuit. He badgered Houston, demanding cash outlays and threatening to sue for half of his wife's future income. Stratten, determined to have an amicable parting, met with Snider in late July to discuss a divorce settlement. She agreed to meet him again on August 14. Meanwhile, Snider purchased a secondhand twelve-gauge Mossberg shotgun and a box of shells. Stratten came to the house that they once shared about noon. Later that evening, after several phone calls to Snider went unanswered, friends entered the abode and found two naked bodies and blood everywhere. Snider had shot Stratten point-blank in the side of the head before turning the gun on himself. He also had sexually assaulted her, both before and after her death. The next morning, the *Los Angeles Times* headline blared out news of the horrifying murder-suicide: "Playmate of Year Slain."[28]

This dreadful episode generated shock waves that buffeted Hefner and the Playboy empire. A chorus of criticism described Stratten as a victim of the publisher's exploitative media machine. "It's time someone takes a good hard look behind the glamorous façade of Hugh Hefner and the Playboy organization," declared an indignant letter to a Los Angeles newspaper. Another critic accused *Playboy* of creating an atmosphere in which sleazy characters such as Snider flourished. "If there had been no market for pictures of her, perhaps there would have been no beginning to the 'meal ticket' philosophy that led to her death," he argued. "Hefner created both the Playmate dream and the deadly nightmare."[29]

Feminists blasted Hefner and *Playboy* for nurturing an exploitative attitude toward women. About three months after the murder, for instance, Teresa Carpenter published "Death of a Playmate" in the *Village Voice,* an article that was reprinted in many newspapers and would go on to win the 1981 Pulitzer Prize for Feature Writing. She argued that three men had sought to use Stratten for their own ends—Hefner, Bogdanovich, and Snider—and that while the latter had pulled the trigger, all bore responsibility for the tragedy. The young woman, she wrote, had been the "catalyst for a cycle of ambitions which revealed its players less wicked, perhaps, than pathetic." Her critique of Hefner and his magazine was searing. Stratten was a "corporate treasure," argued Carpenter, whom *Playboy,* which had never really produced a major actress, "thought was going to be the biggest thing they ever had," while Hefner hoped to gain legitimacy in Hollywood by creating a star, a "Marion Davies to call his own." Snider, the author continued, had been a pitiful creature of the Playboy ethos:

> The irony that Hefner does not perceive—or at least fails to acknowledge—is that Stratten was destroyed not by random particulars, but by a germ breeding within the [*Playboy*] ethic. One of the tacit tenets of the *Playboy* philosophy—that women can be possessed—had found a fervent adherent in Paul Snider. He had bought the dream without qualification, and he thought of himself as perhaps one of *Playboy*'s most honest apostles. He acted out dark fantasies never intended to be realized.

Snider, Carpenter claimed, did what many male readers of *Playboy* probably yearned to do: "instead of fondling himself in private, instead of wreaking abstract violence upon a centerfold, he ravaged a playmate in the flesh."[30]

A horrified Hefner denied that *Playboy* had exploited Stratten. "To whatever degree *Playboy* may have benefited, Dorothy benefited a great deal more, and would have continued to benefit a great deal more," he passionately insisted. "The next film she was reading for and likely would have gotten would have brought her $100,000 and without question, the happiest time of her life was in that last year, year and a half." He reminded listeners that Snider had a record of abusive behavior toward Stratten. Hefner also threw himself into a long article on Stratten's life for *Playboy,* large sections of which he personally rewrote and shaped in the first extensive writing he had done since the Playboy Philosophy two decades earlier. The piece contended that *Playboy* had consistently promoted the lifting of female subjugation—"economically, socially, sexually"—and Snider was "a very sick guy" who "couldn't stand to see Dorothy become an independent human being, with a mind of her own, a body of her own, a life of her own." As for the Carpenter article, it was "a viciously anti-Playboy, anti-male diatribe" that "fabricated facts . . . and invented imaginary motivations." Hefner also pointed out that Carpenter had sold the motion picture rights to her article to the director Bob Fosse, who would go on to make *Star 80,* for more than $125,000. "So much for the exploitation of Dorothy Stratten," he concluded.[31]

Stratten's death, and the public reaction to it, hurt Hefner deeply. It joined Bobbie Arnstein's suicide as one of the most "irrational, painful, horrifying" events of his life, he said later. In concert with the Reagan election and the Talese contretemps, it also portended the beginning of a grim era for Hefner and *Playboy.* Increasingly, he appeared cornered into an isolated position in the broader culture. Reviled by the newly triumphant conservative movement, the publisher and his magazine also were increasingly unwelcome among the progressives whose ranks he yearned to lead. These dispiriting developments, in fact, introduced a protracted decade of travail for Hefner in the 1980s. As soon became apparent, the troubling events of 1980 took place against a backdrop of larger financial problems that brought Playboy Enterprises, Inc., to the precipice of collapse.[32]

II

On October 14, 1980, a euphoric Victor Lownes strode out of a London courtroom. More than a year earlier, as head of Playboy Enterprises Inc.'s enormously profitable gaming operation, he had engineered the purchase of the Victoria Sporting Club in London. The acquisition had made Playboy the biggest gambling enterprise in Britain. But English officials had thrown up a temporary roadblock, denying Playboy a gaming license for the facility because of illegal activity by the previous owners. In an appeal before a London court, however, Playboy attorneys successfully argued that the company's unblemished reputation would produce a strict adherence to all gaming rules. After the license was granted, an exultant Lownes cabled the good news to Hefner in Los Angeles. In the manner of Julius Caesar's famous report on his conquest of Gaul (*Veni, vidi, vici*: "I came, I saw, I conquered"), Lownes wrote, "VICTORIA VICTORIOUS, VISION VINDICATED, VALUE VERIFIED, VERILY VICTOR."[33]

Lownes's elation appeared justified. Over the last fifteen years, the indubitable bad boy of PEI had built a gaming empire in England that profited both the company and himself. After functioning as a key operative in the growing Playboy organization in the 1950s, he had left the company for a time, then rejoined in 1964 after convincing Hefner to appoint him an officer in Playboy Clubs International and let him launch Playboy Clubs in England. When Britain regularized gambling laws with the 1968 Gaming Act, Lownes took full advantage. Within a few years he had established casinos at the Playboy Club and the posh Clermont Club in London, opened Playboy casinos in Portsmouth and Manchester, and created a web of betting shops and bingo parlors around the country.[34]

Throughout the 1970s, as the general financial fortunes of PEI declined, those of its English gaming division soared. Much of it came from an influx of Arab oil money as Saudis, in particular, flocked to London to indulge a fondness for gambling. Lownes welcomed them into the Playboy casinos, and soon it was not uncommon to see wealthy Arabs lose $500,000 in a single night's activity. In fiscal 1980, the *Wall Street Journal* calculated, the English Playboy casinos accounted for 85 percent of the company's earnings. As the new decade opened, financial analysts agreed that PEI's English gaming was keeping the company afloat.[35]

This tremendous success made Victor Lownes the talk of English society. As the highest-paid executive in Britain—his yearly salary of $600,000 per year was larger than that of PEI's president, Derick Daniels—he rubbed shoulders with many of England's rich and famous. In 1972 he purchased a country estate, Stocks, about an hour from London, that became the setting for a flamboyant and highly publicized lifestyle. Its stately mansion with nineteen bedrooms, four cottages, several outbuildings, and a stable, soon saw the addition of tennis and squash courts, a whirlpool and Jacuzzi, a pinball arcade, and a swimming pool. Lownes became an avid fox hunter and participated in high-society horse events with the likes of Prince Charles. On weekends he hosted a perpetual party at Stocks attended by actors, musicians, writers, and celebrities such as Peter Sellers, Roman Polanski, Peter Cook, and members of Monty Python. The estate also functioned as a Bunny training school for the clubs and casinos, which meant that PEI covered many of the estate's operating costs. The constant presence of dozens of attractive young women at Stocks contributed to Lownes's legendary love life. By the 1970s, the PEI executive had created a lavish social scene that rivaled Hefner's.[36]

Then Lownes fell victim to his own hubris. In late 1979, he moved against Playboy's biggest competitor in British gaming, Ladbrokes Ltd., headed by the powerful businessman Cyril Stein. A series of investigative reports detailing unethical and illegal activity at Ladbrokes had appeared in a British magazine, and during the resulting uproar Lownes decided to play the reformer. He formally challenged the renewal of his competitor's gambling license and helped force Ladbrokes out of the gambling business. A furious Stein promised retaliation, and he kept his promise. A few weeks later, police and Gaming Board inspectors raided Playboy casinos in London and confiscated records and files. Stein, it turned out, had paid informers to reveal improprieties in the Playboy operation—giving free club membership to hotel porters who steered wealthy guests to Playboy casinos, accepting false checks from wealthy gamblers to extend them credit, and allowing company directors to gamble in their own facility. There were also accusations that wealthy Arabs had procured Bunnies for their friends. The police and the Gaming Board announced that they would challenge the renewal of Playboy's gambling license because of such improprieties.[37]

As this crisis escalated, Hefner, along with Derick Daniels and corporate managers in Chicago, grew increasingly worried. In late March they summoned Lownes to a special meeting at the mansion in Los Angeles to discuss matters. He offered breezy reassurances that his reputation for honest management would prevail, but was rather unconvincing, partly because he was still groggy after suffering a serious concussion in a horseback riding accident. Meanwhile, lawyers and business experts in England told Hefner and Daniels that the situation was beginning to unravel. Complicating matters was the fact that Lownes and Daniels were engaged in a corporate power struggle within PEI. Lownes believed that profits from his division were supporting inept corporate management in Chicago, while Daniels contended that the English operation had been functioning independently without any kind of corporate control from PEI.[38]

Finally, after several weeks of deliberation and conferences, Hefner decided to act. Convinced that loss of English casino revenue would scuttle PEI, and told by the company's English counsel that Lownes's continued presence made that inevitable, he sent Daniels to London to ask the company's chief of operations in England to resign on April 15, 1981. A furious Lownes stalked out of the meeting. He told the press that his sacking was "stupid" and "an absurdity" and lashed out at PEI management as small-minded bureaucrats who spent their time "sorting through Social Security numbers and personnel files." In a bitter letter to Hefner, he accused Daniels and his team of concocting a "plan to destroy my reputation in order to realize their inordinate ambition to take over the gaming operations and thereby justify their existence."[39]

Hefner stuck to his guns. "Your suggestion that all this is some sort of corporate plot to ruin your reputation is simply untrue and ignores the most obvious facts of the situation," he wrote to Lownes. He defended his decision as in the best interests of the company. The decision to fire Lownes, he stated in a press conference, was a painful one because of their long friendship but "the only appropriate action." He admitted that losing its British gaming license would present "a very serious problem" for PEI, but insisted that the objections were minor and could be resolved.[40]

Hefner's optimism proved misplaced. PEI scrambled to salvage the situation by hiring Sir John Treacher, a British businessman and former admiral in the Royal Navy, to replace Lownes. The move backfired. The Gaming Board saw it as proof that the American parent company controlled its British operation, and foreign control of casinos in England was prohibited by the Gaming Act. As a result, British magistrates decided against Playboy in an initial licensing hearing in early October, ruling that the company was "not fit." Less than a month later, PEI announced the sale of its entire English gambling operation to a British company for only $31.4 million, which experts calculated to be about one-tenth of its value. The whole situation was a disaster, an analyst told the *Wall Street Journal:* "The loss of two-thirds of your earnings is never a pleasant prospect."[41]

But the London debacle prefaced an even larger financial calamity for PEI. The company had bet much of its future on a huge casino project in Atlantic City, taking advantage of a 1976 referendum that legalized gambling on the boardwalk. PEI joined with the Elsinore Corporation to build a huge hotel-casino, and in early 1979, construction began on a twenty-four-story, five-hundred-room gambling palace that would cost some $135 million over the next two years. According to *Business Week,* the company had invested "half its total equity" in the project, but with after-tax profits predicted to be around $30 million a year, Hefner, PEI president Derick Daniels, and Victor Lownes deemed it a sound investment.[42]

Many outsiders, however, thought it was a risky venture. They pointed out that strict regulations on advertising, fierce competition among existing casinos in Atlantic City, and a slumping American economy dimmed the chances for success. Playboy's past history—failures with movies, books, and records and evaporating profits in its clubs and resorts—also inspired little confidence that its expansion into gambling would thrive. In the opinion of one business journal, Playboy's plans in Atlantic City "seem about as chancy as Hefner's earlier efforts turned out to be."[43]

The collapse of Playboy's gambling operation in England provided the first sign of trouble. The director of the state's Division of Gaming Enforcement demanded that Lownes and three of his managers step aside from any involvement in Atlantic City before a temporary operating permit would be granted. They did so, the permit was granted, and the Playboy Hotel and Casino began temporary operation in early April. Hefner even visited the new facility later in the month, arriving like a "conquering emperor," in the words of the local newspaper. But the English failure clouded the future. "I find it very difficult to believe that a company that is unlicensable in another jurisdiction would be licensable in New Jersey," noted a business analyst in the *Wall Street Journal.*[44]

In November 1981, the Division of Gaming Enforcement decided to oppose Playboy's request for a permanent gambling license.

It cited concerns about several episodes in the history of Hefner's organization: the old canard about payments to the New York State Liquor Authority in the early 1960s, the Bobbie Arnstein drug investigation in the early 1970s, the loss of the London licenses, and the false change that led Hefner's hiring of a Chicago attorney with links to organized crime. Hefner and PEI management were stunned, having expected a smooth road to approval. Now hearings before the New Jersey Casino Control Commission were scheduled for January 1982, and license approval would require the approval of four of the five commissioners.[45]

Playboy's Atlantic City casino and, perhaps, its future as a company hung in the balance as Hefner journeyed to Atlantic City to appear as the first witness. His testimony, as the public symbol of the corporation, would be crucial. But when the publisher arrived on January 11 for his first day of questioning, things unfolded inauspiciously. He entered in the company of Shannon Tweed, a tall, stunning blonde who was a recent Playmate and his current girlfriend, and she attracted more attention than he did. Dressed in a blue business suit and tie, Hefner looked weary. In fact, he had been up much of the night fighting with Tweed, and had popped a couple of dexies to stay awake.[46]

Hefner's testimony was a disaster. Later he decried his treatment as "the Atlantic City Inquisition," but much of the problem resulted from lack of preparation. State's attorney James Flanagan questioned the publisher on several matters—particularly the payments PEI made to New York officials in the early 1960s to get a liquor license for the New York Playboy Club. Hefner explained, correctly, that they had been a response to extortion rather than an attempt at bribery, but was unable to recall whether he had been granted immunity in the grand jury inquiry and could not remember salient events and policies. When questioned about the London casino collapse, he confessed that "inappropriate and improper" things had been done in England that "we did not know about." When asked about innocent business relationships with Joe DeCarlo and John Dante, friends with shady reputations, he was unable to recollect details about their dealings. Throughout, Hefner referred to having only "islands of recollection" and professed ignorance about ranking officials and major events in his company's history. Once, unable to recall some point, he tried to joke, "Ask me whom I was dating."

Under pressure, he also admitted that he had not even read the DGE report before testifying.[47]

Hefner's inept performance proved fatal. A seasoned observer of these hearings told the press that "never before had he seen a casino executive so ill-prepared, so unable to answer basic facts about his company." The commissioners voted to deny Playboy and Hefner the permanent license, deeming them "unfit and unwelcome to operate a casino in New Jersey." Three of the commissioners voted in favor of the license, recognizing that PEI's payments to the liquor authority had been the result of extortion. But two voted no, describing Hefner's testimony as "insincere" and denouncing him for "a failure . . . to exhibit the forthright candor he had to display." Flanagan agreed that "Hefner was a terrible witness" and observed that when he admitted that he had not bothered to read the investigative report into his own company, it was the beginning of the end. Hefner had been done in not by corruption or dishonesty—his personal ethics were impeccable—but by his absence from the company he had started.[48]

The decision sent Hefner and PEI reeling. While the commission had left an opening—the company could still gain the license if it presented a plan to divorce itself from Hefner—such a course was unthinkable. Thus PEI arranged to sell its interest in the casino and hotel to the Elsinore Corporation for $58.5 million, with only $7.6 million coming in cash while the balance was covered by an unsecured note. The Atlantic City fire sale was a devastating blow that drained funds, sent company stock plunging, and cut off future revenues. Many outsiders thought PEI might collapse entirely.[49]

As financial fallout from this disaster rained down, Hefner took a drastic measure to save his enterprise. Three weeks after the denial of the Atlantic City gambling license, he called in Derick Daniels and asked him to resign. "Fine, Hef. If that's what you think, that's what we're going to do," Daniels replied. With typical flamboyance, he departed the meeting in his white leather jumpsuit, climbed into a chauffeured Mercedes, and was driven to the opera as he sipped champagne from a bottle wrapped in a white towel. Daniels's easy acceptance of the decision came in part from a generous severance package of $470,000. But it also came from knowledge that Hefner already had a replacement in mind—his eldest child, Christie, age twenty-nine. On April 28, 1982, she became the new president of Playboy Enterprises, Inc.[50]

III

Christie Hefner had joined PEI in 1975 as a "special assistant" to her father following graduation from Brandeis, where the English major had been selected for Phi Beta Kappa and graduated summa cum laude. She took on several projects over the next few years. She operated Playtique, a boutique in the Playboy Building, managed public relations for the yearlong twenty-fifth anniversary celebration of *Playboy*, and chaired the New Publications Group, a company committee charged with evaluating new magazine opportunities. According to Daniels, when he became president in 1976, it was understood that training Christie was part of his charge. By 1978 she had became a corporate vice president and publisher of a pair of Playboy consumer guides. While none of these early projects were rousing successes, the younger Hefner gained plaudits throughout PEI for her incisive intelligence, articulate manner, and attention to business detail. "In contrast to 'Hef,' she has an affinity for balance sheets, a tolerance for daylight office hours, and a gregarious personality," *Fortune* noted. Thus she stood poised to take control of the company as the "Hare Apparent," and the casino catastrophes of 1981–1982 cleared the path for her to step in.[51]

Christie brought several compelling attributes to the table. First, she enjoyed the full trust of her father. While he had been far from an ideal parent, leaving his wife and children in the mid-1950s, he stayed on good terms with Millie after their divorce and maintained regular contact with his children, Christie and David, and supported them and their mother financially. In Millie's words, her daughter accepted Hugh as "a self-involved but feeling person" and enjoyed her occasional visits to the Chicago mansion. While the relationship was somewhat distant, Christie admired her father for his intelligence, kindness, and progressive social views. Many long talks during her adolescence strengthened the bond to her father. Midway through college, she decided to change her name back to Hefner, which touched him deeply—her name had been altered when her mother remarried—and father and daughter grew steadily closer. After asking her to join the company, Hugh clearly began to see her as his successor. "She has the qualities I'm looking for. Intelligence, creativity, good communication with me, a good natural leadership style, and a high profile that works to her advantage both inside and outside the company. She's a good communicator," he told the press after appointing her president. To friends and associates, the delighted publisher often commented, "If Christie didn't exist, *Playboy*'s promotion department might want to invent her." Many observers shared his confidence, with one publication describing her as "a no-nonsense executive who was fast becoming the Katharine Graham of the Midwest."[52]

Christie Hefner also offered another attractive asset. As a talented, ambitious, and articulate woman, she helped negate the feminist accusation that *Playboy* embodied sexism and misogyny. In fact, soon after joining PEI she became the leading spokesperson for a new *Playboy* that was sensitive to women's rights. Possessing a savvy political sensibility—particularly influenced by her mother's Democratic activism, she had grown up campaigning for Hubert Humphrey and Illinois senator Paul Douglas—she was a Jimmy Carter delegate to the 1980 Democratic Convention. She publicly backed the ERA and abortion rights with speeches and fund-raisers, causing Gloria Allred of NOW to praise her as "one of the most articulate, committed, hardworking feminists in the entire country." She stood up to critics who insisted that *Playboy* exploited women. "Playboy has been more supportive of feminist politics and philosophies than most other companies I know of—in its attitude toward hiring and promotion of women, through its editorial and financial support of the Equal Rights Amendment and abortion," she replied. "I think people who make the leap that because it chooses to picture women as sexually attractive, that somehow that goes hand in hand with thinking that women are stupid or women belong in the bedroom, are making a leap of faith that has nothing to do with the magazine."[53]

PEI's new president needed every available ounce of talent, energy, and paternal support upon taking the helm in 1982. She faced a tall order. Buffeted by falling stock prices, mounting losses, and predictions of a grim future, the company appeared in desperate straits. Christie embraced the most reasonable strategy available: push the company to divest itself of unprofitable projects and rebuild its base. In 1981, under Daniels, PEI had jettisoned the unprofitable Great Gorge and Lake Geneva resorts, and the younger Hefner continued down this path. She negotiated the sale of Playboy Books and instituted stringent cost-cutting measures that slashed corporate overhead by some $8 million a year during her first few months in office. She also formulated plans to move the company into the new area of cable television and explored publishing a magazine for modern women. The younger Hefner announced publicly that she planned to concentrate on "the restructuring of Playboy from a broadly based corporation to a clearly focused communications company."[54]

Hugh Hefner was pleased and relieved when his daughter tackled the financial problems besetting his beloved enterprise. Her engagement eased his disengagement from the business aspects of PEI, which he found increasingly abhorrent. During the early stages of the London crisis, a frustrated Hefner had exploded: "Do you know what I really wish? I really wish that all of my executives could just . . . go . . . away . . . and the money would keep coming in!" He admitted to the *Wall Street Journal* that "the business world really doesn't appeal to me" and made a curiously revealing confession in a nationally televised interview: "If I have a failure as a businessman, it probably is in the business area." Hefner was delighted to pull back and focus on the big picture while his daughter handled the tough business details of running PEI.[55]

But a growing array of problems refused to release their grip on the publisher. Professionally, with the slamming of casino doors and the popping of critical sniper fire providing a threatening backdrop, Hefner and his assistants attempted to revamp his magazine and make it relevant for a new era. Personally, he showed signs of wanting to settle down in a more conventional romantic relationship. Neither project proved very successful.

17

The Party's Over

In August 1986, Hugh Hefner made the cover of *Newsweek,* but in an unfortunate fashion. The long feature article, titled "The Party's Over," announced that the Playboy empire was in shambles and about to collapse. Over the last couple of decades, it argued, the magazine had fallen from its pinnacle of hipness in American culture as "the publisher and America gradually drifted apart." Now an array of political, economic, and social problems were pressing in from every direction. Clearly, the fun and games had ended as Hefner, "the Peter Pan of porn," faced a challenge that threatened to overwhelm him: "figuring out where he and his vision fit into contemporary society."[1]

The *Newsweek* piece was distressingly typical. Criticism of the Playboy lifestyle built to a crescendo in the 1980s as Hefner and his magazine came under attack, it seemed, from every direction. In the media, among the critics, and for a popular audience that continued to shrink steadily, the publisher increasingly appeared as a pioneering cultural figure whose time had passed.

But Hefner did not go gently into that good night. Along with his editors, he struggled to revamp *Playboy* and make it relevant to a new age. In his private life, he sought to settle down in a traditional, one-on-one pairing in two successive relationships. But frustration mounted as the magazine spun its wheels, the company's losses mounted, and his romantic life became subject to unprecedented turbulence. For Hefner, a dark decade turned a deeper shade of black.

I

"It is Hefner bashing season," *Rolling Stone* announced in 1986. A "disillusionment with Playboyism" had set in, observed the leading journal of America's up-to-the-minute younger set. "Admiration and envy during Hefner's ascendant, golden years . . . have given way to general distaste." In the previous decade, with the waning of 1960s social activism and experimentation, Hefner had blunted criticism and regained some cultural purchase by channeling the introspective energies of the Me Decade. But now a chorus of commentators pictured *Playboy* as not just wrongheaded or ideologically suspect, but something much worse: irrelevant.[2]

Much of the denunciation was familiar. Conservatives emboldened by the Reagan ascendancy attacked Hefner and his magazine as agents of moral decay. *Conservative Digest*, for instance, reviled the publisher's support of recreational sex, legalized drugs, abortion on demand, and homosexuality, contending that such ideas "have been destroying our society." The rise of AIDS added a sense of looming threat as the sexual revolution pioneered by Hefner "has dissolved in confusion and disillusionment" with the spread of this deadly social disease, claimed the *Chicago Tribune*. Many critics added the familiar refrain of sexism. Both conservative defenders of the family and leftist advocates of women's rights denounced what one critic described as Hefner's ethic of "woman as plaything." "The feminist movement has raised a great deal of consciousness about the role of magazines such as *Playboy*," wrote one columnist.[3]

But the censure of the Playboy ethic in the 1980s was not confined to indignant conservatives and angry feminists. Liberals increasingly lined up to take their swings at Hefner as a faux liberator. In October 1985, the *New Republic* published "Man of the Mansion," a sarcastic assessment of "Hef the American Publishing Genius." The Playboy lifestyle never had meant much, it jeered, and now with his magazine in disarray, his company suffering from inertia, and his "fairly empty existence" at his Los Angeles mansion, "Hef the Letch" had revealed his success formula: "naked young girls that can arouse the fantasies of a whole lot of American men." An accompanying Vint Lawrence cartoon showed a naked, scrawny Hefner with drooping bunny ears, pipe clenched in his teeth, surrounded by wilted flowers, empty fried-chicken boxes, and discarded Pepsi cans.[4]

An equally devastating portrait appeared in a liberal newspaper, the *Los Angeles Times*. Written by the veteran journalist Bella Stumbo, a three-part profile subtly pictured Hefner as a study in insipid, self-involved celebrity. The series began with a description of the disheveled, pajama-clad, pipe-smoking, Pepsi-sipping publisher as he sat in his study waiting to be interviewed: "The effect was not sexy. At 57, Hefner looked like a middle-aged man who might have the flu." Hefner, Stumbo reported, yearned to gain respect for his historic achievements, but her account offered little to warrant such recognition. A confirmed homebody with no real hobbies beyond playing games and watching old films, and no interest in seeing the world, the publisher was "a man who appears to neither want nor need an outlet for his own obvious intelligence." When asked about people he admired, he named movie stars, but beyond Hollywood "Hefner was at a total loss." While claiming that *Playboy* was a feminist publication, he struggled to justify the Playmate Data Sheet and confessed that he didn't like *Playboy*'s explicit photos but was forced to include them because of readers' tastes. Stumbo concluded with a snapshot of the publisher at a mansion reception, complaining about the conservative backlash against the sexual revolution as he smooched and nuzzled with his current twenty-one-year-old girlfriend.[5]

Such attacks at least took Hefner and *Playboy* seriously. More distressing were the dismissals that pictured him as obsolete—the victim of the sexual openness characteristic of modern American life. Still fighting battles against phantom opponents, said one, "Hugh Hefner is an anachronism in our time." *Newsweek* callously noted *Playboy*'s appeal to aging Baby Boomers, with ads picturing bald men with the acclamation "Why Hair Transplantation Works." Even the journalist Bob Greene, an old Hefner ally, noted that twenty years ago "guys my age used to breathlessly await *Playboy*'s arrival in the mail every month. Now, in our sex-inundated society, *Playboy* is passé, even irrelevant." As another critic concluded, *Playboy* was "as relevant today as a Nehru jacket."[6]

For many, Hefner's personal lifestyle seemed to embody this obsolescence. Increasingly, critics depicted his mansion activities as frivolous, dissipated, or even worse, an eye-rolling throwback to the rebellion of the 1950s and 1960s. Hefner had become "sort of an anachronism with his pipe and smoking jacket," sadly observed Greene. The publisher's cloistered regimen, once a source of mystery, now "resembles nothing so much as a study in terminal depression," asserted Martin Amis. Even Hefner's legendary love life now seemed distasteful to many. "Give us a break," one commentator snapped. "A 60-year-old man running around with a 20-year-old girl—who wants to read that." Even *Playboy* insiders contributed to the damage, with editor Nat Lehrman confessing, "Hefner is 60 and obviously out of touch."[7]

The closing of many Playboy Clubs in the mid-1980s brought a flood of obituaries. Initiated by Christie Hefner as part of her crusade to prune unprofitable PEI projects, the shuttering of Playboy establishments in New York, Los Angeles, Chicago, and several other cities seemed to underline the pastness of the Playboy ethos. The picture of "grown women in bunny suits and grown men in pajamas began to look more and more ridiculous," asserted one newspaper. In the wake of feminism, the clubs appeared as a relic of "post-war American sexism, reflecting an age when beauty and sexuality were measured by bust size; when sexual freedom meant male sexual freedom," wrote the *Cleveland Plain Dealer*. Even Hefner agreed that it was fruitless "to try to keep alive something really properly perceived as a reflection of the swinging 60s," as he told the *Los Angeles Times*. "Society has moved on."[8]

Despite this chorus of criticism, *Playboy* remained at the top of the heap among men's magazines, but PEI's deteriorating economic fortunes reinforced an image of decline. Despite Christie Hefner's strenuous efforts to rid the company of dead weight, it continued to sink lower in the water. The magazine itself, while modestly profitable, saw its circulation drop below four million by the mid-1980s as merchandising, with a wide range of apparel and consumer goods, became the leading moneymaker for the company. Its cable television initiative floundered. The Playboy Channel, which debuted in 1980, lost droves of subscribers as its soft-core, R-rated format managed both to bore zealots of the sexual revolution and outrage

Christian traditionalists, who succeeded in forcing many local stations to drop it. By 1986, the full extent of the damage became clear. In its annual report, PEI revealed that it had lost an astonishing $62 million, much of it a write-off when payment for sale of the Atlantic City casino did not materialize. Financial experts reacted with woeful analyses of Playboy's prospects. "Playboy Enterprises' fabled rabbit is a cornered creature these days," said one. In an internal memo, Christie Hefner tried to buck up the PEI troops by pointing to the company's continued strengths. While the financial figures were distressing, she wrote, "it is our love affair with the consumer that has made Playboy Enterprises what it is, and which will keep the company going."[9]

In the face of this torrent of bad news, Hefner and his editors turned to the magazine. *Playboy* always had been the heart of the enterprise, and revitalizing it now seemed more crucial than ever before. In an atmosphere of malaise in the 1980s, the publisher and his associates began searching for a new formula that would make the publication appealing to a current, less sympathetic audience.

II

Longtime readers of *Playboy* found much that was familiar in the 1980s. The monthly Playmates continued to lead the parade of erotic pictorials, while a new emphasis on celebrities brought revealing features on figures such as Suzanne Somers, Madonna, Vanna White, Mariel Hemingway, Kim Basinger, LaToya Jackson, and Cindy Crawford. One of the most popular featured actress Bo Derek, whose dynamic, unclad appearance in the hit movie *10* made her the most attention grabbing sex symbol of the age. National politics also provided a new avenue for eroticism, with pictorials on Rita Jenrette, wife of Congressman John Jenrette, and "The Women of Washington." Hefner provided a personal touch with a 1987 retrospective on Marilyn Monroe, whom he described as a "celestial enigma with which every incandescent blonde has been (usually unfavorably) compared. Her style was both timeless and matchless, her elegance ineffable."[10]

Playboy continued offering other traditional items. A collection of distinguished short stories earned the National Magazine Award for fiction in 1985, while a growing focus on sports brought insightful profiles of boxer Mike Tyson and golfer Greg Norman and an analysis of the NFL's scouting camp. Nonfiction included Cameron Crowe's "Fast Times at Ridgemont High," while coverage of celebrity entertainers brought the "Playboy Interview: John Lennon and Yoko Ono"—it appeared on the newsstands the night the former Beatle was killed in 1981—and Bob Woodward's examination of "The Short Life and Fast Times of John Belushi."[11]

As always, the magazine sought to stay on the cutting edge of popular culture. *Playboy* ran several pieces on the 1980s mania for health and fitness, such as "The Brawning of America" (1984) and "The Fitness Myth" (1988). It focused on the home electronics revolution, advising readers on the "home computer" invasion, the terminology of (and uses for) personal computers, sophisticated new video games, and the emergence of VCRs. In 1984, the magazine offered bewildered readers a special "Playboy Guide to Electronic Entertainment" that surveyed televisions, computers, and cameras, with a warning that "with the electronic world changing so quickly, you can use all of the friends you can get." Around the same time it presented centerfold Susie Scott, "our first Playmate to be a computer whiz," in a pictorial titled "Love at First Byte."[12]

All the while, *Playboy*'s politics remained staunchly liberal. Throughout the decade, Hefner and his magazine launched continuing attacks on the Reagan administration and the broader conservative resurgence in America. It accused Reagan of striking a clandestine deal with the Ayatollah Khomeini in order to embarrass President Carter and ensure a Republican victory in the 1980 election. It chastised the new president for encouraging white racism by cutting programs for the working poor, opposing extension of the Voting Rights Act, giving tax breaks to segregated private schools, and emasculating the Civil Rights Commission. It berated his "Jelly Bean Presidency," accusing Reagan of willful ignorance, corruption, wild defense spending, and pandering to the bigotry of the Moral Majority. In 1988 it lauded the candidacy of Jesse Jackson while a special report the following year lamented a revival of white racism on campus, which it described as sending African American students fleeing to historically black colleges.[13]

But the power of the traditional *Playboy* formula was fading, as its editors well knew. "We can no longer contrast ourselves to a gray-flannel Eisenhower society," editor Arthur Kretchmer told the *Wall Street Journal* in 1985. "It's now a lot more difficult for us to offer something unique." Henry Marks, a top advertising executive at the magazine for many years, added, "The common view of *Playboy* is that the publication is getting a bit stale." These comments encapsulated the challenge facing Hefner and his magazine: how to overcome the perception that it had become anachronistic in a liberated age and make it relevant to modern American men.[14]

The renewal project faced two big obstacles. First, *Playboy* was forced to navigate between advocates of the sexual revolution who saw Hefner's publication as quaint, and conservatives who loathed it as a symbol of a sex-saturated culture. Observers noted the "Catch-22 situation in which *Playboy* management finds itself—damned if it becomes too risqué, and damned if it doesn't." In an interview with Charlie Rose, Hefner admitted that sexual liberation, ironically, had undermined *Playboy* and "the magazine would be much more popular in a much more repressed society." As *Newsweek* concluded in its cover story, if he was to survive "Hefner must find a home somewhere between the anti-smut activists and the outright pornographers, if indeed such an estate exists."[15]

Second, *Playboy* confronted a profound shift in mainstream American cultural values. Early in the 1980s, it became clear that the emotional self-absorption of the Me Decade had transformed into the material self-interest of the Gimme Decade. In the age of Reagan, the middle class became preoccupied with material affluence and economic security, more attuned to family values, and less attracted to liberal social reform. "People keep saying that money is the sex of the '80s," observed editor Arthur Cooper of *Gentleman's Quarterly*. "I suspect that's true to a degree." In this new atmosphere the notorious leftist orientation of Hefner's magazine became problematic. As George Will commented acidly, "the most dated aspect of *Playboy* is its relentlessly liberal politics, which resembles the young Marx as misread by the old Mailer." *Playboy*'s leadership was not blind to the challenge. "We feel we should be running fewer social-action pieces now," editor Nat Lehrman admitted in 1984. "Those pieces don't go down well with our current consumers."[16]

Thus Hefner and his associates came face-to-face with the conservative realignment in the 1980s that would transform mainstream American society for the next several decades. They tried to reshape *Playboy* to accommodate the new zeitgeist. Kretchmer explained part of the strategy as "moving away from a monotonous and relentless focus on sex and positioning itself as a general interest men's magazine." The magazine also began to cut back its political articles in favor of more service features and lifestyle pieces on fashion, travel, and popular music. A new physical appearance accompanied this refocusing—a switch from staples to a glued, or so-called "perfect binding"—that attempted to distance *Playboy* from other sex magazines and make it more akin to coffee-table publications such as *Vanity Fair* and *Architectural Digest*. Christie Hefner sketched out the new vision for *Playboy*. "Leisure becomes a way of coping with a crazy world," she said, and noted that many Americans now saw an annual vacation and recreational activities as necessities, and put as much energy into leisure as into work. Moreover, since many men were divorced or waiting longer to get married, *Playboy* increasingly wanted to present more practical articles on home decorating and home electronics, cooking, and clothes. As Christie told one interviewer in 1985, readers could expect to see "a very different publication from the one my father founded."[17]

In a fashion, *Playboy* also sought to make peace with Reagan's America by reaching out to a much-discussed new group. Young urban professionals, or "yuppies," who jettisoned political radicalism and emotional angst for vintage wines, Rolex watches, BMW sports cars, designer clothes, and gourmet foods, became a prototype for 1980s consumption. Declaring 1984 "The Year of the Yuppie," *Newsweek* claimed that these youthful, affluent members of the managerial and professional classes had embraced a state of "transcendental acquisition." *Playboy*, if not exactly jumping on the yuppie bandwagon, nimbly took a seat. While occasionally chastising yuppie greed, it nonetheless attempted to reconnect with the young, prosperous, striving entrepreneurs of the 1980s.[18]

Playboy, for instance, reemphasized its connection with American business. Critical of some of its values yet receptive to its possibilities, the magazine began running pieces on how to thrive in a modern commercial milieu. "To survive in the ruthless corporate world of the eighties, you have to know when to be a lion, and when to be a lamb," Michael Korda advised readers in his 1981 article "When Business Becomes a Blood Sport." The magazine presented a long analysis of sixties activists who had evolved to embrace money and materialism in the 1980s. Jerry Rubin, who transformed himself from Yippie radical to Wall Street stockbroker, exemplified the trend. In 1983,

Playboy launched a new finance column by the investment expert Andrew Tobias. The following years saw a string of articles on topics such as dressing for success in corporate America and the emergence of corporate celebrities such as Donald Trump. By late in the decade, *Playboy* was even reassessing the social and political significance of the 1960s, balancing its traditional view of it as an era of idealistic, benevolent impulses with another proclaiming that "the Age of Aquarius was one long, bad trip by a destructive generation."[19]

This rapprochement with 1980s business even influenced some of *Playboy*'s erotic features. "Taking Stock of Marina" showcased blond, beautiful Marina Verola, a stockbroker for E. F. Hutton. "What she does like is money. She likes making it, spending a little of it and, most of all, managing it for clients across the United States and in five foreign countries." Other pictorials focused on Robin Avener, a Madison Avenue advertising executive for Ogilvy & Mather, and Pam McCann, Linda Delgado, and Diane McDonald, a trio of lovely entrepreneurs who "make a lot of decisions, earn a lot of money, wear a lot of diamonds, and turn a lot of heads." In 1989, *Playboy* presented "The Women of Wall Street." A text by Louis Rukeyser, host of PBS's *Wall Street Week,* accompanied the alluring photographs. After a lengthy discussion of women's steady rise in the business world, he noted, "In the end, let us never forget what bright women have always known: money is sexy."[20]

Playboy also modified its creed of sexual liberation with a turn toward traditional emotions and institutions. It began the decade with a sentimental evocation titled "We'll Take Romance." "Romance is the result of style, of timing, of tiny gestures," this primer informed readers. "If you like women, you are romantic." *Playboy* even began singing the praises of marriage. In 1983 it presented "Meet the Mrs.," a pictorial on Mrs. Oklahoma and Mrs. Georgia that described them as "a pair of living testimonials to the wondrous power of marriage." At mid-decade, Hefner chose Kathy Shower, a thirty-three-year-old with two daughters, as the Playmate of the Year, noting that "with a mom like Kathy Shower—actress and Playmate of the Year—Mindy and Melanie already have roots to make them proud." The new kinder, gentler *Playboy* appeared in full bloom in February 1989 with *Love: A Special Playboy Issue.* Arriving just in time for Valentine's Day, this remarkable number featured articles on the dynamics of male feelings, quotations on love from some of history's great thinkers and writers, and various techniques for pleasing, arguing with, and romancing the woman you love.[21]

A new concern with the complexities of male-female relationships colored the 1980s *Playboy*. Readers encountered traditional warnings about feminine wiles, such as 1989's "The Return of Designing Women," which argued that modern women once again were looking for a husband to guarantee family, children, and economic security. But now, significantly, a woman authored it. More often, *Playboy* began exploring the emotional, psychological, and physiological factors influencing interactions between the sexes. In 1982, a seven-part series titled "Man and Woman" examined research "that is working to unravel the essentials of our nature . . . a broad science of man—of men and women—a science that is trying to find the answers to the riddles that lie at the heart of who we are." *Playboy* increasingly sought the female perspective. In 1983 it began a new column titled "Women" by Cynthia Heimel, author of *Sex Tips for Girls*, which she described as "a lighthearted report from the female front in the so-called sexual revolution." "What Women Talk About When They Talk About Men," by Susan Squires, explained how women dissected and judged males. This new relational emphasis influenced the magazine's erotic images. In 1986, for example, *Playboy* ran "Double Take," a pictorial that featured married actors Don Johnson and Melanie Griffith together, nude, kissing and fondling in sexy poses on a Mexican beach.[22]

Christie Hefner took the lead in explaining *Playboy*'s new approach. "Now there's a much greater sense, and you see it in articles as well as in the columns, of talking about relationships," she told the public. "Not just sexual relationships—work relationships, love relationships." A fresh audience of "New Men," as she termed them, had emerged from the confluence of the sexual revolution and the women's revolution and were more attuned to domestic life. The way men and women "work together, live together, love together, keep a home together, raise children together—is about as impressively progressive in the 1980s as anyone could have imagined." She estimated their numbers at about forty million and defined them as *Playboy*'s target audience.[23]

Inevitably, such concerns nudged *Playboy* to explore what it meant to be a man in the 1980s. Asa Baber inaugurated a column called "Men" that analyzed men's approach to fatherhood, or their struggles to control powerful, primitive sexual drives. Articles began to appear such as "The Modern Man's Guide to Life," which argued that the sensitive New Man of the 1960s and 1970s had failed because the picture of a male "sitting down and weeping about his difficulties on the job or shedding tears of joy at the thought of a Saturday-night dinner date is enough to make most women puke." It argued for "an old-fashioned guy, a reasonably thoughtful fellow" who treated women with gentlemanly regard, kept his emotions under control, worked hard and played hard, set priorities in his life, and stayed in reasonable physical shape. *Playboy* also poked fun at such stereotypes in "Real Men Don't Eat Quiche." It facetiously maintained that America had become "a nation of wimps. Pansies. Alan Alda types who cook and clean and 'relate' to their wives. Phil Donahue types who are 'sensitive' and 'vulnerable' and 'understanding' of their children." Society, it claimed, "can be divided into two categories of men: those who eat quiche and those who don't." Real Men venerated the benchmarks of male history: "1162, Genghis Khan develops role of Genghis Khan for Charles Bronson," "1762, First poker game," "1948, Invention of the chain saw."[24]

Playboy even modified its erotic attitude. The magazine began to approach sex as not just the simplistic pursuit of physical pleasure but a matter of complex needs and desires between men and women. In 1981, "The Age of Sexual Détente," with essays by a male and female author, praised the cease-fire in the war between the sexes as both shrill feminism and die-hard chauvinism had faded. Yet *Playboy* criticized the aura of brokering in modern romance, as men and women haggled over needs and boundaries, rules and procedures, seeming "not so much to fall in love or into bed as to *arrive* there, in the sense that you arrive at a solution after a long series of calculations or consultations." It contended that among college students, sex seemed to be happening more frequently but in the context of committed relationships. "It appears that today's campus offers a strange hybrid of the sexual permissiveness of the Sixties and the conservatism of the Eighties." In 1989, *Playboy* summed up the sexual culture of the decade in a four-part series titled "Burning Desires: Sex in America." After surveying modern sexual mores, it concluded that despite the cooling of the sexual revolution Americans had "reinvented pleasure." This involved finding erotic fulfillment not only within committed relationships but in many wondrous, prudent new forms: phone sex, computer sex, female-produced pornography, and "safe sex."[25]

Any analysis of sexual activity in the 1980s, however, was clouded by a deadly new threat. By mid-decade, AIDS had burst on the national scene as it spread rapidly among homosexuals before leaping into the heterosexual population. As deaths mounted, so did fear. In a series of pieces, *Playboy* became perhaps the first American magazine to disseminate accurate information and combat myths while defending the cause of sexual liberation. Early in the crisis, the magazine condemned conservatives who maintained that this disease was a revenge from God or Nature for homosexuality and heterosexual promiscuity. By 1986, the magazine focused on publicizing scientific facts about the virus and urging preventative measures: do not share needles, avoid anal intercourse and prostitutes, use condoms. It also insisted that Hefner's message of "fearlessly examining society's inhibitions and. . . . trying to raise the curtain on sexual enlightenment" was more relevant than ever. By late in the decade, however, *Playboy* had despaired, conceding that the disease had dramatically chilled enthusiasm for sex among young, single, heterosexual men and women throughout the country. AIDS, in many ways, seemed to symbolize the frustrating new milieu facing Hefner's magazine.[26]

The struggle to reposition *Playboy* and recapture cultural relevance in the 1980s proved to be a long and frustrating task. The magazine's founder, when he wearied of struggling with the woes of his enterprise, turned eagerly to the pursuit of romance and sexual adventure. He had always found sanctuary in his private fantasies, but the haven of female companionship provided no refuge from the storm in this dark decade. If anything, Mr. Playboy's romantic life proved even more dismaying.

III

By 1981, Hefner's relationship with Sondra Theodore had run its course. After five years together, she had become increasingly distraught over the publisher's sexual dalliances, while he had grown impatient with her possessiveness and emotional fragility. An intensifying cycle of breakups and reconciliation made it clear that the romance had lost its heart. Hefner's roving eye turned elsewhere.

It soon focused on Shannon Tweed, a tall, gorgeous blonde from Toronto. Twice rejected as a potential Playmate, she had entered *Playboy* through a spot on a Toronto television show that made contestants' dreams come true. It put her in touch with the organization, and she went on to become Miss November 1981, and then Playmate of the Year. She also became Hefner's new girlfriend. They had met at the mansion during her shoot and became romantically involved at the Midsummer's Night Dream Party in August 1981. Soon they were steady companions.[27]

Tweed had been born in 1957 to a large family of mink ranchers in Newfoundland. After moving to Saskatchewan following a catastrophic car wreck that left her father incapacitated, she dropped out of high school and worked in a variety of coffee shops, restaurants, hotels, department stores, and nightclubs in Ottawa. She won the Miss Ottawa beauty pageant in 1978, competed for Miss Canada, and launched a successful modeling career in Toronto. Eventually, she determined to go to Los Angeles to pursue a career in movies and television, and saw *Playboy* as her ticket.[28]

Tweed made no secret of her professional ambitions. "I think I can make it in the world of entertainment and I'm going to give it my best shot," she told her hometown newspaper after becoming a Playmate. She spoke frankly about using *Playboy* to advance her prospects, and a relationship with Hefner fit comfortably within this larger plan. At their first Christmas together, the independent young woman gave him a romantic card that said, "I belong to you, too, darling," but carefully crossed out the printed word "belong" and hand-wrote in its place, "well, almost." "Going with Hef is a career move," she informed an interviewer. The publisher suffered no illusions, telling *People,* "I find the way she dropped the net over me enchanting." As a Hefner friend described, when Tweed arrived at the mansion "loving the party life and wearing the 'Absolutely NO DOMESTICITY Allowed in My Presence' T-shirt stretched over her perfectly shaped breasts, it was too much for Hef to resist."[29]

Then Hefner and Tweed fell in love. The publisher felt a genuine spark of affection and within a few months was describing her publicly as "the love of my life." He showered her with so many expensive gifts that a friend, after seeing his lavish Christmas list, memorized it and entertained mansion friends with a singing rendition set to "A Partridge in a Pear Tree." Astonishingly, Hefner even uttered the dreaded "M word," telling an old Chicago friend that his Canadian girlfriend was "the first woman I have seriously considered marrying."[30]

Tweed's unabashed careerism seemed to melt in the face of a growing affection for her older suitor. "I can't rely on myself for everything. I need a love in my life," she began to say. The couple tried to maintain a monogamous relationship, and Tweed talked publicly of marriage. But she realized the obstacle facing her. "Marriage is not natural for Hef. It's natural for me to think in those terms since it's the first time I've known it's right," she told *People*. "But it's going to take him longer since he's been through it before." In an interview with the London *Mirror,* she revealed Hefner's promise that "if we were in love in five years' time and I wanted to have a child, he would marry me."[31]

But soon the genuine love in the relationship began to dissolve as complications set in. Tweed's rapidly advancing career provided the initial difficulty. She became host for the new Playboy Channel's magazine show *Playboy on the Scene,* and the first Video Playmate. A regular role on the hit CBS evening soap opera *Falcon Crest* followed, along with two movie parts. Her hectic work schedule demanded frequent absences, and Hefner bridled. When he complained, Tweed replied, "I want to work, I *have* to work. I can't just sit around being the hostess of the Playboy Mansion. It's not enough for me." During one of the big mansion parties, *Falcon Crest* required her to be on location, and after much sparring over her schedule Hefner finally hired a private plane to fly her directly to the location so she could attend the party. "It was the beginning of the end for Hef and me," she commented later. "What he didn't realize was that our schedules would clash more than once."[32]

Tweed's gradual disenchantment with her role as mistress of the Playboy Mansion widened the split. As the novelty wore off, she felt restless, unproductive, and restricted in ways that gnawed at her vaunted independence. The daily round of game playing bored her silly and she grumbled that Hefner's compulsion had made her a "Pacman widow." He grew disturbed by two by-products of her boisterous lifestyle: drugs and infidelities. Hefner claimed that "I couldn't get her to stop using cocaine," and her sexual peccadilloes infuriated him. He discovered that she was having an affair with a movie costar in early 1983, for instance, and confronted her on the morning of a mansion luncheon for television critics. The couple spent an anguished day hiding their feelings behind fake smiles as they escorted the visitors around the mansion grounds and gave interviews.[33]

The relationship crumbled in spring 1983. Invited by Berry Gordy to attend Motown's Twenty-fifth Anniversary Show at the end of March, the couple spent much of the evening bickering and left early. A few weeks later, Tweed gave Hefner a cartoon showing a man and a woman in a boxing ring punching with heart-shaped gloves. "It is an all-too-accurate portrayal of the frequently rocky romance," Hefner commented. With both participants increasingly dissatisfied, they decided to split up and parted on an amicable note.[34]

Hefner, typically, did not tarry. Within two weeks he had become involved with another Canadian, this one a sultry brunette who had come to the mansion for a Playmate test shoot. Carrie Lee Carmichael – soon shortened to Carrie Leigh for professional purposes—had set her sights on the publisher, according to Marilyn Grabowski, *Playboy's* photo editor. On her Playmate Data Sheet, she identified him as the man she most admired because he "started with nothing and built an empire on what he believed." When Hefner first saw the nineteen-year-old beauty, it was "one of those things when you look across the room and something happens," he told *Rolling Stone*. "We fell for each other." Leigh, who had been modeling since age fourteen, spent the night with Hefner several days later, and within a short time she moved in and became the mistress of the mansion.[35]

Leigh quickly established herself in Hefner's world. Young, audacious, and funny, she appeared as a breath of fresh air. She became friends with a number of Playmates from this period and hosted slumber parties full of youthful female hijinks and girl talk. Leigh also became a regular player—and only female—in Hefner's weekly card games, and the others gave her a framed poster of the queen of spades with a caption: "Carrie Is My Name—Gin Rummy Is My Game." Taking quickly to the good life, she followed a routine of sleeping until noon followed by bubble baths, facials, walks around the grounds, and workouts in the exercise room. She served as hostess for weekly parties and film watching, drawing attention with a parade of gaudy, highly revealing outfits that soon began to fill her closets, courtesy of a generous weekly allowance from Hefner. According to the photographer Alison Reynolds, Leigh used outlandish clothes to shock people because "she was more or less an exhibitionist, and

I think that's what made her a good model." She also bluntly spoke her mind. "I'm really honest and straightforward about a lot of things, which sometimes gets me into trouble," she told a reporter. But the couple shared a mutual infatuation. In a 1984 interview with the *Los Angeles Times,* she gushed, "Hef is one of the sweetest, most considerate men in the world!" The publisher smiled and kissed her, adding, "There's nothing sweeter in life than being in love."[36]

More disturbing qualities soon appeared. Leigh's attention-seeking became more extreme and provocative, as she made a show of walking about the mansion grounds with a snake wrapped around her neck. On one notable occasion she broke up a meeting of Playboy executives on the back patio by parading through the yard naked except for a pair of high heels and a gold chain around her waist. She also established a reputation as a party animal whose pleasure-seeking, according to Hefner and many mansion regulars, produced legendary bouts of drinking and recreational drug use. "She out-caroused the champion carouser of all time: Hef," reported Anne Stewart. She also managed to raise eyebrows at the mansion—no mean feat—with a voracious sexual appetite. Stories of her dalliances with men and women alike soon began making the rounds among the mansion circle and Leigh seemed to delight in her reputation, telling *Playboy,* "I think sometimes I like it even more than he does. I like waking him in the middle of the night. 'Hef!' In the morning: 'Hef!' Sometimes, I even try to get him out of his meetings." Leigh's emotional volatility became conspicuous. "There were early signs of instability. She got drunk one night and ran down the hall naked, threatening to throw herself off the balcony," reported Lisa Loving. Marilyn Grabowski noted that Leigh would "act crazy and create a scene just to get Hef's attention." Hefner described a 1985 incident in which his girlfriend left for Toronto for "three delirious weeks of drinking, drugs, and sexual excess." In his words, she phoned "from the bathroom of her Toronto hotel suite because her partners from the night before were still asleep in the bedroom. . . . She wanted to come home."[37]

Leigh desperately sought celebrity. "Basically, I'm insecure and need attention. I want to be a superstar," she confessed to a Los Angeles newspaper. When Jessica Hahn moved into the mansion for several months after toppling Jim Bakker in the PTL Club sex scandal, Leigh declared, "I wish I had the same [publicity] happen to me." She pleaded with Hefner to put her in *Playboy* and he finally arranged a

1986 cover story titled "The First Lady of the Playboy Mansion." She then sought to parlay the publicity into an acting career with a bit of instruction and an impatient wait to be discovered. According to the film director Richard Brooks, however, Leigh's "delusions . . . came to nothing. She did plenty of over-acting around the mansion, but that was about it." Her search for fame also produced much cosmetic surgery. She underwent numerous procedures—several nose operations, cheek implants, breast enhancement, facial peel, lip enhancement—in a quest for physical perfection. This produced a brittle beauty that—in combination with her temperamental personality—earned her a special moniker among regulars and staff at the mansion: Scary Leigh.[38]

Hefner and Leigh's relationship became an emotional yo-yo with wild swings between passion and contention, romantic fulfillment and emotional drain. Her outlandish behavior produced frequent quarrels, usually followed by overwrought apologies such as this one: "I am very sorry for being unkind tonight. You don't deserve that kind of treatment. You have made me happier than I ever thought possible and behaving the way I did is no way to show my gratitude. I love you and I promise that things are just going to get nicer between us. Love forever, Carrie." Hefner believed that alcohol roused darker impulses. In the summer of 1985, after a heavy bout of drinking, she wrote him a disjointed note that hinted of suicide. "Thank you, Hef. I would die for you . . . love is the key to my life and if I can't fulfill that desire and goal then I have nothing to live for," she wrote. "Love is the most important thing in life. If I can't have that then I have no reason for existence and neither do you." In September 1986, Leigh created a public stir when she insisted on wearing—over Hefner's objections—an extremely revealing dress to a fund-raiser for Democratic candidates held at Barbra Streisand's home. Said one published account, it was "as tight as the casing on a Dodger hot dog. The front of this creation consists of two pieces of cloth crisscrossed over her breasts; she looks like a railroad crossing guard in a Russ Meyer movie." According to Hefner, Leigh fled the event after the couple squabbled, lost a very expensive diamond ring he had given her as a gift, and ended up in bed at a friend's apartment.[39]

Leigh's emotional frailty produced endless entreaties, or demands, for reassurances from her boyfriend. Several times a day, she would ask Hefner, "Do you love me? Am I beautiful?" In her *Playboy* cover story, she admitted to "insecurities and changes in mood. Hef is the first man I've ever known who can handle me no matter what mood I'm in." For the publisher, this meant a stream of verbal and financial avowals, sweet talk and credit cards, pet names and furs, endearments and jewels. Hefner gave Leigh daily gifts, which he called "Dr. Bunny" presents, and she would accept or reject them as she wished. Executive assistant Mary O'Connor recorded some of these episodes in her diary. "Hef walked up while Carrie was saying the diamonds on her necklace were lonesome. . . . Hef came down, Carrie depressed—Dr. Bunny took presents, Carrie didn't like them, but she may consider keeping the pants and sweater. . . . Hef took diamonds for Carrie to see. She preferred the baguette. Hef finally selected a stone from Marvin Hime—$18,000." In addition, Hefner gave Leigh a $5,000 a month clothing allowance, several fur coats, a five-carat diamond friendship ring, and a yearly birthday gift that matched her age in thousands of dollars—$22,000 on her twenty-second birthday and so on for the next several years.[40]

The relationship took on a peculiar sexual dynamic. Hefner, increasingly weary of a group-sex scene he now described as "point-less and pathetic" and interested in settling down, became genuinely monogamous. As Leigh told *Newsweek* in 1986, "He doesn't fool around now—I'd kill him. I don't know how the hell he pulled it off with his other girlfriends." Leigh, however, according to many wit-nesses, pursued sex in a variety of venues. Several Playmates reported that she made advances to them—"I know she was into girls a little bit," said one—while Marilyn Grabowski recounted how she would send her love notes and call in the middle of the night. Hefner gained knowledge of several sexual affairs Leigh had with men. In fact, when Leigh got pregnant and had an abortion, the publisher doubted that the child was his. "I'm a responsible and careful guy," he explained. "It's one of the reasons I've never had any paternity suits."[41]

Hefner's friends grew increasingly appalled at Leigh's behavior and his toleration of it. "It was painful to watch. . . . Here he was letting himself be humiliated, even letting her rub his face in affairs with other people," said John Dante. Cis Rundle described the situ-ation as "toxic" while Dick Stewart denounced her as "a nut case." Richard Brooks saw Leigh as a "cuckoo girl" who "mixed a posture of humility with steel claws." Some even confronted Hefner. Both of his children told him they disapproved of Leigh, and Keith Hefner pleaded with his brother to get rid of the young woman, whom he described as "a terrible person who was making faces and jokes about him behind his back and embarrassing him in public." Lisa Loving, an outspoken Hefner assistant, told him frankly that everyone at the mansion was "embarrassed by your association with her. . . . You are degrading yourself beyond belief." Many concluded that the young Canadian was taking her wealthy, older boyfriend for a financial ride. According to Anne Stewart, she once asked Leigh if she was taking acting lessons and the young woman replied that she didn't need them. When Stewart inquired why not, Leigh responded, "If I can make Hef believe I love him, I'm the greatest actress in the world." Leigh seemed unconcerned about her gold-digger image, telling a *Newsweek* reporter who admired her diamond "friendship ring" from Hefner, "if we got engaged it would have to be 10 more carats."[42]

But Hefner insisted on viewing Leigh in gauzy soft focus as a leading lady—part femme fatale and part ingénue—in the movie of his life. He found her sexually exciting, unconventional, and even fun. In interviews, he described their relationship as "especially fulfilling," characterized the period as "one of the best times of my life," and opined that "life is deadly dull when a relationship becomes routine and boring. Carrie Leigh was never boring." When his friends put her down, he angrily rushed to her defense. "How can they say this dynamite-looking woman with this incredible taste in clothes and a flair for fashion, willing to take steps beyond the boundaries, how can they say that she's a source of embarrassment? She is an incredible addition," he countered.[43]

Yet Hefner understood all too well Leigh's flighty mental state. She drove him to distraction with her antics, but her emotional vulnerability powerfully aroused his sympathy. Among confidants, he spoke of her as his "crippled bird" and mused that he could somehow nurture this lost soul to a state of stability and self-worth. The pathos in Leigh's insatiable hunger for affection and praise caused him to see her as emotionally destitute rather than manipulative. Hefner's empathy even led him to understand her sexual indiscretions. "I've never known anybody like her, who used seduction with both guys and girls as a way of reaffirming that she is desirable or worthy," he said years later. Mary O'Connor, who knew her boss well, suspected another factor at work. She saw the ghost of Bobbie Arnstein hovering in the background, causing Hefner to purge some guilt by doing "those things that I think he feels he should have done more of with Bobbie."[44]

Indeed, Leigh ultimately cut a poignant, rather than a malicious, figure as she cavorted about the mansion craving attention. Scarcely educated, emotionally immature, and thrown into a demanding social whirl, this young woman simply was ill-equipped for her role in Hefner's life. She reached for the tools at hand—exhibitionism and shock tactics—to try and gain security in a pressurized environment. As Chuck McCann, an old Hefner friend, put it, Leigh "really didn't have a fix on life yet. She didn't know what she wanted. . . . With someone like Carrie, coming into a person's life like Hef—it's too much, too soon." Playmate Julie McCullough, a friend of Leigh's, attributed her theatrics to confusion about life goals and a sense of place: "She was like a princess in a big house with not a lot to do."[45]

But by the fall of 1987 Leigh's outrageous behavior had worn down even Hefner. "She just got more and more hysterical, making scenes and throwing tantrums, smashing things, running nude around the house—anything to get a rise out of him," reportevd John Dante. In late September a final straw came when an agitated Leigh, in front of a group of guests, threw an expensive Gallo statue off the balcony of the mansion's great hall, smashing it to bits on the marble floor below. She then fled the premises and disappeared with a female friend for five days. Several weeks later, Leigh procured a key to the safe in Hefner's room and took a sex tape of him and several women that had been made in the 1970s. Telling close friend Jessica Hahn, "I'm going to expose him," she hid the tape in Hahn's mansion bedroom. But Hahn, grateful to Hefner for taking her in after the PTL scandal, returned the tape to him and explained what his girlfriend was planning. Leigh, it turned out, already had met with palimony attorney Marvin Mitchelson and the purloined tape seems to have been part of a ruse to force Hefner into a large monetary settlement. A fuming Hefner noted that after this "attempted shake-down . . . Carrie feels betrayed by Jessica and Hef feels betrayed by Carrie. Merry Christmas, everyone!"[46]

The unbearable tension finally snapped in January 1988 when Leigh left with two girlfriends for a trip to New York City. She phoned to say that she would not be returning to the mansion. Hefner was both hurt and relieved. A short time later, Leigh and Mitchelson held a press conference announcing the filing of a palimony suit against

Hefner in the amount of $35 million. After the publisher denounced it as a "publicity stunt" and filed a countersuit, Leigh reacted with typical unpredictability—she suddenly dropped her legal action to marry an antiques dealer she had met in New York. A chagrined Hefner noted that Leigh had loved the 1987 movie *Black Widow*, a thriller about a woman who married several wealthy men and then murdered them for their money. "It didn't occur to me that Carrie might be viewing it as a training film," he said ruefully.[47]

So the publisher's personal life, much like the financial state of his company, fell on hard times in the 1980s. Buffeted by *Playboy*'s growing public problems, a "damaged" Hefner, as he described himself, yearned for genuine amour. Instead, he fell into a tumultuous psychodrama with Carrie Leigh. "I was trying to settle down; I just picked the wrong girl," he said later. But his problems were only beginning. The atmosphere grew even darker as a gathering political storm blew Hefner back into the public limelight and threatened to destroy him.[48]

18

Strange Bedfellows

n the mid-1980s, a political assault gathered force and challenged everything that Hugh Hefner and *Playboy* stood for. An alliance of strange ideological bedfellows, it aimed to exterminate the publisher, his magazine, and his values. In the front ranks stood newly empowered conservatives of the Reagan administration, but close behind them pressed supporting squadrons of radical feminists. On most issues these two groups clashed, but they overlooked differences to mount a common crusade against what they saw as the corrupting influence of degrading erotic images, promiscuous sexuality, and the exploitation of women. Figures as diverse as the Reverend Jerry Falwell and the lesbian activist Andrea Dworkin joined forces and tried to put Hefner out of business. In a bizarre final chapter of this political saga, Peter Bogdanovich, Dorothy Stratten's distraught boyfriend, emerged from mourning to join the assault.

As this political attack built up steam, Hefner mounted a desperate defense. Throwing himself into the fight, he became obsessed with defending his reputation, his life's work, and his principles. The stress took a severe personal toll on the publisher, and in an ultimate symbol of the dark period of the 1980s, his health finally broke down.

I

On May 20, 1985, Attorney General Edwin Meese announced the formation of a special federal panel to study pornography. While a 1970 presidential commission had concluded that there was no link between sexual material and sexual crime or delinquency, Meese insisted that a new study was needed. Pornography had become more pervasive and more violent, he charged. "We no longer must go out of the way to find pornographic materials. With the advent of cable television and video recorders, pornography now is available at home to almost anyone, regardless of age, at the mere touch of a button."[1]

The eleven-person Meese Commission, as it quickly became known, included three liberals: Judith Becker of Columbia University, Park Dietz of the University of Virginia, and Ellen Levine of *Women's Day*. But conservatives dominated the panel. They included several Republican politicos and several antipornography advocates, such as James C. Dobson, religious traditionalist and popular radio-show host of *Focus on the Family,* the Reverend Bruce Ritter, director of a home for runaways who blamed the pornography industry for their plight, and a law professor from the University of Michigan, Frederick Schauer, who had argued that visual pornography was not speech and therefore not subject to First Amendment protection. The chairman was Henry E. Hudson, prosecuting attorney for Arlington County, Virginia, who had successfully banished most pornography from this suburban Washington, D.C., area. The panel was enjoined to determine the nature of pornography's impact on American life, and to make recommendations to the Justice Department about containing its spread.[2]

The political clout of the Reagan administration clearly lay behind this initiative. Religious conservatives and the Moral Majority comprised a powerful part of the new Republican majority, and the president sympathized with their horrified view of a sex-saturated moral decline in America. He had made several speeches denouncing pornography as "a form of pollution" and pledged to clean up these "hazardous-waste sites." Addressing the National Association of Evangelicals in March 1984, Reagan argued that in the 1960s and 1970s America seemed "to lose her religious and moral bearings, to forget that faith and values are what made us good and great." This decline was reflected not only in rampant drug use, legalized abortion, and the banning of prayer from schools, but also in pornography and promiscuity. Sexual images had become available everywhere, he contended. "Liberal attitudes viewed promiscuity as acceptable, even stylish. Indeed, the word itself was replaced by a new term, 'sexually active.'" But now, Reagan concluded, the American people had decided to "put a stop to that long decline" and seek moral renewal. Soon after, the president announced specific plans: the convening of a special commission because "we consider pornography to be a public problem."[3]

Background skirmishing between Hefner and religious fundamentalists had preceded this declaration of war. In 1982, the Reverend Donald Wildmon announced that his National Federation for Decency would bestow a "Pornographer of the Month" award to corporations that advertised in *Playboy* and publish their CEO's name and company phone number. Wildmon also orchestrated demonstrations against including the Playboy Channel on local cable channels and selling the magazine in neighborhood stores. Jerry Falwell also spoke out, calling for Hefner's religious conversion. "Wouldn't it be wonderful," he said, "if Hugh Hefner got saved and shut down Playboy Enterprises and became a spokesman for Jesus Christ? He could be another Saul."[4]

Then in 1984 the Justice Department's Office of Juvenile Justice and Delinquency Prevention funded a controversial study that sought to link *Playboy* and the sexual abuse of children. It awarded a grant for $743,000 to Judith Reisman for a content analysis of cartoons in men's magazines with regard to the sexual portrayal of children. This former producer and writer for the *Captain Kangaroo* show had made a stir when she termed Hefner and other publishers of male magazines as "sexual fascists . . . who are every bit as dangerous as Hitler." In 1983, she charged that the sex investigator Alfred J. Kinsey had engaged in "vicious genital torture" of children and had sex with over eight hundred minors during the course of his research. Now she analyzed hundreds of images in *Playboy, Penthouse,* and *Hustler,* and concluded that they portrayed children sexually to varying degrees, implying a connection to child abuse. The charges were absurdly false regarding *Playboy,* which never depicted children in sexual situations, and experts almost unanimously dismissed Reisman's study as having little social science value. But her effort illustrated the larger ideological conflict that was brewing.[5]

In reply, *Playboy* taunted its fundamentalist oppressors during the early 1980s. In 1982's "Holy Terror," the authors described a new form of terrorism: "America's fundamentalist right, a hybrid of religious and political absolutism led by a small group of preachers and political strategists, has begun to use religion and all that Americans hold sacred to seize power across a broad spectrum of our lives." A *Playboy* editorial skewered the Reagan administration's "porn paranoia" with the Reisman grant, noting her lackluster credentials, and exposing the close ties between Office of Juvenile Justice appointees and Jerry Falwell, anti-ERA activist Phyllis Schlafly, and the Reverend Pat Robertson. *Playboy* also helped form People for the American Way, an advocacy group soon running anticensorship ads in newspapers and magazines around the country.[6]

But the forces of fundamentalism in the Reagan administration gained an unlikely ally from the other end of the political spectrum. By the early 1980s, radical feminists had launched their own assault on pornography, claiming that sexually explicit material denigrated women and led to acts of sexual violence. In the words of the feminist writer Robin Morgan, "Pornography is the theory and rape is the practice." Susan Brownmiller, author of *Against Our Will,* spoke similarly. "Pornography is propaganda against women, and propaganda is a very powerful spur to action—think of the anti-Semitic propaganda in Hitler's Germany," she declared in *Harper's.* Fired by such convictions, antiporn feminists protested the sale of sexual material in cities throughout the United States and formed pressure groups such as Women Against Pornography and Women Against Violence in Pornography and Media. By 1984, they were prepared to join cultural conservatives in a war on smut, including Hefner and *Playboy.*[7]

The feminist antiporn crusade found a focal point in the endeavors of Catharine MacKinnon and Andrea Dworkin. The former, an urbane law professor from the University of Michigan and the University of Chicago, and the latter, a lesbian activist and radical writer habitually dressed in overalls and work shirts, formed a partnership urging legal action to restrict pornography. They took a new constitutional tack in doing so, defining pornography as a violation of the civil rights of women. In the same way that racist speech was linked to racism, they argued, pornography was linked to sex discrimination against women.

"Pornography creates attitudes that keep women second-class citizens," Dworkin contended. MacKinnon defined pornography as "an actual practice of subordinating women. It's a technologically sophisticated form of trafficking in women." These activists served as consultants for the city councils of Minneapolis and Indianapolis, drafting ordinances that allowed women who were injured through pornography to sue for damages. They were found to be unconstitutional, and neither ordinance went into effect, but a larger target still remained: the godfather of the sexual revolution in America. As Dworkin declared, "*Playboy*, both in text and pictures, promotes rape. Its cartoons promote both rape and sexual abuse."[8]

Hefner and *Playboy* confronted their feminist foes. Two 1980 articles, "Women at War" and "Women Against Sex," portrayed antiporn feminists as angry fanatics who sought to abolish First Amendment rights and censor anyone who disagreed with their assessment of sexual material's impact on women. They noted Marcia Womongold, a Boston militant who fired a rifle bullet through the window of a Harvard bookstore because it sold copies of *Playboy*, *Oui*, and *Penthouse*. They pointed out that antiporn feminists denounced sexual images in newspaper ads, fashion magazines such as *Vogue*, and movies and television. They accused Women Against Pornography of collapsing all distinctions between sadistic images of physical harm to women and fashion photos or Playmate pictorials. In 1981, Christie Hefner reviewed one of the key texts of antiporn feminism, *Take Back the Night: Women on Pornography*, edited by Laura Lederer, and dismissed it for failing "to recognize the subtleties and complexities of sexuality, pornography, and violence, coupled with its underlying theme that men have a propensity to rape and beat women." James Petersen critiqued these crusaders as "Big Sister" agents of thought control right out of Orwell's police state with their own brand of newspeak: "Sex is Rape. Desire is Degradation. The Personal is Political. The Public is Private. Pleasure is Oppression. Porn is Thought Crime."[9]

A special controversy erupted in 1980 with the publication of *Ordeal: An Autobiography*, by Linda Lovelace, the star of *Deep Throat*, the hit porn movie from the 1970s. She now claimed that she had been violently intimidated by her husband/manager, Chuck Traynor, and claimed that Hefner had exploited her during a several-day visit to the mansion. Lovelace maintained that Traynor and Hefner had organized an "orgy night" of group sex with Bunnies, Playmates, and hookers, and that Traynor had pushed her into a public sexual act with a young woman before forcing her to have sex with Hefner. Most luridly, she contended that Traynor set up a private scene for Hefner to observe her having sex with a dog, although she claimed to have feigned the act.[10]

Hefner was caught up in the furor of headlines and reviews. He heatedly denied the charges as pure fiction, contending that his relationship with Lovelace "was based on friendship, not sex" and that he had no knowledge of any intimidation. He characterized her claims as a sensational publicity stunt to boost sales. "The suggestion that she did not enjoy her life at this period is preposterous. She carried on in the same manner after she left Traynor. I saw no change in personality, dress, what have you," he contended. But antiporn feminists embraced Lovelace. In her introduction to a second book by the actress titled *Out of Bondage,* Gloria Steinem pictured her as a victim of smut and lashed out at "Hugh Hefner and his Playboy Mansion," contending that the key issue with pornography was "free will." In her words, "pornography is to women of all groups what Nazi literature is to Jews and Ku Klux Klan literature is to Blacks."[11]

Against this backdrop, the Meese Commission emerged as a fundamentalist-feminist partnership determined to create legal restrictions against the distribution, sale, and consumption of pornographic materials. "In an unusual alliance, feminists have joined conservative intellectuals to make a case for a ban," wrote the *New York Times.* *Newsweek* agreed that "radical feminists . . . joined by right-wing fundamentalists" comprised the new "shock troops" assaulting the pornography industry. Dworkin had no qualms about her new allies. "When women get raped they're not asked first if they're Democrats or Republicans," she declared. The liberal toleration of pornography demonstrated "clearly how the left has betrayed women—they are entirely corrupt."[12]

This political alliance of strange bedfellows made *Playboy,* the most prominent symbol of sexual liberation and imagery in postwar America, a leading target. Over the previous thirty years, Hefner had suffered periodic attacks from foes outraged by his advocacy of recreational sex and unconventional morality. But never before had the opposition found such powerful political expression. Clearly, he was in trouble.

II

The Meese Commission, armed with a budget of only $500,000 and facing a twelve-month deadline, quickly convened a series of hearings around the country. In the fall of 1985 and early 1986 they heard some three hundred hours of testimony from over two hundred witnesses, close to 80 percent of whom were critics of pornography. They convened publicly in six cities to focus on preordained topics: Washington (general), Chicago (law enforcement), Houston (social science), Los Angeles (production and distribution), Miami (child pornography), and New York (organized crime). The panel heard graphic testimony from a variety of interested parties concerning pornography: vice cops and victims, prosecutors and producers, born-again Christians and feminist activists, the National Federation for Decency and the FBI, sober researchers and thundering preachers. The panelists watched dozens of movies and videos, saw countless slide shows put together by witnesses, perused innumerable magazines, and heard taped dial-a-porn encounters. They took field trips to sex shops ("Mr. Peepers" in Houston) and sex districts (Times Square in New York), surveyed the most extreme kinds of sexual behavior and fetishes, and discovered during a session on the world of "rubber goods" (dildos and dolls) that the Houston vice squad had confiscated and was storing some twenty-seven thousand items. At times the commission, according to *Time,* seemed to be on a "surrealist mystery tour of sexual perversity, peeping at the most recondite forms of sexual behavior known—though mostly unknown—to society."[13]

Playboy emerged as a key target. In Chicago, company attorney Burt Joseph reminded the commission that the magazine had never "at any time, in any jurisdiction been found to be obscene in a court of law." But the commission quickly erased any positive impressions. In Miami, a middle-aged man carrying a Bible testified that first seeing an issue of *Playboy* at age twelve had sent him down the path to sexual perversion and drug abuse. In Los Angeles, Miki Garcia, a former Playmate, caused a sensation when she denounced Hefner, his organization, and his lifestyle. Miss January 1973, and later director of Playmate Promotions, she accused the *Playboy* publisher of encouraging Playmates to use illegal drugs, coercing them into orgies, and exploiting women for sexual pleasure, all of which were covered up because of Hefner's influence with the Los Angeles

Police Department. She claimed that some Playmates became part of a call-girl ring while others became victims of rape, serial abortions, venereal disease, and unwanted cosmetic surgery. "I want the public to recognize that *Playboy* magazine is not the coffee table literature that Hugh Hefner says it is, but rather a pornographic magazine," she declared. Garcia added the dramatic claim that her testimony would "put my life and those of my family's in danger." Newspapers leaped on her lurid accusations, writing that "rape, attempted suicide, and violent crime were part of the Playboy lifestyle."[14]

Playboy angrily denied all of Garcia's charges. Spokesmen pointed out that she had never made a single complaint about improper or illegal activity during her employment. Instead, she had written in a memo, "It may sound corny, but *Playboy* has been a wonderful influence on my life. I respect and admire Mr. Hefner and what he stands for." They noted that Garcia had been trying, unsuccessfully, to peddle a book manuscript about her *Playboy* days and accused her of using the commission testimony to prompt interest in the stalled project.[15]

Brenda MacKillop, a born-again Bunny who had worked at the Los Angeles Playboy Club from 1973 to 1976 and frequented the Playboy Mansion, also testified. Now a Christian, pastor's wife, and anti-porn activist, she related that her Playboy lifestyle had brought on depression and near-suicide. "I implore the Attorney General's commission to see the connection between sexual promiscuity, venereal disease, abortion, divorce, homosexuality, sexual abuse of children, suicide, drug abuse, rape, and prostitution to pornography," MacKillop stated. She also appeared at antipornography protests around the country, characterizing *Playboy* as "filth," and even sent a letter and a Bible to Hefner. "What is one to say to someone who has publicly vilified me in such a totally distorted and bizarre fashion in front of the Meese Commission, on television, and in various published interviews?" he replied sharply. "I have never treated you with anything but kindness. . . . You claim to be a good Christian, but the form of Christianity that you practice seems to be the equivalent of placing a burning cross on someone's front lawn."[16]

Early in 1986, the Meese Commission directly attacked Hefner's operation. Its executive director, Alan E. Sears, a fervent anti-obscenity prosecutor from the U.S. Attorney's office in western Kentucky, sent letters to twenty-three retailers saying that they had been accused of involvement in the sale or distribution of pornography. The commission asked for a response to the allegation by March 3, and stated that "failure to respond will necessarily be accepted as an indication of no objection." The list of companies, provided by the Reverend Wildmon, included Coca-Cola (it owned Columbia Pictures), Time, Inc. (it presented R-rated movies on HBO and Cinemax), and *Vogue* (for running Calvin Klein's "Obsession" fragrance ads). This ominous missive clearly threatened a flood of adverse publicity from the government if the companies did not cease selling materials that Wildmon considered pornographic. Within weeks, the pressure tactic bore fruit.[17]

The parent company of the 7-Eleven convenience store chain, the Southland Corporation, announced in April that its seventy-five hundred outlets and franchises would stop selling *Playboy, Penthouse,* and *Forum.* Other retailers quickly followed suit. By summer the magazines had been dropped by Revco Drug Stores, People's Drug Stores, Rite Aid Drug Stores, the Dart Drug Corporation, Stop-N-Go, and Lawson's Milk Company, while J. C. Penney decided to stop selling Playboy/Playmate merchandise. The president of Southland explained that the company had grown disturbed by commission testimony indicating "a growing public awareness and concern over a possible connection between adult magazines and crime, violence, and child abuse."[18]

Playboy responded angrily to the commission's prompting of the 7-Eleven ban. Christie Hefner condemned the action as "a response to the hysteria of the moment" while Robert Scheer, in a blistering analysis in *Playboy* titled "Inside the Meese Commission," described the panel as "an evangelical soap opera." PEI also took legal action, joining with the American Booksellers Association and the Magazine Publishers Association to file suit, claiming that the Meese Commission was creating a "blacklist" that was causing companies to pull from its shelves publications that had not been ruled obscene. On July 3, a federal district court judge agreed. He ruled that the Sears letter contained "an implied threat" that violated the First Amendment by creating "a prior restraint of speech, a right so precious in this nation." He ordered the Meese Commission to notify the retailers and retract the threat and forbade it from including Wildmon's list of supposed corporate transgressors in its final report. After this victory, *Playboy* turned the knife. A few months later, it ran a pictorial on "The Women of 7-Eleven," gleefully noting of the Southland ban, "Did we get mad? Did we get even? No. We got *down*." It quoted its alluring subjects decrying how "The religious groups seem to be taking over" and complaining that "we don't have magazines with beautiful women. But we do have magazines on guns and war and violence."[19]

Playboy quickly gained allies. The National Coalition Against Censorship, which listed such notable figures as Kurt Vonnegut, Betty Friedan, and Colleen Dewhurst, characterized the commission as an attempt to restrict the free expression of ideas. The novelists John Updike and John Irving wrote letters decrying the threat to First Amendment rights. Liberal publications such as the *Nation* denounced the commission as a product of cynical Reaganites manipulating misguided feminists while an ACLU spokesman observed, "I'm afraid there is a train marked 'censorship' which has just left the station." Women's rights groups such as the Feminist Anti-Censorship Task Force (FACT) took issue with the antipornography campaign, arguing that restrictions on free expression always rebounded to harm oppressed or less powerful groups. Some conservative newspapers expressed reservations on libertarian grounds. The *Chicago Tribune* observed that opposition to "the unchecked use of government power used to be one of the main tenets of the conservative faith." The *Orange County Register* described the commission as "bluenosed bullies" promoting "a betrayal of the principle of strictly limited government on which our nation was founded."[20]

This conflict galvanized Hefner into action. As had not been the case since the 1950s, he assumed the stance of an outsider battling the hoary forces of moral authority and sexual restriction. "Suddenly *Playboy* is hopping again," the *Chicago Tribune* noted. "The magazine is once again thrust to the ramparts, battling the forces of ignorance and repression." With a renewed sense of relevance, Hefner reemerged as a happy warrior.[21]

The *Playboy* publisher excoriated religious conservatives who sought to turn back the clock on the sexual revolution. Since the 1950s, he insisted, intelligent people had come to see sexuality as a vital part of the human experience. "When I was growing up, continually our society pitted body and mind against one another, and continually suggested that the devil is in the flesh," he said. "It seems to me that we are doing the same thing all over again." Sexual liberation was an irreversible product of historical change and "what we are seeing now is really a reaction to that," he told a radio interviewer. "I think what happens to some extent is that in the changing of society one takes two steps forward and one step back. What we're going through right now is a kind of digesting of the changes."[22]

A rejuvenated Hefner also took on the Meese Commission directly. Taking up the editorial pen as he had not since the Playboy Philosophy frenzy of the early 1960s, he wrote several indignant pieces in *Playboy*. Hefner accused the panel of engaging in "sexual McCarthyism" and "putting on a circus show of misinformation and innuendo" as it tried to convince the public that erotic materials were harmful. Rather than researching the facts and probing the work of social scientists who had studied the subject, the panel "trundled out a parade of born-again basket cases, anti-sex feminists, and fun-hating fundamentalists." After the Sears letter, Hefner accused the commission of becoming "the tool of evangelical terrorists" and described the incident as "the first successful use of a national black-list since the McCarthy era."[23]

Nor did Hefner mince words concerning Meese's feminist allies. A small faction of the women's movement had endorsed an antisexual position, he argued. "I think the fact that the women's movement got sidetracked with its anti-porn, anti-sexuality is very, very hurtful because the women's movement was supposed to be all about free-dom. . . . The notion that sexual imagery is demeaning or that sex itself is somehow demeaning to women, is one of the saddest notions in terms of our sexuality that I can possibly imagine." Hefner main-tained that genuine feminism was about equality in education, the workplace, and the law. But "Puritanism has always been a part of the women's movement. That's why radical feminists wind up on the same side as the Christian right-wingers fighting porn." While vilifi-cation from feminists hurt, he admitted, it mainly came from a radi-cal fringe. If progressivism now involved "the attitude that is often expressed today, that the actual images of the sex act are degrading to women, then we're in serious trouble," Hefner contended.[24]

In July 1986, Attorney General Meese released the commission's final report in a news conference held in the Great Hall of the Justice Department. In an amusingly ironic tableau, he spoke in front of the "Spirit of Justice," a twelve-foot statue of a woman with one breast bared. The commission issued what one newspaper described as "a call to arms against an $8 billion-a-year porn industry," asserting a causal link between violent pornography and "acts of sexual violence" and claiming that nonviolent sexual material had a harmful effect on society by undermining personal character and devaluing family life. The two-volume, nearly two-thousand-page report offered ninety-two recommendations for legal restrictions on pornography. Perhaps most controversially, the commission encouraged religious and political groups to file complaints, join with police to root out law-breakers, and boycott retailers selling objectionable sexual material. Interestingly, however, it failed to list *Playboy* and *Penthouse* among the forty-five hundred titles it cited as pornographic. Meese himself tried to reassure skeptics that the Justice Department "is not going to engage in any censorship that violates the First Amendment."[25]

The attorney general, however, did not discuss the internal split that had divided the commission as it attempted to formulate its final report. The original version, drafted by Sears and the staff, proved so moralistic and heavy-handed that a majority rejected it. Professor Schauer, describing the draft as "one-sided and oversimplified," took it upon himself to write a new one that became the basis for the report. Even so, two commissioners, Judith Becker and Ellen Levine, refused to sign the final product and authored a twenty-page dissenting report. Complaining that a rush to meet deadlines had caused confusion, they sharply disputed the report's claim of a con-nection between pornography and sexual violence. "No self-respect-ing investigator would accept conclusions based on such a study," they wrote. Moreover, many researchers on sexual materials, vio-lence, and crime claimed that the Meese Commission had distorted their work in drawing its conclusions. Edward Donnerstein, from the University of Wisconsin, whose research was cited by the panel, insisted that the commission had reached "bizarre" conclusions, while Neil Malamuth and Murray Strauss, from UCLA and the University of New Hampshire, complained that their work had been misused in an attempt to buttress preordained conclusions.[26]

The report generated immediate controversy. Jerry Falwell and Pat Robertson approved it as "a good and healthy report" and part of "a definite spiritual revival" in America. Catharine MacKinnon and Women Against Pornography endorsed it as "a major breakthrough in raising the consciousness of the country." Some conservative columnists, such as Cal Thomas, also approved, contending that society had a right to establish the minimum standards by which it wished to live.[27]

But most assessments rejected the Meese Commission Report on grounds of free speech and anticensorship. Liberals characterized it as a blunderbuss legal attack on behalf of reactionary moral crusaders. A memorable liberal dismissal came in a *New Republic* article cleverly titled "Big Boobs," by Hendrik Hertzberg. It was accompanied by a hilarious cover drawing of Meese as a pinup in the style of Alberto Vargas: lounging in a sultry pose with one leg bent provocatively, a hand propped demurely behind his head, a come-hither look on his face, tie askew, bare feet arched in anticipation. As editor Michael Kinsley noted puckishly, "Our idea is that in all those empty slots in 7-Elevens where they used to sell *Playboy* and *Penthouse*, now they use them for the *New Republic*." Many conservatives demurred as well. William F. Buckley deplored pornography but chastised the commission for sending the intimidating Sears letter and accepting a mandate it could not possibly fulfill. The *National Review* asserted that while pornography degraded the quality of American life, the panel had failed to establish its thesis empirically. In a special essay, "The Individual Is Sovereign," *Time* argued on behalf of a rule regarding privacy and sexual choices: "Uncle Sam, and all other uninvited guests, keep out."[28]

Hefner reacted scornfully to the Meese Commission Report. In a *Playboy* editorial, he described it as a blueprint for "sex vigilantes" and quoted Supreme Court justice Harry Blackmun, who had described sexuality as an intimate affair involving "the most comprehensive of rights and the most valued by civilized men: namely, the right to be let alone." At issue, Hefner passionately insisted in a radio interview, was sexual freedom. "Whether it's related to censorship or . . . related to personal privacy in the bedroom, that is a fight we have been fighting in *Playboy* for some 32 years, and it is one that I believe in wholeheartedly," he maintained. "The sexual revolution is a quest for sexual freedom, both to read and to do in your bedroom what you want to do. If freedom has become passé, then we are in very serious trouble."[29]

Most observers agreed with Hefner, but their commentary should have unsettled the *Playboy* publisher. Even as they opposed censorship, defended free speech, and denounced moralistic restrictions from extremists on the right or left, most opponents of the

Meese Commission took pains to emphasize that they were bothered by the sexual invasion of American life. They distanced themselves from a *Playboy* ethos they found distasteful. A series of editorials and columns in the liberal *New York Times,* for example, granted, "There *is* a pornography problem in the United States. Offensively explicit sex and violence are dispensed with too little regard for the rights and sensibilities of those who want themselves or their children shielded from such material." They observed that among reasonable citizens "millions do worry, uneasily and conscientiously" about the easy availability of pornographic material in modern America. The columnist Anna Quindlen, while endorsing sexual liberation and opposing censorship, complained that sexual images had become so pervasive that she constantly had to try and explain them to her young child. *Playboy* had the right to depict nudity, she wrote, but "I think the centerfolds are simply silly, and that all those women miming sexual ecstasy in bizarre undergarments succeed only in looking as if they had bad colds." The predominant liberal position on erotic images—lewd, silly, offensive, problematic, but legally protected—did not exactly constitute a ringing endorsement of *Playboy* values.[30]

Thus Hefner's triumph over the Meese Commission played out as a costly victory. The direct political threat largely evaporated, but a significant problem remained. The attorney general's panel, with its two-front ideological assault from the Moral Majority and the feminist left, highlighted how the evolution of American social and cultural values by the 1980s had put the Playboy Philosophy on the defensive. "The current atmosphere does seem to be a part of a national retrenchment from the giddy permissiveness of the 60s and 70s," *Time* observed. The conservative backlash to the Age of Aquarius, the revolution in women's rights, and the liberal retreat from licentiousness increasingly isolated Hefner in the public sphere. Many now saw him as an agent of sexual manipulation: undermining tradition for conservatives, encouraging female subordination for many feminists, and promoting distasteful license for many liberals.[31]

In the middle of this ideological struggle, a beleaguered Hefner suffered an assault from an unexpected direction. A friend launched a brutal surprise attack that denounced him personally, vilified his values, and supported the accusations of exploitation coming from the Moral Majority and radical feminists. Involving as it did the horrific murder of Playmate Dorothy Stratten, this shocking onslaught caused more pain and trauma than perhaps any other single event in Hefner's life.

III

In the summer of 1984, the film director Peter Bogdanovich published *The Killing of the Unicorn: Dorothy Stratten, 1960–1980*. In this emotional and deeply personal book, the boyfriend of the Playmate and budding actress made a stunning allegation. While her estranged husband Paul Snider had murdered her four years earlier, he said, responsibility for the horrifying death lay elsewhere. Most people blamed the "eternal triangle" of husband, wife, and lover:

> But as I tried to find the truth, I discovered a fourth side to the figure—hidden and dark. Eventually there would be no doubt in my mind that if the shadowy Hefner-side of the pyramid had never existed, Dorothy would not have died. She could have dealt with Paul Snider, a small-town pimp who first spotted and sold her, but she could not handle the slick professional machinery of the *Playboy* sex factory, nor the continual efforts of its founder to bring her into his personal fold, no matter what *she* wanted.

In Bogdanovich's words, "As I found out more and more about Hefner's role in the events, my rage toward him grew."[32]

This attack struck Hefner with full force. For page after page, Bogdanovich unfolded a relentless indictment of the publisher and his operation, claiming that they had caused the demise of his beloved girlfriend. He charged this "Walt Disney of pornography" with leading an exploitative lifestyle that destroyed women within it. Orgies at the mansion, he contended, depended on a continuous supply of fresh-faced, naïve females—"the new girl from Iowa, or Missouri, or Montana"—who would be sexually used, passed around among Hefner's friends, and leered at by voyeurs. Stratten had walked into this trap, Bogdanovich argued. Hefner yearned to confirm his entry into Hollywood society and "wanted a real sex goddess to emerge from the pages of *Playboy*." The young woman filled the bill.[33]

Bogdanovich claimed that Stratten tearfully had confided to him that shortly after she had arrived at the mansion, Hefner had forced himself on her sexually during a late-night Jacuzzi session, an incident that left her bereft and bitter. During subsequent magazine shoots, the publisher had pressured her to submit to ever more raunchy photos that brought her to tears as photographers gave her a puppy to calm her frazzled nerves. These experiences finally drove Stratten to marry Paul Snider out of desperation, Bogdanovich wrote, and when Hefner banned the small-time hustler from the mansion, murder had resulted. But the blame spread farther. "In truth, doesn't *Playboy* figuratively seduce and rape young women? Live off them? Ridicule their gender? Destroy their lives?" wrote the director. "*Playboy* and its kindred porno mills continue to grind up women and spit them out for the masturbatory pleasure of men the world over." Bogdanovich's summation pictured Hefner as "a hygienic super-pimp" and his grand sexual revolution little more than a male ruse "under the guise of liberalism and equality. Its true purpose was to make things easier for the men to get laid." *Playboy* made women into sexual objects and encouraged "sordid and violent male crimes like the one which destroyed Dorothy." In Bogdanovich's conclusion, "All of this has been the result of Hefner's great con."[34]

Bogdanovich, ironically, had been a friend of Hefner's. They had become acquainted in 1976, and their shared love of Hollywood movies nurtured a bond. Bogdanovich was put on the "gate list" at the mansion, which meant he could come on the property whenever he pleased, and he visited frequently—fifty-two times between 1976 and 1980. He called Hefner numerous times and attended Thanksgiving dinner in 1977 and Christmas dinner in 1978 along with a small circle of the publisher's friends. Bogdanovich first met Stratten at the mansion, of course, and had confided to Hefner about their developing love affair. When the publisher received the horrible call from the police about Stratten's murder, he immediately phoned Bogdanovich and over subsequent days offered solace and comfort to the devastated director. Thus Hefner was dumbfounded when he perused an advance copy of the manuscript in the spring of 1984. "This is so crazy," he thought. "It will never be published. The basic theme is a lie."[35]

Hefner's shock soon intensified. William Morrow published the book over the objections of Hefner's attorneys—the publisher had hired the prestigious Washington law firm of Edward Bennett Williams to object to the book's libels—by making a few cosmetic changes. Then Bogdanovich launched an eight-city publicity tour that took him to television shows, public talks, and newspaper interviews where he denounced Hefner and *Playboy* on NBC's *Today* show, ABC's *Good Morning America,* and CBS's *Nightwatch*. Throughout, he claimed that while Stratten had been trapped by Paul Snider, "the larger trap was the one he [Hefner] lured her into—the whole Playboy world." The director elaborated on how his disillusioned girlfriend came to feel that "she had been used like a game, like a pinball machine." Hefner and *Playboy* were "a social poison which destroys women like Dorothy Stratten."[36]

Flogging his book, Bogdanovich appeared as a born-again feminist. He told the press that attorneys for the Stratten estate had filed an amicus curiae brief in support of the antipornography legislation in Minneapolis drafted by Andrea Dworkin and Catharine MacKinnon, and testified in behalf of a similar ordinance proposed for Los Angeles. Bogdanovich sent a message to an antipornography rally held at Stanford University that denounced the "*Playboy* pornography mills" and reported that many women appearing in the magazine had contacted him to testify as to "what *Playboy* has really done to them. It exploits them—their minds, their bodies, their dreams."[37]

Bogdanovich's attack appalled and angered Hefner. Throughout the fall of 1984 and early 1985 he issued impassioned denials of culpability, asserting that the director, consumed by grief and guilt, had penned "an outrageous work of fiction which does a terrible injustice to Hugh Hefner and others at Playboy." The distraught publisher described *The Killing of the Unicorn* as a "total fabrication," a "crazy story," and a "guilt trip." He vehemently denied every accusation, insisting that Stratten delighted in her association with *Playboy* and enjoyed a warm friendship with him. Hefner could only explain the book as the author's "pathological obsession. I think that what he has set up and is attacking here is behavior which he himself has done. In effect, what he is calling Hefner is really his own dark side."[38]

Hefner became fixated on refuting *The Killing of the Unicorn*. According to his assistant, Lisa Loving, for months the publisher "never thought about anything else. He was completely consumed." When friends or associates would suggest gently that he should let it go, arguing that no one really believed Bogdanovich and that it would blow over, Hefner angrily rejected the advice. "It truly, truly devastated him," said Loving. "He was worried about how people would perceive him. . . . It was the most horrible thing that anyone could ever say about him. And it truly did work him into a complete frenzy."[39]

Hefner's obsession stemmed from deep sources. He saw the book as an unjust betrayal of friendship from someone he had treated well. The challenge to his personal integrity disturbed him even more. According to Murray Fisher, a *Playboy* editor and friend, *Unicorn* "was his worst nightmare come true. . . . He absolutely had to prove that he was right because this was a personal attack on him." But perhaps most importantly, Hefner understood Bogdanovich's book to be an attack on the meaning of his whole adult life. Bitter criticism from the fundamentalist-feminist alliance had worn Hefner down, and *The Killing of the Unicorn* seemed to penetrate his defenses to reach a soft spot of insecurity. As they combed through the text comma by comma, Loving noticed, "He kept asking, 'Am I really like that?'" Hefner confessed privately, "The way I am perceived by others who are important to me is one of the most important things in my life and always has been. And there is something in this that just hits very close to home in terms of . . . what I'm all about."[40]

Self-righteously angry, Hefner became convinced that mental instability lay behind the assault. He solicited a private evaluation of the author from a prominent Chicago psychiatrist, who concluded that the film director was suffering from severe depression, paranoia, and possibly psychosis. Hefner also got wind of Bogdanovich's odd behavior toward Louise Hoogstraten, Dorothy's thirteen-year-old sister, and Nelly, the girls' mother, from a private security agent who had worked for the director. The improprieties reported by this source were shocking.[41]

As Hefner defended himself, the critical reaction to *The Killing of the Unicorn* came in. Reviews were almost universally negative. A few commentators found the book to be tender, moving, and convincing, but most saw it as maudlin, self-justifying, and exploitative in its own way. Critics complained that Bogdanovich, while pointing the finger of blame, seemed oblivious to his own sexist susceptibility to "the whore/ Madonna complex" in his view of women. Typically, they condemned the book as "simplistic" and concluded that "Bogdanovich's drippy, shrill account fails both as memoir and pseudo-sociology. Self-justification, revenge, and exploitation with a sugary, sanctimonious façade."[42]

Even so, *Playboy* and its publisher took a battering. Both feminists and fundamentalists, of course, in the mold of the Meese Commission, saw the book as confirming the sleazy, destructive immorality of the Playboy lifestyle. The noted feminist author Barbara Ehrenreich wrote that *Unicorn,* while self-delusional and mawkish, lent credence to the central theme of antipornography feminists: "porn leads to rape leads to murder; women are victims; and most men . . . have mayhem on their minds." In her words, "It says something about *Playboy* magazine, Hugh Hefner, and his entire commercial empire that the best-known Playmate of all time is best known for having been tortured and brutally murdered." Conservatives concurred, blaming Hefner for creating a "dark world into which a naïve, innocent Canadian girl . . . could be dragged and ultimately consumed."[43]

More disturbingly for Hefner, however, even hostile reviews of *Unicorn* seemed to accept its depiction of an exploitative Playboy world. While dismissing *Unicorn,* they noted the "scathing indictment of Hefner and his pals" and described him as a "desiccated hedonist" who cavorted in his "tacky baroque crash pad, the Playboy Mansion West." One reviewer observed that while the book failed, its "most fascinating passages come with Bogdanovich's searing behind-the-scenes look at the Playboy lifestyle." The *New Republic* accepted the author's "devastating portrait of Hefner," while the respected critic Charles Champlin, in the *Los Angeles Times,* described *Unicorn* as "overwrought" but granted its "depressing and persuasive indictment—the most accusing yet—of Hugh Hefner, his private life and his public philosophy, and their raunchy confluence in the Playboy Mansion West in Holmby Hills." Bogdanovich's book, for all its weaknesses, he wrote, demonstrated how "the Hefner philosophy looks retrograde, a denial of the real implications of the sexual revolution."[44]

Such assaults finally became more than Hefner could bear. Under tremendous, self-imposed pressure to clear his name, he suffered a stroke that laid him low for several weeks. Then on April 1, 1985, against the advice of his daughter and associates, he held a press conference at the mansion. In front of dozens of reporters and several television crews, he accused Bogdanovich of not only systematically spreading lies, but of seducing both Louise Hoogstraten, Dorothy's underage sister, and Nelly Schaap, her mother, and breaking up the marriage of the latter. When a reporter asked if Bogdanovich actually had made love to the teenage Louise, Hefner replied, "Without question," and opined that he should be prosecuted for the crime. He then introduced Burl Eldridge, Nelly's estranged husband and Louise's stepfather, who made a statement supporting Hefner's charges.[45]

Within days, Louise Hoogstraten filed a lawsuit against Hefner for slander, libel, and invasion of privacy. Securing legal representation from the noted feminist lawyer Gloria Allred, she asked for restitution in the amount of $5 million. A confident Hefner asserted, "It appears the truth will finally be known." Indeed, six months later Hoogstraten dropped the lawsuit. After a handful of depositions were taken, Allred fled the case and, uncharacteristically, had little to say about the decision. "Everything is governed by attorney-client privilege," she noted tersely. Hefner believed he knew the reason: "She thought she had a women's-rights guy on her hands. And what she had was something else again." Then Bogdanovich issued an apology to Hefner as the suit was dropped. "All of us who loved Dorothy, and I know Hugh Hefner was one of these, have been through the roughest of times, and maybe the healing process may now be accelerated. I am sorry if Mr. Hefner's health has suffered because of things I have said or written."[46]

Ultimately, Hefner was vindicated. As the dust settled, it became clear that Bogdanovich's accusations about Hefner were uniformly false. The story of Hefner's supposed seduction/rape of Stratten, as well as much other information in *Unicorn*, it turned out, was a fabrication from Patrick Curtis. The former husband of Raquel Welch, Curtis had frequented the mansion for several years before being banished for dishonesty, and subsequently was caught out in a highly publicized lie when he claimed to be a decorated fighter pilot in the Marine Corps; in actuality he had never served in the military. Apparently in retaliation for the banishment, Curtis had fed Bogdanovich stories that he later retracted in a signed affidavit. The puppy that had allegedly been given to Stratten as a ploy to quell her hysteria over nude photographs turned out to be a gift from *Playboy* photo editor Marilyn Grabowski, who had hoped it would cheer her up during her escalating fights with her husband, Paul Snider. Delighted, she named it Marston after Hefner's middle name. Stratten's supposed despair about her involvement with *Playboy* was belied by a letter of appreciation to Hefner describing her arrival in Los Angeles as the "beginning to a whole new life for me. . . .

I am amazed at the new areas I keep finding in myself, and keep discovering more and more of life. . . . I am so happy that *Playboy* has been, and will be, a part of my life. And, Mr. Hefner, *Playboy*, of course, is you. Love always, Dorothy Stratten." In a footnote to this episode, in 1989 Bogdanovich married Louise Hoogstraten as her mother publicly bewailed the event, while some fifteen years later Louise turned to Hefner for support during an ugly divorce from the film director.[47]

As the Bogdanovich controversy ground to a halt, Hefner expressed delight "that my true relationship with Dorothy Stratten has been clarified." But his victory came with many casualties. This unseemly scandal seemed to grip and damage everyone who touched it. Most commentators were disgusted by the Bogdanovich-Hefner dispute (even as they rushed to write about it), describing it as "a media circus" and a "public relations war." They saw the director as a self-righteous twister of facts, while one wrote, "It was sad, somehow, watching Hugh Hefner . . . maligning the reputation of a teen-age girl and bickering over the bones of a Playboy Playmate five years dead." Even Hefner confessed to *Rolling Stone* that the feud was "just so bad-taste Hollywood" it made him sick.[48]

In a memo written early in the *Unicorn* quarrel, *Playboy* editor Arthur Kretchmer had warned Hefner against overreacting to the book. "In your effort to destroy Bogdanovich's credibility, you will destroy your own," he argued. Ugly sexual accusations against the film director, even if they were true, would only cause people to recoil as they saw a victim "defending himself by accusing his accuser of kiddie sex. Instead of being seen as a good guy, a man victimized by a guilt-ridden, scapegoating parasite, you'll be one of the players in a tawdry story." Kretchmer's crystal ball proved to be accurate. For many, Hefner's vindication was overshadowed by the flurry of accusations and counteraccusations about orgies, underage sex, attempted rape, pornographic media mills, pathological lovers, and jilted, murderous husbands. Far from appearing glamorous, playful, and avant-garde, Hefner's world appeared to many observers through a haze of vulgar, poisonous smog. The frenzied mudslinging of the Bogdanovich controversy, in this larger sense, only contributed to Playboy's troubles in the age of Reagan.[49]

Ultimately, however, the private impact of the Bogdanovich conflict was even more profound for Hefner than its public implications.

Again, Kretchmer proved prescient. Early on, he cautioned Hefner about "the intensity of your feelings" and warned that going after the *Unicorn* author was "almost guaranteed to tear you to pieces." By early 1985, such disintegration became apparent. In the middle of the controversy, before he knew how things would play out, Hefner grimly internalized stress as he absorbed a drubbing in the press and struggled to defend his integrity. Additional pressures came from the disastrous Carrie Leigh relationship and the political bludgeoning from the Meese Commission. Approaching the edge of emotional and physical exhaustion, a beleaguered Hefner finally collapsed.[50]

PART V

RESURGENCE

19

The Bride Wore Clothes

n the early spring of 1985, Hugh Hefner suffered a physical breakdown. This health crisis, caused by escalating stress in his personal and professional life, frightened him badly and marked the nadir of this difficult period. An unorthodox medical treatment orchestrated by his personal physician restored him to normal functioning in a surprisingly short time, but the experience shook him and prompted a reevaluation of priorities. It liberated the publisher to cut through the entanglements of the Dorothy Stratten controversy and hold the press conference exposing his nemesis, Peter Bogdanovich. It also prompted him to adopt a healthier lifestyle as he slowed down, gave up smoking, changed his diet, and began to exercise.

In a deeper sense, however, Hefner's stroke inspired him to reconsider his personal life. Rethinking his priorities, he initiated a search for succor and stability that gradually led to the last thing many people ever expected to see: matrimony, monogamy, and a family. Initially, he tried to create a stable bond with his current girlfriend, Carrie Leigh, but the growing volatility of their relationship bred disenchantment. When that romance crumbled, he turned elsewhere late in the decade and fell deeply in love with a young woman newly arrived at the mansion. To the shock of many observers, they married within a short time.

Mr. Playboy transformed himself once again as he took on the unfamiliar role of husband and father. Just as Hefner and *Playboy* had mirrored American social evolution in earlier decades, now, too, his embrace of an orthodox family life mirrored what some observers termed the "new traditionalism" of the 1990s. As Hefner entered his autumn years, he seemed to come full circle from rebellion to reasonableness, from hedonistic bachelor to dedicated family man. The process proved to be as dramatic as it was unexpected.

I

In the early morning hours of March 7, 1985, Hugh Hefner was perusing the next day's *Los Angeles Times* in his bedroom suite when he found himself unable to follow the article or comprehend the headline. He called his doctor, who told him to take an aspirin and go to sleep. By next morning, however, the symptoms had grown worse. When he phoned his executive assistant, Mary O'Connor, he slurred his speech and struggled to express simple thoughts. Staff rushed to his side and noticed that the right side of his face was palsied. Immediately, they called his doctor and the publisher went for a series of tests that afternoon. A neurologist asked him to name ordinary items—buttons on a shirt, a tie, a belt—but the publisher could not do so. He also lost the ability to read, could use his right hand only clumsily, and appeared mildly disoriented. An MRI at a Pasadena hospital a short time later—he was whisked there by helicopter—confirmed the diagnosis. Hefner had suffered a stroke.[1]

Over the next several days, Hefner's situation remained serious as his neurological signs continued fluctuating. Morbidly afraid of hospitals, he prevailed upon his close friend and physician, Dr. Mark Saginor, to supervise a course of treatment at the mansion. Saginor, concluding that anxiety reduction was crucial to recovery, agreed and moved into a guest bedroom to supervise around-the-clock care. He consulted the noted neurologist Dr. Clark Espy, and they concluded that Hefner had suffered a moderately severe episode of RIND, or reversible ischemic neurological deficit. They also agreed on a plan of treatment that centered on the aggressive administration of high doses of dexamethasone, a research medication. This unusual approach proved remarkably successful, and within a few days Hefner began to recover. Complete recuperation took several months, however. Christie Hefner, who flew to Los Angeles to comfort her father not long after the stroke, entered his bedroom and saw him reading a book in bed. Her surprise turned to despair when it became apparent that he was presenting a brave front—the book was upside down. Carrie Leigh's flightiness also muddied the waters. She devoted herself to nursing Hefner for several weeks, but then in the middle of the crisis presented him with a demand for marriage. When Hefner demurred, she wrote him a "Dear John" letter and fled the mansion in early April, only to return several weeks later.[2]

Hefner, along with his close friends and associates, had little doubt as to what had brought on the stroke—stress, caused both by the turbulent Carrie Leigh relationship and the nasty accusations leveled by Bogdanovich. The former kept his personal life in a constant state of tension, while the latter, as Hefner confessed in an interview later in 1985, "proved absolutely devastating for me." He had heeded his advisers by limiting his response to *The Killing of the Unicorn*, but repressing his anger created enormous tension, especially when some observers suggested, in his words, that "I was avoiding the confrontation because I had something to hide." Moreover, a dynamic of self-punishment seemed to be at work. Worn down by attacks from the Moral Majority and radical feminists, weary from dealing with Leigh's antics, and reeling from the hostile publicity generated by *Unicorn*, Hefner, for one of the few times in his life, began to doubt himself. "I suppose I half-believed what Bogdanovich was saying about me," he admitted later. "That's what brought the stroke on."[3]

But Hefner quickly recovered his equilibrium. On March 20 he released a statement to the press explaining his recovery from this medical trauma, which he described as "'a stroke of luck' that I fully expect will change the direction of my life." Indeed, it did. First, he interpreted it as releasing him emotionally to reply fully to Peter Bogdanovich's accusations, and the mansion press conference was the result. The stroke also prompted Hefner to slow down and adopt a more easygoing attitude toward life. It "gave me permission in a single day to drop the luggage of my lifetime," he explained. "The priorities in a person's life shift very dramatically in the most positive kind of way." Cognizant of his mortality, he quit smoking his pipe, began eating more healthy foods, gave up Pepsi for Diet Pepsi, and began to exercise moderately. He also decided to begin work on an autobiography—"looking for the reasons behind why I've lived my life the way I have," in his words—as a way of understanding himself and his past.[4]

Perhaps most significantly, the stroke prompted Hefner to reconsider his romantic life in all of its emotional and sexual complexity. He began to seriously ponder the possibility of a more lasting relationship. Such an impulse had flickered in the early 1980s, first with Shannon Tweed and then with Carrie Leigh, but now it became more concerted. In the aftermath of the stroke, he intensified his efforts to settle down with Leigh over the next two years, an impulse that partly explained his baffling patience with her erratic behavior. But the effort fizzled as their stormy relationship blew hot and cold, and Leigh departed for good in early 1988.[5]

But Hefner's growing desire for permanence remained in place. His good friends Dick and Anne Stewart once thought they were alone in a room of the mansion as they sat together, smooching and laughing about some incident in years past. "We didn't realize that Hef was standing at the door," Anne recalled. "He came in and said, 'Wow, that's something I've never had—a memory to share with a girlfriend from a long time ago.'" While his tone was joking, she sensed that he envied their closeness. Dick added, "I always had the feeling that he admired our relationship because we were lovers and buddies." Always believing that the best cure for a failed love affair was to find another one quickly, Hefner responded to Carrie Leigh's departure by looking for another romance. He did not have to wait long.[6]

II

Hefner's growing desire for emotional permanence and security soon found an object. Kimberly Conrad, a tall, statuesque, strikingly beautiful twenty-four-year-old honey blonde, had first visited the mansion on May 22, 1987, and spent several days shooting her upcoming centerfold photos. On her Playmate Data Sheet, she listed her ambitions to continue modeling and then become a commercial real estate agent. "I want to lead a fulfilling life," she wrote. "Travel, experience new places, meet lots of people, and do well in my career and personal life." But with Carrie Leigh still around, Conrad kept her distance from Hefner.[7]

On January 19, 1988, however, she returned to the mansion as Miss January to shoot a future *Playboy* pictorial, this time with the famed photographer Helmut Newton. With Leigh now gone for good, Conrad's beauty and pleasant manner caught Hefner's eye. He chatted with her, but she dodged his invitation to screen a movie and kept a girlfriend nearby for emotional protection. He finally said, "Would you like to spend some time with me?" She replied, "Well, I don't really know you." He said, "How are you going to get to know me if you don't spend some time with me?" She conceded his logic, and they spent the next three hours talking; by the end of the evening, in Hefner's words, "we knew that we cared about one another." The publisher had flowers put in her room, and invited her to return to the mansion quickly for another visit. Conrad came back for the Super Bowl weekend ten days later, and went out for dinner with Hefner, Dick and Anne Stewart, John Dante, and Keith Hefner. She found the publisher to be gentlemanly, attentive, and a lot of fun. In her words, "We had a blast and we really liked each other." The spark of romance quickly burst into flame. At Hefner's invitation, she moved into the mansion in early February and the two became a couple.[8]

Like Hefner's last two girlfriends, Conrad was Canadian. Born in Moulton, Alabama, on August 6, 1963, she had moved with her family to Reno, Nevada, four years later, and then to Vancouver. Conrad grew up as the youngest among three sisters and a brother in the affluent suburb of West Vancouver, that city's equivalent of Beverly Hills. Her mother had divorced and remarried, and her stepfather was a successful financier. She experienced a traditional upbringing with a conscientious mother, a love of animals, and days filled with sporting activities such as squash, water skiing, and racquetball. By adolescence, Conrad had developed a reserved manner with a touch of quirky humor, strong family attachments, and a set of conventional, even conservative social values. She began to model in high school and after graduation made it a career. After promoting a host of local and regional products, she spent two stints in New York City and eventually appeared in commercials for McDonald's and Levi's jeans.[9]

She first came into contact with *Playboy* in Vancouver through Ken Honey, the photographer who had discovered a number of Canadian models for the magazine over the years, including Dorothy Stratten. He first noticed Conrad when perusing some modeling shots, but she was only seventeen, so he urged her to contact him in a few years for some test photos. Being rather reserved and traditional, she had little interest. But several years later, after breaking up with a longtime boyfriend and primed for a "shock value" gesture, she called up Honey and said she was ready to pose for test shots. He took the photos, sent them to Los Angeles, and *Playboy* expressed an immediate interest. The young Canadian flew down, met with photo editor Marilyn Grabowski, and was slated to become the first Playmate of 1988.[10]

When she attracted Hefner's attention early that year, Conrad seemed to embody everything that he sought in a woman. A confirmed homebody, she liked nothing more than staying in comfortable domestic surroundings watching movies and tending to animals. Reserved and sweet-tempered, she mixed easily with people but preferred to stay in the background rather than be the center of attention. Gorgeous yet modest in her clothing tastes, she exhibited a natural beauty that contrasted with her predecessor's plastic surgery and glitzy fashion sense. With no interest in a Hollywood career, she appeared content to focus on Hefner and their life together when they became a couple. Conrad reconciled some of the publisher's conflicted desires by being both a stunning centerfold and a devoted, traditional woman. Hefner was smitten. "I can't believe how all of this has worked out," he told *USA Today* in March 1988. "Out of nowhere, to have this angel arrive and change everything. How lucky can a guy get?"[11]

Hefner's circle of mansion friends was almost as infatuated as he was. After the turmoil of the previous half decade, they saw Conrad's calming, caring influence as a godsend. As she sat watching weekend movies with Hefner, while he smilingly welcomed her menagerie of dogs and cats into his home, onlookers were thrilled. They saw her as a warm, wonderful, down-to-earth woman with no agendas and no hang-ups. "Kimberly is perfect for him," observed Hefner's old friend Joni Mattis.[12]

As the romance bloomed, it revived Hefner emotionally. Friends noticed that he seemed to shed ten years overnight as his step quickened and his good-humored enthusiasm for life bubbled up.

In Conrad's company, he seemed happily at peace with the world. Jessica Hahn described them acting like "a couple of teenagers who just got pinned and were going steady," while Hefner crony Richard Brooks observed, "Everything about her is reassuring to him and when he sees her it is like an electric spark hits him, like a twenty year old." The publisher seemed euphoric. "In this relationship, I have found something I never found before," he told the *New York Times*. "I never thought I would find it." An incurable romantic, he saw their love as the essential element that animated his existence: "It is the equivalent of life for me."[13]

Over the next few months, this whirlwind romance gathered speed, and soon Hefner stood ready to do the unthinkable. Notoriously averse to matrimony, he had often repeated the Woody Allen quip that "marriage is the death of hope." But now he threw his past reservations to the wind. On the evening of July 23, 1988, after watching a movie, *White Mischief*, with friends at the mansion and playing foosball together in the gamehouse, the couple took a walk and stopped at the wishing well on the front lawn. "Will you marry me?" Hefner asked. "Do I have to tell you right now?" she replied, and, slightly flustered, he stammered, "No, of course not." Conrad then laughed and said, "I can't imagine life without you. Yes, I will marry you." Later that evening, Conrad wrote down her hope that "Hef and I stay together forever because I love him so much and he adores and loves me." A short time later, Hefner presented her with a five-and-a-half-carat diamond engagement ring.[14]

It was a genuine love match. In the many interviews that accompanied their engagement announcement, the couple appeared "as gooey and mushy as any lovebirds," as one reporter put it. "They finish each other's sentences. They like to putter around the house. It's enough to send a person into insulin shock." Conrad expressed confidence that her famous fiancé was ready to settle down. "I think he has sown his wild oats. I know he has," she said. "If I didn't feel that he has, or if I felt he would cheat on me, then I would not be married to him." Describing him as a "soul mate," she often grew teary-eyed in talking about the closeness of their relationship. Conrad stressed the depth of her commitment, explaining that he had become the "main focus" of her life. Hefner reciprocated her devotion. "This is the way you'd like it to be," he explained to the *Los Angeles Times*. "There's a line in the film *Pennies From Heaven* which goes something like,

'Somewhere there must be a world where the words to the songs are true.' And it's difficult for me to even say that line without getting a little silly, a little teary-eyed."[15]

Hefner justified his decision to wed as an update, not a rejection, of the Playboy Philosophy. He romanticized marriage. In a long interview with a reporter from the *Sacramento Bee,* he argued that his magazine focused on the romantic relationship between men and women, and the sexual pleasure that should invigorate it. Marriage, in and of itself, he now insisted, did not belie that emphasis. "In all of life, we make compromises between the adventure of it and the security of it—the unknown and the known," he mused. "One of the reasons I avoided marriage all these years is that I think in many instances marriage, and the certainty of it, destroys romance. I don't care very much about marriage, per se. I care very much about love and romance." Now, the publisher was convinced, he had found a mate with whom romance would flourish, not wither.[16]

Hefner's former girlfriends saw more practical factors at work. Barbi Benton credited his new fiancée's willingness to mold herself to his wishes. "She likes to stay inside and not go out to dinner. She has no anxiety about being an actress. She has his interests always in mind," she commented. Sondra Theodore sensed social and biological pressures at work. "Everyone he had been involved with is married and having babies," she observed. "He knows it's time to lead a more conventional life." Shannon Tweed, with typical bluntness, attributed it to his desire for a new challenge: "He's done it all and this is what's left."[17]

As the date for the wedding approached, a flurry of activity dominated mansion life. On April 25, 1989, Hefner, in the annual ceremony, announced that Conrad had been chosen as Playmate of the Year. Two months later, the cover of the June issue proclaimed, "This Playmate of the Year Is a Playmate for a Lifetime." The accompanying piece presented a gallery of enticing photographs of Conrad, along with a long description of her romance with Hefner, their engagement, and the closeness of their relationship. As a *Playboy* writer noted breathlessly, "It will be one of the most startling developments of the century if Hef, whose career has symbolized bachelorhood, comes to represent marriage, American style, in the Nineties." Meanwhile, Conrad chose an off-white gown created by the New York designer Jim Hjelm, while the Los Angeles designer and friend Rick Pallack created a 1940s-look tuxedo with white silk bow tie for Hefner. Colin Cowie, a young Englishman, became the wedding coordinator and spent five hectic weeks organizing the affair. Conrad's friends gave her a traditional bridal shower, but Hefner declined the counterpart. "I had a bachelor party for the last 30 years," he joked. "I don't need one now."[18]

Finally, on July 1, 1989, in an event that few observers of Mr. Playboy ever expected to see, Hefner and Conrad were married in a lavish ceremony at the mansion. Some 150 guests attended, sitting in neat rows of chairs in the front yard up by the wishing well where Hefner had proposed. The groom played pinball with his brother, best man Keith Hefner, for a half hour before the ceremony, but as he took his place to await his bride's arrival, he realized he had forgotten to bring the ring. "Probably Freudian in some way," he quipped. When he reappeared after dashing back up the stairs to retrieve it, the guests cheered. A nervous Conrad, after an attack of lightheadedness and crying, composed herself and came down the aisle smiling on the arm of her father. Both bride and groom grew tearful during the ceremony, but a lighthearted mood prevailed. When the presiding clergyman, the Reverend Charles D. Ara, asked the traditional question about heeding her husband, Conrad commented, "That may be going a little too far." And when Hefner said his final "I do," Ara called out jokingly to the crowd, "You heard him say that? Everybody out there—he said it!"[19]

With the ceremony complete, four hundred additional guests arrived for the reception held in a huge white satin tent covering the whole backyard and containing some ten thousand white roses. After enjoying champagne and caviar, guests adjourned to tables set with silver and crystal for an elaborate multicourse meal featuring smoked salmon, imported cheese, watercress salad, roasted baby potatoes, steak medallions, lamb, grilled baby chicken, and elaborate Viennese desserts. Famous guests such as Bill Cosby, Robert Culp, Angie Dickinson, Mark Hamill, James Caan, Berry Gordy, Tony Curtis, and Alexander Godunov strolled through the crowd. All of Hefner's family and old friends—Shel Silverstein, LeRoy Neiman, Art Paul, John Dante, and Eldon Sellers, along with his Chicago club-hopping buddies from the late 1950s—were in attendance, as well as a trio of old girlfriends. As he posed for a photograph with Barbi Benton, Sondra Theodore, and Shannon Tweed, the publisher put his arm around them and joked, "I may have made a terrible mistake."[20]

Hefner's marriage clearly demarcated the end of an era. "Holy Matrimony!" *People* magazine exclaimed on its cover, next to a wedding photo of the happy couple. "The bride wore white. Hey, she wore clothes! Next week: Hell freezes over." Indeed, this pivotal event in the late 1980s opened the door to a new stage in the publisher's life. As he moved to adopt a more customary lifestyle and traditional set of values, Hefner interpreted his return from the frontiers of bachelor hedonism as a variation on the tale of the prodigal son. After starting out with marriage, then abandoning that for three decades of bachelorhood and sexual adventure, he "came full circle" to a kind of belated homecoming. Hefner embraced, even reveled in, the delights of family life. For the press and public, who had witnessed the publisher's sexual escapades for the last three decades, it proved a fascinating sight.[21]

III

As the 1990s began, the new, domesticated Hugh Hefner appeared on full display. Close friends and distant admirers alike saw a man who, to use one of his favorite words, had "reinvented" himself in the mold of a monogamous family man. Always concerned with explaining his life, the publisher reflected publicly, and at length, on this surprising reorientation. In one sense, Hefner, as well as many critics, agreed that his settling down reflected the traditionalist tone of the age. He described the notion of a Playmate for a lifetime as "right for this particular time, which is kind of conservative." Analyzing his decision to wed, the *New York Times* concurred that "certainly the times are at play here, the AIDS-fearing, commitment-oriented times." Another newspaper suggested, "the motto of the 1990s will become, 'Let's go home.' And the aging playboy, who lost a step or two when he suffered a mild stroke, will stay home to live the simple life A.B. (After Bunnies)." Hefner relished the irony, telling *People,* "Wouldn't it be unique if my life became a symbol of the conservative decade ahead, just as it was a symbol of the swinging 60s and 70s?"[22]

Yet it was obvious to all that Hefner and his new bride were deeply in love. His happiness was so complete that "sometimes I think I must be dreaming," he told friends. He underlined the fairy-tale romance by arranging for a European nobleman to conduct a lighthearted ceremony, complete with sword on the shoulder, declaring her Princess "Kimberella." In an interview with the London *Daily Express,* Hefner expressed his complete contentment. "Before I met her, I had always had a sense that there would be another girl on the horizon and the promise of some new romance," he explained. "But with her I feel totally fulfilled."[23]

Hefner even approved as his beautiful, strong-willed young wife began overhauling decades of tradition at the Playboy Mansion. Kimberly Conrad Hefner, despite her appearance as a Playmate, was in many ways a traditional woman whom her husband occasionally compared to his mother—straight, conventional, strict. The breakneck speed of their romance had been a bit overwhelming—they had married within eighteen months of their first date—but now the young woman moved to establish herself as the mistress of the Playboy Mansion. She directed an upgrade of the mansion menu, instructing the staff of chefs and cooks to stress fresh ingredients and innovative cuisine. She redecorated several of the bedrooms, replacing a heavy, gaudy decorative style with lighter, more elegant elements. Kimberly also became a friend and defender of the mansion's many Hispanic employees, whom she felt were treated too harshly by some of their supervisors. She even convinced Hefner to give up his satin sheets—leftovers from the orgiastic 1970s—and adopt sensible cotton ones.[24]

Kimberly also sought to tone down the raucous eroticism that had prevailed for the last two decades. She asked Hefner to send away the gaggle of female friends and Playmates who hung around the mansion as a matter of course. "She's made it clear that this is her home and people just can't wander in and out now like they always have," said a *Playboy* spokesman. "They must be cordially invited." Casual male friends on the prowl for beautiful women, who used the mansion as a kind of resort hotel—Kimberly described how she was "tired of seeing people I don't even know at the breakfast table"—were politely notified that invitations were now required. Mrs. Hefner requested that guests refrain from public nudity at the pool and grotto. "I want this to be more like a real home," she told the press. "The girls still come over, but they're wearing their bathing suits. I think that's nice." The bare-breasted Barbi Benton bust that sat in the library for many years disappeared into basement storage. "This is my house—not Barbi's—so why should I have that sitting in my library?" she explained. Polite but firm, Conrad Hefner made it clear that a new ambiance of family and home would prevail.[25]

Critics and the public were fascinated by the publisher's new lifestyle. *Life* magazine did a full spread titled "Mrs. Bunny," which detailed in words and photos how the Hefner marriage ended "the 30-year bachelorhood of America's most publicized womanizer." *Chatelaine,* the popular Canadian women's magazine, detailed monogamous married bliss at the mansion and concluded that in a society increasingly bored with recreational sex, it would be "the final triumph of Hef's career to live out his life in the company of a devoted helpmate." Reporters from the *Los Angeles Times* blinked in disbelief at the sight of Mr. Playboy biting into a piece of apple cake with whipped cream frosting and joking, "This is what passes for sin at the Playboy Mansion West these days."[26]

Perhaps the most famous commentary on revamped life at the mansion, however, came in *Doonesbury,* the award-winning cartoon series. Garry Trudeau, its creator, first poked fun at Hefner's wedding. He pictured a loudspeaker announcement: "Out of respect for the sanctity of the occasion, we'd like to ask couples to refrain from using the grotto until after the ceremony." As the revelers howled "Aww!" in dissent, one of them muttered sourly, "It's her. She's changed him." Then another cartoon depicted a stricter announcement going out to scantily clad guests lounging at the pool. "May I have your attention please? From now on we're going to have a few new rules around here. I'm getting tired of coming down every morning to a lot of faces I don't even recognize," said a female voice. "No more 'friend of a friend,' okay? Also, no more frontal nudity at breakfast. It's a bit much. And no full frontal nudity until after 5 P.M.! In general, I expect everyone to be a whole lot more discreet, especially in the Jacuzzi! Everybody understand?" As a chorus of "Yes, Mrs. Hefner," "Sorry, Mrs. Hefner," came from the crowd, the same disgruntled guest grumbled, "There go the 70's."[27]

The transformation of Hefner's life became more pronounced with fatherhood. When the couple had first broached the subject of marriage, she had brought up the question of children and he had said "absolutely." Within a few weeks of the wedding Kimberly became pregnant, and on April 9, 1990, Marston Glenn Hefner was born on Hugh's birthday, an occurrence that seemed almost magical to his father. With both parents wanting another child close in age so they could grow up together, Kimberly quickly became pregnant again, and Cooper Bradford Hefner arrived in the world on September 4, 1991.[28]

Hefner found true delight in his sons. Admitting that he had not been much of a father back in the 1950s with his first two children, he now vowed to make up for the lapse. He ordered that the yellow diamond-shaped sign on the mansion driveway be changed from "Playmates at Play" to "Children at Play." The sight of kids' toys scattered about the floor of the great hall became a common one, and it moved him to tears. He played with the boys on the lawn, pushed them on their swing set, and read comic books to them. When they became fascinated with superheroes, he dressed in a Batman costume for their entertainment. "In my entire life, I could not have imagined such happiness and fulfillment in this very traditional way," Hefner confessed to the *Los Angeles Times*. "I cannot express the magic these two children have brought to my life."[29]

The arrival of children strengthened Kimberly's resolve to clean up the mansion. With maternal impulses at full throttle, she determined to create a true family home and prune people she believed were sullying the atmosphere. She had several run-ins with Steve Powers, for instance, a longstanding mansion crony with a legendary playboy reputation. Tired of watching him bring a succession of young women to the mansion for seduction, she finally snapped when it got back to her that he had been seen having sex in the gamehouse over Easter weekend. Deeming this totally inappropriate for a family setting, she confronted him and demanded an end to "the bimbo of the week." Kimberly also clashed with John Dante, another old friend who had lived at the mansion off and on for twenty years and been part of Hefner's sexual escapades in the 1970s. A failed club owner with a penchant for running up gambling debts, Dante had become a kind of mansion pensioner who did not fit into the new family-oriented atmosphere. He departed in the summer of 1993. Kimberly also recast many mansion social events to revolve more around families and committed couples and less around recreational sex. At her request, Hefner discontinued the raucous Midsummer Night's Dream party in 1994. The annual New Year's Eve party switched from pajamas and negligees to black tie and formal gowns, an event that Marston and Cooper, dressed in their own mini-tuxes, attended with their parents. The annual Easter Egg Hunt, originally a risqué holdover from the 1970s where celebrities searched for eggs emblazoned with suggestive slogans, became a genuine child-centered party where kids combed the property for hand-decorated eggs and prizes.[30]

Hefner was too enthralled with his wife and children to take much heed. Proclaiming, "I've managed to romanticize marriage and children," he contended that his present situation belied the famous F. Scott Fitzgerald statement that there are no second acts in American lives. "I've managed to have a third act, and it has turned out to be the most fulfilling of all," he said. He also shaped a new perspective on the frantic, obsessive quality of his earlier, hedonistic days. Hefner now saw them as setting the stage for his final, mature appearance as a family man. His compulsive pursuit of sex and pleasure seemed aimed at trying to prove something to himself and others. "I confess that when I review some of the old film of myself, I start to squirm," he told one interviewer, because he saw "a guy desperate to be desirable to the opposite sex. A guy hungry for acceptance and love. A guy who could be full of shit." But now he had determined to "put all the masks I used to wear, all the games I used to play, behind me," he admitted to another. Kimberly and his young sons provided "the safe harbor that I was searching for all my life." Confessing that he was more content than he had ever been, he saw his "September years" as providing a happily-ever-after ending to the movie of his life.[31]

In the early 1990s, Hefner, incredibly, became a spokesman for many of the values he had decried over the past four decades. When a reporter suggested that he had become a "traditional family-values kind of guy," the publisher responded, "It's true. In my heart, I think I probably always have been. I think I have come full circle to living life very similar to my parents." In November 1993, Hefner appeared in back-to-back episodes of two family-friendly NBC sitcoms, *Blossom* and *The Fresh Prince of Bel-Air*. "The Playboy philosophy is expressed in a way that is positive and family-oriented," he explained of his new public posture. "I've settled down and *Playboy* has become very mainstream." He appreciated the ironic humor attending the situation. When *People* magazine asked if his new family-man image would hurt business, Hefner quipped, "Quite the contrary. America loves a redeemed sinner."[32]

Hefner's family and friends were happy to see his newfound domestic contentment. Keith Hefner noted that his brother didn't "seem to have anything left to prove, to himself or anyone else" and was "much more at peace than he's ever been before. And much more open as a person." Joe Piastro, the crusty longtime head of security at the mansion, joked good-naturedly about his boss's newfound domesticity. "In all the years I've been here, I've signed in governors, mayors of large cities, movie stars, presidential hopefuls, police officers, sports stars, big-time industrialists, and so on," he said. "I never thought I'd see the day when I signed in Dy-Dee Diaper Service. Shit! What's this world coming to?" Even fellow playboy Steve Powers, on Hefner's seventieth birthday in 1996, congratulated him on his ability "to transcend the life of the flesh to go for what is really important: romance, family, love."[33]

Hefner's late-life commitment to traditional values elicited much public commentary. Reporters flocked to the mansion to witness the remarkable images of Mr. Playboy ensconced in family bliss. "Hefner's legendary bachelor days are definitely behind him. There's a baby swing hanging not far from the tree that shades the wishing well where Hefner proposed to Conrad," noted the *Chicago Tribune*. "A playpen fills a corner of the family gymnasium, where a life-sized photograph of Conrad hangs. The dog houses behind the well-stocked game room have moved to make way for the baby's playground and swing set." Periodicals churned out a long list of phrases and headlines to describe the mansion's new domestic bliss: "Hef's Haven," "The Happy Hefners," "Father Knows Best is his way now," "The Taming of a Playboy," "All-American Dream Comes True for Hefner."[34]

The new Hefner also received celluloid commemoration. In the fall of 1992, a documentary film chronicling his life appeared around the country. Titled *Once Upon a Time,* and produced by David Lynch and Mark Frost, it originally had been a half-hour segment in their 1990 *American Chronicles* television series. Hefner liked it so much that he commissioned a ninety-minute version for theaters and cable television. The publisher contributed significantly, and it emerged as something of an autobiography. The film presented his life as an evolution toward his present state of affairs, opening with scenes of his wedding as he commented on his discovery that "happiness could be found in something very traditional, in the love of a special woman and a home and a family." After examining his long career as a prophet of pleasure and liberation, the film closed with idyllic images of Hefner as he sat on the lawn with his wife and their two children. "What I found in the relationship with Kimberly, in the marriage, in at long last having a more traditional family and children, is that to some extent I've come home again to values very similar to those of my parents. But I don't think I could have got there without that other trip," he reflected. "That trip was necessary for me to really find myself and make sense of it all."[35]

The turn toward traditionalism in Hefner's private life also influenced, albeit more subtly, his magazine and his company in the 1990s. After years of championing the cause of liberation during the Age of Aquarius and then battling a strong conservative backlash throughout the 1980s, *Playboy* moved toward an accommodation between the two. Like its founder, indeed, like much of America, Hefner's magazine tacked toward the middle, seeking to carve out a welcoming space for the mature family man as well as the carefree bachelor. It tried to make room for sexual expression and moral restraint, personal pleasure and meaningful relationships, self-fulfillment and family responsibility.

Goo Heffer, the cartoon autobiography that Hefner began as a teenager in the early 1940s

Hefner putting together the first issue of *Playboy* on a card table in his apartment in late 1953

"Playboy's Penthouse Apartment," a 1956 article that exemplified the magazine's message of consumer abundance

a second look at a high, handsome haven—
pre-planned and furnished for the bachelor in town

PLAYBOY'S PENTHOUSE APARTMENT

A MAN'S HOME is not only his castle, it is or should be, the outward reflection of his inner self—a comfortable, livable, and yet exciting expression of the person he is and the life he leads. But the overwhelming percentage of homes are furnished by women. What of the bachelor and his need for a place to call his own? Here's the answer. PLAYBOY's penthouse apartment, home for a sophisticated man of parts, a fit setting for his full life and a compliment to his guests of both sexes. Here a man, perhaps like you, can live in masculine elegance.

At first glance, it obviously looks like a hell of a fine place to live and love and

be merry, a place to relax in alone or to share for intimate hours with some lucky lass, a wonderful setting for big or small parties—in short, a bachelor's dream place. It is all these but it's more, too — thanks to the fact that it doesn't follow the conventional plan of separated rooms for various purposes. Instead, there are two basic areas, an active zone for fun and partying and a quiet zone for relaxation, sleep and such.

The living room, with its cozy shadow-box fireplace suggests a tête-à-tête on the couch — but it's not as inviting to a cordial crowd of fellow hi-fi enthusiasts. The electronic entertainment center, re-

65

Hefner inspecting bunnies for the new Chicago Playboy Club in 1960

Harvey Cox, William F. Buckley, and Hefner at the Chicago Mansion during the filming of the 1967 NBC television special *The Pursuit of Pleasure*

The thirty-seven-story Playboy Building on Chicago's Michigan Avenue with its trademark beacon in the late 1960s

"The Big Bunny,"
Hefner's black,
specially modified
DC-9 jet, in flight

Playboy meets the
counterculture in this
September 1970
cover, with a shapely
peace activist and a
smorgasbord of pieces
on controversial social
issues

The Playboy Mansion West, which Hefner purchased in 1971 and immediately began to overhaul.

Hefner and his girlfriends watch the Village People perform at *The Playboy Roller Disco and Pajama Party*, a 1979 ABC television special filmed at the mansion

Hefner at the Playmate of the Year reunion at *Playboy*'s twenty-fifth anniversary celebration in 1979

Dorothy Stratten with Hefner at the announcement that she had been chosen to be Playmate of the Year in April 1980

Hugh and Christie Hefner, twenty-nine, not long after he appointed her president of Playboy Enterprises, Inc., in 1982

Kimberly Conrad Hefner, Hugh Hefner, and their sons, Marston and Cooper, at the Playboy Mansion in the mid-1990s

Hefner and his "Party Posse" of platinum-haired girlfriends at the unveiling of his likeness at the Hollywood Wax Museum in 2001

A collection of body-painted girls poses with Hefner at his annual Halloween party in 2002

20

All in the Family

I n September 1995, *Playboy* readers encountered "Classic Kimberly," a text-and-photo story depicting Kimberly Conrad Hefner as the ideal modern woman: part loving wife, part devoted mother, and part erotic siren. Striking nude photos of the tall, voluptuous thirty-two-year-old with the light hair and penetrating blue eyes accompanied her extensive reflections on life as Mrs. Playboy. "Hef and the kids are what my life is all about, not the houses and money and all the people that come and go," she said. The scattering of children's toys, the jungle gym, and the swing set reminded everyone that while the Playboy Mansion was her husband's workplace, it had now become a family haven. Hollywood was a tough town, she admitted, but memories of smaller, more intimate communities with "a different mentality, with people helping people and family values" guided her. "Kimberly is all about family," the story concluded. "Hef, Marston and Cooper are blessed indeed."[1]

This article exemplified how *Playboy* trimmed its sails to capture the prevailing cultural winds in America during the last decade of the twentieth century. In the 1990s, a chastened liberalism from the 1960s sought reconciliation with the fervent conservatism of the 1980s.

407

The result was a swing toward the middle in American life that influenced politics, domestic life, and social values. Hugh Hefner's embrace of family beautifully reflected this powerful social impulse, but so too did the broad content of his magazine. *Playboy,* a cultural flagship par excellence, embodied much of the new moderation as it navigated into America's mainstream at the end of the century. Much like Bill Clinton, the dynamic, youthful president elected in 1992 who made this phrase a centerpiece of his campaign, Hefner and *Playboy* reached out to enrich the lives of "those who work hard and play by the rules."

I

In 1988, the publisher and marketing director of *Good Housekeeping* sat on a flight discussing their magazine and current social trends. The upcoming decade, they mused, a new turn: after the upheavals of the 1960s and 1970s, and the conservative yuppie materialism of the 1980s, the 1990s would see a return to family and home, yet in a fashion that encouraged more flexible career goals, a greater sense of social responsibility, and the pursuit of "quality" experiences and humane values. By 1990, *Good Housekeeping* had launched a national advertising campaign centered upon this "new traditionalism." Proclaiming a "decade of decency," it portrayed Americans as striving to "look for what is real, what is honest, what is quality, what is valued, what is important." *Family Circle* joined the parade. Its advertising campaign of 1992 pictured cultural rebels coming full circle. Photos of young women with diamond engagement rings through their noses, and of young men sporting long hair, tattoos, and leather jackets while holding a baby, appeared next to this slogan: "Lately, family values have been showing up in the most unlikely places."[2]

These venerable magazines captured something essential in the popular mood of fin de siècle America. Following the cultural earthquake of the Aquarian Age and the reactionary tsunami of the Reagan years, many Americans indeed yearned to combine hearth and home with personal liberation, social idealism with personal responsibility. Politically, this impulse helped sweep "New Democrat" Bill Clinton, with his embrace of *both* a welfare state safety net and an ethic of hard work and market competition, into the White House.

Socially and culturally, it influenced the shaping of what the sociolo-gist Alan Wolfe, in an insightful book of the same name, described as "one nation, after all." The vast majority of middle-class Americans, Wolfe argued persuasively, had come to embrace a worldview that lay between the extremes of 1960s revolution and 1980s reaction: "an insistence on a set of values capacious enough to be inclusive but demanding enough to uphold standards of personal responsibility." Weary of both hectoring fundamentalist preachers and victim-fixated leftists, the mass of citizens had forged a pragmatic, centrist, nonideo-logical, largely nonjudgmental consensus in the 1990s that sought to reconcile tradition and diversity, religious belief and tolerance, family and feminism, social obligation and personal fulfillment.[3]

A clear indicator of America's new traditionalism came in the 1994 release of *Sex in America,* a massive survey of sexual behavior and values by a University of Chicago research team. The exhaustive questioning of some thirty-four hundred subjects revealed that most Americans, while their erotic horizons had broadened, still led con-ventional sex lives. The vast majority of men and women lived happily in a sexual universe dominated by "monogamy, marriage, and the missionary position," as *Time* observed. Fidelity trumped adultery, monogamy trumped promiscuity, moderate rates of sexual inter-course trumped orgies and abstinence, and marriage trumped the single life. Most Americans, it seemed, had been jolted but not trans-formed by the sexual revolution of the 1960s and '70s, then sobered but not converted by the antisexual piety of the Moral Majority in the 1980s. While practicing and enjoying sex more than their pre-decessors, modern Americans nonetheless did so largely within the confines of traditional restraints.[4]

Hefner and his magazine reacted ambivalently to this evidence of American sexual conformity. "Our Puritan roots are deep," Hefner commented in *Time.* "We're fascinated by sex and afraid of it." In a private memo to *Playboy* editors, he contended that the survey reflected the conservative prejudices and AIDS hysteria of the Reagan era but, nonetheless, accepted the study's core finding that "we are conventional in our sex lives." *Playboy* sniffed that the survey demon-strated how many Americans "embrace conformity, the average. They run screaming from excess, from experimentation." But this impulse overlooked evidence of "just how rich and diverse [American] sex is." Hefner added, "it is the diversity of our sexual behavior that is the real message." This complex reaction suggested that Hefner and his magazine, like most Americans, were trying to combine respect for sexual tradition with enthusiasm for sexual innovation.[5]

In fact, Hefner's warm new family life appeared as a billboard for America's new traditionalism. The domestic aura of the Playboy Mansion, as many observers noted, embodied an image "in sync with the We Decade of the 1990s." In the words of *USA Today*, "the trend is marriage, monogamy, and moderation. Hefner was the symbol of sexual freedom of the baby boomers. Now that generation is hitting 40 and looking beyond transitory pleasures. Sexuality is not as important. Hefner is finally joining the ranks."[6]

Playboy, beginning its fifth decade of publication, responded to the spirit of the times. The magazine had become an institution. "*Playboy* has emerged as a survivor, rolling along with the changing social landscape," noted the *New York Daily News* in 1993. But survival depended on keen social and cultural instincts. Building both upon its liberationist past and its occasional conservative overtures during the previous decade—admittedly, more sullen than heartfelt—the magazine subtly positioned itself in the vanguard of the new traditionalism.[7]

Christie Hefner took the lead. She observed that as more of the sixties generation (and *Playboy* subscribers) became parents, much "focus in the 90s will be on the continuing evolution of the relationship between men and women in a family environment." The Playboy enterprise needed to become an "adult Disney" focused on "home-centered Baby Boomers," and her father's new lifestyle was a natural fit. "Obviously, the Mansion is no longer bachelor heaven," she wrote in a 1992 memo. "Here's a place where two people who've committed themselves to each other, and are raising a family, live. . . . We need some language that links personal dreams and individual freedom and social responsibility . . . to Hef's personal life."[8]

Michael Perlis, hired as *Playboy*'s new publisher in 1990, joined in. "I'm as mainstream as they come," he told a media journal. Perlis sought to distance *Playboy* even further from skin magazines and place it among upscale competitors such as *Esquire*, *Gentleman's Quarterly*, *Rolling Stone*, and *Sports Illustrated*. He helped lure Volkswagen back as an advertiser and sought new ads from Detroit automakers, men's fashion companies, and consumer electronics. *Inside Media* described his agenda succinctly: "In short, re-mainstream *Playboy*."[9]

A revised magazine gradually took shape. Many long-standing elements remained in the 1990s as the Playboy Forum continued to tackle controversial social issues and the Playboy Interview interrogated many of the most talked-about people in public life, including comedian Jerry Seinfeld, filmmaker Spike Lee, political guru James Carville, billionaire entrepreneur Bill Gates, sports star Shaquille O'Neal, and writer Salman Rushdie. The magazine continued annual features such as "Sex in Cinema," college football and basketball prognostications, and the Rock and Jazz poll, as well as the monthly Party Jokes and surveys of fashion and the newest consumer items. *Playboy's* fictional offerings upheld the high standards of the past, with stories by authors such as John Updike and Margaret Atwood, Jane Smiley and William Kennedy, Joyce Carol Oates and Jay McInerney. It explored the latest trends, such as the emergence of Generation X, the youthful cadre that was filled with "antiboomer rage," addicted to pop culture, and given to an intensely ironic, despairing view of modern life.[10]

Playboy's erotic features also maintained its familiar mixture of celebrity and the girl next door. Pictorials appeared on supermodels Cindy Crawford and Elle Macpherson, actresses Sharon Stone and Uma Thurman, and pop culture icons such as the spurious "Swedish Bikini Team" and "The Babes of Baywatch" from the popular television series. An unusually high number of Playmates in the 1990s went on to fame and fortune: Anna Nicole Smith (May 1992), Jenny McCarthy (October 1993), and Kelly Monaco (April 1997) among them. Most notably, Playmate Pamela Anderson, Miss February 1990, became the leading sex symbol of the age. She quickly seized a career in television and movies, had a much-publicized marriage with rocker Tommy Lee, and appeared on the cover of Hefner's magazine eight times by the end of the decade.

For all of these familiar sights, however, *Playboy* slowly sidled up to the new traditionalism in the 1990s. One of the first signals came in its political orientation. Early in the decade, Hefner's magazine maintained a muckraking, cynical liberalism rooted in the dissenting tradition of the 1960s and 1970s. It ran a regular monthly political column by the liberal analyst Robert Scheer, for example, and criticized Charles Keating's savings and loan scandal. Hefner's occasional political commentaries underscored *Playboy's* left-liberal stance. He condemned the Republican Party for its "conservative agenda based on repression, prohibition, and retribution," upheld the happy advance of sexual liberation, and insisted on the protection of personal freedom and the First Amendment.[11]

By mid-decade, however, *Playboy* became more apolitical. Its stringent, leftist critiques of mainstream America disappeared and pieces on public affairs increasingly were relegated to the Playboy Forum, while Scheer's column stopped running after the February 1996 issue. The magazine chose Leonard Maltin, a Disney movie expert and regular critic on *Entertainment Tonight,* as *Playboy's* film reviewer in September 1998 to replace the retiring Bruce Williamson. With Hefner settling down with marriage and children, the magazine also nixed "World of Playboy," a regular feature for years that had highlighted exuberant social activities at the mansion. Overall, *Playboy* increasingly returned to its 1950s roots as lifestyle, relationships, popular culture, and entertainment moved forward and crowded leftist politics into the wings.

Trendy, let's-enjoy-life topics such as computer technology preoccupied the magazine. With characteristic aplomb, *Playboy* covered the arrival of the DVD (digital versatile disc), which promised to sweep the field for video and computer use. It led readers through the dizzying maze of new gadgetry (cellular phones, portable fax machines, voice-mail machines, pagers, laptop computers with modems), the new electronic jargon (CD-ROM, DAT, Photo CD, VCR, Caller ID), and the breathtaking possibilities of the Internet.[12]

Typically, the magazine translated popular fascination with computers into the language of sex. Several nude pictorials of female enthusiasts surpassed the fantasies of any computer geek hunched over his PC keyboard in some dark cubbyhole. "The moment we asked the women of the Net to reveal themselves, sexy GIFs and JPEGs poured into our digital mailbox from around the world," noted "Women of the Internet" in April 1996. That same issue highlighted Miss April, Gillian Bonner, who had founded her own software development company and "hopes someday to create digital erotic fantasies that are more explicit and expansive."[13]

Playboy's neotraditionalism appeared even more clearly in its approach to relationships between men and women. In 1991, the magazine joined with Roper to conduct a survey of the modern male, his values, and his attitudes, and released the findings early the next year. The Playboy/Roper "Man Track" study indicated that men increasingly sought to combine traditional masculine impulses with an enhanced awareness of women's needs and family responsibilities. They wanted to be perceived as sensitive and caring, yet remained very interested in work, sports, and sex. They sought an armistice in the war between the sexes and better communication with women. In response, *Playboy* launched "Mantrack: A Guy's Guide to Changing Times," a new monthly feature that charted this new sensibility. The first installment examined the surprising extent of male-female agreement on issues such as date rape and sexual harassment. It then noted that men were caught between the demands of work and the desire for more leisure time, but most of them valued labor over play. It reported that "the man of the Nineties may be getting sensitive" as males from eighteen to forty-four ranked the top three criteria for a good relationship in the following order: love, a good sexual relationship, the ability to talk about feelings.[14]

Playboy worked to define modern maleness throughout the 1990s. A new monthly column by Asa Baber discussed the many quandaries facing men and defended them against feminist attacks. "Whenever you hear masculinity defined as innately deadly and brutal, remind yourself that most of us are truly good men," he said. "We love our families, work hard to protect them, cherish our children, and live honorably." The magazine offered advice on manly endeavors, including a tongue-in-cheek take on how to create an image as a rugged outdoor type. An impression of mountain biking expertise demanded familiarity with the technology of the sport but "don't mention anything about the bike's basket or its cute little bell." With caving, the macho poseur should casually note his fearless physical endurance and remember that "stalactites pierce your noggin; stalagmites look like the award they give the Proctologist of the Year."[15]

Playboy revised its traditional instruction to men about attracting and seducing women, now stressing the need for understanding the complex relationship between the sexes. Moreover, in a break with its past, much of this advice now came from women. Clarissa Pinkola Estés, author of the best-selling *Women Who Run with the Wolves: Myths and Stories of the Wild Woman Archetype,* gave pointers on how to understand essential feminine inclinations, desires, and values. Julie Rigby critiqued women's talk shows on daytime TV to give readers the inside scoop on how, in the world of Oprah and Sally Jessy, a man was "dressed down as a bad-smelling, bed-hogging, money-wasting, two-timing bozo who doesn't deserve to be trusted." In an essay on the rules of "postmodern romance," Tracey Pepper focused on practical guidelines for conversation, apparel, second dates, the goodnight kiss, and sexual etiquette. Some basic rules: "Have a car, don't live with your parents, don't get shitfaced, wear underwear, and don't have an ass that is smaller than your date's."[16]

The new traditionalist male inspired a huge advertising and marketing campaign for the magazine in the latter half of the 1990s. Taking the old slogan, "What Sort of Man Reads Playboy?" the ads presented modern *Playboy* readers as educated, computer-savvy, healthy and active, well groomed, and interested in leisure endeavors such as cars, vacations, good restaurants, stylish clothes, sports, travel, and romance. As one ad put it, "He works hard during the week and takes his weekend fun seriously." While the series portrayed men with attractive young women as they stood on a yacht or sat at a casino gambling table, they also stressed their commitment to relationships. "Last week he booked an entire restaurant for his girlfriend's birthday," said one. "He's a man who knows how to celebrate romance," said another. "For Valentine's Day he booked the executive suite and ordered roses and vintage champagne before he proposed."[17]

Thus Hefner and his magazine engaged the neotraditionalist male who had emerged from the maelstrom of Aquarian Age revolution and Reaganite reaction. Even more strikingly, *Playboy* jumped into the so-called "culture wars" of the 1990s as an enthusiastic combatant against political correctness. Just as it had opposed the moralistic pieties of the Religious Right, it now opposed the cultural pieties of the Radical Left with its unforgiving demands for PC behavior. *Playboy* and Hefner, drawing upon many of their long-standing principles, articulated a libertarian progressivism in the 1990s that stressed the greatest possible personal freedom within the boundaries of tradition.

II

Early in the decade, *Playboy* walked a treacherous political tightrope. On one side loomed the conservative forces of the Moral Majority, with whom Hefner and his magazine continued to battle. The Reverend Donald Wildmon, for example, an old enemy from the 1980s, persisted in conducting a campaign that persuaded companies such as ABC, Pepsi, Honda, and Chrysler to stop advertising in *Playboy*. Hefner, mocking the evangelical activist as the "American Ayatollah," sustained opposition through a direct-mail campaign to advertising executives, support for First Amendment pressure groups such as People for the American Way, and an eventual lawsuit against Wildmon.[18]

On the other side appeared the leftist forces of political correctness, who loathed *Playboy* for its attitude toward women. By the early 1990s, they had captured many college campuses, media centers, and even some corporate headquarters, creating a welter of elaborate regulations governing sexual actions and offensive speech against women and minorities. Hefner also battled this censorious spirit, condemning speech codes and sex regulations as repressive, even authoritarian, violations of free speech. The infamous "Sexual Offense Policy" of Antioch College, for instance, which mandated that every step of sexual intimacy—kissing, touching the breasts, touching the genitals, intercourse—required separate, clear verbal consent, at the risk of expulsion, drew his ire. "I see this whole politically correct phenomenon as a new form of Puritanism," he declared. "The notion that women are always victims and men are always predators and need 'guidelines' issued to them so they need to know how to behave on a date seems to me to be very much the opposite of liberation."[19]

Entering the emotional "culture wars" that exploded between these ideological opposites in the late 1980s and early 1990s, Hefner and *Playboy* sought a third way. This effort had a model. In the political realm, President Bill Clinton pursued a "New Democrat" strategy of "triangulation" that sought to synthesize elements of Democratic welfare-state regulation with Republican principles of free-market individualism while distancing itself from hard-liners in both camps. In the cultural realm, Hefner and his advisers shaped a similar strategy that sought a middle way between disciples of the Moral Majority and zealots of the Radical Left. The result was a cultural centrism that was equal parts progressive reform, libertarian freedom, and consumerist prosperity.[20]

A clear indicator of *Playboy*'s cultural triangulation appeared in its January 1992 special section devoted to analyzing the decade just under way. "Wake Up and Smell the Nineties" humorously pilloried the previous era as one of conservative greed and corruption. Cringing at "the appalling decade that just ended," it listed the assaults that came from Ronald Reagan, James Watt, federal deficits, supply-side economists, Ivan Boesky, junk bonds, T. Boone Pickens, and the Fox network (for good measure, it also threw in "nine Barbara Mandrell comebacks, 243 John Candy movies, and Regis Philbin"). Items to be thrown out in a "Nineties Garage Sale" included fur coats, granite desk accessories, and *The Art of the Deal,* by Donald Trump. "The nicest thing about the Nineties will be how little they resemble the Eighties," it concluded.[21]

Right next to this conservative-skewering piece sat "Navigating the Nineties: The P.C. Survival Guide," which turned in the opposite direction to mock the priggish pieties of cultural leftists. It instructed readers on the politically correct answers to a farcical multiple-choice quiz. On how to pick up Cindy Crawford in a bar: "I think together we could both reach our full sexual potential, but only if you think it's still possible for two people to celebrate their gender diversity without oppression or subsuming their individuality." On how to act at a men's movement gathering: "Cursing your father, weeping copiously around a campfire, admitting you have tiny genitals, and then beating your hairless chest." How to address females (all are correct): "a) women b) wimmin c) vagino-Americans." Political correctness, *Playboy* instructed, demanded an excruciating sensitivity to oppression and victimization. "Never allow yourself to enjoy the moment without being fully cognizant of the sorrow that lurks around the corner."[22]

The spirit of cultural triangulation guided the magazine throughout the 1990s. *Playboy* regularly attacked conservative extremism. It pilloried Pat Buchanan's run for the White House in 1996 as a religious crusade of paranoid reactionaries and denounced Pat Robertson for leading an army of evangelical Christians in an attempted takeover of the country's political institutions. It followed Timothy McVeigh's twisted ideological journey among right-wing fanatics that led him to the 1995 bombing of a federal building in Oklahoma City. It offered a stinging critique of the conservative campaign to teach creationism in schools, deeming it an anti-intellectual crusade of the ignorant and the malevolent.[23]

Just as frequently, *Playboy* rejected demands for politically correct attitudes and speech. In 1992, it challenged the multicultural bashing of Columbus as a "dead white male" on the five hundredth anniversary of the European discovery of America. A few years later, the magazine angrily disputed the racially charged verdict in the O. J. Simpson trial. *Playboy's* resistance to political correctness frequently focused on college campuses. It denounced the fad for speech codes, with their ban on "offensive" language, and mocked the broader movement to impose attitudes about gender, race, sexual orientation, and social class. In 1995 it surveyed college students' attitudes and portrayed "a fearful student body blindly marching under the banner of PC." College used to be a place where students freely exchanged ideas and learned to think for themselves, the magazine asserted, but now they "sought safety in numbers and regulations, and sidestepped confrontation and hurt feelings." A close examination of the rancorous debate over a proposed faculty-student sex code at the University of Virginia prompted the conclusion that schools had become training grounds where "the politically correct theorists of righteousness put ever-finer points on their blue pencils."[24]

Hefner and *Playboy* upheld libertarian principles. The magazine defended the right of artistic freedom in the uproar over the work of the controversial artist Robert Mapplethorpe in 1991. When an exhibit of his photographs, which featured graphic sexual images and irreligious themes, brought a prosecution for obscenity in Cincinnati, *Playboy* praised an innocent verdict for protecting constitutional rights: "In the end it wasn't easy. If freedom were easy, the whole world would be doing it." In an interview with the *Advocate,* a gay rights magazine, Hefner admitted to some bisexual experiences as part of the swinging scene at the Playboy Mansion in the 1970s and argued that homosexuality should not be stigmatized. In his words, "I don't think heterosexuality should preclude you from trying whatever's out there." This libertarian stress on protection of personal freedom, opposition to government regulation, and respect for the rights of minority groups defined an important part of the Playboy political perspective in the 1990s.[25]

Not surprisingly, one of *Playboy's* major culture-war battlefields appeared on the terrain of women's issues. On the one hand, the magazine continued fighting pro-censorship, antiporn feminists such as Catharine MacKinnon. "Radical feminism is her gospel, the law is her weapon," noted one piece, and she "won't stop until your libido is behind bars." A report on a 1993 feminist legal conference at the University of Chicago characterized it as a "hatefest" where participants wore buttons saying "So Many Men, So Little Ammunition," vied with one another to berate males as predators, abusers, and rapists, and, finally, celebrated Andrea Dworkin's concluding talk by angrily rushing the stage to shred into confetti Madonna's recently published book *Sex. Playboy* opposed "victimization" advocates, such as Susan Faludi in her best-selling book *Backlash: The Undeclared War Against American Women*. It argued that she twisted statistics, chose evidence selectively, and ignored the fact that many women's financial problems were not the result of a male plot but the product of the troubled economy of the 1980s. For *Playboy,* the danger lay in extremists on both sides—"self-appointed demagogues like Pat Buchanan and Susan Faludi."[26]

At the same time, *Playboy* made common cause with moderate advocates of women's rights. It endorsed what the author Christina Hoff Sommers termed "equity feminism." As opposed to "gender feminism," which sought to rescue female victims from male patriarchy, equity feminists stressed equal access to jobs, equality under the law, and nondiscriminatory treatment for women. This formed the heart of Hefner and *Playboy*'s agenda for women's rights in the 1990s. The magazine presented sympathetic interviews with equity feminists who criticized their radical sisters for adopting nineteenth-century attitudes about women's sexual victimization and moral superiority, using patriarchy to fuel a war between the sexes, creating a hysteria over date rape that made men wholly responsible for sexual encounters, and pressuring the courts to demonize men in divorce settlements. Warren Farrell, a disillusioned former board member of the New York chapter of NOW, wrote articles arguing that gender feminism distorted the male character and ignored the pressures facing men. It ran an editorial from the critic Katie Roiphe, who denounced radical feminists as neo-Victorians whose ideology "infantilizes women. . . . Let's not reinforce the images that oppress us, that label us victims, and deny our own agency and intelligence as strong and sensual, as autonomous, pleasure-seeking, sexual beings."[27]

In fact, Hefner established a relationship with two of the most influential, controversial figures in 1990s feminism. First, he effected a rapprochement with Betty Friedan, the pioneering figure who had inspired the postwar women's movement with *The Feminine Mystique* (1963) before breaking with radical gender feminists in the 1980s. *Playboy* successfully engaged her for the Playboy Interview in September 1992, where it praised her "moderate brand of feminism" for pursuing "equal opportunities for women, equal pay for equal work, better child care, better health care, and more." During the discussion, Friedan condemned making women into sex objects, but added, "I definitely don't think feminism needs to be equated with Puritanism and the denial of sexuality." She insisted on the sanctity of free speech, opposed MacKinnon-Dworkin style legislation against pornography, and opposed a patriarchy paradigm for the women's rights movement. "If men and women don't face these things [sexism, inequality] together, nothing will change," she argued. Friedan was adamant that the movement must rid itself of any antifamily bias, declaring, "You want a feminism that includes women who have children and want children because that's the majority of women." When such positions led many gender feminists to denounce her, she admitted, "I'm not going to lie. I'm very hurt when I feel trashed by the leaders of the organizations I helped to start."[28]

Around the same time, Friedan interviewed Hefner for her book *Fountain of Age* (1993), which attempted to combat the debilitating mystique of aging. Old age, she contended, needed to be seen as a unique stage of life with its own benefits and opportunities rather than as a decline from youth. Hefner, with his second marriage and family, seemed to embody "the new adventure of generativity" for older people. "I started looking for a more traditional one-to-one commitment instead of the Playboy lifestyle," he told her. "It took me a long time to get there, but what gives me the most satisfaction now, strangely enough, is my relationship with my wife and my kids." In 1995, Friedan even published an article in *Playboy* titled "Why Men Die Young." It encouraged men to disengage from the careerist rat race and embrace the new emotional opportunities offered by the revolution in women's rights. And women needed to give gender a rest. "Men will live longer when women are strong enough to realize that they don't need men as scapegoats anymore," Friedan concluded. "We need you, and you need us more than ever."[29]

The magazine also inked an alliance with Camille Paglia, the feminist enfant terrible who burst on the national scene in the early 1990s. With an incendiary style and a best-selling book, *Sexual Personae: Art and Decadence from Nefertiti to Emily Dickinson* (1990), she lambasted victimization feminism and upheld an ideal of female choice and independence. In a pair of articles and a Playboy Interview, this outspoken intellectual dropped bomb after rhetorical bomb on modern gender feminism. While supporting a social agenda of "full political, legal, and social equality for all women," Paglia derided speech-code advocates as "thought police" and described MacKinnon and Dworkin as "victim-mongers, ambulance chasers, atrocity addicts." *Playboy* centerfolds, she maintained, were "very sensuous and very physical," and gender feminists who opposed them simply failed to understand the nature of human sexuality. "Pornography is about lust, our animal reality that will never be fully tamed by love. Lust is elemental, aggressive, asocial," Paglia asserted. In a take-no-prisoners style, she condemned the modern women's movement for neglecting women who wanted to stay at home, abandoning children, and fomenting a destructive war between the sexes. When some activists branded her a traitor, Paglia blamed her ostracism on a feminist establishment that feared reform. "Feminism has betrayed women, alienated men, replaced dialogue with political correctness. PC feminism has boxed women in," she asserted. Paglia believed that women needed a bracing agenda of individual responsibility, appreciation for biological differences, tough-minded assertiveness, and vibrant sexuality. "Let's get rid of Infirmary Feminism, with its bedlam of bellyachers, anorexics, bulimics, depressives, rape victims, and incest survivors," she declared. "Feminism has become a catch-all vegetable drawer where bunches of clingy slob sisters can store their moldy neuroses."[30]

Playboy's 1990's erotic pictorials subtly promoted equity feminism and the new traditionalism. Their subjects increasingly appeared as liberated women for whom sex, family, and personal goals were equally important. As one Playmate confessed, "I used to be a wild and crazy girl. I'm not so wild and crazy anymore. I want to get married. I want to have a baby. Marriage comes first, I guess." Miss October 1995 was a serious student and model who saw no conflict between the two. "Meet the postmodern Playmate. She paints. She reads philosophy. She ponders the meaning of life, the meaning of sex, even the socio-politics of appearing in *Playboy*." A special pictorial titled "Domestic Bliss" presented housewives and mothers whose physical attractions rivaled their domestic devotion. "I think it's great that *Playboy* has decided to pay tribute to all the moms out there who aren't actresses, models, or famous—just women who are doing great jobs raising their families, yet haven't lost sight of their individuality, femininity, and sensuality," wrote one. As the magazine concluded, "A woman's place in the Nineties is wherever she wants it to be."[31]

As it negotiated the tricky terrain of male-female relationships in the 1990s, *Playboy* endorsed a modern code of sexual values that was liberated yet responsible, pleasure-seeking yet non-exploitative, vigorous yet playful, innovative yet respectful of tradition. Its ten-part "History of the Sexual Revolution" acclaimed the twentieth-century triumph of those who embraced sex as "a form of enthusiasm, a playground, a wellspring of intimacy, chuckles, and ecstasy," and celebrated the defeat of those who upheld a "single, sacred model of sex: that of intercourse within marriage." *Playboy* endorsed the advance of women's rights and tutored men on faux pas in language and behavior. It offered enlightened common sense: "If you don't want your love life to be a war, stop seeing women as conquests. Because if it comes to a war, you'll be the loser. History is not on your side. . . . And women's equality is the cause of every man who truly loves women."[32]

The ultimate expression of Hefner and *Playboy's* new tradition-alist sexual ethic may have appeared in an article titled "Sex Is Back." Sexual vitality had returned to American life following a long dry spell of restriction and AIDS fear in the age of Reagan, it asserted. The lesson drawn from this trend, however, marked a fascinating evolution in the nation's most famous proponent of erotic recreation.

> The thing of value is not the sex itself but all that sex carries with it: the companionship, the intimacy, the defeat of loneliness that otherwise gets us all.
>
> That old-fashioned kind of sex, the kind that is part of a private and mostly wonderful thing between two people, is what everyone I talked to . . . seemed desperately to want these days. Boyfriends are back. Girlfriends are back. Marriage is back. Even babies, nature's intended result of all this sex, are most emphatically back. . . . What we are looking for is love.

A man who had run the gamut of sexual adventure voiced the article's poignant conclusion. "I want to settle down. I tried to have open relationships, but I found . . . it was painful to all involved," he noted. "There was a kind of empty feeling there all along, like, Geez, this is fun but what am I going to do when I'm forty-five with no family and I'm just a lecherous old asshole?"[33]

Hefner's public statements reinforced *Playboy*'s independent progressivism. Throughout the 1990s, he denounced both the rigid moralism of fundamentalist conservatives and the antisexual bent of political correctness as "a new form of Prohibition." In a special 1996 editorial, he maintained that both "Victorian repression and colonialism" were disappearing while global communication and trade were increasing. In this new world, the American dream held forth great possibilities: "the dream of personal, political, and economic freedom. It is the dream this magazine was founded upon."[34]

As they advocated a third way between conservatism and politically correct liberalism, Hefner and *Playboy* made common cause with President Bill Clinton in the 1990s. When his sexual escapades ignited controversy, he became a cause célèbre in the magazine. During the 1992 election, when rumors of sexual peccadilloes were swirling, *Playboy* advised him to acknowledge his sexual vitality, point to other presidents who had strayed such as Franklin Roosevelt and John Kennedy, and say, "I've lived a full-blooded life. So far as I know, no one got hurt and I was always careful to use a condom, and I urge others, when the need calls, to do the same." A few years later, it praised Clinton as a kind of middle-class everyman who of all presidents was "the most like you and me." When the Monica Lewinsky scandal exploded, the magazine scoffed at the feverish publicity surrounding it, but chastised Clinton for his reckless indiscretion in conducting the affair. Hefner rushed to defend "The Playboy President," as he termed him in a special May 1998 editorial. Against the backdrop of a revised presidential seal that featured the rabbit head logo, the publisher defended Clinton as a symbol of sexual freedom against the "puritan mob" out to get him. Widespread public support for the president, he argued, suggested "we have at last come of age. We do not expect our leaders to be the stuff of *McGuffey's Readers*." As Hefner concluded, "We are human. We are sexual. Now let's get on with life."[35]

In no small way, *Playboy*'s articulation of the new traditionalism and its appeals to the moderate mainstream was eased by the financial stabilization of Playboy Enterprises, Inc. After nearly going under in the 1980s, the company, under the leadership of Christie Hefner, slowly rebuilt itself on solid, if less expansive, ground during the following decade.

III

In September 1988, two months after his engagement to Kimberly Conrad, Hugh Hefner stepped down as chairman and chief executive of Playboy Enterprises, Inc. Although he planned to stay involved in "major strategic decisions," as he termed it, Christie Hefner would assume control of the company. She had his full confidence, the publisher stressed, because of her successful direction of "a restructuring program that has resulted in an overall return to profitability."[36]

A year later, Christie Hefner made another big change. She announced that PEI would leave its ten-floor abode in the Playboy Building on Michigan Avenue, where it had resided for the past twenty years. The new, smaller headquarters in a Lake Shore Drive office building was unveiled at an open house in January 1990. "The move is not simply a face-lift for the company," Christie said. "It reflects our new direction." But the shift to a less expensive site also saved millions of dollars in yearly expenses. It indicated the new downsized, focused, mainstreaming orientation coming to the fore in Hefner's company.[37]

The younger Hefner had spent much of the 1980s struggling to recover from the financial debacle of the casino crashes early in the decade as she cut unprofitable activities, eliminated debt, and stockpiled cash. Now she was determined to move the company into the black in the 1990s. Slowly but surely, PEI reestablished its financial stability over the new decade as Christie, with her father's encouragement, refocused the enterprise on entertainment and communications. "We've spent a lot of time straightening out where the company ought to be," she declared. "But my becoming CEO marks the coming of a new era—an era of growth."[38]

Christie moved on several fronts. She brought on board a new management team, hiring Michael Perlis, from Rodale Press, as publisher, James Spanfeller of *Newsweek* as associate publisher and head of marketing, Steve Cohen as chief of communications and promotions, and Chiat/Day/Mojo as a new advertising agency. They tried to refocus the Playboy appeal for a broader, mainstream audience. According to the company's new catchphrase, the Playboy product was "quality fun for grown-ups."[39]

The new master plan focused PEI's energies into four areas: publishing (*Playboy* magazine and other smaller projects), entertainment (video and television), product marketing (licensing deals), and catalog sales. This array of products and creations, the company hoped, would promote a modern Playboy lifestyle associated with tasteful "consumer sexiness." In Christie's words, it was "sexy but not sexually explicit." With regard to expansion, PEI would acquire only bargain-price properties and seek investment partners to share the financial burden.[40]

This overall approach inspired PEI to purchase the *duPont Registry,* a guide for buying and selling elite cars; Sarah Coventry, a company that featured inexpensive but fashionable jewelry and accessories; and the *Critics Choice* home video catalog. Searching for a successful formula to strengthen the Playboy Channel—it had been opposed by local fundamentalist groups, but also dropped by many subscribers when they discovered that explicit sex has been deleted from its erotic movies—a pay-per-view format was adopted. PEI also made a strong move into global markets with new foreign editions of *Playboy* and a wide variety of licensed products, videos, and pay-per-view. In order to take advantage of advancing telecommunications technology, the company expanded into electronic publishing and sales, opening a free Web site in 1994, a Cyber Club and online Playboy Store in 1997, and a partnership with K-Tel to create an online music store.[41]

Hugh Hefner provided bedrock support for his daughter as she labored to construct a sturdy business structure for the company. He placed great confidence in her business judgment and endorsed her strategy for focused, controlled diversification of PEI. "We have a wonderful partnership," he declared publicly. "Our views and values are just about identical." When pressed about who was really in charge, he claimed, "She's working for me. I'm the guy that owns the company." But he never rejected any of his daughter's projects and happily settled for monthly business updates from her.[42]

But the process of recovery was slow and difficult in the early 1990s. Publishing and television sectors lost money, while younger consumers remained a tough sell, since the magazine's average reader was a thirty-three-year-old, often married, with an above-average income. In 1993, PEI was forced to reduce overhead costs by eliminating 10 percent of its workforce. Around the same time, after only a few years on the job, publisher Michael Perlis left to take a position with Condé Nast Publications. PEI's fluctuating net income revealed its difficulties in achieving consistent gains and growth. It climbed into the black by 1991, but then things turned sour, with profits falling deeply into the red by 1994. At mid-decade, the company appeared to be stagnating.[43]

In the latter half of the 1990s, however, PEI's financial picture brightened. It teamed up with a consortium of Greek investors to build a $40 million casino on the isle of Rhodes and purchased Spice Entertainment, a cluster of adult television channels, for $95 million, giving it a monopoly on the adult pay-per-view TV market. It also reached out to women, establishing female-oriented Web sites for marketing, pushing a women's apparel line with the rabbit logo, and developing cable programs that featured couples acting out fantasies. Money came in, with PEI posting profits from 1995 to 1999.[44]

Overall, PEI found a measure of financial success, albeit on a smaller and more restricted scale, by the end of the decade. Thus a fin de siècle stability characterized the company, the magazine, and the founder as they made peace with neotraditionalist America. Hugh Hefner seemed the picture of contentment. Freed of economic worry and savoring the secure position of his enterprise, he enjoyed a warm domestic life with a beautiful young wife and two adorable sons. A long magazine piece summed up his late-life transformation: "Happily married and settled right down, he seems to be in the vanguard of another new morality which seeks to shore up home and family against the vagaries of the millennium." Upon reaching age seventy, Hefner seemed to be watching the movie of his life come to its final reel with the kind of romantic ending he treasured.[45]

But appearances deceived. In December 1997, the very time when the laudatory magazine article appeared, the secure, comfortable world he had created over the last decade crumbled. Distraught and thrown off stride, an aging Mr. Playboy was forced to reinvent himself a final time.

21

Back in the Game

On December 31, 1997, Hugh Hefner hosted his traditional New Year's Eve party at the Playboy Mansion for several hundred friends, celebrities, and other guests. But things didn't go as planned. Quite unexpectedly—the tables had already been set with nameplates positioned at the head table for the host and his wife—the publisher appeared alone at his own gala. Guests were told that Kimberly Hefner was ill with the flu. In truth, however, she had decided at the last moment to go to Hawaii with their two children. As the attendees watched, the embarrassed *Playboy* publisher walked from table to table and greeted guests with a stiff smile. The usual merrymaking occurred, but a palpable sense of tension colored the atmosphere.[1]

A few weeks later, the Hefners publicly aired their private problems. On January 20, 1998, they announced a trial separation, citing "separate interests" and stressing that they remained devoted to their two children, Marston, seven, and Cooper, six, who would live with their mother in a house adjoining the Playboy Mansion that Hefner had purchased two years earlier. Both parties held out hope for reconciliation. Kimberly mused, "Maybe we will be able to recapture what we lost," and Hefner added, "Sometimes you don't know how important a thing is to you until it isn't there."[2]

Fate, it seemed, had intervened. Back in 1989, a visiting journalist had described the newlyweds as living in a fantasy world where the young wife served as her older husband's "magic talisman," warding off attacks of age and fading charm. It seemed too good to be true, and the writer warned, "Perhaps reality will one day intrude upon this fantastic existence." Indeed, within a few years reality triumphed over fantasy. The legendary lothario, who had embraced the traditional pleasures of marriage and family, suddenly found his life in disarray. The centrifugal force of coming full circle to a more orthodox lifestyle flung Hefner out of his comfortable cocoon of security at age seventy-one. He was devastated.[3]

I

By the mid-1990s, regulars at the Playboy Mansion noticed subtle signs of trouble. Kimberly often failed to attend the weekend screenings of movies or, if she did, frequently got up and left. At the weekly buffet dinners, Hefner sat at the head table flanked by his old friends while his wife sat at a round table off to the side in a bay window, surrounded by a bevy of her companions. When Hefner kissed his wife publicly, it was usually on the forehead. Kimberly increasingly appeared ill at ease or distracted, while her husband seemed dispirited. In 1995, Dick and Anne Stewart, who had moved away to Phoenix, inquired about the tension in a letter. "Are you two lovers still getting along?" they wrote. "I heard word of a spat or two. Mustn't let it faze you as the road to paradise is full of chuck-holes."[4]

Problems had been brewing since early in the decade. For the first few years of marriage, the relationship had flourished, but after the birth of their second son the couple had begun drifting apart over issues of incompatibility and conflicting interests. Kimberly, especially, grew unhappy with the marriage and her life at the mansion. While adamantly refusing to discuss the reasons for the marital breakup, she has dropped hints about the causes of her discontent.[5]

Her husband's rigid schedule seems to have been one source of unhappiness. Hefner had established a routine at the mansion over the previous twenty years that remained nearly impervious to change: showing movies with buffets and guests on Friday, Saturday, and Sunday evenings; dinner and a movie with male friends on Monday evening's "Manly Night"; cards with his old Chicago cronies on Wednesday evenings; and an assortment of games and activities at other scheduled times. Kimberly began to find this structure oppressive, telling one interviewer not long after the separation, "It was the *same thing* every night for ten years. Sometimes I wanted for us not to have plans. Once in a while, it would've been nice for him to say, 'Let's just call and tell everyone not to come on Friday night and have a quiet dinner together and go to a piano bar or something.'" An active young woman, she liked going to bed at a reasonable hour, getting up early to work out and engage in various pursuits. Hefner, a creature of habit, liked to stay home, enjoy his friends in a dependably arranged setting, and watch old movies. As Mark Saginor, Hefner's close friend, explained, "Kimberly wanted to do more things outside the Mansion grounds, and Hef has never been one to leave his property—it's his personal Shangri-La. That's the major problem."[6]

Kimberly, a private person, also grew weary of living in the fishbowl atmosphere of the Playboy Mansion. As the mistress of this legendary establishment, every week she faced dozens of people who observed her every move. Most of the mansion regulars had known her husband for years, and while she became close friends with some of them, others indulged in court gossip, backbiting, and jockeying for position that left her feeling vulnerable and uncomfortable. "People really watch. When we were going through our downswing—all marriages go through ups and downs, and we've been going through a down for the last year—people had a tendency to treat me differently," she said in 1994. Kimberly, especially with the arrival of children, desperately desired a family home marked by privacy and a few close friends. "Sometimes you want to go downstairs and have quiet, as opposed to running into 50 people," she complained to another journalist. Her frustration sometimes produced heavy-handed maneuvers, such as the sign posted prominently in the staff center near the kitchen: "When mama ain't happy, ain't nobody happy." Years later, Kimberly admitted that her inexperience probably led to missteps, and lamented the lack of a seasoned adviser. As her husband defended the social traditions of the mansion, friction mounted and she came to feel, with some bitterness, that he favored his friends over his family.[7]

Finally, Kimberly grew resentful about having to adapt completely to her husband's lifestyle. A vibrant young woman in her twenties and early thirties, an age when people tend to shape their adult identities, she chafed at the restraints imposed by Hefner's routine. "The truth of it became how I fit into *his* life. And I was lonely," she said, before comparing herself to another young wife thwarted by tradition. "It was like Lady Di. She also married young to a famous man set in his ways. You think or hope, at least, that you can change him. But sometimes it's impossible." For her, it became an issue of power in the marriage. "Hef has had a lot of control over me. But I'm breaking away from that," she asserted at mid-decade. Ultimately, Kimberly found it difficult to shape a viable identity within the parameters of the life, the home, and the activities established by her celebrity husband.[8]

Hefner viewed the growing marital discord in an entirely different light. Initially confounded by his young wife's increasing unhappiness, he struggled to understand it before gradually becoming exasperated and defensive. As Kimberly's complaints mounted, he came to believe that she harbored deep-seated emotional insecurities that led her to resent having to stand in his shadow. She was beset by "low self-esteem," in his estimation, which led her to begrudge the attention he received. "No matter what I did, she had some resentment of me," he contended. "Her actions would say, 'Look at me! Look at me!'" Hefner also concluded that his wife suffered from postpartum depression after the birth of their second child, which reinforced her insecurity and nourished a kind of paranoia. When she entered a room during a mansion social event, he observed, she immediately suspected that people conversing at a table were talking critically about her.[9]

He felt aggrieved by Kimberly's pressure to alter his weekly activities. "Before the marriage, one of the things I told her was 'I don't want my life to change.' She agreed, and then exactly the opposite happened," he complained later. He found her continuous goading to cancel movie nights, thin out the social events, and prune the guest list to be tremendously irritating since these features had contributed greatly to his happiness for many years. Hefner believed that they should be able to have *both* family closeness and the routine of friends, movies, and parties that he had come to cherish. He also began to see a power struggle emerging in the relationship. As he said of her demands, *"That* isn't love. That isn't even wanting to spend time with a person. That's a *power play.* The reality is, I wouldn't be spending time with her anyway. I'd be alone. She would be busy doing her own things."[10]

Emotional incompatibility became an issue for Hefner. Romantic, sentimental, and affectionate, he found his wife, as she settled into the marriage, to be reserved, even aloof. An emotional chasm opened between them. In love with the *idea* of marriage, children, and domestic contentment, the publisher overlooked very real problems and could not understand his wife's growing impatience. He became distraught when she quit having sex with him by the mid-1990s, but even then he was willing to soldier on. The separation was her idea, he stressed, and insisted that "the primary reason the marriage failed" was that she was not suited to it.[11]

Finally, a truly toxic factor poisoned the relationship for Hefner. Not long after the birth of their second son, his wife had an affair with a mansion security guard. When he confronted her after observing some suspicious behavior, she confessed immediately and agreed to end the tryst. But another one followed, he asserts. Rumors of Kimberly's infidelities ran rampant among mansion regulars and staff although, of course, they were never talked about openly. Hefner, who insists that he remained faithful throughout the marriage, was devastated. While sensitive to the irony of the situation—the playboy who had clipped his own wings, only to be cuckolded by his mate—he felt a sense of betrayal that dredged up bitter memories of Millie's affair many years earlier before his first marriage. In an attempt to repair their frayed marriage, the couple sought marital counseling on and off for several years but with little success.[12]

In the summer of 1995, a move toward dissolution came when Hefner purchased the house adjoining the Playboy Mansion—it was a smaller version of the legendary residence—as a sanctuary for Kimberly. The abode facilitated a kind of pseudo-separation. She spent increasing amounts of time there, and with unresolved issues festering, the marriage continued to decay. By the summer of 1997 the situation had grown acute as Kimberly pulled away both physically and emotionally and her husband went through cycles of despair, anger, and fear for the future. When the final break came with the debacle at the 1997 New Year's Eve party, it was almost a relief for all concerned.[13]

Emotionally bruised by the ordeal, Hefner retreated to his old belief that marriage is the death of romance. His experience with Kimberly reaffirmed that the promise of matrimony was greater than the actuality. "What I didn't foresee was how much, when you fall in love, you project your own needs and desires onto the other person," he mused. "You see what you want to see." When the romantic attachment begins to wither, the partners take each other for granted, he concluded, and when children arrive, passion turns into parenting.[14]

While relieved that the tension finally broke, the separation nonetheless left Hefner upset, uncertain, and unconfident. Close friends were concerned. Dick and Anne Stewart described him as unhappy and at loose ends. Mark Saginor put it more colorfully. "He was squashed like a june bug. . . . He couldn't move. He was in the bushes. He runs like a whipped puppy whenever she crooks a finger or bats an eyelash." Hefner admitted his heartache, telling an interviewer, "We've all been there. We've all had our punches in the gut." Even years later, he declared, "She put me through Hell." But he tried to retain his characteristic optimism. Not long after the separation, he characterized it as "more a new beginning than an ending" and claimed—with some irony, since he had said the same thing when he married Kimberly— that F. Scott Fitzgerald's famous quote—"there are no second acts in American lives"—needed revision.[15]

But for a man whose self-image had always been wrapped up with his attraction to women, advancing age posed a grave fear. As he pondered the future, he was haunted by a comment from a close friend, who had observed that as he got older, attractive young women had a way of looking right through him. Hefner feared that he had become similarly transparent. But the publisher quickly recovered his confidence, and within a few weeks of the separation he was spotted at several trendy Los Angeles clubs, dancing and nuzzling with a number of beautiful young women. A short time later, he began dating several Playmates—Carrie Stevens, Jamie Ferrell, and Jaime Bergman. "It's nice to discover that you're still a babe magnet in your 70s and the action has been incredible," he wrote John Dante in May 1998. "It's a whole new world out there—and age isn't even a consideration."[16]

Gradually, *Playboy* began to publicize its publisher's regenerated bachelorhood. A December 1998 article observed, "After a decade of devoted family life, the legendary Mansion madness is back, replete with Playmates prowling the grounds." "The World of Playboy" returned with images of an exuberant Hefner in the company of attractive, buxom young women. "Do these photos look like Hef is suffering from separation anxiety? Since his marital status changed, he has been stepping out again for retro Rat Pack nights of cocktails, swing dancing, and healthy blondes," said one caption. A *Playboy* Christmas cartoon showed a smiling Hefner with his arm around several unclad young beauties as a perplexed Santa Claus asked, "No, seriously. What could you possibly want?"[17]

A pharmaceutical advancement aided Hefner's rebirth as a party animal. In April 1998, on his seventy-second birthday, the publisher was introduced to Viagra, and after celebrating in the grotto Jacuzzi with four young women, he never looked back. "I'd say that it is as close as anyone can imagine to the fountain of youth," he enthused. "It's really a recreational drug that takes all the uncertainty out of the moment. . . . There's nothing physical holding you back." In his zeal, Hefner titled one of his scrapbook volumes "Viva Viagra." Over the next year, he also spruced up his physical presence by having cosmetic neck surgery and by jettisoning the thick aviator glasses he had sported over much of the previous decade.[18]

Rejuvenated both emotionally and physically, Hefner embraced his liberated life with gusto. By the late summer of 1998 he had entered into a relationship with several young women who moved into the mansion as his girlfriends. The "Brande, Sandy, and Mandy" period began as he dated aspiring actress Brande Roderick, and then met a pair of twins, Sandy and Mandy Bentley, at a club. When the sisters disappeared that first evening, he hired a private investigator, who chased them down, one in Las Vegas and the other near Chicago. A friend of the twins, Jessica Paisley, often joined the group. For the next two years, Hefner club-hopped around Los Angeles with his bevy of girlfriends, occasionally meeting close friends such as Alison Reynolds and Joel Berliner.[19]

Hefner delighted in his new life as a man about town. He eagerly soaked up the adulation of young men and women alike at trendy nightclubs such as Barfly, Garden of Eden, Snatch, Las Palmas, the Opium Den, and Bliss. Journalists could be snide. "When Hef, a living, breathing remnant of the Rat Pack era, walked into the club there was a collective gasp," wrote one. "The scene was pure Austin

Powers—Hef was hermetically unsealed and absolutely swinging, baby!" Hefner happily ignored the condescension. With his "Party Posse" in tow, he cracked jokes about being a "babe magnet" and about his girlfriends' platinum locks: "Picasso had his blue period. I'm in my blonde period." When skeptics scoffed at his multiple girlfriends, Hefner shrugged. "There's a bonding here, a romantic connection in which we do what we do together and have a wonderful time," he said. "It's just not politically correct." Surviving a marital crack-up to reenter the social scene, he joyfully discovered "a whole new generation has grown up and was waiting for me to come out and play."[20]

Within a couple of years, the girlfriend scene at the mansion shifted. In May 2000 Brande Roderick moved out to take a full-time television role, and a short time later, Sandy Bentley became mired in a sex-and-money scandal. Unbeknownst to Hefner, she was consorting with Mark Yagalla, a young, unscrupulous hedge fund manager in Las Vegas who showered her with over $6 million in gifts before an FBI investigation led to his arrest for misappropriation of investors' funds. When controversy erupted and Yagalla headed to jail, a disenchanted Hefner asked both Bentleys and Paisley to leave.[21]

A new phase began when Tina Jordan hooked up with Hefner in the late summer of 2000. A buxom blonde with a small daughter, she met the publisher at a mansion pool party and they hit it off immediately. Soon she moved in and became the publisher's primary girlfriend. A new constellation of girlfriends gathered around her with the arrival of Buffy Tyler, Katie Lohmann, Tiffany Holliday, Stephanie Heinrich, Cathi O'Malley, and several others. When Jordan departed in 2002, Holly Madison, who had arrived the year before, came to the fore as Hefner's chief girlfriend. By 2003, yet another platinum "Hef Troop" was in place that included Bridget Marquardt, Zoe Gregory-Paul, Cristal Camden, Sheila Levell, Renee Sloan, and Izabella Kasprzyk. As had been the case since the late 1990s, Hefner's female companions were given a yearly allowance for their appearances in support of the publisher and *Playboy,* provided an expense account for clothing, and given a curfew.[22]

Hefner viewed this kaleidoscopic girlfriend scene as a restorative replay of the 1970s. Delighted that young women still found him attractive, he enjoyed their favors as a soothing balm after the protracted pain of his failed marriage. He saw no reason for commitment.

This exciting, unorthodox new life was not only "fulfilling beyond words," as he put it later, but more genuine and authentic in terms of his own nature. "In the 1990s, with the family, I was trying to live the way I had been taught," he explained. "The way I'm living now is who I really am." Hefner felt young again, and the physical benefits were considerable. Fortified with Viagra, the septuagenarian publisher enjoyed regular sessions of group sex. "He's a wonderful lover, regardless of his age," Madison told the press. "You don't spend fifty years being Mr. Playboy and not learn a few things."[23]

The rejuvenated social scene at the Playboy Mansion elicited much commentary. The picture of seven platinum blondes in their twenties being squired and serviced by a seventysomething Hefner aroused divergent opinions, as did the rush of young celebrities to attend Mr. Playboy's celebrated parties. Some saw it as an embarrassing case of postmodern irony. "He is Unfrozen Caveman Swinger, cryogenically preserved since the 70s," wrote David Plotz in *Slate*. But many found the publisher's resurgent life to be fascinatingly retro cool. "The Playboy bunny has been reenergized, and Hef's house is hopping again," noted *Harper's Bazaar* in a special 1999 story. "Publicists are dialing like crazy to get their clients into parties at the Playboy Mansion, which is the hot list to be on once again." *Vanity Fair* awarded Hefner a place in its "1999 Hall of Fame." A two-page photo by Annie Leibovitz showed Hefner and two girlfriends sprawled on his oversized bed while two others stood behind embracing. He was "presiding anew over the pagan splendors of his pleasure palace," the caption noted.[24]

Hefner relished the attention. "It's like discovering Elvis is alive and well and living in your supermarket," he joked. "There is a younger generation that relates to me, to *Playboy* and the Mansion, the swinging Sixties and Seventies. They are excited that they might be able to revisit a time they missed." People could think what they wanted. Emerging from the ruins of his collapsed marriage with a renewed commitment to the Playboy lifestyle, he was thrilled to preside over a revitalized scene at the mansion.[25]

The public regeneration that characterized Hefner's personal life after his marriage ended also marked his company and magazine. Facing equally trying circumstances as they left the 1990s, they made strides toward reviving the Playboy brand. In the new century, it would appear more vibrant than it had in a quarter century.

II

In late 2003, Hefner and *Playboy* launched a lengthy celebration of the magazine's fiftieth anniversary. A voluminous "Collector's Edition" issue appeared on the heels of a national advertising campaign that touted it as "The Magazine That Changed America." On November 30, Hefner hosted a television special on the A&E Network. Cohosted by Drew Carey and Jenny McCarthy, the show took place at the mansion and featured comedy and musical acts to entertain hundreds of guests. Film footage and images from *Playboy's* half century of history spiced this homage to Hefner, and Ray Bradbury got off the line of the evening. Describing how the magazine's nude photos usually drew attention from its excellent array of articles, he quipped that most people "couldn't see the forest for the tease."[26]

The fiftieth anniversary celebration triggered an outpouring of commentary on Hefner and *Playboy's* impact on American life. Newspapers, magazines, television stations, and web journals throughout the United States tried to make sense, often at some length, of Mr. Playboy and his publication's influence on modern values. Assessments differed widely.[27]

Social conservatives, religious fundamentalists, and feminists denounced the *Playboy* influence. The conservative pundit Cal Thomas complained that Hefner's magazine had helped shape "a culture without rules, without signposts, and without meaning," while Connie Schultz, a feminist columnist, mocked *Playboy* for idealizing freakish females with "a waist the size of a bottle cap and breasts that would keep them afloat in a tsunami." Townhall.com, an influential conservative Web site, blamed Hefner for a "demoralization of the culture" that vulgarized male-female relationships and corroded "an appreciation of intimacy through trust, the basis for every good relationship and every good marriage." *Christianity Today* concluded that Hefner had won a "hollow victory" by mainstreaming pornography. *Playboy's* warped view of women, relationships, and sex, it argued, had created a moral "toxic dump" that would take many decades to clean up.[28]

But most critics offered a more respectful reading of the *Playboy* legacy. Enthusiastically in some cases, grudgingly in others, most commentators granted Hefner's success in liberating America's sexual values from outdated, stultifying moral restraints. "*Playboy* has arguably become one of the half-dozen or so most influential magazines in publishing history," claimed the *Los Angeles Times*, while *Newsday* described the magazine as "the unofficial publication of the sexual revolution." The *Times Magazine* in London placed it among a trio of influences—along with the Pill and rock 'n' roll—that most shaped the changing sexual standards of postwar America. A long essay by Richard Corliss in *Time* contended that Hefner's magazine not only initiated several generations of men into the mysteries of sex, but also influenced the shape of American society. "That's because Hefner had more than a business model; he had a philosophy," wrote Corliss. "He may have been after something more enlightened than an empire. A republic. Playboy's Republic." Even the conservative *National Review* admitted that *Playboy* had advanced the cause of freedom. "A society that allows *Playboy* is not a society that allows women to be stoned to death for adultery," argued Catherine Seipp. "Human nature being what it is, we're probably stuck with either burkas or naked balloon breasts forever. I know which I prefer."[29]

Yet many observers agreed that *Playboy*'s contemporary impact had declined. The sexual revolution had been won long ago and erotic material was available everywhere. Noted one thoughtful critic of the fiftieth anniversary, "It's impossible not to hear the baleful strumming of nostalgia in the ceremonies. The Mansion may be swinging, but it's full of ghosts . . . there's no question that its brightest glory days are behind it." Even Corliss, while fondly praising *Playboy*, admitted that the long-running magazine had tended to "calcify." After a half century, *Playboy* had become an institution, with all the positive and negative baggage that entailed.[30]

While still stylish and intelligent, the magazine appeared predictable, almost staid, in the new century. With the end of Hefner's marriage, the 1990s new traditionalist orientation faded as it attempted to recapture the spirit of an earlier age. The Playmate of the Month remained, of course, as did the erotic pictorials on attractive actresses, entertainers, and celebrities. The Playboy Interview, Playboy Forum, and Playboy Advisor retained their traditional place in the format, along with the charting of new movies, CDs, fashion trends, and leisure fads. New monthly features—"Wired" and "Living Online"— gave a nod to the Internet age. Overall, *Playboy* arrived every month like a visit from an old friend—pleasant, agreeable, unsurprising. It offered a well-written, visually pleasing mélange of pieces on lifestyle, popular culture, and sex for middle-class, middle-aged men. The good life had become the comfortable life.

But a cohort of brash new challengers had arisen to under-cut *Playboy's* appeal and audience. By the late 1990s, the so-called "lad books" had burst onto the magazine scene with great fanfare. Publications such as *Maxim, FHM,* and *Stuff* appealed to younger male readers with an irreverent, ironic, intentionally unsophisticated sensibility. Sporting a beer-and-babes attitude, they discussed "How to Score at Funerals," the finer points of chugging contests at parties, and frat-boy enjoyment of life's animal pleasures. They also featured erotic pictorials of scantily clad young women, although actual nudity seldom appeared. As one critic snorted, the lad books provided "short lessons in ways to become even more shallow than you already are." Despite their crudities, these Generation X magazines grew increasingly popu-lar with the coveted eighteen-to-thirty-four male readers.[31]

Hefner felt the heat. Although sales still placed *Playboy* first among men's magazines—its average sales of 3.2 million per issue outdistanced the lad books by quite a bit—he grew increasingly con-cerned that his aged publication had lost touch with youth values. Supported by many staffers, he pondered an overhaul of the maga-zine. "Quite frankly, what I'm looking for is contemporary version of what *Playboy* meant in the 60s and 70s," he noted. As this crisis of confidence mounted, Arthur Kretchmer, the editorial director of *Playboy* since the early 1970s, decided to retire. He also had grown weary of trying to stay conversant with current trends, and sensed the growing pressure for change. "At this point in my life, I don't care who Weezer is," he confessed. "And that's not fair to Weezer, that's not fair to *Playboy* magazine." Choosing Kretchmer's replacement offered an opportunity to recharge the publication.[32]

Hefner responded by stealing into the challenger's encamp-ment and carrying off a willing hostage. In September 2002, Hefner approved the hiring of James Kaminsky, an editor at *Maxim,* as the new editorial director of *Playboy,* and charged him with updating the magazine. Hefner wanted a revived *Playboy* that would be more lifestyle and less explicit sexuality: "A fresh eye. Better nonfiction. More must-read pieces. More humor." He coveted some of the lad books' irreverence without being "intentionally dumb." For youthful readers, Hefner hoped, *Playboy* would provide "the next step after *Maxim.* It's martinis instead of beer."[33]

Kaminsky promised to revise the magazine while respecting its traditions. *Playboy,* he told the press, had first fired his imagination for journalism as an adolescent and now he hoped to recapture its greatness. "My goal is to take this great editorial package that has worked for 50 years and move it forward for a new generation," he noted. Describing himself as a "change agent," he explained that he wanted to make *Playboy* relevant to "a 25-year-old guy who's never seen this magazine before and may be picking it up for the first time." Kaminsky agreed that the ultimate goal was to capture lad-book readers when they became a bit older, more sophisticated, and more serious.[34]

Despite his endorsement of "an evolution, not a revolution," Kaminsky moved quickly—brutally, many insiders thought—to change the magazine. He elbowed Kretchmer aside during the transition period, and by mid-2003 his influence became evident. *Playboy* began to feature shorter, snappier articles with more photographs, sidebars, boxes, and charts. A growing number of humor pieces appeared, as did younger writers doing investigative pieces on topics such as the murder of rap star Jam Master Jay, the SARS virus, and Wal-Mart's labor practices. New sections on video games and electronics appeared, along with hipper male fashion spreads with skateboarders and surfers as models.

The results were greeted skeptically. A humor magazine satirized *Playboy*'s overhaul: (1) "Scaling back from boobies, boobies, boobies, to just boobies, boobies"; (2) "Aggressively referring to men as 'guys'"; (3) "Stealing *New Yorker* staff writer Seymour Hersh, having him write comprehensive piece on history of the thong"; (4) "Finding out what's in FHM, doing that." The twenty-five-year-old art director at the *Chicago Tribune*—one of Kaminsky's targeted readers—examined the reworked *Playboy* and scoffed that its much-publicized changes amounted to "nothing more than a fresh coat of paint" covering "a schizophrenic desire to appeal to multiple generations." The resulting hodgepodge reeked of "Old Man Poser. . . . *Playboy*'s half stuck in the last century, while trying to get some footing in this one."[35]

The Kaminsky experiment soon collapsed. While his moves had freshened the *Playboy* appeal, his heavy-handed managerial style alienated almost everyone working at the magazine. There had been signs of trouble from the beginning. The day before Kaminsky started, according to Hefner, a dismayed Kretchmer, who had been meeting with the new director, called to say, "We have made a terrible mistake. This guy is a nut case." Indeed, Kaminsky's bulldozer-style maneuvers produced numerous personality clashes that left him widely loathed. "He couldn't get along with anybody," Hefner concluded. Low morale turned to outright rebellion as the new editor disparaged longtime staffers as out of touch or incompetent, and fired many of them. Those who remained saw his "Maximizing" of *Playboy* as taking it downmarket, and Hefner grew concerned that *Playboy* "was losing its soul." Finally, the publisher dismissed Kaminsky in April 2004 and replaced him with a trio of young in-house editors: Christopher Napolitano as the editorial director, with Lee Froehlich and Steve Randall as associate editors. With Hefner's backing, they continued the project of updating the venerable publication, but proceeded in a slower, more subtle fashion and sought to retain elements of *Playboy's* traditional sophistication.[36]

Thus *Playboy* struggled to define itself in the new century. No longer a trendsetter in shaping American values, it faced the problem of how to attract younger readers while retaining the loyalty of longtime ones. This proved a daunting task in an age when print readership was dropping, the Internet was expanding explosively, and advertisers were drawn to the new technology. Moreover, the magazine's message of pleasurable living and personal liberation no longer quickened the pulse, having become part of the common wisdom in modern America. Despite Hefner's hopes, the magazine would never again be the force it had been in the 1960s and 1970s. As even he admitted, it was fated to be a "loss leader" for PEI, a symbol of the Playboy lifestyle for the entertainment and licensing endeavors of the company.[37]

Playboy Enterprises, Inc., also faced fresh challenges in the new century. After enjoying steady, moderate profits throughout the 1990s, it encountered difficulties by decade's end. A December 2000 analysis in *Business Week* pointed to several problems: unprofitable forays into the Internet and television, declining stock prices, a perception among investors that *Playboy* had lost touch with younger consumers. An angry Christie Hefner retorted that the company's long-term, costly investments in online business and cable television would bear fruit shortly. Both disputants were partly right: while the company was losing money as the 2000s began, its strategy held out the possibility of recovery and future prosperity.[38]

Under the younger Hefner's leadership, PEI built its future on a two-part foundation: multimedia entertainment, and the strong licensing potential of the Playboy brand. The company had discovered the potential of the Internet early, launching Playboy.com as a platform for erotic material and e-commerce. Web sales of Playboy merchandise grew slowly and steadily, but the Internet audience for its mild entertainment fare remained small. PEI's forays into cable television were more profitable. From 1999 to 2001, it purchased several pay-TV channels of the Spice Network, which offered explicit sexual films. These deals undercut Playboy's long-standing reputation for fresh-scrubbed, innocent sexuality, but Hugh and Christie Hefner justified the purchase as a diversification of the company, much like Disney's creation of Touchstone Pictures to distribute its R-rated movies. Wall Street applauded the move as PEI began making money from the new acquisitions.[39]

By 2004, PEI was showing a profit. Hopes for the future rested with several new ventures: gaming, as in the recently opened Playboy Club complex in Las Vegas in partnership with the Palms, and in a casino project in Macau, recently described as "the vortex of Asia's resurgent gaming craze;" and Playboy U, a MySpace-type Internet social network. As technology and global markets lead PEI into the future, according to a recent assessment, the company's three divisions have clear goals: television and Internet projects aimed at a younger audience, *Playboy* targeting yuppie males, and licensed products projected toward women. PEI management remains optimistic that digital technology, global markets, licensing opportunities, and location-based entertainment hold the key to future growth and profit. Only time will tell.[40]

Midway through the first decade of the twenty-first century, the Playboy brand is hotter than it has been in years. At the same time, PEI remains a midsize communications and entertainment company with a trajectory of modest growth, while the value of its stock has remained fairly low and the rabbit's appeal seems mostly "retro cool" rather than genuinely vibrant in terms of contemporary influence. But whatever the future may hold, Hefner's position is secure. He has become a legend.[41]

III

On a typical Friday evening in March 2005, Hugh Hefner perched on a leather sofa at the front of his living room movie theater and faced a crowd of about one hundred friends who were settling back in chairs after an elegant buffet dinner. He began to read from carefully prepared, handwritten notes on the evening's film from the early 1930s. Engrossed in the lore of old movies, one of his great passions, Hefner related details about the making of the film, its star, Barbara Stanwyck, its producer, Darryl F. Zanuck, and its reception by the public and the critics. An uncut version of the movie had recently been discovered at the Library of Congress, he reported, and was being shown by special arrangement. As Hefner concluded his talk—"And now, from 1933, *Baby Face*"—and waved his hand for the projectionist to roll the film, the appreciative audience clapped.[42]

The Friday evening classic film has anchored the schedule of life at the Playboy Mansion since the early 1990s. On Saturday evenings, Hefner shows movies of 1930s–1950s vintage, while Sundays see screenings of just-released films, both attended by dozens of regular guests. The publisher plays gin rummy with a small group of old Chicago buddies on Wednesday evenings, and then goes out with his girlfriends to a restaurant and a club on Tuesdays and Thursdays. Perhaps Hefner's favorite evening comes on Monday's "Manly Night," when about a dozen male friends convene for dinner and an old movie. The group includes Keith Hefner, jazz trumpeter Ray Anthony, comedian Chuck McCann, actors Robert Culp and Johnny Crawford, producer Bill Shepard, documentary filmmaker Kevin Burns, producer-director Peter Vieira, entertainer Dick Stewart, and film historians Richard Bann, Ron Borst, and Mark Cantor (until their deaths a few years ago, singer Mel Tormé and actor-comedian Bob Ridgely also were members of the group). Male camaraderie rules the day as the old friends banter, argue about movies and music, and exchange good-natured insults. Even the big, glitzy mansion parties occur on a clockwork schedule: New Year's Eve, Casablanca Night/Hefner's birthday in April, Midsummer Night's Dream in early August, and Halloween in late October. Hefner's life unfolds according to a carefully regulated routine, where several dozen friends in regular attendance create a pseudo-family atmosphere.

But this image of domestic contentment muffles the fact that Hefner has reemerged as a bigger public figure than at any time since his heyday in the 1960s and 1970s. When he ventured out to trendy Los Angeles clubs with a bevy of female companions after his separation, Generation Xers flocked to his table chanting, "You're the man! You're the god! You rule!" "He is the most famous man, with the most famous house, in the most famous neighborhood in the world. He has the most famous parties, with the most famous guests, and their fame is the source of his own," wrote *Rolling Stone* in 2000. "Famous for being famous among the famous."[43]

Confirmation of Hefner's legendary status has rolled in from every direction. He was inducted into the Magazine Hall of Fame on April 28, 1998, along with, ironically, Gloria Steinem. The following year brought a roast at the Friars Club in New York City and the year after that a special fete by the *Harvard Lampoon,* which dubbed him "Lampoon's Greatest Life Force in the History of the Universe." In the summer of 2005 the Discovery Channel chose Hefner as one of the "Hundred Greatest Americans." Public honors also came to the publisher in this period for his contribution of almost $1 million to the UCLA Archives and for an even larger gift to the USC School of Cinema for the preservation and restoration of old Hollywood films.[44]

Hefner's renewed cachet also inspired a spate of appearances in advertising campaigns. He was featured in a television ad for Motorola in 2000, and a magazine ad for Tanqueray gin the following year, in which two Playmates stared lustfully at a gin bottle ("Distinctive Since 1830") while Hefner, in his trademark smoking jacket ("Distinctive Since 1953"), gave them a look of mock admonishment. In 2003, he posed with blond triplets in a print ad for Ecko clothing, and then created a minor controversy in a television campaign for Carl's Jr. Preparing to take a bite out of a burger, he said, "People always ask me, hey Hef, do you have favorites? I tell them no, it's not like that . . . I love them all. It just depends on what I'm in the mood for." Then a voice-over completed the double entendre: "One of six five-dollar burgers at Carl's Jr. Because some guys don't like the same thing, night after night." Conservatives were outraged.[45]

Hefner became a sought-after figure for appearances in television series. From 2001 to 2005 he had cameo roles in the comedies *Just Shoot Me, The Bernie Mac Show,* and *Curb Your Enthusiasm,* as well as the dramas *Las Vegas,* with old friend James Caan, and *Entourage.* Popular musical artists also sought out the Playboy Mansion, making it a site for videos starring Justin Timberlake, Nelly, and Weezer.[46]

Hefner even raised some political hackles. At the 2000 Democratic Convention in Los Angeles, "Bunnygate" erupted when U.S. Congresswoman Loretta Sanchez scheduled a fund-raising event at the Playboy Mansion. The campaign of nominee Al Gore, keen to distance itself from *Playboy,* tried to force a change of venue. When Sanchez refused to alter the event, Gore managers took away her speaking spot at the upcoming convention. She finally relented and relocated the fund-raiser to Universal Studios, while Hefner berated the Democrats for "acting like a bunch of right-wing Republicans."[47]

The biggest sign of Hefner's resurgence, however, came with a hit television series. *The Girls Next Door* debuted in the fall of 2005 on the E! channel as a "reality show" depicting daily life at the Playboy Mansion through the eyes of the publisher's youthful girlfriends. After several of Hefner's blonde companions departed during an acrimonious split the previous year, he had settled into a relationship with three young women. With the show, they quickly emerged as television celebrities in their own right.[48]

Holly Madison had come to the mansion in 2001. After stints at college in Portland and Los Angeles, where she studied psychology and theater, she dropped out of school to gauge other opportunities. A Hefner friend saw her in a bikini contest—she was working for Hawaiian Tropic and at Hooters—and invited her to a mansion party where she met Hefner. At his bequest, she joined his group of girlfriends, and when Tina Jordan decided to leave in 2002, Madison became the publisher's "head girlfriend." They became devoted to one another, and by 2005 she was talking publicly about wanting marriage and children. More recently she has become an assistant photo editor for *Playboy* helping with Playmate shoots.[49]

Bridget Marquardt entered Hefner's orbit after earning a bachelor's degree in communications and public relations from Sacramento State, followed by a master's degree from the University of the Pacific. She had dreamed of being a Playmate, and first came to the mansion while doing a photo shoot for the millennial Playmate search in 1998, where she met Hefner and attended several parties. Following a brief marriage that ended in a friendly separation, she moved to Los Angeles in 2002 to pursue her *Playboy* dreams. Hefner asked her to go out with him and his female companions, and she moved into the mansion as a girlfriend. She became close friends with Madison and deferred to her housemate's romantic involvement with Hefner. Delighted at being part of the mansion's social whirl, she has pursued a career in broadcast journalism at UCLA and now hosts her own radio show.[50]

Kendra Wilkinson, the youngest of the trio, became one of Hefner's girlfriends in 2004 at age eighteen following a serendipitous chain of events. He was struck by her photograph as one of the "body-painted" girls for a mansion party, and made a point of meeting her at the festivities. The following week, he invited her to move into the mansion. Born and raised in San Diego, Wilkinson had been traumatized as a child when her father walked out on the family. She had run away as an adolescent, dropping out of school, abandoning her athletic talent in soccer and softball, and spiraling downward into street-kid destitution, suicidal gestures, and drug dependency. After hitting rock bottom at age seventeen, she dropped the drug habit, returned home, and went back to school to earn her high school degree. She was working as a dental assistant when the Playboy opportunity appeared unexpectedly, and she came to the mansion as a dyed-in-the-wool sports fan with a strong attraction to the hip-hop culture. "Hef saved me," Wilkinson claims of this transformation in her life.[51]

The Girls Next Door, produced and directed by Kevin Burns, who had done a documentary film on Hefner in the 1990s, focuses on this trio of young women and their daily experiences at the Playboy Mansion. Hefner remains at the margins, making intermittent appearances as a fatherly (or grandfatherly) figure dispensing advice and support to his platinum trio. The show emphasizes two themes. First, it presents the activities of Holly, Bridget, and Kendra as a fantasy where the girls enjoy a pampered regimen of fun: planning a mystery-themed birthday party at the mansion, preparing elaborate costumes for the Midsummer Night's Dream Party, flying off to Las Vegas to help a friend celebrate her Playmate of the Year selection, enduring a grueling shoot for their first-ever *Playboy* pictorial, enjoying a ski trip on the slopes of Colorado, taking in the sights of Chicago and New York City on promotional trips. Second, it consistently plays the girlfriends' contrasting personalities against one another. Madison moves through the show as a grounded, cool, and calculating presence who is protective of Hefner and zealous in securing her position as mistress of the mansion. Marquardt, with her pink confection, bedroom and bubbly fascination with mysteries and the occult, offers an emotional, vulnerable disposition that alternates between bouts of girlish delight and tearful disappointment. Breezing through the various segments with a tomboy athleticism and brash, in-your-face sensibility, Wilkinson displays an instinctive comic touch that creates amusement from upending social convention Lucille Ball style.

By turns sexy and outlandish, human and slightly surreal, funny and sweet, the show presents a curiously compelling inside look at the world of the rich and famous. As ads for the show proclaim, "We call it a fantasy. They call it home."[52]

Equally striking, however, is the audience for *The Girls Next Door*. Network executives expected it to be predominantly male, so early promotional efforts focused on sex appeal: "We're about to take you into the lives and the bedrooms of three women who all call magazine mogul Hugh Hefner their boyfriend. . . . From the slumber parties upstairs to the washing of dirty laundry downstairs . . . we're about to get intimate." But surveys indicated that the audience was 70 percent female, and overwhelmingly in the fifteen-to-forty age range. Even more surprisingly, the show has garnered a positive response from many liberated women. Daphne Merkin, a prominent feminist critic, publicly confessed her "secret and somewhat worrying fascination with a retrograde show about the mindless adventures of three Barbies . . . [who are] positively antediluvian in their embrace of unliberated femininity" and "the ancient Sugar Daddy who funds their fun." Much comment and reaction suggests the show's twofold attraction for females.[53]

On the one hand, *The Girls Next Door* presents a retro appeal typical of the larger Playboy revival in the early 2000s. It offers a prefeminist fantasy of women being provided for, loved, and showcased by an elderly, wealthy gentleman. As Merkin has put it, the show updates the old "mutually accommodating (or mutually exploitive) fantasies of what men and women can expect from each other circa an idealized '50s prototype . . . a version of sexism that is benevolent rather than hostile." Women are idealized and protected, adored and sustained in return for being loyal, good-looking, and noncompetitive. This "Cinderella fantasy," Merkin suggests, has a secret, momentary appeal to even the most hardened feminist advocates of gender equality. "It's good fun," she notes, and "we all need time off from Hillary Clinton models of femaleness." Marquardt's fan mail seems to confirm this as correspondents identify with "normal girls leading a fantasy lifestyle." Young females (or some part of them) are enticed by the parties, the clothes, the manicures, the shopping, the mansion, the butlers, and the traveling. "Hef's life has always been a fantasy for men; this is the first time it's become a fantasy for women," says Marquardt.[54]

On the other hand, *The Girls Next Door,* in its own unorthodox fashion, makes a statement of female empowerment. These three young women make decisions and struggle to shape their own lives. "I think that they're strong women . . . making choices and taking advantage of the opportunities that come their way," says one female lawyer of the show's stars. From Holly's determined effort to claim her place as Hefner's mate and work for the magazine, to Bridget's quest for a Playmate pictorial and a future in the communications field, to Kendra's demonstrations of athletic prowess and prudent purchase of her own condominium, the trio pursue their own dreams as Hefner stands in the wings, affectionately providing encouragement and funds but never issuing directives. Merkin finds intriguing the notion that the show is "strangely empowering in that it's the women who are in charge." Again, Marquardt's fan letters support this point. Women tell her that the show has inspired them to work out, go to college, follow their dreams, and pursue their own versions of happiness.[55]

The female fascination with the show confirms just how much Hefner and the Playboy ethos have entered the mainstream after a half century of endeavor. It suggests that the publisher, as his long and controversial career enters its final stage, has emerged victorious in a decades-long cultural war. As George Will, the respected conservative columnist, told Hefner when he arrived at the mansion for an interview in 2003, "Congratulations. You won." But the statement encloses larger questions. What exactly has Hefner won and what is the nature of his triumph?[56]

EPILOGUE

Playboy Nation

The black, leather-bound volumes sit silently in specially constructed oak bookcases that line the rooms and hallways of the Playboy Mansion's third floor. Numbering over eighteen hundred, and still growing, these "scrapbooks" memorialize Hugh Hefner's life. Begun when he was a teenager in Chicago, they detail nearly everything that has happened to, and been said about, the *Playboy* publisher over the last seven decades. Kevin Burns, a close friend, once quipped that the publisher "documents his life more than the Library of Congress," while an associate joked, "Hef is living his life posthumously."

But the very existence of this huge archive reveals something essential about its subject. Hefner, clearly, has been preoccupied with his own life since adolescence. He views it, along with *Playboy*, as his greatest creation. In fact, however, the two cannot be separated. "The magazine has always been an extension of my own dreams and fantasies," Hefner admits. Like intertwined strands of cultural DNA, both *Playboy* and the life of its creator embody some of the deepest desires, values, and impulses at work in modern America over the last half century.[1]

447

From the beginning, Hefner's personal experiences provided the stuff of his public career. The private man relentlessly pursued his dream of "personal, political, and economic freedom" and viewed his pursuit of fun not as immature, something critics often charged, but as a happy embodiment of childhood optimism in a cynical world. He challenged traditional institutions such as marriage, the family, and religion because he had experienced them as impediments, not aids, to individual happiness. In Hefner's calculus, the crucial component was individual desire, not social expectation. He saw his own life as demonstrating that "you don't have to live by somebody else's rules."[2]

This ethic of self-fulfillment came from deep roots in the publisher's complex personality. Hefner has exercised a compulsive control over every aspect of his existence since gaining a measure of independence when *Playboy* began to flourish. From diet to dress to hobbies to social schedules, the Hefner way became one of orderly, unchanging habits. Creating and superintending his living environment down to the tiniest detail, he ignored usual conventions of night and day, work and play, custom and convention when they conflicted with his wishes. He became an efficiency expert focused on his own desire.

But alongside the obsessive controller stood the romantic. Optimistic about human nature and deeply sentimental about human relations, Hefner often quoted the playwright Dennis Potter to describe his approach to the world: "I want to find a place where the words to the songs are true." This romanticism inspired a serial wooing of young women—it was always about emotional connection as much as sex—because the relationships allowed him to experience over and over the ecstasy of youthful romance. This romanticism flowered with equal lushness in his lifelong love affair with the movies. The glamour, adventure, and drama of those larger-than-life images on the silver screen captured his imagination as a boy and never relinquished their hold. Hefner's favorite films provide glimpses into his private world. He sees himself as Jimmy Stewart in *Mr. Smith Goes to Washington* (1939), the lonely, noble hero taking on the system in the interests of justice and liberty. He identifies with Henry Fonda in *The Male Animal* (1942), the slightly nerdy protagonist who wins the girl from a popular athlete, takes on the establishment, and triumphs over the forces of censorship. He idolizes Humphrey Bogart in *Casablanca* (1942), the proprietor of a famous establishment where "everybody comes to Rick's place" yet he never sits down with the customers, an apparent cynic who finally appears as a sentimental idealist who gives up everything for the woman he loves. For Hefner, film is a romantic metaphor for life as he would like it to be.[3]

Thus the *Playboy* publisher, much like Jay Gatsby, F. Scott Fitzgerald's memorable character, is a man of internal ambiguities: a controlling figure who yearns for romance and connection, an organizer of revelry who remains a step outside the ongoing party, a sweet-natured and generous man who is nonetheless determined to pursue his own gratification. Never a devil-may-care hedonist, Hefner has sought his pleasure systematically, doggedly, even frantically in certain periods. This compulsion to have fun, in many ways, represents a modern inversion of the old Protestant ethic with its compulsion to work. Mr. Playboy is a serious sybarite, a sentimental seducer, a disciplined devotee of desire.

But what makes Hefner significant, not just interesting, is that his personal dreams and desires have resonated so broadly. For over fifty years, he has touched something basic in the modern psyche while coming to represent the quintessential American individual. The Hefnerian creed of personal liberation, sexual freedom, and material abundance, articulated in the pages of *Playboy* and promoted in his highly publicized lifestyle, has played a leading role in reshaping modern social values. But only sporadically has Hefner's victory been a case of rousing triumph and acclaim. While periodically enjoying a popular cachet, particularly from the late 1950s through the mid-1970s, Hefner also suffered a repeated battering from many traditionalists and certain feminists over the decades. Yet his resiliency and passionate, indefatigable advocacy kept him afloat. Hefner and his *Playboy* worldview stood on the forward edge of history and persevered as the American mainstream gradually, often unwittingly, digested and assimilated its key tenets. As a commentary recently conceded, "After 50 years of *Playboy*, we all live in Hef's world."[4]

Mr. Playboy has prevailed because of victories—usually slow-gathering in pace and complex in nature—in four key campaigns. First, and most obviously, Hefner survives as the most enduring symbol of the sexual revolution and deserves considerable credit for the sexual openness that has become so characteristic of modern America. It is hard to remember that even in the 1960s married characters in television sitcoms slept in twin beds and were forced to keep one foot on the floor at all times while kissing or embracing. Now premarital sex appears as the norm, sexual advice books sit on the best-seller list, most repressive statutes forbidding sexual activity have been repealed, and sexual frankness in entertainment has become ubiquitous. An American president's misadventures with oral sex inspire graphic newspaper headlines and unembarrassed anatomical disquisitions. Wal-Mart sells *The Girls Next Door* DVDs and Hooters offers a children's menu. In a popular newspaper cartoon, two teenage boys peruse a *Playboy* as one of them whispers, "Pssst, the new 'Abercrombie and Fitch' Catalog's hidden inside.'" Clearly, the forces of sexual restraint have been pushed into enclaves of dissent. Probably more than any other individual, Hefner has been responsible for making relaxed, candid attitudes about sexuality standard fare in modern America.[5]

Playboy offered a stylish model for the modern male in this new world of sexual openness. Under Hefner's leadership, the magazine promoted a sophisticated approach for postwar men that occasionally veered into crassness, but more often urged a standard of urbane, gentlemanly behavior. It is easy, of course, to make fun of the *Playboy* sensibility as a shallow sexual ploy, as in this imagined 1950s conversation: "Female Acquaintance, lowering the volume on Miles Davis' 'Kind of Blue': 'So are you personally persuaded by the critique of Christian ethics that Nietzsche posits in *The Genealogy of Morals?* And by the way, isn't that a lithograph of 'Les Demoiselles d'Avignon' next to your hi-fi?' Swinging Playboy Bachelor: 'Um, can you take off your bra now?'" But Hefner broke the mold by abandoning the old rough-and-ready, outdoorsman ideal for, in Camille Paglia's words, "a new kind of man, a European-style man interested in fine stereo equipment, good wine, sophisticated conversation, and progressive ideas." The *Playboy* style, almost always, urged men to treat the women in their lives sensitively and not shabbily. As the *Atlantic* observed, while men's magazines such as *Maxim* and *FHM* encourage "a lot of boyish grab-assing," Hefner and *Playboy* always presented a more mature, cosmopolitan vision: "finding a nifty chick and sharing the good life with her."[6]

Second, Hefner has been a crucial influence on the ascendancy of consumer culture over the last half of the twentieth century. After a period of pent-up demand during the Great Depression and World

War II, which had slowed the surge of consumer capitalism begun in the early 1900s, Americans stood poised to resume their love affair with material affluence. Hefner captured this yearning. From the outset, he portrayed abundance, as well as relaxed sexual standards, as keys to the good life idealized in his magazine. Readers concurred, and so did the broader society. Enjoyment of a cornucopia of commodities became synonymous with the American Way of Life, and *Playboy* provided monthly guidance on stylish consumption. Readers "enjoyed imagining themselves as the Hefner male: the man who wanted fine wines, chic cars, and smart clothes to go with his beautiful women," noted *Time* magazine. "*Playboy* was the ultimate consumer magazine: the editorial and the advertising were one."[7]

Third, and most controversially, Hefner and his magazine have played a vital, if complicated, role in the feminist revolution that has transformed modern gender relations. On one hand, *Playboy* overturned traditional standards by promoting women's freedom to enjoy sex and advocating economic opportunity, social equality, and abortion rights for them. Hefner's dream of "personal, political, and economic freedom" became part and parcel of the great crusade for women's rights that marched on to legal, social, and cultural triumph. On the other hand, radical gender feminists attacked *Playboy* for degrading women as sexual objects, portraying it as a bastion of male patriarchy and oppression. They branded Hefner as the enemy.

From this tangle of competing claims, the publisher and his magazine emerged as neither heroes nor goats. Instead, they served as a catalyst for the feminist revolution, raising hackles even as they reflected the evolution of mainstream attitudes. Like most Americans, men as well as women, Hefner and *Playboy* came to support the equity feminist movement for equal rights and opportunities while retaining traditional notions of differences between the sexes and rejecting gender warfare. In this dominant consensus by the end of the twentieth century, Hefner, ironically, became a symbol of women's freedom to make choices, whether that meant pursuing a business career or displaying their bodily charms, or both. Standing amid the maelstrom of debate over feminism for much of his career, he proved to be a pivotal figure in the mainstream movement's triumph.

Hefner's important contributions to sexual liberation, consumerism, and women's rights ultimately created his fourth, and largest, role of all. From a long-term historical perspective, he stands as a major architect of America's dominant culture of self-fulfillment during the twentieth century, a value system that replaced the Victorian code of self-control from an earlier age. His significance stands on par with such major figures as Henry Ford and Walt Disney. The popular automobile maker, of course, pioneered a compelling ideology of consumer values, abundance, and self-fulfillment in the early 1900s and transported it into mainstream culture in his legendary Model T. In the middle decades of the century, the beloved Hollywood filmmaker, television pioneer, and theme park creator built upon this foundation by utilizing elements of magic, sentiment, leisure, and consumer marketing to help forge the American Way of Life. Over the last few decades of the twentieth century, Hefner brought the trend to a culmination. More than any other single figure in this latter era, he has symbolized the combination of sexual liberation, material affluence, and personal self-fulfillment that characterizes the modern American dream.[8]

But utopias, of course, do not exist in real life. Thus Hefner's legacy—the modern America he did so much to shape—has created perils as well as promises. The sexual revolution, for instance, has relieved individuals from the burden of excessive repression and ventilated the stifling atmosphere of guilt and shame that long surrounded this powerful human urge. But it also has opened the floodgates, in ways that the *Playboy* publisher never intended, for a great wave of crude sexual imagery and moneymaking exploitation that too often cheapened what it meant to honor. Moreover, sexual freedom fighters such as Hefner tend to see only the beautiful, creative, civilizing capacities of Eros. In trying to chain this animal impulse with reason, they overlook its dark capacities for inciting jealousy and lust, rage and rejection, power and possession. Ironically, as Henry Louis Gates Jr. has observed, sexual liberationists often appear as innocents who advance "the truly bizarre notion that sex could ever be rendered safe, anodyne, biodegradable, predictable, guilt-free, domesticated, wholesome." Thus the sexual revolution, like any successful insurrection, has opened new possibilities for destruction as well as liberation.[9]

Similarly, the triumph of modern consumer culture has created mixed blessings. Realizing what Franklin Roosevelt famously termed "freedom from want," the great mass of Americans since the 1950s have come to enjoy a standard of living that is the envy of the world.

But this mantle of materialism has been suffocating as well as sustaining. Ranging from the environmental left to the religious right, with many variants in between, critics have pointed out that the worship of economic abundance has encouraged a shallow materialism that tends to measure everything—personal happiness, political achievement, social relations, educational goals, religious or philosophical standards—according to a yardstick of unfettered consumption. Not only has this encouraged a worldview too often marked by spiritual sterility and social greed, but it has undermined the work ethic and made the notion of meaningful, creative, productive labor nearly obsolete. Modern consumer culture confirms that in human affairs, new forms of liberation almost always create new forms of imprisonment.

Troubling issues also persist with regard to women's rights. Equity feminism represents the best in the American dream and Hefner and *Playboy* deserve applause for helping to liberate females for sexual pleasure, advocating their full legal and political rights, and staunchly insisting that gender equality must not erase gender differences. At the same time, and primarily due to the torrent of sexual images that inundate modern life, both Hefner and modern America have walked a precarious line regarding humane, democratic principles. Men seeing women (and vice versa) as sex objects is perfectly natural and in accordance with the biological imperatives of the species. But seeing women *only* as sexual creatures diminishes them and threatens to undermine a larger creed of human equality. With its unwavering emphasis on female nudity and sexual appeal, *Playboy* tends to slight other valuable dimensions of female life and experience in favor of the erotic. Hefner and the American mainstream, while reasonably rejecting overheated claims of male sexual tyranny and gender warfare, must be careful to recognize the full humanity of women.

Most broadly, America's modern culture of self-fulfillment has delivered mixed blessings. Unquestionably, the crusade to satisfy emotional and physical desires has brought enrichment and joy to individual lives previously restrained in the iron cage of self-denial. Yet it also has created new difficulties. In a society of playboys and playgirls, for instance, family attachment, the basis of any society, has grown more difficult as gratification-seeking individuals find the sacrifices of marriage and childrearing increasingly hard to justify. Even more importantly, the culture of self-fulfillment molded by

Playboy and others has made it difficult to conceive of the public good. Maintaining commitments beyond the self, for many modern citizens, has become an alien, if not incomprehensible, notion.

Ultimately, however, the allure of fantasy has bound Hefner and the *Playboy* nation to the possibilities, rather than the problems, of modern self-fulfillment. The publisher's dreams of intense romantic love, material abundance, a perfectly ordered life, and complete sexual and emotional gratification have defined the pursuit of happiness in modern America. "The fantasy in *Playboy* became a reality for society," Hefner has observed. Indeed, since World War II citizens of the world's most abundant nation increasingly envisioned their society as one of endless possibilities. The *Playboy* ethos has become mainstream, with its powerful current pulling along many, perhaps most, modern Americans toward a common destination: self-fulfillment in every way imaginable in a world with few restraints. This has become the essence of the modern American dream "where the dark fields of the republic rolled on under the night," in Fitzgerald's phrase. For good or ill—and the publisher would be the first to agree that each individual must be free to judge—we do live in a *Playboy* world in modern America. And what we think of Hugh Hefner is what we think of us.[10]

NOTES

Several matters in the notes require brief explanation. HH stands for Hugh Hefner. HP refers to the Hefner Papers, a very large collection of documents, interview transcripts, company memos, and various historical papers housed at the Playboy Mansion in Los Angeles. HS, followed by a volume number, indicates the Hefner Scrapbooks, some eighteen hundred bound, numbered volumes that Hefner has been accumulating since his adolescence, also housed in the Playboy Mansion. HHIA indicates Hugh Hefner interview with the author, a battery of nearly forty hours of interviews that I conducted with Mr. Hefner from 2003 to 2007. PP stands for Playboy Papers, a collection of the company's historical records and documents on file at the headquarters of Playboy Enterprises, Inc., in Chicago. Unless otherwise indicated, the numerous interviews with friends, family, and associates of Hefner refer to tapes or transcripts that are part of the HP holdings.

My analysis of Hugh Hefner, *Playboy,* and their impact on modern American values has relied upon a very large body of scholarly literature on topics such as consumerism, the sexual revolution, postwar American culture, the 1960s, the age of Reagan, and so on. Because of space limitations, the notes indicate only the most salient secondary sources that have been consulted.

INTRODUCTION. THE BOY NEXT DOOR

1. HHIA, Nov. 6, 2003.
2. *The Pursuit of Pleasure,* NBC, May 8, 1967, videotape, HP.
3. Daniel Boorstin, *The Image: A Guide to Pseudo-Events in America* (New York, 1973 [1961]), 37, 240.

CHAPTER 1. A BOY AT PLAY

1. HH, quoted in Malcolm Boyd, *My Fellow Americans* (New York, 1970), 38; Glenn Hefner file, HH Memo titled "Dad Dies," August 3, 1992, 6; and HHIA, November 6, 2003.
2. Grace C. Hefner, *Remembering: A Collection of Memories* (privately printed, 1994), 37–38, 10–11, 28–29, 13, 33.
3. Ibid., 18, 31–32, 37–38.
4. Ibid., 35–39, 45–46, 52, 54–56, and HS, Vol. 25.

5. Grace Hefner, *Remembering*, 59–62.

6. Ibid., 62, 65–67, and HS, Vol. 25.

7. HS, Vol. 25; Keith Hefner interview with Lynch/Frost Productions, April 19, 1991, 3; and HHIA, Nov. 6, 2003.

8. Keith Hefner interview with Hal Higdon, 1967; HS, Vol. 25; HHIA, Nov. 6, 2003.

9. Grace, quoted in Boyd, *My Fellow Americans*, 39, and Jim Brophy, "Other Voices," March 18, 1986, 1.

10. HS, Vols. 25 and 26, and Jim Brophy, "Other Voices," March 18, 1986, 1.

11. HS, Vols. 25 and 26.

12. Ibid.

13. HS, Vol. 26.

14. HHIA, Nov. 6, 2003.

15. Ibid.; Keith Hefner interview with Hal Higdon, 1967; and Mildred Williams Gunn interview, Jan. 1987, Side 5, 9.

16. Grace Hefner file, undated interview, 3; Grace, quoted in Boyd, *My Fellow Americans*, 40; and Grace Hefner interview, Dec. 1986.

17. Keith Hefner interview with Leo Janos, 1987, 58–60; Keith Hefner interview with Lynch/Frost Productions, 1; Keith Hefner interview with Hal Higdon, 1967.

18. A vast literature on Victorian culture and its traditions includes Daniel Walker Howe, ed., *Victorian America* (Philadelphia, 1976); Karen Halttunen, *Confidence Men and Painted Women: A Study of Middle-Class Culture in America, 1830–1870* (New Haven, 1982); and John F. Kasson, *Rudeness and Civility: Manners in Nineteenth-Century America* (New York, 1990).

19. Salient works on cultural change in the early 1900s include Warren Susman, *Culture as History: The Transformation of American Culture in the Twentieth Century* (New York, 1984); T. J. Jackson Lears, "From Salvation to Self-Realization: Advertising and the Therapeutic Roots of the Consumer Culture, 1880–1930," in Jackson Lears and Richard Fox, eds., *The Culture of Consumption: Critical Essays in American History, 1880–1980* (New York, 1983); Lary May, *Screening Out the Past: The Birth of Mass Culture and the Motion Picture Industry* (Chicago, 1983); John Kasson, *Amusing the Million: Coney Island at the Turn of the Century* (New York, 1978); and Steven Watts, *The People's Tycoon: Henry Ford and the American Century* (New York, 2005).

20. HHIA, Nov. 6, 2003; Keith Hefner interview with Lynch/Frost Productions, 1; Keith Hefner interview with Leo Janos, 4–5; and Mildred Williams Gunn interview, Jan. 1987, Side 5, 10.

21. HHIA, Nov. 6, 2003, and Keith Hefner interview with Leo Janos, 1, 3, 5–6.

22. HHIA, Nov. 6, 2003; Grace Hefner interview, June 30, 1989, 4–5; "Other Voices: Keith Hefner," Keith Hefner file; Keith Hefner interview with Leo Janos, 4; and Grace Hefner interview, 1986, 29–30.

23. HHIA, Nov. 6, 2003; "Conversations of Hef and Keith on Sex and Repression," March 27, 1990, Keith Hefner file, 1–2; "Other Voices: Keith Hefner," Keith Hefner file.

24. Keith Hefner interview with Leo Janos, 1, 67; interview with Grace Hefner, HH, and Keith Hefner, 1986, Grace Hefner file, 26.

25. HHIA, Nov. 6, 2003; Keith Hefner interview with Leo Janos, 14; Grace Hefner interview, undated, 5; and HH, quoted in Marilyn Cole, "The Oldest Swinger in Town," *Times Magazine* (London), Nov. 1, 2003, 29.

26. HHIA, Nov. 6, 2003.

27. Keith Hefner interview with Lynch/Frost Productions, 5, and Keith Hefner interview with Leo Janos, 32, 28.

28. Grace Hefner interview, undated, 3; Grace Hefner interview, June 30, 1989, 14–15; and Grace Hefner, *Remembering*, 75.

29. Ann Hulbert, *Raising America: Experts, Parents, and a Century of Advice About Children* (New York, 2003), 5. See also Julia Grant, *Raising Baby by the Book: The Education of American Mothers* (New Haven, 1998).

30. See the following three articles by Steven L. Schlossman: "Perils of Populariza-tion: The Founding of *Parents' Magazine*," in Alice B. Smuts and John W. Hagen, eds., *History of Research in Child Development* (Monographs of the Society for Research in Child Development), Vol. 50 (1986), 65–67, 77; "The Formative Era in American Parent Education: Overview and Interpretation," in Ron Haskins and Diane Adams, eds., *Parent Education and Public Policy* (Norwood, NJ, 1983), 10–20, 25–32; and "Before Home Start: Notes Toward a History of Parent Educa-tion in America, 1897–1929," *Harvard Educational Review*, Aug. 1976, 452–465.

31. Undated letter from Grace to grade school teacher and 1934 letter to grade school teacher, both in HS, Vol. 25, and Grace Hefner interview, undated, 4.

32. Grace Hefner interview, undated, 6; Keith Hefner interview with Leo Janos, 30; Keith Hefner interview with Lynch/Frost Productions, 1; and Grace, quoted in Malcolm Boyd, *My Fellow Americans* (New York, 1970), 41.

33. HHIA, Nov. 6, 2003, and Keith Hefner interview with Leo Janos, 33–34, 62.

34. HH interview with the author, Nov. 6, 2003, and Grace, quoted in Malcolm Boyd, *My Fellow Americans* (New York, 1970), 43.

35. Court of the Fourth Judicial District of the State of Colorado, 1931, and District Attorney's Information Sheets, J. M. Hefner case, Carson County Clerk's Office, documents in HP; HHIA, Nov. 6, 2003. See also Grace Hefner interview, 1986, 38–39; Grace Hefner interview, June 30, 1989, 45, 47–48; and Keith Hefner inter-view with Leo Janos, 9.

36. HH letter to "Dear Folks," dated Sept. 26, 1948, HP; Mildred Williams Gunn interview, Jan. 1987, Side 5, 11; and HHIA, Nov. 6, 2003.

37. Mildred Williams Gunn interview, Jan. 1987, Tape 1, Side 1, 6, and Side 7, 1–2; Grace, quoted in Malcolm Boyd, *My Fellow Americans* (New York, 1970), 45; and Keith Hefner interview with Leo Janos, 21–22.

38. Grace, quoted in Malcolm Boyd, *My Fellow Americans*, 42–43; interview with Grace Hefner, HH, and Keith Hefner, 1986, Grace Hefner file, 21; *Remembering*, 74–75; and HS, Vol. 25.

39. Grace, quoted in *My Fellow Americans*, 42–43; HHIA, Nov. 6, 2003; Keith Hefner interview with Lynch/Frost Productions, 5; and "Other Voices: Keith Hefner," Keith Hefner file.

40. HHIA, Nov. 6, 2003, and HS, Vol. 25.

41. Ibid.

42. HHIA, Nov. 6 and Nov. 8, 2003.

43. HHIA, Nov. 6, 2003.

44. HS, Vols. 27, 29, and 1.

45. HS, Vols. 28 and 1, and Jim Brophy, "Other Voices," 2, 4.

46. HS, Vols. 5 and 3, and Jim Brophy, "Other Voices," 6.

47. HHIA, Nov. 6, 2003, and HS, Vol. 7.

48. HHIA, Nov. 6, 2003; Janie Sellers to HH, May 24, 1987, Janie Sellers file, HP; and HS, Vols. 4 and 7.

49. HS, Vol. 1, and HHIA, Nov. 6, 2003.

50. HS, Vol. 26; Jim Brophy, "Other Voices," 4, 3; HHIA, Nov. 6, 2003; and HS, Vol. 5.

51. HS, Vol. 1 and 4, and HHIA, Nov. 6, 2003.

52. HS, Vols. 26, 28, 30, and HHIA, Nov. 6, 2003.

53. "A Tragedy of Youth," *Life*, June 6, 1938; HHIA, Nov. 8, 2003; and Grace Hefner interview, 8–9.

54. HHIA, Nov. 6, 2003; Keith Hefner interview #85–58, 4–5; Grace Hefner interview, 6; and HS, Vol. 26. On the Petty Girls and Vargas Girls, see James R. Petersen, *The Century of Sex: Playboy's History of the Sexual Revolution, 1900–1999* (New York, 1999), 126, 167.

55. Jim Brophy, "Other Voices," 5; Janie Borson Sellers interview in Janie Sellers file; and HH cartoon dated Jan. 8, 1944, in HS, Vol. 7.

56. HHIA, Nov. 6 and Nov. 8, 2003.

CHAPTER 2. BOOT CAMP, COLLEGE, AND KINSEY

1. HS, Vol. 8, and HHIA, Nov. 8, 2003.

2. Mildred Williams Gunn interview, Jan. 1987, Side 5, 3–4, and HHIA, Nov. 8, 2003.

3. HHIA, Nov. 8, 2003, and Millie Rohrbach interview, Oct. 1989, Tape 1-B, 21–22.

4. HHIA, Nov. 8, 2003.

5. HS, Vol. 9.

6. HS, Vols. 9–11.

7. The letter is in HS, Vol. 11.

8. Ibid.; Keith Hefner interview with Leo Janos, 1987, 57; and HHIA, Nov. 8, 2003.

9. HS, Vols. 12–13.

10. HS, Vols. 14–24.

11. HHIA, Nov. 8, 2003, and HS, Vols. 14–24. The "Atomic Age" quote is in Vol. 22.

12. See the wartime letters from HH to Mildred Williams in the Millie Gunn file, HP.

13. HS, Vols. 12, 13, 9–11, and HHIA, Nov. 8, 2003.

14. HS, Vols. 31–34.

15. HS, Vols. 35–36, HHIA, Nov. 8, 2003.

16. HS, Vols. 36–38, and HHIA, Nov. 8, 2003.

17. HHIA, Nov. 8, 2003.

18. HS, Vol. 38, and HHIA, Nov. 8, 2003.

19. HS, Vol. 36, and HHIA, Nov. 8, 2003.

20. HS, Vol. 41, and HHIA, Nov. 8, 2003.

21. HS, Vol. 38, and Bob Preuss interview with Leo Janos, 1987.

22. HS, Vol. 43; Bob Preuss interview with Leo Janos, 1987; and HHIA, Nov. 8, 2003.

23. The play is contained in HS, Vol. 41.

24. HH letter to "Dear Folks," dated Oct 11, 1948, HP.

25. HS, Vol. 35, especially HH to Janie Borson Sellers, dated Aug. 5, 1946.

26. Mildred Williams Gunn interview, Jan. 1987, Tape 1, Side 1, 1–2, 18; Millie Rohrbach interview with Murray Fisher, Oct. 1989, 1–2; and HHIA, Nov. 8, 2003.

27. Mildred Williams Gunn interview, Jan. 1987, Side 1, 16–17, and Side 5, 15–16; HHIA, Nov. 8, 2003; and HS, Vol. 41.

28. Millie Rohrbach interview with Murray Fisher, Oct. 1989, 1–2; HHIA, Nov. 8, 2003; Mildred Williams Gunn interview, Jan. 1987, Tape 1, Side 1, 10, 18, and Tape 1, Side 2, 1–2.

29. Regina Markell Morantz, "The Scientist as Sex Crusader: Alfred C. Kinsey and American Culture," *American Quarterly* (Winter 1977), 564. See also James H. Jones, *Alfred C. Kinsey: A Public/Private Life* (New York, 1997).

30. Morantz, "Sex Crusader," 568–575, 582–583.

31. Morantz, "Sex Crusader," 575–582, and *Time*, August 24, 1953.

32. HH to Janie Borson Sellers, dated Aug. 5, 1946, HS, Vol. 35.

33. HS, Vols. 40, 42, 36, 38.

34. HS, Vols. 41 and 42.

35. Bob Preuss interview with Leo Janos, 1987, and Mildred Williams Gunn interview, Jan. 1987, Side 5, 12, 15.

36. Hefner's review is in HS, Vol. 41.

37. HS, Vol. 42.
38. Mildred Williams Gunn interview, Jan. 1987, Tape 1, Side 1, 10–11, and HHIA, Nov. 8, 2003.
39. HHIA, Nov. 8, 2003, and Millie's explanation of the affair in Mildred Williams Gunn interview, Jan. 1987, Tape 1, Side 2, 2; Tape 1, Side 1, 17; Tape 1, Side 5, 18, 20. Young Hefner would have been truly devastated if he knew the truth—that Millie had sex with the coach many times, that she enjoyed it very much, and that she went back and continued the affair even after confessing. Hefner would not learn this until many years later.
40. HHIA on Nov. 8, 2003, and May 26, 2004.
41. HH's note can be found in HS, Vol. 24.

CHAPTER 3. THE TIE THAT BINDS

1. HH to "Dear Folks," Sept. 26, 1948, HP.
2. HS, Vol. 44, and HHIA, Jan. 3, 2004.
3. HH, "Hugh Hefner Story" memo dated Sept. 12, 1995, and HHIA, Jan. 3, 2004.
4. HS, Vols. 44, 46, 47, and HHIA, Jan. 3, 2004.
5. HHIA, Jan. 3, 2004; HH letter dated Christmas 1951 in HS, Vol. 49; and HH, "Hugh Hefner Story" memo dated Sept. 12, 1995.
6. Ibid., and HH letter dated Jan. 1, 1953, in HS, Vol. 51.
7. HH note dated Sept. 1949, in HS, Vol. 46.
8. Mildred Williams Gunn interview, Jan. 1987, and HS, Vols. 44 and 46.
9. HS, Vol. 47, and Millie Gunn interview with Leo Janos, Jan. 1987.
10. *Chicago Daily Tribune,* April 4, 1951, and *Chicago Herald-American,* April 16, 1951, in HS, Vol. 48, and HH letter dated March 1951, HS, Vol. 48.
11. HH letters dated June 1, 1951, and Aug. 19, 1951, in HS, Vol. 49.
12. HH letter dated Christmas 1951, HS, Vol. 49; HH letter dated May 1, 1952, HS, Vol. 50; and HHIA, Jan. 3, 2004.
13. HHIA, Nov. 8, 2003, and Jan. 3, 2004.
14. HH, quoted in Richard Gehman, "The Fabulous Hef" ms. (1962), 404–405.
15. Ibid., 406–407; "Playboy Interview: Ayn Rand," *Playboy,* March 1964; and HHIA, Jan. 7, 2004.
16. HH, "Sex Behavior and the U.S. Law," in HP, 4, 73–77.
17. HH memo, June 17, 1987, in HP, and HHIA, Jan. 3, 2004.
18. HH, quoted in Richard Gehman, "The Fabulous Hef" ms. (1962), 406–407, and HHIA, Jan. 3, 2004.
19. HHIA, Jan. 3, 2004; Mildred Williams Gunn interview, Jan. 1987, Side 5, 11; and HH Christmas 1950 Letter, HS, Vol. 47.
20. HS, Vols. 50 and 51; HH, "Hugh Hefner Story" memo dated Sept. 12, 1995, in HP; Mildred Williams Gunn interview, Jan. 1987; and HHIA, Jan. 23, 2004.
21. HHIA, Jan. 3, 2004.
22. HHIA, Jan. 3, 2004; Millie Rohrbach interview, Oct. 1989; and Eldon Sellers, undated memoir, Eldon Sellers file, HP.
23. Mildred Williams Gunn interview, Jan. 1987, and HHIA, Jan. 3, 2004.
24. Eldon Sellers memoir; HS, Vol. 51; HH, "Hugh Hefner Story" memo dated Sept. 12, 1995, in HP, 11; and HHIA, Jan. 3, 2004.
25. Millie Rohrbach interview, Oct. 1989; letter dated May 1, 1952, HS, Vol. 50; HS, Vol. 51; and Eldon Sellers memoir.
26. Millie Rohrbach interview, Oct. 1989; Mildred Williams Gunn interview, Jan. 1987; and Eldon Sellers memoir.
27. Mildred Williams Gunn interview, Jan. 1987; Eldon Sellers memoir; Millie Rohrbach interview, Oct. 1989.

28. Eldon Sellers memoir.
29. Ibid.
30. Eldon Sellers memoir, and Mildred Williams Gunn interview, Jan. 1987.
31. Eldon Sellers memoir, and HHIA, Jan. 3, 2004.
32. "Hugh Hefner Story," 11, and HHIA, Jan. 3, 2004.
33. HS, Vol. 51, and HH, "Hugh Hefner Story," 11.
34. Cartoon segments dated Aug. 6, 1944, in HS, Vol. 12; "Hugh Hefner Story," 11–12; and HHIA, Jan. 3, 2004.
35. HHIA, Jan. 3, 2004.
36. "Other Voices: Eldon Sellers," Eldon Sellers file, HP, and cartoon dated March 1953, in HS, Vol. 52.
37. HS, Vol. 52.
38. HS, Vol. 52; Millie Rohrbach interview, Oct. 1989; and "Notes from Interview with Burt Zollo," Aug. 18, 1988, Burt Zollo file, HP.
39. "Hugh Hefner Story," 12–13; "Notes from Interview with Burt Zollo"; letter to parents dated Sept. 5, 1953, in HS, Vol. 52; Millie Rohrbach interview, Oct. 1989; and Eldon Sellers memoir.
40. HHIA, Jan. 3, 2004; "Hugh Hefner Story," 13; "Art Paul interview with Leo Janos, 1986, HP; and "The Fabulous Hef" ms., 241–243.
41. HS, Vol. 50; "Hugh Hefner Story," 12; and HH, "Golden Dreams," *Playboy*, Jan. 1994, 121.
42. HHIA, Jan. 3, 2004; HS, Vol. 52; "Golden Dreams," 265; and "Art Paul interview with Leo Janos, 1986, HP.

CHAPTER 4. HOW TO WIN FRIENDS AND TITILLATE PEOPLE

1. HH, "Golden Dreams," *Playboy*, Jan. 1994, 271, and his letter to posterity dated Jan. 1954, in HS, Vol. 53.
2. "Golden Dreams," 271–272.
3. Ibid.
4. Ibid., 270–271, and HHIA, Jan. 3, 2004.
5. *Playboy*, undated first issue, 3.
6. Ibid.
7. Ibid., 17–19.
8. David Halberstam, *The Fifties* (New York, 1993), 116–130, 173–187; Kenneth Jackson, *Crabgrass Frontier: The Suburbanization of the United States* (New York, 1985); "What a Country!" *Fortune*, Oct. 1956; David Potter, *People of Plenty* (Chicago, 1954); and "Special Issue: The Good Life," *Life*, Dec. 28, 1959, 13–14.
9. See Elaine Tyler May, *Homeward Bound: American Families in the Cold War Era* (New York, 1988). The quote appears on p. 11.
10. The classic analysis of this transformation is Warren I. Susman, "'Personality' and the Making of Twentieth-Century Culture," in his *Culture as History* (New York, 1984), 271–285.
11. See Stephen J. Whitfield, *The Culture of the Cold War* (Baltimore, 1991), for an interesting analysis of this trend.
12. See the essays in Lary May, ed., *Recasting America: Culture and Politics in the Age of the Cold War* (Chicago, 1988), for an exploration of many of these dissenting impulses.
13. HH letter to posterity, Jan. 1954, in HS, Vol. 53, and HHIA, Jan. 3, 2004.
14. HHIA, Jan. 3, 2004.
15. "An Impolite Interview with Hugh Hefner," *Realist*, May 1961, 11.
16. Letter from Ray Russell, *Playboy* Associate Editor, published in the April 1954 *Writer's Digest*, in HS, Vol. 53, and "The Good Life," *Playboy*, Sept. 1955, 63.

17. "Playbill," *Playboy,* Nov. 1954, 2, and "They Call Me Playboy," 1955 ad solicitation published in *Advertising Age,* in HS, Vol. 56.
18. "The Playboy Reader," *Playboy,* Sept. 1955, 36–37.
19. "What is a Playboy?" *Playboy,* Apr. 1956, 73.
20. HH, quoted in Alan Whitney, "Playboy: Sex on a Skyrocket," *Chicago,* Oct. 1955, 37.
21. "Nudity and the Foreign Film," *Playboy,* Oct. 1954, 40–44.
22. HH, quoted in "Playboy: Sex on a Skyrocket," 36–37.
23. See in *Playboy:* Bob Norman [Burt Zollo], "Miss Gold-digger of 1953" (undated first issue), and "Dear Playboy," Jan. 1954; Burt Zollo, "Open Season on Bachelors," June 1954; and Jay Smith, "A Vote for Polygamy," July 1955.
24. See in *Playboy*: Julien Dedman, "That Brooks Brothers Look," Feb. 1954; Thomas Mario, "Pleasures of the Oyster," April 1954); and Thomas Mario, "How to Play with Fire," July 1954.
25. See in *Playboy*: Dave Brubeck, "The New Jazz Audience," Aug. 1955; "Playbill" and "Playboy After Hours," Nov. 1955; and "Playbill," Oct. 1956.
26. See in *Playboy*: Shepherd Mead, "How to Apply for a Job," May 1954; Thomas Mario, "Is She Your Kind of Dish?" Oct. 1954; and Evelyn Waugh, "The Death of Painting," Aug. 1956.
27. Ray Bradbury, "Fahrenheit 451," serialized in *Playboy,* March–May 1954; Charles Beaumont, "Black Country," *Playboy,* Sept. 1954; and letter from Ray Russell, *Playboy* Associate Editor, published in the April 1954 *Writer's Digest,* in HS, Vol. 53. For other examples of *Playboy's* early fiction, see W. Somerset Maugham, "Appearance and Reality," Oct. 1954; John Steinbeck, "The Ears of Johnny Bear," Jan. 1955; and James Jones, "The King," Oct. 1955.
28. Jackson Lears, "A Matter of Taste: Corporate Cultural Hegemony in a Mass-Consumption Society," in May, *Recasting America,* 38–57.
29. HH letter to posterity, Jan. 1955, in HS, Vol. 55; HH letter to posterity, summer 1955, in HS, Vol. 56; and HH letter to investors, December, 1956, in HS, Vol. 57.
30. HH letter to posterity, Jan. 1954, in HS, Vol. 53.
31. Eldon Sellers memoir (undated), Eldon Sellers file, HP, and HH letter to posterity, Jan. 1955.
32. HH, quoted in "Playboy: Sex on a Skyrocket," *Chicago,* Oct. 1955, 37; transcript of HH on TV show *Night Beat,* with Mike Wallace, fall 1956, HS, Vol. 58; and HH letter to posterity, Jan. 1955.
33. HH letter to posterity, Jan. 1955.
34. HH letter to posterity, Jan. 1954, and HH letter to posterity, summer 1955.
35. "Playboy: Sex on a Skyrocket," *Chicago,* Oct. 1955, 35, and HH, quoted on 37; "Sassy Newcomer," *Time,* Sept. 24, 1956; "For Young City Guys," *Newsweek,* Nov. 7, 1955; and 1956 *Night Beat* transcript.
36. "Playboy Goes to Court Challenging Ban by Summerfield," *New York Post,* Nov. 18, 1955; "Playboy, Post Office in 2nd-class Hassle," *Printer's Ink,* Dec. 2, 1955; and "Press Release," Nov. 1955, in HP.
37. Articles in the *Daily Northwestern*: "Playboy Gets the Axe in Campus Bookstore," Jan. 13, 1956; "A Story of People Who Weren't There," Jan. 30, 1956; and HH, "Playboy Editor Argues Against Bookstore Ban," Jan. 19, 1956.

CHAPTER 5. HEDONISM, INC.

1. Marge Pitner interview, July 8, 1988, HP.
2. Marge Pitner interview, July 8, 1988, HP, and Patricia Pappangelis interview with Trikilis Productions, Pat Pappas file, HP.
3. John Mastro interview with Trikilis Productions, Mastro file, HP, and Vince Tajiri interview with Murray Fisher, Dec. 18, 1989, Tajiri file, HP.

4. Art Paul interview with Leo Janos (1986), Art Paul File, HP, pp. 12–16.

5. "Arthur Paul and Friend," *Journal of Commercial Art,* Aug. 1960, n.p., and Richard Gehman, "The Fabulous Hef" ms. 1962, HP, 242–244. Gehman's unpublished manuscript relies heavily on interviews, from which he quotes extensively.

6. Art Paul interview with Leo Janos, 1986, Art Paul file, HP, 2–4, and "Arthur Paul and Friend," *Journal of Commercial Art,* Aug. 1960, n.p.

7. Ray Russell to Leo Janos, Jan. 20, 1987, Ray Russell file, HP, and Gehman, quoting Russell in "The Fabulous Hef" ms., 1962, 438–442.

8. Ray Russell to Leo Janos, Jan. 20, 1987, Ray Russell file, HP.

9. Ray Russell to Leo Janos, Jan. 20, 1987, Ray Russell file, HP, and Russell, quoted in Gehman, "The Fabulous Hef" ms., 1962, 443–444.

10. Vince Tajiri, undated interview, Vince Tajiri file, HP, and "Famed Nisei Photographer Vincent Tajiri Dies," *Rafu Shimpo,* Feb. 9, 1993.

11. Vince Tajiri, undated interview, Vince Tajiri file, HP, and Tajiri, quoted in Gehman, "The Fabulous Hef" ms., 1962, 244–247.

12. HS, Vol. 57, and HH to Keith and Rae Hefner, April 2, 1956, Keith Hefner file, HP.

13. Ray Russell to Leo Janos, Jan. 20, 1987, Ray Russell file, HP, and Spectorsky, quoted in Gehman, "The Fabulous Hef" ms., 1962, 218–220.

14. Spectorsky to HH, Feb. 18, 1956, HP; HH to Keith and Rae Hefner, April 2, 1956, Keith Hefner file, HP; Murray Fisher, quoting Spectorsky when interviewing Arlene Bouras, May 10, 1989, 18–19, HP; and Spectorsky memo to Vic Lownes, May 14, 1956, HP.

15. Spectorsky interview, quoted in Richard Lehman, "The Fabulous Hef" ms., 1962, 221–224, and interview with Theo Spectorsky, Theo Spectorsky file, HP. Hefner noted Spectorsky's influence in HHIA, May 2004.

16. Theo Spectorsky interview with Murray Fisher, May 8, 1989, HP.

17. Theo Spectorsky interview with Murray Fisher, May 8, 1989; Arlene Bouras interview with Murray Fisher, May 10, 1989, 5–6; Murray Fisher, quoted in Gehman, "The Fabulous Hef" ms., 1962, 227–228; and "A Revealing Interview with A. C. Spectorsky," *Word Business,* April 1967, 45.

18. Spectorsky, quoted in Gehman, "The Fabulous Hef" ms., 1962, 229, and Theo Spectorsky interview with Murray Fisher, May 8, 1989.

19. Theo Spectorsky interview with Murray Fisher, May 8, 1989; Arlene Bouras interview with Murray Fisher, May 10, 1989, 16–18. The Trilling story was related by *Playboy* editor Walter Goodman and repeated in Thomas Weyr, *Reaching for Paradise: The Playboy Vision of America* (New York, 1978), 39.

20. Spectorsky, quoted in Gehman, "The Fabulous Hef" ms., 1962, 193; Spec to Hef memo on "The Manipulators," Sept. 25, 1957, HP; "Highlights of Interview with Ray Russell," June 8, 1989, Ray Russell file, HP.

21. Theo Spectorsky interview with Murray Fisher, May 8, 1989; "Highlights of Interview with Ray Russell," June 8, 1989, Ray Russell file, HP; and Spectorsky, quoted in the Rev. Malcolm Boyd, "The Late Spectorsky on *Playboy,*" *Variety,* Feb. 2, 1972.

22. "Gleanings from Conversation with Eldon Sellers," Jan. 3, 1989, Eldon Sellers file, HP.

23. Victor Lownes interview with Lynch/Frost, April 13, 1991, Victor Lownes file, HP, and "Gleanings from Conversation with Eldon Sellers," Jan. 3, 1989, Eldon Sellers file, HP.

24. Theo Spectorsky interview with Murray Fisher, May 8, 1989; Betty Zuziak interview with Leo Janos, 1988; and Victor Lownes interview with Murray Fisher, March 10, 1989.

25. Lownes, quoted in Gehman, "The Fabulous Hef" ms., 1962, 261–262; and Shel Silverstein interview, with HH present, Nov. 26, 1986, Shel Silverstein file, HP.

26. Victor Lownes interview with Murray Fisher, March 10, 1989, HP; and Eldon Sellers memoir, 1989, Eldon Sellers file, HP.

27. Victor Lownes interview with Murray Fisher, March 12, 1989; Dick Rosenzweig, "Rosenzweig on Vic at Work," Victor Lownes file, HP; "Theo Spectorsky on Anson Mount," Anson Mount file, HP; and "Vince Tajiri on Vic Lownes," Vince Tajiri file, HP.

28. Victor Lownes interview with Murray Fisher, Mar. 12, 1989, Victor Lownes file, HP, and HH to Victor Lownes, Dec. 1959 memo, Victor Lownes file, HP.

29. Betty Zuziak interview with Leo Janos, 1988, 51; Theo Spectorsky interview with Murray Fisher, May 8, 1989; Eleanor Bradley interview with Murray Fisher, Sept. 27, 1989; Jean Parker interview with Murray Fisher, June 14, 1989, 33; Russell Miller, *Bunny: The Real Story of Playboy* (New York, 1984), 56; and "Eldon Sellers on Vic at Work," Victor Lownes file, HP.

30. Dick Rosenzweig, "Rosenzweig on Vic at Work," Victor Lownes file, HP; Gehman, "The Fabulous Hef" ms., 1962, 257; Mike Shea, "Mike Shea on Vic," Victor Lownes file, HP; and HHIA, May 2004.

31. Eleanor Bradley interview with Murray Fisher, Sept. 27, 1989, HP, and Shel Silverstein interview, with HH present, Nov. 26, 1986, HP.

32. Theo Spectorsky, Jack Kessie File, HP, and Joe Paczek on "Life at 232," Joe Paczek file, HP.

33. Nancy Mount interview with Murray Fisher, June 7, 1989, HP, and "Theo Spectorsky on Anson Mount," Anson Mount file, HP.

34. *LeRoy Neiman, Art and Lifestyle* booklet, Neiman file, HP; LeRoy Neiman interview with Lynch/Frost Productions, May 23, 1991, HP; "LeRoy Neiman on the Genesis of 'Man at His Leisure,'" Neiman file, HP; and "Other Voices: LeRoy Neiman," Neiman file, HP.

35. Joe Paczek on "Life at 232," Joe Paczek file, HH Papers; HHIA, May 2004; and HH, Memo on "The Hugh Hefner Story," 1995, 15, HP.

36. HHIA, May 2004.

37. Arlene Bouras, undated statement, Bouras file, HP; Patricia Pappangelis interview with Trikilis Productions, Pat Pappas file, HP; Vince Tajiri, undated statement, Vince Tajiri file, HP; and Marge Pitner interview with Trikilis Productions, HP.

38. HHIA, May 2004; Arlene Bouras, undated statement, Bouras file, HP; John Mastro, undated interview, John Mastro file, HP; Ernest Tucker, "The Playboy Behind Playboy," *Chicago American Pictorial Living*, June 5, 1960; and Shel Silverstein, undated comments, Silverstein file, HP.

39. LeRoy Neiman, undated statement, Neiman file, HP.

40. Arlene Bouras, quoted in Nina Liu, "Meet the Purist in Hef's Domain," *Copy Editor*, Dec. 1990/Jan. 1991, 5, and John Mastro, undated interview, John Mastro file, HP.

41. Marge Pitner interview July 8, 1988, HP; Pat Pappangelis interview, July 7, 1988, Pat Pappas file, HP; John Mastro, undated interview, John Mastro file, HP; Eldon Sellers memoir (undated), Eldon Sellers file, HP; and Gehman, "The Fabulous Hef" ms., 1962, 206, 207–208, HP.

42. Gehman, "The Fabulous Hef" ms., 1962, 207–208, and Art Paul interview with Leo Janos, 1986, Art Paul file, HP.

43. Art Paul interview with Leo Janos, 1986, Art Paul file, HP; Ray Russell to Leo Janos, Jan. 20, 1987, Ray Russell file, HP; and HH and Shel Silverstein, interview with Leo Janos, 1989, Shel Silverstein file, HP.

44. HH memo to Ray Russell, A. C. Spectorsky, Jack Kessie, Nov. 19, 1956, HP.

45. Vince Tajiri, undated interview, Vince Tajiri file, HP; Arlene Bouras, undated statement, Bouras file, HP; and HH memo to Fred Crawford, Apr. 2, 1957, HP.
46. HH to Perkins Bailey, Sept. 4, 1956, HP; HH memo to A. C. Spectorsky, June 21. 1956, HP; and HH memo to Ray Russell, Dec. 4, 1959, HP.
47. HH memo to Spectorsky, Oct. 9, 1956, HP, and HH memo to Spectorsky, Russell, Kessie, June 27, 1956, HP.
48. HH to Burt Zollo, March 21, 1956, HP.
49. Jack Kessie, quoted in Weyr, *Reaching for Paradise*, 33; Victor Lownes interview with Lynch/Frost, April 13, 1991; A. C. Spectorsky and Art Paul, quoted in Richard Gehman, "The Fabulous Hef" ms., 1962, 197, 204–205, HP; HH, quoted in Will Jones, "Hefner's a Playboy—and a Workhorse: In Chicago a Bit of Rome," *Minneapolis Sunday Tribune*, Feb. 26, 1961; and HHIA, May 2004.
50. "Confidential Vocational Audit of Hugh M. Hefner," dated August 13, 1956, in HS, Vol. 57.
51. HH memo to Fred Crawford, May 20, 1956, HP; and HH's 1959 Year-End Letter, HS, Vol. 63.
52. Gehman, "The Fabulous Hef" ms., 1962, 206–207, and HH's Year-End Letter, Dec. 1958, in HS, Vol. 60.
53. HHIA, May 2004.

CHAPTER 6. THE PURSUIT OF HAPPINESS

1. Transcript, HH on *Mike Wallace Interview*, fall 1956, HS, Vol. 58.
2. Beth Bailey has disentangled and analyzed many of the threads of the sexual revolution in her "Sexual Revolution(s)," in David Farber, ed., *The Sixties: From Memory to History* (Chapel Hill, NC, 1994), 235–262, and *Sex in the Heartland* (Cambridge, MA, 1999).
3. *New Yorker* cover, June 22, 1957, and David Cort, "Sophistication in America," *Nation*, Feb. 2, 1957, 96–97.
4. HH, "The Playboy Philosophy," *Playboy*, Sept. 1963, 81; Feb. 1963, 45; and Feb. 1965, 177, and "Playboy Interview: Hugh M. Hefner," *Playboy*, Jan. 1974, 65–66.
5. The secondary literature on Victorian culture is enormous, but a good starting point is Daniel Walker Howe, ed., *Victorian America* (Philadelphia, 1976). See also Jayme A. Sokolow, *Eros and Modernization: Sylvester Graham, Health Reform, and the Origins of Victorian Sexuality in America* (Rutherford, NJ, 1983), and, on Comstock, Helen Lefkowitz Horowitz, *Rereading Sex: Battles over Sexual Knowledge and Suppression in Nineteenth-Century America* (New York, 2002), 367–403.
6. Among many fine works on the turn-of-the-century shift away from a Victorian culture of self-denial to a modern consumer culture of self-fulfillment, see T. J. Jackson Lears, "From Salvation to Self-Realization: Advertising and the Therapeutic Roots of the Consumer Culture, 1880–1930," in Jackson Lears and Richard Fox, eds., *The Culture of Consumption: Critical Essays in American History, 1880–1980* (New York, 1983); Lary May, *Screening Out the Past: The Birth of Mass Culture and the Motion Picture Industry* (Chicago, 1983); John Kasson, *Amusing the Million: Coney Island at the Turn of the Century* (New York, 1978); and Lewis Erenberg, *Steppin' Out: New York Nightlife and the Transformation of American Culture, 1890–1930* (Chicago, 1981). Elaine Tyler May, *Homeward Bound: American Families in the Cold War Era* (New York, 1988), provides a compelling analysis of the connections between family formulations and politics during the Cold War era.
7. See Beth Bailey, *Sex in the Heartland*, 75–80, for a perceptive analysis of the sexual orthodoxy.
8. David Halberstam, *The Fifties* (New York, 1993), 59–61, 272–281, 455–462, 471–478, and 576–584, discusses many sexual countercurrents in the decade.

9. Alan Whitney, "Playboy: Sex on a Skyrocket," *Chicago,* Oct. 1955, 36–37, and HHIA, Jan. 3, 2004, and May 26, 2004.

10. See in *Playboy*: reply to reader's letter, Aug. 1954, 3; Jules Archer, "Don't Hate Yourself in the Morning," Aug. 1955; Harrison Case, "Contour Contact," June 1957; and Jay Smith, "The Big Bosom Battle," Sept. 1955.

11. See in *Playboy*: "Playboy's Yacht Party," July 1957; "Playboy's House Party," May 1959; "The Girls of Hollywood," Oct. 1960; and "Minsky in Vegas," April 1958.

12. HH, quoted in "Sex on a Skyrocket," 36, and Frankenstein Smith (HH pseudonym), "Virginity," *Playboy,* Sept. 1954.

13. Shepherd Mead, "The First Sap of Manhood and How It Rises," *Playboy,* Dec. 1955.

14. See in *Playboy*: Thomas Mario, "The Breaking of the Fast: Morning Menus for Two," June 1957; Blake Rutherford, "The Marks of the Well-Dressed Man," March 1957; "Playboy's Penthouse Apartment," Sept. and Oct. 1956; and "Playboy After Hours," *Playboy,* Nov. 1955.

15. HH, quoted in Hal Higdon, "Playboying Around the Clock with Hugh Hefner," *Climax,* Feb. 1962, and in transcript for the Canadian Broadcasting Company's radio documentary *Project '62: Playboy of the Modern World,* 1962, 10, HP.

16. HH, quoted in "About the Nudes in Playboy," *U.S. Camera,* April 1962, 69, and in *Playboy of the Modern World* transcript, 10.

17. HH, in "About the Nudes in Playboy," April 1962, 69; HH, quoted in Hal Higdon, "Playboying Around the Clock with Hugh Hefner," *Climax,* Feb. 1962.

18. HH on Irv Kupcinet's *At Random,* CBS television show, Chicago, July 3, 1962.

19. HH, "The Playboy Philosophy," *Playboy,* Feb. 1965, 184.

20. HHIA, May 26, 2004, and Ivor Williams, "The Pious Pornographers," *Playboy,* Oct. 1957.

21. HH to Larry Silverstein, A. Stein and Company, Oct. 26, 1959, HP.

22. HH, "The Playboy Philosophy," *Playboy,* Dec. 1964, 160, and Sept. 1963, 233.

23. HHIA, Jan. 3, 2004.

24. *Playboy,* July 1955, 27.

25. *Playboy,* Dec. 1955, 29–32; *Playboy,* Oct. 1956, 40–46; and *Playboy,* Oct. 1957, 85.

26. See Ralph Stein, *The Pin-Up: From 1852 to Now* (Chicago, 1974); Mark Gabor, *The Pin-Up: A Modest History* (New York, 1972); and Joanne Meyerowitz, "Women, Cheesecake, and Borderline Material: Responses to Girlie Pictures in the Mid-Twentieth Century U.S.," *Journal of Women's History* (Fall 1996), 11–13.

27. HH on *Mike Wallace Interview,* and HHIA, May 26, 2004.

28. "Requirements for Playboy's Playmate of the Month," 1956, 1, HP, and HH to George J. Abrams, Vice President for Advertising, Revlon Products Corp., March 23, 1956, HP.

29. HH, in "About the Nudes in Playboy," *U.S. Camera,* April 1962, 70–71, and "Playboy Interview: Hugh M. Hefner," *Playboy,* Jan. 1974, 69.

30. Joe Paczek interview with Murray Fisher, July 8, 1988, HP.

31. *Playboy,* Dec. 1956, 41–47.

32. *Playboy,* Jan. 1959, 39–43.

33. Bob Norman [Burt Zollo], "Miss Gold-digger of 1953," *Playboy,* Dec. 1953, 6–8, and Burt Zollo, "Open Season on Bachelors," *Playboy,* June 1954, 37–38.

34. Jay Smith, "A Vote for Polygamy," *Playboy,* July 1955, 15–16, and "Meet the Playboy Reader," *Playboy,* April 1958, 76.

35. "An Impolite Interview with Hugh Hefner," *Realist,* 14, and HH, quoted in *Playboy of the Modern World* radio documentary, 1962, transcript, 13–14, HP.

36. HH, "The Playboy Philosophy," *Playboy,* Feb. 1965, 176, 179–180.

37. Jackson Lears, "From Salvation to Self-Realization: Advertising and the Thera-peutic Roots of the Consumer Culture, 1880–1930," in Jackson Lears and Richard Wightman Fox, eds., *The Culture of Consumption: Critical Essays in American History, 1880–1980* (New York, 1983), 4. HH is quoted in "The Playboy Philoso-phy," *Playboy*, Feb. 1963, 45.
38. HH, "The Playboy Philosophy," *Playboy*, Jan. 1965, 172, and Martha Wolfenstein, "Fun Morality: An Analysis of Recent American Child-Training Literature," in Margaret Mead and Martha Wolfenstein, eds., *Childhood in Contemporary Cul-tures* (Chicago, 1955), 168.
39. HH, "The Playboy Philosophy," *Playboy*, Feb. 1965, 179.

CHAPTER 7. AN ABUNDANT LIFE

1. "Playboy Interview: Hugh M. Hefner," *Playboy*, Jan. 1974, 65, 82.
2. Vic Lownes interview with Lynch/Frost, April 13, 1991.
3. "The Men's Shop," *Playboy*, Dec. 1953.
4. David Potter, *People of Plenty: Economic Abundance and the American Character* (Chicago, 1954); David Riesman, *Abundance for What? and Other Essays* (Garden City, NY, 1964); John Kenneth Galbraith, *The Affluent Society* (Boston, 1958); and Lizabeth Cohen, *A Consumer's Republic: The Politics of Mass Consumption in Postwar America* (New York, 2003), 11–15.
5. "Playboy Interview: Hugh M. Hefner," *Playboy*, Jan. 1974, 66.
6. "They Call Me Playboy," 1955 ad solicitation in *Advertising Age*, HS, Vol. 56.
7. See in *Playboy*: "The Basic Bar," Jan. 1958; "The Compleat Fidelitarian," Oct. 1957; "The Stereo Scene," Oct. 1958; "The Verities of Vino," Oct. 1958; "The Compleat Sports Car Stable," April 1957; "The Playboy Sports Car," Sept. 1960; and "Mixing the Perfect Martini," Sept. 1955.
8. "Playboy's Penthouse Apartment," *Playboy*, Sept. 1956, 53–60, and Oct. 1956, 65–70.
9. See in *Playboy*: Frederic A. Birmingham, "The Well-Clad Undergrad," Sept. 1958; Blake Rutherford, "Fashion Afoot," March 1959; Blake Rutherford, "The Marks for the Well-Dressed Man," March 1957; and Robert L. Green, "A Formal Affair," June 1959.
10. Gretchen Edgeren, *The Playboy Book: Forty Years* (Los Angeles, 1994), 35, and HH to Peter L. Postelnek of Bentley, Barnes, and Lynn, Inc., Feb. 24, 1959, HP.
11. Edgeren, *Playboy Book*, 35, and "Gleanings from Conversation with Eldon Sellers," Jan. 3, 1989, Eldon Sellers file, HP.
12. The ads listed in the previous three paragraphs were noted in the author's close survey of the June 1959 issue of *Playboy*.
13. "Playboy Reader Service," *Playboy*, Oct. 1957, 87.
14. See in *Playboy*: John Moss, "Playboy on Poker," Nov. 1957; Patrick Chase, "The Art of Travel," May 1959; "Invitation to Yachting: Playboy's Guide to Fun Afloat," July 1959; and nightclub ads appearing in the Nov. 1959 issue.
15. See in *Playboy*: Richard Gehman and Robert Reisner, "Bird," Jan. 1957; Leonard Feather, "Ella Meets the Duke," Nov. 1957; Robert George Reisner, "Sinatra," Nov. 1958; and "The 1957 Playboy All-Stars," Feb. 1957.
16. See in *Playboy*: Ed Pazdur, "Boxing 1956," Feb. 1956; Anson Mount, "Playboy's Pigskin Preview," Sept. 1958; and "Yuletide for the Playboy Sportsman," Dec. 1958. See also HH, "The Magazine 1955–1959," Sept. 16, 1987, 18, on the "Pigskin Pre-view," HP.
17. See in *Playboy*: Hollis Alpert and Charles Beaumont, "The Horror of It All," March 1959; Charles Beaumont, "Chaplin: The Chronicle of a Man and His Genius,"

March 1960; Richard Gehman, "Charming Billy," Dec. 1960; and Wolcott Gibbs and Ward Morehouse, "Broadway: The Season Just Past, the Season to Come," Dec. 1956.

18. "Silverstein: Sketches from the Satirical Pen of a Talented New Artist," *Playboy*, Aug. 1956, 52, and "The Sick Little World of Jules Feiffer," *Playboy*, Aug. 1958, 25–27. For a sampling of these cartoonists, see *Playboy: 50 Years of Cartoons* (San Francisco, 2004).

19. "Playbill," *Playboy*, July 1957, 2, and "Playbill," *Playboy*, Jan. 1958, 2.

20. HH, "The Magazine, 1955–1959," Sept. 16, 1987, 6, 16, HP; HH's 1959 Year-End Letter, HS, Vol. 63; and HH's 1960 Year-End Letter, HS, Vol. 65.

21. HH letter to posterity, July 1957, HS, Vol. 58. For inside pictures of the financial crisis, see "Highlights of March 2, 1989, Eldon Sellers Interview," Eldon Sellers file, HP, and John Mastro interview with Murray Fisher, HP.

22. "Meet the Playboy Reader," *Playboy*, April 1958.

23. "What Sort of Man Reads Playboy?" subscription ads in *Playboy*: May 1958, 82; Nov. 1958, 98; and Jan. 1959, 82.

24. "The Beat Mystique," *Playboy*, Feb. 1958, with Herbert Gold, "What It Is— Whence It Came," 20, 84–87; Sam Boal, "Cool Swinging in New York," 21, 26, 50; and Noel Clad, "A Frigid Frolic in Frisco," 21, 22, 74–75. Also Jack Kerouac, "The Origins of the Beat Generation," *Playboy*, June 1959, 31–32, 42, 79. A descriptive account of the Beats can be found in David Halberstam, *The Fifties* (New York, 1993), 295–307, while more scholarly analyses appear in Steven Watson, *The Birth of the Beat Generation: Visionaries, Rebels, and Hipsters, 1944–1960* (New York, 1995), and Preston Whaley, *Blows Like a Horn: Beat Writing, Jazz, Style, and Markets in the Transformation of U.S. Culture* (Cambridge, MA, 2004).

25. "Beat Playmate," *Playboy*, July 1959.

26. HH in "Playbill," *Playboy*, Dec. 1958, 3, on the fifth anniversary of the magazine, repeated in HH letter for posterity, Dec. 1958, HS, Vol. 60.

27. HHIA, Jan. 3 and May 26, 2004.

28. HH to Homer Hargrove, May 13, 1960, HS, Vol. 64, and HH in *Project '62: Playboy of the Modern World*, 1962, transcript of radio documentary broadcast by the Canadian Broadcasting Company, HP.

29. HH, quoted in Hal Higdon, "Playboying Around the Clock with Hugh Hefner," *Climax*, Feb. 1962.

30. HH to Jean Shepherd, June 8, 1961, HP, and HH, quoted in Higdon, "Playboying Around the Clock."

31. See a number of articles from the *Chicago Sun-Times* and *Chicago American* in April and May 1959, and "Playboy Mag Scrams Jazz Fest at Soldier Field," *Variety*, May 20, 1959, all in HS, Vol. 61, for background on the booking problems with the event. HH noted the connection between the Playboy Jazz Festival and the Upbeat Generation in "The Magazine 1955–1959," Sept. 16, 1987, 22, HP.

32. See the raft of newspaper and magazine articles in HS, Vol. 62.

33. See "Chi Jazz Fest: A Plus for Playboy," *Variety*, undated, and Lownes's statement in undated article from *Billboard*, both in HS, Vol. 62.

34. HH, quoted in Bill Davidson, "Czar of the Bunny Empire," *Saturday Evening Post*, Apr. 28, 1962, 34.

35. For an insightful description of the Kitchen Debates, see Elaine Tyler May, *Homeward Bound: American Families in the Cold War Era* (New York, 1988), 16–18.

36. HH in *Project '62: Playboy of the Modern World*, 1962, transcript of radio documentary broadcast by the Canadian Broadcasting Company, HP.

37. HHIA, May 26, 2004, and HH, "Playboy Philosophy," *Playboy*, Jan. 1965, 171–172.

38. HH, "Playboy Philosophy," *Playboy*, Jan. 1965, 172, and HHIA, May 26, 2004.

39. HH memo to Ray Russell, Dec. 4, 1959, HP, and HH to Homer Hargrove Jr., May 15, 1960, HP.
40. See the raft of newspaper clippings about this incident in HS, Vol. 62.
41. HH's rejoinder in "Dear Playboy," *Playboy,* July 1960, 6.
42. HH, "The Hugh Hefner Story," Sept. 12, 1995, 16–17, HP, and internal FBI memo dated Oct. 27, 1955, and copy of post office memo dated Feb. 11, 1955, both in HH/Playboy FBI file released under Freedom of Information Act.
43. HH letters to posterity, dated May 1 and Sept. 1952, both in HS, Vol. 50; HH to Homer Hargrove Jr., May 15, 1960, HP; and HH, "Playboy Philosophy," *Playboy,* Jan. 1965, 171.
44. HH memo titled "Jules Feiffer, Mort Sahl, and Lenny Bruce," Dec. 17, 1987, 1–20, HP; Rolf Malcolm, "A Real Free-Form Guy: The Egghead Humor of Mort Sahl," *Playboy,* June 1957; and Larry Siegel, "Rebel with a Caustic Cause: Sick Comic Lenny Bruce," *Playboy,* Feb. 1959.
45. Ibid.
46. See in *Playboy*: Vance Packard, "The Manipulators," Dec. 1957; John Keats, "Eros and Unreason in Detroit," Aug. 1958; Ralph Ginzburg, "The Cult of the Aged Leader," August 1959; and "The Contaminators: A Statement by the Editors of Playboy," October 1959.
47. HH to Ronald Reagan, May 13, 1960, HP.
48. Ernest Tucker, "The Playboy Behind Playboy," *Chicago American Pictorial Living,* June 5, 1960.
49. HH, quoted in Bill Davidson, "Czar of the Bunny Empire," *Saturday Evening Post,* Apr. 28, 1962, 36.
50. HH, quoted in Malcolm Boyd, *My Fellow Americans* (New York, 1970), 60, and HH in "About the Nudes in Playboy," *U.S. Camera,* April 1962, 68.

CHAPTER 8. LIVING THE FANTASY

1. "Highlights of Interview with Ray Russell," June 8, 1989, Ray Russell file, HP.
2. Vic Lownes, Lynch/Frost interview, April 13, 1991, HP.
3. Daniel Boorstin, *The Image: Or, What Happened to the American Dream* (New York, 1962), 57, and Richard Schickel, *Intimate Strangers: The Culture of Celebrity in America* (Chicago, 2000 [1985]), 29. A fine book that discusses the broader historical evolution of fame is Leo Braudy, *The Frenzy of Renown: Fame and Its History* (New York, 1986).
4. HHIA, May 26, 2004; Shelly Kasten, "Other Voices," HP; Skip Krask, "Other Voices," HP; and Don Adams, 1989 interview, HP.
5. Kasten, "Other Voices," and Krask, "Other Voices."
6. Arlene Bouras on Ray Russell, Arlene Bouras file, HP; Bev Chamberlain interview with Murray Fisher, Oct. 26, 1989; HH, "Personal Reflections on the 1950s," Oct. 5, 1987, HP; "Gleanings from Conversation with Eldon Sellers," Jan. 3, 1989, Eldon Sellers file, HP; Marge Pitner interview, HP; Arlene Bouras on Joe Paczek, Arlene Bouras file, HP; and "Highlights of Interview with Ray Russell," June 8, 1989, Ray Russell file, HP.
7. The record of these liaisons is in HS, Vols. 57, 58, 59. See also HH, "The Magazine, 1955–1959," Sept. 16, 1987, 9, HP; HH, "Personal Reflections on the 1950s," Oct. 5, 1987, HP; Bev Chamberlain interview with Murray Fisher, Oct. 26, 1989; Janie Borson Sellers interview, Janie Sellers file, HP; and HH to Larry DuBois and Murray Fisher, Oct. 24, 1989, HP.
8. Art Paul interview with Leo Janos, 1986, Art Paul file, HP, and Marge Pitner interview, HP.

9. Millie Gunn interview with Leo Janos, Jan. 1987; and HH to Keith and Rae Hefner, April 2, 1956, Keith Hefner file, HP.

10. HH's 1959 Year-End Letter, HS, Vol. 63; Marge Pitner interview, HP; HH, quoted in "Betty Zuziak," Betty Zuziak file, HP; and Betty Zuziak interview with Leo Janos, 1988.

11. HH, "Sophistication in America," Dec. 4, 1989, HP; HS, Vols. 59 and 60; and *Playboy,* Dec. 1958, 51–54.

12. Joni Mattis interview with Leo Janos, 1988, and HH, interoffice memo, March 1, 1990, Joni Mattis file, HP.

13. Betty Zuziak interview with Leo Janos, 1988; Joni Mattis interview with Leo Janos, 1988; and Connie Chancellor, "Other Voices," HP.

14. Betty Zuziak interview with Leo Janos, 1988, and Joni Mattis interview with Murray Fisher, Jan. 19, 1990, 11–18.

15. Betty Zuziak interview with Leo Janos, 1988, 83.

16. Marge Pitner interview, HP, and Betty Zuziak interview with Leo Janos, 1988.

17. Joni Mattis interview with Murray Fisher, Jan. 19, 1990; Betty Zuziak interview with Leo Janos, 1988; and Joni Mattis interview with Leo Janos, 1988.

18. Marge Pitner interview, HP, and Betty Zuziak interview with Leo Janos, 1988; Joni Mattis interview with Murray Fisher, Jan. 19, 1990; Zuziak interview with Leo Janos, 1988; Joni Mattis interview with Leo Janos, 1988; Mattis interview with Fisher, Jan. 19, 1990.

19. Millie Gunn interview with Leo Janos, Jan. 1987, and Marge Pitner interview, HP.

20. HH letter to posterity, July 1957, HS, Vol. 58; Millie Rohrbach interview with Murray Fisher, Oct. 1989; and Millie Gunn Rohrbach interview with Leo Janos, 1986.

21. "Hugh Hefner Sued by Wife for Divorce," *Chicago Daily Tribune,* March 19, 1959, and HH's 1959 Year-End Letter, HS, Vol. 63.

22. "Playbill," *Playboy,* June 1957, 2–3.

23. HH to Leo Janos, memo on "The Magazine 1955–1959," Sept. 16, 1987, 19, HP.

24. "Playbill" and "The Hildebrand Rarity," *Playboy,* March 1960; "Chronology for Ian Fleming/James Bond/Sean Connery," Oct. 12, 1990, HP; "James Bond's Girls," *Playboy,* Nov. 1965, 133; and HHIA, Nov. 11, 2004. See also Gretchen Edgren, *The Playboy Book: Forty Years* (Los Angeles, 1994), 76, 103. Ian Fleming was the subject of the "Playboy Interview" in *Playboy,* Dec. 1964, while Sean Connery appeared in the same venue in Nov. 1965. Serializations of James Bond novels began in *Playboy* as follows: *On Her Majesty's Secret Service* in April 1963; *You Only Live Twice* in April 1964; and *The Man with the Golden Gun* in April 1965.

25. Robert George Reisner, "Sinatra," *Playboy,* Nov. 1958, and Robert Legare, "Meeting at the Summit: Sinatra and His Buddies Bust 'Em Up in Vegas," *Playboy,* June 1960. Sinatra would appear as the subject of a Playboy Interview in *Playboy,* Feb. 1963.

26. HHIA, Nov. 11, 2004, and HH, "My Card File—Mid-1959 to Jan. 1961," Dec. 21, 1987, 15–17.

27. HHIA, Nov. 11, 2004; HH, "My Card File—Mid-1959 to Jan. 1961," Dec. 21, 1987, 19; and HH, memo titled "If You Don't Swing," Feb. 14, 1990, 15.

28. HS, Vol. 66, and HH, "My Card File—Mid-1959 to Jan. 1961," Dec. 21, 1987, 25.

29. Ad titled "It Pays to Know" for Walther Motor Company, Fall 1959, HS, Vol. 62, and HH to Howard Lederer, March 2, 1959, HP.

30. Ernest Tucker, "The Playboy Behind Playboy," *Chicago American Pictorial Living,* June 5, 1960; Will Jones, "Hefner's a Playboy—and a Workhorse: In Chicago a Bit of Rome," *Minneapolis Sunday Tribune,* Feb. 26, 1961; and wire service newspaper articles in HS, Vol. 68.

31. Ray Russell to Leo Janos, Feb. 2, 1987, HP; and Betty Zuziak interview with Leo Janos, 1988, 10, HP.

32. Betty Zuziak interview with Leo Janos, 1988, 63–64, 85.

33. HH, "My Card File—Mid-1959 to Jan. 1961," Dec. 21, 1987, 2; and HH memo to Larry DuBois and Murray Fisher, April 3, 1989.

34. *Chicago Sun-Times*, Aug. 13, 1959.

35. HS, Vol. 62.

36. HH, "My Card File—Mid-1959 to Jan. 1961," Dec. 21, 1987, and Victor Lownes, quoted in *Sales Management*, Oct. 16, 1959, 108.

37. HH memo to Dan Schuffman, Dec. 8, 1959, HP; and Vic Lownes interview with Murray Fisher, March 12, 1989.

38. HH memo to Larry DuBois and Murray Fisher, Oct. 24, 1989; and HH memo to Larry DuBois and Murray Fisher, April 17, 1989.

39. HH memo to Larry DuBois and Murray Fisher, Oct. 24, 1989; "Playboy's TV Penthouse," *Playboy*, March 1960, 41–43; ad in *Playboy*, Jan. 1960, 6; and ad in *TV Guide*, Dec. 26, 1959, 28.

40. *Chicago Daily Tribune* and *Variety* clippings, HS, Vol. 63, and HH memo to Larry DuBois and Murray Fisher, Oct. 24, 1989.

41. HS, Vols. 63, 64, and 65, and "Playboy's More Polished," *Chicago Sun-Times*, Sept. 21, 1960.

42. HH memo to Larry DuBois and Murray Fisher, Oct. 24, 1989, HP, and Gretchen Edgren, *Inside the Playboy Mansion* (Los Angeles, 1998), 8–9.

43. HH's 1959 Year-End Letter, HS, Vol. 63, and Theo Spectorsky recollection, unmarked document in Victor Lownes file, HP.

44. HH memo to Larry DuBois and Murray Fisher, Oct. 24, 1989, 18–20, and HH, "The Hugh Hefner Story," Sept. 12, 1995, 22–23.

45. Ibid., and Edgren, *Inside the Playboy Mansion*, 66–67.

46. HH, "My Card File—Mid-1959 to Jan. 1961," Dec. 21, 1987, 11, 14–15; and HH, "The Hugh Hefner Story," Sept. 12, 1995, 22–23.

47. Kathryn Loring, "A Bachelor's Dream," *Chicago Sunday Tribune Magazine*, March 5, 1961; "The Boss of Taste City," *Time*, March 24, 1961, 55–56; Bill Davidson, "Czar of the Bunny Empire," *Saturday Evening Post*, April 28, 1962, 34–38; and "Playmate Holiday House Party," *Playboy*, Dec. 1961, 120–129, 209.

48. HH memo to Jack Kessie titled "Playboy Key Club," July 28, 1959, HP, and Vic Lownes, Lynch/Frost interview, April 13, 1991.

49. HH memo to Larry DuBois and Murray Fisher, April 19, 1989; and Vic Lownes interview with Murray Fisher, March 12, 1989.

50. Arnold Morton interview with Hal Higdon, 1967; Arnold Morton interview with Leo Janos, 1986; and Arnold Morton interview with Murray Fisher, Oct. 20, 1989.

51. See materials on the Chicago Club in HH memo to Larry DuBois and Murray Fisher, April 19, 1989; HS, Vol. 64; and "The Playboy Club," *Playboy*, Aug. 1960, 40–44. Abundant materials on *VIP* are in HS, Vols. 102–104.

52. "The Playboy Club"; HH memo to Larry DuBois and Murray Fisher, April 19, 1989; and Vic Lownes, Lynch/Frost interview, April 13, 1991.

53. HH, "The Hugh Hefner Story," Sept. 12, 1995, 23; Keith Hefner interview, April 19, 1991, HP; and Will Jones, "Hefner's a Playboy and a Workhorse: In Chicago a Bit of Rome," *Minneapolis Sunday Tribune*, Feb. 26, 1961.

54. Keith Hefner interview, April 19, 1991, and "The Playboy Club," 41.

55. "Advertising: Playboy Maps New Magazine," *New York Times*, Feb. 10, 1961, and Will Jones, "Hefner's a Playboy—and a Workhorse: In Chicago a Bit of Rome," *Minneapolis Sunday Tribune*, Feb. 26, 1961. Material on the brief history of

the magazine appears in HS, Vols. 68–71. Critical reactions can be sampled in *Newsweek*, Aug. 28, 1961, 72; *Time*, Aug. 28, 1961, 39; and *Saturday Review*, Sept. 9, 1961, 79.

56. "Playbill," *Playboy*, Nov. 1961, 3, and *Variety*, Jan. 11, 1962. Much material on the film project can be found in HS, Vol. 68.
57. Tony Curtis interview, June 6, 1991, HP, and "1960–61 Chronology of the Tony Curtis Movie" and "Chronology of Tony Curtis Movie for 1962 and 1963," HP.
58. HH to Tony Curtis, Jan. 10, 1961, HP.
59. See documents and letters in "1960–61 Chronology of the Tony Curtis Movie" and "Chronology of Tony Curtis Movie for 1962 and 1963," HP; Norman Lear interview with Murray Fisher, April 8, 1991; and HH memo to Larry DuBois and Murray Fisher, May 28. 1990
60. HH, year-end letter dated Dec. 1961, HS, Vol. 70.

CHAPTER 9. THE PHILOSOPHER KING

1. *The Most*, Inter Video Production, produced by Richard Ballentine, directed by Gordon Sheppard, 1961, HP.
2. "Prince of Playmates," *Newsweek*, Sept. 2, 1963.
3. "The Boss of Taste City," *Time*, March 24, 1961, 55–56, and Bill Davidson, "Czar of the Bunny Empire," *Saturday Evening Post*, April 1962, 34–38.
4. "World of Playboy: Magazine, Key Clubs Thrive on Formula of Sex, Sophistication," *Wall Street Journal*, March 22, 1962; *New Yorker*, Feb. 17, 1962; "Playboy's No. 1 Playboy," *Pageant*, July 1961; and "An Impolite Interview with Hugh Hefner," *Realist*, May 1961. For copies of the international articles, see HS, Vol. 68.
5. Art Buchwald, "Tomorrow the World!" *New York Herald Tribune*, March 8, 1962; *Mad*, March 1960, in HS, Vol. 66; and 1962 number of *Aardvark: The Intercollegiate Magazine of Satire & Parody*, in HS, Vol. 68.
6. See the following transcripts and/or videotapes in HP: *Project '62: Playboy of the Modern World*, Canadian Broadcasting Company; *Keyhole* and *Today* from 1961; Irv Kupcinet's *At Random* CBS television talk show, July 3, 1962; Mike Wallace's *PM East*, August 18, 1961; and *The Steve Allen Show*, Nov. 6, 1963, noted in HS, Vol. 92. Many clippings about radio and television publicity appear in HS, Vols. 90–92.
7. P. T. Barnum, *Struggles and Triumphs* (New York, 1981 [1869]), 120.
8. HH on Irv Kupcinet's *At Random* CBS television talk show, July 3, 1962, HP. For typical HH statements of the *Playboy* ethos, see his comments in Hal Higdon, "Playboying Around the Clock with Hugh Hefner," *Climax*, Feb. 1962, 17, and Robin Douglas-Home, "Bosom Friends," *Queen*, Apr. 24, 1962, 50–51.
9. HH, quoted in Douglas-Home, "Bosom Friends," 51, and on Kupcinet, *At Random* television show. A typical HH explication of his sexual views came in Hal Higdon, "Playboying Around the Clock with Hugh Hefner," 17.
10. HH, quoted in Hal Higdon, "Playboying Around the Clock with Hugh Hefner," *Climax*, Feb. 1962, 12, 17–18; "World of Playboy," *Wall Street Journal*, March 22, 1962; and *The Most*, award-winning 28-minute documentary film, 1962.
11. Russell Kirk, "Bunny Ears Are Symptoms of a Sick Society," *San Francisco News Call Bulletin*, July 9, 1963; John Ciardi, "Reflections of a Square," *Saturday Review*, Nov. 2, 1963, 56; and Benjamin DeMott, "The Anatomy of 'Playboy,'" *Commentary*, Aug. 1962, 113.
12. HH, "The Playboy Philosophy," *Playboy*, Dec. 1962, 73, and HH to Milburn P. Akers of the *Chicago Sun-Times*, Sept. 23, 1963, HP.
13. HH to Milburn P. Akers of the *Chicago Sun-Times*, Sept. 23, 1963, HP.

14. HH to Milburn P. Akers of the *Chicago Sun-Times*, Sept. 23, 1963, HP, and HH memos to A. C. Spectorsky titled "Philosophy Research," dated Nov. 4, 1963, April 17, 1963, Jan. 25, 1963, March 19, and April 12, 1963. A substantial number of such memos can be found in HP.

15. Nat Lehrman interview with Trikilis Productions, 1–2; and Nat Lehrman, "Notes Toward Hefner's Autobiography," 1991, 2, 4–8; Richard Gehman, "The Fabulous Hef," ms., HP.

16. Keith Hefner interview with Murray Fisher, Feb. 22, 1991; "Highlights of Interview with Ray Russell," June 8, 1989; and Theo Spectorsky interview with Murray Fisher, May 8, 1989.

17. The Playboy Philosophy appeared in *Playboy* in twenty-five installments. Following the opening essay in December 1962, twelve appeared in 1963, six in 1964, five in 1965, and one in 1966.

18. "The Playboy Philosophy," *Playboy,* installment seven, June 1963; installment ten, Sept. 1963; installment two, Jan. 1963; and "Mort Sahl on the Philosophy," Mort Sahl file, HP.

19. See letters in "Dear Playboy," *Playboy,* June 1963, 12–13; "Dear Playboy," *Playboy,* March 1963; and "Playboy Forum," *Playboy,* Sept. 1963, 66, 77.

20. Paul F. Hoye, "An Open Letter to Mr. Hefner on Philosophy," *Providence Evening Bulletin*, Feb. 16, 1963; Robert A. Wilson, "Negative Thinking," *Realist,* June 1963, 25; and Gary Gerlach, "This Bunny Business—Playboy or 'Payboy'?" *Iowa City Iowan,* Apr. 25, 1963.

21. "Playboy," *Notre Dame Scholastic,* Mar. 8, 1963; "Statement Good, Source Questionable," *Portland (OR) Reporter,* May10, 1963; "Playboy Ethic Assailed as Infantile by Priest," *New Haven Journal-Courier,* Feb. 12, 1964; and J. A. Ward, "Hugh M. Hefner: Guardian of the Faith," *Antioch Review* (Summer 1963), 215.

22. Harvey Meyerson, "The Playboy Philosophy: Bunnies in a Tinseled Thinksville," *Chicago Sunday Sun-Times,* April 21, 1963.

23. Gary Gerlach, "This Bunny Business—Playboy or 'Payboy'?" *Iowa City Iowan,* Apr. 25, 1963; *Esquire,* Jan. 1964; and "An Infinite Number of Monkeys," *Christian Century,* Aug. 28, 1963.

24. HH to Jack Kessie, memo on "Philosophy Letters," April 24, 1963, HP, and "Playboy Forum," *Playboy,* July 1963, 41. HS, Vol. 110, contains a list of Hefner's 1965 campus engagements, along with participating panelists, several local newspaper accounts of the proceedings, and a list of the dozens of campus invitations from all around the country that he was unable to accept. On the Playboy Foundation, see James R. Petersen, *The Century of Sex* (New York, 1999), 297–298, and HH to author, Nov. 9, 2007.

25. See the following installments of the "Playboy Philosophy" in *Playboy*: Dec. 1962; Dec. 1964; Jan. 1965; Feb. 1965; and May 1965.

26. "The Playboy Philosophy," *Playboy,* March 1963.

27. "The Playboy Philosophy," *Playboy,* Jan. 1963, 52.

28. "The Playboy Philosophy," *Playboy,* Sept. 1963, Aug. 1963, and July 1963.

29. "The Playboy Philosophy," *Playboy,* March 1963, July 1963, April 1963, Jan. 1964, and Feb. 1964.

30. "The Playboy Philosophy," *Playboy,* Dec. 1963 and Jan. 1965.

31. "The Playboy Philosophy," *Playboy,* March 1963, 58.

32. HH, quoted in Malcolm Boyd, *My Fellow Americans* (New York, 1970), 55–56. On the religious ferment of the 1960s, see, for example, George M. Marsden, *Religion and American Culture* (Belmont, CA, 2001), 249–271; Leonard Sweet, "The 1960s: The Crisis of Liberal Christianity and the Public Emergence of Evangelicalism,"

in George Marsden, *Evangelicalism and Modern America* (Grand Rapids, 1984); and Robert Wuthnow, *After Heaven: Spirituality in America Since the 1950s* (Berkeley, 1998).

33. Theodore Peterson, "Playboy and the Preachers," *Columbia Journalism Review,* Spring 1966, 32–35, and J. W. MacGorman, "Playboy Philosophy Exposed," *Baptist Program,* Aug. 1965, 17.

34. J. James Thomas, "The Playboy Ethic," *Dimension,* Nov. 4, 1963, 3; J.Claude Evans, "Playboy Philosophy," *Catholic World,* Oct. 1964, 44–45; Evans, "The Playboy Philosophy," 44; and William Hamilton, "Hefner's Hasty Pudding," *Motive,* May 1963, 20–21.

35. Allen J. Moore, "Playboy Goes Religious," *Christian Advocate,* July 15, 1965, 7, and Roy Larson, "The Lowdown on the Upbeats," *Motive,* April 1960, 40. See also Darrell L. Guder, "Who Is Man and What Is Love," *Eternity,* Oct. 1964, 23.

36. Moore, "Playboy Goes Religious," 8; Larson, "Lowdown on Upbeats," 41; Cox, "Playboy's Doctrine of Male," *Christianity and Crisis,* April 17, 1961; 58–59; Frank E. Houser, "Dehumanizing the American Male," *Eternity,* Oct. 1964, 28, 30; and J. Claude Evans, "The Playboy Philosophy," 46.

37. Cox, "Playboy's Doctrine of Male," 57, 59; Guder, "Who Is Man and What Is Love," 24–25, and Houser, "Dehumanizing the American Male," 28, 29, 30.

38. "Religion and the Playboy Philosophy," *National Observer,* July 19, 1965, 15, and John Graham, "The Playboy Philosophy," 1964 sermon, HP.

39. "The Playboy Philosophy," *Playboy* Jan. 1965, 169–170; and Moore, "Playboy Goes Religious," 7.

40. "The Playboy Philosophy," *Playboy,* May 1965, 193.

41. The Reverend William Hamilton, "The Death of God," *Playboy,* August 1966, 137, 139; and "The Playboy Panel: Religion and the New Morality," *Playboy,* June 1967, 55–78, 148–161.

42. The transcript of Cox and HH at Cornell is reprinted in "Hefner and Cox: Sex— Myths and Realities," *Motive,* Nov. 1965, 7–11. See also Harvey Cox, "Revolt in the Church," *Playboy,* Jan. 1967, 129, 211; and Harvey Cox, "For Christ's Sake," *Playboy,* Jan. 1970, 117, 238.

CHAPTER 10. THE HAPPINESS EXPLOSION

1. Tom Wolfe, "Hugh Hefner, Chicago Recluse—King of the Status Drop-Outs," *New York: The Sunday Herald Tribune Magazine,* Nov. 7, 1965, 7–11, 22, 24.

2. Ibid., 22, 24, and Tom Wolfe, *The Pump House Gang* (New York, 1968), 9, 14.

3. "An Empire Built on Sex," *Life,* Oct. 29, 1965, 68A; Oriana Fallaci, "Hugh Hefner: 'I Am in the Center of the World,'" *Look,* Jan. 10, 1967, 55, 56; and "Interview with Hugh M. Hefner by Malcolm Muggeridge," 1964, HP.

4. David Farber, *The Sixties: From Memory to History* (Chapel Hill, NC, 1994), 2.

5. See, for example, Sidney Tillim, "The Fine Art of Acquiring Fine Art," *Playboy,* Jan. 1962; Ronald Jaye, "The Playboy Town House," *Playboy,* May 1962; and "Playbill," *Playboy,* Sept. 1960, 1.

6. Joseph Wood Krutch, "Life, Liberty, and the Pursuit of Unhappiness," *Playboy,* Dec. 1964; Alfred Kazin, "The Love Cult," *Playboy,* Mar. 1962; and Leslie A. Fiedler, "The Literati of the Four-Letter Word, *Playboy,* June 1961.

7. "Playbill," *Playboy,* Nov. 1960, 3; "The Playboy Panel: Sex and Censorship in Literature and the Arts," *Playboy,* July 1961; "The Playboy Panel: Uses and Abuses of the New Leisure," *Playboy,* Nov. 1965; "The Playboy Panel: "Business Ethics and Morality," *Playboy,* Nov. 1962; and "The Playboy Panel: TV's Problems and Prospects," *Playboy,* Nov. 1961.

8. Dates for these interviews in *Playboy* were: Davis, Sept. 1962; Wilder, June 1963; Sinatra, Feb. 1963; Burton, Sept. 1963; Nehru, Oct. 1963; Sartre, May 1965; Hoffa, Nov. 1963; Schweitzer, Dec. 1963; Dali, July 1964; the Beatles, Feb. 1965.

9. On the growth of the Playboy Clubs, see "Disneyland for Adults," *Playboy*, Oct. 1963. On the Lownes departure, see "Gleanings from Conversation with Eldon Sellers," Jan. 3, 1989, Eldon Sellers file, HP; Shelley Kasten interview with Murray Fisher, Jan. 30, 1991, 6; and HH, notation in HS, Vol. 75.

10. See "Corruption Uncorked in New York," *Life,* Apr. 5, 1963, and a raft of newspaper stories from the *New York Herald Tribune, New York Times,* and *Chicago Sun-Times* in HS, Vols. 80, 82, 86, 104, and 105. HH presented a detailed explanation of his magazine's role in the scandal in "The Playboy Forum," *Playboy,* Aug. 1963.

11. HS, Vol. 104; "Hefner Taking Over Palmolive Building," *Chicago American,* Apr. 24, 1965; and "The Cosmo Club," *New York Herald Tribune,* June 23, 1965.

12. HH's annual progress report dated Nov. 30, 1964, HS, Vol. 105.

13. HH memo to Jack Kessie, May 16, 1960, HP; HH memo to Jack Kessie, Jan. 24, 1963, HP; HH memo to A. C. Spectorsky, 1964; HH memo to A. C. Spectorsky, Art Paul, and Vince Tajiri, Oct. 28, 1964; and HH, "Sex in Cinema, Parts VI and VIII," Aug. 17, 1965.

14. HH memo to A. C. Spectorsky, Jack Kessie, Vince Tajiri, Bev Chamberlain, and Art Paul, Nov. 6, 1962; HH memo to Art Paul, Reid Austin, and Phil Kaplan on "Comment on Current Playboy Design," July 31, 1962; and HH memo to Harvey Kurtzman, Feb. 22, 1962.

15. HH memo on "Club Atmosphere," Nov. 12, 1962; HH memo on "Miami-Chicago Manager," Nov. 29, 1962; HH memo on "Playboy Book Publishing Schedule," Feb. 20, 1963; and HH memo on "Increasing Acceptance of Executive Responsibilities," April 8, 1965.

16. HH memo on "Receptionists," Nov. 16, 1961; HH memo on "Miscellaneous Matters at 1340," March 17, 1961; and HH memo on "Rooms at 1340," Nov. 9, 1962.

17. HH, quoted in Thomas Weyr, *Reaching for Paradise: The Playboy Vision of America* (New York, 1978), 167.

18. See Thomas Weyr, *Reaching for Paradise,* 147–155, 169–174, and Nat Lehrman interview with Lynch/Frost, May 28, 1991.

19. Paul Goodman, "The Deadly Halls of Ivy," *Playboy,* Sept. 1964; J. Paul Getty, "Money and Conformity," *Playboy,* Feb. 1961, and "The Homogenized Man," *Playboy,* Aug. 1964; and Sir Julian Huxley, "The Age of Overbreed," *Playboy,* Jan. 1965.

20. Terry Southern, "Seeing Is Believing," *Playboy,* Jan. 1965; Dan Wakefield, "The Prodigal Power of Pot," *Playboy,* Aug. 1962; and Richard Carter, "The Pursuit of Perfection," *Playboy,* Sept. 1961.

21. "Opposing Statements on the Role of the Right Wing in America Today," *Playboy,* Jan. 1963, and Marquis Childs, "The Liberal Dilemma," *Playboy,* May 1965.

22. *Variety* clipping in HS, Vol. 63, and Lownes, quoted in *Chicago Daily News,* Feb. 5, 1960.

23. News clippings and memorabilia in HS, Vols. 65 and 66; HH, "My Card File—Mid-1959 to Jan. 1961," Dec. 21, 1987; John Wilcock, "Can a Negro Be a Playboy," *Village Voice,* Oct. 19, 1961; and HH, Letter to the Editor, *Village Voice,* Nov. 9, 1961.

24. L. F. Palmer Jr., "Playboy Magazine Job Policy Bared: Playboy Employs the Best Regardless of Race," *National Courier,* March 3, 1962, and clippings in HS, Vols. 71 and 72.

25. HH, "My Card File—Mid-1959 to Jan. 1961," Dec. 21, 1987; Dick Gregory interview with Lynch/Frost, May 21, 1991; and "Hefner Guarantees Miss. Hunt Reward," *Chicago Sun-Times,* June 25, 1964.

26. HH memo to Vince Tajiri and Bev Chamberlain, March 5, 1962. See interviews in *Playboy* on the following dates: Gregory, Aug. 1964; Clay, Oct. 1964; and King, Jan. 1965.

27. See "Playboy Interview: Malcolm X," May 1963, and "Playboy Interview: George Lincoln Rockwell," April 1966.

28. Nat Hentoff, "Through the Racial Looking Glass," *Playboy,* July 1962, and James Baldwin, "Words of a Native Son," *Playboy,* Dec. 1964.

29. Norman Mailer, *The Presidential Papers* (New York, 1963), 260.

30. Keith Hefner, quoted in Gretchen Edgren, *Inside the Playboy Mansion* (Santa Monica, CA, 1998), 27, 40, and in Keith Hefner interview dated April 19, 1991. Fisher and Hope are quoted in *Inside the Playboy Mansion,* 46, 29.

31. HH, "Introduction," *Inside the Playboy Mansion,* 12.

32. HH, quoted in "Chronology of Sleep and Dexedrine-Induced Wakefulness," Oct. 11, 1990, and Victor Lownes interview with Murray Fisher, March 12, 1989, HP.

33. HH memo to Victor Lownes, June 24, 1958, HP, and HH memo to Victor Lownes, Nov. 3, 1958, HP. See other, similar memos to Lownes dated Aug. 20, 1958, and July 22, 1959.

34. Spectorsky memo to HH on "The Manipulators," Sept. 25, 1957.

35. Ray Russell to Leo Janos, Jan. 20, 1987, and Richard Rosenzweig, "Other Voices," Rosenzweig file.

36. Victor Lownes interview with Murray Fisher, March 12, 1989; "Ray Russell on the Editorial Meetings," Ray Russell file, HP; Arlene Bouras interview with Bob Carr, March 1990; and Richard Rosenzweig, "Other Voices," Rosenzweig file.

37. See memos from HH to Spectorsky from Oct. 1965 in "Mansion Story" file, and Spectorsky memo to HH on "Mansion Copy," Nov. 2, 1965.

38. "Murray Fisher on the Chicago Mansion Story," HP. The piece appeared as "The Playboy Mansion," *Playboy,* Jan. 1966.

39. "Hefner Arrested on Obscenity Charge," *Chicago Tribune,* June 5, 1963; "Two Definitions of Obscenity," *Time,* June 21, 1963; Hugh Hefner, "Freedom of Religion in Chicago," *Freethinker,* Dec. 13, 1963, 394, 398–399; Murray Rosenfeld memoir in "Mansfield Bust" file, HP; "Franklin, Freud Invoked in Hefner Obscenity Trial," *Chicago Sun-Times,* Nov. 22, 1963; "Hefner's Attorney Brands Franklin a Playboy of '76," *Chicago American,* Nov. 21, 1963; "Hefner defends Playboy," *Chicago Tribune,* Dec. 6, 1963; "Judge Rules Mistrial in Hefner Case," *Chicago Tribune,* Dec. 7, 1963; and Colin McCall, "*Playboy* and the Catholics," *Freethinker,* Dec. 13, 1963, 393–394.

40. HH memo "1961 Scrapbook Memories," to Larry DuBois, Murray Fisher, and Reg Potterson, June 15, 1990.

41. HH memo "1961 Scrapbook Memories," to Larry DuBois, Murray Fisher, and Reg Potterson, June 15, 1990; Joni Mattis and HH, quoted in *Inside the Playboy Mansion,* 40, 58; and HS, Vol. 96, which is filled with stories about, and nude snapshots of, Ms. Michele.

42. *Inside the Playboy Mansion,* 42, and HH memo, June 15, 1990.

43. HH memo, Nov. 14, 1989, and HH memo, June 15, 1990.

44. Maddox, quoted in *Inside the Playboy Mansion,* 42, and HH memo to Larry DuBois and Murray Fisher, Oct. 2, 1990.

45. HH, quoted in *Inside the Playboy Mansion,* 43, and HH memo to Larry DuBois and Murray Fisher, Oct. 2, 1990.

46. Cynthia Maddox, quoted in *Inside the Playboy Mansion,* 44, and in "Sex Is Here to Pay," *Weekend,* July 19–25, 1966.

47. Cynthia Maddox, quoted in "Sex Is Here to Pay,". *Weekend,* July 19–25, 1966.

48. Cynthia Maddox, quoted in "Sex Is Here to Pay," *Weekend,* July 19–25, 1966; HH and Cynthia Maddox, quoted in *Inside the Playboy Mansion,* 43–44; and HH memo "1961 Scrapbook Memories," to Larry DuBois, Murray Fisher, and Reg Potterson, June 15, 1990.

49. Mary Warren file, HP, and HH interview with Patrick Anderson, Nov. 2, 1991.

50. Richard Rosenzweig interview with the author, Aug. 5, 2005, and Nat Lehrman and HH, quoted in *Inside the Playboy Mansion*, 65, 64.

51. Shel Silverstein in 1968 statement, Mary Warren file, HP; Warren, quoted in 1968 statement, Mary Warren file, HP; and HH, quoted in *Inside the Playboy Mansion*, 65.

52. "An Empire Built on Sex," *Life*, Oct. 29, 1965, 68–70. Warren's changing hair color can be seen in the dozens of snapshots in HS volumes on the period from 1963 to 1968.

53. Sally Bealls interview with Murray Fisher, fall 1989; HH, quoted in Oriana Fallaci, "Hugh Hefner: 'I Am in the Center of the World,'" *Look*, Jan. 10, 1967, 57; and HH memo to Larry DuBois and Murray Fisher, Oct. 23, 1990.

54. HH in 1968 statement, Mary Warren file, HP; Humphrey's party noted in HS, Vol. 103; and "An Empire Built on Sex," 68–70.

55. See photos of Mary Warren, and cards from her to HH, in HS, Vols. 91, 93, 99, and 114.

56. 1968 statement in Mary Warren file, HP; Warren and HH's dating activity as detailed in HS, Vols. 132, 135, 136, 137; Warren's 1968 card in Vol. 138.

CHAPTER 11. MAKE LOVE, NOT WAR

1. See HHIA, Nov. 3, 2005; HH to Larry DuBois and Murray Fisher, Dec. 10, 1990; and "Swinging London: 'You Can Walk Across It on the Grass,'" cover story, *Time*, April 15, 1966, 30–34.

2. "Anything Goes: The Permissive Society," *Newsweek*, Nov. 13, 1967, 74–76.

3. Max Lerner, "The Pleasure Society," *New York Post*, Oct. 11, 1967.

4. For the classic treatment of this theme, see Tom Wolfe, *Radical Chic & Mau-Mauing the Flak Catchers* (New York, 1970).

5. See cover, introductory "Letter from the Publisher," and "Think Clean," pp. 76–82, all in *Time*, March 3, 1967.

6. HS 131 and videotape of *The Pursuit of Pleasure*, NBC News Special, broadcast May 8, 1967, HP.

7. Dennis Dugan, "Empire Run from a Round Bed," *Newsday*, Aug. 13, 1968; *Playboy Progress Report 1968*, HP; "Playboy Puts a Glint in the Admen's Eye," *Business Week*, June 28, 1969, 142–144; "No Playboys Work for Hugh," *Generation: The Magazine of Young Businessmen*, Sept. 1968, 21–24; and "On Passing 5,000,000," *Barron's*, March 25, 1968, 1.

8. See photographs and articles on the Playboy Building in HS, Vol. 131; Gene Siskel, "A Big Bunny Joyride," *Chicago Tribune*, Feb. 19, 1970; Phil Casey, "Airborne Playboy," *Washington Post*, Feb. 8, 1970; "Hugh Hefner's Jet Black Bunny in the Sky," *Look*, June 2, 1970; and HS, Vol. 132.

9. See the following erotic articles in *Playboy*: "The French Fonda," Aug. 1966; "The Bunnies of Missouri," March 1967; and "Brush-On Fashions," March 1968. On literature, see the following in *Playboy*: Jean-Paul Sartre, "The Parisians and the Germans," Jan. 1966; Isaac Bashevis Singer, "The Courtship," Sept. 1967; Saul Bellow, "The Old System," Jan. 1968; Kurt Vonnegut Jr., "Fortitude," Sept. 1968; John Updike, "I Am Dying, Egypt, Dying," Sept. 1969; Graham Greene, "Crook's Tour," Nov. 1969; and Joyce Carol Oates, "Saul Bird Says: Relate, Communicate," Oct. 1970.

10. See the following consumer articles in *Playboy*: "The Sophisticated Planesman," March 1966; "Building a Business Wardrobe," Nov. 1966; and "Playboy's Guide to a Continental Holiday," May 1968. See the following Playboy Interviews: Federico Fellini, Feb. 1966; Bob Dylan, March 1966; Woody Allen, May 1967; Michelangelo Antonioni, Nov. 1967; and Stanley Kubrick, Sept. 1968.

11. See in *Playboy*: James Farmer, "Mood Ebony," Feb. 1966; "Playboy Panel: The Crisis in Law Enforcement," March 1966; and Max Lerner, "Red China, the United States, and the United Nations," July 1966.

12. See in *Playboy*: Edward Bentley, "Conscience Versus Conformity," Jan. 1967; Max Lerner, "Climate of Violence," June 1967; and Kenneth Roxroth, "The Fuzz," July 1967.

13. See Playboy Interviews with: Arthur Schlesinger Jr., May 1966; Fidel Castro, Jan. 1967; and Timothy Leary, Sept. 1966. See also Jacob Brackman, "The Underground Press," *Playboy*, Aug. 1967.

14. See the stories in *Playboy*, Dec. 1967.

15. On the turbulent Democratic Convention in Chicago, see David Farber, *Chicago '68* (Chicago, 1988).

16. On Hefner's experiences with the Chicago Democratic Convention and the Chicago police, see articles in HS, Vols. 139 and 140; Charlotte Curtis, "Guests Flock to Weeklong Party Given by Playboy's Publisher," *New York Times*, Aug. 29, 1968; "Street Violence Invades Playboy Empire," *Chicago American*, Aug. 28, 1968; and Hefner's press conference remarks as reprinted in *Law and Disorder: The Chicago Convention and Its Aftermath* (New York, 1968), 86.

17. The best treatment of the events surrounding the Democratic Convention is David Farber, *Chicago '68* (Chicago, 1988). See two other books by Farber for insightful treatments of late 1960s America: *The Age of Great Dreams: America in the 1960s* (New York, 1994), chaps. 8–10, and his edited collection of essays, *The Sixties: From Memory to History* (Chapel Hill, NC, 1994).

18. HH, quoted in "Lord of the Bunnies," *San Francisco Chronicle-Examiner*, July 10, 1966, and in "The APME Red Book 1967," An Account of the Annual Convention of the Associated Press Managing Editors Assn. at Chicago, Oct. 17–20, 1967, 74–75.

19. HH, quoted in the following: Calvin Tompkins, "Mr. Playboy of the Western World," *Saturday Evening Post*, April 23, 1966, 101; "The APME Red Book 1967," 67; William Tusher, "Hefner Sees Link Sex Ban with Racial Bias," *Hollywood Reporter*, Dec. 1, 1969, 8; "Phone Dialogue: The American Sex Revolution," with Dr. Albert Ellis, *Voices: The Art and Science of Psychotherapy*, Spring 1967, 90; and "Why Not Pornography?" a forum discussion on University of Chicago TV program *Roundtable*, broadcast Oct. 3, 1969.

20. See HH's statements in "Mr. Playboy of the Western World," 101; David Farr, "The Night the Bishop Dropped In at Sex HQ," *The People*, Aug. 17, 1969; and Malcolm Boyd, *My Fellow Americans* (New York, 1970), 30–33.

21. HH, quoted in Boyd, *My Fellow Americans*, 33; HH to Larry DuBois and Murray Fisher, Dec. 10, 1990. He reaffirmed this political sensibility in HIA, Nov. 3, 2005.

22. See in *Playboy*: Jack Lind, "The Sexual Freedom League," Nov. 1966; Richard Warren Lewis, "The Swingers," April 1969; "A Swinger's Guide to Academe," Sept. 1968; "The Playboy Interview: Masters and Johnson," May 1968; and "The Playboy Interview: Dr. Mary Calderone," April 1970.

23. See in *Playboy*: Howard Junker, "Theater of the Nude," Nov. 1968; "Sweet Paula," Aug. 1969; and Bruce Williamson, "Oh! Calcutta!" Oct. 1969.

24. See "Playboy Forum," *Playboy*, Sept. 1968 and March 1969.

25. See in *Playboy*: "Hang One On," Aug. 1968; "Enter the Nonsuit," May 1970; and "Back to Campus," Sept. 1970.

26. See in *Playboy*: R. E. L. Masters, "Sex, Ecstasy, and Drugs," Nov. 1967; "Pot: A Rational Approach," Oct. 1969; and Playboy Panel on "The Drug Revolution," Feb. 1970.

27. See in *Playboy*: Nat Hentoff, "Youth—The Oppressed Majority," Sept. 1967; "Playboy Panel: The Student Revolt," Sept. 1969; Nat Hentoff, "The War Against Dissent," Sept. 1968; David Halberstam, "The Americanization of Vietnam," Jan. 1970; Geoffrey Norman, "Project Survival," July 1970; and Harvey Cox, "For Christ's Sake," Jan. 1970.

28. See in *Playboy*: Senator Jacob Javits, "Lower the Voting Age," Feb. 1968; Senator J. William Fulbright, "A New Order of Priorities," July 1968; Senator Joseph D. Tydings, "Americans and the Gun," March 1969; Senator Frank Church, "The Global Crunch," Aug. 1969; Justice William O. Douglas, "An Inquest on Our Lakes and Rivers," June 1968; and the Honorable Arthur J. Goldberg, "Our Besieged Bill of Rights," Jan. 1970. On King, see HH to Larry DuBois and Murray Fisher, Dec. 10, 1990.

29. See the following Playboy Interviews: William Sloane Coffin, Aug. 1968; Ralph Nader, Oct. 1968; Jesse Jackson, Nov. 1969; and William Kunstler, Oct. 1970. See also Michael Horowitz, "Portrait of the Marxist as an Old Trouper," *Playboy*, Sept. 1970.

30. In *Playboy*, see: "Turned On," Playmate Debbie Hooper, Aug. 1969; "Revolutionary Discovery," Playmate Gloria Root, Dec. 1969; and "Tuned-In Dropout," Elaine Morton, June 1970.

31. See in *Playboy*: "Martyrs of Hope: Martin Luther King and Robert Kennedy," Jan. 1969; "The Decent Society," Jan. 1969; "Bring Us Together," Jan. 1970; and "Playboy's Political Preference Chart," Nov. 1970.

32. On *Playboy*'s strong libertarian bent, see Nat Hentoff interview with Murray Fisher, Sept. 2, 1989, 3, HP.

33. Lee Winfrey, "Have the Times Outrun the World of Playboy?" *Detroit Free Press*, March 2, 1970, and Morton L. Ross, "Poor Richard and Playboy: Brothers Under the Flesh," *Colorado Quarterly* (Spring 1967), 355–360.

34. Student quoted in Malcolm Boyd, *My Fellow Americans*, 16, and another quoted in "Playboy Puts a Glint in the Admen's Eye," *Business Week*, June 28, 1969, 144.

35. "The Playboy Forum," *Playboy*, Nov. 1969.

36. See, for instance, two of J. Paul Getty's pieces in *Playboy*: "The Educated Executive," Sept. 1968, and "Two Paths to the Top," Dec. 1969. See also in *Playboy*, Nov. 1970: "West of Eden," and "Presents Perfect."

37. HH, quoted in the following: Malcolm Boyd, *My Fellow Americans*, 27, 31; "Hugh Hefner's Jet Black Bunny in the Sky," *Look*, June 2, 1970; and Wayne Warga, "Hefner Hops Aboard the TV Bandwagon," *Los Angeles Times*, Aug. 11, 1968.

38. Christopher Lasch, *The Culture of Narcissism* (New York, 1978), especially 12–16, 81–83, offers the most powerful rendering of this critique. For other versions, see Thomas Frank, *The Conquest of Cool: Business Culture, Counterculture, and the Rise of Hip Consumerism* (Chicago, 1997); David Brooks, *Bobos in Paradise: The New Upper Class and How They Got There* (New York, 2001); and Joseph Heath and Andrew Potter, *Nation of Rebels: Why Counterculture Became Consumer Culture* (New York, 2005).

39. HH, quoted in Malcolm Boyd, *My Fellow Americans*, 32–33; Harvey Cox, "God and the Hippies," *Playboy*, Jan. 1968; and "Leisure in the Seventies," *Playboy*, Dec. 1970.

40. HH, quoted in Boyd, *My Fellow Americans*, 21.

41. HH, quoted in Stephanie Fuller, "Hefner: Old Age and the Playboy Philosophy," *Chicago Tribune*, April 24, 1968; "Hugh Hefner Faces Middle Age," *Time*, Feb. 14, 1969, 69–70; and HHIA, Nov. 3, 2005.

42. See Hefner's comments in "The New Hugh Hefner—An Edwardian Look," *Midwest: Magazine of the Chicago Sun-Times*, May 5, 1968, and in "Hefner: Old Age and the Playboy Philosophy."

43. HH, quoted in Stephanie Fuller, "Hefner: Old Age and the Playboy Philosophy," *Chicago Tribune,* April 24, 1968; "The New Hugh Hefner—An Edwardian Look," *Midwest: Magazine of the Chicago Sun-Times,* May 5, 1968; and HHIA, Nov. 3, 2005.

44. HH to Larry DuBois and Murray Fisher, Dec. 10, 1990; HH to Larry DuBois and Murray Fisher, Jan. 15, 1991; HS, Vols. 138–142; and HHIA, Nov. 3, 2005.

45. HH to Larry DuBois and Murray Fisher, Dec. 10, 1990.

46. See HH to Larry DuBois and Murray Fisher, Dec. 10, 1990, 17–18.

47. See HS, Vol. 136.

48. HHIA, Nov. 3, 2005; Bill Cosby interview with Murray Fisher, Aug. 27, 1989; and HH to Larry DuBois and Murray Fisher, Dec. 10, 1990. On the Lake Geneva resort, see HS, Vol. 137, and "Every Man's Eden," *Institutions: Magazine of the Service World,* Aug. 1968, 85–100.

49. HHIA, Nov. 3, 2005, and HH, quoted in Wayne Warga, "Hefner Hops Aboard TV Bandwagon," *Los Angeles Times,* Aug. 11, 1968.

50. HH, quoted in Boyd, *My Fellow Americans,* 59; HS, Vols. 138–140; and HH, quoted, in "Playboy Nocturnal Syndi to Air Hefner, Advanced Sex," *Variety,* Aug. 1, 1968, 10.

51. HH to DuBois and Fisher, Jan. 15, 1991; Lee Wolfberg, "Other Voices," HP; HS, Vol. 139; and HHIA, Nov. 3, 2005.

52. Barbi Benton, "Other Voices," HP; HH to DuBois and Fisher, Jan 15, 1991; and HHIA, Nov. 3, 2005.

53. HS, Vol. 139, which contains Klein's map; HH to DuBois and Fisher, Jan 15, 1991; and Barbi Benton interview with Murray Fisher, Mar. 12, 1991.

54. HS, Vol. 139; Barbi Benton interview with Murray Fisher, Mar. 12, 1991; HH to DuBois and Fisher, Jan 15, 1991; HHIA, Nov. 3, 2005; and Bill Cosby interview with Murray Fisher, Aug. 27, 1989.

55. Barbi Benton interview with Murray Fisher, Mar. 12, 1991; HH to DuBois and Fisher, Jan. 15, 1991; and HHIA, Nov. 3, 2005.

56. HS, Vols. 145, 146, 148, 149; "Hefner Calls Barbara His First Love," *Sacramento Union,* Aug. 8, 1969; "Playboy's Playboy Grooms Playmate," *Columbus (OH) Citizen-Journal,* Aug. 8, 1969; and Barbi Benton interview with Murray Fisher, Mar. 12, 1991.

57. Barbi Benton interview with Murray Fisher, Mar. 12, 1991, 17–18.

58. BB quoted in "Barbi Is a Doll—Hugh Hefner's, That Is," *Chicago Tribune,* Jan. 18, 1970; "Barbi Doll," *Playboy,* March 1970; BB quoted in "Barbi Is a Doll—Hugh Hefner's, That Is," *Chicago Tribune,* Jan. 18, 1970; and Barbi Benton interview with Murray Fisher, Mar. 12, 1991.

CHAPTER 12. WHAT DO WOMEN WANT?

1. "10 at College Strip During Playboy Talk," *Chicago Tribune,* Feb. 6, 1969.

2. "Playboy Plus Antioch Plus Protest," *Chicago Sun-Times,* May 21, 1969, and Gene Siskel, "Feminist Strikes at Playboy," *Chicago Sun-Times,* Dec. 15, 1969.

3. On domestic containment, see Elaine Tyler May, *Homeward Bound: American Families in the Cold War Era* (New York, 1988). See also Alice Echols, "Nothing Distant About It: Women's Liberation and Sixties Radicalism," in David Farber, ed., *The Sixties: From Memory to History* (Chapel Hill, NC, 1999), 151–152, who described this same female role as "ultradomesticity."

4. This situation is discussed in May, *Homeward Bound*; Ruth Rosen, *The World Split Open*; and Alice Kessler-Harris, *Out to Work: A History of Wage-Earning Women in the United States* (New York, 1982).

5. The *Babs and Shirley* cartoon was reprinted in *Playboy: 50 Years, the Cartoons* (San Francisco, 2004), 32.

6. HH, quoted in Robin Douglas-Home, "Bosom Friends," *Queen,* Apr. 24, 1962, 51; and HH comments on Irv Kupcinet's *At Random,* CBS television show in Chicago, July 3, 1962.

7. See in *Playboy*: Shepherd Mead, "Beware of Hasty Marriage," Sept. 1962, and "The Playboy Coloring Book," Jan. 1963.

8. Shepherd Mead, "The Handling of Women in Business," *Playboy,* Jan. 1957, 54; "Give Your Wife the Pink Pedestal" advertisement, offered by "The Tycoon" in Philadelphia, *Playboy,* Sept. 1956; and Lownes, quoted in Bill Davidson, "Czar of the Bunny Empire," *Saturday Evening Post,* Apr. 28, 1962, 36.

9. HH, quoted in "About the Nudes in Playboy," *U.S. Camera,* April 1962, 69; HH on Irv Kupcinet's *At Random,* CBS television show in Chicago, July 3, 1962; and HH to Jean Shepherd, June 8, 1961, HP.

10. See in *Playboy*: Bob Norman [Burt Zollo], "Miss Gold-digger of 1953," Dec. 1953; Jules Archer, "The Great Guessing Game," March 1956; and William Iversen, "I Only Want a Sweetheart, Not a Buddy," July 1960.

11. See the following articles by Philip Wylie in *Playboy*: "The Abdicating Male," Nov. 1956; "The Womanization of America," Sept. 1958; and "The Career Woman," Jan. 1963.

12. "The Playboy Panel: The Womanization of America," *Playboy,* June 1962.

13. HH, quoted in "Banned Program," *Mademoiselle,* Oct. 1963, 113. (This 1958 Susskind television show on "The Sexual Revolution in America" was killed at the time because of its frankness, but the transcript was later reprinted in *Mademoiselle*.); HH in "About the Nudes in Playboy," *U.S. Camera,* April 1962, 68; and "An Impolite Interview with Hugh Hefner," *Realist,* May, 1961, 9–10. See similar comments from HH in Robin Douglas-Home, "Bosom Friends," *Queen,* Apr. 24, 1962, 51, and in HH to Jean Shepherd, June 8, 1961, HP, where he asserted "a real and crying need for an antidote to the female-dominated, castrated society in which we live."

14. HH, quoted in *Project '62: Playboy of the Modern World,* 1962, transcript of radio documentary broadcast by the Canadian Broadcasting Company, HP.

15. HH's statements on Irv Kupcinet, *At Random* CBS television talk show, July 3, 1962, HP.

16. Transcript of *The Dick Cavett Show* No. 1, 1970, HP.

17. Transcript of *The Dick Cavett Show* No. 2, 1970, HP. See a report on the incident in "Cavett Gets an Added Lib," *New York Post,* May 27, 1970.

18. Gloria Steinem, "A Bunny's Tale," *Show,* May and June 1963. Steinem's recollections of the project can be found in Carolyn G. Heilbrun, *The Education of a Woman: The Life of Gloria Steinem* (New York, 1995), 104–107. A forerunner of the Steinem article came in Jane Kramer, "Dreams of a Playboy: Bunnies on the Rabbit Run," *Village Voice,* Nov. 29, 1962, a skeptical, sarcastic report on the training of bunnies for the about-to-open NYC Playboy Club.

19. Steinem, "A Bunny's Tale."

20. Ibid.

21. Kathryn Leigh Scott, *The Bunny Years: The Surprising Inside Story of the Playboy Clubs, the Women Who Worked as Bunnies, and Where They Are Now* (Los Angeles, 1998), 6, 184, 144, 147.

22. Gloria Steinem, *The Beach Book* (New York, 1963), and Gloria Steinem to HH, July 7, 1962, HP.

23. Marie Torre, "A Woman Looks at the Girly-Girly Magazines," *Cosmopolitan,* May 1963, 42, 43; Diane Lurie, "In Hefnerland, Women Are Status Symbols," *Life,* Oct. 29, 1965, 70; and Gregor Roy, "Plato, the Penthouse, and the Girl Who Hesitates," *Mademoiselle,* March 1965, 249.

24. Theodore Irwin, "Cosmopolitan Interviews Hugh M. Hefner, Playboy's Controversial Editor," *Cosmopolitan,* May 1966, 79–80; Oriana Fallaci, "Hugh Hefner: 'I Am in the Center of the World,'" *Look,* Jan. 1967, 56; "The Playboy Philosophy . . . Hefner Analyzes Women," *San Francisco Examiner,* Nov. 15, 1965; and HH interviewed by Dr. Albert Ellis on Sept. 22, 1966, in "The American Sex Revolution," *Voices,* Spring 1967, 94, 95. HH also offered a clear explanation of this argument in Malcolm Boyd, *My Fellow Americans,* 35.

25. Marjorie Proops, "At the Court of the Playboy King," *New York Daily Mirror,* May 29, 1968; "Hugh Hefner Raps," *Eye,* July 1968, 67; and "Playboy Mansion Hopping with Bunny Prospects," *Chicago Tribune,* Feb. 9, 1969.

26. See in *Playboy:* John Clellon Holmes, "The New Girl," Jan. 1968; "The No-Bra Look," Sept. 1970; and Robert Hall, "The Abortion Revolution," Sept. 1970.

27. "Playboy Forum," *Playboy,* April 1970, 60. See "Playboy Forum," *Playboy,* April 1968, 61–62, for an earlier statement.

28. "Playboy Attacked by Student Feminists," *Daily Trojan,* April 9, 1970; "Women Seen as 'House Niggers' and Victims of Hugh Hefner," *Little Rock Democrat,* Nov. 11, 1970; Guy Livingston, "Femme Liberation Group Pickets Hub Playboy to Protest Bunnies," *Variety,* April 2, 1970.

29. Gloria Steinem, "What Playboy Doesn't Know About Women Could Fill a Book," *McCall's,* Oct. 1970.

30. Susan Braudy, "The Article I Wrote on Women That *Playboy* Wouldn't Publish," *Glamour,* May 1971, and Morton Hunt, "Up Against the Wall, Male Chauvinist Pig!" *Playboy,* May 1970. The magazine offered additional defense of its position in the August 1970 issue in "Playboy Forum," 52, and "Dear Playboy," 8.

31. "Confrontation at Hefner's Pad," *Chicago Daily News,* April 16, 1970; "Antibunnies Jeer at Hefner Peace Bash," *Los Angeles Times,* April 17, 1970; "Women Shake Up Peace Establishment," *Voices,* May 1970; and "Playboy's Gal Bucks Her Boss," *Chicago Sun-Times,* April 16, 1970.

32. HH to A. C. Spectorsky, Jan. 6, 1970, PP. The memo was extracted nearly in its entirety in "New Feminists Are the 'Natural Enemy,'" *Voices,* May 1970, 1–2.

33. "Women's Liberation Adherents Go to War with Playboy Again," *Chicago Tribune,* April 24, 1970; "Liberation Sisters Unite to Take the Play out of Playboy," *Chicago Sun-Times,* April 24, 1970; and "Male and Female," *Newsweek,* May 18, 1970.

34. "Playboy Interview: Germaine Greer," *Playboy,* Jan. 1972; "Playboy Interview: Betty Friedan," *Playboy,* Sept. 1992; and HH, quoted in Malcolm Boyd, *My Fellow Americans,* 53–54.

35. Oriana Fallaci, "Hugh Hefner: 'I Am in the Center of the World,'" *Look,* Jan. 1967, 57.

36. HH, quoted in "Sex Is Here to Pay," *Weekend,* July 19–25, 1966.

37. Fallaci, "Center of the World," 56–57; "Hugh Hefner Raps," *Eye,* July 1968, 67; and HH, quoted in Malcolm Boyd, *My Fellow Americans,* 65.

38. Maddox, quoted in "Sex Is Here to Pay"; Fallaci, "Center of the World," 57; and HH, quoted in Malcolm Boyd, *My Fellow Americans,* 61–62.

39. "Playboy Interview: Hugh M. Hefner," *Playboy,* Jan. 1974, 68, 70.

40. See Barbara Ehrenreich, *The Hearts of Men: American Dreams and the Flight from Commitment* (New York, 1983), 50–51, and Betty Friedan, *The Feminine Mystique* (New York, 1963), especially chapter 1, "The Problem That Has No Name," and chapter 12, "Progressive Dehumanization: The Comfortable Concentration Camp."

41. Ehrenreich, *Hearts of Men,* 49, and Friedan, *Feminine Mystique,* 322–332. On the culture of self-fulfillment, see T. J. Jackson Lears, "From Salvation to Self-Realization: Advertising and the Therapeutic Roots of the Consumer Culture, 1880–1930," in Lears and Richard Wightman Fox, *The Culture of Consumption: Critical Essays in American History, 1880–1980* (New York, 1983), 3–38.

42. On the split between equity and gender feminism, see Christina Hoff Sommers, *Who Stole Feminism? How Women Have Betrayed Women* (New York, 1994), 22–29, 131–136. On disputes within feminism over lesbianism, see Ruth Rosen, *The World Split Open: How the Modern Women's Movement Changed America* (New York, 2000), 164–175.

43. Joyce Carol Oates, "Playboy Forum," *Playboy,* Jan. 1975, 18.

CHAPTER 13. DOWN THE RABBIT HOLE

1. The "world on a string" comment came in HH memo to Larry DuBois, Murray Fisher, and Patrick Anderson, Dec. 9, 1991, HP.

2. Bruce J. Schulman, *The Seventies: The Great Shift in American Culture, Society, and Politics* (Cambridge, MA, 2002), 80. Other useful assessments of the 1970s include David Frum, *How We Got Here: The 70s, the Decade That Brought You Modern Life—For Better or Worse* (New York, 2000), and Beth Bailey and David Farber, eds., *America in the Seventies* (Lawrence, KS, 2004).

3. HH memo to Larry DuBois and Murray Fisher, July 10, 1991, HP.

4. HH memos to DuBois, Fisher, and Anderson, Jan. 28, 1992, and Dec. 17, 1991, HP.

5. HH memo to DuBois, Fisher, and Anderson, Jan. 28, 1992, HP, and "Barbi File," HP.

6. Barbi Benton interview with Murray Fisher, Mar. 12, 1991, and HH memo to DuBois, Fisher, and Anderson, Jan. 28, 1992, HP.

7. HH memo to DuBois and Fisher, July 10, 1991, HP; HH memo to DuBois, Fisher, and Anderson, Jan. 28, 1992, HP; and Benton quoted in Tom Burke, "Here's Barbi: Hugh Hefner's Playmate," *Cosmopolitan,* Sept. 1973, 67.

8. Carlton Stowers, "Karen Christy: A Visit with Miss December," *Dallas Morning News Sunday Magazine,* Feb. 27, 1972, 5–7, and Karen Christy interview with Larry DuBois, Feb. 1992.

9. HH memo to DuBois and Fisher, July 10, 1991, HP.

10. HH memo to DuBois, Fisher, and Anderson, Jan. 28, 1992, HP, and HH memo to DuBois and Fisher, July 10, 1991, HP.

11. Karen Christy interview with Larry DuBois, Feb. 1992; HH memo to DuBois and Fisher, July 10, 1991, HP; and HH memo to DuBois, Fisher, and Anderson, Jan. 28, 1992, HP.

12. Karen Christy interview with Larry DuBois, Feb. 1992; and HH memo to DuBois, Fisher, and Anderson, Jan. 28, 1992, HP.

13. HH memo to Bobbie Arnstein, Sept. 25, 1972, noted in "Karen Christy File," HP, and HH quoted in Gretchen Edgren, *Inside the Playboy Mansion* (Santa Monica, CA, 1998), 132.

14. Karen Christy interview with Larry DuBois, Feb. 1992; HH memo to DuBois, Fisher, and Anderson, Jan. 28, 1992, HP; and HH memo to DuBois and Fisher, July 10, 1991, HP.

15. Barbi Benton interview with Murray Fisher, Mar. 12, 1991, and "Adventures in the Skin Trade," *Time,* July 30, 1973, 52.

16. Barbi Benton, quoted in "Hef in Hot Water," *People,* Oct. 22, 1973, and in "Barbi, the Girl of the Golden West," *Los Angeles Times,* Sept. 7, 1973; "The Blond Who Stole Hefner from Barbi," *San Francisco Examiner,* Oct. 22, 1973; "Surprise—Karen Is Hefner's No. 1 Now," *Chicago Daily News,* June 14, 1973; and HH memo to DuBois, Fisher, and Anderson, Jan. 28, 1992, HP.

17. HH, memo to DuBois, Fisher, and Anderson, Jan. 28, 1992, HP, and Christy interview with Larry DuBois, Feb. 1992.

18. Christy interview with Larry DuBois, Feb. 1992; and HH memo to DuBois, Fisher, and Anderson, Jan. 28, 1992, HP.

19. Ibid.

20. Barbi Benton interview with Murray Fisher, Mar. 12, 1991; and Barbi Benton, "Other Voices," HP.

21. "Federal Drug Probers Zeroing In on Hefner," *Chicago Tribune,* Dec. 8, 1974; and "Hollywood Figures Tied to Playboy Drug Probe," *Chicago Sun-Times,* Dec. 9, 1974.

22. HH memo to Patrick Anderson, Larry DuBois, and Murray Fisher, Jan. 28, 1992.

23. "Hef's Secretary Faces Drug Case," *Chicago Tribune,* March 22, 1974.

24. For *Playboy* insiders' conviction that government authorities were out to get them, see HH interview with Joe Wiesman in "An Embattled King in the Playboy Empire," *Washington Post,* Jan. 26, 1975, and Arthur Kretchmer, "Other Voices," HP.

25. HH memo to Patrick Anderson, March 11, 1992.

26. On the government's belief that "The illegal trafficking of narcotics permeated the Playboy organization," see Douglas P. Roller and Gary S. Shapiro, Chicago Strike Force, U.S. Government Memo to Edward T. Joyce, Dept. of Justice, Dec. 18, 1974, copy in HP. On Arnstein's April suicide attempt, see Larry DuBois, "Remembering Bobbie" ms., 2000, HP.

27. Pat Colander, "The Life and Death of Bobbie Arnstein," *Reader: Chicago's Free Weekly,* Aug. 15, 1975; Shirley Hillman interview with Larry DuBois, June 6, 1991; and Barbara Kerr, "Bobbie Arnstein" ms., 1978, HP.

28. Colander, "The Life and Death of Bobbie Arnstein."

29. Kerr, "Bobbie Arnstein"; "Crash in Indiana Kills an Editor of Playboy Magazine," *Chicago Sun-Times,* August 10, 1963; Shirley Hillman interview with Larry DuBois, June 6, 1991; and Colander, "The Life and Death of Bobbie Arnstein."

30. Kerr, "Bobbie Arnstein," and DuBois, "Remembering Bobbie."

31. Michelle Urry interview with Lynch/Frost, April 25, 1991; Becky Strick interview with Larry DuBois and Murray Fisher, June 19, 1991; Hillman interview with DuBois.

32. Hillman interview with DuBois; and Bobbie Arnstein, "Memo to New Bunny Mothers," undated, HP.

33. Karen Christy interview with Larry DuBois, Feb. 1992; Hillman interview with DuBois; Strick interview with DuBois and Fisher; and Urry interview with Lynch/Frost.

34. Christy interview with DuBois, Feb. 1992; Kerr, "Bobbie Arnstein"; and DuBois, "Remembering Bobbie," which contains the HH quote.

35. Hillman interview with DuBois; Strick interview with DuBois and Fisher; Phyllis Mahoney to Dick Rozensweig, July 20, 1993, HP; Michelle Urry interview with Murray Fisher, April 5, 1991; and Urry interview with Lynch/Frost.

36. Hillman interview with DuBois, and Urry interview with Fisher.

37. Bobbie Arnstein to John Dante, Dec. 30, 1971, HP, and Bobbie Arnstein to Dick Rosenzweig, Feb. 13, 1974, HP.

38. Colander, "The Life and Death of Bobbie Arnstein"; Bobbie Arnstein to Phyllis Mahoney, undated, HP; and Kerr, "Bobbie Arnstein."

39. Kerr, "Bobbie Arnstein"; Colander, "The Life and Death of Bobbie Arnstein"; and Strick interview with DuBois and Fisher.

40. "Hef's Secretary Faces Drug Case," *Chicago Tribune,* March 22, 1974; Colander, "The Life and Death of Bobbie Arnstein"; Strick interview with DuBois and Fisher; Hillman interview with DuBois; and Urry interview with Lynch/Frost.

41. HH memo to Patrick Anderson, March 11, 1992; "Voluntary Statement" given to DEA by William Noel, June 15, 1974, HP; and Department of Justice Memorandum, Chicago Strike Force to Edward T. Joyce, Deputy Chief of Criminal Division, Dec. 18, 1974, copy in HP.

42. "Playboy Connection Told at Trial," *Chicago Daily News,* Oct. 22, 1974; "Dope Sale to Hefner Aide Told," *Chicago Tribune,* Oct. 22, 1974; "Hefner Aide Found Guilty," *Chicago Sun-Times,* Oct. 31, 1974; "Playboy Aide Gets 15 Years," *Chicago Tribune,* Nov. 27, 1974; HH memo to Patrick Anderson, March 11, 1992; and Patrick Anderson, *High in America: The True Story Behind NORML and the Politics of Marijuana* (New York, 1981), chap. 8. Anderson's book relies upon extensive conversations with Keith Stroup, head of NORML and close friend of, and attorney for, Bobbie Arnstein.

43. "Federal Drug Probers Zeroing In on Hefner"; "Hollywood Figures Tied to Playboy Drug Probe"; "Playboy Ex-Security Aide Says Drugs Used at Mansion," *Chicago Tribune,* Dec. 9, 1974; "New Quiz by Carey in Playboy Girl Death," *Chicago Daily News,* Dec. 11, 1974; "Call Hefner in Death Quiz," *Chicago Tribune,* Dec. 12, 1974; and "Playboy Bunny Murdered, Mother Says; Tells of Clues," *Chicago Daily News,* Dec. 12, 1974.

44. "Hefner Called Drug Probe Target," *Los Angeles Times,* Dec. 8, 1974; "The Playboy Connection?" *Newsweek,* Dec. 23, 1974; Alexander Cockburn, "Who's After Hef?" *Village Voice,* Dec. 23, 1974; and Bob Greene, "Won't You Come Home, Hugh Hefner?" *Chicago Sun-Times,* Dec. 17, 1974.

45. "Party Promotes Pot Law Reform," *Santa Monica Outlook,* Aug. 3, 1974; "Who's After Hef?" *Village Voice;* "News in Brief," *Los Angeles Times,* Dec. 24, 1974; and Richard Rhodes, "A Very Expensive High," *Playboy,* Jan. 1975, 131.

46. Hillman interview with DuBois; Urry interview with Lynch/Frost; and Les Marshall interview with Murray Fisher, Mar. 26, 1991.

47. Hillman interview with DuBois; Colander, "The Life and Death of Bobbie Arnstein"; DuBois, "Remembering Bobbie"; transcript of Arnstein suicide note, addressed to Keith Stroup, HS 263. See also "Hefner's Aide Kills Herself," *Los Angeles Times,* Jan. 13, 1975, and "Hefner Aide Found Dead; Blame Drugs," *Chicago Tribune,* Jan. 14, 1975.

48. HH to Anderson, March 11, 1992.

49. "Hugh M. Hefner's Statement to the Press on January 14, 1975," transcript, HP. Stories on the press conference include "Hefner Hits Probers in Suicide," *Chicago Sun-Times,* Jan. 15, 1975; "Hefner Blames Government for Bobbie's Death," *Chicago Tribune,* Jan. 15, 1975; and "Hefner Blames Witch-Hunt for Suicide," *Los Angeles Times,* Jan. 15, 1975.

50. "Hefner Blast Clouds Playboy Drug Probe," *Chicago Tribune,* Jan. 19, 1975; "Hefner Sheds the Playboy Image," *Chicago Sun-Times,* Jan. 16, 1975; "Puzzling Revelations Bared in Arnstein Case," *Chicago Sun-Times,* Jan. 26, 1975; "An Embattled King in the Playboy Empire," *Washington Post,* Jan. 26, 1975; "The Death of Bobbie," *Newsweek,* Jan 27, 1975; "Clouds Over Bunnyland," *Time,* Jan. 27, 1975; and William Safire, "Mayday and Playboy," *New York Times,* Jan. 27, 1975.

51. "U.S. Drug Chief Quits in Scandal," *Chicago Daily News,* May 30, 1975; "Hefner Drug Quiz Dropped by U.S.," *Chicago Tribune,* Dec. 30, 1975; and Samuel K. Skinner to Hugh Hefner, Jan. 30, 1976, HP. Hefner's views on the collapse of the case are fully expressed in HH memo to Anderson, DuBois, and Fisher, April 30, 1992.

52. Anthony J. Lukas, "The 'Alternative Lifestyle' of Playboys and Playmates," *New York Times,* June 11, 1972, and "Can You Bare It?" *Forbes,* March 1, 1971, 17–21.

53. "Playboy After Hefner," *Dun's Review,* Feb. 1974, 46; "Big Problems for Playboy's Empire," *Business Week,* April 13, 1974; and Bryce Nelson, "Playboy Faces Naked Truth on Revenues," *Los Angeles Times,* April 8, 1975.

54. "The World of Hef: Playboy Rabbit Seen Biting Off Too Much; Critics Say Empire is a 'Managerial Muddle,'" *Wall Street Journal,* March 2, 1971, and "Playboy After Hefner," *Dun's Review,* Feb. 1974, 45, 47. See also "Woes of Playboy Empire

Continuing to Mount," *Advertising Age,* Jan. 20, 1975, and "Trouble in Bunnyland," *Newsweek,* Sept. 2, 1974.

55. HH, "Notes on Captain's Paradise," HP; "Playboy After Hefner," *Dun's Review,* Feb. 1974, 45–46, 49; Robert Gutwillig, memo to Bob Preuss, April 30, 1974, HP; Robert Gutwillig, "Other Voices," HP; "Playboy Enterprises Realigns," *Chicago Sun-Times,* Feb. 26, 1975; and "Playboy Shuffle: Exec Re-Align, Office of the President Formed," *Variety,* Feb. 26, 1975.

CHAPTER 14. DISNEYLAND FOR ADULTS

1. Many of the stories and O'Connor's memo are reproduced in Gretchen Edgren, *Inside the Playboy Mansion* (Santa Monica, CA, 1998), 122–123, while the poster was noted in Bob Greene, "A Week at Hef's," *Midwest: The Chicago Sun-Times Magazine,* Nov. 25, 1973. See also Robert Greenfield, "The Rolling Stones Go South," *Rolling Stone,* Aug. 3, 1972.

2. HH, quoted in "Q & A Hugh Hefner," *Los Angeles Times,* Feb. 27, 1970.

3. HH memo to Larry DuBois and Murray Fisher, July 10, 1991.

4. Ibid.

5. HH memo to Patrick Anderson, Larry DuBois, and Murray Fisher, Jan. 28, 1992.

6. Ron Dirsmith interview with Bob Carr, March 1990, and HH memo to Larry DuBois and Murray Fisher, July 10, 1991.

7. "Hefner Housewarming a Benefit for ACLU," *Los Angeles Times,* Nov. 23, 1971, Harvey Markowitz to Dick Rosenzweig, "Notes and Comments on a Meeting with Attorney Jerome Mayo," Sept. 28, 1972, and Jerome J. Mayo to Judge John B. Milliken, Nov. 14, 1972, both in HP.

8. Ron Dirsmith interview with Bob Carr, March 1990.

9. James Bacon, "Just a Little Mansion in the Hills," *Los Angeles Herald Examiner,* Nov. 23, 1971; Anthony Haden-Guest, "The Pubic Hair Papers and Hugh Hefner," *Rolling Stone,* Dec. 20, 1973, 64; and HH memo to DuBois, Fisher, and Anderson, Jan. 28, 1992, HP.

10. HH, quoted in Pax Quigley, "Playboy Mansion: Architectural and Other Delights," *Beverly Hills,* Sept.–Oct. 1978, and in Haden-Guest, "The Pubic Hair Papers and Hugh Hefner," 66.

11. HH, quoted in "Chicagoland Interview: Hugh M. Hefner," *Chicagoland,* Dec. 1978, 24. See also "Playboy Mansion West," *Playboy,* Jan. 1975.

12. HH memo to DuBois, Fisher, and Anderson, Jan. 28, 1992, HP; Kenneth Turan, "Foldout Fantasy: Playmates Galore on Playboy's 25th Year, *Washington Post,* Sept. 10, 1979; HS, Vol. 362; and Edgren, *Inside the Playboy Mansion,* 168, 244.

13. HH memo to DuBois, Fisher, and Anderson, Jan. 28, 1992; HS, Vol. 362; and HS, Vol. 372.

14. *Inside the Playboy Mansion,* 186–189, 231–234; *The Playboy Roller Disco and Pajama Party* advertisement, *Hollywood Reporter,* Nov. 23, 1979; and Tom Shales, "Cashing In on the Beatles and Yawning Through Hefner's Pajama Party," *Washington Post,* Nov. 23, 1979.

15. "Mansion Parties" memo; "Playboy Bunnies Missing at Brown's Fund-Raiser," *New York Times,* May 24, 1976; "Some Find Splendor in the Grass," *Los Angeles Herald Examiner,* Aug. 4, 1977; and "Playboy Contributes Food, Funds for ERA," *Chicago Tribune,* Mar. 13, 1978.

16. "Playboy's Playmate House Party," *Playboy,* Dec. 1977.

17. HH memo to DuBois, Fisher, and Anderson, Jan. 28, 1992, and HH to David Wolper, Sept. 12, 1995, HP.

18. HH memo to DuBois, Fisher, and Anderson, Jan. 28, 1992; *Inside the Playboy Mansion,* 157; "Mike Trikilis File," HP.

19. Lee Wolfberg interview with Murray Fisher and Larry DuBois, May 1989; HH memo to Patrick Anderson, and Murray Fisher, Oct. 13, 1992; and HH memo to DuBois, Fisher, and Anderson, Jan. 28, 1992.

20. HH memo to Patrick Anderson and Murray Fisher, Oct. 13, 1992.

21. Debra Svensk, "Other Voices," and Marcy Hanson, "Other Voices," HP.

22. Monique St. Pierre interview with Lynch/Frost, May 21, 1991, and with Murray Fisher, June 1, 1992.

23. Leann Moen interview with Murray Fisher, Sept. 4, 1994; Debra Svensk, "Other Voices"; Marcy Hanson, "Other Voices"; and Alison Reynolds interview with Murray Fisher, May 15, 1992.

24. See HS volumes 286–447 for Hefner's massive photographic and textual record of many of these sexual relationships. See also HH memo to Patrick Anderson and Murray Fisher, Oct. 13, 1992.

25. Sondra Theodore, "Other Voices"; Theodore's interview in "From Miss Bicentennial to Playmate," *Fontana (CA) Herald-News*, June 25, 1977, and "She Went from Girl-Next-Door to Centerfold," *San Bernardino Sun-Telegram*, June 18, 1977.

26. Theodore, "Other Voices"; Sondra Theodore, undated interview, HP; Theodore interview in "From Miss Bicentennial to Playmate"; and HH memo to Patrick Anderson and Murray Fisher, Oct. 13, 1992.

27. HH memo to Patrick Anderson and Murray Fisher, Oct. 13, 1992, and HHIA, August 9, 2006.

28. Theodore interview in "From Miss Bicentennial to Playmate"; Theodore quoted in "She Went from Girl-Next-Door to Centerfold"; and Theodore, undated interview, HP.

29. Sondra Theodore, undated interview, HP; Leann Moen interview with Murray Fisher, Sept. 4, 1994; and *Inside the Playboy Mansion*, 198–199.

30. Leann Moen interview with Murray Fisher, Sept. 4, 1994; Heather Waite interview with Murray Fisher, May 12, 1992; Alison Reynolds interview with Murray Fisher, May 15, 1992; and Sondra Theodore, undated interview, HP.

31. Monique St. Pierre interview with Murray Fisher, June 1, 1992, and Marcy Hanson, "Other Voices," HP.

32. "Benwa File," HP, and *Inside the Playboy Mansion*, 178.

33. HH, quoted in Jack Mabley, "Hef Glories in the Flesh," *Chicago Tribune*, Dec. 20, 1978, and HH to Patrick Anderson and Murray Fisher, April 16, 1992.

34. Haden-Guest, "Pubic Hair Papers," 64; HH memo to DuBois, Fisher, and Anderson, Jan. 28, 1992; HHIA, August 9, 2006; and Sondra Theodore, undated interview, HP.

35. HH memo to DuBois, Fisher, and Anderson, Jan. 28, 1992, and HHIA, Aug. 9, 2006.

36. HH memo to DuBois, Fisher, and Anderson, Jan. 28, 1992, and Billy Eisenberg, "Other Voices," HP.

37. HH memo to DuBois, Fisher, and Anderson, Jan. 28, 1992; Billy Eisenberg, "Other Voices," HP; and Larry DuBois, "Other Voices," HP.

38. "Playboy Interview: Hugh M. Hefner," *Playboy*, Jan. 1974, 78; Sondra Theodore, undated interview; and Billy Eisenberg, "Other Voices," HP.

39. Tom Wolfe, "The 'Me' Decade and the Third Great Awakening," *New York*, Aug. 23, 1976, 26–40.

40. The quote is from Christopher Lasch, *The Culture of Narcissism: American Life in an Age of Diminishing Expectations* (New York, 1978), xvi. See also Peter Clecak, *America's Quest for the Ideal Self: Dissent and Fulfillment in the 60s and 70s* (New York, 1983); Philip Slater, *The Pursuit of Loneliness: American Culture at the Breaking Point* (Boston, 1970); Robert N. Bellah et al., *Habits of the Heart: Individualism and Commitment in American Life* (New York, 1985); and Richard

Sennett, *The Fall of Public Man: On the Social Psychology of Capitalism* (New York, 1974).

41. HH, quoted in "25 Years of Playboy," *Toronto Globe and Mail,* Dec. 9, 1978; "Esquire Interview: Hugh M. Hefner," *Esquire,* Dec. 1970, 42; HH, quoted in Anthony Haden-Guest, "The Pubic Hair Papers and Hugh Hefner," *Rolling Stone,* Dec. 20, 1973, 66; HH, quoted in "Chicagoland Interview: Hugh M. Hefner," *Chicagoland,* Dec. 1978, 15; and "Playboy Interview: Hugh M. Hefner," *Playboy,* Jan. 1974, 72, 82.

42. Christie Hefner, *John Calloway Program,* television station WTTW in Chicago, Jan. 24, 1979, HP, and HH memo to DuBois, Fisher, and Anderson, Jan. 28, 1992.

43. J. Anthony Lukas, "The 'Alternative Life-Style' of Playboys and Playmates," *New York Times Magazine,* June 11, 1972, 13, 16; "Playboy's Quarter Century," *Newsweek,* Jan. 1, 1979, 68; Bob Greene, "A Week at Hef's," *Midwest: The Chicago Sun-Times Magazine,* Nov. 25, 1973, 23; and "Hugh Hefner," *People,* Dec. 2, 1974, 6–9.

44. "Playboy Interview: Hugh M. Hefner," *Playboy,* Jan. 1974, 64; "Playboy Mansion West," *Playboy,* Jan. 1975; "Playboy's Playmate House Party," *Playboy,* Dec. 1977; and "The World of Playboy," *Playboy,* Sept. 1978, 9–10.

45. "Playboy Interview: Hugh M. Hefner," *Playboy,* Jan. 1974, 80; "Sun-Times Interview: Hugh Hefner," *Chicago Sun-Times,* Dec. 21, 1978; Boris Weintraub, "Hugh Hefner and Playboy—At 25 They're Still Having Fun," *Washington Star,* Jan. 4, 1979; and HH, quoted in "The Youngest Rabbit," *Miami Herald,* Dec. 26, 1978.

46. Program tape, *Saturday Night Live,* October 15, 1977, HP; and Don Rogers memo on "HMH/Saturday Night Live," Nov. 2, 1977, HP.

47. *Playboy: Twenty-Fifth Anniversary Issue,* Jan. 1979; *Inside the Playboy Mansion,* 224–233; and HH to author, Nov. 27, 2007.

48. Bob Greene, *Spectrum,* CBS Radio Network, Dec. 12, 1978; "25 Years of Playboy," *Eden (NC) News,* Dec. 5, 1978; Max Lerner, "Playboy: An American Revolution of Morality," *New York Post,* Jan. 10, 1979; "Playboy at 25: It Shaped a Revolution That May Have Passed It By," *Crain's Chicago Business,* Dec. 11, 1978; "Playboy's Quarter Century," *Newsweek,* Jan. 1, 1979, 68; and "Proclamation" from Office of the Mayor, City of Chicago, Dec. 20, 1978, HS 397.

49. Alton Slagle, "Reality Crashes the Playboy Party," *New York News,* Feb. 2, 1975; "Wretched Excess," *Boulder Camera,* Feb. 2, 1975; and Bob Greene, "There It Goes . . . Myth America," *Chicago Sun-Times,* July 30, 1975.

50. M. J. Sobran, "The Sage and Serious Doctrine of Hugh Hefner," *National Review,* Feb. 1, 1974, 134, 136; George Will, "Playboy of the Gatsby World," *Newsday,* March 25, 1975; and George Will, transcript of *Assignment America: Hugh Hefner at 49,* WNET, television broadcast May 6, 1975, HP.

51. Rick Soll, "Prince Hef of Playboy Protects Seat of Power," *Chicago Tribune,* July 31, 1975; "Sweet Seventeen and Rocking—and Hugh?" *Dallas Times Herald,* Aug. 7, 1977; Gary Streff, "In My Opinion," *Milwaukee Journal,* July 17, 1979; Tom E. Roy, "The Ledger Balance Sheet," *Ballinger (TX) Ledger,* Dec. 4, 1978; Thomas BeVier, "Playboy's Empire: Pushing 25," *Detroit Free Press,* Oct. 15, 1978; and "Q & A: Hefner Is Still a Fantasy After All These Years," *Chicago Tribune,* May 3, 1976.

52. Anthony Haden-Guest, "The Pubic Hair Papers and Hugh Hefner," *Rolling Stone,* Dec. 20, 1973, 70; "Trouble in Wonderland," *Dayton Daily News,* Feb. 12, 1975; Tim Patterson, "Playboyism: Consumerism Run Amok," *The Guardian: An Independent Radical Newsweekly,* Dec. 27, 1978; Ned Comstock, "What Bugs Bunny," *Barrington (RI) Times,* Sept. 9, 1976; and "Does the Middle Class Finance Pornucopia?" *Christian Science Monitor,* Oct. 16, 1978.

53. The quip appears in the "Charles McDermid File," HP.

CHAPTER 15. A HUTCH DIVIDED

1. HS, Vol. 193; Richard Todd, "Gathering at Bunnymeade," *Atlantic,* Jan. 1972; and Paul Galloway, "Convening Hugh Hefner's Literature 101," *Midwest: Sunday Magazine of the Chicago Sun-Times,* Nov. 28, 1971.

2. HH memo to Patrick Anderson, Larry DuBois, and Murray Fisher, Dec. 9, 1991. The fullest account of the post-Spectorsky editorial transition, and one that was based on interviews with many of the participants, appears in Thomas Weyr, *Reaching for Paradise: The Playboy Vision of America* (New York, 1978), 179–193.

3. Arthur Kretchmer, undated interview with Trikilis Productions, HP; "Arthur Kretchmer: Other Voices," HP; HH memo to Anderson, DuBois, and Fisher, Dec. 9, 1991; and Charles Leroux, "Mr. Kretchmer's Wild Ride," *Chicago Tribune,* Nov. 15, 2002.

4. Kretchmer, quoted in J. Anthony Lukas, "The 'Alternative Life-Style' of Playboys and Playmates," *New York Times Magazine,* June 11, 1972, and Mike Laurence, quoted in J. Madeleine Nash, "Male Magazines: The Assault on Bunny Heights," *Chicago Tribune Magazine,* Sept. 9, 1973.

5. "Chasing Playboy's Golden Bunny," *Business Week,* Aug. 9, 1969, and Anthony Haden-Guest, "The Pubic Hair Papers," *Rolling Stone,* Dec. 20, 1973, 60. The fullest analysis of the *Playboy-Penthouse* conflict can be found in chap. 3, "The Pubic Wars," in Douglas K. Ramsey, *The Corporate Warriors: Six Classic Cases in American Business* (New York, 1987).

6. Al Goldstein and Jim Buckley, "An Exclusive Interview with Bob Guccione, Keeper of the Penthouse," *Screw,* Sept. 17, 1973.

7. Ibid.

8. Ibid.; Robert Guccione, quoted in Anthony Haden-Guest, "The Pubic Hair Papers," *Rolling Stone,* Dec. 20, 1973, 60; "Playboy Interview: Hugh M. Hefner," *Playboy,* Jan. 1974, 84; and Guccione, quoted in Ramsey, *Corporate Warriors,* 121.

9. HH, quoted in Anthony Haden-Guest, "The Pubic Hair Papers," 61; HH memo to Vince Tajiri and Art Paul, June 8, 1970, PA; HH, quoted in "Q & A Hugh Hefner," *Los Angeles Times,* Feb. 27, 1970; and Bryce Nelson, "Playboy Faces Naked Truth on Revenues," *Los Angeles Times,* April 8, 1975.

10. Ramsey, *The Corporate Warriors,* 115, 118, 120, 126, 129, 138.

11. "Playboy Will Publish New Magazine, 'Oui,' with European Slant," *Wall Street Journal,* March 22, 1972; "Hefner's Grandchild," *Time,* Aug. 28, 1972; "Son of Playboy," *Newsweek,* Aug. 28, 1972; "Playboy After Hefner," *Dun's Review,* Feb. 1974, 48–49; and HH memo to Patrick Anderson, Larry DuBois, and Murray Fisher, Dec. 9, 1991.

12. "Adventures in the Skin Trade," *Time,* July 30, 1973, 49, and "The Skin-Book Boom: What Have They Done to the Girl Next Door?" *Esquire,* Nov. 1976. For another contemporary analysis of these publications, see J. Madeleine Nash, "Male Magazines: The Assault on Bunny Heights," *Chicago Tribune Magazine,* Sept. 9, 1973.

13. "Playboy Interview: Hugh M. Hefner," *Playboy,* Jan. 1974, 63, 84; Guccione, quoted in "Prodigal Son Makes It Big," *Forbes,* March 1, 1971, 19; David Shaw, "Penthouse—A Challenge to Playboy," *Los Angeles Times,* Sept. 29, 1971; "Hefner's Grandchild," *Time,* Aug. 28, 1972; and Kenneth Koyen, "Has Hef's Vision Gone Dim?" *Wall Street Journal,* Jan. 26, 1972.

14. "Porno Chic," *New York Times Magazine,* Jan. 21, 1973; chap. 7, "The Joy of Sex, 1970–1979," in James R. Petersen, *The Century of Sex* (New York, 1999), 321–375; "The Porno Plague," *Time,* April 5, 1976, 58; and Bob Greene, "Beyond the Sexual Revolution," *Newsweek,* Sept. 29, 1975, 13.

15. Morton Hunt, "Sexual Behavior in the 1970s," *Playboy,* Oct. 1973. The subsequent five installments appeared in November 1973; December 1973; Jan. 1974;

February 1974; and March 1974. For an example of the publicity attending the survey, see "A Sex Poll (1973)," *Time,* Oct. 1, 1973, 48.

16. HH, quoted in "Adventures in the Skin Trade," *Time,* July 30, 1973, 51.

17. "From Here to Obscenity," *Newsweek,* Nov. 17, 1975.

18. See the discussion of Howard Lederer in Ramsey, *Corporate Warriors,* 136; Arthur Kretchmer, quoted in Philip K. Dougherty, "Playboy Drawing a Line on Sex," *New York Times,* Oct. 31, 1975; and HH to David Wolper, "The Hugh Hefner Story," Sept. 12, 1995, 42.

19. HH, quoted in Ramsey, *The Corporate Warriors,* 137; "New Format in Offing for Playboy Magazine," *Gallagher Report,* Nov. 1975; Philip K. Dougherty, "Playboy Drawing a Line on Sex," *New York Times,* Oct. 31, 1975; "Playboy Opts for Retreat in Pubic Wars," *Los Angeles Times,* Dec. 3, 1975; "From Here to Obscenity," *Newsweek,* Nov. 17, 1975; "Playboy Courting a Family Image," *Washington Post,* Sept. 19, 1976; and "Playboy's Non-Nude Cover Program," speech delivered by Ben Goldberg on July 22, 1976, and reprinted in *Impact: The Voice of the Newsstand Publisher,* August 1976.

20. Weyl, *Reaching for Paradise,* 289, and Kretchmer, quoted in "The Editor in Charge of Overhauling Playboy," *Chicago Daily News,* March 20–21, 1976.

21. HH, quoted in "Daily News Interview: Hugh M. Hefner," *Chicago Daily News,* Nov. 12, 1976, and the following articles in *Playboy*: "Johnny Carson, Watch Your Ass: There's a Revolution Going On," Nov. 1976; "Pinball . . . and Other Electronic Indoor Sports," Dec. 1978; Norman Mailer, "The Fight," May and June 1975; and "Playboy Interview: Francis Ford Coppola," July 1975.

22. See in *Playboy*: Kathy Lowry, "Me and the Other Girls," August 1976; Dan Greenburg, "My Weekend of Flashy Orgasms," April 1977; "Swingers Scrapbook," Dec. 1977; and "The Great Playboy Sex-Aids Road Test," March 1978.

23. Kretchmer, quoted in Abe Peck, "Playboy: The First 25 Years," *Chicago Sun-Times,* Dec. 20, 1978, and in "Playboy Plans for the'80s," *San Diego Union,* Dec. 3, 1978.

24. Alexander Cockburn, "Press Clips," *Village Voice,* April 21, 1975; "Hugh Marston Hefner Says He Is a Very Moral Man," *Faces,* Dec. 16, 1975, 22; and "A Conversation with Hugh Hefner," *Advertising Age,* July 21, 1975.

25. Kretchmer, quoted in Peck, "Playboy: The First 25 Years."

26. "Daily News Interview: Hugh M. Hefner," *Chicago Daily News,* Nov. 12, 1976, and Andrew Kretchmer quoted in "Publisher's Page," *Folio: The Magazine for Magazine Management,* Oct. 1977, 3. See also HH's comments in "Playboy: The Empire at 25," *Detroit News Magazine,* March 25, 1979.

27. Kretchmer, quoted in Peck, "Playboy: The First 25 Years;" "Daily News Interview: Hugh M. Hefner," *Chicago Daily News,* Nov. 12, 1976; "Playboy's Pipeline" and "Playboy on the Scene," *Playboy,* April 1978; and HH, quoted in "Hugh Hefner of Playboy Enterprises, Inc.," *Madison Avenue,* Jan. 1979. See also Kretchmer, quoted in "From Here to Obscenity," *Newsweek,* Nov. 17, 1975.

28. "Lust for Life" ads reproduced in Jack Feuer, "The Playboy Difference," *Marketing Communications,* May/June 1977, 38–40, and in Barbara G. Harrison, "Reimagifying Playboy," *More: The Media Magazine,* Nov. 1977, 26–28. For other treatments of the ad campaign, see "Lusting for More Life: Playboy's Strategic Change," *Client/Media News,* Sept. 19, 1977, and "Playboy's New 'Lust for Life' Media Campaign," *Madison Avenue Magazine,* June 1977, 26–28.

29. See in *Playboy*: Carl Bernstein and Bob Woodward, "All the President's Men," serialized in May and June 1974; Nat Hentoff, "If You Liked '1984,' You'll Love 1973," May 1973; Roger Rapoport, "It's Enough to Make You Sick," Sept. 1973; Laurence Gonzales, "You Gotta Believe," July 1975, and Playboy Editorial, "Some Tough Questions About Airline Safety," Sept. 1979; Scott Burns, "America Is Going

Broke," Jan. 1976; Dan E. Moldea, "The Hoffa Wars," Nov. 1978; and Larry DuBois and Laurence Gonzales, "The Puppet and the Puppetmasters: Uncovering the Secret World of Nixon, Hughes, and the CIA," Sept. 1976.

30. See in *Playboy*: "Playbill," Dec. 1972; Richard Rhodes, "A Very Expensive High," Jan. 1975; Dan Greenburg, "My First Orgy," Dec. 1972; and Hunter S. Thompson, "The Great Shark Hunt," Dec. 1974. On the New Journalism, see Tom Wolfe, *The New Journalism* (New York, 1973), and Marc Weingarten, *The Gang That Wouldn't Write Straight: Wolfe, Thompson, Didion and the New Journalism Revolution* (New York, 2005).

31. A. C. Spectorsky to Nat Lehrman, April 23, 1969, PA; A. C. Spectorsky to Jim Goode, Arthur Kretchmer, Dec. 3, 1969, PA; HH to Vince Tajiri, Bev Chamberlain, June 12, 1969, PA; and "A Report on Plans, Projects, Proposals," by A. C. Spectorsky for "The Executive Committee," March 30, 1970, PA.

32. "Playbill," *Playboy*, Jan. 1971.

33. See in *Playboy*: Saul Braun, "Nearer, Silent Majority, to Thee," Feb. 1971; Sen. Philip Hart, "Swindling and Knavery, Inc.," August 1972; E. L. Doctorow, "The Bomb Lives!" March 1974; "Playboy Interview: Jane Fonda and Tom Hayden," April 1974; Robert Scheer, "Nelson Rockefeller Takes Care of Everybody," Oct. 1975; Robert Sherrill, "Injustices of the Burger Court," April 1979; and "The Playboy Enemies List," Oct. 1977.

34. See in *Playboy*: Richard Reeves, "Hustling the Youth Vote," Nov. 1972; Robert Scheer, "Death of the Salesman," June 1974; Craig Vetter, "Bring Me the Head of Timothy Leary," Sept. 1975; and Jim Harwood, "Saint Jane and the Hollywood Dragon," July 1978.

35. See "Playboy Interview: Jimmy Carter," *Playboy*, Nov. 1976. Robert Scheer's account of the interview appeared in his "The Ruling Class," *New York Times*, Oct. 1976, 14–15, while his editorial assistant from *Playboy*, Barry Golson, offered his recollection in "When Carter and Playboy Spoke in Plains," *New York Times*, Sept. 30, 1976.

36. "The Great Playboy Furor," *Newsweek*, Oct. 4, 1976, 70–71; "Carter's Comments on Sex Stir Disparate Reactions of Concern," *New York Times*, Sept. 23, 1976; "Trying to Be One of the Boys," *Time*, Oct. 4, 1976, 33–34; George F. Will, "Not For Everyone's Coffee Table," *Chicago Sun-Times*, Sept. 30, 1976; William Safire, "Carter in Playboy," *New York Times*, Sept. 23, 1976; "Carter on Sin," *Washington Post*, Sept. 21, 1976; Mary McGrory, "A Guided Tour of Carter's Soul," *Chicago Tribune*, Sept. 24, 1976; and Max Lerner, "That Playboy Interview," *New York Post*, Sept. 24, 1976. See Richard Cohen, "Carter, Sex, and Much Ado," *Chicago Sun-Times*, Sept. 27, 1976, and Carl T. Rowan, "Carter Vs. the Sanctimonious Ones," *Chicago Daily News*, Oct. 14, 1976, for liberals who supported Carter.

37. *Chicago Sun-Times*, Sept. 22, 1976; *Dayton Daily News*, Sept. 27, 1976; Ford ad in *Chicago Sun-Times*, Oct. 23, 1976; "Ford and Carter Forces Dispute GOP Ad Showing Playboy Cover," *New York Times*, Oct. 22, 1976; and "Carter Regrets Interview in Playboy, Wouldn't Do It Again," *Los Angeles Herald Examiner*, Oct. 24, 1976.

38. "Romance: An Idea Whose Time Has Come," memo from Arthur Kretchmer to Shel Wax and Barry Golson, Jan. 30, 1979.

39. "The Rousing Return of Romance," *Playboy*, Dec. 1978, and cartoon, *Playboy*, Jan. 1979, 207.

40. Tom Wolfe, "The Me Decade and the Third Great Awakening," *New York*, Aug. 23, 1976, 26–40; HH, quoted in "Hugh Hefner of Playboy Enterprises, Inc.," *Madison Avenue*, Jan. 1979; and HH, quoted in "Chicagoland Interview: Hugh M. Hefner," *Chicagoland*, Dec. 1978, 23.

41. See "Lust for Life" ads reproduced in Jack Feuer, "The Playboy Difference," *Marketing Communications,* May/June 1977, 40; in Barbara G. Harrison, "Reimagifying Playboy," *More: The Media Magazine,* Nov. 1977, 32; and in "Playboy's New 'Lust for Life' Media Campaign," *Madison Avenue Magazine,* June, 1977, 27.

42. "Leisure in the Seventies," *Playboy,* Dec. 1970; G. Barry Golson, "I'm OK, You're So-So," *Playboy,* Jan. 1974; and Robert Shea, "The Inner Game of Sex," *Playboy,* Oct. 1978.

43. See "Playmate of the Month" in *Playboy,* Aug. 1976 and April 1978.

44. See "The Playboy Report on American Men: A Study of the Values, Attitudes, and Goals of U.S. Males 18-to-49 Years Old," conducted for Playboy Enterprises, Inc. by Louis Harris and Associates, Inc. (1979), HP. A condensed version of the study appeared as "The Playboy Report on American Men," *Playboy,* Mar. 1979.

45. Dr. William Simon, quoted on *Good Morning America,* ABC TV, Jan. 19, 1979, transcript, HP; Simon, quoted in "How Important Is Sex?" *Houston Post,* Jan. 21, 1979; Christie Hefner, quoted on *John Calloway Program,* television station WTTW in Chicago, Jan. 24, 1979, transcript, HP. See also press commentary in Nadine Brozan, "A Study of the American Man," *New York Times,* Jan. 19, 1979; "Playboy Poll Plots Pursuit of Pleasure," *Cleveland Plain Dealer,* Jan. 17, 1979; and Abe Peck, "New American Male: Values Center More on Self," *Chicago Sun-Times,* Jan. 19, 1979.

46. F. C. Klein and J. R. Laing, "Playboy's Slide: Hotel Losses, Decline in Circulation Weaken Hugh Hefner's Empire," *Wall Street Journal,* April 13, 1976.

47. "Middle-Aged Rabbit," *Forbes,* June 1, 1977; "A Conversation with Hugh Hefner," *Advertising Age,* July 21, 1975; and Dan Stone, quoted in "Business Chronology for the Derick Daniels Era," July 8, 1992, HP.

48. HH memo to Anderson, DuBois, and Fisher, April 30, 1992; Wayne Dunham, "Playboy Exec Aims for Upswing in Profits," *Chicago Tribune,* July 15, 1975; Larry Ingrassia, "Hef Gives Up His Jet and His Mansion," *Chicago Sun-Times,* July 30, 1975; and John McCarron, "Hefner to Hold the Fort in Playboy Cost-Cutting," *Chicago Tribune,* July 30, 1975.

49. Klein and Laing, "Playboy's Slide." See also "Hefner Gives Up His Biggest Bunny," *Chicago Tribune,* April 3, 1976, and "Playboy Gets $7.7 Million Tax Bill," *Chicago Daily News,* July 26, 1976.

50. Don Parker interview with Murray Fisher, undated, HP.

51. Niles Howard, "Playboy's President Search Has Deadline of June 30," *Advertising Age,* April 19, 1976, and Parker interview with Fisher.

52. Susan Britton, "New Man at Playboy," *New York Times,* Oct. 31, 1976, and Diana McLellan, "Derick J. Daniels: The Prince of Playboy," *Washington Star Portfolio,* Oct. 31, 1976.

53. "An Ailing Playboy Gets a New Manager," *Business Week,* Sept. 27, 1976, 58, and Derick Daniels interview with Larry DuBois, April 21, 1992.

54. "Hefner Turns Reins over to News Executive," *Chicago Tribune,* Sept. 9, 1976; "Playboy Names D.J. Daniels President," *Wall Street Journal,* Sept. 9, 1976; Niles Howard, "Daniels in the Bunny Den," *Advertising Age,* Sept. 27, 1976, 4, 80; and "Prince of Playboy."

55. "New Man at Playboy;" Clifford Terry, "He's Pushing the Bunny Back into the Black," *Chicago Tribune Magazine,* Aug. 12, 1979; and Lew Powell, "From N.C. Hutch, the Chief Bunny," *Charlotte Observer,* April 8, 1979.

56. "The Prince of Playboy."

57. Lawrence T. Mahoney, "Knight Errant in the Kingdom of the Hedonists," *Miami Magazine,* Mar. 1977, 28–30, 54–55; Gottlieb, quoted in Russell Miller, *Bunny: The Real Story of Playboy* (New York, 1984), 273; and HH, quoted in Larry DuBois, memo to Hefner, Anderson, and Fisher, July 8, 1992.

58. Clifford Terry, "Derick Daniels: The Man Behind Playboy's Financial Turnaround," *Chicago Tribune Magazine,* Aug. 12, 1979; Lew Powell, "From N.C. Hutch, the Chief Bunny," *Charlotte Observer,* Apr. 8, 1979; *Bunny,* 273; and Nat Lehrman interview with Murray Fisher, Oct. 16, 1989.

59. Bob Guttwillig interview with Murray Fisher and Larry DuBois, July 22, 1989; Dan Stone, "Other Voices," HP; and Victor Lownes, "Other Voices," HP.

60. "Hefner Turns Reins over to News Exec," *Chicago Tribune,* Sept. 9, 1976; HH memo to Victor Lownes, dated Oct. 7. 1976, quoted in DuBois to Hefner, Anderson, and Fisher, July 8, 1992; and Daniels, quoted in "The Prince of Playboy," "New Man at Playboy," and "Daniels: The Man Behind Playboy's Financial Turnaround."

61. Derick Daniels interview with Larry DuBois, April 21, 1992.

62. Niles Howard, "Playboy Building New Empire on Redefined Priorities," *Advertising Age,* May 9, 1977; "Dozens Are Fired in Playboy Shake-Up," *Chicago Sun-Times,* Sept. 10, 1977; "Playboy Fires 70 Employees in Shakeup," *Chicago Daily News,* Sept. 9, 1977; "Pink Slips Save $1,000,000: Playboy," *Advertising Age,* Sept. 19, 1977; and "Another Playboy Hutch Cleaning," *Time,* Sept. 26, 1977, 64.

63. "Skinning the Rabbit," *Newsweek,* Sept. 26, 1977; "The Bunny Battles Back," *Forbes,* June 26, 1978, 38; and N. R. Kleinfeld, "Playboy Settles Down to Work," *New York Times,* Dec. 8, 1978. See also "Middle-Aged Rabbit," *Forbes,* June 1, 1977, 48–50.

64. Mike Royko, "Why Hef Is a Real Pill," *Chicago Sun-Times,* Dec. 22, 1978; Richard Cohen, "You're a Genius Today If You Make a Million," *Washington Post,* Jan. 2, 1979; and "Playboyism: Consumerism Run Amok," *Guardian,* Dec. 27, 1978.

65. David Handler, "Hefner Is His Own Best Putdown," *Milwaukee Journal,* Dec. 4, 1978; Arnold Rosenfeld, "Playboy, Now Grown Heavy With Child," *Dayton Daily News,* Dec. 5, 1978; "Inflation May Deflate the Playboy Philosophy," *Pittsburg* (KS) *Morning Sun,* Dec. 6, 1978; "Cultivating Ostentation," *Bethlehem* (PA) *Globe-Times,* Dec. 9, 1978; "Let's Hope There's No 50th," *Red Wing* (MN) *Republican-Eagle,* Dec. 21, 1978; "Helped to Relieve Insecurity," *Medford* (MA) *Mercury,* Dec. 22, 1978; "What Hath Hef Wrought?" *Greensboro* (NC) *Record,* Dec. 26, 1978; and "Playboy Deserves No Accolades," *Champaign-Urbana News-Gazette,* Dec. 8, 1978.

CHAPTER 16. THE DARK DECADE

1. Cis Rundle interview with Lynch/Frost, May 1, 1991.

2. Ibid., and Lisa Loving, Trikilis interview, undated.

3. Anti-*Playboy* ad, *Chicago Tribune,* Oct. 19, 1980, and *Chicago Sun-Times,* Oct. 23, 1980, sponsored by the National Heritage Foundation, and "Playboy Views Protest as Recurring Nuisance," *Advertising Age,* Oct. 27, 1980, 38. See also "The Chicago Statement: A Response to the Effect of the Playboy Mentality on Our Society," published by the Chicago Statement Foundation, 1979, HP.

4. Among many books on the rise of conservatism and the Reagan Revolution, see Jerome L. Himmelstein, *To the Right: The Transformation of American Conservatism* (Berkeley, CA, 1990); Steven F. Hayward, *The Age of Reagan: The Fall of the Old Liberal Order, 1964–1980* (New York, 2001); Paul Gottfried, *The Conservative Movement* (New York, 1993); Mark Gerson, *The Neoconservative Vision: From the Cold War to the Culture Wars* (Lanham, MD, 1997); Lisa McGirr, *Suburban Warriors: The Origins of the New American Right* (Princeton, NJ, 2001); and Robert C. Liebman and Robert Wuthnow, eds., *The New Christian Right* (New York, 1983).

5. "Play It Again, Phyllis," *Sacramento Bee,* April 13, 1978. See HS 286 for Hefner's defense of Harry Reems during his prosecution for *Deep Throat* in 1976;

Goldstein's prosecution in Wichita; and Flynt's prosecution in Cincinnati. In Oct. 1976, *Playboy* ran a sympathetic piece on the Reems case.

6. Ronald Reagan, Announcement of Presidential Candidacy, Nov. 13, 1979, Ronald Reagan Presidential Library Web site; Howell Raines, "Reagan Backs Evangelicals in Their Political Activities," *New York Times*, Aug. 23, 1980; "Politics from the Pulpit," *Time*, Oct. 13, 1980, 28, 35; and William F. Buckley, "Sex Omnia Vincit: With Friends Like This Man, The First Amendment Doesn't Need Enemies," *Los Angeles Herald Examiner*, Sept. 5, 1980.

7. See Jeffrey Hart, "America's New 'Moral Majority,'" *Los Angeles Herald Examiner*, July 24, 1980; "Politics from the Pulpit"; "Reagan Beneficiary of Evangelical Tide," *Los Angeles Herald Examiner*, Oct. 6, 1980; Falwell's *Listen America!* quoted in "50 Years Later, Playboy Still Swinging," *Chicago Sun-Times*, Nov. 28, 2003; Falwell, quoted in Johnny Greene, "The Astonishing Wrongs of the New Moral Right," *Playboy*, Jan. 1981, 260; Falwell, quoted in Jeffrey K. Hadden and Charles E. Swann, *Prime Time Preachers* (Reading, MA, 1981), 167; "We Can 'Clean Up' TV in a Year, Predicts Moral Majority's Falwell," *Chicago Sun-Times*, Jan. 10, 1981; and "How the Porn Industry Set Up the Dope Lobby," *Moral Majority Report*, March 16, 1981, 18–20.

8. HH in Malcolm Boyd, *My Fellow Americans*, 29; HH interview with Philip Walters, WBBM TV, Nov. 11, 1981; and Christie Hefner, interview on *Mike Miller Show*, WXYZ Detroit, Nov. 7, 1980.

9. See in *Playboy*: Robert Scheer, "The Reagan Question," Aug. 1980; Johnny Greene, "The Astonishing Wrongs of the New Moral Right," Jan. 1981; Peter Ross Range, "Inside the New Right War Machine," Aug. 1981. See also *Playboy* advertisement attacking the "New Moral Right," *New York Times*, Dec. 9, 1990. Other attacks on the Moral Majority in *Playboy* included Peter Ross Range, "Illegalizing Abortion," June 1981, and Kevin Cook, "Georgia on Our Minds," Dec. 1981.

10. "Prayboy," *Playboy*, Dec. 1981.

11. Gay Talese, *Thy Neighbor's Wife* (New York, 1980), 428–429. On the money and publicity attending this project, see "Caught in the Coils of Sex," *Newsweek*, April 28, 1980, 85–86.

12. The biographical sections on HH appear in *Thy Neighbor's Wife*, 20–41, 56–73, 367–412, while the generalizations appear on 73, 367–368.

13. See Joan Beck, "A Skin-Deep Peek at Our New Sexual 'Freedom,'" *Chicago Tribune*, April 25, 1980; Barbara Harrison, "Thy Neighbor's Wife," *New Republic*, May 3, 1980; Mordechai Richler, "Bad Vibrations," *New York*, April 28, 1980. Other complaints about the book's "pontifical solemnity" and tedium can be found in Anatole Broyard, "Books of the Times," *New York Times*, April 30, 1980, and Kenneth Turan, "Sex With the Proper Stranger," *New West*, May 5, 1980, 93–94. The partisanship quote comes from Turan, "Sex with the Proper Stranger." The impoverished quote comes from Richler, "Bad Vibrations."

14. Harvey Mindess, *Los Angeles Times Book Review*, April 2, 1980, and Kenneth Turan, "Sex With the Proper Stranger," *New West*, May 5, 1980, 93–94. See Robert Coles, "Transforming American Sexuality," *New York Times Book Review*, May 4, 1980, for similar criticism.

15. See liberal criticism in "Caught in the Coils of Sex," *Newsweek*, April 28, 1980, 85–86; Barbara Harrison, "Thy Neighbor's Wife," *New Republic*, May 3, 1980; Ellen Goodman, "The Unlovable Talese," *Chicago Sun-Times*, May 20, 1980; Robert Coles, "Transforming American Sexuality," *New York Times Book Review*, May 4, 1980; and Alexander Cockburn, "Mr. P, Mrs. V, and Mr. T," *New York Review of Books*, May 29, 1980. See conservative criticism in Joan Beck, "A Skin-Deep Peek at Our New Sexual 'Freedom,'" *Chicago Tribune*, April 25, 1980; "Plumbing the

Shallows," *Time,* April 28, 1980; and Ernest Van Den Haag, "Once More, Without Feeling," *National Review,* Mar. 6, 1981, 225–226. Many of the reviews seemed to take on a nasty personal edge, as analyzed in Henry Allen, "Thy Neighbor's Wife and Thy Critics' Knife," *Washington Post,* May 7, 1980.

16. Barbara Harrison, "Thy Neighbor's Wife," *New Republic,* May 3, 1980, and Alexander Cockburn, "Mr. P, Mrs. V, and Mr. T," *New York Review of Books,* May 29, 1980.

17. Mordechai Richler, "Bad Vibrations," *New York,* April 28, 1980; Robert Coles, "Transforming American Sexuality," *New York Times Book Review,* May 4, 1980; and Ellen Goodman, "The Unlovable Talese," *Chicago Sun-Times,* May 20, 1980.

18. Mordechai Richler, "Bad Vibrations," *New York,* April 28, 1980, and Ernest Van Den Haag, "Once More, Without Feeling," *National Review,* Mar. 6, 1981, 225–226.

19. See John Leonard, "A Reviewer's Notebook: Thy Neighbor's Wife," *Playboy,* May 1980, 56–58, Talese's reaction in Philip Nobile, "Sexual Politics: L'Affaire Talese," *New York,* April 21, 1980, 42–43, and "Playboy Interview: Gay Talese," *Playboy,* May 1980, 75–116. HH was quoted in Nobile, "Sexual Politics: L'Affaire Talese," *New York,* 42, 44.

20. For details on Dorothy Stratten's life, see Richard Rhodes, "Dorothy Stratten: Her Story," *Playboy,* May 1981. Perhaps the longest article ever published in the magazine, it was based on the work of Rhodes, *Playboy* editors, and the exhaustive research of John Riley and Laura Bernstein.

21. Ibid.

22. Ibid.

23. Ibid.

24. Ibid.

25. Ibid.

26. Ibid.

27. Ibid.

28. Ibid., and "Playmate of the Year Slain," *Los Angeles Times,* Aug. 15, 1980.

29. See Letters to the Editor, *Los Angeles Herald Examiner,* from John M. Ertle on Nov. 24, 1980, and George Hughes on Nov. 26, 1980.

30. Teresa Carpenter, "Death of a Playmate," *Village Voice,* Nov. 5 and 11, 1980.

31. HH interview with Rona Barrett, KNBC TV Los Angeles, April 8, 1981, transcript, HP, and "Dorothy Stratten: Her Story," 248–250.

32. HH's comment came in HHIA, Jan. 9, 2007.

33. Victor Lownes, "Other Voices," HP. Also see Lownes's account of the incident in his memoir, *The Day the Bunny Died* (Secaucus, NJ, 1982), 302–305.

34. Lownes, *The Day the Bunny Died,* 61–94.

35. Sally Quinn, "Kismet at the Gaming Tables Spells Profit for Victor Lownes," *Washington Post,* July 22, 1977; Daniel Heneghan, "Playboy Licenses Challenged," *Atlantic City Press,* April 11, 1981; and Terri Minsky, "Playboy Could Meet Only Fraction of Costs If It Loses Profitable Casino Operations," *Wall Street Journal,* Oct. 7, 1981.

36. Henry Hanson, "You Want Gambling? Here's Gambling," *Chicago,* Nov. 1979, 174; "Kismet at the Gaming Tables"; and Lownes, *The Day the Bunny Died,* 106–121.

37. Lownes, *The Day the Bunny Died,* 146–157; "Raid Playboy's London Casinos," *London Daily News,* Feb. 21, 1981; and "Playboy Says Permits for Its London Casinos Are Being Challenged," *Wall Street Journal,* April 13, 1981. Russell Miller, *Bunny: The Real Story of Playboy* (New York, 1984), 287–315, provides a detailed analysis of Lownes's and Playboy's escalating problems with its gambling operation in England.

38. Lownes, *The Day the Bunny Died,* 157–165; HHIA, Jan 9, 2007; and Derick Daniels interview with Larry DuBois, April 21, 1992.

39. "Playboy Boss Is Fired," *London Daily News*, April 16, 1981, and Lownes to Hefner, May 6, 1981, HP.

40. HH to Lownes, June 20, 1981, HP, and "Hefner Feels Badly About Lownes Firing," *Atlantic City Press*, Apr. 29, 1981.

41. "Admiral Will Direct Playboy's British Group," *New York Times*, July 9, 1981; "Admiral of the Bunnies," *London Daily Mirror*, July 9, 1981; "Playboy's Run of Hard Luck," *Newsweek*, Oct. 19, 1981, 64; "Playboy to Sell British Casinos for $31.4 Million," *Wall Street Journal*, Nov. 4, 1981; and quote from "Playboy Loses 2 London Casino Licenses," *Wall Street Journal*, Oct. 6, 1981. See Russell Miller, *Bunny*, 315–332, for a detailed analysis of the final collapse of Playboy's British gaming operation.

42. "Playboy Discloses Plan for a Hotel-Casino in Atlantic City, NJ," *Wall Street Journal*, March 7, 1977; "Playboy Settles Down to Work," *New York Times*, Dec. 8, 1978; "Playboy's Risky Bet on Atlantic City Gambling," *Business Week*, March 16, 1981; and "Playboy's Work on Atlantic City Casino Is More Hurdle Race Than Sprint to Gold," *Wall Street Journal*, April 15, 1980.

43. "Playboy Bets More on Casinos," *Chicago Tribune*, Feb. 8, 1981, and "Playboy's Risky Bet on Atlantic City Gambling," *Business Week*, March 16, 1981.

44. "State Pressures Playboy to Shelve 4 Executives," *Atlantic City Bulletin*, April 2, 1981; "Playboy's Casino Gets Panel's OK," *New Jersey Press*, April 4, 1981; "Hef Arrives in Atlantic City Like a Conquering Emperor," *Atlantic City Bulletin*, April 29, 1981; and "Playboy Loses 2 London Casino Licenses, Clouding Plan for Atlantic City Operation," *Wall Street Journal*, Oct. 6, 1981.

45. See Russell Miller, *Bunny*, 333–334, for an extensive summary of the Division of Gaming Enforcement investigative report.

46. HS 551, "The Atlantic City Inquisition"; "Atlantic City Hearings" file, HP; HHIA, Jan. 9, 2007; and "Since 'Hefner Is Playboy,' His Testimony Was Crucial," *Philadelphia Inquirer*, April 18, 1982.

47. "Atlantic City Hearings" file, HP; "Hefner Testifies at Casino Hearing," *Los Angeles Times*, Jan. 12, 1982; "Hef Didn't Know Clubs Misbehaved," *Atlantic City Bulletin*, Jan. 12, 1982; "Hefner: I Was Misled about London," *New Jersey Press*, Jan. 14, 1982; and "Since 'Hefner Is Playboy,' His Testimony Was Crucial," *Philadelphia Inquirer*, April 18, 1982.

48. "New Jersey Agency Objects to Playboy as Casino License," *Wall Street Journal*, March 10, 1982; "Hefner Is Refused Permit for Casino," *New York Times*, April 8, 1982; "Hefner Ruled Unfit to Hold Casino License," *Wall Street Journal*, April 8, 1982; "Since 'Hefner Is Playboy,' His Testimony Was Crucial," *Philadelphia Inquirer*, April 18, 1982; and Flanagan, quoted in Russell Miller, *Bunny*, 341.

49. Eleanor J. Tracy, "Playboy Takes Another Hit in Atlantic City," *Fortune*, Dec. 9, 1985, 95; Russell Miller, *Bunny*, 341–342; and HHIA, Jan. 9, 2007.

50. Derick Daniels, "Other Voices", HP; Shawn Tully, "Playboy Makes the Boss's Daughter Boss," *Fortune*, Aug. 23, 1982, 114; and "Miss Hefner Is President at Playboy," *New York Times*, April 29, 1982.

51. Jesse Kornbluth, "The Education of Christie Hefner," *Savvy*, Mar. 1980, 17–18; Lally Weymouth, "The Princess of Playboy," *New York*, June 21, 1982, 37; Daniels, quoted in "Playboy Enterprises Names Christie Hefner to Post of President," *Wall Street Journal*, April 29, 1982; and Shawn Tully, "Playboy Makes the Boss's Daughter Boss," *Fortune*, Aug. 23, 1982, 107–108.

52. "Princess of Playboy," 37, 40, and "Education of Christie Hefner," 18, 20.

53. Gloria Allred to Christie Hefner, Oct. 13, 1978, HS 380; full-page invitation/advertisement to NARAL fund-raiser in *Variety*, Oct. 5, 1978, along with *NARAL Newsletter*, Nov. 1978, both in HS 380; and "Princess of Playboy," 35, 39.

54. "Playboy Selling Two Resort Hotels for $42 Million," *New York Times*, Nov. 21, 1981; Shawn Tully, "Playboy Makes the Boss's Daughter Boss," *Fortune*, Aug. 23, 1982, 115; and CH, quoted in "Miss Hefner Is President at Playboy," *New York Times*, April 29, 1982.

55. HH, quoted in "Executives" file, HP; "Playboy Chief Hefner Devotes Little Time to His Company Now," *Wall Street Journal*, April 7, 1981; HH interview with Tom Jarrid and *20/20*, ABC TV, Feb. 14, 1983, transcript in HP; HH, quoted in "Princess of Playboy," 34.

CHAPTER 17. THE PARTY'S OVER

1. "The Party's Over," *Newsweek*, Aug. 4, 1986.

2. Hillary Johnson, "Blows Against the Empire," *Rolling Stone*, March 27, 1986, 70, 72, and "'I Am a Warm and Caring Person': Hugh Hefner Talks to Martin Amis," *Observer*, Sept. 22, 1985, 12.

3. Cliff Kincaid, "Playboy Hugh Hefner's Politics of Hedonism," *Conservative Digest*, Aug. 1986, 22, 24; Steve Daley, "Playboy as Relevant Today as a Nehru Jacket," *Chicago Tribune*, May 13, 1986; "Playboy Empire Faces Midlife Crisis," *San Diego Union*, July 5, 1986; and Robert Maynard, "Playboy Has Lost Touch With Sexual Tastes of 80s," *Virginia Daily News*, Aug. 11, 1986.

4. Joseph Nocera, "Man of the Mansion," *New Republic*, Oct. 14, 1985, 36–41.

5. By Bella Stumbo in the *Los Angeles Times:* "Hugh Hefner at 57—He Wants Respect," Dec. 26, 1984; "Hefner the Homebody: The World Comes to Him," Dec. 27, 1984; and "Hefner on Hefner: Real Guy Is a Very Moral Man," Dec. 28, 1984.

6. "Playboy Empire Faces Midlife Crisis," *San Diego Union*, July 5, 1986; Robert Maynard, "Playboy Has Lost Touch With Sexual Tastes of 80s," *Virginia Daily News*, Aug. 11, 1986; "Playboy Falls on Hard Times," *Miami Herald*, July 13, 1986; "Sex Losing Its Appeal for Playboy," *Los Angeles Times*, Aug. 25, 1986; "The Party's Over," *Newsweek*, Aug. 4, 1986, 56; Bob Greene, "Presley, Hefner: Two Who Molded America," *Chicago Tribune*, Oct. 20, 1981; Bob Greene, quoted in "Playboy Empire Faces Midlife Crisis," *San Diego Union*, July 5, 1986; and Steve Daley, "Playboy as Relevant Today as a Nehru Jacket," *Chicago Tribune*, May 13, 1986.

7. Bob Greene, quoted in "Playboy Empire Faces Midlife Crisis," *San Diego Union*, July 5, 1986; Martin Amis, "'I Am a Warm and Caring Person': Hugh Hefner Talks to Martin Amis," *Observer*, Sept. 22, 1985, 14; "Playboy Falls on Hard Times," *Miami Herald*, July 13, 1986; "As Men's Values Shift, Playboy Seeks a Way to Still Seem Exciting," *Wall Street Journal*, Sept. 12, 1985; and Lehrman, quoted in "Sex Losing Its Appeal for Playboy," *Los Angeles Times*, Aug. 25, 1986.

8. "Killed by Laughter," *Rochester Democrat and Chronicle*, July 5, 1986; "Bunny Bones," *Cleveland Plain Dealer*, July 5, 1986; and HH, quoted in "Playboy Bunny Reunion Closes Door to a Key Era," *Los Angeles Times*, June 30, 1986. See similar critiques in Joe Cohen, "Out-of-Date Bunnies' Last Hops Are Playboy Clubs' Closing Act," *Variety*, July 2, 1986, and "As Hutches Vanish, Playboy Bunnies Share the Memories," *Wall Street Journal*, June 23, 1986.

9. Richard E. Smith to Arthur Kretchmer, interoffice correspondence, Aug. 18, 1986, HP; "Playboy Empire Faces Midlife Crisis," *San Diego Union*, July 5, 1986; "The Cupboard's Not Yet Bare at Playboy," *Chicago Tribune*, Aug. 17, 1986; "Playboy Bunny in a Hole," *New York Daily News*, Aug. 19, 1986; and Christie Hefner to all employees, "Fiscal 1986 Results," Aug. 15, 1986, HP. On PEI's record loss, see also "Playboy Enterprises Suffers Loss of $62 Million in Fiscal Year," *Los Angeles Times*, Aug. 16, 1986; "Playboy Closes Book on Fiscal '86 with a $62.2 Million Loss," *Chicago Sun-Times*, Aug. 16, 1986; "Playboy Posts Loss," *New York Times*,

Aug. 16, 1986; and "Playboy Loses Mount; Club Shutterings Hurt," *Variety*, Aug. 20, 1986.

10. See in *Playboy*: "Bo," March 1980; "The Liberation of a Congressional Wife," April 1981; "The Women of Washington," Nov. 1980; and "Marilyn: A Loving Tribute by Hugh M. Hefner," Jan. 1987.

11. See in *Playboy*: Cameron Crowe, "Fast Times at Ridgemont High," Sept. 1981; "Playboy Interview: John Lennon and Yoko Ono," Jan. 1981; and Bob Woodward, "The Short Life and Fast Times of John Belushi," July 1984.

12. See in *Playboy*: Kevin Cook, "The Brawning of America," May 1984; William Barry Furlong, "The Fitness Myth," May 1988; "Playmate Linda Mays," Feb. 1983; Robert E. Carr, "A Guerrilla Guide to the Computer Revolution," May 1981; Peter A. McWilliams, "Where the Joys Are: A User-Friendly Computer Primer," Nov. 1983; Walter Lowe Jr., "How to Survive in the Video Game Jungle," March 1982; Kevin Cooke, Teresa Grosch, James R. Petersen, Anne Beatts, P. J. O'Rourke, and Bruce Williamson, "The VCR Date," Sept. 1986; "Playboy Guide to Electronic Entertainment," May 1984; and "Love at First Byte," May 1983.

13. See in *Playboy*: Abbie Hoffman and Jonathan Silvers, "An Election Held Hostage," Oct. 1988; Hodding Carter III, "Reagan and the Revival of Racism," Jan. 1986; Peter Moore, "The Jelly Bean Presidency," July 1988; Amiri Baraka, "What Makes Jesse Run," July 1988; Robert Scheer, "The Men Who Would Be President," Nov. 1988; and Trey Ellis and David J. Dent, "Campus Racism: A Special Report," June 1989.

14. Arthur Kretchmer, quoted in "As Men's Values Shift," and Henry Marks, quoted in "The Graying of Hugh Hefner," *Chicago Tribune Magazine*, May 27, 1984.

15. "Playboy Empire Faces Midlife Crisis," *San Diego Union*, July 5, 1986; "Playboy Falls on Hard Times," *Miami Herald*, July 13, 1986; George Will, "Playboy Tries to Adjust to World It Created," *Chicago Sun-Times*, Sept. 19, 1985; HH interview with Charlie Rose, CBS News *Nightwatch*, Oct. 30, 1985, HP; and "The Party's Over," *Newsweek*, Aug. 4, 1986.

16. "Playboy Falls on Hard Times," *Miami Herald*, July 13, 1986; George Will, "Playboy Tries to Adjust to World It Created"; and Lehrman, quoted in "The Graying of Hugh Hefner."

17. "Sex Losing Its Appeal for Playboy," *Los Angeles Times*, Aug. 25, 1986; "Playboy Empire Faces Midlife Crisis," *San Diego Union*, July 5, 1986; "Fantasy Has Given Way to Reality in Playboy, Hefner Daughter Says," *Southern Illinoisan*, May 3, 1978; Jim Shahin, "Chronicle Interview: Christie Hefner," *Austin Chronicle*, Sept. 20, 1985; J. Ellis, G. Fabrikant, and E. Ames, "Playboy Heiress Remodels Sagging Empire," *Australian Business*, May 29, 1985; and Lisa Gubernick, "Daddy's Girl," *Us*, July 29, 1985.

18. See "The Year of the Yuppie," *Newsweek*, Dec. 31, 1984. For other insightful commentary, see Hendrik Hertzberg, "The Short Happy Life of the American Yuppie," in Nicolaus Mills, ed., *Culture in an Age of Money: The Legacy of the 1980s in America* (Chicago, 1988), 66–82; and Marissa Piesman and Marilee Hartley, *The Yuppie Handbook* (New York, 1984).

19. See in *Playboy*: Michael Korda, "When Business Becomes Blood Sport," June 1981; Donald R. Katz, "Ruthless Mothers: Money, Values, and the Gimme Decade," Sept. 1981; Andrew Tobias, "Quarterly Reports," Mar. 1983; Hollis Wayne, "Success Story," Feb. 1986; Laurence Shames, "Yikes! Business Superstars!" Aug. 1986; and essays by Harlan Ellison, and by David Horowitz and Peter Collier, in "The Sixties: A Reappraisal," Jan. 1988.

20. See in *Playboy*: "Taking Stock of Marina," March 1983; "Ad Ventures with Robin," July 1984; "$ucce$$ $torie$," August 1984; and "The Women of Wall Street," August 1989.

21. See in *Playboy*: "We'll Take Romance," Sept. 1980; "Meet the Mrs.," May 1983; "Playmate of the Year," June 1986; "Kathy Goes to Hollywood," May 1985; and *Love: A Special Playboy Issue*, Feb. 1989.

22. See in *Playboy*: Marcia Froelke Coburn, "The Return of Designing Women," June 1989; Jo Durden-Smith and Diane DeSimone, "Man and Woman," Jan. 1982 to July 1982, quote from Jan. 1982 installment, 287; Cynthia Heimel, "Fact or Best Seller," Feb. 1987; Susan Squires, "What Women Talk About When They Talk About Men," Feb. 1986; and "Double Take," Jan. 1986.

23. "Reason Interview: Christie Hefner," *Reason*, June 1986, 37, and Christie Hefner, quoted in Ron Grossman, "This Hef Thinks She Has Men Pegged," *Spokane Chronicle*, Jan. 11, 1986.

24. See in *Playboy*: Asa Baber, "Men," April 1982, Aug. 1982, and Nov. 1982, 53; Denis Boyles, Alan Rose, and Alan Wellikoff, "The Modern Man's Guide to Life," Dec. 1987; and Bruce Feirstein, "Real Men Don't Eat Quiche," May 1982.

25. See in *Playboy*: "The Age of Sexual Détente," Oct. 1981; Laurence Shames, "Sex in the Age of Negotiation," Nov. 1983; "Sex on Campus 1982," Oct. 1982; and Steve Chapple and David Talbot, "Burning Desires: Sex in America," Part I: "The World's First Safe-Sex Orgy," April 1989; Part II: "The Right to Party," May 1989; Part III: "The Changing of the Feminist Guard," June 1989; Part IV: "Porn Minds Its Manners," August 1989.

26. See in *Playboy*: Craig Vetter, "The Desexing of America," Dec. 1983; "AIDS Update: Myths and Realities," June 1986; Arthur Kretchmer, "Can Sex Survive AIDS?" Feb. 1986; and David Seeley, "Night Life in the Age of AIDS," July 1987.

27. "Shannon Tweed" file, HP; "Newfoundland Miss Is Playboy Playmate," *St. John's* (Newfoundland) *Evening Telegram*, Oct. 9, 1981; Shannon Tweed, *Kiss and Tell* (Beverly Hills, 2006), xiii–xxi, 61–67; and Sondra Theodore, quoted in *Inside the Playboy Mansion*, 250.

28. *Kiss and Tell*, 1–61; "Shannon Tweed" file; and "Newfoundland Miss."

29. "Newfoundland Miss"; HS 548; *Kiss and Tell*, 69–71; Shannon Tweed interview with Jack Cafferty, WNBC TV in NYC, May 13, 1982; Tweed, quoted in "Shannon Tweed" file; HHIA, Jan. 9, 2007; "That New Bird on Hugh Hefner's Arm," *People*, Dec. 6, 1982, 113–115; HHIA, Jan. 9, 2007; and Anne Randall Stewart, draft article titled "Palimony, Smalimony," HP.

30. HH interview with Scott St. James, KMPC Radio, May 5, 1982; "Palimony, Smalimony"; and HH, quoted in "Shannon Tweed" file, HP.

31. "Shannon Tweed" file; *Kiss and Tell*, 69; "Life After Hef," *Starweek*, July 30–Aug. 6, 1983; "That New Bird on Hugh Hefner's Arm," *People*, Dec. 6, 1982, 113–115; and Tweed, quoted in "Shannon Tweed" file, HP.

32. "Shannon Tweed" file, HP; Byron de Arakel, "Hanging Around with Shannon Tweed, Falcon Crest's Confident Belle," *Orange Coast*, April 1983; "Life After Hef," *Starweek*, July 30–Aug. 6, 1983; and Trudy Pacter, "How 'Skinny' Shannon Hit the Big Time," *London Sunday Mirror*, May 6, 1984. See also Tweed, quoted in *Inside the Playboy Mansion*, 259, and *Kiss and Tell*, 85–89, on growing tensions with HH over her work schedule.

33. "Life After Hef," *Starweek*, July 30–Aug. 6, 1983; Tweed, quoted in *Inside the Playboy Mansion*, 250; HHIA, Jan. 9, 2007; HS 601 and 602. See *Kiss and Tell*, 84–85, 74, 90–92, where Tweed gives an account of her disenchantment with mansion life, her growing cocaine use, and her affair with Peter Weller.

34. HS 610 and 611; "Shannon Tweed" file, HP; *Kiss and Tell*, 92–94. Tweed would go on to establish a long-term relationship with rock 'n' roller Gene Simmons of Kiss.

35. Marilyn Grabowski, quoted in "Great Palimony Caper," *Playboy*, Aug. 1988, 64; HH, quoted in Hillary Johnson, "Blows Against the Empire," *Rolling Stone*, Mar. 27, 1986,

147; and "Playboy: The Party's Over," *Newsweek,* Aug. 4, 1986, 56. In HS 616, HH noted that in early May 1983 "Carrie Lee Carmichael (AKA Carrie Leigh) returns from Canada. She will change Hef's life—and not for the better." In HS 617, a note says that on May 8, 1983, "Carrie Leigh and Lorraine Michaels spent the night with Hef." Carrie Leigh declined to be interviewed for this book.

36.　"Carrie Leigh: First Lady of the Playboy Mansion," *Playboy,* July 1986, 120; Alison Reynolds, quoted in *Inside the Playboy Mansion,* 261; "First Person: Carrie Leigh," *Los Angeles Herald,* July 20, 1986; and Leigh and HH, quoted in Bella Strumbo, "Hefner on Hefner," *Los Angeles Times,* Dec. 28, 1984. For favorable comments on Leigh from two other Playmates, see Julie McCullough and Monique St. Pierre, quoted in *Inside the Playboy Mansion,* 282, 280.

37.　*Inside the Playboy Mansion,* 280; photos of Leigh on April 27, 1985, in HS 700; Anne Randall Stewart, "Palimony, Smalimony" article ms.; HHIA, Jan. 9, 2007; Leigh, quoted in "First Lady of the Playboy Mansion," 166; and Loving, Grabowski, and HH, quoted in "The Great Palimony Caper," 64, 67.

38.　Leigh, quoted in *Los Angeles Daily Breeze,* July 8, 1986; Michael Roche, quoted in "Besides Multiplying, Bunnies Sometimes Sue," *People,* Feb. 29, 1988, 62; "First Person: Carrie Leigh," *Los Angeles Herald,* July 20, 1986; Richard Brooks, "Other Voices," HP; "Great Palimony Caper," 67–68; and Anne and Dick Stewart interview with Murray Fisher, Dec. 1992.

39.　Carrie Leigh to HH, Dec. 26, 1985, HP; Carrie Leigh, note reproduced in HH to DuBois and Fisher, July 1, 1991, HP; "Barbra Streisand Fundraiser," *People,* Sept. 22, 1986; and "Great Palimony Caper," 68.

40.　HH, interview with DuBois and Fisher, 1989; Leigh, quoted in "Carrie Leigh: First Lady of the Playboy Mansion," *Playboy,* July 1986, 166; Mary O'Connor interview with Murray Fisher, April 22, 1991; and "Great Palimony Caper," 67. Lisa Loving interview with Murray Fisher, Jan. 18, 1993, confirmed that Leigh would demand daily "Dr. Bunny" gifts from HH.

41.　HH, quoted in "Hugh Hefner: The Father of the Sexual Revolution Still Thinks He Knows Best," *Details,* April 1993; Anne and Dick Stewart interview with Murray Fisher, Dec. 1992; Joni Mattis interview with Leo Janos, 1988; Leigh, quoted in "The Party's Over," 56; Julie McCullough and Marilyn Grabowski, quoted in *Inside the Playboy Mansion,* 282, 261; Kimberly Conrad Hefner interview with Kevin Burns in 2000 noted that Leigh made a pass at her when she first arrived at the mansion; HHIA, Jan. 9, 2007; and HH, quoted in "Besides Multiplying, Bunnies Sometimes Sue," *People,* Feb. 29, 1988, 62.

42.　John Dante, "Other Voices," HP; Cis Rundle, "Other Voices," HP; Anne and Dick Stewart, interview with Murray Fisher, Dec. 1992; Richard Brooks interview with Lynch/Frost, May 1, 1991; Richard Brooks interview with Murray Fisher, July 23, 1989; Keith Hefner, "Other Voices," HP; Lisa Loving interview with Murray Fisher, Jan. 18, 1993; Mary O'Connor interview with Murray Fisher, April 18, 1991; Anne Randall Stewart, "Palimony, Smalimony" article ms., HP; and Leigh, quoted in "The Party's Over," *Newsweek,* Aug. 4, 1986, 55.

43.　HH interview on *Larry King Live* with guest host Geraldo Rivera, CNN, March 26, 1986; HH, quoted in "The Great Palimony Caper," 64; and Lisa Loving interview with Murray Fisher, Jan. 18, 1993.

44.　HH interview with DuBois and Fisher, 1989, and Mary O'Connor interview with Murray Fisher, April 18, 1991.

45.　Chuck McCann interview with Geoff Miller, winter 1989, and Julie McCullough, quoted in *Inside the Playboy Mansion,* 282.

46.　John Dante, "Other Voices," HP; HH interview with DuBois and Fisher, 1989, with HH's loss of sexual interest confirmed by Anne and Dick Stewart interview with Murray Fisher, Dec. 1992, and John Dante, "Other Voices," HP; HH's notation on the statue-smashing on Sept. 27, 1987, in HS 795 and two guests' recollection of the episode in Anne and Dick Stewart interview with Murray Fisher, Dec. 1992; Jessica Hahn quoted at length on the tape caper in *Inside the Playboy Mansion,* 286, with her story confirmed in "Great Palimony Caper," 146, and "Palimony, Smalimony" article; and HH notation on Dec. 20, 1987, HS 804.

47. HH notation on Jan. 9, 1988, in HS 805; "Great Palimony Caper," 148, 68, 64, 146; and HHIA, Jan. 9, 2007.
48. HHIA, Jan. 9, 2007.

CHAPTER 18. STRANGE BEDFELLOWS

1. "Pornography Commission Appointed," *Washington Times,* May 21, 1985, and "Meese Names Panel to Seek Methods to Control Pornography," *New York Times,* May 21, 1985.
2. Ibid., and Martin Morse Wooster, "Reagan's Smutstompers," *Reason,* April 1986, 32–33. See also an interview with Hudson: "Q & A: Is New Action Needed on Pornography?" *New York Times,* June 23, 1985.
3. Ronald Reagan, quoted in James Petersen and Hugh Hefner, *The Century of Sex* (New York, 1999), 409; Ronald Reagan, "Remarks at the Annual Convention of the National Association of Evangelicals in Columbus, Ohio, March 6, 1984," and "Remarks on Signing the Child Protection Act of 1984, May 21, 1984," both on Web site for *The Public Papers of President Ronald W. Reagan*: www.reagan.utexas. edu/archives.com.
4. Donald Wildmon to Yamaha Motor Corporation, June 18, 1982, and subsequent letter from Yamaha to Hefner, July 14, 1982, informing him of the campaign, both in HP; "Thunder on the Right: The Growth of Fundamentalism," *Time,* Sept. 2, 1985, 55.
5. Judith Reisman's remarks noted in Martin Morse Wooster, "Reagan's Smutstompers," *Reason,* April 1986, 28; Philip Shenon, "Projects of a Provoking Sort," *New York Times,* May 23, 1985; Philip Shenon, "Child Abuse and Photos Linked by a Researcher," *New York Times,* Sept. 23, 1986; Howard Kurtz, "$743,371 Later,'" *Washington Post,* Sept. 12, 1986; and Judith A. Reisman, "About My Study of 'Dirty Pictures,'" *Washington Post,* June 18, 1985.
6. See in *Playboy*: Flo Conway and Jim Siegelman, "Holy Terror," June 1982, and Larry Bush, "Fat Grants and Sleazy Politics: Reagan's Porn Paranoia," Aug. 1984.
7. Robin Morgan, quoted in "Free Speech vs. the Smutbusters," *National Law Journal,* Dec. 22, 1980, 47, and in "The War Against Pornography: Feminists, Free Speech, and the Law," *Newsweek,* March 18, 1985, 60, and Brownmiller quoted in "The Place of Pornography," a round-table forum in *Harper's,* Nov. 1984, 36. *Newsweek's* "The War Against Pornography" provided a clear overview of the feminist antiporn movement, while other useful descriptions appeared in Robert Shea, "Women at War," *Playboy,* Feb. 1980, and Lindsay Van Gelder, "Pornography Goes to Washington," *Ms.,* June 1986.
8. Andrea Dworkin and Catharine MacKinnon, quoted in "The War Against Pornography," 60, 66, and in Sharon Bernstein, "Even Feminists Can't Agree on Sex-Violence Link," *Los Angeles Herald Examiner,* May 4, 1988, and Andrea Dworkin, quoted in "Reagan's Smutstompers," 30.
9. See in *Playboy*: Robert Shea, "Women at War," Feb. 1980; John Gordon, "Women Against Sex," Oct. 1980; Christie Hefner, "By Sex Possessed," Aug. 1981; and James Petersen, "Politically Correct Sex," Oct. 1986.
10. Linda Lovelace, *Ordeal: An Autobiography* (Secaucus, NJ, 1980), 189–190, 198–201.
11. Liz Smith, News Center Four, 5 O'clock Report, Dec. 18, 1979, Burrelle's TV Clips, HP; "Linda Lovelace's 'Ordeal': Beatings, Rape, and Terror," *Philadelphia*

Sunday Bulletin, Feb. 24, 1980; HH, quoted in statement on "ORDEAL, by Linda Lovelace," Jan. 29, 1980, HP, and in "Linda Lovelace on her Ordeal," *Newsday,* April 14, 1980; and Gloria Steinem, "Introduction" to Linda Lovelace, *Out of Bondage* (Secaucus, NJ, 1986), 9–10.

12. Walter Goodman, "Battle on Pornography Spurred by New Tactics," *New York Times,* July 3, 1984, and "The War Against Pornography," *Newsweek,* March 18, 1985, 58, 66.

13. Carol S. Vance, "The Meese Commission on the Road," *Nation,* August 2–9, 1986; "Porno Panel Given Graphic Testimony," *Los Angeles Times,* Oct. 18, 1985; Robert Scheer, "Inside the Meese Commission," *Playboy,* Aug. 1986; and "Sex Busters," *Time,* July 21, 1986. The fullest, if highly critical, account of the Meese Commission's endeavors appears in Philip Nobile and Eric Nadler, *United States of America vs. Sex: How the Meese Commission Lied About Pornography* (New York, 1986).

14. Burt Joseph, quoted in "Junk Pornography Panel, Playboy Says," *Chicago Sun-Times,* April 24, 1986; witness quoted in Hendrik Hertzberg, "Big Boobs: Ed Meese and His Pornography Commission," *New Republic,* July 14 and 21, 1986, 22; Transcript, Miki Garcia Statement to U.S. Attorney General's Commission on Pornography, Oct. 17, 1985, HP; "Playboy Says Unsold Book Motive for Centerfold Allegations," Associated Press, Oct. 18, 1985; and "Playboy Testifies Before Pornography Commission," United Press International, Oct. 18, 1985.

15. Burton Joseph, Special Counsel for *Playboy,* to Alan Sears, Executive Director, Attorney General's Commission on Pornography, Nov. 6, 1985, HP, and Miki Garcia memo to Les Marshall, Sept. 7, 1977, HP.

16. Brenda MacKillop's testimony quoted in HH, "Sexual McCarthyism," *Playboy,* Jan. 1986, 58, and at greater length in Nobile and Nadler, *United States of America vs. Sex,* 107–108; MacKillop, quoted in "Ex-Bunny: Depravity Starts with Playboy," *Cedar Rapids Gazette,* Oct. 25, 1986, and in "Ex-Playboy Bunny Leads Antipornography Rally," *Washington Post,* Aug. 7, 1986; and HH to Brenda MacKillop, July 25, 1986, HP.

17. Form letter sent to companies from Alan E. Sears, Executive Director, Attorney General's Commission on Pornography, Feb. 11, 1986, HP; "Chill Factor," *Time,* June 23, 1986, 46; and "Meese Commission on the Road," 77.

18. "Adult Magazines Lose Sales as 8,000 Stores Forbid Them," *New York Times,* June 16, 1986; "7-Elevens Act to Stop Adult Magazine Sales," *Los Angeles Times,* April 11, 1986; and Thompson, quoted in "7-11 Won't Sell Adult Magazines," *Chicago Tribune,* April 11, 1986.

19. Christie Hefner, quoted in "7-11s Act to Stop Adult Magazine Sales," *Los Angeles Times,* April 11, 1986; "Inside the Meese Commission"; "Pornography Panel Barred from Publicizing Retailers," *New York Times,* July 4, 1986; "Pornography Case Judge Rebukes Panel," *Los Angeles Times,* July 4, 1986; and "The Women of 7-Eleven," *Playboy,* Dec. 1986.

20. Robert H. Burger, "The Meese Report on Pornography and Its Respondents," *Library Quarterly,* 1987; Updike and Irving letters included in full in Nobile and Nadler, *United States of America vs. Sex,* 194–197; Marcia Pally, "Ban Sexism, Not Pornography," *Nation,* June 29, 1985, which included the ACLU quote; Lisa Duggan, "The Dubious Porn War Alliance," *Washington Post,* Sept. 1, 1985; "The Higher Morality of Power," *Chicago Tribune,* May 2, 1986; and "Bluenosed Bullies," *Orange County Register,* April 30, 1986.

21. "The 'Rev. Ed' Puts His Foot Down, and Suddenly Playboy Is Hopping Again," *Chicago Tribune,* July 27, 1986.

22. HH, quoted in *Sandi Freeman Report,* CNN, Dec. 12, 1984, HP, and in interview, *American Focus,* KPWR FM radio, April 13, 1986. See a similar expression of sentiments in HH interview with Charlie Rose, CBS News *Nightwatch,* Oct. 30,

1985, HP, and HH, quoted in "All-American Playboy," *San Antonio Light,* April 13, 1986.

23. "Sexual McCarthyism," 58–59, and Hugh M. Hefner, "The Blacklist," *Playboy,* July 1986.

24. Jonathan Roberts, "Hugh Hefner," *Interview,* December 1985; HH, quoted on *Larry King Live,* CNN, March 26, 1986, HP; "Hugh Hefner: The Father of the Sexual Revolution Still Thinks He Knows Best," *Details,* April 1983, 131; and HH interview, KCBS News, Dec. 5, 1985. See also HH interview with Charlie Rose, CBS News *Nightwatch,* Oct. 30, 1985, HP.

25. "Meese's Anti-Porn Battle Plan," *Los Angeles Herald Examiner,* July 10, 1986; "Pornography Commission's Report Calls for Nationwide Crackdown on Obscenity," *Wall Street Journal,* July 10, 1986; "Panel Calls on Citizens to Wage National Assault on Pornography," *New York Times,* July 10, 1986; and "A Salvo in the Porn War," *Newsweek,* July 21, 1986.

26. Schauer, quoted in "Big Boobs"; "2 on U.S. Panel Dissent on Pornography's Impact," *New York Times,* May 19, 1986; "Researchers Dispute Pornography Report on Link to Violence," *New York Times,* May 17, 1986; and "The Pornography Panel's Controversial Last Days," *Washington Post,* May 30, 1986. See E. I. Donnerstein and D. G. Linz, "The Question of Pornography," *Psychology Today,* Dec. 1986, for a fuller airing of complaints about the commission's misuse of research findings.

27. Jerry Falwell, quoted in "Report Draws Strong Praise and Criticism," *New York Times,* July 10, 1986; Pat Robertson, quoted in "Sexbusters," 17; radical feminists quoted in "A Second Opinion on Pornography's Impact," *New York Times,* May 18, 1986, and "Sexbusters," 18; and Cal Thomas, "Society Has a Moral Right to Act Against Pornography," *Los Angeles Times,* July 11, 1986.

28. Liberal dismissals included "Not Smut, Just Trash," *Los Angeles Times,* July 10, 1986; Ellen Goodman, "Will the Bunny Killer Also Kill Pornography?" *Chicago Tribune,* July 4, 1986; "The Porno Proposals," *Washington Post,* July 11, 1986; "Porn Commission Report Misses the Larger Points," *Philadelphia Inquirer,* July 13, 1986; and "The Story of X," *New York Times,* July 13, 1986. See "Big Boobs," while Kinsley was quoted in 'Personalities," *Washington Post,* June 28, 1986. See William F. Buckley, "Porno Panel's Report Bares Errors, Lacks Solutions," *New York Daily News,* July 14, 1986; "Meese vs. Playboy," *National Review,* Aug. 1, 1986, 13–14; and "Sexbusters" and "The Individual Is Sovereign," *Time,* July 21, 1986, 80.

29. Hugh M. Hefner, "Sex and the State," *Playboy,* Oct. 1986, 53, and HH on *Newsweek on the Air,* WFYR Radio in Chicago, July 27, 1986, HP.

30. See the following in the *New York Times*: "Defeated by Pornography," June 2, 1986; "The Story of X," July 13, 1986; and Anna Quindlen, "Defining Obscenity: Not for Blind Justice," July 23, 1986. For similar pieces opposing the Meese Commission proposals but acknowledging a pornography problem, see "The Porno Proposals," *Washington Post,* July 11, 1986; "Porn Commission Report Misses the Larger Point," *Philadelphia Inquirer,* July 13, 1986; Ellen Goodman, "Will the Bunny Killer Also Kill Pornography?" *Chicago Tribune,* July 4, 1986; "An Issue of Consent," *Los Angeles Times,* June 9, 1986; Jim Courter, "Protect Families From Pornography," *Philadelphia Inquirer,* July 16, 1986; and "A Salvo in the Porn War," *Newsweek,* July 21, 1986, 18.

31. "Sex Busters," *Time,* July 21, 1986, 13.

32. Peter Bogdanovich, *The Killing of the Unicorn: Dorothy Stratten, 1960–1980* (New York, 1984), 9.

33. Ibid., 5, 7, 18, 21.

34. Ibid., 29, 32, 174–175, 176, 184.

35. "Peter Bogdanovich: Visits to the Mansion" document, HP; HH interview with Playboy lawyer Paul Ciotti, Nov. 16, 1984, Document No. 11, Dorothy Stratten File, HP; HHIA, Jan. 9, 2007; and HH, quoted in Paul Ciotti, "Doing Right by Dorothy," *California,* July 1985, 96.

36. HH's statement to Paul Ciotti, Nov. 16, 1984, Document No. 11, Dorothy Stratten File, HP; Edward Bennett Williams to Harvey L. Lipton, General Counsel for the Hearst Corporation, June 28, 1984, HP; *Today,* NBC, Aug. 27, 1984, transcript, HP; *Good Morning America,* ABC, Aug. 27, 1984, transcript, HP; *Nightwatch,* CBS, August 31, 1984, transcript, HP; and George Christian, "Bogdanovich Relates His Side of Dorothy Stratten's Story," *Houston Chronicle,* Sept. 4, 1984. See also Peter Bogdanovich interview, *The David Newman Show,* WJR-AM Radio, Detroit, Nov. 29, 1984, transcript, HP. *Unicorn* was serialized in five installments in the *New York Daily News*: Sept. 1, 3, 4, 5, and 6, 1984.

37. Bogdanovich, quoted in Gregg Kilday, "The Bunny Hop, Part II," *Los Angeles Herald Examiner,* April 1, 1985, and in "Doing Right by Dorothy," 96.

38. "Hefner Responds," Playboy statement on *Unicorn,* printed in *USA Today,* Aug. 2, 1984, and "Hefner Counters Bogdanovich View of Stratten Killing," *Chicago Sun-Times,* Aug. 22, 1984. See HH interview with Paul Ciotti, Nov. 16, 1984, Document No. 11, Dorothy Stratten File, HP, for a private expression of such sentiments.

39. Lisa Loving interview with Murray Fisher, Jan. 18, 1993, and with Michael Trikilis, undated, both in HP.

40. Cis Rundle interview with Lynch/Frost, May 1, 1991; Lisa Loving interview with Murray Fisher, Jan. 18, 1993; Loving quoted in "Doing Right by Dorothy," 82; and HH interview with Paul Ciotti, Nov. 16, 1984, Document No. 11, Dorothy Stratten File, HP.

41. "A Psychiatric Appraisal of Peter Bogdanovich's *The Killing of the Unicorn,*" Aug. 28, 1984, Document No. 10, Dorothy Stratten File, HP, and "Notes from a Meeting with Mary O'Connor, Lisa Loving, and Bill Jordan of WCJ Investigative Consultants," June 29, 1984, HP.

42. Nancy Evans, "How the Playmate Was Murdered," *Glamour,* Feb. 1984, and "Review: Killing of the Unicorn," *Kirkus Reviews,* July 1, 1984. For positive reviews, see Roxanne T. Mueller, "A Moving Tribute to a Slain Beauty," *Cleveland Plain Dealer,* Aug. 19, 1984, and Darrell Shoults, "The Killing of Dorothy Stratten: A Story Bogdanovich Has to Tell," *St. Louis Globe-Democrat,* Aug. 18–19, 1984.

43. Lyda Hurst, "Exploitation of Slain Playmate Continues," *Toronto Star,* Aug. 23, 1984; Barbara Ehrenreich, "The Stratten Story," *American Film,* Nov. 1984, 75; and Shoults, "Killing of Dorothy Stratten."

44. Sneed and Lavin, "Hugh Who?" *Chicago Tribune,* Aug. 5, 1984; Matt Roush, "Bogdanovich on the Stratten Tragedy," *USA Today,* Aug. 2, 1984; James Wolcott, "The Killing of the Unicorn," *Vanity Fair,* Aug. 1984, 38; Lee Grant, "Love and Death, Hollywood Style," *San Jose Mercury News,* Sept. 9, 1984; Joseph Nocera, "Man of the Mansion," *New Republic,* Oct. 14, 1985, 38; and Charles Champlin, "The Killing of the Unicorn," *Los Angeles Times,* Aug. 5, 1984. See Joel E. Siegel, "A Cracked Pot," *Washington City Paper,* Aug. 17–23, 1984, and Eleanor Ringel, "Stratten Memoir Clouded by Love," *Atlanta Constitution,* Aug. 19, 1984, for other examples of negative book reviews that nonetheless pilloried Hefner.

45. HS 697 presents a full record of the press conference. HH was quoted in many newspapers, including "New Charges Fly in Playmate's Murder," *Boston Herald,* April 2, 1985; "Hef: 'Film Big Seduced My Playmate's Teen Sister,'" *New York Post,* April 2, 1985; and "Hefner Refutes Bogdanovich's Accusations Re Stratten Death," *Variety,* April 2, 1985.

46. "Actress' Sister Sues Hefner for $5 Million," *Chicago Sun-Times*, April 9, 1985, and Gregg Kilday, "Page 2: The Bunny Hop, Part III," *Los Angeles Herald Examiner*, April 9, 1985, with HH quoted in both; Allred and HH, quoted in "Blows Against the Empire," 144; Gregg Kilday, "Page Two: Truce or Consequences," *Los Angeles Herald Examiner*, Sept. 4, 1986; "The Region," *Los Angeles Times*, Aug. 30, 1985; and "Playboy Enterprises Press Release," Aug. 29, 1985, HP.

47. Patrick Curtis described in Ciotti, "Doing Right by Dorothy," 83, and "Blows Against the Empire," 142; Marilyn Grabowski, "Stratten's Playboy Years," *Los Angeles Times*, Aug. 19, 1984; Dorothy Stratten to HH, April 8, 1979, HP; "Bogdanovich Weds Stratten's Sister," *USA Today*, Jan. 4, 1989; "Bride's Mom Rips Love-Triangle Director," *New York Post*, Jan. 5, 1989; "Bogdanovich Takes Stratten's Little Sister as His New Bride," *Los Angeles Herald Examiner*, Jan. 3, 1989; and HH to author, Nov. 28, 2007.

48. "Playboy Enterprises Press Release," Aug. 29, 1985; Barry Koltnow, "Hefner Puts Stratten's Story in Center Ring—Again," *Santa Ana Register*, April 3, 1985; "Blows Against the Empire," 72; Gregg Kilday, "Page 2: Surrender Dorothy!" *Los Angeles Herald Examiner*, April 2, 1985; Gordon Diller, "Hefner Mystique Lives Only in Boyhood Dreams," *Los Angeles Herald Examiner*, April 8, 1985; and HH, quoted in Hillary Johnson, "Blows Against the Empire," *Rolling Stone*, March 27, 1986, 71.

49. Arthur Kretchmer to Hugh Hefner, memo on "Bogdanovich," July 6, 1984, HP.

50. Ibid.

CHAPTER 19. THE BRIDE WORE CLOTHES

1. HH interview with Charlie Rose, CBS News *Nightwatch*, Oct. 30, 1985, HP; HHIA, Apr. 11, 2007; and Lisa Loving interview with Michael Trikilis, undated, HP.

2. Mark Saginor, "Letter to the Editor," *Chicago Sun-Times*, March 26, 1985, HP; Mark Saginor on "Hef's Stroke," and Joe Piastro on "Hef's Stroke," Gretchen Edgren, *Inside the Playboy Mansion* (Santa Monica, CA, 1998), 272–273; Christie Hefner, quoted in *Inside the Playboy Mansion*, documentary film (E!, 2002); HHIA, April 11, 2007; and Leigh's "Dear John" letter, April 5, 1985, HP.

3. Mary O'Connor interview with Murray Fisher, April 22, 1991; HH interview with Charlie Rose, CBS News *Nightwatch*, Oct. 30, 1985, HP; and Murray Fisher, quoting Hefner during his interview with Joni Mattis, Jan. 19, 1990.

4. HH press release, March 20, 1985, HP; HH, quoted in "Hefner Puts Stratten Story in Center Ring—Again," *Santa Ana Register*, April 3, 1985; HH interview with Charlie Rose, CBS News *Nightwatch*, Oct. 30, 1985, HP; HH interview, *American Focus*, KPWR FM radio, April 13, 1986; and "Def Hef: Hugh Hefner on Feminism, Fatherhood, and Forty Years of Centerfolds," *Buzz*, Nov./Dec. 1992, 115.

5. HHIA, April 11, 2007.

6. Anne and Dick Stewart interview with Murray Fisher, Dec. 1992, and HHIA, April 11, 2007.

7. HS 785; HS 786; and Kimberly Conrad Hefner interview with the author, May 30, 2007.

8. Hefner and Conrad, quoted in Jeannine Stein, "Mrs. Hef?" *Los Angeles Times*, Oct. 21, 1988; Secretary Lisa Loving's notebook entry for Jan. 20, in HS 806; and HS 807.

9. HS 785, and Kimberly Conrad, Hefner interview with the author, May 30, 2007.

10. Ibid.

11. HHIA, April 11, 2007; Kimberly Conrad Hefner interview with the author, May 30, 2007; "Kimberly Conrad Gets Her Playboy," *USA Today*, April 25, 1989; and HH, quoted in "Love Burns Anew for This Playboy," *USA Today*, March 8, 1988.

12. Dick and Anne Stewart interview with Murray Fisher, Dec. 1992; Anne Stewart, "Palimony, Smalimony" article ms., undated, 13–14, HP; Chuck McCann interview with Geoff Miller, winter 1989; Lisa Loving interview with Murray Fisher, Jan. 18, 1993; Jessica Hahn, "Other Voices," HP; and Joni Mattis, quoted in "Hugh Hefner, Husband," *USA Weekend,* June 9–11, 1989.

13. Jessica Hahn, "Other Voices," HP; Hahn quoted in "Kimberly Conrad Gets Her Playboy," *USA Today,* April 25, 1989; Richard Brooks, "Other Voices," HP; HH quoted in Robert Reinhold, "Hefner Says Playing Days Are Over," *New York Times,* July 28, 1988; and HH, quoted in "Love Burns Anew for This Playboy."

14. HH, quoted in "Love Burns Anew for This Playboy"; HH, quoted in "Mrs. Hef?" *Los Angeles Times,* Oct. 21, 1988; Kimberly Conrad notes on HH's proposal, in HH to Patrick Anderson and Murray Fisher, July 6, 1992; and HS 821.

15. "Mrs. Hef?" *Los Angeles Times,* Oct. 21, 1988; Conrad, quoted in "Cinderella and the Playboy," *Chicago Tribune,* May 4, 1989, and in "C'mon Hef," *Sacramento Bee Magazine,* Jan. 15, 1989, 9; and HH, quoted in "Mrs. Hef?"

16. HH, quoted in "C'mon Hef."

17. Barbi Benton, Sondra Theodore, and Shannon Tweed, quoted in "Hugh Hefner, Husband," *USA Weekend,* June 9–11, 1989.

18. HS 846, "This Playmate of the Year Is a Playmate for a Lifetime," *Playboy,* June 1989, 128–136, and quote on 152; Jeannine Stein, "Hefner Wedding: Strictly Top Hat, Tails," *Los Angeles Times,* June 27, 1989; and HH, quoted in "Hef Gains a Bride, Loses a Reputation," *People,* July 17, 1989, 38.

19. HS 854 and 855; Shannon Nix, "Inside Hefner's Wedding," *San Francisco Chronicle,* July 3, 1989; and "Hef Gains a Bride, Loses a Reputation."

20. Ibid.

21. Cover of *People,* July 19, 1989, and HHIA, April 11, 2007.

22. HH, quoted in Luaine Lee, "Stargazing: Hefner's Finally Hooked," *Pasadena Star-News,* April 28, 1989; Anne Taylor Fleming, "Ramparts Tremble When Hefner Says 'I Do,'" *New York Times,* July 5, 1989; Suzanne Fields, "Hefner a Herald of the 90s?" *Washington Times,* July 6, 1989; and HH, quoted in "Hef Gains a Bride, Loses a Reputation," *People,* July 17, 1989.

23. HH to Larry DuBois and Murray Fisher, June 4, 1990; *Inside the Playboy Mansion,* 292–293; and "Hef Swaps Bunnies for Babies," *London Daily Express,* Dec. 2, 1993.

24. Lisa Loving interview with Murray Fisher, Jan. 18, 1993; Kimberly Conrad Hefner interview with the author, May 30, 2007; and "Queen of the Hutch," *Vancouver,* Nov. 1988, 42.

25. "Changes at the Mansion," *Edmonton Sun,* July 4, 1989; "Hef Gains a Bride, Loses a Reputation," *People,* July 17, 1989, 39; "Mrs. Bunny," *Life,* 104; and Kimberly Conrad Hefner interview with the author, May 30, 2007.

26. "Mrs. Bunny," *Life,* Sept. 1989, 102–107; Philip Marchand, "Hef and the Missus," *Chatelaine,* Sept. 1989, 64–69, 117; and Roger Simon, "Sin Is a Piece of Cake at Playboy Mansion," *Los Angeles Times,* Oct. 4, 1992.

27. *Doonesbury, Los Angeles Times,* June 29, 1989, and August 19, 1989.

28. Kimberly Conrad Hefner, 2000 interview for *E! Hollywood Story,* HP; Kimberly Conrad Hefner interview with the author, August 10, 2007; "Hef, Wife Expecting," *Hollywood Reporter,* Aug. 31, 1989; and HS 876, 910.

29. HHIA, April 11, 2007; Jeff Yarborough, "Hugh Hefner: The Advocate Interview," *Advocate,* March 8, 1994, 41; HS 897; *Inside the Playboy Mansion,* 303, 313; and HH, quoted in "Sin Is a Piece of Cake at the Playboy Mansion," *Los Angeles Times,* Oct. 4, 1992.

30. Kimberly Conrad Hefner interview with the author, May 30, 2007; Steve Powers interview with Bob Carr, March 1990; Steve Powers, quoted in *Inside the Playboy*

Mansion, 301; Dante departure note in HS 974; Kimberly Conrad Hefner, 2000 interview for *E! Hollywood Story,* HP; and *Inside the Playboy Mansion,* 304, 312.

31. HH, quoted in the following: Joe Chidley, "Hef at Home," *Maclean's,* Aug. 15, 1994, 40; "Hugh Hefner: The Father of the Sexual Revolution Still Thinks He Knows Best," *Details,* April 1993, 131; "Playboy Interviewed: Hugh Hefner Talks of Life," *Miami Herald,* Nov. 18, 1992; Roger Simon, "All-American Dream Comes True for Hefner," *Arlington Heights Daily Herald,* Oct. 3, 1992; "Partying with Hugh Hefner, *Chicago Southtown Economist,* Oct. 18, 1992; "Def Hef: Hugh Hefner on Feminism, Fatherhood, and Forty Years of Centerfolds," *Buzz,* Nov./Dec. 1992, 115; Daniel Ritz, "Hugh Hefner: Right Hand Man," *Arena,* Autumn 1994, 64; "Playboy Founder Hugh Hefner Enjoys Life at 70," Reuters World Service news release, April 8, 1996; and HH to Murray Fisher, March 1, 1991, HP. See also HH's statements in *Inside the Playboy Mansion,* 303, 308.

32. "Playboy Interviewed: Hugh Hefner Talks of Life," *Miami Herald,* Nov. 18, 1992; "Hef Lifestyle Blossoms into Prime Time," *Chicago Sun-Times,* Nov. 8, 1993; and "Hef's Newest Playmate," *People,* May 7, 1990.

33. Keith Hefner, "Other Voices," HP; Joe Piastro interview, April 6, 1990, HP; and Steve Powers to HH, April 9, 1996, HP.

34. "Hef's Haven," *Chicago Tribune,* Sept. 22, 1991; Cheryl Lavin, "The Happy Hefners," *Chicago Tribune,* March 28, 1990; "The Taming of a Playboy," *Los Angeles Times,* Nov. 11, 1992; and Roger Simon, "All-American Dream Comes True for Hefner," *Buffalo Daily Herald,* Oct. 3, 1992.

35. The genesis of *Once Upon a Time* is explained by Hefner in Chris Willman, "Hugh Hefner: The Taming of a Playboy," *Los Angeles Times,* Nov. 11, 1992, and in "Chronology of Events, 1988–1992," 14–15, HP. Hefner, quoted in *Once Upon a Time,* 1992, produced by David Lynch and Mark Frost, directed by Gary Grossman and Bob Heath. The film drew a mixed critical response. See "'Hugh Hefner: Once Upon a Time,' An Airbrushed Life," *Los Angeles Times,* Nov. 13, 1992, and other reviews in HS 946, 947. Another documentary, this time for A&E Biography, would appear in 1996: *Hugh Hefner: American Playboy,* produced and directed by Kevin Burns.

CHAPTER 20. ALL IN THE FAMILY

1. "Classic Kimberly," *Playboy,* Sept. 1995.

2. See the following in the *New York Times*: Philip K. Dougherty, "Social Analysis From Good Housekeeping," Aug. 11, 1988; Randall Rothenberg, "Proclaiming a Decade of Decency," Jan. 2, 1990; Stuart Elliott, "Good Housekeeping Modifies Its Campaign Celebrating Families," Mar. 29, 1993; and Stuart Elliott, "A Family Circle Campaign with Unexpected Images," Jan. 4, 1992. For leftist, feminist critiques of these campaigns, see Marcy Darnovsky, "The New Traditionalism: Repackaging Ms. Consumer," *Social Text,* 29 (1991): 72–91, and D. A. Leslie, "Femininity, Post-Fordism, and the New Traditionalism," *Environment and Planning D: Society and Space* 11 (1993): 689–708.

3. Alan Wolfe, *One Nation, After All: What Middle-Class Americans Really Think About God, Country, Family, Welfare, Immigration, Homosexuality, Work, the Right, the Left, and Each Other* (New York, 1998), 322. For two perceptive reviews of Wolfe's book, see Richard Bernstein, "Finding Harmony Amid the Diversity," *New York Times,* Feb. 25, 1998, and Jonathan Rieder, "The Muddled Middle," *Slate,* March 11, 1998. For a similar analysis of the 1990s from a political scientist that links a new traditionalism to Clintonian politics, see Edward Ashbee, "'Remoralization': American Society and Politics in the 1990s," *Political Quarterly,* April–June 2000, 192–201. An amusing variant of this interpretation came in David Brooks, *Bobos in Paradise: The New Upper Class and How They Got There*

(New York, 2000), which analyzed the "bourgeois bohemian" as the predominant style of America's elite establishment in the 1990s—the individual who has "wedded the bourgeois world of capitalist enterprise to the hippie values of the bohemian counterculture."

4. See "Sex in America," cover story in *U.S. News and World Report,* Oct. 17, 1994, 74–81; "Sex in America," cover story in *Time,* Oct. 17, 1994, 62–71; and "Not Frenzied, But Fulfilled," *Newsweek,* Oct. 17, 1994, 70–71. For the popular version of the report, see Robert T. Michael, John H. Gagnon, Edward O. Laumann, and Gina Kolata, *Sex in America: A Definitive Survey* (New York, 1994). The lengthier, full report was published as *The Social Organization of Sexuality* by the University of Chicago Press.

5. HH, quoted in "Sex in America," *Time,* 64; HH memo, "Two Books on Sex," Oct. 12, 1994, HP; and James R. Petersen, "The Great Sex Survey Hoopla," *Playboy,* Feb. 1995, 42–43.

6. "Queen of the Hutch," *Vancouver,* Nov. 1988, 42; Joe Chidley, "Hef at Home," *Maclean's,* Aug. 15, 1994, 40; and "Hugh Hefner, Husband," *USA Weekend,* June 9–11, 1989.

7. Tom Lowry, "The Naked Truth About Playboy: It's Forty Years Old," *New York Daily News,* Dec. 5, 1993.

8. Christie Hefner, quoted in the following: "Inside Hefner's Wedding," *San Francisco Chronicle,* July 3, 1989; "Promoting Pleasure for Profit," *World Link,* May 1989, 67; "Playboy and Leisure Time Marketing in the 1990s," *Town Hall Journal,* Aug. 8, 1989, 123; "Christie Hefner Is Reshaping and Reviving Her Father's Adult Empire," *Washington Post,* Aug. 3, 1997; and Memo to Playboy List titled "Mansion and Hef Positioning," Sept. 4, 1992, HP.

9. "The Mike Who Would Be Hef," *Inside Media,* Jan. 10, 1990, cover, 27–31.

10. "Generation X," *Playboy,* Dec. 1992.

11. See in *Playboy*: Roger Simon, "See Ross Run," Aug. 1992; David Heilbroner, "Blundering Toward Waco," Sept. 1993; Joe Morgenstern, "Profit Without Honor," April 1992; Hugh Hefner, "Just Say No," Nov. 1992; HH on Bill Maher's *Politically Incorrect,* Feb. 6, 1997, HS 1169 and tape of show in HP; and HH on *Larry King Live,* April 17, 1997, HS 1181, and tape of show in HP.

12. See in *Playboy*: Rogier van Bakel, "Digital Rush," Sept. 1996; Dawn Gordon, "Are You Sure S. Bull Has an Unlisted Number?" March 1990; Jonathan Takiff, "Playboy's Electronic Lexicon," May 1994; J. C. Herz, "Confessions of an Internet Junkie," June 1994; and Ted C. Fishman, "Ten Cool Things You Can Do With Your Computer," June 1996.

13. See in *Playboy,* April 1996: "Women of the Internet" and "Virtually Gillian."

14. See two PEI press releases dated Feb. 13, 1992, both in HP—"Playboy Exposes the Real Man to Madison Avenue" and "What Men's Movement?"—and *Playboy,* Sept. 1992, 3, and "Mantrack," 31–34.

15. See in *Playboy*: Asa Baber, "Men," Oct. 1994; and Dennis Boyles and Mathew Childs, "Manly Pursuits," May 1993.

16. See in *Playboy*: Gene Stone, "Clarissa Explains It All," July 1994; Julie Rigby, "A Man's Guide to TV Talk Shows," Aug. 1994; and Tracey Pepper, "Finally, the Rules of Dating," July 1994.

17. "What Sort of Man Reads Playboy?" *Playboy,* April 1998, 65, and Feb. 1998, 59.

18. On Wildmon's controversial endeavors, see "The Gospel on Trash TV," *Chicago Tribune,* May 22, 1989, and "Religious Right May Be in for a Fight," *Los Angeles Times,* May 20, 1991. On *Playboy's* initial reaction, see the following memos in HP: HH to Christie Hefner, May 22, 1989; Arthur Kretchmer to Christie Hefner, May 16, 1989; and Christie Hefner to HH, May 25, 1989. *Playboy's* subsequent actions are listed in "Chronology of Events, 1988–1992," HP.

19. See "Sexual Correctness: Has It Gone Too Far?" cover story, *Newsweek*, October 25, 1993, for good background on this phenomenon, while HH was quoted in Jeff Yarbrough, "Hugh Hefner: The Advocate Interview," *Advocate*, March 8, 1994, 43.

20. See Dick Morris's explication of the "Triangulation" strategy in his book *Behind the Oval Office: Winning the Presidency in the Nineties* (New York, 1997), and in "The Clinton Years: Interview with Dick Morris," *PBS Frontline* (2000), www.pbs.org.

21. Joe Queenan, "Wake Up and Smell the Nineties," *Playboy*, Jan. 1992.

22. Peter Nelson, "Navigating the Nineties: The P.C. Survival Guide," *Playboy*, Jan. 1992.

23. See in *Playboy*: Jonathan Franklin, "Inside Buchanan's Bunker," April 1996; Mark Bowden, "Holy Terror," February 1999; Ben Fenwick, "The Road to Oklahoma City," June 1997; and Colin Campbell and Deborah Scroggins, "Very Weird Science," Dec. 1995.

24. See in *Playboy*: Garry Wills, "Columbus Go Home," Jan. 1992; Vincent Bugliosi, "Outrage: The Reasons O. J. Simpson Got Away With Murder," July 1996; Mathew Child, "Politically Correct Speech: A Guide to Who Can Say What to Whom on Campus," Oct. 1991; Chip Rowe, "The Safe Generation," June 1995; and Doug Hornig, "The Big Chill on Campus Sex," Nov. 1993.

25. James R. Petersen, "Showdown in Cincinnati," *Playboy*, March 1991, and "Hugh Hefner: The Advocate Interview," *Advocate*, March 8, 1994, 42.

26. See in *Playboy*: Pete Hamill, "Woman on the Verge of a Legal Breakdown," Jan. 1993; Ted Fishman, "Hatefest: Hanging Out at a Feminist Legal Conference," Aug. 1993; and James R. Petersen and Linda Strom, "Forum: Whiplash," July 1992. See also James Petersen, "Catharine McKinnon: Again," Aug. 1992. For similar mainstream liberal rejections of MacKinnon and her ilk, see John Irving, "Pornography and the New Puritans," *New York Times Book Review*, March 29, 1992, and Carlin Romano, "Between the Motion and the Act," *Nation*, Nov. 15, 1993, which concludes, "The first settlers in America came here to get away from people like Catharine MacKinnon. . . . She is an authoritarian in the guise of a progressive."

27. Christina Hoff Sommers, *Who Stole Feminism? How Women Have Betrayed Women* (New York, 1994), 22, 134–135, 224–226, 230. In *Playboy*, see Jack Kammer, "Interviews with Feminists on the War Between the Sexes," Feb. 1994; Warren Farrell, "The Myth of Male Power," July and August 1993; and Katie Roiphe, "Date-Rape Hysteria: The Feminist Resurrection of Victorian Morals," May 1992.

28. "Playboy Interview: Betty Friedan," *Playboy*, Sept. 1992.

29. Betty Friedan, *Fountain of Age* (New York, 1993), 623–624; "Now, the Second Revolution," *Newsweek*, Oct. 4, 1993, 78; and Betty Friedan, "Why Men Die Young," *Playboy*, April 1995.

30. See in *Playboy*: "20 Questions: Camille Paglia," Oct. 1991; "Playboy Interview: Camille Paglia," May 1995; and Camille Paglia, "The Return of Carrie Nation," Oct. 1992.

31. See in *Playboy*: Tawni Cable, "Cable Ready," Miss June 1989, 117; Alicia Rickter, "Earth Shaker," Miss October 1995; and "Domestic Bliss," August 1992.

32. "Playboy's History of the Sexual Revolution," by James R. Petersen, ran from Nov. 1996 to Nov. 1999. The quotes come from the final installment, "Who Won the Sex War?" *Playboy*, Nov. 1999. See also Glenn O'Brien, "Flirting With Feminists," *Playboy*, April 1993.

33. Michael Kelly, "Sex Is Back," *Playboy*, May 1990.

34. "Hef Swaps Bunnies for Babies," London *Daily Express*, Dec. 2, 1993, and HH, "Playboy 2000: A Celebration of the Postfeminist, Postmodern Man," *Playboy*, April 1996, 47.

35. See in *Playboy:* Robert Scheer, "Lust in the White House," May 1992, 39; Asa Baber, "A Good Man," Sept. 1995, 30; Ted Fishman, "The Playboy Forum: By Our Scandals We Are Known," *Playboy,* July 1998, 55; James R. Petersen, "The Rules of an Affair," *Playboy,* February 1999, 49; and Hugh Hefner, "The Playboy President," *Playboy,* May 1998, 11.

36. "Playboy's Hefner to Step Down," *Chicago Sun-Times,* Sept. 13, 1988. See also "Playboy Founder Hugh Hefner Plans to Name Daughter to Firm's Top Job," *Wall Street Journal,* Sept. 13, 1988, and "Hefner's 35-Year Reign at Playboy Drawing to an End," *Chicago Tribune,* Sept. 13, 1988.

37. HS 871; "Playboy Interview: Christie Hefner," *Playboy Enterprises Inc.,* special publication, 1990; and "Troubled Playboy Enterprises Streamlining for '90s," *Dallas Morning News,* Sept. 23, 1989.

38. "Goodbye to Bunny Girls," *Business Week,* Nov. 14, 1988.

39. "Playboy Brings in New Management," *Publishing News,* June–July 1989; "Playboy Expected to Hire Chiat to Put Ad-Buyers in the Mood," *Wall Street Journal,* May 16, 1990; and Karen Stabiner, "Hef II," *Los Angeles Times Magazine,* Sept. 10, 1989, 10.

40. "Christie Hefner Is Reshaping and Reviving Her Father's Adult Empire," *Washington Post,* Aug. 3, 1997, and Karen Stabiner, "Hef II," *Los Angeles Times Magazine,* Sept. 10, 1989, 10.

41. On PEI's business strategy, see "Christie Hefner Takes Reins of Tamer Playboy," *Chicago Sun-Times,* Nov. 14, 1988; Karen Stabiner, "Hef II," *Los Angeles Times Magazine,* Sept. 10, 1989, 10; "Playboy Trying New Poses to Improve Growth Picture," *Crain's Chicago Business,* Nov. 14, 1988; "Goodbye to Bunny Girls," *Business Week,* Nov. 14, 1988; "Playboy Reports $3.8 Million Loss for Fiscal '89," *Magazine Week,* Sept. 4, 1989; and "Playboy to Split Shares into Voting, Nonvoting Classes," *Wall Street Journal,* May 8, 1990. On foreign markets, see "Troubled Playboy Enterprises Streamlining for '90s," *Dallas Morning News,* Sept. 23, 1989; "Christie Hefner," *Chicago Tribune,* Jan. 7, 1990; "Playboy Enterprises Refocuses the Dream," *Bloomberg,* Sept. 1993, 65–66; and "Playboy Looks Overseas as U.S. Climate Grows Hostile," *Wall Street Journal,* Sept. 29, 1993. On electronic projects, see "Playboy Enterprises Refocuses the Dream," *Bloomberg,* Sept. 1993, 65–66; "Playboy Seeks a Place in the Electronic Future," *New York Times,* Dec. 21, 1993; "Playboy Pins Hopes on Net," CNET News.com, March 19, 1998; and "K-Tel Gets Into Bed with Playboy Online," *New York Post,* Nov. 4, 1998.

42. "Christie Hefner Is Reshaping and Reviving Her Father's Adult Empire," *Washington Post,* Aug. 3, 1997, and Karen Stabiner, "Hef II," *Los Angeles Times Magazine,* Sept. 10, 1989, 16.

43. See "Playboy's Strategic Overhaul Has Wall St. Talking Turnaround," *Crain's Chicago Business,* Sept. 25, 1989; "Playboy Looks Overseas as U.S. Climate Grows Hostile," *Wall Street Journal,* Sept. 29, 1993; "Playboy's Fortunes Tied to the Bunny," *Advertising Age,* Oct. 24, 1994; "Playboy Cuts Work Force," *New York Times,* Sept. 29, 1993; "Playboy to Cut 60 Jobs, Post Operating Loss in Quarter," *Chicago Sun-Times,* Sept. 28, 1993; "Playboy Trying New Poses to Improve Growth Picture," *Crain's Chicago Business,* Nov. 14, 1988; "Playboy Reports $3.8 Million Loss for Fiscal '89, *Magazine Week,* Sept. 4, 1989; "Earnings," *Chicago Sun-Times,* Aug. 6, 1992; and "Earnings," *Chicago Tribune,* Aug. 5, 1993.

44. On PEI projects, see "Bunny's Gamble," *Crain's Chicago Business,* Aug. 25, 1997; "Spicing Up Playboy," *Cable,* Feb. 9, 1998; "Playboy Spices Up Its Adult Business," *Multichannel News,* Feb. 9, 1998; "Deal Gives Playboy Monopoly on Adult TV," *USA Today,* Feb. 5, 1998; "Playboy Tries to Pick Up Women," CNET News.com, Nov. 10, 1998; and "Can Aging Playboy Lure Women?" *Wall Street Journal,* Nov. 10, 1998.

On profit figures, see "Playboy Hires Creative Artists to Find Investors to Fuel Ambitious Expansion," *Wall Street Journal,* Nov. 7, 1995; "A Titillating Takeoff for '97 Earnings at Playboy," *Hollywood Reporter,* Aug. 16, 1997; and "Pulling Rabbits out of Hats," *Chief Executive,* Sept. 1999, 48–49.

45. Joanna Piros, "Paradise Found," *Vancouver Lifestyle,* Dec. 1997, 50, 53.

CHAPTER 21. BACK IN THE GAME

1. See *Mr. Playboy,* A&E Biography, for film segments of the New Year's Eve 1997 party. HH's scrapbook volume for the event, HS 214, is titled "New Year's Eve without Kimber," while a picture of the publisher with a bunch of pretty girls has the caption "Hef alone in a crowd." HS 1215 is titled "Alone and Lonely."
2. "Hefners to Split," *Chicago Sun-Times,* Jan. 21, 1998; "Playboy King, Wife Split," *New York Post,* Jan. 21, 1998; and "Splitting Hares," *People,* Feb. 9, 1998.
3. Philip Marchand, "Hef and the Missus," *Chatelaine,* Sept. 1989, 117.
4. Dick and Anne Stewart to HH and Kimberly Conrad Hefner, May 6, 1995, HS 1064.
5. Kimberly Conrad Hefner in an interview with the author on August 10, 2007, politely but firmly refused to discuss anything regarding the breakup of the marriage. She spoke similarly in a 2000 interview for *E! Hollywood Story,* tape in HP.
6. Kimberly Conrad Hefner, quoted in Bill Zehme, "The Man Who Loved Women," *Esquire,* Aug. 1998, 66; an unnamed "Mansion source," quoted in "Hefners to Split," *Chicago Sun-Times,* Jan. 21, 1998; Kimberly Conrad Hefner and Mark Saginor, quoted in "Splitting Hares," *People,* Feb. 9, 1998, 147–148. Dick and Anne Stewart, in an interview with the author on August 7, 2007, confirmed this point.
7. Kimberly Conrad Hefner, quoted in Joe Chidley, "Hef at Home," *Maclean's,* Aug. 15, 1994, 40, and in "Splitting Hares," *People,* Feb. 9, 1998, 148; Kimberly Conrad Hefner, interview with the author, May 30, 2007; and Bill Zehme, "The Man Who Loved Women," 141. Dick and Anne Stewart, interview with author, Aug. 7, 2007, discussed Conrad Hefner's frustrations about creating a home at the mansion.
8. Kimberly Conrad Hefner, quoted in Bill Zehme, "The Man Who Loved Women," *Esquire,* Aug. 1998, 66, and in Joe Chidley, "Hef at Home," *Maclean's,* Aug. 15, 1994, 40. Conrad Hefner also raised the Lady Diana analogy in an interview with the author, May 30, 2007.
9. HHIA, April 11 and Aug. 7, 2007.
10. HHIA, April 11, 2007, and HH, quoted in Bill Zehme, "The Man Who Loved Women," *Esquire,* Aug. 1998, 140.
11. HHIA, April 11, 2007, and HH, quoted in Lydia Martin, "Original Playboy Back in Action," *Miami Herald,* Nov. 22, 1999. HH also discussed his perceptions of the marital collapse in "Playboy Interview: Hugh M. Hefner," *Playboy,* Jan. 2000, 244.
12. HHIA, April 11, 2007, and August 9, 2006, and author's interviews with several regular mansion guests, who spoke on condition of anonymity. In 1997, according to published press reports, Mark Speers, a security employee at the mansion, sued Kimberly Hefner for sexual harassment, claiming that he had been fired from his position because he had rejected her sexual advances. The lawsuit was settled out of court in September 1997. HH defends his wife and says that this situation is unrelated to the earlier affairs that helped erode their marriage. On the Speer lawsuit, see "Splitting Hares," 147, and "Playboy King, Wife Split," *New York Post,* Jan. 21, 1998.
13. HHIA, April 11, 2007, and HS 1135, 1137, and 1197, the latter of which is titled "A Long, Lonely Summer."
14. HHIA, April 11, 2007, and HH, quoted in Lydia Martin, "Original Playboy Back in Action," *Miami Herald,* Nov. 22, 1999, and in "Echoes of a Bunnyman," interview with Bob Guccione Jr., *Gear,* Sept./Oct. 1998, 87.

15. Dick and Anne Stewart interview with the author, Aug. 7, 2007; HHIA, Aug. 7, 2007; and Bill Zehme, "The Man Who Loved Women," *Esquire*, Aug. 1998, 61, 66, 60, 65, 63.

16. HHIA, Aug. 7, 2007; HS 1218, 1223, 1241; and HH to John Dante, May 18, 1998, in HS 1242.

17. See in *Playboy*: Bill Zehme, "Inside the Playboy Mansion," Dec. 1998; "The World of Playboy," Jan. 1999, 19; and cartoon, Dec. 1999, 120.

18. HH, quoted in Marilyn Cole Lownes, "In It for the Bunnies," *Esquire* (British Edition), July 1999, 139, and in "Once Again, I'm a Babe Magnet," *London Daily Telegraph*, July 27, 1998; HS 1236, titled "Viva Viagra"; and HS 1280 and 1344. See "The Potency Pill," cover story in *Time*, May 4, 1998, 50–57, for an analysis of Viagra's arrival on the American scene.

19. See HS 1244, 1372, 1253, and 1270.

20. Mark Seal, "The Big Bunny Hops Again," *American Way*, March 15, 2001, 64–65; HH, quoted in Marilyn Cole Lownes, "In It for the Bunnies," *Esquire* (British Edition), July 1999, 139, in "Once Again, I'm a Babe Magnet," *London Daily Telegraph*, July 27, 1998, in Lydia Martin, "Original Playboy Back in Action," *Miami Herald*, Nov. 22, 1999, and in "Razor Interview: Hugh Hefner," *Razor*, April/May 2001, 42.

21. See HS 1425 and 1445, and Brande Roderick to HH, undated, probably in late June 2000, and HH to Brande Roderick, June 30, 2000, both in HP. Yagalla had met Sandy Bentley in the fall of 1999 and, according to published reports, began to shower her with lavish gifts such as cars, diamonds, vacations, and a Las Vegas residence. He also gave her a platinum American Express card on which she ran up some $1 million in clothes, meals, travel, food, and collectibles. Mandy Bentley also received a car and other gifts. After Yagalla's arrest by the FBI, investors mounted a lawsuit against him and tried to get their money back. The judge issued an injunction barring the Bentleys from selling the gifts. See "Attorney Targets Gifts to Model from Arrested Fund Manager," *USA Today*, March 8, 2001; "Taking Playmate's Toys," *New York Daily News*, March 27, 2001; and especially Benjamin Wallace, "The Prodigy and the Playmate," *Philadelphia*, June 2001, 95–103, for the full story of the relationship and the scandal.

22. Tina Jordan, quoted in Lucy Broadbent, "The Toughest Part of Being a Hef Babe Is Getting Dressed," *Personal*, Sept. 16, 2001, 8, and HS 1444, 1445, 1486, 1492, 1548, 1600, 1651, and 1699.

23. "Sexy at 75," *New York Post*, March 12, 2001; "Citizen Hef," *Chicago Tribune Magazine*, Dec. 12, 1999, 16; HHIA, Aug. 7, 2007; "Playboy Interview: Hugh M. Hefner," *Playboy*, Jan. 2000, 65; and Holly Madison, quoted in "Playboy's First Lady Tells All," London *Sunday Mirror*, Dec. 7, 2003.

24. David Plotz, "Hugh Hefner: He Swings, He Misses," *Slate*, July 21, 2000; "Playboy or Bust" and "Party Politics," *Harper's Bazaar*, Dec. 1999, 207, 225; and "The 1999 Hall of Fame," *Vanity Fair*, Dec. 1999, 316–317.

25. HH, quoted in Marilyn Cole Lownes, "In It for the Bunnies," *Esquire* (British Edition), July 1999, 139.

26. *Playboy*: *50th Anniversary Issue*, Jan. 2004; advertisement, "Playboy: The Magazine That Changed America," *New York Times*, Dec. 1, 2003; and *Playboy's 50th Anniversary Celebration*, A&E, Nov. 30, 2003, HP.

27. For reviews of *Playboy's 50th Anniversary Celebration* on A&E, see Noel Holston, "From Playboy to Platoon," *Newsday*, Dec. 5, 2003, and David Bianculli, "Hef Wins Booby Prize," *New York Daily News*, Dec. 3, 2003.

28. Cal Thomas, "Only One Side of Hugh Hefner's Playboy Legacy Is Being Told," *Dallas Morning News*, Jan. 5, 2004; Connie Schultz, "Sorry, Hef, But It Takes a

Real Man to Celebrate the Beauty of Real Women," *Cleveland Plain Dealer,* Oct. 1, 2003; Suzanne Fields, "Yearning for a Glimpse of Shocking Stocking," Townhall. com, Dec. 15, 2003; and "The Hollow Victory of Hugh Hefner," *Christianity Today,* Dec. 2003, reprinted at christianitytoday.com.

29. "Playboy at 50: A Man's Notes," *Los Angeles Times,* Nov. 28, 2003; "Playboy at 50," *Newsday,* Oct. 2, 2003; Marilyn Cole Lownes, "The Oldest Swinger in Town," *Times Magazine* (London), Nov. 1, 2003, 29; Richard Corliss, "That Old Feeling: Your Grandfather's Playboy," *Time,* Jan. 3, 2004; and Catherine Seipp, "Living with Playboy," *National Review Online,* Jan. 13, 2004. For other respectful, largely positive critiques: "Playboy Turns 50," *Houston Chronicle,* Dec. 14, 2003; "50 Years Later, Playboy Still Swinging," *Chicago Sun-Times,* Nov. 28, 2003; "Forget T&A," *San Francisco Chronicle,* Dec. 11, 2003; and "The Original Playboy," *Ottawa Citizen,* Dec. 6, 2003.

30. "Playboy at 50: Cutting-Edge Becomes Almost Quaint," *Dayton,* Dec. 8, 2003; Brian McCoy, "Playboy's Maturity Makes It Outdated," *Stockton Record,* Dec. 19, 2003; Geoff Pevere, "Playboy Bunny Running Low on Batteries," *Toronto Star,* Jan. 3, 2004; and Richard Corliss, "That Old Feeling: Your Grandfather's Playboy," *Time,* Jan. 3, 2004.

31. David Brooks, "The Return of the Pig," *Atlantic Monthly,* April 2003, reprinted in TheAtlantic.com.

32. HH, quoted in "Hefner Decrees: Less Sex Better in New *Playboy,*" *New York Observer,* Oct. 7, 2002, and Kretchmer, quoted in Greg Lindsay, "Rethinking a Great American Magazine," *Folio,* Nov. 1, 2002, at Foliomag.com.

33. HH, quoted in "Hefner Decrees: Less Sex Better in New *Playboy,*" *New York Observer,* Oct. 7, 2002.

34. Kaminsky, quoted in the following: "Playboy's Mr. October," *Newsday,* Sept. 23, 2002; "Playboy's New Editor Reshapes Aging Bunny," Reuters, May 6, 2003; "Defining 'Cool' for a New Age: Playboy Tries to Modernize in Face of Competition," *New York Times,* April 23, 2003; "The Original Playboy," *Ottawa Citizen,* Dec. 8, 2002; "What Playboy Means to Sex and Pop Culture," *Kansas City Star,* Dec. 2, 2003; and "Playboy Makeover Aims to Lure Younger Readers," *Chicago Tribune,* Nov. 30, 2003.

35. "Playboy's Overhaul," *Onion,* Oct. 30, 2002, reprinted in theonion.com, and "An Uneasy Alliance in Revised Playboy," *Chicago Tribune,* June 29, 2003.

36. HHIA, Aug. 7, 2007.

37. Ibid.

38. "Playboy's Not-So-Energized Bunny," *Business Week,* Dec. 4, 2000, 44, and CH to Stephen Shepard, Editor-in-Chief, *Business Week,* Nov. 28, 2000, HP, later published in *Business Week,* Dec. 18, 2000. At a business forum in Los Angeles in December 2000, Christie Hefner also vented her anger at the article, bluntly calling it "full of shit." See "Playboy CEO Is Hopping Mad," Wirednews.com., Dec. 8, 2000.

39. For a comprehensive, insightful analysis of PEI's business strategy since the early 1980s, see Greg Burns, "Adventures in the Skin Trade," *Chicago Tribune Magazine,* Oct. 16, 2005. CH discussed aspects of the company's strategy in an interview with the author on Sept. 14, 2007. On the controversial Spice TV purchase, see "Playboy Gets More Explicit," *Washington Post,* July 3, 2001; "Playboy Sheds Gentleman's Cloak, Buys XX TV Channels," *Los Angeles Times,* July3, 2001; "Playboy to Acquire 3 Cable Purveyors of Hard-Core Sex," *Wall Street Journal,* July 2, 2001; "Playboy Goes XXX," *Newsweek,* July 16, 2001; and "Publishing," *Delaney Report: International Newsletter for Marketing, Advertising, and Media Executives,* July 9, 2001.

40. Among a host of articles on PEI's profits, restructuring, and projects in recent years, see "Playboy Boots Publishing Executives as Ad Market Wanes," *USA Today,*

Dec. 4, 2000; "Playboy to Slash Headcount at Its Online Operations," *Wall Street Journal,* Oct. 11, 2001; "Playboy Enterprises, Inc. Announces Restructuring," PEI press release, Nov. 21, 2002, HP; "Playboy to Revive Club, and Bunnies, in Las Vegas," *Wall Street Journal,* Oct. 6, 2004; "Playboy Enterprises Reports Strong 2005 Results," Lexdon.com, Feb. 14, 2006; "Playboy Says It's Not for Sale," CNNMoney.com, Feb. 13, 2007; and "Playboy Perks Up Its Ears," *Chicago Sun-Times,* Aug. 28, 2007. A convenient chart of PEI's net income/loss year-by-year from 1971 to 2004 is in Greg Burns, "Adventures in the Skin Trade," *Chicago Tribune Magazine,* October 16, 2005, 18, and the quote comes from that same page. Christie Hefner discussed the company's most recent projects, and her hopes for a prosperous future, in an interview with the author, Sept. 14, 2007.

41. On *Playboy's* revived appeal, see HH in "Razor Interview: Hugh Hefner," *Razor,* April/May 2001, 42.

42. "Friday Night Movie Notes," March 4, 2005, HS 1895. Richard Bann, Hefner's good friend and a film historian, assists with research and sketches rough drafts of the publisher's weekly film talks.

43. Bill Zehme, "The Man Who Loved Women," *Esquire,* Aug. 1998, 60, and Wil Hylton, "Hugh Hefner," *Rolling Stone,* Aug. 31, 2000, 60.

44. See HS 1237, 1567, 1604, 1913, and "It's Hugh Hefner to the Rescue," *Los Angeles Times,* July 25, 2002.

45. See HS 1398, 1567, 1754, 1755, "HH's Carl's Jr. Advertisement" tape, HP. On the conservative outcry against the Carl's Jr. ad, see "Hefner Ads Too Close for College's Comfort," *Los Angeles Times,* Nov. 21, 2003.

46. See HS 1489, 1685, 1759, 1783, 1890, 1897, and 1893.

47. "Gore Confronted by New Issue: Playboy," *New York Times,* Aug. 12, 2000; "Mentioning Playboy Gives Democrats the Jitters," *Chicago Tribune,* Aug. 12, 2000; "Sanchez Out Again as Convention Speaker," *Los Angeles Times,* Aug. 15, 2000; and HH, quoted in "Hefner Calls Dems Hypocrites," *USA Today,* Aug. 14, 2000, and "When Mansion Can Barely Be Mentioned," *Los Angeles Times,* Aug. 12, 2000.

48. On the changing of the guard among HH's girlfriends, see HS 1816 and 1823.

49. Holly Madison interview with author, August 11, 2007. See also Holly Madison to Tina Jordan, Sept. 1, 2002, HS 1651, and "Playboy's First Lady Tells All," London *Sunday Mirror,* Dec. 7, 2003.

50. Bridget Marquardt interview with the author, Aug. 6, 2007.

51. Kendra Wilkinson interview with the author, Aug. 6, 2007.

52. Ad for premiere of *The Girls Next Door* in summer 2005, HP.

53. "E! Entertainment Television Unveils Its Most Aggressive Slate," press release, May 11, 2005, HS 1911, and Daphne Merkin, "I Dream of Holly (and Bridget, and Kendra)," *Elle,* June 2007, 201. The show's appeal to professional women and feminists is also examined in "Why Women Love 'Girls Next Door,'" *New York Post,* Aug. 6, 2007.

54. "I Dream of Holly," 260, and Marquardt interview with author, Aug. 6, 2007.

55. Lawyer quoted in "Why Women Love the 'Girl Next Door'"; "I Dream of Holly," 260; and Marquardt interview with author, Aug. 6, 2007.

56. HHIA, April 11, 2007. The columnist's reflection on Hefner "winning" appeared in George Will, "At 77, Hefner's the Life of the Party," syndicated column printed in, for example, the *Columbia Daily Tribune,* June 3, 2003.

EPILOGUE. PLAYBOY NATION

1. Kevin Burns, quoted in Daphne Merkin, "I Dream of Holly (and Bridget, and Kendra)," *Elle,* June 2007, 201; HH on the magazine and his life as his greatest creation in "Razor Interview: Hugh Hefner," *Razor,* April/May 2001, 42; and HH, quoted in "Playboy Interview: Hugh M. Hefner," *Playboy,* Jan. 1974, 70.

2. HH to author, Oct. 18, 2007, and HH, quoted in "Citizen Hef," *Chicago Tribune Magazine,* Dec. 12, 1999, 15. For other HH statements on the need for personal liberation, see "Def Hef: Hugh Hefner on Feminism, Fatherhood, and Forty Years of Centerfolds," *Buzz,* Nov./Dec. 1992, 68; "Playboy Interview: Hugh M. Hefner," *Playboy,* Jan. 1974, 72; "Hugh Hefner: The Father of the Sexual Revolution Still Thinks He Knows Best," *Details,* April 1993, 131; and "Playboy Interview: Hugh M. Hefner," *Playboy,* Jan. 2000, 245.

3. HH, quoted in "Citizen Hef," *Chicago Tribune Magazine,* Dec. 12, 1999, 23.

4. David Shaw, "After 50 Years of Playboy, We All Live in Hef's World," *Los Angeles Times,* May 4, 2003.

5. Cartoon by Mike Luckovich, *Atlanta Journal-Constitution,* Dec. 4, 2003.

6. Reed Johnson, "Playboy at 50: A Man's Notes," *Los Angeles Times,* Nov. 28, 2003; "Camille Paglia: Playboy Interview," *Playboy,* May 1995, 62; and John Zobenica, "Are We Not Men? Down the Ladder from Playboy to Maxim," TheAtlantic.com, January/February 2007.

7. The phrase "consumer's republic" is from Elizabeth Cohen, *The Consumer's Republic: The Politics of Mass Consumption in Postwar America* (New York, 2003), while the quote is from Richard Corliss, "That Old Feeling: Your Grandfather's Playboy," *Time,* Jan. 3, 2004.

8. See the author's *The People's Tycoon: Henry Ford and the American Century* (New York, 2005) and *The Magic Kingdom: Walt Disney and the American Way of Life* (New York, 1997).

9. Robert Coles, "Transforming American Sexuality," *New York Times Book Review,* May 4, 1980, 6, and Henry Louis Gates Jr., "The Naked Republic," *New Yorker,* Aug. 25 and Sept. 1, 1997, 123.

10. HH, quoted in "Hugh Hefner: The Man Who Started It All Speaks Boldly," *Bold,* Dec. 2000, 29, and F. Scott Fitgerald, *The Great Gatsby* (New York, 1925 [2004]), 180.

INDEX